For

*Jim
Rachele and Katherine
and for
My Sister Fellows at the Bunting Institute, '91–'92*

Contents

List of Illustrations/ix
Acknowledgments/xiii
Dating/xv
On Translating Cartoons/xvii
A Note on Transliteration/xix

I
Introduction/1
a. Historical Background/1
b. Method/10

II
Publishing, Format, Images, and Readers/25

III
The Voice and Image of the Public, and Its Targets/51

IV
Revolutionary Exemplars: France and Iran/73

V
The Comic Sovereign: The Satirical Critique of Authority/113

VI
The Comic Aggressor: The Critique of European Political and Economic Hegemony/149

VII
The Comic Culture: The Critique of Society, Culture, and European Influence/189

VIII
Fashion Satire and the Honor of the Nation/221

Contents

IX
Dogs, Crime, Women, Cholera, and Other Menaces
in the Streets/259

X
Technology, Transport, and the "Modern" Street/289

XI
Conclusion: Revolutionary Options, Satiric Imagery,
and the Historiographic Frame/317

Appendices
Appendix 1. List of Gazettes/333
Appendix 2. Price and Post/335
Appendix 3. Location of Publishers/339

Notes/341
Bibliography/439
Index/461

Illustrations

1.1	The Press as Protector of Freedom	6
1.2	"Funeral" for a Gazette	7
1.3	Loosing the Censor	8
2.1	Unreliable Post: "One for you and one for me"	42
2.2	Female Readers Depicted in Advertising	44
2.3	A Gazette Contest Coupon	49
3.1	Karagöz and Hacivat	55
3.2	The Drummer	58
3.3	Züğürt	59
3.4	Züğürt and the Unemployed Bureaucrats	61
3.5	Enver Bey	62
3.6	Masthead Old Nags	64
4.1	Mother Liberty	76
4.2	"Marianne" and the Dragon	81
4.3	Insurance for the Motherland	82
4.4	Abd ül-Hamid, Sans Souci	85
4.5	The Trials of Freedom	88
4.6	Freedom Comes of Age	90
4.7	Iranian Shahs and Attendants	94
4.8	The New Year's Present	97
4.9	The Shah's Tobacco	99
4.10	Muhammad Ali Shah and Despotism	101
4.11	Sultan Abd ül-Hamid and Despotism	102
4.12	Free Ottomans and the Oppressive Shah	103
4.13	Sattar Khan and Muhammad Ali Shah	104
4.14	The Czar's Fatherly Administration	107
4.15	Bathing in the Constitutional Waters	108
5.1	Outcasts' Club	119
5.2	At the Museum: "Dinosaurs" of the Past	120
5.3	The Shaky Foundations of Monarchy	122
5.4	The "Spoils" of War	125
5.5	Tyranny Personified	126
5.6	The Bloody Sultan	127
5.7	The Suffering of Anatolia	129
5.8	The Sultan in Exile	131

List of Illustrations

5.9	Cavid Bey and the Powers	134
5.10	Old Amusements and New	137
5.11	The Constitutional Struggle	138
5.12	The Ottoman Elections in Istanbul	142
5.13	Deputies at Work	143
5.14	The London Delegation	145
5.15	"What Did You Bring Us From London?"	146
6.1	The English Occupation of Egypt	156
6.2	No Room for the Mother Tongue	157
6.3	John Bull as "Venus" in the Persian Gulf	159
6.4	The European Powers in Morocco	163
6.5	When is a Czar Not a Czar?	166
6.6	Eating the Balkans	168
6.7	Austria, Bulgaria, and the Young Turks	169
6.8	The Ottoman Milk Cow	172
6.9	The War Trumpet	174
6.10	The Ottoman Boycott of Austrian Goods	177
6.11	Leaping the Tobacco Régie	179
6.12	Asking Haci Ağa For a Raise	182
6.13	The Beggar at the Ball	184
6.14	Régie Strikers	186
6.15	Tünel Car Construction	187
7.1	Consigning the Nişan Defters to the Museum	196
7.2	"Which Alphabet Do You Prefer?"	197
7.3	Alafranga Couple	204
7.4	Burhan üd-Din the Actor	208
7.5	Fraternité	211
7.6	"The Naked Woman"	212
7.7	Going Skating	215
7.8	Getting It Right	217
8.1	Straight from Paris to Anatolia	229
8.2	Imported Corsets	231
8.3	Conspicuous Consumption	233
8.4	Young Turk at Marienbad	234
8.5	Gift for the Harem	236
8.6	Crete and Her Protectors	238
8.7	Dirty Old Man Austria	240
8.8	Liberty and Despotism	242
8.9	Breaking Her Chains	244
8.10	The Mother Nation	246
8.11	Women's World Bureau	251
8.12	The Balance of Chastity	254
8.13	Uniform Sale	256
9.1	Istanbul Fifty Years Later	260
9.2	Petitioning Against Their Eradication	265

9.3	Police Academy	269
9.4	Pursuing a Thief	270
9.5	Safety in the Streets	272
9.6	The "Look" of Cholera	279
9.7	Old Era and New	280
9.8	Gift of Czar Nicholas	282
9.9	Austria as Cholera	283
9.10	Cholera and the Lady	284
9.11	A Play in Two Acts: Act I, Stricken	285
9.12	A Play in Two Acts: Act II, The Delivery	286
10.1	Abd ül-Hamid and the Airplane	291
10.2	The Sultan's Planned Modes of Escape	292
10.3	Turtle-Pulled Tram	295
10.4	Doubling the Population	297
10.5	Broken-Down Auto	299
10.6	The Vezirs' Dirigibles	306
10.7	Circumventing the Empire's Bad Roads	307
10.8	"Rain" from a Plane	309
10.9	Phone Wire War Zone	310
10.10	Telling Time	312

Acknowledgments

The idea for this book came not from persons, or at least not from persons alive, but from cartoons. Their power and humor survived the years (which claimed their often anonymous authors) and the changes that have transformed the Istanbul streets that, often enough, were their setting. The creation of this book, however, was greatly facilitated by the assistance of colleagues, family, and friends. My first debt is to Bruce Craig and Mark Stein, friends who provided materials, advice, and encouragement. My second debt is to the Bunting Institute which provided those things that Virginia Woolf long since deemed necessary, and more. The sisters who made up the '91–'92 Bunting community provided exercises in narrative, visualizing, analysis, and fellowship. The insight and imagination of their company can never be duplicated. Among them, I particularly wish to acknowledge Linda Eisenmann, Gabby Friedler, Alice Freidman, Karen Hansen, Jahan Kuhn, Florence Ladd, Katie Park, Liz Rosenblum, Susan Sibbet, and Connie Soja. Colleagues have provided me with many forms of assistance: references, discussion, insights, encouragement, a critical eye, a cartoon. For these tangible and intangible aids, I wish especially to thank Walter Andrews who has a great eye for weeding out theoretical confusions and non-sequitur thoughts, and Feroz Ahmad and Carter Findley for their generous and thoughtful readings. I also wish to thank Rifat Abou El-Hajj, Ginny Aksan, Bill Blair, Roderic Davison, Selim Deringil, Alice Diab, Elizabeth Frierson, Jim Gelvin, Müge Goçek, Sheila Katz, Hasan Kayalı, Sinan Kuneralp, Susan Miller, Chris Murphy, Afsaneh Najmabadi, Andras Riedlmayer, and Mohamad Tavakoli. Rob Williams and Jessica Jones provided research assistance. I was influenced by the experimentation on frameworks for Ottoman historiography in the works of Şerif Mardin and Zeyneb Çelik. I wish to acknowledge the Atatürk Kütüphanesi and the University of Chicago Library for the use of their wonderful collections. The Institute of Turkish Studies, Washington D.C., provided generous funding for figures. The University of Tennessee Department of History, and the Exhibit, Performance, and Publication Expense Fund of the U.T.K. Office of Research also provided generous support. Thanks to Joe Rader and Hua Li of the University of Tennessee Archive for the production of the digitally scanned images used in this work. Finally, I am grateful for the love and support of my family,

Acknowledgments

the forbearance and considerable assistance of my husband James Fitzgerald, and the cheery smile of my daughter Rachele Brummett.

Earlier versions of parts of this work have appeared in the *International Journal of Middle East Studies* (November 1995) and *Princeton Papers* (Spring/Summer 1997).

Like all historians, I am engaged in a project that is both recollective and inventive. I submit this combination of ideas and images in the hopes that others will reconceive my imaginings and loose or retie my knots. May you read it with the good humor and audacity of Karagöz and with the conjurer's eye of Nekregû and Pişekâr. Any errors are the sole responsibility of the author.

Dating

Dating Ottoman serials requires the manipulation of a three tiered dating schema: *malî* (Ottoman fiscal year), *hicrî* (A.H.), *milâdî* (C.E., Gregorian calendar). The primary dating schema used on Ottoman serials is the Ottoman *malî* fiscal year, ubiquitous in the periodical press and based on, "The Hijra era overlaid on a Julian Old Style calendar, with some peculiarities deriving from its adaptation for the Ottoman environment."* This schema presents a series of problems for dating and for identifying Ottoman serials. First, references, citations, and library cataloging have often misidentified *malî* periodical dating as *hicrî*, creating a two and sometimes three year mistranslation into C.E. dating. Second, some gazettes include both a *malî* and a *milâdî* date. Such a dual dating scheme might, for example, provide the following dates: 11 Ağustos 1324 (*malî*) / 24 August 1908 (*milâdî*); or 20 Haziran 1324 / 3 July 1908. There is a standard date divergence of thirteen days, with the *milâdî* calendar date thirteen days later than the *malî* calendar date. Unfortunately, every gazette was not always scrupulous about the thirteen day difference and so one will occasionally find an issue marked with a twelve or fourteen day difference between the *malî* and *milâdî* dates.

Another dilemma with the use of the *malî* year on periodicals for translation into C.E. dating is the question of when the year changes. On late Ottoman periodicals, the *malî* calendar year ordinarily changed in late Şubat (February) or early Mart (March). But, in some cases, the year listed on a given publication might not change until April or even May. This could result, for example, in an issue with the date Nisan 1324 (apparently published before the constitutional revolution and equivalent to April 1908 C.E.), which was actually published in April 1909, after the counter-revolution. It is important to remember in Ottoman periodical dating that translations from standard dating tables will not necessarily work to provide exact date equivalents; and dates of individual issues must be scrutinized and compared to contents in order to check for errors and to ascertain the

---

*Richard B. Rose, "The Ottoman Fiscal Calendar," *Middle East Studies Association Bulletin* 25, no. 2 (1991): 159, 157–167. In Ottoman publishing, the dating confusion which Rose notes from 1916 (162) applies to the earlier years of the century as well. See also Niyazi Berkes, *The Development of Secularism in Turkey* (Montreal: McGill University Press, 1964), 421–422, who notes that the malî calendar was devised in 1790, or 1205 A.H.

dating and year change systems in use for that particular periodical. [For a major dating schema that includes *malî* year, see Faik Reşit Unat, *Hicrî Tarihleri Miladî Tarihe Çevirme Kılavuzu* (Ankara: T.T.K. Basımevi, 1984).]

I have indicated the *malî* and C.E. dates (separated by a slash /) for the periodicals cited here. On the rare occasions when *hicrî* dates are used, I have included them. When the exact date of a periodical is in question (usually because covers of the issue have been removed), I have estimated the date and enclosed it in brackets [ ]. Some periodicals were published with continuous numbering, not restarting the pagination from page one with each new issue. In those cases, when the date of the individual issue is unclear, I have indicated the full range of publication dates for that title (e.g., March to October 1908).

On Translating Cartoons

The work of translation requires art, knowledge, and the realization that the act of translation itself transforms indelibly. In attempting to translate Ottoman cartoons into English, I have struggled with all three of those requirements. Sometimes the very topical nature of the cartoon message, combined with my imperfect knowledge of Ottoman affairs, has caused me to throw up my hands and say, "What exactly is going on here?" Sometimes I have decided not to include cartoons because they were, for me, incomprehensible. In those cartoons which I have included, I have surely missed some of the multiple framings of message, text, and image. Or, the rich, evolutionary characteristics of the Ottoman Turkish language may have been communicated only dimly in the translation, some evocations captured, others missed. I have attempted to translate the captions here as literally as possible. I have not tried to duplicate rhyming prose and, hence, the English captions are often less artful than the originals. Cartoon captions, however, lend themselves to the use of expressions, verse, slogans, and vulgarisms more than do other forms of narrative prose. Therefore, where slang or expressions were used, I have often been somewhat less literal, attempting to transmit that expressionistic nature of the caption. Sometimes a nearly equivalent expression in English serves better than a very literal translation from the Ottoman, which may end up sounding like pidgin English. Where some element of the caption was particularly problematic, I have indicated it in the footnotes. In every case, where captions were given in Ottoman and in French (or in some other language), I have translated the Ottoman caption. The French versions are often significantly different.

A Note on Transliteration

There is no single standard for transliterating Ottoman Turkish. Ottomanist scholarship has employed a wide variety of systems for rendering the Ottoman into languages written in the Latin script. Decisions on transliteration have also been influenced by nationalist ideological positions that wish to privilege certain forms as more or less "Turkish" (or more or less "Arabic") than others. The transliteration system I have employed here is an attempt to preserve to a certain extent some of the distinctiveness of the Ottoman Turkish. It is based primarily on that found in the Redhouse dictionaries: James W. Redhouse, *A Turkish and English Lexicon* (Beirut: Librairie du Liban, 1974, reprint from 1890 edition); and *Redhouse Yeni Türkçe-İngilizce Sözlük* (İstanbul: Redhouse Press, 1968). This system results in transliterations which approximate but do not always duplicate modern Turkish usage. I have preserved, for example, breaks in the script words that are not preserved in modern Turkish. Names (Abd ül-Hamid rather than Abdülhamid) are sometimes slightly different from current modern Turkish configurations. Also, Ottoman Turkish, unlike much of modern Turkish, often does not conform to vowel harmony, and my transliterations will reflect that difference (preferring a romanization of the letter to its transformation to produce exact vowel harmony). On a somewhat different note, I have utilized the English versions of certain words that have become Anglicized (e.g., pasha, rather than paşa) except where they appear in direct citations. Similarly, for the cities Izmir and Istanbul, I have used the dotted capital *I* only in citations.

I
Introduction

*Hacivat: Hey, have you seen what the papers are writing, now that the age of freedom (*hürriyet*) has begun?*
Karagöz: They write and talk about everything, everything that's going on, in sum, they are continually spouting off on everything, from start to finish, from old to new, from sweet to salty, Hacivat Baba!
Karagöz: Again and again, a lot of gazettes have come out. Thus, we are immersed [up to our asses] in our gazettes. The age of freedom for us has indeed been bountiful. . . .
—[Dialogue in the gazette *Hacivat*,
one month after the revolution][1]

HISTORICAL BACKGROUND

In July 1908, a relatively bloodless revolution toppled the notorious autocrat Sultan Abd ül-Hamid, effectively ending his thirty-two-year reign and nearly five centuries of Ottoman monarchical rule in Istanbul. The gag of censorship fell, and the voice of the Ottoman press echoed throughout the sultan's dominions and thence to the capitals of Europe. The revolution in thought that had precipitated the revolution of arms at last found its way into print. It had not always been so. When Abd ül-Hamid, heir to the conquerors of Constantinople and Cairo, ascended the throne in 1876, the Ottoman empire had surrendered much of its past glory, and some of its territory, to the ascendant military powers of Europe. The Ottoman lands still stretched from the Balkans to Arabia and included the holy cities of Mecca, Medina, and Jerusalem. But the empire was nearly bankrupt. European trading partners benefited from favored nation trade status under a capitulatory regime which debilitated the economy of the once prosperous Ottoman state. The Ottoman Public Debt was established in 1881, under French direction, to administer directly the meeting of payments for the enormous Ottoman foreign debt. European and American entrepreneurs had invaded the empire developing German-owned railroads, building

British-owned textile mills, and setting up Singer sewing machine dealerships. Britain and France were locked in a conflict, from which Britian would emerge the victor, to see which would annex the sultan's Egyptian territory. Bosnia and Herzegovina were occupied by Austria, Cyprus (in 1878) and Egypt (in 1882) by Britain, and Tunis by France. Russia declared war the year after Abd ül-Hamid's accession, invading eastern Anatolia and also advancing troops to within ten miles of Istanbul. In the aftermath of this conflict, the Ottomans were forced to recognize the independence of Rumania, Serbia, and Montenegro and to pay a 300 million ruble indemnity to Russia.

In this context of heightened foreign domination and intervention, Abd ül-Hamid (ruled 1876–1909) was brought to power by the fledgling Ottoman constitutionalists who deposed his predecessor and wrote for the empire a constitution based on a Belgian model. But constitutional government was not destined to become a nineteenth-century Ottoman phenomenon. Once Abd ül-Hamid consolidated his power, he dissolved the newly installed Ottoman parliament after less than two years, banished and imprisoned his detractors, and established one of the most elaborate spy systems in the history of the monarchy. His reign, progressive in some areas, was considered synonymous with political repression and censorship of the press. Espousing Pan-Islam in an attempt to bolster his political legitimacy as successor to the caliphs, the sultan instead found his legitimacy challenged by a growing array of opponents who characterized his regime with the word *istibdad* (despotism).

Many frustrated constitutionalists were exiled or became voluntary expatriates. Some among their number founded the Committee for Union and Progress (CUP) or *İttihad ve Terakki Cemiyeti,* in 1889. The success of CUP recruiting, especially among military officers, eventually brought about the army revolt that precipitated the constitutional revolution of 1908. The CUP's program was based roughly on Ottomanism (the preservation of the empire and an attempt to create unity around the symbols provided by the Ottoman dynasty), opposition to foreign intervention, and the reinstatement of the constitution.[2] In July 1908, Abd ül-Hamid agreed, under military pressure, to reinstate the constitution. That fall, a Chamber of Deputies was elected and, in December, met, electing Ahmet Rıza (editor of the expatriate CUP gazette *Meşveret*) as Chairman of the Chamber.[3] The revolutionary regime was immediately faced with serious challenges to the sovereignty of the Ottoman state. Capitalizing on the period of interregnum following the the revolution, Bulgaria proclaimed its independence and Austria annexed Bosnia and Herzegovina. When certain elements from the military, the palace, and the religious establishment cooperated in an abortive counter-revolution in April 1909, Abd ül-Hamid was deposed and Mehmet V Reşad was installed as sultan. Although Ottoman sultans would

Introduction

remain titular heads of the empire until the aftermath of World War I, never after Abd ül-Hamid would they again wield sovereign power. That passed to the cadre of military and civil bureaucrats who brought about the 1908 revolution.[4]

The Revolution, Censorship, and the Press

In the European press, responses to the Ottoman revolution ranged from reserved to enthusiastic. Some observers were skeptical, others equated Ottoman constitutionalism with Western-style enlightenment, and took credit for setting the example.[5] The Ottoman language press, however, was not content to view the proposed demise of sultanic power as equivalent to the march of progress. Its reticence is not surprising. The year following the July 1908 revolution was an interregnum both in terms of freedom of the press and in terms of the functioning of a new Ottoman regime. The limits of both had yet to be tested. The Ottoman press, as noted by the shadow puppet characters Karagöz and Hacivat, had a field day after the revolution, and nowhere were the critiques of revolution, of imperialism, and of culture more pointed than in the satirical gazettes. For Ottoman journalists, 1908 was a year of euphoria and of disillusionment. In the satirical press, this ambiguity resulted in the crafting of an Ottoman "reality" which did not duplicate the "reality" reflected in the pages of the serious (non-satirical) press. Satire was already a well-established genre in the Ottoman literary tradition; but after the revolution, a public print version of these satiric traditions was allowed to flourish. Ottoman revolutionary cartoons synthesized a variety of Asian and European satiric styles in image and narrative. Using cartoons, satirists created an Ottoman cartoon space where the crisis of the revolution could be played out, where the merging of the real and the imagined was natural and inevitable. If human folly is the object of satire, then revolution, perhaps, is the perfect vehicle for the satirical voice. Revolution is the exchange of the old familiar follies for unknown and untested follies. In the Ottoman satirical gazettes (*mizah mecmuaları*) we find the suspicion that practicing constitutional government might not be as easy as imagining it—that the new follies might be just as bad as the old. Thus, when the revolution launched a two-year period of journalistic license unprecedented in Ottoman history, satirists targeted the new constitutional government as well as the old autocratic regime. They also suggested that the revolution would facilitate a European annexation of the Ottoman intellect and identity through cultural imperialism.

The revolution allowed for an immediate boom in Ottoman serial publication. This "democratization of the printed word" was similar to or perhaps even more dramatic than that which accompanied the French revolution.[6] Under Sultan Abd ül-Hamid, publishing had been tightly controlled rather than completely suppressed. The Ottoman official yearbook for 1908 lists ninety-seven publishers active in Istanbul and that list is not

Introduction

complete.[7] Another source compares the approximately 103 Turkish language gazettes published in the twenty-eight years between 1879 and 1907 with 240 new gazettes published in a single year immediately following the revolution.[8] While the new government struggled with the logistics of electing deputies for the assembly (*meclis*), the press mobilized to ensure that its newfound license would not be rescinded. It went to work challenging the primary symbol of autocracy, the sultan, and the concrete manifestation of his oppressive regime, the Press Law.

This law required government authorization for all publications, in whatever language, either through the Ministry of Public Instruction (for Ottoman applicants) or through the Foreign Ministry (for foreigners). A copy of each issue of every periodical had to be sent to the Press Bureau which had been established in 1862. By 1908 the Domestic Press Bureau included a director with five assistants, five examining clerks, more than a dozen inspectors (responsible for the supervision of newspapers, printing establishments, and theaters), plus clerks and secretaries.[9] Acts (or rather words) of aggression, compromising the security of the state, outraging public morals, customs, or one of the empire's religions, or offending the sultan, his family, government officials, or Ottoman allies were offenses punishable with fines, imprisonment, and suspension of the publication.[10] Theatrical performances were also censored with performers forbidden the use of certain words, such as *sultan*. When a European gazette published a caricature of Abd ül-Hamid as a lobster, the word *lobster* was also banned from performances.[11]

Censorship, although never more than partially successful, was a standard of life and of communication in Abd ül-Hamid's realm; similar conditions characterized the regimes of counterpart autocracies such as that of the Shah of Iran.[12] Abd ül-Hamid had ordered that no mention of his own health or family could be made in the Ottoman press, and all references to foreign affairs were carefully edited. As one foreign resident of Istanbul noted in 1903:

> The Turkish Press Censor confiscates all European journals containing references to the internal affairs of Turkey, or her relations with the Powers, and prohibits the publication in the native Press of any news of practical importance to the Turkish public. And it is only, therefore, by intercourse with European acquaintances, who receive their correspondence and newspapers through the medium of the foreign post offices—English, French and Austrian—that an intelligent Turk is enabled to obtain a knowledge of current political events.[13]

Abd ül-Hamid's press control measures included the periodic seizure of issues that reported on affairs that might show the regime in a bad light.[14] He also banished those who were thought to have inspired unfavorable comments in the press and pressured his officials and ministers to limit what was printed. The sultan accused the press of "leading public opinion astray."[15] Abd ül-Hamid and his opponents were thus agreed that public opinion constituted an important locus of struggle. Monarch and gazette each attempted to capture and hold that terrain.

Under the dual pressures of despotism (*istibdad*) and of European cultural and economic penetration, the press gained the potential to become an instrument that would define a new political and social order. Censorship restrained this potential, but the revolution loosed the penmen of Istanbul and gave them a public forum.[16] The press then addressed both the anxieties created by the disestablishment of the old regime and the underlying forces and conditions that had produced the revolution in the first place: the lack of political and social freedom, the debilitated economy, the obsolete military, the perceived corruption of officials at all levels of the government, the dearth of opportunity for a new class of Western-educated bureaucrats, the prostitution of the Ottoman economy to European economic interests, and the cultural schizophrenia created by Ottoman reform programs and by European dominance.[17] These themes were neither novel nor unique to the post-revolutionary era; they had been the subject of considerable debate in Ottoman political and literary circles for some time. What was new in this era was the opportunity to explore such issues more widely, more freely, and more vigorously. Once the revolution took place, the resurrection of the press, at least temporarily, was not to be denied.[18]

Numerous cartoons portrayed the unshackled press emerging as a vigorous agent of literary and political action. *Alem*, for example, showed the Ottoman gazettes in the form of a lion, labeled "Protector of Freedom" [Figure 1.1]. He was tearing at a register labeled "new publishing regulations (*yeni matbuat nizamnamesi*).[19] Where nineteenth-century French satire had used scissors as the quintessential symbol of press censorship, the Ottoman cartoonists used tombstones, coffins, and images of resurrection to characterize their release from the Hamidian censor.[20] They also depicted funerals and burials for gazettes that closed down. Some examples of such cartoons are *Davul*'s frame showing a funeral for the gazette *Demet* (Bouquet) a women's magazine that "expired" after only seven issues [Figure 1.2]; and *Kalem*'s image of the censor as a (vampire) skeleton emerging from its coffin [Figure 1.3]. In this latter cartoon, the Press Law is used as a lever to pry off the coffin's lid.[21]

The sultan, the meclis, and the European powers received the lion's share of barbs in revolutionary satire. Abd ül-Hamid was much more than a symbol of dynastic rule. He was a crass reminder of the tenuous nature of constitutional government. In the nine months before he was deposed in April 1909, he was the object of persistent and virulent attacks in the press. Cartoon images of the sultan ranged from that of a spoiled child to bloody murderer to traitor. Nor was the symbol of a new age in Ottoman government, the meclis, free from satirical critique. After all, why should the press expect miracles from a hodge-podge of untried deputies whose potential

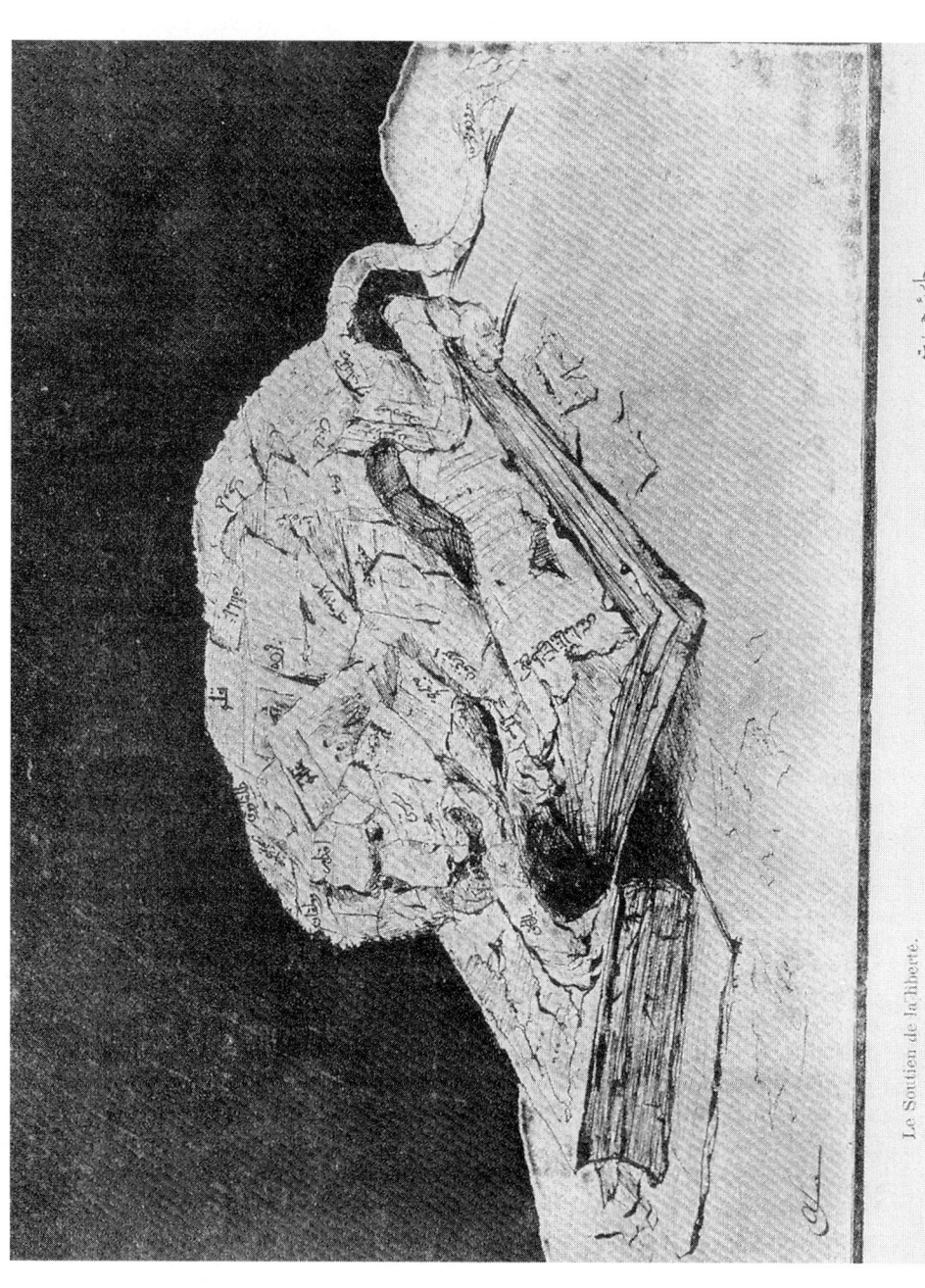

Figure 1.1 The Press as Protector of Freedom

La funérailles de Démet.

Figure 1.2 "Funeral" for a Gazette

Figure 1.3 Loosing the Censor

Introduction

for warding off European territorial aggression was seriously in doubt? While the journal *Musavver Muhit* printed pictures and laudatory mini-biographies of the newly elected meclis members ("our deputies"), the satirical gazette *Davul (Drum)* portrayed them as cocks fighting while the hawks of Europe swooped down to steal the chickens from the barnyard.[22] In lieu of idealistic declarations of unqualified support for constitutional government, *Kalem* revealed a vision of revolutionary chaos and parliamentary malaise: an inept, corrupt, or hopelessly fragmented parliament wasting time while foreign enemies devoured the empire.

This is not to say that satirical journals opposed the implementation of constitutional government. Their own existence, like that of the meclis, was a function of the revolution. Satire, however, admitted a skepticism prompted by the grim realities of the external Ottoman political situation. The critique of the meclis centered on the inability of the government to counter the aggressions of the European powers. Parliamentary government in Istanbul signified territorial expansion for Austria-Hungary, Bulgaria, Russia, and Britian. This opportunism, and the inability of an Ottoman government that was in the process of formation to stop it, was the third major target of Ottoman satire after the sultan and the meclis. In many gazettes, social satire (ranging from critiques of fashion to lampoons of disease control and working conditions) also shared space with attacks on government. Here too, European imperialism or influence, which affected economic conditions and dictated fashion, was perceived to play an essential role in the articulation of a new Ottoman social order.

For some, freedom of the press symbolized the new era of freedom from despotism that the revolution was supposed to engender. For others, freedom of the press represented license that would ultimately undermine Ottoman state and society.[23] Fear of the power of the press led to the destruction of the offices of the pro-Unionist gazettes *Tanin* and *Şurayı Ümmet* during the abortive counter-revolution of April 13, 1909, and to the assassinations of Hasan Fehmi, editor of *Serbesti* (March 6, 1909), and Ahmet Samim, writer for *Sada-i Millet* (June 1910). In the aftermath of the counter-revolution, the daily Islamic gazette *Volkan* was shut down and its editor, Derviş Vahdeti, executed for sedition.[24] Other gazettes were also suppressed and a new press law implemented that summer of 1909. Vigorous political satire continued after the counter-revolution was put down, but press censorship resumed as the CUP struggled to dominate the government and as the Ottoman state suffered a series of defeats in the Balkan and North African wars, which ultimately culminated in the empire's dismemberment in World War I.[25] In any case, the period 1908 to 1911 was unique in Ottoman publishing. It provides a window on the maelstrom of Ottoman thought just when survival and imagination hung in the balance, and when untried revolutionary options poured forth from the pens of Istanbul journalists, only to be reworked in the cartoon space by Ottoman satirists.

Introduction

METHOD

This work analyzes narrative and cartoon satire published in Ottoman language gazettes during the second Ottoman constitutional revolution. It focuses on the critiques of autocracy, of revolutionary idealism, and of European political and cultural hegemony in the period of transition from empire to nation-state. No book in English has been produced on the Ottoman press during the second constitutional revolution of 1908. Work in Turkish is limited to general studies (primarily on the prerevolutionary press), reference works, analyses of the expatriate press in Europe, and picture books on Ottoman cartoons. The exception here is the three volume work by Turgut Çeviker on caricature, *Gelişim Sürecinde Türk Karikatürü*.[26] The sophistication and sheer volume of the historiography generated on European states such as France, England, and Germany cannot yet be matched in Ottoman studies where the first catalog of the Istanbul periodical press was published only in 1986.[27] Scholarly energies on the press in revolutionary contexts have been devoted primarily to France. Major contributors in this area are Jack Censer with his quantitative study of the French radical press, *Prelude to Power: The Parisian Radical Press;* Roger Chartier with his exploration of the themes, uses, and logistics of press production and readership, *The Cultural Uses of Print in Early Modern France;* Richard Terdiman, *Discourse/Counter-Discourse: The Theory and Practice of Symbolic Resistance in Nineteenth Century France,* on a discourse model for the French press and satirical literature; Jeremy Popkin's work on the press, the market, and political ideology; and Robert Darnton with his various assessments of the sociology of press culture, authors, and writers.[28] Theoretical works not restricted to France that include the role of the press in constructing "national" identity and public consciousness, such as Jürgen Habermas, *The Structural Transformation of the Public Sphere: An Inquiry into a Category of Bourgeois Society,* and Eric Hobsbawm, *The Invention of Tradition,* are also useful for this project.[29] Though such works provide substantial methodological guidelines for scholars utilizing the abundant Ottoman periodical sources, they are not readily translatable in their entirety to the Asian or Ottoman milieu because their models are concerned with disparate time frames, are applied to comparatively homogenous populations, or lack the appropriate colonial context.[30]

I will argue that the Ottoman revolution took place in colonial context and, thus, comparisons located in India, Mexico, and Brazil may prove more useful for analyzing the Ottoman revolution than those based on Britian or France. In this regard, Benedict Anderson's *Imagined Communities* is a useful work because Anderson alters the boundaries and frameworks of historiographic analysis. He takes areas such as the Americas or Southeast Asia as starting points for analyzing the nature of late-nineteenth- and early-twentieth-century nation building, rather than presuming the centrality of western Europe. We Ottomanists have not yet learned to take the Ottoman empire itself as our starting point.

Introduction

Ottoman publishing was not comparable to contemporaneous French, English, or German publishing, either in scope of circulation of mass dailies and weeklies or in duration of press history. Press journalism came late to Istanbul. The first Ottoman Turkish language gazette was not launched until the early nineteenth century (1831). Even in the arena of imperialist critique, the Turkish language press was a latecomer compared, for example, to the Indian press.[31] India, with its century-long history of subjugation, had both the European infrastructure and the accumulated grievances to provide the format and (emotional) force for such a critical press. Further, the Ottoman press, at the time of the constitutional revolution was in a stage of development geared primarily to the articulation of political position rather than to profit, although the inclusion of advertising (in addition to announcements called *i'lan*) had begun by 1908 to reflect a more market-based orientation. Ottoman revolutionary gazettes, in narrative and cartoon, tended to reflect the political orientations, skepticism, and idealism of the editors and publishers. They were financial liabilities more often than sources of profit for their investors.[32]

Although, in 1908, the Ottoman press, like the eighteenth-century French press, was still in experimental stages of development and technology, world economic and political relations had changed drastically since 1789. By 1908, France was many stages removed from the "romantic," ideological vision of revolution, which it still personified in the symbolism of the Ottoman gazettes. The Ottoman press had to translate its own revolution into a context in which European imperialism already dictated the economic fortunes of the empire. A struggle between the three estates was not adequate to express or symbolize this revolutionary reality. The Istanbul press had to represent revolution in the context of empire reborn or empire dismembered, rather than simply selecting alternatives for defining the national identity. In 1908, the Ottoman press was still debating the desirability of European infrastructure while contrasting the glories of European empire with the memories of the Ottoman imperial past.[33]

European nation-state models of identity formation are also not readily translatable to the Ottoman case. A "citizen" Frenchman or Englishman (even if an imaginary one) was far easier to construct than the "citizen" Ottoman, who resided anywhere from Macedonia to Arabia. Scholarly debate over when and whether the discourse of nationalism became dominant in Ottoman territories obscures the complexity of the Ottoman situation. Identity, for the subjects of the Porte, was never merely a question of linking one's destiny to an Ottomanist or nationalist program. Nowhere has it ever been demonstrated that any but a few of the sultan's subjects ever identified themselves primarily as *Osmanlı* (Ottoman). At the height of Ottoman power, in the sixteenth century, the predominant identities for those resident within the empire were local identities. These identities of place outlived the displacement of one empire and the advent of another, and nationalist discourse called forth these local identities, as if newly born, at the end of the nineteenth century. In 1908 Istanbul, options perceived by the revolutionary press were not reducible to dichotomies of modern vs. traditional, monarchical vs. parliamentary, or ethnic-national vs. polyglot empire. Nor, despite the caliphal pretensions of sultan Abd ül-Hamid, was Islamic discourse represented as inextricably tied to the fortunes of the monarchy. Religious identity has always been hyper-emphasized by scholars dealing with the Ottoman empire, but in the cartoon space, religious and "national" identities were only two (albeit two highly significant) possibilities among many. Identities based on function, class, education, and locale represented the significance and continuity of group, family, and task above and beyond recognition of any specific nation, religion, or governmental form.

Unlike France or England, the Ottoman state experienced its revolution at a time when its political and cultural sovereignty were already irrevocably compromised by European hegemony. As Edmund Burke has noted (for India and Algeria): "Since European power was based on the local elites, this had a distorting impact on internal processes of change, working to undermine the legitimacy of collaborating groups and/or diverting social movements from their internal targets to the European rulers."[34] This distorting impact on processes of change applied also in the case of states, such as Iran and the Ottoman empire, which were not fully colonized. The Ottoman press's assessment of the form and content of the new domestic reality (government and society) was possible only with the admission that a primary alternative was no sovereignty at all. This colonial alternative might take the form of formal annexation of parts of the Ottoman empire or the more insidious forms of economic and cultural surrender. Further, this latter possibility was already well advanced and carried considerable weight in Ottoman literary circles by virtue of the European (especially French) language education of many Ottoman publishers and writers. Early in the twentieth century, European states, banks, concessionaires, and merchants already controlled much of the Ottoman economy. The question the Ottoman press was forced to address was whether these same outsiders controlled or would control the Ottoman territory and intellect. This preoccupation with foreign dominance shifted emphasis, in Ottoman revolutionary satire, away from possible internal targets, such as the elite ulema, and muted attacks on the new government.

The revolution took place at the end of a uniquely long period of dynastic rule, in a very cosmopolitan capital. Ottoman society possessed a memory of imperial grandeur that linked, in that same capital, the twentieth to the fifteenth century. At the same time, it was afflicted by the experience of watching the impetus to conquest pass to others who now dominated the globe and the Ottomans themselves. Still a vast empire, the Ottoman state was subject to the colonial ambitions of these newly dominant powers. Yet, the presumption of colonial context does not mean that Ottoman revolutionary satire was a genre strictly of doom and skepticism. The revolution suggested many possibilities, from resurrection to morbidity.

Although Western imperialism was an important organizing principle in Ottoman revolutionary satire, representation of the West in satire was far from unidimensional. Representations were as multiple and complex as the long history of transactions and cultural exchange between the Ottoman domains and Europe. Only within that context of cultural, commercial, artistic, and intellectual exchange can these images and their production be understood. In 1908, "Europe" constituted a serious threat to the empire's survival. Western powers were militarily and economically dominant; but money and violence were only two of the most obvious forces operating in the intricate web of Euro-Asian relations. Others emerge, as will be demonstrated here, in the cartoon frames, serialized romances, and advertising pages of the Ottoman gazettes.

With the above circumstances in mind, I am addressing the Ottoman satirical press output as a measure of confrontation with European political and cultural hegemony. This study is informed by an approach that takes the colonial context as its basic premise. By colonial context I mean that although the Ottoman state was not directly conquered and "colonized" in the sense that India was colonized, its systems (education, communication, transport), economy, and culture had been colonized as surely as had those of India. I am not proposing, thereby, that the late Ottoman empire was essentially the same type of entity as colonized nations such as India or Brazil, for example. Each was "possessed" by Europe and resisted that possession in its own distinctive fashion. Rather, I wish to draw attention to the possiblities for comparison and to the complex position within the world system that the late Ottoman empire held. We have been too inclined to think of empire as empire and to believe that we know the nature and boundaries of the Ottoman state, its essential identity fixed somewhere in the time of Süleyman. But the empire was a dynamic entity, no more static in the early twentieth century than in the sixteenth.

My research focuses attention on the roles of two political cultures contending for hegemony in early-twentieth-century Istanbul, one dominated by the sultanate and one by the proponents of European-style constitutionalism, as expressed in the revolutionary press. At this time, the nature of the new political system was neither fully determined nor fully apparent. This study of the press reveals that the threat of European political and cultural hegemony restricted the commitment to a constitutional system of government. The suspense generated by the threat of Austrian, British, or even Russian invasion and by Ottoman military and financial weakness made many writers skeptical that a parliament could effectively replace the authority of the sultan. Nor can a simple dichotomy be drawn on the basis of dominant (sultanic) and counter (constitutional) discourses, with the constitutional position becoming dominant in the first year of the revolution.[35] Such a bipolar model, as suggested in Terdiman's study of nineteenth-century France, requires, at least, a third component, based on the colonial context of the Ottoman press.[36] Hence, I would propose a schematization of the discourses in the Ottoman revolutionary press drawn on, but not rigidly limited to these: dominant (sultanic) discourse, counter discourse (a range of alternatives resistant to sultanic order) and a third anti-imperialist option (a discourse that takes as its primary defining characteristic the consideration of the threat of submission to European hegemony in all its forms). The latter discourse overlaps and infects the oppositions of the dominant and counter discourses such that, for example, the constitutional discourse cannot be assumed to represent a single philosophy of political and social order, the success of which is gauged by its approximation to European constructs. Further, the contention for the symbolic repertoire, in images and narrative, cannot be reduced to the challenge of a single "modern and progressive" counter discourse to the apparently traditional, inert, and reactionary dominant discourse's monopolizing of legitimizing symbols. The creation, appropriation, allocation, and use of symbols is not readily divisible into two such mutually exclusive realms of ancient and modern in the Ottoman cartoon space where the anti-imperialist discourse intrudes upon and distorts the selection of symbols.

David Laitin's *Hegemony and Culture: Politics and Religious Change among the Yoruba,* has factored the colonial context into an assessment of the allocation of symbols and its relation to religious and political identities.[37] Laitin developed a modified version of Antonio Gramsci's concept of hegemony to address the inadequacies of social systems and rational-choice theory.[38] He argues that hegemonic power is not completely free to forge identities. Rather it must have a real basis in the symbolic repertoire of the society. Challenges to hegemonic power must attempt to delegitimize what their own society sees as obviously and eternally legitimate. The "political culture" of a society can be thought of as a function of the "points of concern" embedded in the dominant cultural subsystem.

It is exactly these "points of concern" that are captured in the Ottoman satirical press. In the cartoon, symbols were contested and created. Ottoman satirists during the revolution expressed the confusion of competing symbolic repertoires (European, "traditional," recombinant) in realms of sovereignty, fashion, thought, education, manners, bureaucracy, and technology. This study approaches Ottoman "points of concern" and style of presentation, in both narrative and images, through focusing on the satirical press. Satire concentrated specifically on the concerns, threats, and fears afflicting Istanbul rather than magnifying the euphoria and hopes prevalent in the immediate aftermath of the revolution, as did much of the non-satirical press. Satirical images (cartoons) represented these concerns in immediate and dramatic ways.[39]

During the revolution, the hegemonic (or dominant) subsystem, in this case based on the authority of the Ottoman sultanate, was in the process

Introduction

of being disestablished. The press attempted to articulate and to shape a sense of the spectrum of political and social possibility. In this attempt, Ottoman writers sought tangible examples to represent and predict the unseen Ottoman future. France and Iran became these predictors, revolutionary exemplars manipulated in the Istanbul press to represent the poles of advantage and humiliation possible in the aftermath of revolution. The French revolution provided an ideal of the vision of progressive political transformation resulting in "*Liberté, Fraternité, Égalité.*" The Iranian revolution of 1905–1906 posed the specter of disastrous territorial losses to European imperial powers and of the reassertion of despotic kingship as under Muhammad Ali Shah, (a scenario that would be reenacted under the Pahlavis). India and Japan were also employed as Ottoman alter egos: India representing the culmination of the colonial experience and Japan representing the "modern" Asian state with the military capacity to whip a "European" bully, the old Ottoman nemesis, Russia.[40]

The revolutionary press also distilled the struggle for cultural hegemony into images of dress where France was, again, an exemplar. Fashion satire provided a symbolic repertoire pitting "traditional" dress (representing alternately obsolescence and military incompetence, or security, honor, and the preservation of Ottoman identity) against French fashion (representing alternately modernity and a revolution in manners, or moral decay and European dominance). Technology was also an important area of contention in the Istanbul press, not, as has been suggested, because of religious opposition to innovation but because progress in the form of imported European technology was associated with the financial ruin of the state and with inefficiency and corruption in government.

The revolutionary Ottoman satirical press, unlike the French revolutionary press, did not generally adopt religion as a major target of criticism. While the new parliament came under varying degrees of attack, the press was often silent on the issue of organized religion. I suggest that this reticence was partly the result of the historical co-optation of the Islamic ulema by the Ottoman state, but mainly a result of the fear that the Ottoman social order was already sufficiently threatened by European cultural hegemony. As Şerif Mardin has pointed out, Islam was viewed as "social cement."[41] Islam was a vital element of Ottoman identity and political tradition. It could neither be dismissed nor subjected lightly to attack.[42] Rather than critique Islam outright, the press more often than not, challenged it indirectly by means of "enlightenment" science. It may be argued that the colonial context helped preserve Islam against attacks that it might otherwise have suffered in the changing political order. Yet, its omission as a primary target—and hence the existence of alternatives to an Islam/tradition/reaction vs. secular/progressive dichotomy—suggests that religion was only one among many determining factors in the articulation of revolutionary thought in the Ottoman satirical press. If this seems obvious, one need only take note of the historiographic language used to articulate

15

Introduction

the peoples and nations of the Middle East. Too much of scholarship on the Middle East and on Muslim majority areas relies on uncritical assumptions about religion as the driving force for political decision making and as the sole, definitive regulator of options for the construction of social identity.

Sources

The basic sources for this study are sixty-eight gazettes, published in Istanbul, with initial publication dates ranging from July 1908 to 1911. This was a crucial period during which the stringent censorship of Abd ül-Hamid was lifted, remained suspended through the election of the new parliament, and then again was gradually brought to bear on the press following the counter-revolution and imposition of martial law in April 1909, the deposition of the sultan, and the consolidation of CUP power. I include only the Istanbul Ottoman Turkish language press, thus omitting the provincial press, gazettes in other languages, the expatriate press, and the foreign-language press, all of which are important.[43] My focus on publications in the capital is both pragmatic (limiting the number and scope of the publications surveyed) and intentional (reflecting the political and cultural center of the empire where publication output was remarkably high, and avoiding provincial publications, which are less accessible and which might concentrate on local affairs or target separatist interests). I also take into consideration some of the genre predecessors of these revolutionary satires such as *Çıngıraklı Tatar, Kara Sinan,* and *Mizan* along with a few later gazettes.

Of the sixty-eight gazettes surveyed, thirty-six are entirely satirical. Another twelve either include some satire and cartoons, or include "*mizah*" as one of the major content areas in the subtitle. Nearly one-third contain no cartoons or satire (although even these may contain an occasional joke or humourous poem/story). Included are two non-satirical annuals (*salname*) and seven political daily papers. These two latter categories are not treated at all in depth; they do not truly fit the periodical classification of the other publications, but they are included to provide price and content contrast, to supplement the discussion based on the main periodicals, and to provide a link to other studies of the serious daily press. The other fifty-nine titles are gazettes (understood as periodical literature) published monthly (3), twice monthly (1), weekly (30), twice weekly (18), in single issue only/no frequency given on title page (6), and a gazette that called itself a daily but appeared roughly twice a week (1). Weekly and twice-weekly formats were easily the most common frequencies for satirical gazettes. But, frequency, as listed on the title page of these gazettes, was often a reflection of intent rather than publication schedule. *İştirak*, for example, though called a weekly, actually appeared approximately three times per month. The gazette *Perde*, which ran for eight issues, began as a twice weekly publication and shifted to a weekly format. Dailies in particular were subject to

Introduction

missed issues, but other periodicals, particularly those published in brief runs, were also subject to schedule irregularities.

The cartoon illustrations in this work are taken from a variety of gazettes, their selection determined in part by availability for reproduction. Most of the gazettes I surveyed were housed in the Atatürk Kütüphanesi in Istanbul and could not be photographed. A certain core of gazettes, because of their cartoon range and thematic focus, provide the bulk of examples herein. Cartoons from the gazette *Kalem* are disproportionately represented because it was accessible and because *Kalem* employed a wide variety of styles and cartoonists. Some of the most spectacular post-revolutionary cartoons are to be found in the gazette *Yeni geveze* but, unfortunately, I was unable to obtain a copy for duplication. Thus, the cartoon illustrations found in this work cannot be considered truly representative in the sense of providing examples of the entire range of the Ottoman press's cartoon production. They do, however, illustrate many of the styles and themes found in a whole range of satiric gazettes produced in Istanbul in the period in question. More importantly, each of the themes, targets, and ideas suggested in the cartoons here used were repeated in other gazettes of the period. Examples from gazettes that were not available for reproduction are either alluded to in the text or referenced in the endnotes. Many of the illustrations, here, are produced through digital scanning, a process that holds great promise both for preservation of rare materials and for capabilites of enhancing faded or damaged images.

Mizah Mecumaları (Satirical Gazettes)

The basic set used for analysis in this study is satire, particularly cartoon satire. Focus on satire allows the most skeptical and most flexible of a broad range of press perspectives to take center stage. In the Ottoman case (an example of Laitin's "incomplete hegemonies") the alternatives and symbols selected by the press required the utmost resilience against a background of the void. Satire provided a ready-made antidote to possible chaos and an already familiar set of symbols for resisting or recreating both inertia and change. I have purposefully not typed cartoons and satirists by political party because such a typology suggests an already understood and overly rigid demarcation of the cartoon space that does not really apply. The Istanbul press in 1908 was not really a party press, although there were party organs and cartoons that represented party positions. Political affiliation is not a negligible factor; but in a preliminary study such as this one, presenting a range of images available in the satirical press is, I think, more important than trying to force those images into rigid categories that carry with them their own interpretative baggage.

The term *mizah* was most commonly used to identify the Ottoman satirical gazettes. Often translated as *humor* or *joking, mizah,* in the context of the revolutionary press, is better translated as "satirical." *Mizah,* in all cases, assumes a component of political or social criticism. The terms "*latife*" (humorous anecdote, witticism) or "*eğlence*" (amusement) are occasionally found, identifying genre. These, however, may imply a lighter vein, often devoid of political criticism, they personify one type of the contemporary notion of a *humor* magazine.

The focus on satire, here, is intentional because this study is concerned with images, narrative and cartoon, which the revolution disbursed throughout Istanbul and beyond: picked up at publishing houses, delivered to the literate, passed hand to hand, and plastered on office walls. It is concerned with the jaundiced eye, which saw in revolution not solely the ideal-induced euphoria of freedom but the reality-induced skepticism of imperialist innovation and bureaucratic paralysis. This skepticism, taking its characteristic form in the dialogues of the shadow puppet character, Karagöz, and his cronies, found its visual counterpart in cartoons of the man on the street and his various nemeses: sultan, meclis, posturing European monarchs, and broken-down trams.[44] The cartoon mascots, or cartoon spokespersons, of these gazettes (*buffoon, destitute-*one, *conjurer*) were precisely chosen, for some buffoonery was required to wring humor out of the bankrupt empire, and no less than a conjurer seemed required to resurrect its honor and status.

The *mizah* gazettes voiced a rhetoric whose intent was not solely either instructional or political polemic, but a warding off of the pain of blows, anticipated and apparently unavoidable. These purveyors of skepticism are complemented in this study by samples of non-satirical gazettes—identified as *siyasi* (political), *edebi* (literary), *iktisadi* (economic), *ilmi* (religious or scientific). Their images reflect the variety of options in the currents of thought loosed into print, however briefly, in July of 1908. This study has consciously attempted to avoid taking the most well-known gazettes such as *Tanin, Sabah,* and *Tercüman-ı hakikat* as a unique or comprehensive standard of the press. Critics of this selection might note the failure to employ such major political dailies, arguing, perhaps with some justification, that such gazettes represent the best circulated and most popular currents of thought in Istanbul. But the most prominent and mainstream newspapers do not tell the whole story. I wish to direct attention to that part of the press that was more visual and in some ways, by virtue of the license provided by the cartoon, more skeptical. Arguably, the most popular and most circulated product of the Ottoman press was not the editorial, but the cartoon.

The Satiric Image

Cartoons are, by their very nature, designed to confound the dimensions of time, space, language, and perceived reality.[45] The effect of a cartoon is dependent both upon its invoking a perceived "reality" and upon its subsequently breaking the boundaries of that perception. That is, cartoons are expected to alter reality, radically or subtly, in ways which are both familiar and startling. To do so, cartoons employ tropes that are themselves caricatures of character, dress, aspect, setting, and situation. The cartoon mocks the attempt to bound signifier and signified; it serves as a mediator, for the viewer/reader, between chaos and culture, between the old and the new order. For each cartoon, the press fixed meaning as it stamped ink to paper. Then, as the cartoon passed from hand to hand, it evoked, from the recombinant languages and societies of Ottoman Istanbul, a series of responses, thoughts, and images, either anticipated or unanticipated.

It is difficult to assess the effects of a cartoon, to know what exactly it accomplished.[46] When a gazette is shut down because a particular cartoon or editorial is published, then a fairly (but only a fairly) direct cause and effect can be established. Otherwise, the response of an individual or group to the press's output is a function of a complex set of socio-cultural variables.[47] The editor can only calculate and try to manipulate the possible responses any cartoon symbol might evoke. The audience for any given cartoon may first be imagined, but then it is transformed again and again as the cartoon circulates, becomes the topic of discussion, and becomes distanced in time and space from its point of creation and the events or ideas that it depicts.

Charles Press, in his analysis of American political satire, has separated the elements of the cartoon into those that affect the intellect, the conscience, and the emotion: (1) *the picture of reality,* an attempt to demonstrate the essence of truth; (2) *the message,* a recommendation; (3) *the mood,* an indication of how the viewer should feel.[48] These elements are linked to the cartoons' content (characters, dress, setting, gesture), and derive from the cartoonists' (or publishers') loyalties, goals, and methods, or how they tell the viewer to look at something. Press focuses on the agency of the cartoonist and the political and social contexts of cartoon production. But, the symbols by which viewer responses are evoked, the alternatives for "reading" the cartoon, and the framing of the cartoon in the context of the gazette are also important material considerations in constructing the meaning of Ottoman satire.

In certain ways, Press's model of the function of cartoons mirrors Laitin's model of the interfaces between available symbols, people's points of concern, and their perceived options regarding how to address those concerns.[49] The cartoonist employs what Laitin would call the symbolic repertoire of the society in order to attack either the dominant discourse or one of the competing counter discourses.[50] The successful cartoon, using familiar symbols, creates a picture of reality with which its public can identify.[51] Then, through focusing on that particular society's "points of concern," the cartoon delivers its message and suggests an appropriate mood, with the ultimate objective of either challenging or affirming the dominant discourse.[52] If the chosen symbols are not familiar, if the chosen picture of reality does not capture the imagination of the public, then the cartoon fails and the message and mood recommendations are wasted. Ibn Khaldun made a similar point regarding another form of narrative, history. He argued that good, successful history was that which made sense, which constructed its story within the realm of possibility.[53] Historical evidence, like the cartoon's "picture of reality," and like the social identities that contending discourses attempt to construct, is limited by the symbolic repertoire that a given society can and will recognize.

Cartoons speak in the language of symbols—a sort of "something old, something new, something borrowed, something blue," as the old saying about a bride's garb goes. They do not have to be original, a quality which, in any case, is not a preeminent value in traditional Middle Eastern arts. As Giulio Argan has noted on the iconology of images:

> The image which is worn out, consumed, recited for the thousandth time, or deformed by the careless habit by which it has been adapted to the most varied occasions is often much more eloquent for the historian of the image than the scholarly, purified, controlled version which is established by the lucid structure of a formal system.[54]

The images of the satirical press were just such worn out, consumed, habitual images, adapted from many genres for many occasions. Their effect was based more on the familiarity than on the novelty of symbols. Nor did the symbolic repertoire of cartoons need necessarily to evoke responses that were conscious or spoken, on the part either of the cartoonist or of the reader/viewer. The symbols (the sultan's coat, a woman's veil), which might be so familiar that they seemed part of the scenery of the cartoon space, were still possessed of great power.[55]

Nor is there any rigid dichotomy between the symbols of the elite classes and "popular" symbols, or between "popular" culture and "high" culture.[56] The press under consideration in this study was a press produced by elites; but their symbolic repertoire was not a discretely elite one. The satiric press evolved out of Ottoman literary, artistic, and theatrical cultures. One is hard put to trace these cultures back to purely elite historical antecedents somewhere in an imagined past. Certainly, the images of Ottoman satire can never readily be assigned to categories based on a division between aristocrats and masses. Chartier is worth quoting at length on this subject because he staunchly and eloquently refrains from reductionist paradigms where culture is concerned:

> First and foremost, it no longer seems tenable to try to establish strict correspondences between cultural cleavages and social hierarchies, creating simplistic relationships between particular cultural objects or forms and specific social groups. On the contrary, it is necessary to recognize the fluid circulation and shared practices that cross social boundaries. . . . The materials that convey the practices and thought of ordinary people are always mixed, blending forms and themes, invention and tradition, literate culture and folklore.[57]

Introduction

Chartier rejects what he calls cultural history's "reductive definition of society, seen strictly in terms of the hierarchy of wealth and condition . . . popular culture is too simplistic—rather there are intricate mixtures of discipline and invention, revitalizations and innovations, models imposed . . . and freedoms preserved."[58] Ottoman cartoon culture reflects this mixed and dynamic model of Chartier's. It combines what historical analysts might label as elite, folk, mass, or popular cultural icons (in images, verse, songs, slogans), thus giving the lie to rigid assumptions about the elite nature of print culture. - nice point

Even the layout of a revolutionary gazette reflects the hodge-podge nature of its symbolic repertoire and presentational mode: part memory, part prediction of an uncertain future, part come-on. In each issue of a gazette, there is a layering (like that of the fossil record) of text, image, and meaning, within and around cartoon images. The cartoon may be embedded in the narrative, particularly if it is linked to an opening essay or dialogue on page one or two.[59] Often, however, the cartoon is detached from the surrounding print, its connections to the narrative left to the imagination of the reader. The captions, long, short, or translated into French, may add to, alter, or distort the visual meaning of the image. In gazettes that are not entirely satirical, the cartoons are often part of the appended matter: announcements, letters, and ads that are arranged after the primary content of the gazette (news, editorials, and essays). This appending suggests the secondary nature of humor or satire. In the satirical gazette, on the other hand, "serious" content such as news, editorials, essays, and even letters is subordinated to the satiric project, suggesting the essentially subversive nature of satire.[60]

Looking at Images

How does one read a revolution or look at revolutionary imagery almost a century after its printing? Press satire is, after all, a medium that depends upon an immediate understanding of day-to-day changes, the nuances of politics and the "in" jokes of the day. The simple answer to this question is that much is lost. We have no direct translation of the revolution; it is not immediately accessible. On the other hand, even the Ottoman reading public in 1908 did not know all the "in" jokes of the day. Thus, we become readers or viewers of Ottoman satire in a cohort of those once-removed, twice-removed, and so on, like cousins in a disbursed and large family. Narrative escapes the historian of satire more often than does image; language has been too radically altered or knowledge of historic interactions has been communicated in too scant or distorted a way. The language of cartoon captions or satiric dialogue can be obscure, complicated, bilingual, or highly sophisticated, even though satire often simplifies language in order to maximize its comprehending public. Satiric imagery, perhaps more so than dialogue, is essentially a mode of communication that flourishes

21

Introduction

when the message is direct, the impact immediate. Thus, the "picture" in Ottoman cartoons was often charged with evoking powerful images, memories, or reactions, without benefit of distracting or complicating narrative.

To assess these images, one must lay the Ottoman cartoon before a new set of viewers to see what effects it provokes. I can trace sets of symbols, or alterations in language; I can speculate on the meaning of images within certain better or lesser known political and social contexts. I cannot, for the most part, state what was the Ottoman editor's intent or what was the Ottoman viewer's interpretation. I cannot measure the effect of cartoons on the Ottoman public.[61] But I do not believe that the human experience is so disparate, from the beginning of the twentieth century to its end or from the Ottoman to the American empire, that it is impossible to "read" and give meaning to a ninety-year-old cartoon or indeed to that cartoon's public. This work is just such an exercise in presuming (or attempting to translate) meaning, an exploration in how and where and to what purposes satire worked.

The Ottoman historian is not a trained reader of pictures (although the Ottoman historian reads script as image, not only as text). Thus, this work is also an experiment, a struggle and, finally, an invitation to those who practice the decoding of images to direct their attentions to the Ottomans. The Ottoman revolutionary press was translating images and their symbolic content into a new medium, recasting those symbols and creating new ones. The forms taken by that translation process point up past traditional ways of looking at images (such as the shadow puppet theater). I am reappropriating those images and retranslating them. I began by thinking the images would tell me something about Ottoman politics, but I end by thinking that they tell something about imagination and cultural comparisons. Surveying the images in a wide range of satiric or partly satiric gazettes, I found that cartoon satire focused on certain targets and grouped itself along certain thematic lines. Two overarching themes tended to dominate the images. First, a preoccupation with the threat of European imperialism in its various forms. Second, an attempt to divide the Ottoman situation or condition into three paradoxes or polarizations; the empire and its citizens were represented as entrapped (or at least positioned) between (1) the old (*eski*) and the new (*yeni*), (2) the glory of revolution as embodied in the rather temporally distant French Revolution and the humiliation of revolution as embodied in the recent Iranian Revolution, and (3) the promise of freedom on the one hand and, on the other, the subordination to sultanic tyranny (*istibdad*) and European imperialism.

The compelling nature of these themes, repeated in many cartoons across various types of gazettes, determined the organization of materials in this work. The dichotomy between old and new runs throughout the chapters that follow the three introductory chapters on the revolution, the press, and its public. Chapter 4 focuses on the two revolutionary exemplars of France and Iran; the outcome of the former's revolution is represented as

Introduction

liberty and the outcome of the latter's as subordination to despotism and imperialism. Chapter 5 looks at the satiric critique of old and new forms of authority: the traditional sultanic order and the new parliamentary government. Chapters 6, 7, and 8 focus on the critique of European political, economic, and cultural hegemony and on the ways in which cartoons suggest that post-revolutionary Ottoman society was evolving in a European-dominated world order. Chapter 9 looks at the various menaces that satirists suggested were plaguing Ottoman society and the Istanbul streets. Chapter 10 analyzes representations of technological change and its role in social transformation, again with particular emphasis on European mediated innovations. Using the representations in chapters 4–10, which illuminate these themes and paradoxes, the final chapter contains some thoughts on issues that have intrigued historians of the late Ottoman period, the issues of identity, nationalism, and revolutionary ideology.

The cartoon images in the gazettes surveyed pushed me out of my original categories and classifications; but they have yet to teach me an ideal way to read images. Having established the organizational schema noted above, based on a surface reading of the cartoons, how further have I deciphered these images and to what purpose? I have examined the aspect, dress, settings, accessories, gender, ethnic indicators, and other identity typings of the characters in Ottoman cartoons, along with the juxtaposition (in the cartoon frame) of these characters to inanimate objects and to slogans and dialogue. These elements provide not only a parade of familiar and less familiar symbols, they provide the opportunity to speculate on the ways in which Ottoman gazettes envisioned and evaluated the past, present, and future of Ottoman society, and its connections to other societies. There is always the question of how deeply one can presume to read these pictures. This is a preliminary study. As such, it cannot begin to trace the multilayered history and evolution of individual symbols in Ottoman cartoons. I have attempted to identify some symbols and tropes in the Ottoman cartoon frame, and to group them thematically. The cartoon, in some ways, attempts to reduce society to its symbols. But these cartoons, I believe, demonstrate that those symbols are the result of a complex cultural synthesis; they function as part of an evolutionary process in which the press was participant. I have tried, then, to analyze the picture of reality, the message, and the mood that the selected cartoons suggest. My reading is one of many possible readings and, as such, it can be neither definitive nor authoritative. It, and the accompanying reproductions of Ottoman cartoons, are designed to emphasize the themes delineated above and to provoke alternative readings.

II

Publishing, Format, Images, and Readers

The Ottoman revolution, and the ensuing transition from autocracy to constitutional monarchy, provided the conditions for a unique period in Ottoman press history, a roughly two-year period during which censorship was initially nonexistent, and then limited. Editors and journalists responded with an outpouring of gazettes and pamphlets. Over two hundred new periodicals were published in Istanbul alone in the first year of the revolution. Of these, numerous examples were entirely satirical and others included satire among the themes identified in their mastheads. Satiric gazettes (*mizah mecmualan*) were published monthly, bi-monthly, weekly, or even daily, some surviving for years and others for only a few issues.[1] Their publishers were an eclectic group, often deriving from the well-educated class of men whose affairs included both literature and politics and who were, often but not always, literate in French. Writers in the Ottoman state had been imagining a new social and political order for some time, one that might dispense with kingship, explore new freedoms and, they hoped, survive the enmity of the various European states that were threatening to dismember the empire. Their satiric gazettes, in this period of minimal censorship, internal political turmoil, and maximum threat of foreign invasion became the voices of Ottoman anxiety. On this unstable ground they created a cartoon revolution.

My project is necessarily circumscribed by focusing on gazettes of a political and satirical nature. Print and cartoon images, although for a time unconstrained by state censorship in the Istanbul press, were subject to political, economic, and cultural limiters.[2] Their expression can shed light on certain conjunctures among press, public, and state in a period of crisis when the "natural" order of things had come irrevocably to be transformed and its immediate, let alone its final, shape remained undetermined. I cannot claim to answer the question of what exactly the journalists were thinking. The objective here is rather to present what areas of concern Ottoman satirists thought worthy of a public forum and what images, symbols, and narrative journalists used to attempt to alter the consciousness of the Ottoman government, people, outsiders, and themselves in order to prepare for and to dictate the direction of the political and cultural transformation of the empire. I see the press neither as merely reflective nor as strictly manipulative (there was after all a price to be paid for a gazette).

There is also the question of attempting to visualize society by analyzing print culture. The long-standing debate on the nature of the press as an "elite" source, particularly in a society where the bulk of the population is illiterate, has yet to be resolved. My own view is that strenuous efforts to differentiate elite and popular culture, and the accompanying turf battle for hegemony over the voice of the masses, diverts the historian from a task that is already highly representational. The press was not invented in an antiseptic environment comprising only the myths, symbols, material culture, and objectives of the wealthy and learned classes. Nor was it, particularly in satiric form, aimed only at converting, amusing, and selling those elites. Thus, the study of print culture, particularly in the form of images and especially in cartoon satire, reveals much about the nature of Ottoman society, both elite and popular.[3] The cartoon, the essence of which is to blur the boundaries between the real and the imagined, served to make the already porous boundaries between elite and popular even more fluid. Cartoons, especially, bridged the gap between literate and illiterate culture because cartoons (as quickly grasped and powerfully communicative visual fields) provided a common ground on which the ideologies and symbols of literate and illiterate were mingled. Some cartoons were absolutely incomprehensible without their captions; they relied on long and laborious captions paired with images that were dull or coincidental. But many cartoons relied on dramatic visual imagery, drawing on instincts and common symbols that relayed an immediate message wordlessly. Cartoons were freer, more mobile, than their constraining or complementary surrounding text; they were torn out, passed around, hung up, and posted in the streets.

That said, the satirical press neither advocated a classless society nor polarized society into elites and masses. Journalists in Istanbul, like those in revolutionary Paris, were a very important group of opinion makers; they were promulgating and reflecting ideology.[4] Yet the polarization between "people" and "*aristocratie*" that has been applied to the French revolutionary press was not duplicated in Istanbul.[5] Ottoman journalists attempted to construct political, economic, and cultural ideals, but these were not simplistically aligned by class alone. This study cannot demonstrate an Ottoman collective imagination. Rather it can show the ways in which individual gazettes used thematic appeals, such as innovation vs. regeneration, to construct or preserve shared national objectives and a notion of the Ottoman "citizen," without necessarily attempting to break down traditional social ranks. Some themes, such as the fear of foreign invasion or the dissatisfaction with transport systems, could be used to suggest a national unity. Journalists, for example, critiqued European technology, as a manifestation of European imperialism, for undermining the "people" and their cultural sense of wholeness as well as for disrupting their day-to-day lives. Ultimately, the foreign threat and "national" survival provided the primary mode in the satiric press for promoting the solidarity of Ottoman state and culture. Outside of that sphere of imminent danger, Ottoman society as portrayed by the *gazeteciler* (newspapermen) was a society fragmented along the lines of class, education, rank, religion, gender, and ethnicity. Command of many types of knowledge, science, and culture, in 1908, was not within the grasp of the everyday Ottoman. Instead, the journalists, those who did command knowledge and culture, placed within the grasp of their less enlightened brother and sister citizens newspaper satires of the ordering of their universe: past, present, and to come. Theirs was the freedom to determine wrongs, to disseminate doctrines and, through relatively uncensored narrative and cartoon, to reach a hitherto less reachable audience.

PUBLISHING AND PUBLISHERS

Of course, not everyone viewed the output of the revolutionary press as a project of enlightenment. In the eyes of some observers, satirists went too far. The freedom of the press that characterized the empire after the revolution seemed little more than journalistic license, enabling Ottoman writers and publishers to spread whatever scurrilous stories and pictures they pleased to the public. Some blamed this on the influence of the foreign press. Mark Sykes, a British officer traveling from Izmir to Bursa in 1909, noted the cartoons of an Ottoman official in the town of Balat: "I found a mudir sitting in a sarai with the most extraordinary political cartoons—among others one from a filthy Italian paper of H.I.M. [Abd ül-Hamid] drunk on the floor of his palace surrounded by the ladies of the harem."[6] Others lay the blame on irresponsible and vulgar Ottoman publishers and writers: "Everyone wrote whatever came to him. In these writings there was no discipline of thought or of spirit. In fact the names of some of the gazettes expressed this, for example '*Eşek* [Ass].' In no country that I know of is it possible to find in publications of quality such filth and commonness as in the caricatures published in *Eşek*."[7]

Freedom of the press was clearly not to everyone's taste. In revolutionary context, journalistic license could be seen as enfeebling the revolution and delegitimating the revolutionaries before the eyes of foreign observers. Such critiques of the press were echoed in Tehran as well as in Istanbul. A British observer, commenting on the Iranian revolutionary press at about the same time, expressed sentiments similar to those above:

> Meanwhile there arose in Tehran a Press that for unbridled license in the discussion of things and people could not have been rivalled. Vituperation was its strong point, and the heights attained in the abuse of the Shah, Government, parliament, politicians, rival publications and finally private individuals, were calculated to shame the Yellow Press of the most civilized countries.

Foreigners have from time to time said many hard things of Persians, but no outsider has ever said of them such unmerciful things as appeared daily in the Tehran papers. . . . But the Teheran papers and their many imitators in the provincial towns penetrated far into the country districts and were widely read.[8]

Ottoman publishers, like the observers above, were anxious to determine the proper place, voice, and function of journalism in revolutionary context. Striking in an examination of the Ottoman revolutionary press is the degree to which the press was self-conscious. The Ottoman journalists and publishers were their own audience, preoccupied with articulating, imagining, and debating the role of "The Press" in the Ottoman gazettes. A gazette carried on a dialogue with itself and its peers. This self-analysis took a variety of forms: humorous representations of journalists, serial essays on press history, critiques of the content of other gazettes, articles and editorials on the press and on its responsibilities and past and present failures, and borrowings (excerpts, cartoons or letters) from other gazettes.[9] There was no dilemma of copyright or qualms about imitation as evil as such in this literary form. The early-twentieth-century press was not so proprietary as it later became, and did not preclude the duplication of either narratives or images from the pages of competitors. This freedom allowed the gazettes to print serious and satiric dialogues featuring the positions of various journalists and gazettes; revolutionary journalism was a highly dialogic process, facilitated by the absense of copyright.

The press's dialogue functioned not only in space (an internal repartee among the literati and gazettes of the revolutionary era) but in time. That is, the satirists and satire of the revolution were not newly born out of the revoutionary situation. They carried on traditions of the prerevolutionary era press, but in freer and more elaborate forms. These traditions were borne, often, by the same men who published prerevolutionary gazettes, and other literary forms, both within and outside the empire. The noted author, Hüseyin Rahmi (Gürpınar), who published the novel *Şik* (Chic), which satirized the Westernized Ottoman, in 1887, began publication of the satirical *Boşboğaz* immediately after the revolution in 1908. One of that gazette's writers was the well-known author, Ahmed Rasim. Men who had produced opposition gazettes abroad before the revolution relocated their publishing activities to Istanbul. The gazette *Şurayı Ümmet* (1902–1910), for example, which began publication in Cairo and Paris, moved to Istanbul. Ahmed Rıza who published the CUP expatriate organ, *Meşveret*, in Paris, became the head of the new constitutional regime.[10] Mahmud Nedim, writer for the satirical *İncili çavuş*, also wrote for the single issue gazette *Adalet* (Justice), published in Paris about six months before the revolution. Mehmed Fazlı began publication of his satirical gazette, *Lâklâk*, in Cairo, then shifted to Istanbul a year after the revolution. Others shifted their activities to Istanbul from within the empire, launched new gazettes, or transformed old ones. Baha Tevfik, for example, was writing the gazette *İzmir* (published in Izmir) during the year before the revolution. He edited, also in Izmir, a single issue gazette called *11 Temmuz 1324* (24 July 1908) celebrating the revolution and, shortly thereafter, transferred his operations to Istanbul where he was editor of the satirical *Eşek* and active in the production of various post-revolutionary gazettes. Mehmed Rauf, one of the concessionaires of the classic prerevolutionary Istanbul satirical gazette *Hayal*, published a subsequent satirical paper called *Hayal-i cedid* from 1910 to 1911.[11]

The revolutionary press thus capitalized on the ideas, models, resources, and personnel of the prerevoutionary era to produce a striking flourescence of gazettes and of satire in 1908. Although statistics on the number of books and gazettes published in the empire, as already noted, can be highly variable and impressionistic, it is clear that the Ottoman publishing industry was gearing up in the latter half of the nineteenth century. Censorship, however, decisively limited what could be published, at least legally.[12] That is what changed so dramatically in 1908. The revolution and the constitutional regime that it promised and delivered brought to the literati and satirists of Istanbul the opportunity to run with the ball, so to speak, and they took full advantage. Teams of writers and editors were invented, reconfigured, and resurrected, as were "new" formats and an explosion of images.

The writers, editors, and publishers of the revolutionary press were a mixed group with varying political objectives. All were produced and formed in the context of the autocracy and censorship fostered by Abd ül-Hamid. All were influenced by the educational and cultural transformations, welcome or unwelcome, that were reconstructing the Ottoman intellectual space.[13] Their interpretations, urgings, and reactions to a new revolutionary political and social order, however, differed considerably. There follow a few brief biographies of penmen treated in this study, to illustrate the diversity of Ottoman journalists who, by the way, were not simply and only journalists as we have come to understand that term in conjunction with late-twentieth-century newspapers and television. I add a disclaimer that biographical information on Ottoman journalists, with the exception of certain men who were either prominent members of the literati or of the government (or both), is often difficult and sometimes impossible to assemble.[14] There is no compilation of journalists indicating their origins, schooling, occupations, and political service, and the history of Ottoman literary "officialdom" has yet to be written. As is illustrated in the biographical sketches found in Turgut Çeviker's work on caricature, such information comes piecemeal from biographies, memoirs, anecdotes, and encyclopediae.[15] I do not attempt biographies of the agents of satirical production in this work; but illustrations of the positions taken by editors and writers on various issues and of the internal dynamics of the Ottoman publishing industry are incorporated throughout the body of this study.

One well-known publisher was Celal Esad (Arseven), born in 1875 and the son of a pasha.[16] He was educated in the military and government service schools (Askeri Rüşdiye, Galatasaray Sultanısı, and Mülkiye-i Şahane) where he learned French. In 1908 he launched the satirical gazette *Kalem* (1908–1911), which catered to an audience conversant in both Ottoman and French. *Kalem* vigorously supported constitutionalism but reserved the right to criticize both the parliament and the dominant CUP (Committee for Union and Progress). Highly Europeanized in format, tone, and imagery, it was often critical of the effects of Europeanization on Ottoman society. The primary target of *Kalem*'s early issues was the sultan, portrayed as everything from a spoiled child to a butcher with his throne resting on a pile of skulls.[17] Esad remained a public servant into the Republican Period, holding a variety of posts in arts and education. He exemplifies the Ottoman publisher with a Westernized educaton, emerging from the Ottoman elite *askeri* (military/bureaucratic) class, whose career was tied to the success of the new constitutional regime. His partner Salah Cimcöz (1877–1947), also from a pasha family, was elected to the constitutional assembly in 1914.[18] Together Esad and Cimcöz wrote a play on the reformer, "Sultan Selim III," which was first staged in 1910.[19]

Some of the most striking cartoons found in the Ottoman revolutionary press were produced by an editor, Mehmet Fazlı, who drew his own cartoons. Little is known about his life or death. Apparently he studied drawing in Europe and was the brother of Mahmut Hakkı, head of the Mahmud Bey Publishing House.[20] He began publication of the gazette *Lâklâk* in Cairo, publishing five issues in 1907. After the Ottoman constitutional revolution, he published fourteen more issues under the same title in Istanbul. In addition to producing and illustrating his own gazette, Fazlı also penned many of the cartoons in the gazette *Püsküllü bela*, published weekly for seven issues before the counter-revolution in 1909. That same year he published *Resimli Afgan Seyahatnamesi*, an illustrated travel account. Fazlı is notable not only for combining the editorial and cartoonist tasks, but also for his particularly biting social satire.

One of the pioneering publishers of political satire in Istanbul was Kirkor Faik, who edited, managed, financed, and wrote for multiple gazettes in the years 1885 to 1914: *Geveze, Gülşen, Hazine-i fünun, Mecmua-i lisan, Musavver geveze, Musavver terakki, Perde*, and *Yeni geveze*. These gazettes, of different frequencies and types, covered the topics of satire, literature, science, history, and political affairs. Some were illustrated, one was a daily, and one, *Yeni geveze*, had a spectacular range of cartoons, perhaps unequalled in the constitutional period. Like other journalists of this time, Faik was involved in the production of several types of gazette simultaneously. He was a publisher of books and translations, as well as gazettes, and was associated with the Alem and Asır publishing houses.[21] Decorated by the sultan, Kirkor Faik is an example of a publisher who could survive and prosper both under the revolutionary and the prerevolutionary regimes.

Kıbrıslı Derviş Vahdeti, editor of the Islamic daily *Volkan* (Volcano), was a journalist of a different stripe.[22] Indeed Vahdeti was one of the popular targets for caricature in the satirical press. Born on Cyprus in 1870, Vahdeti had come to Istanbul as a young man for study in the *medrese* (Islamic university) system. Capitalizing on the suspension of censorship that coincided with the revolution, he used *Volkan* as an organ for political and religious criticism of the new regime and of Ottoman society. Apparently a real firebrand (judging by the response his critiques engendered), Vahdeti's campaign of religious reaction (or affirmation depending on one's point of view) was cut short when he was implicated in the abortive counter-revolution of 1909. *Volkan* was shut down after the issue of 21 April, 1909, and Vahdeti was imprisoned and executed. The significance of his career as a journalist lies in the fact that the revolution briefly allowed a cacaphony of different print voices to reach the Istanbul streets. The revolutionary press was not limited to representing the viewpoints of the CUP, nor, indeed, were even its most liberal organs unified in their vision of what Ottoman society should become. Neither before nor after the first year of the revolution could a periodical like *Volkan* be published, but for the duration of its brief run, it gave Vahdeti the power to communicate and to mobilize sectarian sentiments that neither the new government (once established) nor the more secular press could ignore.

Finally, there is the journalist Hüseyin Nazmi, who was associated with the publications *Afacan, Cadaloz, Çekirge, Eşref, Hale, Hande,* and *Musavver hale*. I single out Nazmi because he worked on some particularly scathing satirical gazettes, but also because I have been able to find out so little about him, despite the fact that he was very actively involved in publishing in Istanbul between 1909 and 1911.[23] Some men's names were included in the mastheads of gazettes primarily for their financial rather than journalistic contributions, but this does not appear to be entirely the case with Nazmi. In fact, most of those included on the mastheads of revolutionary gazettes, whether as *sahib* (concessionaire), *müdür* (manager/editor), or *muharrir* (writer/editor), were engaged in writing tasks as well as in other roles in the production of the gazette.

Publishers operated independently, in association, and as organs of various political parties. Clearly not every editor with a political or literary agenda could afford to finance a gazette alone.[24] Partnerships and associations could provide an editor with financial as well as political and intellectual support. An Ottoman publishing association (*Matbuat-ı Osmaniye Cemiyeti*) was founded in Istanbul shortly after the revolution. Its founding membership reflected the political association of the publishers, a committment to forming a constitutional regime, and the shared editorial interests of their gazettes. Charter members and their gazettes were Ahmed Cevdet Bey (*İkdam*), İsmail Hakkı Bey (*Tanin*), Pozant Efendi (*Pozantiyon*), Selanikli Tevfik Efendi (*Sabah*), Cenap Şehab üd-Din Bey (*Servet-i fünun*), Hüseyin Cahid Bey (*Yalçın*) (*Tanin*), Samih Bey (*İttifak*), Abdullah Zühtü Bey (*El*

Tiempo), Mahmud Sadîk Bey (*Servet-i fünun*), Murad Bey (*Mizan*), Mihran Efendi (*Sabah*), Nikolaidis Efendi (*Konstantinopolis*).

Yet many publishers were highly independent; and the level of organization suggested by the formation of the Ottoman Publishing Association does not signify that the revolutionary press was in any way unified, coherent, or well ordered. Periodicals were often ephemeral and idiosyncratic—outbursts of passion or energy coarsely inscribed and soon lost—seldom making it into the repositories of the latter-day institutions of preservation.[25] Even those publications that endured cannot necessarily be neatly typed by party affiliation. There were party organs, particularly dailies, in the Ottoman press of the time. But it would be wrong to assume that all gazettes and all editorial positions followed readily discernible party lines. That assumption would tend to obscure the fluid qualities of narrative and cartoon in the revolutionary press.

PUBLISHING HOUSES—PRODUCTION, LOCATION, AND DISTRIBUTION

The history of the Ottoman publishing industry has yet to be written and this study does not undertake that task.[26] Research still needs to be done on the history of individual publishing houses, the adoption of new presses, the development, financing and utilization of printing techniques, the organization of the labor force and production, and distribution and advertising arrangements. Ottoman publishing was not fixed in space such that the production history of any one gazette is static or completely predictable. Many periodicals were issued in single-issue or very limited runs; gazettes sometimes underwent multiple title changes; and some writers used pseudonyms for political satire gazettes. There was a tendency to shift printing house, editor, or head writer (often several times) during the run of a single gazette. Also certain book publishers founded and published their own gazettes, as illustrated by the following announcement from the Ahmet İhsan Company which was combining operations for its printing house and the publication offices of its gazette: "We have the honor to bring to your attention that our Establishment is preparing to relocate to a site on Vâlide Mekteb Street, near the Tomb of Sultan Mahmud. Our state of the art Printing House, thus installed in its modern locale, assures its clients a better calibre of work. We have, as well, the pleasure of informing you that . . . . we will inaugurate our new installation, reuniting the friends of our House and of our Journal, *Servet-i fünun*."[27] Gazettes, in turn, advertised the book productions of the publishing houses. Ottoman serial publishing was a highly personal and individual enterprise, with some aggressive publishers or editors involved in multiple publications and the activities of multiple publishing houses. Limited runs, plus the ephemeral nature of the periodical press, contribute to the difficulty of assembling complete publication information on any given title.

Steam and even electric presses had become increasingly common in Europe at the turn of the twentieth century, but they were limited to the larger newspaper establishments.[28] In Istanbul, at the time of the revolution, electric presses were still viewed as innovative technology. In 1890, the Ottoman yearbook, *Takvim-i Bahar,* following accounts of the 1889 Paris exposition, the Eiffel Tower, electrical wonders like the velocipede, and other uses for electrical power, reported enthusiastically on the new printing technologies employed in Europe and America. The article was called "The Biggest and the Smallest Newspapers."

> In New York City a newspaper called *World* is published, composed of forty pages, each with 7 columns and each column with 2,000 words. The Sunday edition prints 400,000 copies using 100, 000 *okka* [2.83 lbs/*okka*] of new paper and 1,000 *okka* of ink. If this much paper were bound into volumes it would produce 4 million books, that is to say twice the number found in the National Library in Paris. For this vast production, *World* employs 12 presses of the latest model, the biggest and most advanced presses available. Each one of these presses in an hour prints 48,000 sixteen-page forms, folds, cuts, and bundles them into batches of 50 each![29]

Earlier in the century, the Moroccan traveler, Muḥammad as-Saffār, had been equally impressed by the development of the foreign press and printing in Paris. In his account of a trip to France in 1845–1846, he included a lengthy description of printing processes in a publishing house employing "eight hundred" workers. There he observed both hand and automated presses (the latter run by steam and water power), lithographic reproduction, and typesetting in both Arabic and Latin scripts. As-Saffār was extremely interested in the possibilities such presses provided for mass dissemination of books; he also remarked on the mass consumption of newspapers in Paris:

> All the leaders of France, and especially in Paris, make a contract with the owner of a newspaper to receive a new gazette each day, in return for a fixed sum paid annually. Likewise, all the cafés receive numerous gazettes each day from many places. When someone enters a café, first the waiter brings him a newspaper so he may learn what is new, and then he serves him his coffee. The newspapers are handed back and kept there. Whoever wishes to know what has happened in the past can hunt around in the café for a gazette from that time, and read about it.[30]

In Istanbul, no gazette approached the *World*'s circulation volume or technological advancement. Electricity, in Istanbul in the revolutionary era, was only in its earliest stages of development.[31] Gas and electric services for lighting were still restricted to limited areas of the city in 1908 and, in general, the conversion of machinery to electrical power seems to have been

Publishing, Format, Images, and Readers

a post-revolutionary development. The Ottoman Ferry/Steamship company, for instance converted its dockyards to electric power between 1910 and 1912. Tickets for boat travel, however, were still printed on hand presses by the company's employees.[32] Indeed, electricity in general was considered a novelty for day-to-day use in Istanbul as in other Middle Eastern cities where streets, factories, and transport systems were still not electrified at the time of the revolution.[33] Circulation numbers for a few Istanbul gazettes indicate that some printers must have had gas or steam-run presses in Istanbul by 1908 but the standard press, apparently, remained the hand press.[34]

The revolution, and the boom it brought to the Ottoman publishing industry provided the framework for revolutionary developments in publishing technology. When Ahmet İhsan, one of the major publishers in Istanbul, opened up his new printing house in 1912, it was equipped with electricity. This development was announced in the pages of *Servet-i fünun;* the new establishment was:

> . . . unequalled in Istanbul. Lighted by electricity and heated with *kalorifler* [radiators], our publishing house is engaged in the production of work for Rumeli, Bagdad, Manastir, the Mersin railroad, the Şirket-i Hayriye, the Haliç Steamship Companies, the Tünel Company, Bomonti Factory and for many government departmental offices. We employ the latest English printing presses for every type of document and the most excellent colored illustrations, [producing] the most exact copy (*en müstakimâne bir suret*).[35]

This announcement of expansion and modernization by one of Istanbul's larger publishing houses reflects the increased availablility of electrical resources in Istanbul in the years after the revolution as well as the technical demands of high volume printing.

Many of the revolutionary gazettes considered in this study, however, were much smaller operations. Printing houses produced the publications of multiple publishers, and it was a rare publication that had its own exclusive printing house. Many gazettes changed printing house more than once, indicating that the printers often functioned as multi-task jobbers, each printing house producing a variety of books and serial publications. Thus a print organization did not ordinarily consist of an individual gazette and its subsidiary publications monopolizing the output of a press. Instead, individual publishers switched printing houses to suit the needs or finances of their gazettes or, as was the case with several powerful publishers, an individual owned his own publishing house and press and issued a series of publications, books, and periodicals.[36] Publisher and printing house, then, in early-twentieth-century Istanbul cannot be considered coterminous, nor can the production location of most gazettes be considered fixed. Periodicals did have editorial offices, however, for purposes of communication and subscription; and these offices were usually indicated on the gazettes' mastheads.

Less problematic than the production mechanisms of Ottoman publishers is the location of the Ottoman publishing industry, which tended to be focused in two main areas of Istanbul: Bab-ı Âli Street and environs, and Pera/Beyoğlu (see Appendix). Among the sixty-eight core publications in this study, for example, of thirty-four publishers named on the initial issue of each title, fourteen list their address as Bab-ı Âli Street; many others were located nearby.[37] This concentration provided the opportunity for shared facilities, and a logistic ease to switching publishing house. Some publications listed multiple offices or changed address several times in the space of a few issues. Others listed alternate addresses for production, editorial, and distribution services. A few of the publications surveyed listed distribution points for their gazettes, although most did not. This omission suggests perhaps that such information was common knowledge.

Enver Şapolyo gives an impressionistic account of the distribution of the daily paper *Tercüman-ı hakikat*. He conjures an image of the Istanbul streets and of Ottoman consumption of the press in the period after the revolution.

> *Tercüman* still came out in the evenings in Ebussuud Caddesi. It was a beautiful printing of medium size. It emphasized internal and foreign affairs. Hundreds of paper-sellers (*müvezzi*) waited at the door of the publishing house. They bought the papers, and sold them, shouting 'Tercüman.' I myself saw the way the gazettes were snatched up. The paper-sellers were scattered all over Istanbul. Once, during the school holiday, I too worked selling the paper.[38]

FORMAT

A four-page format was the most common form for revolutionary gazettes with eight or sixteen page formats less common. Periodicals printed monthly, bimonthly, or annually often had over one hundred pages, sometimes with pages continuously numbered from issue to issue. Print size and quality varied as did page size; common page sizes ranged from 25.7 mm. high by 18.7 mm. wide to 40 mm. high by 27.4 mm. wide.

The text content of the gazettes considered here included: news; educational/informational pieces, and technical writing on a variety of scientific topics; rhetorical content (letters, editorials, speeches); entertainment content (humor, literature, gossip, theater); official documents (parliamentary proceedings, edicts, reports, and letters from officials); and publisher/reader interaction content (announcements, advertisements, and contests). The distribution of these sections was not uniform across gazettes but there was a common pattern. Title pages generally included subscriber information and an essay, dialogue, or editorial expressing the point of view of the editor. Illustrated gazettes often included a cartoon (sometimes illustrating the introductory essay) or photograph on page 1.

Middle pages included news, reports, more dialogues, letters, and literature. Page 4 (or the last page) was often reserved for announcements, cartoons and other forms of humor, and advertisements. Some satirical gazettes had cartoons throughout.

IMAGES AND PHOTOGRAPHY

There were three basic types of illustration in the Ottoman revolutionary gazettes: photographs, line illustrations, and cartoons. Line illustrations could take the form of title page mastheads and decoration, portraits and other types of narrative illustration, or simple decorative motifs (scrolls, flowers, etc.) in margins. Photographs were limited to the more established and expensive publications (often monthlies or annuals) although a few gazettes would publish an occasional photograph, often to commemorate a special event.[39] Invariably, the publications with regular and numerous photographs were priced in the upper cost range of 1 *kuruş*, or more, per issue.

Photographic houses gained currency in Istanbul in the latter half of the nineteenth century; and the sultan himself was an avid patron of photography. The sultan's primary photographer was M. Karagapoulos, whose shop (along with those of Sebah and Joallier, Abdullah Frères, Apollon, and Phoebus) was in Pera.[40] A symbiotic relationship developed between some of these photographers and the Ottoman publishing industry. The photographers would advertise in gazettes that utilized their services for photographic illustrations. The prospective customer could thus peruse in his gazette not only the photographer's ad but also samples of his work. It is possible that photographic services were provided free in exchange for this publicity. In the case of the gazette *Resimli kitab*, which contained numerous photographs and sold for the hefty price of 5 *kuruş* per issue, two photographers shared billing space with the editor on the title pages of each issue. These were Apollon and Kenan Bey.[41] Apollon, whose advertising slogan was "perfection, excellence, and low price / *mükemmelliyet, nefaset, ehveniyet,*" was located on the Grande Rue de Péra, also called Beyoğlu Cadde-i Kebir, opposite the German Bazaar.[42] Kenan Bey provided some of the prizes (photographs and photographic postcards) for *Resimli kitab*'s subscriber contests. In this way the periodical press provided him with an indirect form of advertising.[43]

Another photographer, Phoebus, advertised prominently in the pages of *Kalem* and he too benefited from the gazette's subscription mechanisms. In its seventh issue, published October 15, 1908, *Kalem* announced a price increase from 1 *piastre* per issue to 50 *para* per issue. (Note that 1 *piastre* = 1 *kuruş* = 40 *para*.)[44] The editor noted, however, that its readers would be compensated in the following ways: the length of each issue had been increased from twelve to sixteen pages, a series of portraits (executed in Europe) of famous people would soon be published, and *Kalem* intended to award premiums to its first one thousand subscribers. These premiums would be displayed in the Décugis Store, number 471 on the Grand Rue de Péra on Friday, Saturday, and Sunday and their allocation to subscribers would be decided by lot. In addition, the first five hundred subscribers would receive, along with their confirmation of subscription, a coupon good for "one cabinet-portrait to be executed at the atelier of Phoebus, the photographic studio well known in Pera."[45] In this fashion, the commercial interests of the gazette, the photographer, and the department store in Pera which displayed the prizes were combined and articulated for the edification of the reading public.

CARTOONS AND CARTOONISTS

The most common form of illustration in the satirical gazettes was the cartoon. Cartoons varied considerably in sophistication of art work. Some were completely dependent on lengthy captions and had little immediate visual impact; that is, the picture without the caption did not convey the cartoon's message. Many, however, were immediately funny or telling without benefit of caption. Although a significant number of cartoonists did sign their work, many more remained anonymous, suggesting a continuity of traditional artistic practice that emphasized message and function rather than author. No cartoonist received masthead billing as did the photographic studios of Apollon and Kenan Bey in *Resimli kitab*. Thus, the cartoon's message was not that of the cartoonist alone. Rather, the cartoons, to a greater or lesser degree, reflected the editorial policies of the gazettes they inhabited. Some editors, like Mehmed Fazlı in the periodical *Lâklâk* (Stork), drew their own cartoons. Some cartoonists produced cartoons for several gazettes. Cartoons were also reprinted from one gazette to another, and cartoons from foreign gazettes were reprinted, suggesting that the cartoonists had no proprietary rights as such.

Cartoons signed "*İttihad ve Terakki Atelyesi*" and "Soresco" suggest that there was studio cartoon production, with stables of artists generating images on demand instead of working individually. Soresco was an "*Atelier de Photo-Zincographie*," in Galata, which advertised itself as producing various types of work for gazettes.[46] The Soresco name is found on many cartoons (sometimes in conjunction with cartoonists' signatures like Scham and Scarselli). Non-Turkish names like Soresco have prompted speculation on the provenance of Ottoman cartoons; but Ottoman artists were, after all, of many ethnic derivations. There is no indication that Ottoman editors were importing cartoons from abroad; indeed the immediacy of gazette response to the news of the day would make regular importation of cartoons impractical. Unlike other cartoon production operations, Soresco credited its work on the cartoon plates.

While many Ottoman cartoonists remained anonymous, even signed cartoons do not automatically reveal a great deal about the men producing

Ottoman satirical images. Turgut Çeviker includes a brief list of cartoonists in his study of Ottoman caricature but, with few exceptions, details on the lives and backgrounds of these men (and one woman) are scanty at best.[47] Çeviker's list notes the following cartoonists during the period 1908–1918: Cemil Cem, Sedad Nuri (İleri), Ali Dino, İzzet Ziya, Ali Sami (Boyar), Halit Naci Bey, Mehmet Baha Bey, Mehmet Fazlı, Damat Fahir Bey, Münir (Osman), D. Mazlum, Cevat Nuri, Sedat Simavi, Fatma Zehra, A. Enver, Ali Fuat Bey, Kenan Bey, Celil Safvet, İskender, Ramiz (Gökçe), Ahmet Lütfi, Ahmet Cemil, Lâl, A. Scarselli, d'Ostoya, A. Rigopulos, Pahatrekas, Ion, Pleicek, Fellah, İdis, L. Andrès, Couros, Redleb, C. P., Aram, Andonyan, and a cartoonist who employed a slashed S signature.[48] (Note, that cartoonists with non-Turkish names cannot be assumed to be foreigners, but are, most likely, Ottoman citizens or residents.) Only a few of these cartoonists are extensively represented in the gazettes I have surveyed. Their very anonymity suggests that only a few of the gazettes' artistic craftsmen were granted much formal recognition in the ideological production of the Ottoman revolutionary press.[49] There were indeed satiric "geniuses," like Sedad Nuri; but the ordinary cartoonist was apparently not at liberty to follow only the dictates of his own imagination. Satirical gazettes were often one- or two-man editing/publishing operations and, as such, the editors had considerable influence over cartoon content. This admission does not suggest that certain cartoonists did not have their preferred themes, but cartoonist themes were constrained by editorial preferences and by events. Nor could cartooning escape, or wish to, the symbol sets of representational reference. Cartoons were full of echoes and recreations, literary and pictorial, drawing on historical memory or derived from last night's or last week's edition.

STYLE AND CONTENT

Ottoman cartoons come in a range of artistic styles, shapes, and sorts, circumscribed by printing and engraving technologies, by cultural delimiters, by financial constraints, and by the limited page space available. Cartoons had to reflect the immediate concerns of the day, and they had to be generated in time for weekly or biweekly deadlines (most satiric gazettes were not dailies). Stylistically, they ranged from highly sophisticated to very primitive. That is, some cartoons were little more than stick drawings or rough, fuzzy sketches of one or two people. Others contained a rich development of facial and costume detail as well as elaborate background material. Most cartoons, however, fell somewhere between these two extremes. Often the most effective cartoons were those with a stark and dramatic central character, juxtaposed to a fairly simple background (containing a few telling symbols) and requiring a minimal caption. Engraving and lithographic techniques permitted considerable depth and tone variation in some cartoons. Color was used as an overlay in some of the more elaborately cartooned gazettes, like *Kalem*, but the standard for images and print was black and white; not until the World War I era did satirical gazettes with multiple color cartoons come into more common use. Of course, black and white, here, cannot be taken too literally since ink type and printing technique meant that "black" ranged from brown to grey to black to almost purple. "White" was really some form of buff color, for the most part. While some, especially large-page format, gazettes specialized in striking full-page cartoons, most cartoons were either half- or quarter-page in size. Captions were generally written below the cartoons, many cartoons having (in addition) brief introductory captions at the top of the page or labels on various parts of the cartoon. Although long elaborate captions were still fairly common, Ottoman gazettes of the revolutionary period were moving away from the lengthy captions commonly found in nineteenth-century cartoons.

One could argue that, in terms of form, Ottoman cartooning was an imitative art, taking its models from European gazettes.[50] That argument, however, would be a gross oversimplification of the nature of an evolving art form. Indeed, many cartoons in the revolutionary press were quite similar (in subject matter, style, depiction of character, and decor) to cartoons found in such European gazettes as *Punch* and *La Caricature*. For example, two cartoons by Daumier, "European Equilibrium," showing the world balanced on the points of rifles, and "Galileo surprised at the surface of the earth," showing Galileo tiptoeing through an earth bristling with bayonet points, are reproduced with modifications in Ottoman cartoons expressing the precarious military position of the empire.[51] If one compares Ottoman and Iranian satire for this same period, one is struck by the degree to which Ottoman cartoons approximate European ones (particularly in the depiction of sexual themes) and Iranian cartoons do not. It is clear that the pervasive European cultural influences in the capital had provided Ottoman cartoonists with a variety of European models; French, English, Italian, and German gazettes were significant in this regard.[52] But these same cartoonists were merging these European influences with other (Ottoman, Persian, Arabic, Mediterranean) satiric and artistic models (stylistic, narrative, and thematic) available in the cosmopolitan world of Istanbul.[53] For every cartoon that might almost be straight out of *Punch,* except for the caption, there were many others (in *Al-Üfürük* or *Geveze,* for instance) that owed little or nothing to the cartooning styles of European gazettes. Poetry, caligraphy, and puppet theatre, for example, were important "indigenous" (or non-European) influences on Ottoman cartoon art.[54] One need only compare the styles of cartoonists like Sedad Nuri, Mehmed Fazlı, Cemil Cem, and D. Mazlum (not to mention many anonymous cartoonists) to see that Ottoman cartooning was a diverse and evolving art form with a memory for various traditions. It reflected the culturally diverse and culturally combative atmosphere of the city in which it was produced. Like the empire itself, Ottoman satire was also multilingual. Although this study examines Ottoman language satire, it is important to keep in mind that the Istanbul press produced satire in the Armenian, Greek, French, Arabic, and Persian languages (among others) as well.

PRICE AND POST

What did it cost to read? Often, nothing. As Ottoman and foreign gazettes were passed hand to hand, read aloud in gatherings, or tacked up on walls, their words or pictures might not even cost the price and effort of literacy. But there were subscribers who paid for their gazettes in amounts that varied with the distance from the centers of production, printing houses, and editorial offices. Demand and censorship were also factors in the price of reading. Ismail Kemal Bey commented in his memoirs that he published the late-nineteenth-century organ, "*Medjra-Efkiar*," in Philippopolis (outside the empire's boundaries) because the sultan forbade its publication in Istanbul. Nonetheless, it found a ready market in the Ottoman capital: "In spite of the seizures of the paper by the police on its arrival in Constantinople, there was no lack of copies in the capital, and the public bought them up at double and treble their price."[55] After the revolution, such banning and censorship were not a major factor in driving up the price of periodicals. Limited printings, however, combined with the popularity of some (especially illustrated) issues, could result in prices being raised over the original issue price for certain back issues.

Subscription prices varied depending on where the subscriber lived: Istanbul (*dar üs-saadet*), the provinces (*vilâyet, dışarı*), and foreign lands (*memalik-i ecnebiye*). Various combinations or elaborations on the above division were made, sometimes distinguishing only between Ottoman (*memalik-i mahruse*) and non-Ottoman (*memalik-i ecnebiye*) territories. Subscription prices were given for six as well as twelve month periods, often at a slightly higher price per issue for the former. More detailed subscription information might include whether prices given included postage, where subscriptions could be picked up to avoid postage costs, and other types of circulation information. Besides subscription prices, costs for advertising, per page or per line, might also be given on the title page, although ad information was more commonly listed in the back of an issue.[56] Publication and subscription information not given in the title header was often printed either on the first page or, more often, on the last page under subtitles such as "announcements (*ilânat*)" or "notes to readers."

Prices were ordinarily given in *para* per single issue (*nüsha*) and in *kuruş* (*piastre*) or *francs* per subscription. The expected readership was reflected in the gazette's pricing information: inclusion of information in French, prices given for non-Ottoman territories, and prices given in other currencies besides Ottoman and French (for example, rubles, dinars, or pounds sterling). The average revolutionary gazette price was 10 *para* for an issue numbering four to eight pages. The single most apparent reason for a given title's price exceeding this amount was the inclusion of photographs, which could dramatically increase the cost of a publication. This was the case with gazettes like *Devr-i cedid, Musavver Muhit* (50 *para* per issue each) and *Şahika* (1 *kuruş* per issue). Other reasons for higher pricing were length, bilingual publication, and sometimes (but more often not) numerous illustrations. The pen was clearly cheaper than the photographic lens for conveying either information or satire.

Price was also a reflection of the market, as illustrated by price changes in some gazettes. Thus, for example, the first issue of *Papağan* cost 40 *para* but subsequent issues were only 20 *para* each, suggesting that the market would not bear a 40 *para* price for a four page gazette. *Sebat* dropped its issue price on a four page gazette from 20 *para* to 10 *para* after five issues at the higher price. Although daily papers may have been available at a lower price once they were a day old, back issues of the periodical press, at least for some titles, sold for more than the original issue price. This pricing encouraged subscriptions and suggests the editors' assessment that certain issues, once circulated, would generate a demand that outweighed the inconvenience of producing and retaining extra issues over the number required for subscriptions and initial sales.[57]

Of course subscriptions brought with them their own problems of delays and losses. The satirical gazettes made great sport of the deficiencies of the Ottoman postal service and mail subscribers might wait some time for the latest gazette. According to one cartoon in the satirical *Alem*, the "loss" of gazettes in the mail was not always innocent. In a scene entitled "Our Mail," *Alem* shows two postal clerks pocketing illustrated gazettes handed in at the post office window (Figure 2.1). While one slips a gazette into his jacket, the other reaches for a gazette being posted by a customer. The first man winks at the other, "This one for me and that one coming in for you."[58] Behind the counter is a wastebasket full of discarded letters. The illustrated gazettes were both the most expensive and in some sense the most popular of the periodicals. This cartoon suggests the nature of the illustrated gazette as a desirable commodity, as well as indicating the satirist's jaundiced view of the notion "lost in the mail."

READERSHIP

The audience for the Ottoman revolutionary press is difficult to pinpoint, count, and identify.[59] Much of this identification is based on conjecture from content and remains squarely in the realm of speculation, a realm, in any case, which is the inevitable habitat of the cultural historian. There are, however, certain avenues of evidence that reveal in a more concrete fashion the Ottoman press's reading and "looking" public. One avenue is the editor/reader communications that are found sometimes on the title page but most often on the concluding page or pages of Ottoman gazettes. These

Figure 2.1 Unreliable Post: "One for you and one for me"

communications take a variety of forms: identifying or advertising information about new gazettes, subscription information, circulation and distribution information, letters, contests, and general "advice to readers" remarks. A second avenue is memoirs or other narrative sources concerning who was reading what, when. A third avenue is documentation found in publications lists, government regulations, and licensing, censorship, and regulatory orders or forms.[60] Regulations on the press have been published by Server İskit, although a systematic study of the Ottoman archives' Yıldız collections and holdings of the various bureaus is likely to reveal further substantial documentation on the Ottoman press.[61] This study generally will employ evidence from content, narrative statements, and editor/reader communications found in the gazettes. The gazettes themselves envisioned their readers, as is evident, for example, in the pages of *Kalem*, where male and female readers were depicted in ads and in cartoons (Figure 2.2).[62]

Most gazettes did not include circulation statistics as an integral part of the published subscriber information. The gazette *Kalem*, a weekly that began publication on 3 September 1908, solicited advertisers, beginning in issue seven (15 October, 1908), by asserting that its press run was 10,000 issues. By issue nine (29 October, 1908) the press run claims had been boosted to 13,000 copies. Many publications had much smaller runs.[63] Şapolyo mentions circulations between 5,000 and 25,000 in the constitutional period, adding that *Eşek* (published 1910–1912) was "the biggest seller," and that *İkdam* sometimes had a daily run of 50,000, but he cites no source for this information.[64] It seems unlikely that *Eşek* (a biting satiric gazette that survived a series of name changes) had the largest run, although it may have been very popular.

Circulation statistics and reader counts, of course, do not tell the entire story of Ottoman reading. Roger Chartier has suggested the dangers of imagining readers and the amount, nature, or outcomes, of their reading.[65] Like Chartier's reporters on eighteenth-century French peasant reading, the Ottoman press's own assessments of readership, or the accounts in memoirs of gazette reading, are impressionistic and themselves participate in the process of "creating" the Ottoman reading public. Still, again like Chartier's descriptions, such Ottoman representations reflect the "still somewhat vague awareness that the Revolution was in the process of upsetting deep-seated cultural habits."[66] Cartoons on Ottoman reading suggest this awareness. A 1909 cartoon in *Kalem* for example contrasts readers in the "West" and in the "East," showing a European and his child avidly reading, surrounded by piles of books. That frame is contrasted to one of the Ottoman and his child, "after the July 1908" revolution. The Ottoman reads as well, but he has only one book.[67] This theme was repeated in another cartoon that combined the notion of the revolutionary "awakening," with a depiction of the ready availability of gazettes after the revolution. This cartoon, from October 1908, shows a row of men, yawning and nodding on a bench. The caption, asks, "Why weren't they speaking before?" and

CAPITAL:

Lstg. 400,000

Siège Central:

SMYRNE

sur les quais

SUCCURSALE DE CONSTANTINOPLE:

PÉRA, Grande Rue de Péra (*nouvel immeuble St-Antoine*).
STAMBOUL, Stambollian Han, Bagtché-Capou.

Tapis de Smyrne

Si vous cherchez un tapis qui sort de l'ordinaire qui diffère de tout ce que vous avez déjà vu, venez nous visiter.

Nous avons en exposition un choix merveilleux des plus beaux exemplaires de notre fabrication, nous avons la spécialité de tapis artistiques, que nous plaçons par leurs prix modérés à la portée de toutes les bourses

HABILLEMENTS
pour
Hommes, Dames et Enfants
Bonneterie et Lingerie
chez
MAYER
Galata   Stamboul

Vient de paraître:

PLAN ARCHÉOLOGIQUE

de Constantinople

par Djélal Essad Bey.

Figure 2.2   Female Readers Depicted in Advertising

answers, "Because they were asleep." The second frame shows the same lineup of men on the same bench. Each man is deeply engrossed in his gazette. The caption asks, "Why can't they speak now?" and answers, "Because they're reading."[68] The five men are drawn to represent different classes: a soldier, an efendi, a religious man, a worker. This cartoon suggests the new freedom of the press and reflects the press's preoccupation with its readers, its own role in the revolution, and distinctions between then and now, old and new.

Consumption of mass periodicals remained a predominantly urban phenomenon in the immediate aftermath of the revolution, but developments in transportation enhanced the possibilities for wider press distribution; and papers could and did reach the countryside.[69] Soon provincial presses, too, became more common so that, as Weber noted of early twentieth-century France, "the press had fully assumed its role of conducting social electricity to the whole of the nation."[70] Still, the pace of Istanbul gazette consumption at the center was much swifter than that of provincial consumption where readers had to await subscriptions or the arrival of travelers from the capital.

Males from the elite classes in Istanbul remained the primary readers and the primary target audience (gauged by content, style, and tone) of the revolutionary periodical press. The press was essentially a male-centered and driven operation. Despite the existence, as early as the nineteenth century, of an Ottoman women's press (designed for a female audience and employing some female editors and writers), the editors, writers, and cartoonists of the revolutionary press were overwhelmingly male.[71] Men, also, generally controlled household budgets, which paid for gazettes and subscriptions.[72] Although education and literacy especially for elite women had advanced considerably in the century preceeding the revolution, education as an avenue of access to the periodical press was still predominantly a male preserve.[73] Women were, however, consumers, both of goods and of reading, even if they were not the initial purchasers. Thus a few new gazettes, often with male editors, did specifically target the female reader, and others included her. All of the gazettes in this study targeted a predominantly male audience. Some did, however, address women in ads and special women's sections (*Resimli kitab* and *Kalem* for example) while others, in essays and polemics addressed to Ottomans (*Osmanlılar*), included women as well as men.[74]

Irrespective of gender, Ottoman readers often relied on foreign newspapers for world news before the revolution. The alternatives were expatriate Ottoman organs smuggled into the city, or the vigorously controlled Ottoman publications allowed by the sultan. The relatively free circulation of the foreign press in Istanbul during the reign of Abd ül-Hamid is well documented. A story from 1901 by Demetra Vaka, an Ottoman citizen of Greek extraction, illustrates at once newspaper readership among elite Ottoman women, the availability of foreign newspapers, and the intercourse between Ottomans and Europeans at the turn of the century. Vaka's Turkish friend, "Hilme" (probably Halime), was raised in Asia Minor by her maternal grandfather, a man whom Vaka described as "a Turk of the new school which believes that women ought to be educated to be the companions of men."[75] Until the age of fourteen, when she took the veil, Hilme studied English, French, German, and Western literature with her male cousin, Murad. Elite Ottoman women had access to such an education, especially in literature and poetry. Some, however, were taught to read but not to write in order to discourage the penning of love letters.[76] At eighteen, Hilme was betrothed to Murad. While he served in diplomatic posts and studied in Paris, Vienna, and England for three years, she continued studying Western literature, aided by the books Murad sent her. During this time, she also took, "one daily paper [each] from Paris, Vienna, Berlin and London" as well as "several monthly periodicals." This consumption indicates the wealthy status of Hilme's family. Her education and relationship with Murad, though, indicate the social and political milieu in Istanbul, which provided both the demand for and the access to foreign and Ottoman language serials in the years before the revolution. Istanbul had an appetite for news of the world, and this appetite was not limited to men. The motivation for such reading was both practical and educational. Istanbul's upper classes were taking part in a "world" cultural system the center of which was no longer Istanbul itself. The readers were already in place; the revolution suspended the censorship that left them relatively little to read but the foreign press.

There were also non-elite readers and even illiterate "readers" for the Ottoman periodical press.[77] Even before the revolution this audience had access to the press through public readings: "Coffee houses . . . form the chief centers of union and conversation for the middle and lower classes. Here those who can read impart to their unlettered neighbors the news of the day,—or at least as much of it as has been approved by the Press Censor . . . [written in Istanbul, 1904]."[78] Such readings were a public institution in the Ottoman empire, and also in Iran where Edward G. Browne noted that the Iranian revolution of 1905–1906 not only encouraged a flourescence of the press similar to that prompted by the Ottoman revolution but also prompted a change in material for professional readers in coffee-houses:

> The people are awake and slowly learning. The most remarkable manifestation of the popular awakening is the large increase in the number of newspapers. Not the old, stilted, futile style of paper, but popular journals, written in comparatively simple language. Everyone seems to read a paper now. In many of the coffee-houses professional readers are engaged, who, instead of reciting the legendary tales of the Sháh-náma, now regale their clients with political news.[79]

Ottomans who could afford neither the price of an issue or of a subscription had access, like their Iranian counterparts, to such public readings.[80]

Ahmet Rasim wrote of the *kıraathaneler* (coffeeshops where gazettes were provided, or reading rooms) at the Galata bridge, where a man might while away the hours.[81] Newspapers were also passed around, scavenged, sent out to the provinces, and posted on walls.[82]

Thus, the consumers of the Ottoman press were of various sorts: male and female, elite and pedestrian, literate, semi-literate and even illiterate. Their desires and objectives were mirrored in the content of the gazettes, which cannot be considered merely an expression of the rhetorical and commercial objectives of the editors. They demanded the news, which for so long had been denied to them. They demanded information, education, and enlightenment, which were sometimes associated with Europe. They also wanted entertainment; and the revolutionary press gave them that entertainment in the form of *mizah mecmuaları*, so they could laugh at themselves and others, and so they could see their fears about the world, the empire, and their culture reproduced in the cartoon space.

THE KNOWLEDGE CONTEST / *BILMECE*

"*Bilin bakalım?*" (Let's see what you know?) read the last section in an issue of the gazette *Musavver Muhit*—a four question game with the answers right there on the page, printed upside down. In other gazettes, puzzles were more difficult and the rewards more substantial than simple self-satisfaction. The *bilmece* (riddle, puzzle, guessing game) evolved as a special section in the gazettes, located usually on the last page, juxtaposed or in proximity to letters and announcements—a printed, direct communication between the press and its readers.[83] These became at once a marketing tool and a knowledge contest, with printed coupons to be cut out and submitted along with the readers' answers to the questions or puzzles. Answers and winners' names were published in subsequent issues. Prizes appropriate to a knowledge contest were awarded: books, subscriptions, even stamped post cards. The *bilmece* was a riddle to be solved—visual or narrative—and the coupon was a permit of entitlement to enter: one issue entitled the reader to one entry. To see the solution, or who won, a reader needed to buy the next issue. The gazettes, through the *bilmece*, established a dialogue with readers in the course of which winners were named publicly, their ages, neighborhoods, professions, and education sometimes designated as well. The reader lost his (though not always *his*) passivity, and his knowledge or cleverness was honored in print.

Bilmece were not necessarily published in every issue, probably to allow time for reader response and the processing of entries. Of the sixty-eight periodicals surveyed, almost one fourth (fifteen) had formal *bilmece* sections with answers published in later issues and, of these, ten had coupons for submission with the reader's entry.[84] Besides these, several other gazettes had less formal *bilmece* sections comprising an occasional puzzle section (sometimes humorous) entitled "*bilmece*," which did not require an entry submission.[85] The *bilmece*, then, was a significant representation of the developing Ottoman serial publication industry's articulation of itself and of its readership. These contests reflect a middle ground in the types of communication characteristic of revolutionary gazettes—a middle ground that was neither political rhetoric or instructional literature on the one hand, nor purely entertainment on the other, but rather an attempt to orchestrate the commercial space around participating consumers who were not content to remain simply passive.

The *bilmece* provide one of the limited avenues of access to the readership of the Ottoman press. This avenue is not representative. First of all, the contests privileged certain kinds of knowledge.[86] Second, only some readers entered. Many of the publications consulted still contain *bilmece* coupons, intact and unclipped; the voices of the non-entering public, thus, remain unheard. Further, only the winners names were published—other entrants were sometimes reflected in anonymous entry counts. Yet the winners lists give the Ottoman press readership a name, a gender, and a profession, things which are found only accidentally or incidentally in other sources.

Bilmece coupons were often simple affairs consisting only of the gazette's name and the issue number. One fairly elaborate example, from the periodical *Resimli kitab*, illustrates not only the target Ottoman audience but also the commercial implications of the knowledge contest (Figure 2.3). This coupon was divided into two parts, on both of which the entrant was to write his or her name and address. The larger section was the entry form and the smaller was a receipt to be used in case a prize was won. The illustrated coupon advised all potential participants: "Those who have given the right answer will be placed in a drawing. . . . In order to conform to the contest conditions, the entry must be sent within twenty days to Kenan Bey at our Istanbul office. Solution sheets not attached to the bilmece coupon for that issue will not be included in the drawing."[87] Thus, the knowledge contest was circumscribed in time. The twenty-day limit permitted the announcement of winners in a timely fashion in the second issue after the printing of that particular contest. The prizes suggest *Resimli kitab*'s imagined audience:

> First prize: an enamelled timepiece especially for women.
> Second prize: an elegant sun parasol.
> Third prize: a complete set of compasses [for drawing].
> Fourth through twentieth prizes: our special photographic cards, by Kenan Bey.
> Twenty-first through fiftieth prizes: 3 post cards.

The content and advertising of *Resimli kitab* did not specifically target women, but the first prizes in its *bilmece* suggest that the contests might be designed to appeal to the female reader. The fact that Kenan Bey was not

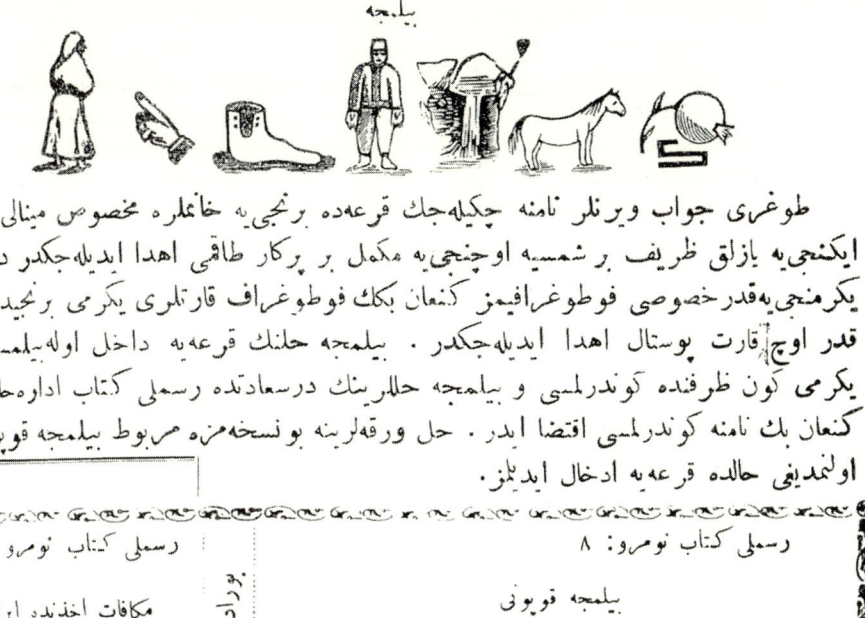

Figure 2.3 A Gazette Contest Coupon

only the gazette's designated recipient of entries but also the photographer responsible for the illustrated postcard prizes (sixteen winners in each contest) suggests that the *bilmece* had a secondary commercial objective besides boosting sales of the publication. The photographic post card prizes circulated examples of Kenan Bey's work to an audience capable of paying the high (5 *piastre* per issue) price of *Resimli kitab;* they were potential customers for the newly burgeoning photographic industry.

A list of winners, from a previous contest, in this same issue of May 1909, provides the names, addresses and occupations of readers. The major prizes were awarded to (1st) Âsım Paşazade Rauf Bey, Salonica; (2nd) Kemal Bey, grandson of Yaver Bey, an assiduous student [*müdavemlerinden*] at the Beyoğlu German School; (3rd) Hadice İclâl Hanım [a female] from Gedik Paşa. Winners of the photographic cards included students, bureaucrats, military personnel, two merchants (*tüccar*) and a special correspondent for the gazette *Yeni asır.* Following the names of male winners (on the list of the twenty-first to fiftieth prizes) were those of three women: A. Naciye, a Kanlıca teacher; Saadet, daughter of the *Doğancı* (Falconer) Miralay Ârif Bey, from Üsküdar; and, also from Üsküdar, Hadice Hanım, daughter of the late *Mirahor* (Master of the Horse) Ziya Bey. Gender distinctions superseded those of rank in this list. Only Hadice İclâl Hanım, winner of the third prize, earned the right to have her name listed before those of the men. The other three female winners were listed after men of lower social rank. Within prize categories, the male winners were not listed in any apparent order, either alphabetically or by rank. Entrants were primarily from the Istanbul area, but the winners included one participant from Edirne and several from Salonica. For five winners, only initials were given. Somewhat fewer than the fifty prizes were awarded, indicating either insufficient entries or a dearth of correct answers.

This knowledge contest was a minor reflection of the struggle then galvanizing the empire: a struggle in which certain kinds of knowledge, and certain kinds of literacy were rewarded, a struggle over rank, gender, occupation, and social order. The rhebuses and word/picture problems tried the audience's abilities to read pictures.[88] For the Ottoman state the answers to its own riddles were either upside down or, like so many of the stories and essays in the gazettes, "to be continued." The outcome of the constitutional transformation was not yet apparent but guesses to the riddles of European imperialism had to be made immediately—one per customer, in effect— with victory or defeat revealed only in some later installment.

III

The Voice and Image of The Public, and its Targets

There is no such thing as a completely free and original cultural product which uses none of the materials imposed by tradition, authority or the market and which is not subject to the surveillance or censure of those who hold sway over things and word.[1]
—Roger Chartier, *The Cultural Uses of Print*

I don't care a straw for your newspaper articles, my constituents don't know how to read, but they can't help seeing them damned pictures.[2]
—Boss Tweed

VOX POPULI

Much has been written on the press and its intimate relationship with the imagined entity called the public.[3] For pupuses of this study, the public remains as elusive as illiteracy and a lack of first hand accounts and circulation statistics make it. Yet there is a public; the press creates the public by assuming and addressing it and the public creates the press by consuming it. Without the public there would be no advertising.[4] The public is real because it is embodied in cartoon characters who engage in satiric interaction with the gazettes, with the other inhabitants of the cartoon space, and with the public at large. The press addresses the public directly, as in a lead article in the serious weekly, *Beyan ül-hak*, entitled "To Our People" or, elsewhere in the same gazette, "*karilerimize*" (to our readers).[5] The press at once creates, imagines, and attempts to capture that illusory public by capturing its symbols. As Laitin has noted, elites in all subsystems try to make their subsystem the privileged locus of symbolic production in their society. The press was one mechanism of those subsystems and each gazette was an organ in the struggle of various elite groups for the high ground in symbol production.[6]

Gazettes, like politicians, contend on a terrain of symbolic representation; sometimes they are trying to capture the voice of the "people," although who that people is may be differentially defined. To claim (or even recognize) that voice, Ottoman revolutionary gazettes employed specific strategies which combined the novel and the familiar. They used language and images which were assumed to be "popular," that is having a long and familiar cultural past in the minds of their readers. As Robert Philippe puts it: "The synthesizing power of the print expresses both what is visible and what is concealed. To what is, it adds what has been and what will be. The image is thus liberated from the grammar of space and time and the print remains dynamic, aggressive, fertile, and creative."[7] Revolutionary gazettes also attempted to monopolize the public by gaining the authority to create or determine what would become popular and familiar - the new cultural symbols. In the satiric gazettes, a mastery of the old cultural symbols and an understanding of just how far those symbols could be warped or broken, gave the writers and editors authority. They spoke in the language of the people, whoever those people happened to be, and their readers granted them the authority to push that language in novel directions.[8]

The voice of the people was also an evolving voice. Language was not fixed and the press used dialog to show the confusion of concepts inherent in the revolution, as is illustrated in this dialog between two children:[9]

Vatan ne dir?	What is homeland (*vatan*)?
Tiyatro oyunu.	A play.
Hürriyet ne dir?	What is freedom (*hürriyet*)?
Gazete ismi.	The name of a gazette.
Uhuvvet ne dir?	What is brotherhood (*uhuvvet*)?
Daha göremedimki bileyim . . .	I still can't tell.
Adalet?	Justice (*Adalet*)?
Teyzemin kızının adı.	The name of my aunt's daughter.
Meşveret?	Consultation (*Meşveret*)?
Ne olduğunu anlayamiyorum.	I have no idea.

The public, in Ottoman satire, was often represented as a bewildered public, and the children, here, were symbols of a certain public naivete in the face of social and political change. There was, indeed, a popular play entitled "*Vatan*," and *Adalet* could be used as a name; but the paradox that this simple punning dialogue suggests is that of finding corresponding words and meanings for political and social "novelties."

The revolutionary press was a singularly dialogic form, a medium that connected the press, the government, and the public in a series of intimate ways no longer generally employed in big city newspapers today (but still employed in some variants in small, local gazettes). There is a long tradition of the use of dialogue as a device for political criticism and philosophical debate in Middle Eastern and European literatures.[10] Ottoman dialogues used comparisons with the "other," East vs. West, or modern vs. traditional, to critique their own political and cultural systems.[11] This dialogic criticism was endemic in the revolutionary press. It could be skillful or clumsy, and it came in a whole series of forms, such as cartoon captions, conversations, and debates. The government made announcements in the press; the proceedings of the assembly were published in newspapers; letters columns contained vivid and continuing debates (often between prominent figures) on the affairs of the day; apologies were demanded and issued in print; and editorials were often written in dialogue form.[12] Political factions used the newly won freedom of the press to mobilize support, influence public opinion, and even spread rumors via their newspaper organs. In February 1909, when the Chamber of Deputies was attempting to force Kâmil Pasha to resign, he threatened to publish his own version of their conflict in the press, adding that it would not be his responsibility if this jeopardized the state.[13] The Chamber called Kâmil's bluff, but his threat indicates a clear appreciation for the power of the press to influence public opinion. The press was thus a forum for intimate and aggressive "public" participation that took place at a variety of levels.

Dialogue approximated print culture to verbal culture; it preferred the gazette as a form of conversation.[14] Announcements, advertisements, editorials, spoofs, even cartoons all retained to a certain degree this oral, conversational mode. That mode, in turn, proposed the gazette as a forum for the voices of the "people," as if voices, somehow snatched from the air, the street-corner, the coffee-shop, the meclis, had suddenly metamorphosed directly onto the printed page. As if to reinforce that image of the print voice of the people, illustrations and headers showed this imagined "public" talking. *Kalem*, in its "*Haftalık Dedikodu*," (Weekly Gossip) section, showed tongues wagging, men talking to women, women talking to men.[15] Other gazettes had similar sections.

The satirical press participated in these creative dialogic functions by publishing imaginary letters of protest, invented dialogues attributed to various public figures, fake telegraph communications, and phony extracts from other newspapers. It even participated in media events, like the opening of the meclis and the assassination of the journalist Hasan Fehmi, which captured the emotions of the populace (at least according to the press) and allowed the dialogic relationship of press and public to become even more intimate. These uses of the press are partly a result of the limited forms of "mass" communication available and partly a function of the stage of development of the Istanbul press at the time of the revolution. The Istanbul press was just beginning to discover the possibilities of mass distribution and of market orientation; it was still a press that employed a very personal and individual tone, not yet mediated by notions of the press as supposedly impartial observer. Gazettes, for the time being, were constrained neither by demands for detachment, by censorship, nor by rules against plagiarism.

GAZETTE MASCOTS AND IMAGES OF THE PUBLIC

What did the voice of the people look like? The Ottoman revolutionary gazettes did not have to look far to find mascots and spokespersons for the imagined public. The symbolic repertoire of the revolutionary press demonstrates the press's dependence upon and determination to rearticulate traditional cultural symbols. Far and away the most prominent mascot symbol in the satirical press was the shadow puppet character, Karagöz (Blackeye).[16] Karagöz was "Everyman," the voice of the people, the voice of reason, a journalist, a member of parliament, sly, sardonic, silly, expectant, skeptical, the quintessential "innocent" bystander.[17] Karagöz and his host of supporting characters inhabit the pages of the revolutionary gazettes, delivering alternately sound political and cultural editorials or scathing political and cultural critiques. A good example is in *Perde*, which used Karagöz and Hacivat both as its mascots and as the main characters in its cartoons.[18] There was even a *Karagöz Yearbook*, a take-off on the *salname* (yearbook or almanac) genre which was very popular in the empire at this time.[19] Shadow puppet theater was a traditional vehicle for both political and social satire; and Karagöz was the natural choice for the voice of the satirical press (Figure 3.1). Like the press, shadow theater had been rigorously censored during the reign of Abd ül-Hamid.[20] Indeed, the satirical press was equated with shadow theatre, as demonstrated by the selection of titles like *Hayal* (Shade, Imagination), *Karagöz*, and *Bebe ruhi* (The Dwarf, a shadow play character).[21]

Not only were puppet theater characters ubiquitous in the satirical press, but Karagöz-type dialogue was the most common narrative form employed for political and social critique, in the satirical press and also in the political diatribes of the serious press.[22] The dialogic form (employing a series of rhetorical questions, quick repartee, and a straight man requiring enlightenment) was such an institution in Istanbul society that it had a direct and immediate appeal to readers of various classes. Its language was often deceptively simple. Karagöz dialogue was not only extremely effective, it was a class leveler (or, at least a meeting place of the classes).[23] Dialogic criticism placed in the mouths of Karagöz and his cohort was used to castigate the meclis, bemoan the inefficiency of municipal services, or to poke fun at the foibles of Ottoman culture and of humankind in general. Often it provided a vehicle for vigorous but "anonymous" (or at least unsigned) criticism of the regime. The participants could be Karagöz and Hacivat, the Old and the New, man and woman, the Europeanized vs. the traditional Ottoman, and so on. Where the Karagöz figures themselves were commonly used in late-nineteenth- and early-twentieth-century satire, post-revolutionary satire could also retain the Karagöz format while employing names of real or imaginary people. For example, an "innocent bystander" type would ask questions of a cabinet member or deputy who had been given a fictitious name.

Figure 3.1   Karagöz and Hacivat

The Voice and Image of The Public

The "*Muhavere*" (argument, conversation, dialogue), the second formal element in Karagöz plays, was adapted in many satirical gazettes into a standard feature of each issue, with a variety of social and political concerns treated in dialogue form under the generic subhead "*muhavere*."[24] For example the mascot of *Nekregû* (The Wit), engaged in dialogues with partners like Zarifi and Çelebi; but *Nekregû*, as gazette, also engaged in dialogues with other gazettes like *Sabah* and *Tanin*. This intra-gazette dialogue form was endemic in the satiric press. In *Perde*, there were dialogues between Karagöz and Hacivat, and also among the various gazettes of the day. *Yuha* ran a comic dialogue between two asses: "Big Ears" and "Mangy Ass," and *Boşboğaz* ran dialogues among the various satiric gazettes.[25] As in the shadow puppet plays, gazette dialogues often had fixed locales. A favorite one, particularly for the critique of city services, was the Galata Bridge, a meeting place and point of transit. "On the Bridge," became a category of literature, a neutral space where the public met and where anonymous critics could ply their trade and then move on. Bridge dialogues are found, for example in *Lâla, Ton ton risalesi, Geveze,* and *Zevzek*.[26] Dialogues range from dead serious to completely silly and reflect traditional Karagöz language to a greater or lesser degree. They illustrate the commitment to dialogue format as a standard vehicle for polemic, humor, and criticism. Frequently they are used to address some of the most repeated questions of the revolutionary era: "Now that the constitution has been revived, will the empire survive?" "What is the meaning of *hürriyet* (freedom) and of *meşrutiyet* (constitutionalism)?" "What are the practical day-to-day implications of this great transformation?"

There were other "voices of the people" besides Karagöz, some of them female. The Ottoman revolution, like other revolutions before and since, provoked notions that the people must be stirred to action, wakened from their lethargy, forced to see that their "chains" must be shed. To accomplish these tasks, the satiric press used noise: drummers, bell-ringers, and nags. The "people," however, were not necessarily represented as inert. An alternative was the image of the long-suffering people as world-weary and wise, possessed of a certain type of folk wisdom and pragmatism, moved to near silence but provoked to speak out by the inevitabilty of suffering and oppression. These alternative visions of the "people" were reflected in the mascots, the John and Jane Q. Publics, who prowled the pages of revolutionary satire. Two such characters were Züğürt (Destitute One) and Cadaloz (Old Nag), mascots of gazettes of the same names. Often such mascots were represented as people of the lower classes; they were dressed in "traditional" forms of clothing (like turbans and cloaks), or they represented actual "traditional" figures, like the *falakacı*, keeper of the bastinado, *hocas*, traditional musicians, and magicians. Another sort of mascot found in the pages of satiric gazettes was Don Quixote (*Don Kişot*), symbol at once of cynicism, idealism, and the absurd. The use of Don Quixote illustrates one form of the influence of Western literature on the Ottoman literati; he represented the irony of the revolutionary situation (tilting at windmills) and was sometimes listed as an editor, contributor, or letter writer.[27]

One traditional humorous character, Nasr üd-Din Hoca, a wise buffoon of the low level clergy, was not particularly prominent in revolutionary satire. The Hoca, in various forms, is found in folk literature throughout the Afro-Eurasian Oikumene.[28] His lack of prominence in revolutionary satire may well be due to his generally mild manner.[29] The revolution seemed to want more biting spokepersons, those who were aggressive (even violent) as well as complaining, those who fought back with words rather than resignation, those who acted rather than observed. This is not to say that there was no place in the Ottoman cartoon space for the simple buffoon or the passive sad sack. But the feisty and vehement Karagöz was a more likely heroic buffoon. Clearly, Pope did not have "shadows" like Karagöz in mind when he wrote: "To attack vices in the abstract, without touching persons, may be safe fighting indeed, but it is fighting with shadows."[30] In the Ottoman satirical press, Karagöz and his cronies were shadows who fought back; they were expert at touching persons and ideas.

Other mascots were born of a combination of folk literature and revolutionary necessity. One was the Davulcı (Drummer), mascot for the gazette *Davul* (Drum). Like other spokespersons of his sort, the Drummer both announced and participated in the cartoon revolution (Figure 3.2).[31] He was shown in every issue as the awakener of the people, drumming to announce the gazette, the revolution, and the news to his fellow citizens. He was also a key figure in the gazette's cartoons, commenting on the nature of monarchy or the foibles of politics. The drummer was a vigorous, noble-looking fellow, dressed in traditional costume, a spokeman from the lower ranks of the social order. He was a symbol of the press, which envisioned itself as rousing the populace and enlightening it at the same time. Of course there is a certain paradox in the press assimilating to itself both the image of a modern, Western style, enlightener as well as that of the presumably illiterate, traditional drummer; but this paradox was not invented in the Ottoman revolutionary press. In the press, the vigorous, lower-class citizen was a symbol of revolution for the Ottoman as for the French, Iranian, and (later) Russian revolutions. The Ottoman press did not advocate a restructuring of social classes; rather it appropriated the lower classes to symbolize vigor or oppression and to satirize the foibles of the elite classes.

Another voice of the people drawn from the lower classes was the peasant Züğürt (Destitute One).[32] Züğürt was an itch that would not go away (Figure 3.3). Poor, like Nasr üd-Din, Züğürt did not have the facility for compromise and placation that the Hoca possessed in abundance. Instead he confronted the powers that were and told them what they had done wrong. These confrontations were not physical. Züğürt was aged, small in stature, and unprepossessing, but he did not back off. Leading his donkey and dressed in patched pantaloons and beat-up fez, Züğürt was a spokesman

Figure 3.2 The Drummer

Figure 3.3   Züğürt

for the poor and for all those Ottomans oppressed by institutions and autocrats.

Thus, for example, Züğürt, in a 1911 cartoon, confronted the Ottoman regime with the *kadro hariciler*, the masses of bureaucrats thrown out of work by the massive reorganization of government launched after the revolution. This frame showed the downcast and ragged unemployed pleading with Halil Menteşe Bey, the Interior Minister, "Mercy Sir, deign to keep your promise; we remain shut out; we await your favor." But, the intrepid Züğürt wryly comments, "Mercy, friends, you come at the wrong time. They are struggling with their own afflictions. . . . you can no longer be assured of your old, accustomed security."[33] In this cartoon, Züğürt not only takes up the problems of bureaucratic unemployment and unfulfilled government promises, he also takes a sardonic poke at the bureaucratic classes (Figure 3.4). They were naive to assume their sinecures would last forever. Now they are more like their lower class "brother" citizens; forced to depend on the "charity" of the state.

Of course, Züğürt was not designed by the poor; he was an appropriation, forging bonds of unity or at least sympathy across class lines.[34] His satire focused on internal rather than foreign affairs. He did not necessarily expect things to change, but the revolution had granted him a print voice and he would not be silent. Züğürt was a cartoon "hero," a figure who stood in marked contrast to the "heroes" of the revolution portrayed so proudly in the serious press. Gazettes like *Resimli kitab* (Illustrated Book) filled their pages with studio photographs of "the heroes of liberty," like the one included here of Enver Bey, a dominant figure in the post-revolutionary regime (Figure 3.5). Such photographs "staged" an heroic revolution that would bring freedom, order, success, and prosperity to Ottoman society.[35] Enver appeared strong, solid, secure; his pose, rifle, and expression spoke confidence to the viewers. Züğürt was a different kind of hero; he conjured an alternative view of the revolution, a view in which the Ottoman citizens were suffering at the hands of a regime that might prove no better, or even worse, than the autocratic regime which preceded it. Like Enver in his studio portrait, the cartoon Züğürt was calm and confident, but his confidence was borne of experience and of fearless desperation, a certainty that neither liberty nor justice were easily obtained.

The public spoke in female as well as male voice. One of the most scathing of the revolutionary press's tongues was located in the mouth of Cadaloz (the Old Nag), mascot for the gazette published in 1910 of the same name. Cadaloz, a strikingly androgynous figure, suggests, like Züğürt, that with age comes a certain license. Indeed, the daring voice in Ottoman satire is often an aging voice. With age, too, comes a certain blurring of the lines between women (who may then be viewed as something besides sexual beings) and men.[36] Freed from a sexual role, Cadaloz was perhaps also free to take on what was ordinarily a male voice, a venomous satiric voice, in what was ordinarily a male space.[37] Her dress (a significant indicator of character

قادرو خارجاری — امان افندم ، وعد بیورمشدیکز . حالا آجقدهمز . لطفکره منتظرز .
زوکورت — امان آرقداشلر ، یاکاش وقتده کلدك . اونلر کندی دردلریله اوغراشیورلر . زی دیکارلریمکه . . . بن بیلیرم ، ناظر
کله برلواده مأمور بولندم. ایی آدمدر اما . . . هله بر دفعه اسکی راحتی تأمین ایتـوزده . . .

Figure 3.4 Züğürt and the Unemployed Bureaucrats

قهرمان حريت بيكباشی انور بك
Le Héros de la liberté : Le Commandent Enver Bey

Figure 3.5　Enver Bey

in cartoons) also approximated male dress, in direct contrast to that of the ordinary Ottoman cartoon woman, which often exaggerated sexuality and femininity. Cadaloz represented the disgust and discouragement of the public; she had no faith in the benevolence of political and social transformation.[38]

Cadaloz, spoke a transcendant and universal wisdom. She was not the mythic madonna mother of the nation, holding the infant "Freedom" in her arms, but the scarred and skeptical mother whose children had grown up, and not turned out right. She was the long-suffering, enduring Jane Q. Public, viewing the revolution with jaundiced eye, who had yet to solve the dilemmas of the old hegemonies much less to address the bewildering array of new cultural options and their effects. This cartoon mother was not fooled by the euphoria or the promises of "*Liberté, Fraternité, Égalité.*" She knew that Europe's assault on the empire was only the latest in an endless cycle of the strong imposing their will upon the weak. She was the mirror image of the male "everyman," Karagöz. She thought European influences could be good, bad, or indifferent – but the human condition remained the same. This mother was satire's answer to the idealized vision of revolution. She asked the reader to remember suffering, want, and folly. She was the voice and image of the fears of the revolution, of the cultural anxiety that considered the threats faced by the empire: the undermining of its bases for social unity, its political ineptitude, and its economic dependence. Like her shadow puppet predecessors for generations past, she expected the worst.

Cadaloz is perhaps the most powerful image, the most compelling voice, among the woman forms in the Ottoman satirical press. She defends neither Islam, nor the monarchy, nor the republic. She knows that the revolution will not bring glory or readily disarticulate customary social bounds. She is neither enamored of the constitutional project nor deceived by the illusion of her own role in it. She has been engaged in the patriarchal bargain for many generations.[39] And when she imagines woman, community, and nation, she believes that she knows them already, and that there is no such thing as progress, only change.

The old nag came in different forms (Figure 3.6). Her figures were utilized in satiric dialogue, humorous skits, and cartoons. But always, she had an insistent voice.[40] In satiric dialogue, she might be *Büyük Hanım* (literally *Big Lady*, but meaning Old Lady or Granny), bemoaning conditions for the woman (and man) in the street: bridge tolls, the price of bread, the fact that the government's loudly touted *hürriyet* (freedom) did not seem to bring the promised benefits.[41] Her image appears in the mastheads of several gazettes. For example, the masthead of the periodical *Geveze* (Blabbermouth) contains two characters: one a jovial and talkative man, the other a scowling and scolding old nag.[42] A later Ottoman gazette, called *Diken* (Thorn or Barb), and published between 1918 and 1920 while the empire disintegrated in the aftermath of World War I, also had an old nag as its mascot.[43] Her specialty was social satire.

Figure 3.6 Masthead Old Nags

All of these mascots in the Ottoman cartoon space generated criticism and reflected critical sentiments already in place. They were familiar figures in general; but their success, like the longevity of the shadow puppet theater, was based on the predictability of the characters and the unpredictability of events. The titles and mascots of many of the *mizah mecmuaları* reveal the tone and style (complaint, silliness, or resignation) through which they proposed to expose the political and social ramifications of revolution: *Şikâyet* (Complaint), *Cadaloz* (Old Nag), *Körük* (Bellows, Agitator), *Latife* (Joke), *Nekregû ile Pişekâr* (Conjurer and His Raggedy Sidekick), *Şakacı* (Jester), *Zevzek* (Giddy or Talkative One), *Dalkavuk* (Toady, Buffoon), *Eşek* (Ass). Many titles express (tongue in cheek) a position of misery of one form or another: *Cellad* (Executioner), *Dertli ile garib* (Pained, Complaining and Destitute), *Falaka* (Bastinado), *Mahkûm* (Condemned One), *Şaka* (Wretched, also Indolent, Joke), *Züğürt* (Destitute One). Others sound the call to inform and stir up with a variety of sounds: *Davul* (Drum), *Cart beyim* (Tearing Noise), *Curcuna* (Noisy Confusion, Carousal), *Çıngırak* (Bell), *Hande* (Laughter), *Nay* (Reed Flute), *Tokmak* (Mallet or Knocker), *Ton ton risalesi* (onomatopoetic - Vapur Horn Gazette), *Geveze* (Blabbermouth). The titles that depict misery or wretchedness point up the skeptical nature of the critiques often found in the satirical gazettes; they see the Ottoman people as under the gun. These titles are in marked contrast to the often idealistic titles of serious gazettes like *Serbesti* (Freedom), and *Hürriyet* (Freedom).

In Ottoman narrative and cartoon, the public is shown as caught between internal and external threats or "evils": autocracy, oppression, poverty, European imperialism, foreign invasion. Who would meet the demands of the "people," as proclaimed by the complainers, the drummers, the conjurers? To answer this question, satire drew from the forces (virtue, freedom, god, past heroes and warriors, glory, inertia, and fate), which moved the human characters of the revolutionary drama. It suggested that the voice of the people might well go unanswered. But as long as there was a press to drum and buzz and mutter, the "people" would not succumb silently to either the internal or external threats.

TARGETS

While the press created images of the public, that public did not exist in an idyllic cartoon vacuum. Rather, the public and the satiric mascots who often represented that public, occupied a cartoon space that was frought with danger, aggravations, and sources of bewilderment. The satiric press translated the enemies of the empire, its problems, and its anxieties, into a series of targets. Facing these opponents, the new Ottoman regime and its citizens could triumph, endure, or be overwhelmed. Sometimes the new regime and the public were themselves the targets of the press. The targets of Ottoman satire were linked directly to the crisis of new and old orders, which the revolution seems to have symbolized or precipitated, and to the imminent threats of the day: bankruptcy and conquest. Within these frames, the satiric gazettes crafted their own visions of the sultanic and constitutional orders, and of the European "other."

Charles Press, in his work on American cartoons, divides political cartoons into four categories dependent upon the way in which the cartoon approaches its target; these ways are descriptive (fatalistic), laughing satirical, destructive satirical, and heroic or glorifying.[44] All of these styles of taking on targets were evident in the Ottoman revolutionary press. Some gazettes specialized in the laughing satirical style; most of the gazettes examined here at least occasionally employed the heroic or glorifying mode (for the new government, the heroes of the revolution, or even the Ottoman citizen). The destructive satirical mode was employed liberally in the early days of the revolution when many editors were preoccupied with disarticulating the sultanic discourse. Later, satire employing this same mode was leveled at the CUP. Perhaps a most characteristic mode of Ottoman satire was what Press calls the descriptive, fatalistic mode. The descriptive, fatalistic cartoon image creates a picture for the "reader" of what is going on, but it is skeptical of the possible remedies for the situation depicted.[45] The satiric genres of the Karagöz dialogue and the Nasr üd-Din tale roughly match this category of the descriptive, fatalistic cartoon. Given these satiric genre predecessors and given the precarious position of the Ottoman state in the aftermath of its revolution, it is no wonder that the descriptive, fatalistic mode holds a prominent place in the Ottoman cartoon space.[46]

The way a gazette manipulated its pictures of reality, messages, and moods, suggested the extent to which that publication was willing to grant or withhold legitimacy from a specific vision of political and social order. But the recommendation and mood were complicated by apprehension that neither the new order nor the old were calculated to offer salvation from European imperialism. Charles Press has proposed that "the revolutionary technique follows a predictable routine: to paint the social (including religious), political, and economic leaders as inhuman monsters while conjuring up pictures of the atrocities that flow from their malevolence. The rules and symbols of that system are to be regarded with contempt at every opportunity while those who oppose it, domestic or foreign, are to be feted as heroes."[47] Once an authoritarian system comes under severe criticism, according to Press, it is a no-win game. That is, there is no room for mild mannered monsters in this type of satire. Once demonized, the old regime cannot then be exorcised and viewed in a more benevolent light. Press's model finds its echo in the Ottoman revolutionary press. Abd ül-Hamid, like Louis-Phillipe as Gargantua in Daumier's cartoon, and Muhammad Ali Shah in Iranian satire, took on monstrous proportions in the pages of the Istanbul gazettes.[48] Initially, the sultan was the revolutionary press's public enemy number one. The press, however, had still larger monsters than the sultan to parade before the public eye: the Gargantuas of Europe swallowing the empire piecemeal.[49] Both foreign support and foreign opposition to the Istanbul regime were clearly recognized as self-interested, hegemonic, and scarcely motivated by altruistic notions of the spread of cultural progress. There lay the dilemma. Athough Ottoman satirists wished to command the symbolic repertoire in order to articulate and shape a "new" Ottoman identity (one not associated with defeat and bankruptcy), they did not wish to surrender this process of creation to Europe. Then too, one could not simply attack the sultan alone, because the sultan was the representative, the symbol, of an entire traditional system, of a dominant discourse. Once the sultan came under attack, so too could all the social and political structures of the empire.[50] Satirists then were caught in what could be a paradoxical position, intent on destroying the hegemonic system of the sultanate and (at least) parts of what that system represented while, at the same time, defending that system from "foreign" attacks.[51]

The construction of targets in the Ottoman revolutionary press, then, was done against the background of European imperialism as the target that could not be ignored. That said, the major internal target of satire was the government. Echoing Charles Press's schema (which is based on the revolutions of America, England, and France) the Ottoman revolutionary press savaged the primary symbol of the old regime and of the old dominant discourse, the sultan (and his ministers). To do so, satirists employed images and symbols drawn from the art of Germany, England, Italy, and especially France, such as the cartoons of *Punch* or *La Caricature*'s cartoons showing vegetables metamorphosing into the king or government figures.[52] The sultan became the monster of *istibdad* (despotism). But, not long after the revolution, the sultan became a puppet, devoid of compelling power; with the establishment of a new government and later with the deposition of Abd ül-Hamid, Ottoman political satire turned to the meclis, the CUP, and the new ministers of state as its primary targets. Satire was drawn to power, and the new dominant discourse was not a sultanic one.[53]

While satire was galvanized by external threats and by the debate over the nature of sovereignty, it did not limit itself to political themes. Economic conditions in the empire were a primary target: mismanagement of resources, foreign interests and intervention, the sad state of Ottoman labor. Social satire was also prominent in the revolutionary press, which lampooned manners, education, theater, gender roles, and the struggle between old and new cultural mores. Part of this perceived cultural transformation of the Ottoman state and the Ottoman mind was the infiltration of European culture: new literature, new fashions, new morals, new ways of telling time. Women, in particular their bodies and their dress, became a cartoon foil for debates over cultural hegemony and the honor of the nation. Urban problems, such as crime (and crime control), disease, and dog packs were standard targets of revolutionary satire, and so were technological changes. Cartoons noted that new technologies often failed to function, especially in the area of transport systems. Thus, comparisons of the donkey to the tram, the skif to the steamship, and the pedestrian to the automobile were standard fare for readers of Ottoman cartoons. Together these varied targets were paraded across the Ottoman cartoon space to reflect the nature of Ottoman anxieties and to suggest the directions in which state and society might move.

In the gazette *Davul,* for instance, which was published in twenty-four issues between 1908 and 1909, the targets of cartoons break down roughly as follows:

Internal Politics—The Meclis	46%
Foreign Relations with Europe	15%
The Sultan	13%
Social Criticism	05%
Dress	05%
Economy	04%
European Economic Intervention	04%
The Bureaucracy	03%
The Press	02%
Education	01%
Arts and Culture	01%
Religion	01%

This is a very rough classification and is based on a small set of cartoons, but it does reflect the priorities in *Davul*'s satire. Unlike some gazettes, which focused on foreign affairs, *Davul* suggested that the fate of the empire depended upon the behavior, style, and evolution of the new government. Each gazette had its own particular focus, some generalist gazettes evoking multiple targets and others sticking to the same specific area of satire week after week. Thus, for example, *Lâla* (published in 1910–1911) targeted internal affairs exclusively, and *Musavver Papağan* (1908–1909) focused on foreign affairs, especially in Austria and the Balkans. Of course domestic and foreign affairs were often intimately and inextricably connected so that a critique of the regime might well include a critique of its internal and foreign policies.

Themes that might be expected in the context of constitutional revolution but that play a decidedly secondary role in revolutionary press satire are religion and ethnicity. Although there was considerable religious rhetoric in the serious press concerning the nature of piety and the shape revolutionary government should take (Derviş Vahdeti's rhetoric in *Volkan* is a good example), the satiric press was quite reticent about communal struggle. Attacks on the clergy, or scenes that pit Muslims against Christians or Jews, are singularly absent from the Ottoman cartoons I observed.[54] This absence is not, however, as some accounts of the early days of the revolution would suggest, a result of Ottomans discarding their communal animosities as a new age of catholicity and freedom dawned. Even though the empire had, over all, been a tolerant one, localism, communalism, and ethnocentrism were elements of Ottoman culture before and after the revolution. Rather, the satirical press's restraint concerning religious conflicts reflected both the high value it placed on Ottoman social unity in the face of foreign threats and the strong current of religious piety running through the press establishment.[55] Piety is, of course, difficult to measure, but the power of religion as a force in Ottoman society is undeniable. The personnel, hierarchies, and institutions of the dominant and minority faiths might be subject to criticism, but the satirical press tended to abstain from general attacks on religion.[56] Often, in revolutions, the relative chaos of the revolutionary situation and the traditional association of religious hierarchies with members of the elite classes tended to provoke attacks on religious institutions (as they did during the French Revolution). But, in the Ottoman case, the transfer of power was relatively less chaotic, and the threat of foreign invasion relatively more pressing. Nor did the *ulema* (clergy) command as high a degree of political power within the Ottoman state system in 1908; they were, thus, a less significant target than they might once have been.[57]

In an era when ethnic nationalisms were apparently gaining power, ethnic typecasting or slurring was not a dominant mode of satire in the gazettes examined.[58] Again, the failure to make ethnic slurs a primary focus may signal the satiric press's attempt to preserve the bonds of social unity in a multi-ethnic state.[59] There is, however, perhaps a simpler answer. That is, for the very reason that the Ottoman state was ethnically very diverse and very mixed, it possessed a series of traditional tropes for ethnic caricature and felt no particular urgency to develop new ones.[60] This is not to say that the Ottoman cartoon space was devoid of ethnic types. On the contrary, ethnic markers, usually in the form of dress, were fairly common in Ottoman cartoons. Ethnic marking did not, however, require a targeting or critiquing of one particular ethnic group. Ordinarily, where ethnic marking did occur, it was to produce comic effect, not necessarily at the expense of one ethnic group versus another. Where all the "ethnics" were Ottomans, this became a form of self-satire; Ottoman cartoons were expert at self-satire. The possible exception may be found in cartoon satire of Balkan types, particularly Bulgarians. Ethnic Balkan "types" were caricatured by exaggerated "traditional" dress: Greek, Albanian, Bulgarian. These "types" were usually employed for identification of place (dress also identified functional types like peasant or minister) rather than for ethnic satire. But, because Bulgaria capitalized on the revolution to declare its independence, it came in for particular scrutiny in the satirical press, as a secessionist state and collaborator with the European powers. In this context, the Bulgarian king and some of his subjects became targets in the satirical press, not so much because of their ethnicity but because of their political behavior. Thus, ethnic satire became a satire of "nations."

Arabs, on the other hand, who might or might not be typed by dress, were seldom the subject of ethnic slurring in the satirical press (the primary exception was Abd ül-Hamid's finance minister, İzzet Pasha).[61] İzzet was shown, for example, in *Dalkavuk,* as a huge figure, one foot on the Ottoman Cabinet, dispensing money and medals to reaching hands on both sides of the Bosphorus.[62] The press also satirized the succession struggles in Morocco. But, much more common were cartoons showing Arabs (especially those in Egypt) in a sympathetic light, as suffering at the hands of European imperialists.[63] None of this is meant to imply that ethnic animosities were not expressed and exercised among the empire's inhabitants; it would be interesting, for example, to compare the language and images of the press in the capital with those of the press in the Arab provinces to see what differences existed in the presentation of ethnicity as subject.

The portrayal of Arabs as victims of imperialism illustrates an important aspect of the nature of ethnic typing in the Ottoman satirical press. Although relatively few ethnic slurs were directed at internal ethnic groups, external ethnic groups, particularly Europeans, were fair game. Dress, exaggerated to suggest ethnic type and ethnic allegiance, was employed to type foreigners. The imperialist powers and their citizens were the subjects of regular and scathing attacks in the Ottoman cartoon space (rapacious Austrians, greedy Britons, militaristic Russians), although, often these images did not represent images of the people per se, but personifications of the enemy states. The colonial context proved to be a significant influence on the nature of cartoon identity formation. It was not simply a question of which targets were available for satirization, it was also a question of which targets were to be protected and which targets it was expedient to attack. Again, satire was drawn to power, and it was where ethnicity was associated with various forms of power, that it was most exploited for satiric purpose. The image of the "European," of course, was not solely an object of attack in the Ottoman cartoon space; he could also stand for that which was free, admired, and desirable. But generally, the "European," in Ottoman satire, was a threat and, as such, subject to ethnic typing and to attack.

Class was an important denominator in cartoon images but it was utilized primarily in very stereotyped and formalistic ways. Class was reflected in the selection of gazette mascots, in critiques of municipal administration, and in social and economic satire. It was evoked to suggest the impoverishment to which the empire was subjected by the oppression of monarchy and of imperialism. Use of comic spokemen or women from the lower classes was a standard mode for expressing the skeptical nature of the satiric voice; in Ottoman cartoons the poor got poorer and the rich got richer. Even though satire attempted to draw lines of Ottoman brotherhood, and sisterhood, across class lines, in order to promote "national" unity, there was a tacit understanding in the cartoon space that the lower and upper classes (in general) neither spoke the same "language" nor understood revolution in the same ways.[64] The revolutionary press was faced with the paradox of creating revolutionary bonds of unity with the lower classes in a society that was very class conscious while, at the same time, deploring the ignorance and inertia of those very classes. As Neil McWilliam has observed in his thought provoking analysis of the connections between art and class in post-revolutionary France:

> [L]aying claim to a cultural identity was no easy matter and no one strategy could be pursued without paying a price. Throughout the 1830's and 1840's bourgeois commentators increasingly probed the working-class habitus for evidence of a collective moral being, and inclined to treat alleged cultural preferences as elements in a broader social etiology. For some, increasing literacy brought with it the threat of insubordination provoked by lurid and immoral works through whose corrupt appeal the people became "insolent, cavilling, impudent, blasphemously cynical, rebellious, unruly, mad on debauchery, and consumed by impious fever".[65]

One might argue that Ottoman satire's impressions of the "people" were more tolerant than those McWilliams cites on the French masses. Ottoman satire automatically granted the "working-class" a collective moral being. Also, "insolent, blasphemously cynical, and unruly" certainly sounds like an apt characterization of Karagöz, the hero of Ottoman satire. Nonetheless, the revolutionary impetus to rhetorics of unity did pose a dilemma to Ottoman satirists when they turned to topics of social evolution. Cartoons, because they breached the boundaries of physical, social, and intellectual space, could help the "bourgeois" press resolve this dilemma. But, in the end, that press was generally engaged in cross-class caricature rather than in a revolutionary disarticulation of class boundaries. In the Ottoman cartoon, as in the boulevard theaters of nineteenth-century Paris, "popular audiences could easily be subborned into applauding their own grotesque caricatures."[66]

In 1911, *Cadaloz* expressed this class disjuncture through a confrontation between a gentleman and a street sweeper. In this cartoon the gentleman, "Mr. Chic," a dandy with bow tie, spats, and goosehead cane, berates the sweeper who has just swept dirt on his pants: "Hey, you've soiled me, is that any way to clean!?" The annoyed young sweeper, undaunted, retorts, "What are you yelling about? Everyone is free now (*her kesin hürriyeti var*). I can sweep any way I want!" Off to the side, an observer, the old nag, Cadaloz, shrugs. She knows this misunderstanding is not likely to be resolved. "Ah," she says, "We'll never get used to this freedom business, we just don't understand it."[67] Thus, the voice of the people was a voice that was snatched up in revolutionary rhetorics, even in the satirical press, for purposes of mobilizing the Ottoman citizenry and shoring up "national" unity. But the satirists never forgot for long just how far Istanbul society was from such visions of unity and a shared revolutionary project.

IV
Revolutionary Exemplars: France and Iran

For years, virtually total despotism had crushed the wretched [Iranian] people. . . . but in Iran, slowly slowly, constitutionalism (meşrutiyet) . . . had begun.
—*Nevsal-ı Osmanî*, "Iran"[1]

The Ottoman press appropriated, modified, reproduced, and invented revolution, using the precedents of the French and Iranian revolutions for inspiration. These concrete examples were focal points around which the Ottoman press organized its messages about revolutionary outcomes. France provided a distant revolution that took on mythic proportions and was idealized in the Ottoman press. The appropriation of French political and satiric models was only one manifestation of a preoccupation with European political organization, literature, education, and society, which had been gathering force in Istanbul during the nineteenth century, a preoccupation with the image of success.[2] Iran, conversely, represented a revolution that was near in time and in space, one which suggested the twin disasters of subjugation to reactionary monarchy and to rapacious foreign intervention.

Emerging from a milieu wedded to the hegemonic system of sultanic autocracy and empire, how was the Istanbul press to articulate revolution in 1908? The Ottoman system still traced its heritage to the "*gazi*" steppe confederations and to the "slave" elites that directed the imperial armies and bureaucracies of Selim I and Süleiman the Magnificant in the sixteenth century. In the sultanic system's model of obedience exchanged for justice and promotion, the press found little precedent for identities forged around notions of "popular" sovereignty.[3] Once the perceptions of both justice and gain were no longer present to legitimize the hegemonic system, Abd ül-Hamid found it expedient rigidly to control the press to deter the public exploration of alternative systems of sovereignty. But, after the revolution, the press, relatively uncensored and fueled by the silenced speculations of decades, sought its revolutionary precedents in the idealized past of France and in the stark and immediate reality of Iran.

Various authors have assessed the development of political language in the Middle East and traced the expressions of revolution in that area to European antecedents, particularly to the French revolution and to Western political philosophies.[4] This "imitationist" school has drawn assenting and dissenting responses, particularly from scholars working on Arab nationalism.[5] Among the counter arguments to the notion that European patterns were applied whole hog (then roughly tailored) to Muslim states is the argument that the Middle Eastern peoples needed no model of revolution, of consensual rule, or of popular sovereignty, because there were long-standing historical precedents for all of these within the context of classical Islamic government and law. The French, (or English) therefore, did not "discover" popular sovereignty or create a new notion of state.

What may be more significant than the above debate, however, is the way in which political concepts were construed by each people in each period, or the ways in which these concepts were appropriated and subsequently evolved. The argument over the French revolution, for example, still needs to be refined in accordance with the extent, depth, manner, and nature of that revolution's influence. At issue is not so much who invented consensus or the "rights of man" but, rather, what groups were effected, through what modalities, and in what areas of Ottoman society.[6] What can be said, here, is that the image of the French revolution was clearly before the eyes of many of the literati active in publishing before and after the Ottoman revolution and, through the cartoon press, before the eyes of the non-literate as well. What cannot be said from examining this image is how literally the writers took the comparison, how exactly the image called up in the press matched the writers' beliefs about the eventual articulation of an Ottoman political and social system, or what part of that image was rhetorical and what part "real."[7] Discussion in the empire of European thought, literature, and actions could have been purely academic or informational. It could have served as preparation to combat a perceived political or cultural threat from abroad. It could have served as rhetoric, pure and simple, without benefit of intent to implement; or it could have represented a sincere commitment to produce a French-like society in Istanbul. Each of these options is suggested in the Ottoman cartoon space, where picturing France or picturing the Empire were not constrained by the boundaries of political reality. My purpose here is not to accept or refute some fixed degree of magnitude by which European models were imposed on a "helpless" or "backward" Asian empire, or to settle for good and all what institutions were and were not invented by Europe. My purpose, rather, is to show that the Ottoman state's cartoon vision of itself was diverse and evolving, as were the language and images chosen to reflect that evolutionary process. Satirists chose selectively from among the available images of revolution, and that selection was strongly influenced by highly particularistic, distinctly Ottoman, versions of France and of Iran.

For example, shortly after the Ottoman revolution, the first issue of the daily, *Üç gazete,* dated September 11, 1908, ran an article entitled "The Politics of Muhammad Ali Shah."[8] It was signed, simply, "Musa." This author states that, since the French revolution, constitutionalism has not yet been properly established in the world, even though England serves as an example of constitutional rule achieved. He begins his piece by noting that, in what he calls an "era of *hürriyet* (freedom)," Muhammad Ali Shah must surely be paramount among the kings of the world who are hostile to constitutionalism (*meşrutiyet*). The shah's absolutism, Musa writes, is said to surpass even that of Louis XVI. France, here, as in many other articles, stood for the launching of revolutionary freedoms and the escape from the tyranny of the *ancien regime* while Iran stood for the perpetuation and exaggeration of an obsolete absolutism.

FRANCE

On December 2, 1909, about one year after the Ottoman revolutionary regime held elections for a new Chamber of Deputies, the Istanbul gazette *Kalem* published a cartoon. It shows a small child climbing to the top of a flag staff borne by an Ottoman soldier and bearing the Ottoman flag (Figure 4.1). The child shades its eyes to gaze off into a brilliant sun rising over Istanbul. In the midst of this sun stands the Eiffel Tower—its top metamorphosed into a womanly figure, who, in turn, gazes maternally at the child. The cartoon's caption reads: "facing mother liberty" (*māder hürriyete karşı*). There can be no doubt, in this cartoon, that it is France that has given birth to the Ottoman revolution, that the Ottoman child is seeking its French mother. But the concerned matron is not the France of 1909. It is the idealized revolutionary France of 1789; it is freedom. Just as Mother Liberty, in this frame, appears to hover in a vision over the Ottoman capital, so too the Istanbul press created an illusion to serve its own image of the Ottoman political transformation. In this particular version of that image, the Ottoman state is drawn in a relation of dependence, as a child. The child figure symbolizes the newness and fragility of the Ottoman experiment in freedom, a fragility that is, however, fortified by the Ottoman soldier on whose shoulders the child climbs. The mother figure suggests the wisdom and experience of France in matters of liberty; she will be the teacher and the child looks to her for guidance.[9] Although this cartoon suggests a dream or a vision, that dream is rooted in a known place, Paris, the outlines of which are vaguely suggested in the sun's rays around the Eiffel Tower. It is also directed to a known place, Istanbul, the foundation upon which the standard bearer and the flag rest.

French revolutionary ideology had a significant impact on the development of constitutionalist discourse in the Ottoman Empire and Iran in

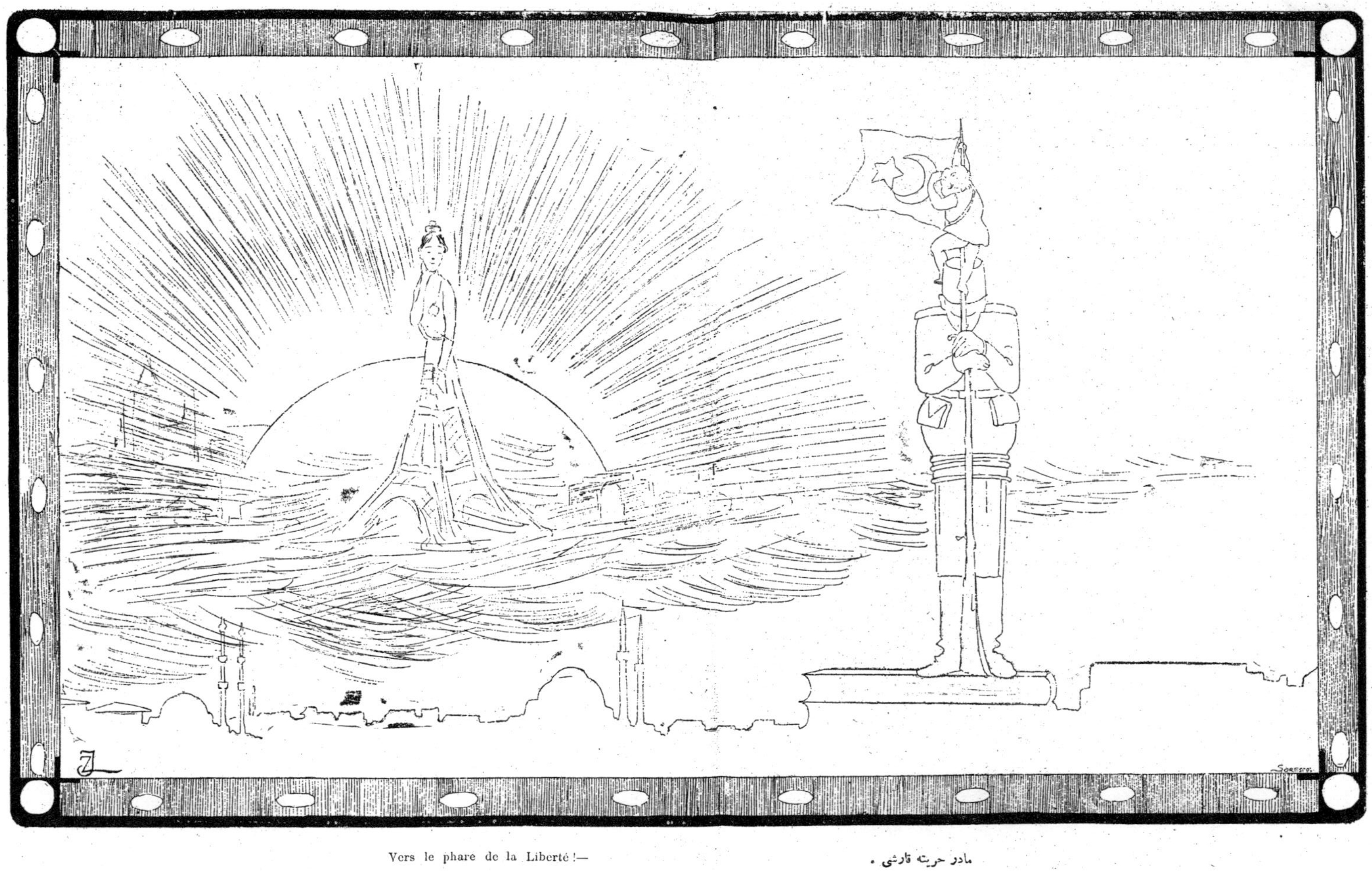

Vers le phare de la Liberté!—

Figure 4.1 Mother Liberty

the nineteenth and early twentieth centuries.[10] Ottoman intellectuals had long debated the nature and efficacy of constitutionalism and the relevance or desirability of France as model. "*Liberté, Fraternité, Égalité*" found its echo in the Turkish, Persian, and Arabic press during the 1905–1909 constitutional revolutions along with both explicit and implied references to France as exemplar.[11] The press and other literary forms adapted the language and slogans of the French revolution to signify opposition to sovereign power (*hâkimiyet*). In this discourse, France, as symbol of a "new" and progressive political ideology, joined more traditional images of resistance to injustice, such as the *Karagöz* shadow puppet characters, in Turkish language publications. Not everyone, though, was so sanguine about the French Revolution and a constitutional regime. Derviş Vahdeti, in a January 1909 article entitled "Out with the Old, In with the New" (*Eskiler Gitsin, Yeniler Gelsin*), pointed out the bloodbath associated with the French Revolution

Images of the French revolution in the Istanbul press often provide a euphoric vision.[12] Thus, for example, *Davul* ran a tongue-in-cheek cartoon of figures representing the empire's diverse communal groups after the revolution, they are arm in arm, shouting "Long live brotherhood" (*vive la fraternité*).[13] This vision of revolution anticipated a new prosperity, the modern counterpart of what the classical Ottoman system of sovereignty had once promised in return for the acceptance of autocratic rule. The French revolution was a rhetorical ideal in the Ottoman press, stripped of its historic reality and symbolic of the potential for all the good of a new social and political order.

In direct opposition to this image was the specter of Iran, emerging from the 1905–1906 constitutional revolution, its territorial integrity compromised by rapacious Britian and Russia, and its people encumbered by the reassertion of tyrannical and ineffectual kingship under Muhammad Ali Shah. Too close, temporally and spatially, to Istanbul's own revolution, Iran symbolized the inability of revolution to achieve freedom, prosperity, or constitutional rule. In Iran, as in France, a counter-revolution had signified the vitality of the traditonal hegemonic system and the society's anxiety about the competence of the citizens to rule. The resilience of the dominant sovereign system, in Iran as in the Ottoman state, was enhanced by the long tradition of a universal law (the *Shariah*) that provided a force for unity in the society and for legitimation of the sovereign systems that had co-opted or tried to co-opt its agents, the ulema (religious authorities). Where, in France, this universal law was associated with the challenge to the dominant subsystem, in the Ottoman empire it was one of the mainstays of sultanic order.

Iran was the nearest and most likely model for constitutional revolution; its revolutionaries, in 1906, had imposed a constitution on Muzaffar al-Din Shah. But the Ottoman press chose to render its own history using a European model, many miles and years removed from the cries of jubilation in the streets of Istanbul. Why France? The Iranian revolution symbolized reality, the reality of internal chaos and of Britain and Russsia moving in to seize territory as the new government struggled to establish itself. The French revolution symbolized the ideal, an image of freedom, justice, prosperity, and a comraderie of spirit as antithesis to the oppression, military weakness, economic default, and moral bankruptcy of the monarchical regime under which, the press suggested, Ottoman society was suffering. France was also a great power; Iran was not.

Another reason for choosing France as model was the training and education of the corps of journalists and politicians who constructed the revolution in the press. The emergence of a French-literate intelligentsia began in earnest in the nineteenth century, in part the result of Ottoman (and Qajar) attempts to ward off political and economic collapse through diplomatic efforts and educational reforms. The Ottoman Translation Bureau was created and its staff members often sent to France to complete their training.[14] Besides the formation of the Ottoman Translation Bureau, several factors had contributed to the formation of a French literate public in Istanbul in the late nineteenth century. These factors were the incorporation of French-language into Ottoman civil education systems, the sending of Ottoman youths to Paris for training, the development of a French language Ottoman expatriate press by exiled Young Turks, the use of French tutors by upper-class Ottoman families, and the popularization of French literature and culture by Istanbul journals like *Servet-i fünun* (*Treasury of Science*), published by Ahmed İhsan in 1891–1928.[15] A Francophone class of intellectuals was thus created, which, in turn, played a dominant role in constitutionalist publications before and after the revolution.

The lives of three important nineteenth century Ottoman thinkers, İbrahim Şinasi (1824–1871), Ziya Paşa, and Namık Kemal (1840–1888), illustrate the various avenues for the transmission of French ideas and culture.[16] Şinasi learned French from a French renegade in the Ottoman military service and later joined an Ottoman student mission to Paris where he lived for five years. Ziya Paşa studied French as a member of the Imperial household service, lived as an exile in Paris from 1867 to 1872, and translated various French works into Ottoman Turkish. Namık Kemal was educated in French at home, joined the Ottoman Translation Offices of the Customs and of the Porte, and also lived as an exile in Paris. After his return in 1871, he produced the patriotic drama *Vatan* (Homeland).[17] The careers of these literati suggest the ways in which the French language and French political culture had come to influence Ottoman elites by the latter half of the nineteenth century. Many of those men whose positions in the military, bureaucracy, or publishing industry gave them a voice in articulating the 1908 revolution were the products of this Francophone influenced education.[18] Once revolution unshackled the press, the crisis over how specifically to define an Ottoman constitutional regime was complicated by the bilingual philosophy of revolution that such men constructed.[19]

Having chosen France as revolutionary exemplar, the press was not unaware of the other image of France, the image of imperial power, of military threat, of territorial ambition, the France of Napoleon. Just as there was a movement to imitate French politics, language, and culture, there was a counter-movement to resist the influence of France, which provided the symbols, both of attaining freedom and of losing it absolutely: the Revolution and Napoleonesque imperialism.[20] Juxtaposing the two options intellectually was not an easy task but the polarization was made readily in cartoon images. In cartoons, twentieth-century France, run by the "heirs" of Napoleon, was a polity that represented victory, the impulse to conquest, and the means to subjugate other peoples.[21] But, the "other" France was Marianne, the revolution, the spirit of liberty. The Ottoman satiric press separated these images of France; like Ebenezer Scrooge's ghosts in Charles Dickens's famous tale, one was the image of France past (revolution), the other of France present (colonial threat). If only the Ottomans could merge the two into an Ottoman constitutional regime that brought both freedom and strength, then the state could be an equal of France, sharer in both revolutionary and imperial glory rather than a victim of French imperialism, like Morocco. Many Ottoman literati were, of course, quite conversant with the third Republic, its history, and its evolution; but in the rhetorics of the Ottoman revoutionary press and the Ottoman cartoon space, it was the tropes of the French revolution and contemporary French imperialism that took center stage.

The negative image of France, that of European imperial power and aggressor will be dealt with in subsequent chapters. The positive image, that of leader in the struggle for political freedom and civilizational excellence, took several forms in the cartoon space. Cartoons of the Ottoman revolution depicted the slogans, banners, and street demonstrations of the French revolution as well as images of Marianne and of the French revolutionary style cap. Concepts associated with the French revolution (such as constitutionalism, elections, freedom of speech, a free press) were also juxtaposed to visual symbols suggesting France or French civilization.

The slogan "*liberté, fraternité, égalité,*" (*hürriyet, uhuvvet, müsavat*), for example, was endemic in the Ottoman revolutionary rhetorics, a clearly well-known catchphrase for the freedoms and privileges of constitutional government.[22] In a speech on February 16, 1909, for example, the Grand Vezir Hilmî Pasha called upon "liberty and equality for all the citizens, and justice for all, in order that [the empire] might occupy a place of honor among the civilized nations."[23] In the cartoon space, this phrase alone suggested revolution, a free press, and government by the people.[24] A cartoon in *Nekregû* showed a sun labeled "freedom" bursting up through the pavement and scattering the old regime; above the sun were stars labeled "fraternity," and "justice."[25] In a cartoon in *Kalem,* this slogan was enscribed on the base of a monument bearing the figure of the constitution (*kanun-ı esasî*), shown in the form of a lion.[26] It suggested the ideals upon which constitutional government should be based. The gazette *Lâklâk* showed a pyramid of Ottoman citizens, waving Ottoman flags and banners reading "*hürriyet, müsavat,* and *adalet*" (justice). At the top of the pyramid stood a staunch citizen with a banner marked *meşrutiyet* (constitutionalism).[27] Other symbols of French freedoms, like the Marseillaise, were also called up in the Ottoman press to suggest the new Ottoman era of liberty.[28] Indeed the word freedom (*hürriyet*) became the symbol for the opening of all doors, as aptly satirized in a cartoon in *Kalem*. This cartoon shows a boy selling roses, hustling after a well-dressed citizen. "Bey Efendi, roses, roses," he urges.[29] The man looks skeptical. "Freedom roses, efendi," proclaims the boy. "Well then . . . ," the man relents, reaching for his wallet. Satirists, capitalizing on the prevalence of words like *hürriyet* and *müsavat* in the serious revolutionary press, poked fun at the concepts themselves. *Boşboğaz* ran a serialized "Freedom Dictionary" (*Kamus-i Hürriyet*) which consisted of a series of silly definitions for Ottoman words and phrases.[30] *Şakacı*, depicted its own version of "*müsavat*" (equality): putting a short man on stilts so that he could be just as tall as his neighbor.

The figurative heroine of the French revolution, Marianne, was also found in many variations in Ottoman cartoons. One such cartoon, shows "*Hürriyet,*" as a nubile "Marianne" type, sheltering under the arm of a noble figure representing the Ottoman army (Figure 4.2). He is protecting her from a two-headed dragon representing the forces of reaction. "Don't fear, my Dear," he says, "I'm by your side and my sword is sharp."[31] In this recreation of the St. George myth, *Hürriyet* wears a pseudo-classical costume and the French revolutionary cap. She is youthful and fragile, suggesting the newness and vulnerability of the Ottoman political order. One can argue that this figure is not sufficiently sexually evolved to represent Marianne; but I would argue that this is a sexually charged figure and, further, that the Ottoman cartoonists used the Phrygian cap as a trope to suggest the French Revolution, very often in conjunction with a female figure. (Some viewers would pick up the allusions of this symbol and many, presumably, would not.) No compunction was felt to adhere strictly to the symbols of revolution as they had been employed in France. This cartoon at once associates the Ottoman Revolution with its French forebear, and suggests that the fruits of the Revolution may only be preserved through vigilance and force. The army here is a bastion for the defense of freedom; it is the nation's sword, its manhood. The army will keep order and avert the anarchy associated with the French revolution. This particular image is a precursor to those depicting the Third Army's *Hareket Ordusu* (Action Army), which "saved the nation" after the counter-revolution of April 1909.[32]

Marianne figures were not the only female incarnations of the nation found in the Ottoman cartoon space (see chapter 8).[33] They may be contrasted to a more "Turkish" version found in the gazette *Davul*, in a cartoon called "Constitutionalism Insurance." Also in "classical" robes, *Davul*'s female nation is being examined by a European male physician; she wears a crescent in her hair rather than the French cap (Figure 4.3).[34] What is

Figure 4.2 "Marianne" and the Dragon

Figure 4.3   Insurance for the Motherland

important here is that symbols, in image and narrative, of the French revolution were commonplace in the Ottoman cartoon space. Their emplacement there suggests not only that the cartoons' producers were familiar with French culture, language, and imagery, but that they expected these symbols to strike a familiar chord in at least parts of their audiences as well.

At least one cartoonist used a Marianne figure in a frame that celebrated the Ottoman revolution as opposed to its violent European counterparts. In a frame entitled "You Compare," *İncili çavuş* contrasted a picture of dancing in the street labeled "Revolution in the Ottoman lands," to a drawing labeled, "Revolution Abroad," which showed a street battle and a Marianne-like figure raising her arms in an attempt to stop the conflict.[35] This image is pointing out the relatively bloodless nature of the Ottoman constitutional revolution, drawing a contrast to the bloody aftermath of the French revolution and more recent nationalist revolutions in Europe. It suggests that the Ottomans are the true successors to the ideal of revolution as embodied in the figure of the idealized female nation. The Marianne figure in this cartoon is much closer than the adolescent Marianne figure in the dragon cartoon to the grown-up figure of the beloved found in French revolutionary imagery. But, even in French artisty, Marianne was an evolving figure. In any case, it was not so important to Ottoman satirists that their female liberty symbols exactly approximated Marianne, as long as a cap or a bare breast associated with a female figure could suggest the glorious freedoms of the French revolution.

The ideal France found expression in three major themes in the Ottoman press: the conquest of tyranny, the liberation of culture, and the granting, with constitutionalism, of a voice to the previously voiceless "people." Before a society could be liberated, its tyrants had to be neutralized. This capturing of sovereign power was suggested in cartoons showing Abd ül-Hamid caged and juxtaposed to symbols of the French revolution.

A powerful example of this type of cartoon is found in the gazette *Papağan,* a publication in which elaborate, full-page cartoons tended to emphasize the Ottoman "alliance" with Western European powers rather than its conflicts with them. The publisher, "Kitabcı Karabet," was clearly in sympathy with Britian and France; his animosity was directed at Austria. This particular cartoon appeared shortly after the deposition of the sultan. It shows noble-looking Ottoman freedom fighters parading along, pulling Abd ül-Hamid who is dressed in a topcoat and seated in a cage.[36] To add insult to injury, a street dog barks at the caged sultan. The procession seems to be taking place for the benefit of the foreign powers, who are shown dressed in military uniform and viewing the spectacle from behind a low wall. In this frame, all of the foreign powers look somewhat sinister. The cartoon, in its entirety, suggests not only the triumph of the revolution, but also the necessity of demonstrating to the European states that the revolution has triumphed over tyranny.

A second cartoon makes the comparison to the French revolution explicit. It shows a small and angry looking Abd ül-Hamid peering out of a cage-like jail cell, while street celebrations are going on below (Figure 4.4). The triumphant crowds march under banners labeled "*liberté*," "Union and Progress," and "Mehmed V," Abd ül-Hamid's successor. The deposed sultan is watching the procession go by and bemoaning the fleeting nature of time and of mores. Over the bars through which he peers is enscribed the slogan, "*Sans Souci*" (without care).[37] Thus the triumph of the Ottoman revolution over autocracy is portrayed in a frame in which Abd ül-Hamid is surrounded by the slogans and symbols of the French revolution. The frame reminds the viewer, as do many such cartoons, of the apparent indifference of the palace to the woes of the populace. The main task of the French revolution, according to the Istanbul press, had been the removal of the autocrat; this, in turn, would pave the way for effective government, social freedom, and the unleashing of political, cultural, and intellectual progress and enlightenment.[38]

One such aspect of social freedom where France served as exemplar was the theater. The Ottoman revolutionary press saw the theater not merely as entertainment but as an art form for popular freedom of expression that France had perfected. (Satire and criticism of the theater will be taken up in chapter 7.) The new Ottoman theater became a forum for the expression of ideas, and it was symbolic of what was portrayed as a "new" freedom to socialize, to walk the streets, to meet and discuss freely. France was also the model for "advanced" mingling of the sexes, suggested in the Ottoman cartoon space by Western fashion, feminism, and by modes of entertainment like the cafe concert. France, in short, had (to quote one article) "*la vie moderne.*" The cartoon space showed French-style freedom as characteristic of the new Ottoman regime; its members were shown at the theater, socializing with women, and patronizing Western-style venues. A cartoon satirizing this French inspired liberalism asks: "How can you tell that the Young Turks are civilized?" The answer is: "They follow the (French) fashions, they drink whiskey, they have a fondness for things foreign, they fight and shout at each other in Parliament."[39] Civilization was apparently a mixed blessing; but France was clearly a model for freedom of expression and the development of education, which in turn led to scientific thinking and progress.[40]

In the Ottoman press, the comparison of the empire to France found expression in a whole series of comparisons between the old era of tyranny and the new era of constitutionalism and freedom. Typical of numerous articles with titles like "Yesterday and Today" or "Before and After" is one serialized under the header "İstanbul" in the journal *Resimli kitab*. It is by İzzet Fuad Pasha, translated from the French and entitled, "Before and After Constitutionalism."[41] This article, like many other Ottoman essays, is cast in dialogue form, its protagonists are an Istanbulite and a Parisian, and its setting is "the Istanbul bridge." It contains a series of questions asked about Ottoman constitutionalism. The answers emphasize the great floures-

Hamid — O tempara!. ô mores!!...   زمان ده‌كيشدكه اخلاق ده كيشير .

Figure 4.4 Abd ül-Hamid, Sans Souci

cence of the press, the freedom of exchange of ideas, and the promotion and dissemination of scientific knowledge. The Ottomans, in short, had dutifully followed the enlightened example of the French and looked to the constitutional regime to bring them the fruits of freedom. In another article in the same gazette, Mahmud Sadık held up France as an example of a nation where the various "nations," (*millet*s) learned each other's languages, a skill he saw as essential.[42] *İnkılâb* defended unity and freedom against the oppression of the old regime and the palace in an editorial entitled "In the Name of Constitutionalism," and signed, simply, "An Ottoman."[43] Other articles examined in great detail and from different perspectives the concepts of nation, constitutionalism, and freedom.[44]

The satirical press responded to such articles with its own dialogues, humorous versions of what was going on in the era of *meşrutiyet* and *hürriyet*. *Hokkabaz* for example, ran a humorous poetic list of "the ages of *hürriyet*," authored by "Herodotus."[45] *İncili çavuş* ran a satiric dialogue between *Hürriyet* and *İstibdad* (Liberty and Despotism), which begins with *İstibdad* hailing *Hürriyet*, who asks: "What, are you still around?"[46] Another piece in the same gazette characterized the old regime as "a thirty-two year era of slavery, despotism, and oppression," and the era of *hürriyet* as one of "reanimation" for the press.[47] *Kalem* published a cartoon celebrating the proclamation of the constitution, and the method by which it was achieved; it showed a soldier with a sword (labeled "constitution") popping out of a shipping box marked, "from Salonica to Istanbul."[48] The army, here again, was the instrument through which the nation's freedom would be attained.

The revolutionary press suggested that the new regime would be one in which the "people" had a significant place. In 1789, presaging the French revolution, Emmanuel Sieyes wrote, in a widely circulated pamphlet: "What is the third estate? Everything. What has it been heretofore in the political order? Nothing."[49] These sentiments, suggesting the newly won power of the "people," were echoed in an issue of the journal *Meram* (Design), published on November 12, 1908. The lead article was entitled, "*Dün, Bugün*," (Yesterday, Today); it began: "We Ottomans, yesterday what were we? Nothing! Today, what are we? Everything!"[50] The Ottoman press, then, had not only adopted the vision of the French revolution, but its language as well. The "people," in this idealized vision, were to be a new force in the Ottoman state.

But freedom, in the Ottoman revolution as in the French, was not to be absolute, and the political reality of the third estate never lived up to its ideal. The sovereign state, even without a powerful sovereign, still required that the "people" remain the people, subordinate to the regime. But the rhetoric of the will of the people was firmly incorporated into Ottoman political language, and into the language of Ottoman cartoons (see chapter 3).

Clearly the Ottoman revolution was not "popular" in the sense that it was the culmination of mass provincial revolts or of widespread peasant rebellion. Nor was the revolutionary press strictly "popular." Many revolutionary gazettes, with their French-language inserts and sophisticated political imagery were primarily aimed at the well educated and literate. But, in words and symbols, they portrayed themselves as representing the voice of the "people." They used traditional figures, like *Karagöz* and the *Davulcı* (drummer), to represent the new Ottoman "citizens" of the constitutional empire. These figures delivered the message that the constitutional regime would indeed bring *liberté, fraternité, égalité* to all men. And the medium for this message of freedom would be the French literate Ottoman press, as the bearer of the French revolution to the Ottoman masses. Tyranny had brought censorship and revolution would bring representative government, freedom of information, freedom of thought, freedom of the press, even freedom to demonstrate as illustrated by photos of student demonstrations and workers strikes in France.[51]

Nonetheless, it is unclear how many of the "people" were glad to see traditional government go, or how many thought the change in the course of the nation's history would be for the better. The idea of a new age of *hürriyet* inspired the cartoonists as it inspired the leaders of the revolution. The cartoonists, however, suggested that the new era of freedom might be a little too modern for the Ottomans and that not everyone was enthusiastic about the cultural advantages supposedly derivative from European constitutionalism. This ambiguity is suggested in cartoons in *Kalem* and *Alem*. Both play on conventional scenes and settings to satirize the "people's" understanding of *hürriyet*.

One cartoon, dated October 22, 1908, satirizes the electoral process. The Chamber of Deputies was originally scheduled to assemble on November 1 but its opening was actually delayed until December 17.[52] An old *muhtar* (local official, headman), in turban and pantaloons, sits smoking his narghile; he is confronted by two district organizers, in "modern" dress. One of them protests that he cannot seem to get through to the muhtar; he cannot understand why he is sitting smoking when the parliament is supposed to open in ten days and the electoral list remains unfinished (Figure 4.5). "Sir," replies the muhtar, "What's the point of this 'freedom' of yours if I can't enjoy my Ramadan water-pipe."[53] The contrast here is between the old Ottoman "ease" and the apparent revolutionary fervor, a theme that traced through various types of Ottoman literature. It is a contrast between the old patronage elites of the sultanic order and the new Western-educated elites of the constitutional order. The emergence of these elites coincided in the latter nineteenth century with a transformation in the dress (symbolized by the European frock coat) and furnishings of Ottoman civil officialdom.[54] The reinstatement of the constitution meant a shift in the centers of authority as well as in the traditional methods for approaching that authority. The cartoons used contrasts in dress style to emphasize the radical nature of that shift.

The second cartoon also shows a traditional scene: the young man of

Figure 4.5 The Trials of Freedom

the house preparing for a fling. The frame shows an angry older man, switch in hand, running towards a couple in front of what looks like a garden shed (Figure 4.6). The young man has seized his (possibly willing) accomplice. She has lost a shoe, but has what might be a sly smile on her face. "What are you up to with the girl?" shouts the elder, who appears to have dashed out in his house slippers. "None of your business?" replies the boy, ". . . I'm of age; time to assert my freedom (*hürriyet*)!"[55] Here, as in the *muhtar* cartoon, the point is that the notion of freedom is subject to interpretation, and that (as with all grand schemes) there may be negative effects as well as positive ones. Freedom might not be as appealing an idea as it seemed; and the rhetorics of revolution might not correspond to the realities. The "people," in effect, had not produced the revolution, and might not be ready to internalize its ideals.[56] They might respond instead with indifference or license.

Another cartoon criticism of the new era of *hürriyet* was the criticism that freedom brought weakness, that the empire might fall prey to the real France and its European cronies while it was busy celebrating its newfound "freedoms" (see chapter 6). The Ottoman situation and its colonial context could not be forgotten, despite the promise of a transformed and modern state and society. Thus, the revolutionary "gift" from France, for the Ottoman satirist, could look something like a Trojan Horse. He had to reconcile the France of the romanticized Lady Liberty and the twentieth-century imperial France, which was trying to claw out its share of Ottoman territory. He had to reconcile his empire's own glorious imperial past, embodied in sultanic sovereignty, with its parliamentary present, which threatened to surrender its hard-won liberty to European armies.

This paradox is apparent in a flag that was marketed in Istanbul for the opening of the new parliament on December 17, 1908. On the bottom it read, *Kanun-ı esasî*, the fundmental law. In the center was inscribed, along with the star and crescent: *uhuvvet, hürriyet, müsavat* (fraternity, liberty, equality). In each corner was a word: *vatan, servet, adalet, nizam* (homeland, wealth, justice, order), the desired outcomes of the revolution, and on the top edge: *liberté, fraternité, égalité*.[57] The flag gave the date (in Ottoman and French) of the revolution. Here was a concrete illustration that France had a powerful influence on crafting the symbols of revolution. The flag was waved by the people in the streets of the capital on the day of the triumph of Ottoman constitutionalism There is, too, a final irony of this flag, a reminder that the power of Europe lay not only in words and symbols. The flag was manufactured in Britian. His Majesty's empire benefited economically when the Ottoman crowd purchased flags emblazoned with French slogans to celebrate its freedom.

By 1911, fairly stringent censorship had been reinstated. Three years after the revolution it was clear that constitutionalism and freedom were not synonymous. In that same year a five *para* Ottoman tin coin was minted. The tin itself symbolizes the devaluation of the "currency" of the Ottoman state

Mais tu n'as pas honte Petit Malheureux.
Comment mon Oncle, mais ce n'est pas la Liberté.

- نزه یه کوربیورسك قیزی .ف
- سندن صورارز ... رشدی ؛ حریتی اثبات ایده جکم !.

Figure 4.6   Freedom Comes of Age

since its glory days when the treasury was full and the Janissary corps was paid in silver *akçe*. Still, the minting of coinage in the ruler's name is a traditional symbol of sovereignty in the Islamic state—and this coin bore the tughra device of the sultan on the front and the traditional designation of state (*devlet-i Osmaniye*) on the back. But, circling the tughra, was the slogan: *hürriyet, müsavat, adalet* (liberty, equality, justice).[58] The press, which had waved the banner of the French revolution, was now more or less gagged again, but the language of that revolution was stamped into the coinage itself, in the hands and pockets of the people in the street.

IRAN

The Ottoman press watched events in Iran with a blend of interest, fascination, and horror. Iran was represented in part as a more primitive version of the Ottoman empire, a traditional agrarian state that had not benefited, as the Ottoman state had, from a cosmopolitan culture and from contacts with Europe. It was also sketched with bonds of sympathy, as a state which suffered, as the Ottoman state did, from the twin afflictions of autocratic rule and European imperialism.[59] For the Ottoman press, the events of the Iranian revolution, still unfolding in 1908, provided a case study for the Ottoman experiment in revolution and in constitutional government. Unlike France, and its distant mythologized revolution, Iran was close, immediate, and threatening. If it failed, so too might the Ottoman revolution fail.

Coverage of Iran in the Ottoman press was not a priority in terms of space, but it was, nonetheless, significant. Iran appeared in the pages of Ottoman gazettes in various forms which can be roughly divided as follows: (1) news coverage of foreign dignitaries and world events, usually in the form of brief notices or captioned pictures; (2) satirization of the shah and of the idea of tyrannical rule; and (3) images of Iran as victim of European imperialism, a sympathetic satire prompted by the perception of shared weakness. These categories were a function of the newly liberated Ottoman press's preoccupation with covering the (previously suppressed) news of the world, the Empire's long historical relationship of competition and contact with Iran, and the dramatic nature of the events unfolding in the Iranian revolution.

The Iranian revolution had begun with a series of protests against the government, culminating in a general strike in December of 1905 in Tehran and mass demonstrations, a massacre by the Cossack brigade, and a strike by the ulema in the summer of 1906. Ultimately, on August 5, 1906, Muzaffar al-Din Shah signed a proclamation convening a Constituent National Assembly.[60] This announcement and the ensuing elections were accompanied by a dramatic increase in the number of gazettes published in Iran.[61] On December 30, 1906, the shah, only five days before his death, signed the Fundamental Laws drafted by the new assembly. But this auspicious beginning for Iranian constitutional government did not signal a new and peaceful era of constitutional rule. The shah's successor, Muhammad Ali Shah, soon clashed with the constitutionalists and became a symbol of reactionary autocratic rule. It was he who would become the butt of many of the Ottoman satirists' barbs on Iran.

The struggle between Muhammad Ali Shah and the constitutional forces led to civil war, beginning in June 1908 when the shah led a successful military coup, shelled the parliament building, and declared martial law. In the aftermath of his coup, the shah, "banned all societies and public meetings, including passion plays, dissolved the National Assembly, and seized thirty-nine of his opponents who had failed to escape or take sanctuary in the Ottoman embassy."[62] The shah's success was assured with Cossack aid, and Russian troops capitalized upon the chaotic conditions of this counter-revolution to intervene in northern Iran. The shah's tyranny and the slaughter of Muslims by Russian troops prompted some of the Iranian clerics to send a telegram to Abd ül-Hamid, beseeching his aid as "Sultan of Islam," and asking him to provide the Muslims, "safety from the victory of the infidel."[63] This telegram suggests the bonds of sympathy that might be drawn between Ottomans and Iranians on religious grounds if not on those of shared political ideology. Ottoman satirists took up those bonds of sympathy and viewed Muhammad Ali Shah's collaboration with the Russians with contempt and dismay.[64] In August 1908, *Karagöz* targeted the Czar's tyrannical power and collaboration with foreigners. Commenting on the peculiar nature of communications, he noted that the most direct route to Muhammad Ali Shah in Iran was through Russia.[65] *Geveze* sneered at the shah paying the "loyal" Cossacks to protect him.[66] In the end, however, the shah lost this year-long struggle. In July 1909, the triumphant constitutionalists deposed him and he took refuge in the Russian embassy; but the Russian troops remained in Iran. Meanwhile, the shah's twelve-year-old son, Ahmad, was elevated to the throne.[67] His accession was met in the Ottoman press with a combination of interest and amusement. He was the "Little Shah (*Küçük Shah*), his crown too big for his head, symbol of a weak monarchy and a weakened state.[68]

Even before he was deposed, the Ottoman cartoon space had predicted the defeat of the shah. In October 1908, *Al-Üfürük* published a cartoon showing Muhammad Ali Shah pulling a vehicle labeled "Despotism Wagon," while an automobile labeled "Freedom" smashed into it.[69] The juxtaposition of cart and auto enhances the impression that despotism is obsolete and that freedom characterizes the modern era. A telling cartoon in *Püsküllü belâ* suggested that Muhammad Ali Shah would end up on a bench in the Luxembourg Gardens in Paris, an object of curiosity to passersby. The frame shows the shah, looking depressed, a tear falling from his eye. A ragged man approaches him and speaks: "What are you mulling? You got off easy again. Have you forgotten those who gave their lives in this affair? Don't worry, tomorrow you can come with me and make five francs a day breaking rocks!"⁷⁰ This interesting placement of the despot in Paris, the site of idealized revolutionary glory, expresses not only Ottoman sympathy for Iran's revolutionary martyrs but illustrates the sentiment that Muhammad Ali Shah might escape the punishment he truly deserved.

After the shah was deposed, *Kalem* neatly satirized both his humiliation and Iran's continued dependence on European loans. This clever satire, entitled "Iran's New Loan," showed an Iranian bringing his pawn (the shah's uniform, hat, and sword) to a decidedly European-looking pawnbroker. On a side table stands the bound and naked Muhammad Ali Shah, holding his severed head, which neatly covers his genitals. The pawnbroker, surveying the offered clothes, looks unimpressed. "This is not sufficient security for the amount of money you want," he says. "What do you say we throw in the head of the ex-shah?" replies the Iranian.[71]

News Coverage

In Ottoman coverage of world events, some items on Iran were more comprehensive than others. The gazette *Hikmet* devoted considerable ink to the Russian intervention in Iran; and the daily, *Millet,* included "news of Iran" as a regular part of its coverage.[72] The annual, *Salname-i servet-i fünun,* briefly covered events in Iran as part of world news.[73] Elsewhere the "news" might consist solely of a picture and a brief caption. For example, *Eşref* carried a picture of the new shah, Ahmad, in September 1909, after the deposition of Muhammad Ali Shah.[74] *Resimli kitab* carried pictures of the Persian ambassador, Reza Daneş Khan, and of the Ottoman ambassador to Tehran, Husein Hassib Beg. Neither of these illustrations was accompanied by additional commentary. In December 1909, the same gazette ran a photograph of Najdi Beg in Trabzon. This man is identified as having returned from Iran where he was engaged in "aiding the self-sacrificing struggle for the acquisition of *meşrutiyet.*"[75] He is called *vatanperver,* caretaker of the homeland. Thus, some of the news coverage of Iran in the Ottoman press became more than just an avenue for satisfying the curious, it became a vehicle for crafting political ideology and for dividing the global social space into those fighting for the right (constitutionalism and patriotism) and those intent on preventing those expressions of freedom. Here the political commentary was captured in the language of a few brief phrases. Constitutional government had to be preserved and the faces in the photograph, the adjectives in the caption, and the sentiments of the editors all documented the nobility of the constitutional struggle.

Some news coverage of Iran served either to illustrate the quaintness of Iranian society and its culture or to represent Iran as one of the various "foreign" monarchies about which the educated Ottoman should be informed. The photographs in the journal *Resimli kitab,* for example, serve as a lesson in history and culture (Figure 4.7). On one page, containing three plates, the top photos show Muhammad Ali Shah, dressed in a highly elabo-

ایران شاهی محمد علی شاه
Mehmed Ali Chah de Perse

ایران شاهی مرحوم مظفرالدین شاه
Feu Mouzaffereddin Chah da Perse

شاهك معیت مأمورلرندن

Figure 4.7   Iranian Shahs and Attendants

rate and bemedalled uniform, and his predecessor, Muzaffar al-Din Shah (reigned 1896–1907).[76] The latter is distinguished by the simplicity of his dress and by the breadth of his waxed mustache. Under their images is a picture of two members of the shah's suite. In their pointed caps and leggings, they look like apparitions from a past era, conjuring the same image of obsolescence that, in cartoons, Abd ül-Hamid's eunuchs were used to produce.[77]

Resimli kitab's photos also trace the evolution of the Iranian civil war. Issue two, from October 1908, shows a photo of chained Iranian captives held prisoner at the shah's "Bagçe Saray."[78] The March 1909 issue contains images of the meclis members and of the Iranian parliament building, shut down since Muhammad Ali Shah's coup.[79] A whole series of photographs concerning Iran appear in the June issue of that same year, just prior to the shah's being deposed. Among these are portraits of the shah's brother, who had claimed asylum with the Ottomans, the shah himself, and his cabinet. Naib al-Saltana is identified in one photo as the shah's uncle and one of those "directing the tyranny" in Iran. In another photgraph is Shaykh Fazallah, a prominent molla and early supporter of the constitutional movement who later joined the royalist camp and was executed; he is identified as a key figure in the Iranian crisis.[80] None of these images was embedded in related narrative text. Nonetheless, each one could serve to evoke both the curiosity and the sympathy that events in Iran inspired in the Ottoman empire. The Iranian civil war, coincident as it was with the first year of the Ottoman constitutional revolution, and with its concommitant foreign intervention, could not fail to peak the interest of the Ottoman reading public.[81] Indeed, one of the early acts of the Ottoman assembly, once constituted, was to vote a resolution supporting the constitutional revolution in Iran.

The "news" in Iran was also satirized in Ottoman cartoons, in: phony dialogues, imaginary interviews, and fake news reports. A supposed telegraph communique in *Davul,* for example, read as follows: "From Tabriz, 23 Kanun-ı sani 1324 malî (5 February 1909): The Shah this evening had a frightening dream. It is rumored in political circles that it will be referred to the honorable Abu ül-Hüda Efendi for an interpretation."[82] This "report" was a take-off on the real telegraphed news reports, which were printed in Ottoman gazettes to advise the public of foreign affairs. The telegraph was a relatively new phenomenon in the the empire and an important source of foreign news. Abu ül-Hüda was Abd ül-Hamid's notorious advisor and, some said, conjurer; a sort of "mad monk" of the late Ottoman period, he was often lampooned in the Ottoman press.[83] Perhaps Muhammad Ali Shah was dreaming that his regime was about to come to an end in five short months. Certainly he had good concrete reasons for disturbing visions. In any case, the fake news of his dream and its interpretation in the Ottoman court served to point up the affinities between the autocrat in Istanbul and his counterpart in Tehran.[84]

Images as well as narrative were used to suggest fake communiques. A cartoon in *Kalem* showed a supposed phone call between Czar Nicholas and Muhammad Ali Shah on April 29, 1909. The phone call concerns the deposition of Abd ül-Hamid. The Czar speaks into the phone, "Yes, it's true. He's abdicated." Muhammad Ali replies, "I'm astounded. This discredits us all!"[85] In this image, another symbol of modernity, the telephone (Abd ül-Hamid was rumored to be superstitious about the phone) became the mechanism that conveyed the news of the end of autocracy. Other cartoons and narrative satire also used the idea of wire communications to satirize the shah and his links to the czar, and the sultan.[86]

Satire of the Shah

Muhammad Ali Shah held the distinction in the Ottoman cartoon space of representing monarchy at its worst. Although he was grouped with Abd ül-Hamid as a tyrannical autocrat, he did not share in the sympathy and association with ancient glories that partly redeemed the cartoon images of Abd ül-Hamid. When it came to images of a Muslim ruler who oppressed and slaughtered his people, Muhammad Ali Shah was without peer; his only close rival was a non-Muslim ruler, Czar Nicholas of Russia. This privilege of place in the Ottoman press's rogue's gallery was illustrated in many cartoons. The shah's regime was associated with deceit and brutality in a two-part cartoon that ran in *Boşboğaz* shortly after the Ottoman revolution. In part one, the shah's "announcement of *hürriyet*," was represented by a smoking cannon and the shah, sheathing his sword, standing beside a sliced-up Iranian on the ground; in part two the shah "gave his assurances," while sitting inside a ring of cannons facing outward.[87] A cartoon in *Coşkun kalender* warned Sattar Khan (an Iranian constitutionalist hero) not to trust the shah, who claimed to accept the constitution with "perfect and generous cordiality" while holding a sword behind his back.[88] These and many other frames imagined the shah as something more than an autocrat: he was a duplicitous and murderous villain.[89] Sometimes these frames used Persian or Persianized language in the captions, as in one cartoon of a contented looking shah sitting on a pile of bodies and skulls.[90] Such "graveyard" imagery was typical in cartoons of the shah.

The image of the shah as assassin was forcefully illustrated by two cartoons published during the Iranian civil war in 1909. The first is entitled, "The New Year's Present" (*nevruz hediyesi*). It shows an exchange (Figure 4.8). The shah, in uniform and clutching his sword, receives his New Year's gift from his minister, 'Ain al-Dawla. The gift is a plate bearing three bloody heads. In return, the shah presents his man with a medal. The caption is in Persian. 'Ain al-Dawla says : "As God is my witness, I killed the owners of these with my own hands." Practically slavering over his gift, the shah replies: "Praise to you, well done!"[91] The message is clear, the shah and his minister collude in bloody tyranny and the shah rewards those who slaugh-

Figure 4.8 The New Year's Present

Revolutionary Exemplars

ter his own people. Such images of the Iranian shah went beyond simple charges of oppression. The timing of this cartoon is significant. *Nevruz* fell very close to the date of the Ottoman counter-revolution and the accompanying bloodshed for which Abd ül-Hamid was held responsible. Thus, this cartoon not only condemned the brutality of the shah, it implied at least some equation of the autocratic regimes in Tehran and Istanbul.

The second cartoon, a color plate in *Kalem* published shortly before Muhammad Ali Shah was deposed, brought an economic dimension to the critique of the shah's tyranny. This cartoon's caption, in French, reads: "The extra tobacco of the shah." It shows the shah in uniform with his huge and ubiquitous sword in hand (Figure 4.9). With it, he is slicing through the Iranian Chamber of Deputies as if it were a large block of tobacco. Pieces of the bloody deputies are scattered on the floor beneath. The caption is a mock Persian verse in Ottoman. It reads like a history of the revolution, (with a bit of poetic license): "A gun fired, the smoke of the nation ascended to the heavens, the Iran shah chopped the delegates like tobacco."[92]

This image is full of visual clues suggesting traditional rule and culture. In the background are the rising sun and lion symbols of the Persian empire. One of the lions is peeking at the shah and the other hides his eyes from the hideous act. The motif of the lion and sun are repeated on the shah's crown.[93] The shah wears the baggy pants and upturned-toe shoes meant to suggest traditional dress, and on the floor is a flowered carpet. In the foreground, a houka lies ready to receive the newly cut "tobacco." The shah looks happy in his work. As in the cartoon of the New Year's gift, it is the barbarous act itself that seems to satisfy Muhammad Ali Shah. There is also a certain playing with the borders between reality and representation in this cartoon. Behind the shah is what appears to be a curtain, suggesting perhaps that this is a performance. The deputies become a commodity and the shah becomes an actor, reciting verse, all for the edification of the Ottoman audience. The understated economic message in this cartoon again relates the shah's regime indirectly to that of the Ottoman empire, because both sold their tobacco interests to foreign consortia. Both suffered the taint of collaboration with Europe's economic exploitation of the Middle East.[94]

In the Ottoman satirical press, the sultan was blamed for weakening the political, social, and economic structure of the empire by monopolizing power and colluding with foreign exploiters in Europe. The shah was blamed for exactly the same faults: civil strife and collaboration. Abd ül-Hamid and Muhammad Ali Shah were very closely associated as rulers formed in the same mold; they had become threats to the security of the state.

This association is illustrated in a matched set of very striking cartoons, drawn by Ali Cemali, and produced in the gazette *Alem* (World).[95] The two cartoons, each comprising an entire page and juxtaposed one to the other, were run shortly before the deposition of the shah. Each monarch is shown

Figure 4.9   The Shah's Tobacco

confronted by the figure of Despotism, depicted as a bearded demon king who holds a sword and has two snakes emerging from his shoulders.[96] (This same placement of snakes was, by the way, used in images attacking Muhammad Reza Shah during the Iranian Revolution of the latter twentieth century.) The cartoons are captioned, but what is most interesting here is the clear intention of equating the despotic regimes of Abd ül-Hamid and Muhammad Ali Shah. As one opened the gazette, the right-hand image showed a seated and grim Abd ül-Hamid, already deposed; the standing figure of Despotism is asking his advice because there is no longer anything for him to do in the empire (Figure 4.10). That grouping is juxtaposed to the left-hand image in which the shah, standing with his back turned to the viewer, is pictured as a minion summoned to an audience with Despotism, who is seated on a throne (Figure 4.11). Together, the two images (in setting and pose) called upon the traditional iconography of kingship, and delivered a single message on the precarious nature of tyrannical rule.

These images shared the Ottoman cartoon space with another set of images of the Iranian revolution. The Ottoman satirical press saw itself, and the Ottoman revolutionary regime, as serving a paternal or brotherly role, that of enlightened role model, in the Iranian struggle for freedom from despotic rule. While the shah had been successful in closing down the Iranian meclis, the Ottoman meclis, despite internal conflicts, remained open.[97] Cartoons in the gazette *Musavver Papağan* (Parrot Illustrated) suggested that the Ottoman revolutionaries were symbolic liberators, standing as a beacon of freedom for the Iranians who were being denied their rights to liberty by the oppressive shah. This sentiment reflected the CUP's stated support for the Iranian revolutionaries. Two very impressionistic cartoons in *Papağan*, published in the first year of the revolution, juxtapose the shah as depot, his suffering subjects, and the "free" Ottomans. The first shows the shah on an ass, waving a bloody sword and riding roughshod over the backs of the Iranian people (Figure 4.12).[98] These suffering Iranians are pleading with three noble looking Ottoman constitutionalists bearing the star and crescent flag; they are the *"hür Osmanlılar,"* the free Ottomans, offering the Iranians hope for an end to tyranny.

The second cartoon is similar, but more telling. In it the shah sits atop a stone tower (bristling with cannon and circled by crows) from which hang the bloody corpses of those he has murdered (Figure 4.13).[99] Help is on the way, however, with Iranian freedom fighters ascending the tower to liberate the Iranian people. This cartoon seems to refer specifically to the heroic defense against the long seige of Tabriz mounted by the shah's armies during the civil war. The figure leading the revolutionaries against the shah is Sattar Khan, a leading constitutionalist and hero of the defense of Tabriz.[100] Once again, in the background of this frame, the Ottoman constitutionalists stand with their flags, an example of the triumph of freedom over despotism, lending support to the Iranian revolutionaries.

Dis moi moi ce que je dois faire pour ne pas subir les mêmes conséquences que toi.

Figure 4.10 Muhammad Ali Shah and Despotism

Le despotisme. Altesse, il me semble que je n'ai rien à faire ici dorénavant; je vous prie de me donner vos conseils? . . . . .

Figure 4.11 Sultan Abd ül-Hamid and Despotism

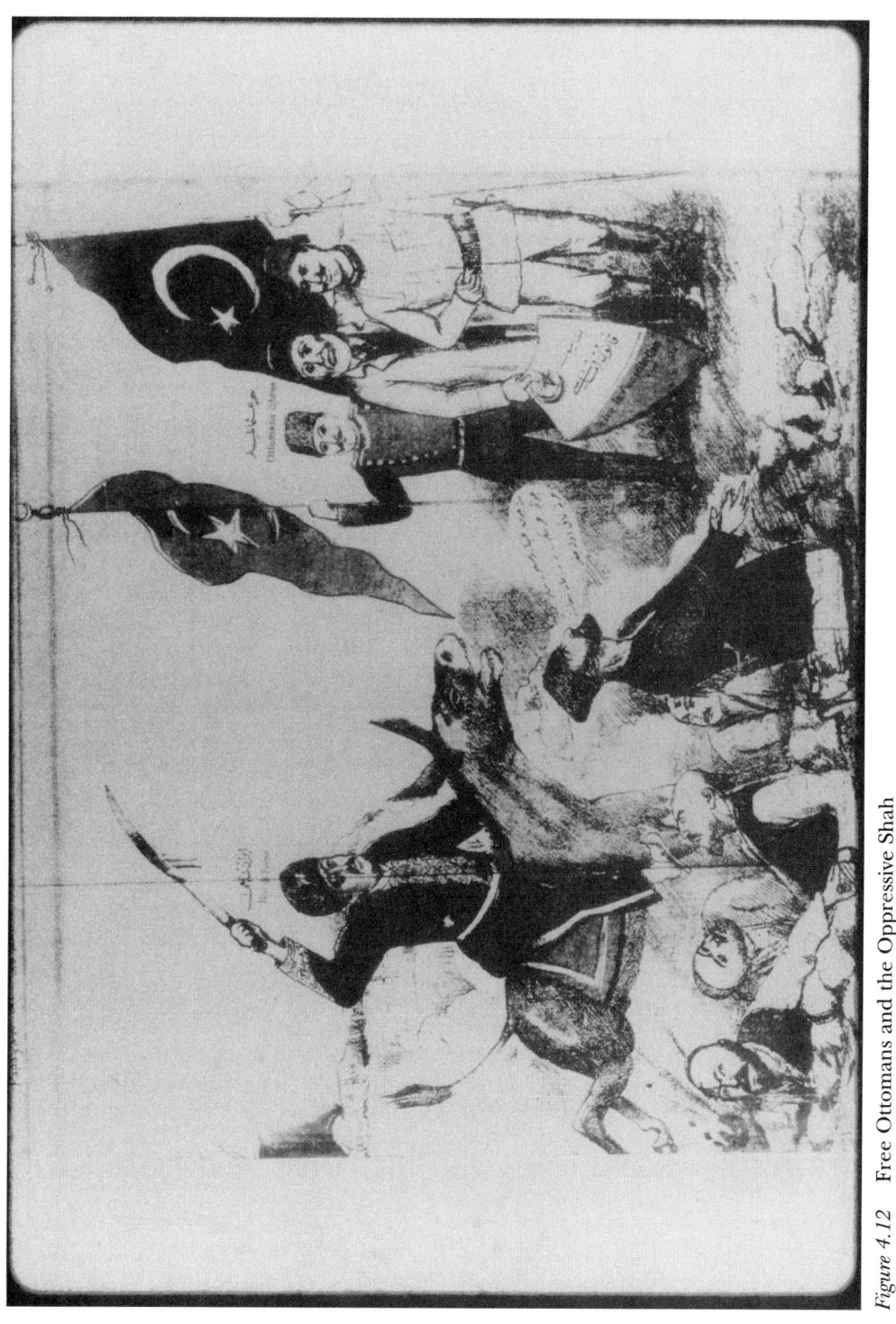

Figure 4.12 Free Ottomans and the Oppressive Shah

Figure 4.13 Sattar Khan and Muhammad Ali Shah

The gazette *Eşref* ran a photograph and piece on "the courageous" Sattar Khan in its first issue; and *Muhit* also ran a photo of the heroic figure of Sattar Khan.[101] But the triumph of Sattar Khan and the deposition of Muhammad Ali Shah did not bring the bounty of peace and *hürriyet* irrevocably to the Iranian people. In 1911, *Cadaloz* printed a cartoon of "Iran" as a ruined city full of skulls, the Iranian sun symbol sticking out its tongue in the background and Muhammad Ali Shah in the foreground.[102] Two weeks later, the gazette *Afacan* (using Persianized cartoon captions) satirized the machinations of the deposed shah, his thug supporters, and the "traitor" forces of despotism.[103] *Falaka* implicated Russia, Britain, and the ex-shah for stirring "the fires of rebellion" in Iran in one cartoon. In another, it showed the Russian bear shoving the shah on a sled down an icy slope to fuel the fires of a burning Iran. The *falakacı*, watching nearby and smoking his pipe, recites what may be a proverb: "A hide does not turn into a fur rug, an old enemy does not turn into a friend . . . . whoever doesn't take warning is doomed to destruction."[104] Thus, the Ottoman satirists were not overly sanguine about the constitutional "victory" in Iran. They envisioned their own empire as a refuge for Iranian patriots and a model of constitutional success; but they also looked to Iran with some anxiety for a vision of post-revolutionary cataclysm.

The image of Ottoman support and sympathy for the Iranian struggle, which these cartoons suggest, is mirrored in a photograph reproduced in the gazette *Resimli kitab* in June 1909.[105] The photo shows a large group of Irainians who had sought asylum in the Ottoman embassy in Tehran during the civil war.[106] Prominently displayed in the frame is the Ottoman flag with its star and crescent. Just as in *Papağan's* cartoons, this flag functioned as a symbol of freedom from despotic rule. It bespoke a commitment to constitutionalism that extended beyond the boundaries of the empire and embraced the Iranian struggle for freedom. This imagery of shared ideals, despite its divergence from day-to-day political realities, linked the representations of Iran in the Ottoman cartoon space to those in the serious press. While waving the flag of freedom for Iran, both venues were also waving a flag of patriotism and self-celebration for the audiences at home.[107]

Finally the bonds of sympathy for Iran could be drawn using the notion of brotherhood vested in the community of Muslims, even though the satirical press, as usual, was skeptical of such trans-national unities. *Yeni geveze* published a cartoon frame featuring a *hoca* addressing a crowd, apparently of Iranians, while the mascot, Geveze, looked on. The *hoca* rallied the crowd: "If foreigners are meddling in Iran, let's ask the whole Islamic world for assistance."[108] Geveze, however, wryly retorts that while the Islamic world may be ready to help, the real problem is despotism. He is not sanguine that Pan-Islamic rhetoric will save Iran. This joke could include an oblique shot at the Ottoman regime as well, a reminder that the foreign threat would not be warded off with rhetoric alone.

105

Iran as Victim

The empires of sultan and shah were also linked spiritually by their subordination to European states; it was this position of shared suffering that provided the third category of Ottoman satire of Iran. Iran served as an example of European imperialist exploitation of the revolutionary situation, an exploitation that the Ottoman cartoonists could readily envision as directed against themselves. In Ottoman satire's scenario of Iran's political victimization, Russia (with good reason) was the main villain. The czar, in his treatment of Iran, was drawn using the same symbols of death and brutality that were used in the illustrations from *Papağan* to suggest the brutality of the shah. Thus, in a cartoon entitled (in French) "The Pacifist's Dream," the czar is shown sitting on a skull-throne before row upon row of gallows (Figure 4.14). Hanged men dangle from the gallows and the sky is full of ravens (symbols of death) that also walk beneath the rows of the executed. Pointing to the hanged men, the czar says, "Let me rush off to Iran, there too to establish my fatherly administration."[109] This cartoon signifies not only Nicholas's participation in the brutalization of his own people but also the immediate threat of the Russian occupation and invasion of Iran. An analogous cartoon, showing a skull, crows in the background, and a Russian soldier, gun in hand, riding over a ground littered with bodies, appeared in *Kalem;* it was entitled, "Russian civilization in Iran."[110] While the British threat to Iran in the south was most often characterized in Ottoman cartoons in terms of economic rape, the Russian threat in the north was most often associated with murder and mayhem. *Alem,* in February 1909, showed the figures of both the Czar and John Bull mugging the shah, stabbing him with a long bloody blade. The caption reads, "Enough . . . too much . . ."[111]

While the constitutionalists struggled to liberate Iran from the shah's tyranny, Russia and Britain had capitalized on the resultant political instability, signing a pact in 1907 that divided Iran into spheres of influence.[112] This agreement was later noted in a long informational article on Iran published in one of the Ottoman yearbooks, *Nevsal-ı Osmanî*.[113] But a contemporary Ottoman cartoon "commemorated" the interventionist policies of Britain and Russia in a different way. It warned its readers that constitutionalism meant vulnerability. The cartoon shows Iran as a man bathing naked in the "constitutional waters" while Britain and Russia run off with his clothes (labeled Bouchire and Azerbaican). Sitting and watching from the shore is an Ottoman soldier, symbol of the empire (Figure 4.15). The Iranian cries out to him, "Help, Help, ... While I was bathing in the constitutional waters (which for me was like the Water of Life) they stole my clothes !"[114] In this cartoon the Ottoman figure remains an observer not a participant. The overt lesson of this frame was that the Ottomans were not eager to help the victimized Iran. The underlying message was that the Ottomans themselves might suffer the same fate, a fate embodied in an-

Nicolas II.--Cette malheureuse Perse a besoin d'être pacifiée.. Je ne ferais pas mal d'y étendre mon administration paternelle.

Figure 4.14 The Czar's Fatherly Administration

Le Persan. — Pendant que je me plongeais dans la Jouvence Constitutionnelle, on m'a volé mes effets.... Au secours! Au secours!

Figure 4.15   Bathing in the Constitutional Waters

other cartoon, in *İncili çavuş*, which showed "Turkey" as a drowning man, trying to crawl out of the "sea of despotism" while ugly sea creatures (Germany, Austria, Italy and Russia) attacked him.[115]

A Persian poem of the time repeated the theme of foreign rapacity depicted in these Ottoman cartoons, portraying Iran as "trampled by the wrath of the English and the Russians. . . . two man-eating wolves."[116] The poet Ja'far-i Khāmna'ī (Khameneh'i) suggested that even Hippocrates and Galen would be unable to cure the ills of Iran. In the Ottoman empire, it was the fear of similar ills and of the humiliation associated with foreign domination that drove the pens of satirists to focus on Iran. As Khāmna'ī so eloquently expressed it: "I see the Nation clothed in the garb of poverty and misery. / With the yoke of servitude on the neck, with the rod of abasement overhead. / I see it politely kissing the fetters of its subjection."[117]

Certain stock cartoon images were often used to portray such subordination in the interactions of the powerful European states and the Middle Eastern empires. These representations were sometimes subtle but often they were quite direct, using imagery of eating or cutting up to demonstrate what was being done to the Ottoman and Persian states. The Empire and Iran shared the dubious honor in the cartoon space of being the objects either of Europe's desire or at least of its unwanted attentions. In the process, they would be consumed or destroyed.[118] A typical format for such imagery was the representation of patient and physician. One cartoon in *Kalem* showed Iran as the unfortunate patient. He is surrounded by "The European Doctors" (Russian, British, and one other) who are in the process of cutting off his arms and legs. While Iran, crying out, tries to get up from the operating table, the Russian "surgeon" admonishes him, "Take courage! We're doing these things for your own good."[119] This juxtaposition of physician as imperialist and patient as Middle Eastern victim is common in Ottoman cartoons. Here the patient is Iran and the amputations are a metaphor for the inroads of the Powers in Qajar territorial space. Elsewhere, Ottoman cartoonists used the same juxtaposition to demonstrate what the Powers proposed for their own territorial integrity.[120]

The metaphor of physician and patient here is a particularly apt one because the physician represents a caretaker, someone who will do the patient good. Unlike those cartoons which represent the European Powers in military uniform, the physician-patient cartoons suggest that the Ottoman and Iranian empires had turned to Europe for aid and a cure for their ills. They suggest that those who were obligated to be responsible and benevolent had, instead, used their positions of authority to dismember the weak. Thus, in the Ottoman cartoon space, Britain, Austria, Russia (and others) represented not only the power to kill but the power to deceive. The Ottomans felt an affinity for the suffering of the Iranians who, like themselves, were depicted as weak and sick. Like Iran, the "Sick Man of Europe" might not survive the European "cure." It is worth noting here that the unwilling patient is a common trope in Ottoman poetry in which the lover begs the physician not to destroy him with his cure. In Ottoman cartoons, the European could be either physician or beloved, each one capable of destroying the "lover."

INDIA AND JAPAN

If France and Iran were the two poles between which the Ottoman press constructed its revolutionary reality, then India and Japan were secondary referential poles. Japan was idealized as a one-time traditional Asian power that had successfully modernized, and, more to the point, had decisively defeated a "European" power, Russia, in battle. This image of the defeat of its long time mortal foe galvanized the Ottoman imagination. Japan still had an emperor, but it also had a constitution and an effective military. That military was treated in one of the early issues of the Ottoman gazette *Meram*.[121] Ottoman Unionists envisioned the empire as becoming a West Asian Japan, militarily strong and technologically modern. India, on the other hand, was the model, par excellance, of a one-time imperial Muslim power which had been thoroughly subordinated and colonized by another European power, England.[122] Britian was the most successful imperialist nation of the time, and India was the symbol of that success, the "jewel in the crown." Victoria, monarch of the conquering British, had been crowned "empress" of India in 1877. The image of the conquered India was, perhaps, particularly poignant for the Ottomans because the former dominant power in India had been a Turkic empire of long-standing, the Mughuls. Of course India had its own nationalist movement at this time and the Indian press was a significant organ for the spread of Indian nationalism. But, for the Ottoman press, India served primarily in the role of negative model, an example of how complete and how extensive Britain's imperial conquests could be.[123]

An interesting side note, here, on the drawing of bonds of sympathy and anti-imperialism between the Ottoman Empire and India, can be found in the memoirs of one Edwin De Leon, a traveler, ambassador, and one-time emissary of the Confederacy. De Leon, speaking of Syria and Palestine, noted that the Sepoy Rebellion in mid-nineteenth-century India had created quite a stir in the empire. It had, "disturbed the whole Mussulman world, and through . . . verbal communication . . . had become generally known."[124] News of the British slaughter of their rebellious Muslim troops was, then, apparently common knowledge, at least in certain areas of the empire. The message of the enforcement of British order through violence, according to De Leon, prompted both fear and anger among the Muslim inhabitants of the "Holy Land," such that the English Bishop of Jerusalem felt compelled to issue a pastoral letter explaining the events in India in the hope of avoiding Christian–Muslim tensions. This anecdote suggests that the population of the Ottoman empire, even in the nineteenth century, was

Revolutionary Exemplars

not so removed from news of events in India as one might suppose. Images of British imperialism and of the sufferings of "fellow" Muslims could then, as in 1908, generate rhetorics of unity and resistance that transcended national and ethnic lines.

Japan, on the other hand, was attractive not only for its victories, but also for its style of rule, which melded the traditional and the modern.[125] In the second volume of the *Treasury of Science Yearbook* (*Salname-i servet-i fünun*), in a section giving brief resumés of various states and their rulers, Japan's form of government (*hükûmet*) is given as *meşrute,* constitutional monarchy; *payitaht* (literally foot of the throne) was the Ottoman term for the capital city, Tokyo. The designation *meşrute* distinguished Japan from France, whose form of government was given as republic (*cumhuriyet*), and approximated it to Iran, whose form of government was also *meşrute.*[126] But unlike Iran, Japan was perceived as modern and, unlike France, it was decidedly non-Western.

In the Ottoman cartoon space, Japan's victory over Russia allowed for the construction of a sort of pan-Asian, or at least anti-Russian affinity. *Kalem* reprinted a German cartoon called "The Sino-Japanese Comedy."[127] It showed an audience of one, a squat and buffoonish Russia, applauding a Punch and Judy type show in which Japan and China beat upon each other with sticks. But then the two performers embraced and, sticks in hand, turned on Russia who jumped up to flee the theater. Thus, an Ottoman gazette imported European imagery to satirize the Asian triumph over a "European" state. The boundaries of the Ottoman cartoon space were porous; they permitted the passage of multiple artistic influences and allowed the imagining of affinities with states as disparate as France, Japan (which had very limited direct connection with Ottoman political realities), and Iran (which had a long history of both conflict and cultural affinity with the Ottoman empire.)[128] Each state was participant in a world system where artistic influences and economic interests had long been shared and where shared political realities were now inevitable.

V

The Comic Sovereign:
The Satirical Critique of Authority

I usually fled from the contemptibleness of this infamous infant who was agitated like a vagrant, captainless, rudderless ship among the ruinous European waves . . .
—Ahmed Şerif, *Anadolu Tanin*, 1909[1]

In this way, the Ottoman writer, Ahmed Şerif, characterized the Ottoman state in the days after the revolution. His sentiments point out that the ideal of replacing autocratic rule did not produce the reality of a secure government confidently meeting the challenges of European arms and investments. The metaphor of the rudderless ship-of-state is a tired one, but it illustrates that neither "people" nor *meclis* (assembly) were quite prepared to occupy the helm vacated by Abd ül-Hamid. The revolution had both provoked and derived from a crisis of confidence in traditional government, and the Ottoman press struggled with the paradox of a revolution that had neither destroyed the monarchy nor fully vested authority in a constitutional regime. Three years after the new regime was seated, a cartoon in the satiric gazette, *Perde*, suggested that Şerif's metaphor still held true; it showed Karagöz and Hacivat rowing out to sea with a life preserver marked "*hürriyet* (freedom) to rescue the ship of state."[2]

It is not surprising that the images of monarchy in the revolutionary press were multiple and conflicting. The press, after all, had only recently become accustomed to manipulating the language of resistance to sovereignty. In 1901, when the United States president, McKinley, was assassinated, "the papers printed in Turkey were only permitted to say that he had died of indigestion."[3] Rulers were not killed by their own people in the Ottoman order of things, at least not in print. After the revolution, in 1908, the press was in a stage of experimentation where the articulation of sovereignty was concerned. The cartoon space, in this regard, provided a clear (or at least a sheltered) field upon which alternative forms of sovereignty could be played out. Where authority itself was, at best, an ambiguous concept, quicksilver images of a noble or ludicrous monarch, citizen, nation, and parliament danced across the cartoon frames of revolutionary gazettes like shadow puppets caught in an evolving set of freeze-frames.

Of course, the cartoon field, like the contested political space was never clear of the baggage of memory and symbol. It was a field of combat, full of axes to grind, grudges, flashbacks, and entrenched positions. Like the cartoon, the sultanate was more then its physical reality. The sultan was both ruler and symbol of the state. Because of the unique longevity of the Ottoman dynasty, it was extremely difficult for the Ottomans (constitutionalist and modernist rhetoric notwithstanding) to disassociate the idea of the state from the figure of the sultan. The deposition and even killing of individual monarchs had become fairly commonplace, but the Ottoman dynasty itself was inextricably woven into the Ottoman consciousness as symbol of the enduring state.[4]

Enduring monarchies were associated with the prosperity of the people and with the preservation of the state. This association between the survival of a people and the person of the king is embodied in the Sassanid circle of justice theory, a theory consciously cultivated by the Ottoman dynasty. Now, almost a century after the fall of Abd ül-Hamid, there remain few monarchies in the Euro-Asian sphere. Those that do remain, however, still retain or at least assert this association of the monarchy with the prosperity (and the history) of their people. Monarchies can be tenacious things. One such survivor, the British monarchy, though long deprived of actual rule, maintains a preservation myth in the form of the Tower of London ravens. The tradition holds that when the ravens leave the Tower (which dates from the early days of the Norman kings) the monarchy will fall. In the Ottoman satirical press, ravens also symbolized the monarchy in powerful imagery that directly linked the raven (or crow) to the person of the sovereign. But, in the Ottoman case, equating the sultan with the raven symbolized the morbidity rather than the longevity of the state. The crow was a symbol of death.[5] Traditionally, the carrion crow (*gurab*) was contrasted to the royal falcon (*şahbaz*). There is a tremendous irony in reversing that imagery. The revolution had produced a crisis of identity and of authority in which the sultan (symbol of the state, and of Ottoman glory) could become instead a symbol of the state's demise. Linking images of the sultan to those of ravens expressed this crisis. The sultan, having endured past the point at which he could provide life to the kingdom, became a symbol of death, preserving his sovereignty only at the expense of his people. The imagery of the Ottoman monarchy had come full circle. Where Osman, the founder of the dynasty, was associated with prosperity and expansion, as symbolized, in the chronicle of Âşıkpaşa, by a tree of life and flowing streams, Abd ül-Hamid was associated with the choking off of the life of the empire.[6] Where Süleiman Kanuni was the "Lawgiver," Abd ül-Hamid was the violator of the law and of the circle of justice.

It is not easy to explain the emergence of a new Ottoman polity, its birth agonies and the elite and popular responses thereto. Studies of the turn of the twentieth century have suggested (directly or obliquely) that the compelling, and Western, notion of popular sovereignty had come of age and, through the agency of a series of nationalist movements, had come inevitably to sweep aside the monarchies of the large agrarian empires.[7] Attention has focused on the channels by which Western-style revolutionary ideology and political language were transferred to the Ottomans. But European imperialism, the power of Ottoman cultural traditions, and the world political and economic contexts out of which the new Ottoman regime emerged are also important factors. The alternatives for the empire in 1908 were not necessarily sovereignty to the sultan or sovereignty to the "people." The alternatives, rather, were autonomy or subordination, a state that endured or one that was swallowed up by its enemies. Public confidence in the sultan had eroded. Still, there was neither experience of, nor general confidence in, the idea of an elected government. Who or what would supply a political solution that bridged the gap between traditional monarchy and an imagined and imitative Western form of electoral regime? The Ottoman satirical press illustrates that there was no one clear answer to that question.

Revolutionary political debate, as embodied in the Istanbul press, focused on what measures were necessary to refashion the political system and to prevent colonial subjugation and the disintegration of empire. Ottoman political analysts, unlike those of the French revolution, did not have a tradition of discourse on "to have a king" or "not to have a king." What they did have was over one hundred years of perspective on the aftermath of the French Revolution and, more importantly, on the results of European imperialism in Asia. Here, India served as a model of the combined effects of the displacement of (Mughul) sultanic authority and the acquisition by a European state of control of the economic resources of a one-time imperial power.[8] Ottoman political options were forged in this context, and only in this context can the exercise of those options be understood. Hence an analysis of the Ottoman revolution must add to the assessment of European Great Power diplomacy and military might a history of Ottoman political thought that does not assume that it necessarily recognized parliamentary sovereignty as inevitable, efficient, or even adequate.[9] This study does not presume to take on that task.[10] But it does propose to suggest certain strains in Ottoman political thought through a presentation of the satire of monarch and of meclis. This satire was heavily influenced by the threat of foreign domination. It viewed the Ottoman monarch as both unique and as one in a company of similar sovereigns who were being pushed out, gently or violently, by a new world order of things.[11]

115

THE OBSOLETE MONARCH

Monarchy represented traditions of empire, a kind of power that was supposedly unshared and unique. Of course absolute power is a myth and an ideal rather than an expression of the actual workings of kingship. But it was the very uniqueness that monarchy suggests that was coming under attack (or being subverted) in the modern era. In his study on political graphics, subtitled "Art as Weapon," Robert Phillipe argues, "The modern age began with this negation of uniqueness."[12] Phillipe, here, is actually discussing the printing of multiple images, but his words can also be used for the negation of kingship. In the "mass" culture that the twentieth century press was trying to create, or at least beginning to experience, the images of kingship and its alternative forms of government multiplied. With the revolution, not only did the government lose its monopoly over the production of images of kingship, but cartoon kings multiplied in the cartoon space, seizing the option of making monarchy ridiculous, redundant, or obsolete. Of course the government never had a complete monopoly on the images of kingship, but it did attempt to regulate what people could and could not see or read about the sultan and, for that matter, about other monarchs.

Obsolescence, indeed, was a notion of which the Ottoman press was very conscious. This preoccupation with obsolescence derived not only from the sense of a world competion in which the Ottoman state was losing to European contenders, but from the unique position of the empire. It remained a vast, poly-ethnic, traditionally governed, agricultural empire in an era when most such empires had either been fragmented from within or dominated from without. It was surrounded with examples of the ways in which monarchies could be disposed of, yet its monarchy represented an unbroken and unconquered line reaching back to an era of security, prosperity, and glory or, at least, to an era imagined so to be.[13] Thus, it cannot be assumed that the Ottoman form of monarchy simply became obsolete in the face of European "modernity," or that Ottoman minds moved inexorably toward constitutionalism simply because new structures were necessarily or already being put in place. It is true that the old, once successful strategies of Ottoman rule were no longer working; but which political and cultural forms would replace them was still unclear.

The concept of obsolescence was one gentle alternative to that of violent removal of the monarch.[14] Abd ül-Hamid would not be the Charles I or the Louis XVI of the modern era. He would not be beheaded in fact; rather, he was represented in the press as set aside, along with other symbols of the past, by the inevitable march of modernity. This notion of gradual obsolescence suggested that the Ottoman empire, in transforming its government and its king, might avoid the violence of the French Revolution while, at the same time, avoiding the violence of foreign conquest. Nor would the Ottoman sultan become another Mughul emperor, turned out by powers that had learned the lessons of modernity. For the Ottoman press, the monarchy would endure, at least for the moment, although in diminished form. It was both anachronism and survivor.[15]

In revolutionary satire, this paradox of the sultan as anachronism and survivor was expressed in cartoons that featured the solidarity of Abd ül-Hamid and the monarchs of other large agrarian empires, like Iran and Russia. Abd ül-Hamid was characteristically portrayed as one of a series of autocratic monarchs on the road to oblivion as the new political order made their style of rule a thing of the past. One cartoon, for example, pictured the "Caravan of the rejected monarchs," in which the shah is shown packing up and joining the caravan while the Greek king shouts to him from the window above "Wait a second, please, I'm coming too."[16] In this type of association, there was no necessary distinction between Asian and European monarchs. Rather, the autocrats, of whatever "nation," assumed a collective identity; they were dinosaurs, symbols of an old and oppressive past that had no place in the modern world order. These autocrats were museum pieces to be viewed by succeeding generations as oddities of a dead past. Yet their day was not quite past. Their cartoon images show them still resident in their palaces, though under seige, speaking together on the phone, and consulting over "retirement" options for monarchs whose power had been usurped.[17]

A cartoon in *Cingöz*, for example, right after the revolution, showed Abd ül-Hamid and Muhammad Ali Shah seated on a bench, inviting the standing Czar Nicholas to join them:

Shah and Sultan:	Hey. Why not sit down like us?
Czar:	Am I a fool like you? One needs to take the air.
Shah and Sultan:	True, but sometimes the air turns violent.[18]

The term for air or wind here, "*rüzgâr*," can also mean time or fortune; hence "fortune can change violently," as indeed it did for all three of these monarchs.

Especially after Abd ül-Hamid was deposed, the Ottoman press suggested that Muhammad Ali Shah, too, must follow him into monarchical oblivion. *Davul*, immediately after the sultan was deposed, ran one such cartoon.[19] The shah's downfall was also traced in the satire of the journal *Karagöz*. In May of 1909, the gazette showed Abd ül-Hamid and the shah clasping hands across Anatolia. The sultan, already in exile in Salonica, may as well have been drawing the shah after him.[20] In another cartoon, dated July 1909, the month the shah was deposed, *Karagöz* depicted Abd ül-Hamid, peering from his window, an odd Juliet to Muhammad Ali Shah's Romeo, standing below. The caption read: "meeting of the former couple."[21]

These are just a few of the many cartoon juxtapositions that showed the monarchs of the old traditional era sharing or about to share a similar fate. Abd ül-Hamid served as a model of resignation. In the cartoon space, the transfer of power, from monarchs to constitutionalists, seemed inevitable. What made it inevitable was not the will of the people but the forceful coming of a modern era to which neither the old regimes nor the public could fully relate. In any case, the satirists suggested, Muhammad Ali Shah was a good example of the fact that the transfer of power, inevitable as it may be, would not take place without a struggle and without a variety of unexpected or undesirable effects.

Elsewhere, the king of Morocco was included in the ranks of the deposed or soon to be deposed autocrats. *Alafranga,* for example, ran a cartoon called "The Outcasts Club," which featured Mulla Hâfız of Morocco, Abd ül-Hamid, Muhammad Ali Shah, and an undesignated East Asian ruler (Figure 5.1).[22] The scene suggests a men's club, a game of bowls, and insider joking among the club's "brothers." Cartoons that grouped the Moroccan king with other Middle Eastern rulers, however, usually focused on these sovereigns as targets of European imperialism. *Resimli kitab,* for example, printed (or reprinted) a cartoon showing the warring royal brothers of Morocco, Mulla Hâfız and Abd al-Aziz. Both were mounted on hobby horses, and one said to the other, "Let's make like we're battling, we'll amuse the Europeans."[23] This image emphasized the subordinate position of the Moroccans and their apparent reduction to childlike dependency. Short years later, in 1911, France took Morocco as a protectorate.

Perhaps the most dramatic cartoon highlighting the idea of the obsolete autocrat is one shown in *Kalem*. It employs the idea of the museum as a repository for the rulers of the past. The cartoon shows "Doctor of Philosophy Rıza Tevfik Bey," a renowned writer and thinker, giving a lesson in natural history to a group of attentive young scholars (Figure 5.2). He stands in a hall with diagrams of archaic beasts on the wall. Before him are two museum cases, one containing "dinosaur" bones, and the other the figures of autocratic rulers. "What you see before you," he states, pointing to the figures of the rulers, "are the most terrible of the beasts of the archaic age. They ate a hundred times more than the present-day elephant eats. They were insatiable. It's very lucky that today all that is left of them is their fossilized remains."[24] In his hand, Rıza Tevfik grasps a copy of "Darwin." The message here is clear. The Ottoman state is evolving and evolution cannot be stopped. The young scholars, civil servants trained in the new Ottoman schools, dressed in jackets and ties, are symbols of the modern enlightened new order. For them, the autocrats, in their uniforms and medals, are merely the latest in a long line of fossils, the objects of scientific study. They are museum pieces; but, for the "teacher," symbol of the Young Turk revolution, they still symbolize the "tyranny" of recent times. He is grateful that these "voracious beasts" have now become a memory. In this cartoon, the museum becomes the frame for the imagined, fearsome past, the noble present, and the enlightened future of the empire.[25]

118

Figure 5.1   Outcasts' Club

Figure 5.2 At the Museum: "Dinosaurs" of the Past

OTHER REPRESENTATIONS OF SOVEREIGNTY

But obsolescence was only one among the ideas associated with monarchy in satiric imagery. Sovereignty was treated in a variety of ways; it engendered feelings ranging from loyalty and sympathy, to condemnation and loathing. Heads of state like Abd ül-Hamid and his foreign counterparts (along with their spouses and children, pets, clothes, and forms of entertainment) populated the pages of the Ottoman yearbooks, newspapers, and journals.[26] They showed noble or touching photographs of Ottoman princes or European royal families, bedecked with medals, gazing off into the future. Such images were offset in satire by humorous or abusive portrayals of kings and monarchy.

In the Ottoman cartoon space there were several kinds of "kings." First, there were the concepts of monarchy in general and the particular Ottoman brand of monarchy, the sultanate. The gazette *Davul* showed monarchy itself as resting on a shaky foundation with the monarchs of the world trying to repair it (Figure 5.3).[27] *Davul*'s satire shows a huge crown resting on scaffolding, with "workers" of various nationalities exerting their best efforts to build it up. The drummer mascot of the gazette, arm raised, stands off to the side and warns that the "foundations are rotten," and that the monarchs themselves will expose monarchy's defective nature.

Then, there were specific kings: Abd ül-Hamid, his successor Mehmed Reşad, and the current monarchs of Europe and Asia. These latter were grouped in the cartoon space into those most resembling the sultan (the Russian czar and the Persian shah), those who represented imperialist Western powers (the English, Austrian, and German kings, and also the czar), those who were already subordinated to Western Powers (the Egyptian and Moroccan kings), upstart rivals in one-time Ottoman territories (like the Bulgarian and Greek kings), and other, more distant kings, who played only an occasional role in Ottoman cartoons (like the Japanese emperor).

One gazette had a regular column entitled "*Büyük Başlar*," literally *Big Heads*, each installment providing a satirical cartoon and political analysis of the chosen ruler.[28] This notion of kings as exaggerated heads can be juxtaposed to images of the headless state such as that in the introductory quote in this chapter by Ahmed Şerif. Such varied images of sovereignty depict the unease of transition from traditional monarchy. On the one hand, there is the humanizing of kings through pictoral representation of monarchs at home, with their families, domestic and smiling. On the other hand, there is the caricature of monarchy, big-headed, vain, and laughable, the object of humor.

The imagining of Abd ül-Hamid in the satiric press was an evolutionary process. The iconography of kingship changed from 1908 to 1909, from the formidable despot to the stooped and defeated Abd ül-Hamid, moody in his carriage or perched on a donkey, the object of ridicule. Representations of the sultanic order in the Ottoman satirical press fall roughly into

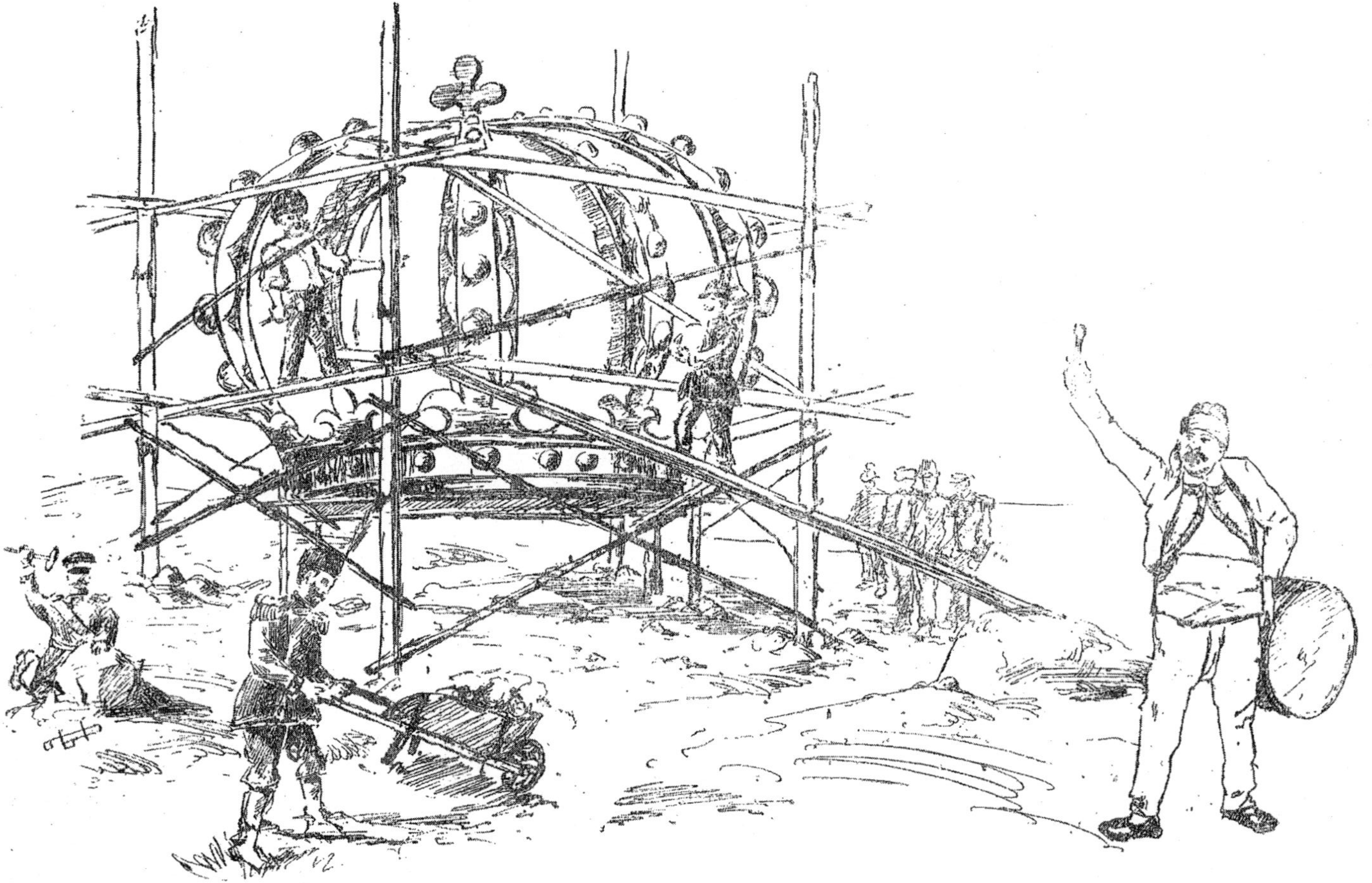

Figure 5.3 The Shaky Foundations of Monarchy

three categories, which reflect the external threats to the regime and the internal progression from sultanic to constitutional order. These images overlap in the Ottoman cartoon space. At first, the sultan was sometimes associated with benign cooperation for restoring the constitution. But, one insistent satiric image of Abd ül-Hamid in the early months of the revolution was that of oppressor. The sultanic order was associated with tyranny (*istibdad*). That image was compounded, especially in the aftermath of the spring 1909 counter-revolution, with visions of Abd ül Hamid as sullied with the blood of his people; the implication was that Abd ül-Hamid's reign could no longer be legitimated. Once elected, the new government itself became a primary target for the political critiques of the press, replacing the sultan as agent responsible for warding off the demons of want and defeat. Yet the sultan remained a secondary target to the extent that he still wielded much of the power that the CUP had not yet had the temerity or expertise to seize. A second image was that of the sovereign as collaborator, selling the resources of his empire to foreign imperialists and the offices of state to the highest bidder. This representation charged the sultan not simply with corruption, but with treason. A third image was that of the sultan as symbol of a lost imperial glory and of a secure and traditional order that could never be recovered. There was fear of a future where no figure had emerged to synthesize the might once distilled into one sovereign lord.[29] Abd ül-Hamid became a symbol of power lost. This image surfaced after his deposition, when it became apparent that the constitutional regime could not easily resurrect the bankrupt Ottoman state.[30] The images of a pitiable old sultan, thin, and melancholic, with only the company of cats and eunuchs was contrasted to the images of a robust "new" sultan, Mehmed Reşad, a man who traveled outside the palace, who was apparently noble and serene, but no longer a symbol of real power.[31]

Although the satiric press allowed the new regime a delay of indeterminate length for replacing the sultanic order with something more dependable than the rhetoric of *liberté, fraternité, égalité,* it found the disassociation of Abd ül-Hamid from the notion of Ottoman sovereignty generally expedient. Hence, the sultan became the oppressor, his rule of *istibdad* (despotism) contrasted to *meşrutiyet* (constitutionalism). In fact, the Hamidian era, in the revolutionary press, was often simply referred to as "the age of *istibdad*.i"[32] It was no accident that the CUP in exile had translated V. Alfieri's book on despotism into an Ottoman version, called *İstibdad,* in 1899; or that Charles Kool's history (in French) of parliamentary governments was published in Istanbul in 1908.[33] Abd ül-Hamid represented the main internal impediment to a new political order. Without either replacing traditional sovereignty or promoting the fearsome notion of sovereign power to the people, the press could exercise its fury on the head of Abd ül-Hamid as individual, a sovereign who had forfeited his entitlement to rule by failing to provide justice.

The images of Abd ül-Hamid as bloody tyrant are predictable; he is demonized and delegitimated in a variety of cartoon frames. One cartoon,

The Comic Sovereign

for example, shows an empty crown atop Abd ül-Hamid's throne around which is piled a tower of skulls (Figure 5.4). This striking, unsigned image is entitled "the results of war," directly associating Abd ül-Hamid with the past (and possibly future) suffering of his people in battle.[34] But, even without caption, this stark imagery takes the two most prominent symbols of the sultanate, the crown and throne, and associates them directly with death and human misery. Where the classical sultanate stood for triumph and prosperity, this sultan, not even present in the frame, was made to stand for defeat and destruction.

Another image assailing the monarchy does use the figure of Abd ül-Hamid, associating him directly with the bloodshed of the counter-revolution, the final blow to his legitimacy. This cartoon is entitled, "*istibdad müşahhas*" (tyranny personified).[35] Again, the picture is quite explicit without caption. It is the same type of vision of illegitimate kingship that Shakespeare conjured so eloquently in "Macbeth." Abd ül-Hamid is shown in the foreground, a sword in a pool of blood at his feet and blood dripping from both his hands (Figure 5.5). He gazes out the window, where a scaffold and noose stand, stark white against a black background. Here the sultan is charged with the murder of his own people; the frame suggests that he deserves the fate meted out to other such criminals, the same fate that awaited some of the failed counter-revolutionaries. His sword is no longer the straight and noble symbol of protection for his people but a warped symbol of impotence and treachery.

Finally, in a cartoon that employs traditional motifs and wordplay, *Davul* portrayed Abd ül-Hamid as a bloodthirsty tyrant (Figure 5.6).[36] This image of a belligerent and beleaguered sultan appeared one day after the National Assembly declared him deposed.[37] It shows Abd ül-Hamid posed before a cloth held up by human skulls. This backdrop (which suggests theatricals or shadow play) is splashed with red (blood), a particularly striking device because only a handful of cartoons in *Davul* employed colors beyond black and white. The title reads: "The former *Hünkâr* and *Hunkâr.*" *Hünkâr* was a traditional title of the sultan meaning sovereign or commander and *Hunkâr* meant the bloody one or doer of bloody deeds. This image implicated Abd ül-Hamid in the bloodshed of the counter-revolution. Underneath the sultan's image, the caption asks: "[Is he] one of the readers of the novel, *The Red Mill Murders,* or its protagonist?" This caption is a reference to the thriller, *Le Moulin Rouge*, by Xavier de Montépin, a popular nineteenth-century French novel that had been translated into Ottoman Turkish.[38] It seconds the top caption's charge that Abd ül-Hamid was a murderer and reveals the literary background against which much of Ottoman cartooning was framed. The cartoonist clearly expected his audience to be aware of the novel and its contents. This image illustrates how Ottoman cartooning combined "traditional" and "modern" devices in satiric presentation. Abd ül-Hamid, here, is posed before a backdrop as if he is having his photograph taken. But the skulls, his title, and the use of rhyming

124

Figure 5.4 The "Spoils" of War

Figure 5.5 Tyranny Personified

Figure 5.6 The Bloody Sultan

prose in the caption are all taken from iconographic and narrative styles with a much longer history than photography had. The skulls, the blood, the crown, the throne, before and after the revolution, remained standards of the anti-monarchical repertoire.[39]

Such images, in effect, sanctioned the deposition of Abd ül-Hamid. Lesser measures were seen as frought with peril; the empire might end up like Iran or Russia. In fact, such images approximated the sultan to Muhammad Ali Shah in Iran and Czar Nicholas in Russia. Both were the subject of vitriolic satire in the Ottoman press. Their despotic brand of monarchy (along with that of Abd ül-Hamid) was contrasted to the Ottoman hopes for constitutionalism and liberty as embodied in images of the Young Turks.

Images of Abd ül-Hamid as despot, however, went beyond equating him with some generic form of tyranny shared by other monarchs of agrarian empires. The sultan was also charged with specific acts of oppression. A cartoon in *Geveze* showed a starving Anatolian peasant tied to a column on which the woes of Anatolia were inscribed (Figure 5.7). In the foreground, Abd ül-Hamid, speaking to the new grand vizir, Hilmi Pasha, denied all responsibility for the starvation and misery of his people: "In my time, such things could never be!"[40] This cartoon illustrates how satirists linked the suffering of the population in the provinces to the corrupt administration of Abd ül-Hamid and his ministers. These conditions of privation were not necessarily ameliorated by the Young Turk Revolution, but the autocratic sultan (by the logic of traditional kingship) was held accountable for the maintenance of justice and prosperity for the people. In the cartoon space he became the fountainhead from which the problems of the empire seemed to flow.[41]

The critique of monarchy also derived from the association of the old regime with selling out the empire to foreign interests and from an association of foreign monarchs with attacks on the Ottoman state. That association provided the Ottoman satirists with another form of king cartoon, directed not at the sultan, but at the monarchs who were threatening the survival of the empire. These, in particular, were directed at the kings of England, Austria, Germany, and Russia, those powers thought most likely to invade or to detach parts of Ottoman territory (see chapter 6). European imperialism was also blamed for producing competing kings in one-time Ottoman territory. Abd ül-Hamid was made complicit in the charges against foreign kings because he had not been able to stop their inroads.

Despite all the images of kingly complicity, tyranny, and injustice, the satirical press was not persuaded that the empire must rid itself once and for all of sultanic power. Sultans, however worn, wearing, overbearing, and ineffectual were what the Ottomans were used to. Thus, revolutionary satire also portrayed Abd ül-Hamid, if not as sympathetic, at least as familiar. Especially after his deposition, this familiarity translated into images of the wistful sultan wishing for the olden days and bemoaning the lost era of Ottoman glory.[42] He was shown petting his cat and wondering what was going on in Istanbul, talking to his eunuch, or gazing longingly at a passing

Comment Hilmis, est-ce de cette façon que tu gouvernes en laissant mon peuple mourir de faim! sous mon régime je ne tolérai pas cela!..

Figure 5.7 The Suffering of Anatolia

hot air balloon, imagining it as a mode of escape.[43] A striking cartoon by the well-known cartoonist, Cemil Cem, showed a brooding Abd ül-Hamid immediately after his deposition (Figure 5.8). Head in hand, the sultan is contemplating his troubles and bemoaning the loss of his confidant: "Oh, Abu ül-Hüda, where are you? If you were here I wouldn't be in this fix! [44]

Thus ended the ambitious career of a man who had claimed to be caliph.[45] Abd ül-Hamid had not shown himself ready to accept a radical diminution of his power. Instead, he was implicated in the 1909 counter-revolution. Although the period of Ottoman sultanic glory was clearly over, the office of sultan was maintained past the end of the empire. A struggle over the elimination or rearticulation of sovereignty was going on all over Europe, with widely divergent contexts and histories for each struggle. But neither the sultan nor the Ottoman public was willingly prepared, in 1908, for a king who (as one observer described Vittorio Emanuele of Italy around the same time), "has appropriately described his own conception of his duties as those of a permanent undersecretary to the ministry, holding in his hand the threads of tradition, and constantly ready to assist them with the counsels of his experience."[46] Abd ül-Hamid was, rather, himself the thread of tradition, his long rule both affirming and re-creating the traditions of Ottoman imperial power. For the most part, not even the satirical press was willing to cut that thread if it meant any more than removing the one dynastic strand of Abd ül-Hamid, while keeping in reserve the sultan's brother and sons.

Even under the new and malleable Sultan Mehmed Reşad, Abd ül-Hamid's successor, there was a certain maintenance of sovereign power. The constitution, restored in the summer of 1908, allocated considerable power to the sultan including, via Article 113, the right to banish anyone who was judged to be a threat to the security of the Ottoman state.[47] In 1909, the constitution was modified, first to limit the powers of the sultan and then to expand the powers of parliament at the expense of the ministers of state. So, the recognition of monarchy as despotic, corrupt, or even intolerable, was a gradual process. Nor could attacks on the monarchy be presumed necessarily to be either revolutionary or reform minded.[48] As with the palace politics of Abd ül-Hamid's reign, the politics of the constitutional period were shaped as much by the struggle for power as by the desire for representative government.

In conclusion, the Ottoman press was preocupied with monarchy as reflected in the cartoons, photographs, and stories of gazettes and yearbooks. Sovereigns were ever present, the Ottoman sovereign (and his counterparts elsewhere in the world)—if not the figure of the sultan himself, then his coat, his nose, his tughra. The anxiety produced by trying to rearticulate monarchy in a constitutional context was reflected in the varied representations of sovereignty. There were, of course, the standard demonizations, but there was also sympathy and ironic imagery. Abd ül-Hamid, in the cartoon space, was transformed into a clown, a crow, a monster, a tyrant, a

— O Ebul-Huda où es-tu? Si tu étais encore là, tu aurais pu conjurer ce malheur.

— آه أبو الهدى نرده سين؟ اكر سن اولسه ايدك بو نلر باشمه كلزدى ...

Figure 5.8   The Sultan in Exile

pitiable old man, an obsolete institution, a shade. But, even after his exile, he was still present, inhabiting (some would say tainting) the Ottoman journalistic consciousness and the cartoon memory. No one took his place as padishah, since the real power of that title was gone. Rather, his successor, Mehmed V, sat on the throne as a figurehead, while Abd ül-Hamid remained the symbol of real sultanic power.[49] The revolution could not yet dispense with the sultan. Years later, after the empire was dismembered in World War I, even Atatürk exorcised the ghost of the sultanate with some trepidation.

DEPICTING THE NEW REGIME AND THE CONSTITUTIONAL OPTION

The old regime represented tyranny and a certain internal and external paralysis. As *Kalem* put it, one of the "benefits of constitutionalism," was that the administrative system known as the "*Yavaş, Yavaş* (Slowly, Slowly) System," would be abolished.[50] But, while the Hamidiyan regime was associated in satire with corruption and ineptitude, so too was the new regime, although its corruption and ineptitude might take different forms. As one outsider put it:

> Constantinople is a reactionary city. It has depended too long on Yıldız [the palace]. It contained too many spies-out-of work, cashiered officers, impecunious hodjas and unemployed prophets . . . . Old soldiers spoke too, of the easy times the troops had before this Parliament came into existence. . . . . Now we have young men who speak German half the time, who have been educated in military schools here or abroad, who are apparently half giaours [unbelievers] some of them, who instead of ornamenting their rooms with holy texts from the Koran, hang therein (so their orderlies tell us) picture-post-cards representing unveiled foreign women.[51]

This view of the political transition in the Ottoman state suggests the reservations some segments of the Istanbul population had over vesting authority in the hands of the CUP or its competitors rather than in the hands of the sultan and his coterie.

The satirical press seconded this skepticism in a series of cartoons that shed light on the Ottoman political schizophrenia of this period. Political satire, after all, is an old genre, rooted in the existence of governments, politicians, and their latent or blatant faults. The press continued to direct its barbs at the new regime to the extent that convention and censorship (once the CUP consolidated its power) allowed. What follows, here, though, is not an elaborate description of the press's critique of the new Ottoman government. I am interested, rather, to provide a set of satirical examples that illustrate the unease of the transfer to constitutional monarchy and the readiness of the satirists to scrutinize critically forms of "progress" that later historiography has both glorified and taken for granted.

Initially the overthrow of the old order led not to a general critique of authority but, rather, to a critique of the old elites, the sultan, and the palace power brokers.[52] Once these had been marginalized in a variety of ways, the new elites came increasingly under scrutiny: the new government, the political parties, the meclis, and the Europeanized bourgeoisie, all of whom were represented in the press as centers of authority. Feroz Ahmad has noted that, "The first five years of constitutional government were marked by a constant struggle for power in which the CUP finally emerged victorious."[53] This power struggle centered around two primary divisions of the new government, the cabinet ministers and the assembly (meclis, or Chamber of Deputies), and around the two Young Turk political factions of Liberals (generally cosmopolitan and upper class) and Unionists (generally lower middle class and more radical in their reform ideologies). It also drew in the foreign embassies, the army, and those representing ethnic or religious constituencies. These contending figures and factions provided grist for the satiric press's mill.

Satirists exulted in targeting various ministers of state; one cartoon, for example, in *Dalkavuk* depicted the members of the *Şurayı Devlet* (Council of State) as a bunch of bored yes-men, yawning, reading the paper, and writing letters while thoughtlessly following the lead of the chairman.[54] Elsewhere, the *mizah mecmuaları* represented members of the assembly or of the council of ministers as crying or squabbling children, as indecisive incompetents, and as phonys; ministers were shown playing blind man's bluff, jousting with each other, or trying to perform acrobatics.[55] Certain ministers attracted the cartoonists ire more than others, especially those who seemed to wield the most power in crafting the new constitutional state, such as the grand vezirs Kâmil Pasha and Mahmud Şevket Pasha.[56] A common target was Mehmed Cavid, the Unionist Finance Minister and Minister of Public Works, whose slight frame, glasses, and mustache lent themselves to the caricaturists' art. Cavid was a primary target because he held the purse strings and could thus be blamed directly for financial woes. He was satirized regularly in *Kalem,* as for example in a cartoon showing a frowning Cavid stuck in an "Ottoman Loan" sack. [57] This cartoon reminded the gazette's readers of the unmanageable condition of the empire's finances. It also equated Cavid personally with the Ottoman debt.

Another cartoon of Cavid Bey continued that theme of subordination more directly. It shows the finance minister as a big-eared, unhappy-looking child in knickers, caught between contending adults (Figure 5.9). On one side, a slick male England placates the child, "My Dear, I'd like to give you the money but your "auntie" won't hear of it." The "auntie," here, is a scowling French Marianne. On the other side, Marianne berates the child as a smiling Russia looks on; she scolds: "Impudent child! You want to take money from me only to go and give it to others!"[58] Here, as in other cartoons, the Ottoman empire, in the form of Cavid, is reduced to humiliating childlike acquiescence, while the "adult" powers wield the purse strings

Le ménage franco-anglais.

— Moi je veux bien prêter, mais c'est-à-dire ... كذا يعني استعرت انا عارف ... يارب ، ياد درمك استعرت ... باش اوڏيك
qui a l'argent.

Marianne. — Petit vaurien ! Me demander
de la galette pour entretenir Germania ! Quel
toupet !

والله ، عارم يوش بتت بارة بردك كدب
ابعطك وبردت !

Figure 5.9 Cavid Bey and the Powers

and give the orders. England comes off as deceitful and a maker of false promises. One gets the impression that Cavid was in a no-win situation, both inside and out of the cartoon frame. The context for both these cartoons was Cavid's visit to Paris in the summer of 1910 for purposes of securing a loan. The extensive conditions the French govenment attempted to place on any such loan were designed to subordinate the empire even further and ultimately insured the failure of Cavid's project.[59]

The satirists' images of the new regime stood in direct contrast to some of the new regime glorification going on in the serious press. The latter drew a marked contrast between the old and new eras; it printed photos and lists of the "new" deputies and the "old" ministers of state.[60] It meditated on constitutional government, the responsibilities of citizens, national harmony, and the effectiveness of the meclis.[61] From one point of view, the new regime represented progress, modernity, liberty, the restoration of the constitution, and the reform (if not the abolition) of the old oppressive order. These associations were celebrated in the Ottoman revolutionary press, and even in some of its cartoons. The image of "sweeping out" the old corruptions and problems was a prevalent one, even though many of the old elites remained in positions of power.[62] The idea that the constitution would somehow bring the empire into an enlightened and strong, though European-dominated, sphere was a powerful and alluring one, especially as technological advances and new economic structures seemed to be dividing the globe into a two-tiered system of the progressive imperialists and the traditional imperialized. The Ottomans wished, once again, to be one of those imperial powers. More realistically, though, it was difficult to imagine how the constitution could transform an impoverished empire, surrounded by powerful enemies, into a phoenix, emerging from the ashes into a new era of Ottoman power and prosperity.

The Ottoman satirical press played devil's advocate, scrutinizing the faults and ineffectiveness of the new ministers and parliament, dwelling on the "pathetic" state of Ottoman finances, and suggesting that the new regime's reorganization schemes were merely a set of cruel tricks played on a gullible public. Speculating on post-revolutionary conditions in the city, *Üç gazete* concluded, in an article entitled "Who Are the Istanbul Deputies?" that the new regime, without justice, would resemble "a soldier without a sword, a steamship without a compass."[63] The fragility of the new regime and its constitutional ideology were embodied in numerous cartoon frames showing balancing acts, precarious positions, and tenuous supports. *Boşboğaz*, for example, published two cartoons associating the preservation of *hürriyet* with tightrope walking and kite strings.[64] The implication in both cartoons was that the future of the empire was hanging by a thread, a strong thread, perhaps, but a thread nonetheless. These images neatly combine the optimism and the pessimism of the early revolutionary period.

The critique of the former and present regimes relied on a juxtaposition of "old" and "new" that was comprised both of clear symbols and uncertainties. These symbols and uncertainties are illustrated in a cartoon dated September 24, 1908, and entitled "Old Amusements and New."[65] The cartoon embodies both the critique of the sultanic order and the expectations for its constitutional replacement (Figure 5.10). Among the symbols of the old regime were a gumball-machine type dispenser of medals and decorations and a "yes-man" pasha (*evetci başı*), suggesting how Abd ül-Hamid's officials acquired their positions. There was a toy Hicaz railroad surrounded by dead toy soldiers, symbol of the sultan's Pan-Islamic claims and his running battles with rebellious bedouin, and a toy bank with *Credit Lyonnaise* on the side and the Ottoman council of ministers on the top, symbolizing the government's selling out of the Ottoman state to foreign economic interests. The "new" regime's toys were a broom for sweeping out corruption, a national theater and newspapers for freedom of expression, steamships, a gramophone-headed campaigner exhorting his brother Ottomans, "Long live the nation," and a banner celebrating the new regime. The banner, however, signified the uncertainty of the new constitutional government. In place of the old slogan, "Long live the padishah," was an unfilled space: the banner reads, "Long live ????." This frame was a more down to earth version of Ottoman realities than the paeans to "*hürriyet*," and the "long live *vatan* (homeland), long live *millet* (nation), long live *maarif* (education)," found elsewhere in the press.[66] What exactly would replace the sultan and the old order that he represented was, according to this cartoon, unclear.

In other cartoons, the satirists suggested that perhaps the empire simply was not ready for constitutional government and that there was some wisdom in the old order of things. A cartoon in *Dalkavuk*, for example, pictured the brash, young, "Present Era" as literally dropping constitutional government down upon "Turkey," Iran, and Russia, while the "Former Era," an old man, watched in dismay.[67] In this frame, the Ottoman "national assembly," the Iranian "national assembly," and the Russian "duma" are three eggs which smash when they hit their target states. The Old Era fruitlessly warns the New that he had better be more careful.

A major question was whether an elected government was capable of salvaging the empire and making it strong. Many satirists apparently lacked faith in the new meclis. As W. A. Coupe has noted for the cartoons of the German revolution of 1848: "The favorite conceit was to reduce the principle of popular sovereignty *ad absurdum* by taking the concept literally and representing the Parliament of the Future as an assembly of drunkards, lay abouts and ne'er-do-wells concerned only to prolong their licentious mode of existence with borrowed money."[68] Like the nineteenth-century German satirists, Ottoman cartoonists were fond of presenting elected government as running amok, inept, uncaring, and mired in inertia.

This kind of jaundiced view of the state of the empire was tellingly depicted in a two page cartoon in-the-round in the gazette *Alem*. The cartoon is a series of pie-wedge shaped scenes drawn around a central medallion (Figure 5.11). In the central medallion, labeled "Istanbul" are two

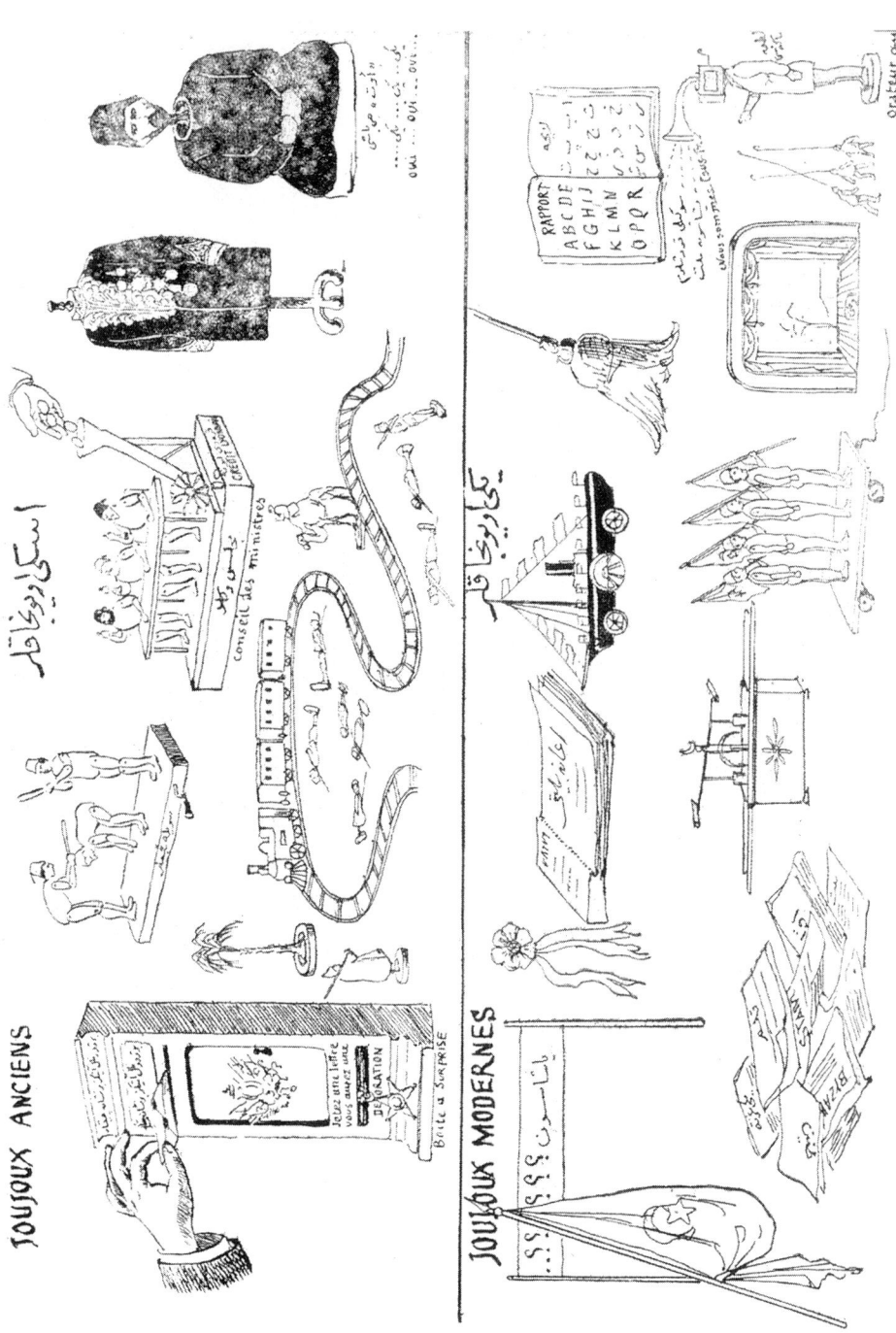

Figure 5.10 Old Amusements and New

Figure 5.11 The Constitutional Struggle

مشروطيتڭزك صوڭ لوحه‌سی!..

figures, representing political parties, locked in combat: the CUP (*İttihad ve Terakki Cemiyeti*) and the Liberal Union (*Fırka-ı Ahrar*); they symbolize the internal divisiveness of the empire and the ongoing struggle for power among various factions. The images circling this central theme are scenes of struggle and devastation: starvation in Anatolia, intercommunal strife, slaughter in Armenia, armed conflict in the Balkans and Arabia, Austria carrying off Bosnia and Herzegovina, Crete being pulled apart, and the newly installed King Ferdinand of Bulgaria, looking smug. The figures of women are used to good effect in this caricature: the naked Crete in a tug of war between male figures, Bosnia and Herzegovina in a scene of abduction, a bloody and bare-breasted woman with her dead baby in Armenia and, finally, the large and lecherous figure of King Ferdinand of Bulgaria holding a tiny weeping woman in his hands. Their images cry out that the empire and its erstwhile territories are piteous and vulnerable. But the figures of the empire's fighting political parties seem not to care. Thus the cartoon space envisioned the prospects facing the new regime. The caption, in French, reads, "Unify us! Unify us!" But the caption in Ottoman Turkish reads, "*Meşrutiyetimizin son levhası!*" (The last page of our constitutionalism!), as if this image were the last plate, the final apocalyptic episode, in an illustrated book.[69]

Another satiric piece suggested that perhaps the empire could escape experiencing its last gasp. This dialogue between the two mascots of the gazette *Cingöz* proposed that, "Every affair, everything of the former era (*devr-i sabık*) was contaminated by iniquity. . . . The Ottomans were breathing their last breaths."[70] But now, Cingöz claimed, in the new era (*devr-i cedid*), things would be put right. This grandiose claim, however, was couched in a series of non-sequiturs and verbal gags, very much tongue-in-cheek. It played upon the prevalent inclination to contrast an imagined new order with an excoriated old order, but it suggested no great faith in the salutary powers of the new revolutionary regime.

While it is true that the cartoon space occasionally painted a more rosy picture of the new regime, usually its officers were imagined with their feet mired in greed, factionalism, corruption, ignorance, and ineptitude.[71] Where elected government was concerned, it was more often the meclis in general and the inefficiency of a parliament, rather than individual delegates, that were the subject of satire in the cartoon space. Satirists suggested that the parliamentary system neither solved old problems nor prevented the onset of new ones, and that delegates from all over the empire could not work together and had not a clue how to run a government.

Many of the serious gazettes ran excerpts from (and reports on) the meclis proceedings.[72] They also ran photos of the elections, the proclamation of the constitution, and the first meeting of parliament. These photos, themselves a symbol of modernity, suggested that the functioning of the new regime would be an ordered, glorious, and praiseworthy process. One photo, for example, showed the elections at Istanbul, a very serious and very masculine affair (Figure 5.12).[73] But the satiric press presented a very different view of the constitutional regime. It suggested, once the meclis was in place, that it was something less than diligent and productive. A cartoon, by Sedad Nuri, is titled "Among Deputies." It shows a pair of parliamentarians, chicly dressed and steeped in ennui (Figure 5.13). Smoking cigarettes, they look bored and disaffected. Shadowy figures of their confreres in the background suggest loitering and gossiping rather than labor and energy. One delegate says to the other, "Mercy (*Aman*), these deliberations .... it's impossible to sleep!"[74] In this frame, Nuri questions more than the training and effectiveness of the meclis members, he questions their motives. His satire is particularly telling when one recalls that the new members of government, in the serious press, tend to be portrayed as noble citizen patriots, ready to work and sacrifice for the good of the country and its glorious constitutional future.

The satiric press also suggested that expecting the European Powers to befriend and support the new Ottoman regime was tantamount to letting the fox into the henhouse. Predators could not be trusted, even if dressed in the garments of freedom and progress.[75] Thus, the new regime was also tainted with the accusation that it pandered to the interests of European states without bringing the empire anything in return. Meclis members (like the sultan before and the Cabinet) were accused of selling out the interests of the empire to the ambitions of foreign governments, the interests of foreign entrepreneurs, and their own seduction by foreign culture and fashions. These latter charges were most often depicted in the cartoon space by showing members in exaggerated Western fashion or by showing Ottoman representatives cavorting in foreign capitals (see chapters 7 and 8). *Kalem* lampooned these connections when it published a poem (in French) entitled "*Vive la Constitution.*"[76] Its rhyme scheme depended upon the juxtaposition of *députés* with *indemnités* (poking fun at the powerlessness of the meclis members before European fiscal dominance) and of *constitution* with *illusion* (suggesting that the promises of the constitutional regime could not be relied upon). The celebrations of the proclamation of the constitution and of the opening of parliament could not disguise the facts that the empire was losing territory to its European "counterparts," was deeply in debt, and dependent for its defense on foreign loans and an inadequate and antiquated army and navy.

A more direct expression of the frustrations embodied in Ottoman economic dependence on Europe can be found in the juxtaposition of two images, one in the serious and one in the satirical press. On the front page of the August 23, 1910 issue of the weekly *Resimli İstanbul* (Illustrated

Photo : Aigle

فوطو : اغل

درسعادتده انتخابات — مکتب سلطانى باغچه‌سنده

Les éléctions à Constantinople — Dans le jardin de Lycée de Galata-Séraï

Photo : Aigle

فوطو : اغل

درسعادتده انتخابات — هیئت تفتیشیه

Les éléctions à Constantinople — les contrôleurs

Figure 5.12 The Ottoman Elections in Istanbul

Entre députés.

مبعوثلر بيننده :

— Ces interpellations sont terribles. On ne peut même pas dormir...

— آمان بو استيضاحلر ... اويومق بيله ممكن دگل !

Figure 5.13 Deputies at Work

The Comic Sovereign

Istanbul), there is a photograph (Figure 5.14).[77] It shows a distinguished-looking group of men, most dressed in topcoats, ties, and fezzes. The caption beneath this photograph identifies the group as the special delegation to London of the Ottoman meclis. Both photo and caption convey information and generate an impression of gravity and seriousness of purpose.

The front page of the September 2, 1910 issue of the satiric gazette *Lâklâk* contains a cartoon of a similar group of dignitaries. Indeed, although some of the figures have been moved, it is clear that the *Lâklâk* cartoon is modeled directly on the photograph of the London delegation. Despite the grave expressions on the faces of the cartoon delegation, however, the mood and the message of the *Lâklâk* cartoon are radically different from those of the photo. In the cartoon frame the delegates have been moved to the background. Superimposed upon them is a large figure; he faces the delegates and has his back to the viewer (Figure 5.15). He is dressed in the clothing of the poor, and his juxtaposition, in size, in dress, and in space, to the delegates, makes this a very striking cartoon. This figure in the foreground is a symbol of the Ottoman public and his stance suggests a question that is "spoken" even without the caption. The cartoon goes beyond the simple representation of the government delegation; it asks about results: What has the government done for the public? The frame is entitled: "On the Return of Our Representatives from Europe." In conventional dialogue format, the cartoon figure of the public, like a child on the return of his parents, asks the delegates, in effect, "What did you bring us from London?" They reply, "Iron samples." Incredulous, he asks, "No gold?" The delegates reply: "This time iron, . . . the gold will come in time."[78]

This cartoon, perhaps more dramatically than any other surveyed here, points up the disjuncture between the hopes for a glorious new Ottoman order, and the realities of administering an impoverished empire with an untried and untrusted form of government.[79] While the serious press might celebrate the elections and the establishment of a new parliament, the satiric press reminded the Ottoman reading and viewing public that the new government could be corrupt, inefficient, and most significantly, unable to deliver on its promises.[80] Thus, although a return to the old sultanic order was impossible, and although the authority of the sultan had, apparently, been irrevocably broken, the authority of the new regime became a major target of satire in the revolutionary press. This was especially so once the revolutionary honeymoon, so to speak, was over, and once Abd ül-Hamid had been exiled into powerlessness. The satirist places in the mouth of John Q. Public his accusations against the delegation and the government. In so doing, he becomes the spokesman for the imagined "people."

The gazette *Zügürt* was also expert at expressing the disillusionment of the "people" with the new regime. One frame, entitled "Ministry without Minister," shows a group of petition-waving citizens standing in the street before a half-opened door. At the door stands an official with his hand

مجلس مبعوثان عثمانی طرفندن لوندره‌یه اعزام قلنان هیئت مخصوصه

[برنجی صره] عبیدالله افندی   عارف بك   زهرزاده احمد پاشا   رشدی پاشا   حقی بك   توفیق بك   طلعت بك   محمدعلی بك   رضا توفیق بك
[ایکنجی صره] خالدی افندی   دیمترووییج افندی   مدحت بك   مازلیاح افندی   صاصون افندی   فاضل افندی   اسماعیل بك   بستانی افندی

Figure 5.14 The London Delegation

Figure 5.15 "What Did You Bring Us From London?"

raised to stop them. The citizens, some ragged and none appearing particularly prosperous, complain to the official, "Hey, we've been standing here at this door for ten days with petitions in our hands; what are we supposed to do?" The official, looking as if he has heard these words before, replies, "What's the big deal your waiting ten days? . . . . We've been waiting for years."[81] This is, of course, the quintessential complaint about the workings of governments and their bureaucracies; it is not a complaint unique to the Ottoman empire. But, in the aftermath of the revolution, frames like these suggested that there would be no radical changes in the responsiveness of the government to the needs of the people. Constitutional government or no, some things would remain very much as they had been under the old regime.

VI

The Comic Aggressor:
The Critique of European Political and Economic Hegemony

During the last few years, our policy, if I may so call it, in Turkey has been, and for some time to come will be, to attempt the impossible task of furthering our commercial interests while pursuing a course . . . . which the Sultan interprets as being pre-eminently hostile in aim and tendency. . . . In a highly centralized theocracy like the Sultanate and Caliphate combined, with its pre-economic conceptions, every big trade and concession is regarded as an Imperial favour to be bestowed on the seemingly friendly, a category in which, needless to say, we are not included.
—Mr. Fitzmaurice in Istanbul to Mr. Tyrrell in London
April 12, 1908[1]

The Near East is the only region in the world not yet appropriated by a Great Power. Nevertheless it is the finest field for colonization.
—Quoted in Moon, *Imperialism and World Politics*[2]

INTRODUCTION

Ottoman cartoons did not call what they depicted imperialism.[3] Rather, they targeted the behavior of a series of aggressors that latter day historiography has labeled imperialist. The Ottoman empire had itself once been a great imperial power, and some of its early-twentieth-century elites hoped to restore that glory. But the imperialism envisioned in the cartoon space was of a somewhat different type; it was the activity of European states, using what were imagined to be modern technologies and modern ideologies, to detach parts of the empire and to control the resources and influence the citizens in those parts that remained. In the Ottoman cartoon, these aggressors, and their henchmen, were made comic in an effort to understand and make them manageable. Where enemies were apparently uncontrollable, they were at least subject to ridicule.

In caricature, Europeans and European states might be reduced to simple images of things that were threatening: menacing armies, cholera, or greedy entrepreneurs sucking the empire dry. It is important to note that the cartoon space often ignored the intricate details of the political situation of the day in favor of gross caricature, timeless imagery, and "patriotic" demonizations. Thus, for example, the actual details of the various Balkan province resistance movements and struggles for autonomy, territory, revenues, and independence were often muted or passed over in favor of targeting Great Power greed, meddling, and aggression. Cartoons could also treat peoples and territories that for all practical purposes had been long since lost or taken as still and indelibly Ottoman "property." Thus, the myth of empire was preserved, in cartoon format, by violating the boundaries of time and of territory.

Nonetheless, the cartoon space, like the realities it proposed or suggested, was neither entirely simple nor unidimensional. Europe was not simply made to represent the grim realities of conquest or subordination; its character was perceived to be complex. While this chapter focuses on the satire of European imperialism, it is worth noting that there were (and had been for some time) clear political and intellectual currents within the empire that actively fostered emulation of the very European systems that these cartoons critique.[4] Those currents of thought and action shared space in the Ottoman press with others that warned of the peril and evils inherent in collaboration with or emulation of the West. Ottoman satire was clearly conscious of this ambiguity in defining and relating to Europe. The unsettled role that European culture played in the Ottoman press's consciousness will be elaborated in later chapters. In this chapter, the precarious political, economic, and military position of the Empire takes center stage. It was that precarious position, and the dominant role of certain European states on the world scene, that cast Europe in one of its characteristic roles, that of villain, in the Ottoman cartoon space.

THE POLITICAL ORDER, BACKGROUND

Simply put, the political situation of the Ottoman empire in 1908 was tenuous. The gazette *Kalem,* in a cartoon showing a funeral for the Eastern Question, suggested that the revolution would transform Ottoman foreign affairs; but the empire remained a pawn in Great Power politics.[5] While the revolution both prompted and reflected an evolution in Ottoman domestic politics, it also precipitated a series of crises.[6] As noted earlier, some of the immediate effects were the final annexation of Bosnia and Herzegovina by Austria, and the declaration of independence by Bulgaria; both were the culmination of processes underway well before 1908.[7] The perceived weakness associated with the revolution can also be linked to the subsequent Italian invasion of Libya (1911) and the Balkan Wars (1912–1913), both aimed at detaching Ottoman territory. Within a more global frame, the balance of power in Europe had been shifting. With Germany ascendant, England firmly ensconced in Egypt, Austria bellicose, and Russia occupying areas of Iran, it was no longer clear that the old "Sick Man of Europe" standoff was either useful or viable.[8]

With this internal and external flux, the revolutionary era was characterized by the notion that new political combinations were possible, necessary, or inevitable. The question was, who would be the winners and who the losers. In the winner category, the Ottoman empire did not look like a promising bet. Its late-nineteenth-century losses and treaties had shown that, for the most part, it had neither the military nor the political clout to control its own destiny. Indeed, a cartoon in the September 24, 1908, issue of *Kalem* proposes that the Ottoman government ponder those very losses. The cartoon shows the bearded figure of "History," urging peace while conjuring up the memory of 1877 in a battle scene that recalled the devastating Ottoman losses to the Russians.[9] The historic memory of the Ottomans did indeed include many victories, but the memories of the more recent past were mostly memories of humiliation. Although the CUP imagined the empire as the future Japan of West Asia, the new regime was clearly hampered by its own internal divisions and, more particularly, by its economic and military weakness. In the cartoon space, all these vulnerabilities were exposed. In the economic sphere, cartoons characterized the empire as bled dry by corrupt officials and as terminally dependent upon foreign powers. In the political arena, the Ottomans were depicted as relatively helpless in the face of European juggernauts like Britian and Austria. The military power of the Ottomans was not necessarily insignificant, but the military and economic power of their enemies was perceived to be formidable. Imitation of Europe had not brought the empire parity, and the subordination, real and perceived, of the Ottoman state to foreign powers, prompted both fascination and defensive aggression in the Ottoman press.

The Ottoman state, at the turn of the twentieth century, found itself drawn into the colonial orbit of European powers.[10] That situation was reflected in the topics and themes chosen for emphasis in the Ottoman press. *Meram,* a journal published between November 1908 and February 1909, for example, had a series of articles on the history, literature, and economy of England and France. Even *Meram's* frank admiration, however, was tempered with an acknowledgment of European imperialist ambitions. One article traced British imperialism through a history of the East India Company. This served as a reminder that conquest naturally followed economic control in the sequence of Western penetration. Other articles contained analyses of Ottoman foreign relations with England, France, and Russia.[11] The purpose of these articles may have been simply educational, but their tracing of history was a tracing of the vagaries of power and of the current privilege of place held by Britain. A similar treatment of European affairs can be found in the conservative *Beyan ül-hak,* the first issue of which contained an analysis of European politics.[12] *İstişare,* which focused on various aspects of European political and social ideologies, also included lengthy discussions of the history of the capitulations, the galling economic concessions by which the empire gradually had subordinated itself to European commercial interests.[13] Thus, the Ottoman press reflected not only on the advancement of European states, but on the ways in which Europe had achieved its dominance, and on the implications of that dominance for the status and viability of the Ottoman state.

After the revolution, the press was cognizant that the success of the new constitutional regime was dependent upon its ability to relieve itself of the burden of the capitulations and to negotiate for itself a more favorable position in a world order dominated by certain European powers. This consciousness was reflected even in the mastheads of the revoltionary press. The editors of *Serbesti* (Freedom), for example, in November 1908, were giving notice of the boundaries of the "new" Ottoman state. In effect, they were outlining its territorial claims and rejecting those of Austria, Great Britain and other states. Their postal rates section on subscription prices noted that (non-foreign) rates were for "*Memalik-i osmaniye ile Bulgaristan, Bosna, Hersek, Mısır, Kıbrıs ve Girid için* . . . ."[14] The "Ottoman lands," in this statement, still included Egypt (long since English turf), Crete (claimed by Greece), Cyprus (occupied by Britain and claimed by Greece), Bosnia / Herzegovina (which had passed into the hands of Austria) and Bulgaria (which claimed independent status). Here *Serbesti* was affirming Ottoman sovereignty, giving notice, in a seemingly innocuous way, of the empire's traditional territories and claims. The message of sovereignty was both a defensive and an offensive one. The new Ottoman regime, founded on the principles of constitutionalism and freedom, should maintain those areas traditionally belonging to the Ottoman empire and reclaim those "usurped" by the governments in Europe. The threat of territorial loss was a real one and the Ottoman press was painfully aware that the empire had more of rhetoric and memories of past glory than it had military force to oppose the armies of Europe mobilizing to dismember the empire of Osman.

IMAGES OF AGGRESSORS, ENGLAND

Once the revolution had lifted the restrictions imposed on the press by Abd ül-Hamid, the instinct for survival replaced censorship as a force affecting Ottoman revolutionary pens. Domestic critique (the satire of sultan, meclis, and society) was complemented by a vigorous critique of foreign intervention and influence. But, especially after Abd ül-Hamid was deposed, Ottoman satirists were visibly aware that the primary threat to Ottoman sovereignty was external rather than internal. In the satirical press, Europe, paragon of success in imperial expansion, capital accumulation, and arms development, became the comic aggressor. This representation expressed the dilemma of the dual nature of Europe as, at once, revolutionary exemplar and chief enemy. The European acquisition of a supposed "pinnacle of civilization" (distilled in such accomplishments as constitutional government, enlightenment thinking, efficient transportation, mixed gender entertainment, and "modern" fashions) brought with it the desire and aptitude for conquest. Familiar with the habits of empire, the Ottomans knew all too well that imperial expansion came at the expense of the weak. This knowledge prompted the satirical press to scrutinize the exercise and outcomes of European hegemonic activity rather than to laud its virtues. The various regimes of Europe were accused of brutality, greed, larceny, injustice, and of making themselves and their imitators ridiculous. Here, a distinction could be (and was) made between the actions of individual states and the "actions" of a generalized, disembodied European "other." That is, Ottoman satire could designate parts of Europe or target an unspecified amorphous Europe as a whole. Primary specified targets were England, Austria, France, Russia, Germany, Bulgaria, and later Italy. In the social realm, the target was often an unspecified Europe or European ("Frank"), or the cultural threat of Europe could be condensed into the single form of its standard bearer, France.

There was a rank order of comic aggressors in images found in the Ottoman press, and this order was determined by the extent and nature of each regime's ability to insult or imperil Ottoman sovereignty. Hence Britain, whose navy and conquests earned it both fear and admiration, was characterized as a swallower of states and dominator of allies. France, posing a less immediate military threat, was still the greedy aggressor in North Africa, especially Morocco. It retained its image of revolutionary exemplar but was also accused of making both men and women frivolous and debauched through its culture of wine, fashion, sex, and cafes. Austria, longtime foe and now militarily potent, symbolized ill fate and the turn of fortunes. A regime lacking in the political enlightenment of Britain or the cultural distinction of France, it wielded the threat of invasion with the authority that once characterized the Ottoman armies bound for Vienna. Its success was particularly galling. The Ottoman boycott of Austrian goods in 1908 was heavily exploited in the press to show that the Ottomans still wielded the power to determine their own destiny when confronted with such an aggressor. Germany too was depicted as an up-and-coming military juggernaut. Less threatening, but equally galling, was the newly proclaimed "king" of Bulgaria. Prince Ferdinand of Saxe-Coburg had been crowned in Bulgaria on August 14, 1887; but it was Bulgaria's proclamation of independence after the Young Turk revolution that elevated Ferdinand as a major target in the Ottoman cartoon space. A buffoon in Ottoman cartoons, too small to bear the weight of crown and insignia, Ferdinand and Bulgaria now symbolized Ottoman emasculation, the inability to control or retain one-time subordinates.

Of course, visions of European imperialism in the context of the Ottoman revolution varied according to who was conjuring those visions. Some English observers, for example, would have it that the Ottoman revolutionaries loved and honored Britain as a constitutional brother and felt nothing but esteem for the British.

> In England in particular the Turkish Revolution was warmly received, partly because it implied a compliment to the result of our own political evolution, and partly from our innate admiration for the qualities displayed by the principal actors—enterprise, courage and moderation. So much for sentiment. In more material aspects there was solid satisfaction in the course of events. Any change in the system of government which would lead to the formation of a strong and independent Turkey was welcome to us from the point of view of Mediterranean strategy; while reformation in Turkey itself, whose principal commercial client we are, could only lead to economic development of a larger market for our industrial products. To round off the situation there was the pleasant knowledge that the Young Turks were full of admiration for British institutions, British ideals, and British people, and that they freely attributed their inspiration to the example of England. Manifestations of their feelings toward us were numerous and sincere, and for the time we held the supreme place in the Turkish heart.[15]

This self-congratualtory speech by one David Fraser reveals some ways in which the Ottoman revolutionaries were framed in Britain: political emulators, providers of markets, and contributors to the strategic interests of Britain. "So much for sentiment," indeed. Fraser's emphases reveal the imperial interests of Britain that provided so much fodder for the pens of Ottoman satirists. His estimation of the British place in "the Turkish heart," however, was perhaps somewhat off the mark, at least where the Ottoman cartoon space was concerned.

Instead of drawing lines of sympathy between Britain and the empire as a sort of constitutional patron and its protege, the Ottoman satirists instead drew bonds of brotherhood among those who suffered jointly the ravages of English imperialism. Egypt, for centuries an Ottoman province, became in the satirical press a symbol of the greed, ambition, and oppression of the English conqueror. England had preserved the fiction that its occupation of Egypt was "temporary," but after twenty-six years no one in the empire imagined the relationship of England and Egypt as anything other than that of master and subordinate. The Ottomans, while throwing off their own oppressive regime and attempting to ward off the evil-eye of European avarice, imagined the Egyptians, who were agitating for independence from England, as brothers-in-arms, fellow nationalists (of sorts).

The Comic Aggressor

These sentiments were vigorously expressed in the gazette *Serbesti,* using the words *vatanperver* (defender or nourisher of the homeland), *vatandaş* (compatriot), and *kardeşimiz* (our brothers.)[16]

These images of "imagined community," to use the terminology of Benedict Anderson, are clearly demonstrated in two cartoons from the gazette *Kalem.*[17] The first cartoon shows a gigantic figure of England (not John Bull, but a capped, plaid-stockinged, pipe-smoking giant). He is leaning against the pyramid, symbol of "the East" and monument to the ancient character of Egyptian identity (Figure 6.1). The very nonchalance with which he smokes his pipe and rests his feet on the pyramid seems to insult the Ottoman viewer, suggesting that whatever claims, Ottoman or Egyptian, there might be to this territory, they are made irrelevant by the power and "size" of Britain. The giant reclines, he does not have to exert himself to hold this territory. In the foreground of the frame stands a group of "Young Egyptians;" they are protesting the English occupation.[18] Although the protest here appears hopeless, the tiny demonstrators are calculated to arouse the sympathy and patriotic indignation of the viewer. The caption is written in Ottoman, French, and Arabic, suggesting that the message is directed at European imperialists (or their sympathizers), at the victims of imperialism, and at those (the Ottomans) who might suffer the same fate.

A variation on this pyramid theme can be found in *Züğürt,* which shows the figure of Egypt trying to get the British lion to jump through a hoop. But, the cartoon notes, "he has forgotten that there is an impediment to this particular maneuver, the pyramids."[19] Those pyramids, labeled in French, "*Moderne Pyramide del Leone,*" consist of huge stockpiles of munitions. They are no longer a symbol of Egyptian glory, but of English military power. As in the previous cartoon, the message here is that might will determine who rules Egypt and that might is in the hands of Britain.

A second cartoon from *Kalem* shows another figure of Egypt which draws lines of affiliation across geographic, linguistic, and ethno-national boundaries (Figure 6.2). It shows an Egyptian, his mouth stuffed with three tongues, labeled (in French), "French, English, and German." In his hand he holds his own tongue, labelled "*maternelle.*" Pointing to it, he says, "My own tongue remains in my hand."[20] The caption, in French, reads, "the languages in Egypt;" but in Ottoman the caption reads, "*mısırda sene-i ecnebiye*" (the year of the foreigner in Egypt). This is a play on the designations of year according to calendar type, such as *sene-i malîye* (Ottoman financial year) or *sene-i milâdîye* (Christian era year). It suggests that, in Egypt, the British occupation had produced a new era, a new kind of counting time that was dictated from abroad.

This cartoon also suggests a certain confusion of identity whereby the crowding in of the foreign tongues has made it difficult for the Egyptian to recognize himself, or to communicate with his own people. Indeed, this representation intimates that the tongues have in fact left the Egyptian without a voice, the three tongues, ironically, becoming a gag. There is a

كنج مصرليلر انكلتره اشغالنى پروتستو ايتديلردر .   شبان المصريون يردون احتلال الانكليز

La protestation des Jeunes Egyptiens contre l'occupation Anglaise.

Figure 6.1 The English Occupation of Egypt

Figure 6.2 No Room for the Mother Tongue

further irony here, embodied in the fact that this satire of linguistic imperialism is produced in an Ottoman gazette that itself produces a bilingual narrative, in Ottoman and in French. The Ottoman press had itself been colonized by French language and culture, and it did not require a great deal of imagination to transpose the figure of the gagged Egyptian into one of a gagged Ottoman.

The question of linguistic identity remained a highly pertinent one for Ottoman and later Turkish, society. The French language, in particular, was prominent in Istanbul society. French slogans were translated into Ottoman on coins, and prices in both *kuruş* and *francs* on newspapers and in shop windows reflected the overall economic and political infiltration of Europe.[21] Today, the booksellers of Istanbul, long-confined to the old ways of the *Sahaflar,* booksellers' street, publish their catalogs in English with prices in dollars, a concession to market demands and to the English-language world order. In 1908, the publishers of Istanbul faced the same imbalances of economic power, but the "world" language was French and the "common" coin was the franc.

By World War I, the CUP was acting to counteract the linguistic encroachment that is suggested in the cartoon of the Egyptian with four tongues. In 1916, the Ottoman government passed a law that imposed Turkish as the language of correspondence for all foreign firms operating in the empire.[22] Harry Stuermer, a correspondent for the *Gazette de Cologne* in Istanbul, complained that the CUP's Talat Bey had decreed that all the signs on the shops in Pera must be written in Ottoman Turkish. Stuermer regarded this decree as a major imposition. In Pera (the "European" section of Istanbul), a place where "not one in a thousand knows how to read Turkish," he wrote, "all the inscriptions on the stores must be replaced with Turkish text, carefully painted in the national colors of white and red."[23] Indeed, such crises of linguistic identity exist today with the French vigorously attempting to eradicate the linguistic imperialism of English and the Quebecquois banning English street and shop signs. So, in the Ottoman case, the war of tongues that was depicted in revolutionary cartoons continued on the streets of Pera. It was a war that was percieved to be vital, a series of battles for turf and for identity.

Ottoman satire, of course, was not without its more humorous side as is clearly evidenced in a rather different cartoon vision of English imperialism, in which the satirist employed the imagery of Western art to lampoon Western domination. The cartoon, which plays with gender distinctions as well as with traditional iconography, portrays John Bull as a hairy-legged version of Boticelli's Venus, rising on the half-shell from the Gulf of Basra (Figure 6.3).[24] Although the image is designed to provoke laughter, its subtext is still the seeming inevitablity of British dominance in the Gulf.

Other representations tended to be more forthrightly sinister, demonstrating the processes by which Britain, quite literally, was gobbling up the globe. A late World War I vintage cartoon in the Ottoman gazette *Diken,*

Figure 6.3 John Bull as "Venus" in the Persian Gulf

made the point dramatically in a series of small frames tracing British imperialism from 1914 to 1918. The little sketches are not sophisticated, but they are telling even without their captions. The smug looking, yet elfin, figure of John Bull is shown, arms crossed, watching his fortunes increase from Egypt, to Baghdad, to Africa, to Istanbul, surveying his ships and counting his commercial receipts. The final two frames show first John Bull as a colossus astride Istanbul, and then the "whole world" as slaves to England, bringing their goods and bowing at John Bull's feet.[25] This was the vision of British domination that was prefigured in the cartoons of the revolutionary period, a vision in which the empire became just one more of the many pawns of a militaristic and ambitious England. For the Ottoman satirists of 1908, an England ensconsed in Cairo was an ill-omen of things to come.

MULTIPLE EUROPEAN POWERS

Britian, of course, as top dog in the imperialist scramble, was a primary target of satire in the Ottoman press; but the other European powers did not escape the satirist's pen, they were lampooned individually or in consort. The Ottomans rightly imagined themselves as surrounded by enemies. That frightening image is suggested in a cartoon showing the "empire," in bed, complaining about the tumult that has awakened him. Meanwhile, Russia, Austria, Germany, and Greece march in on him, rifles drawn.[26] The cartoon space took on each of the empire's foes or threateners, producing customized images to satirize each one's greed and rapacity. The imperialist powers were also often shown collaborating to dismember the empire or swallow it up. They conspired, for reasons that were not always apparent, against Ottoman sovereignty. Each was, in its own way, the symbol of a particular type of threat; each was also part of a menacing and amorphous European "other."

What the European states, in consort, were doing to the Ottoman state was represented in cartoons as acts of pulling apart, cutting up, eating, betraying, seducing, or deceiving. In the cartoon space, European powers cajoled, threatened, or fought over Ottoman territory, as seen in a frame in *Geveze* where each foreign state personified is crying out to the Ottomans: "Come to me, [no] come to me, come, come!"[27] Sometimes the foreign states were shown as physicians, "operating on" the empire, but actually dismembering it.[28] Or, the empire and its parts became the pieces in games played by the European states. Such an image is found in a cartoon entitled, "the new billiards fanatic."[29] The frame shows Franz Joseph of Austria intent on a game of billiards with the czar. Illuminating the playing surface is a lamp, the globes of which contain the "faces" of European powers like John Bull and Wilhelm II. The players chalk their cues with a chalk labeled "status quo" and the billiard balls are Greece, Montenegro, Bulgaria, and Serbia. Little more than a year later, these balls and players would be immersed in the Balkan War. This cartoon portrays the contest among European states, a game in which the empire itself was not depicted as a player. It suggests the satirist's self-image, the Ottomans as powerless pawns. The European leaders calmly amuse themselves, engaging as a matter of course in a competition to determine the fate of the Ottoman state. Ottoman cartoons also sometimes showed individual European powers sharing their own fate, as pawns in a great game. One such example is *Alem's* cartoon of Franz Joseph as the puppet of Germany's Wilhelm.[30]

Elsewhere, this competition is depicted in a clever cartoon that purports to decline the verb "to have." The cartoon, entitled "Foreign Politics," declines "*avoir, indicatif présent*" in French: "*vous avez* (you have), *nous avons* (we have) . . . ."[31] Figures for each element of the declension show who "has" what. The Ottoman figure has nothing; he says, "They have." Franz Joseph holds two globes representing Bosnia and Herzegovina: "I have." The czar points at him angrily, "You have." The message is clear, it is the foreigners who have and the very act of having finds its ultimate expression in foreign politics and in foreign language.

Games can, however, have unexpected outcomes and, occasionally, the European powers were shown getting the worst of it. That is the case in a 1911 cartoon in *Yeniçeri* (Janissary), which shows the European powers not as grown-up soldiers but as schoolboys. The group stands in a semi-circle to watch one of their number, Italy, torment Tripoli, pictured as a turkey wearing a fez. But the tables are turned as the turkey wheels and pursues Italy, who scrambles off yelling, "Mercy, Help, Help, Help . . . ."[32] Italy had invaded Tripolitania in September 1911, at which Enver mobilized Ottoman officers to resist the Italian advances. This satire of Italy's ambitions to expand its territory at Ottoman expense (and of the Ottoman resistance) infantalizes the European states by depicting them as schoolboys. Still, the boys, however ineffective in this scenario, are wearing uniforms, symbols of their military pretensions. This is one of the few cartoons where the empire is portrayed winning in the game of territorial ambition. Once it invaded Tripolitania in 1911, Italy became a major rather than a minor player in Ottoman anti-imperialist frames.[33] That same year, a similar cartoon targeted Garibaldi's ventures in Albania as "the Garibaldi follies," a sort of vaudeville misadventure.[34] Italy thus joined states like Austria and Britian as co-conspirators in the Ottoman cartoon space, a sinister group intent upon robbing and destroying the empire.

The "Great Powers," were not always power brokers in the Ottoman cartoon space. Even though they were usually represented as threats, menaces, and rapacious devourers, sometimes the satirists conspired to portray them as weak or pathetic. One such cartoon played on the notion of spotting the mote in someone else's eye but being unable to see the beam in one's own. It showed raggedy caricatures of the czar, John Bull, and Marianne, gathered around a trunk marked "*Jeune Turquie.*" The czar pulled a cloth from among the clothes inside and exclaimed, "Ugh! I've found a dirty hanky among the Young Turks' linens![35] In this frame, the European powers are reduced to a Dickensian rabble, scrabbling to find faults in others in order to obscure their own sins.

THE IMAGE OF FRANCE

France, as noted in a previous chapter, served in Ottoman satire both as model of revolutionary virtue and as one of the gang of greedy European imperialist states eager to capitalize upon the empire's weakness. In the latter form, France was ordinarily male, uniformed or suited, awaiting his chances for financial or territorial gain. He was not quite in the same league with aggressors like Britain and Austria. But France was targeted for its bloody aggression in Morocco. In the Ottoman cartoon space, French imperialism in Morocco symbolized the subjugation of fellow Muslims, the encroachment in North Africa where the Ottoman sultan still exercised at least nominal sovereignty, and the possibilities for the subjugation of the empire itself.

At the time of the Ottoman revolution, Morocco was at the center of a vigorous struggle between the French and the Germans for strategic position in the Maghreb. The Algeciras conference of 1906 had affirmed Moroccan sovereignty and commercial opportunity for all European powers; but France, in consort with Spain, was permitted to police Morocco and had steadily advanced its interests there. By 1911 it would gain Morocco as a protectorate. This aggression was immortalized in a cartoon showing Mulla Hafiz, who had overthrown his brother, Abd al-Aziz IV, and become ruler of Morocco shortly after the Ottoman revolution (Figure 6.4). Mulla Hafiz is shown facing a group of European powers who stand impatiently outside his gate. He leans out but does not open the gate and tells them that he himself plans to be the master of his house. "If you want to send me your regards," he says, "send me some illustrated postcards and I will respond immediately with perfect ardor."[36] This cartoon is particularly ironic because illustrated postcards were one of the vehicles through which Europeans captured and colonized the North African peoples, objectifying them as exotic "Orientals" for the European viewer.[37] In the forefront of this particular cartoon, just outside Mulla Hafiz's gate, is what looks like a tomb monument with a ball and crescent on the top. Inscribed on it is an epitaph for the Algeciras Pact. In reality though, French ambitions in Morocco could not be entombed as readily as the Algeciras Pact was set aside in this cartoon frame.

Where the French in North Africa were concerned, the Ottoman journalists of the revolutionary period had a long history of confrontation on which to build. The struggle between the French on the one hand, and the Ottomans and North African governors on the other, had been developing throughout the nineteenth century. There had been insults and skirmishes dating to the eighteenth century. As the famous Arabophile, Wilfrid

MOULAY HAFID. — Je veux être le maître dans ma maison... Envoyez-moi des cartes postales illustrées et je vous répondrai de tout cœur !

Figure 6.4 The European Powers in Morocco

Blunt recorded, with typically dry wit: "On April 29, 1827, an undignified little scene, but one not without precedent in oriental courts, took place in a pavilion of the Kasbah at Algiers—the Dey [autonomous governor of Algiers] struck the French Consul in the face with his fly-whisk. This trivial episode, famous to history as the *coup d'éventail*, was to change the destiny of North Africa."[38] In his colorful story of the French conquest of Algeria, Blunt goes on to note that, in the seventeenth century, two successive French consuls were fired from the mouth of a cannon by the Dey of Algiers, "in revenge for French bombardments and demands for indemnities," and that on the latter occasion the French admiral, "retaliated by decapitating seventeen influential Turks whom he had on board."[39] These episodes suggest not only the power of rumor and the intimate associations between Istanbul and the North African centers of power but also the fact that North Africa had long been an object of French intervention and desire.

It was not only in the Ottoman press that French brutality in Morocco was the subject of caricature. In May 1908, French cartoonist Aristide Delannoy and editor Victor Meric published a cartoon on the cover of the gazette, *Les Hommes du jour*, showing "General d'Amade as a bloody butcher, surveying the carnage he had created during the conquest of Morocco."[40] Both journalists were sentenced to a year in jail and fined for insulting the military. Like their French counterparts, Ottoman cartoonists saw the French actions in North Africa as expressions of raw power and greed. The French presence in Algeria and Morocco, like that of the British in Egypt, was a reminder that the Ottoman empire was powerless to aid allies or dependents. Outside of the struggle for North Africa, however, France tended usually to be shown in consort with other powers when it came to Ottoman visions of European imperialism. Unlike Britain, Russia, Germany, and Austria, it tended not to be portrayed alone as a single agressor.

IMAGES OF AUSTRIA, RUSSIA, GERMANY, AND BULGARIA

Austria, in the Ottoman cartoon space was represented, in the figure of its emperor, Franz Joseph, as a potent military threat and a power intent on breaking up the Ottomans' Balkan territories. Austria was actively involved in alienating Ottoman lands. This role is suggested in a cartoon that depicts the serene, crowned head of Franz Joseph as a hot air balloon. The "new delivery balloon of Franz Joseph" floats over a group of tiny uniformed men representing the states of Europe and the Balkans.[41] As they gaze upwards, a figure throws out his deliveries from the dirigible's basket. The packages are labeled "Crete" and "Bosnia." This cartoon proposes that, in effect, Franz Joseph is not only taking Ottoman provinces himself (the annexation of Bosnia and Herzegovina), he is conniving in the carrying off of the *memalik-i osmaniye* by others.[42] Such images, in which the Ottomans are either entirely absent or, at best, helpless witnesses to the partition of their own state, are common in Ottoman cartoons. Frames of Austrian, British, or Russian aggression often suggest a flea market for the sale of the worn, but still valuable, Ottoman goods, a European sale to which the Ottomans had not been invited.

Russia, in the iconography of the revolutionary era, is a power neither entirely Western nor entirely Eastern. For many satirical purposes, Russia was grouped with other states, like Britain and Austria, representing European imperialism. Yet, in other ways, Russia was, in part, a reflection of the Ottoman self.[43] It was a large, traditional, agrarian empire with an autocratic sovereign who was often compared to his counterparts in the Ottoman empire and Iran. Thus Russia holds a somewhat unique place in the rogues' gallery of aggressors in the Ottoman cartoon space. It was a sometime ally of the Western European powers, but it was also a lone and terrible threat, attempting to advance it borders at the expense of the Ottomans, the Hapsburgs, the British, and others.[44] Russia, for cartoon purposes, often acted alone; it was in Europe but not necessarily of Europe. Further, where Britian and France could represent modernity and progress, Russia represented tradition, backwardness, and oppression as well as raw military force. Russia was also the perceived instigator of separatist revolt in the Ottomans' Balkan territories.

The association of Russia with old-style repressive regimes is made clearly in one cartoon frame that, as in the images of Abd ül-Hamid, emphasizes the symbols of crown and throne. This picture shows a huge czar with an outsize crown on his head (Figure 6.5). He sits on a tremendous throne, his hands dripping blood down its front. Beneath his boots are the smashed bodies of his subjects, one, still alive, with his hand raised, entreating. In the background, the city seems to be burning. The czar gazes down at a small figure next to his throne; the man appears to be a minute version of the czar himself (he probably represents Ferdinand of Bulgaria). He carries a sign that says "national assembly, progress, peace." The caption here does not translate felicitously; it plays on the word *naçar*, which means helpless, or *naçar*, not a czar; hence: "Here is another impotent potentate, another czar, not a czar."[45] But the message concerns identity; the small figure is yet another czar who (literally, here) does not measure up. That is, the very notion of czar is incompatible with representative government, progress, and peace. For the Ottoman satirists, such a monarch could not turn into something he was not; whether his violence was aimed inward at his own citizens, or outward at the Ottomans and Iranians, the czar could be counted upon to act as the brutal scion of a past, despotic era.

On its northwestern front, the empire faced a multiplicity of threats from Austria, Germany, and even from the upstart Bulgaria.[46] The close relationship between these two major powers and their Bulgarian protege is neatly summarized in a cartoon in *Alem*, one which equates the exercise of power with the act of eating. This cartoon shows Ferdinand of Bulgaria,

— Ça un Tzar — jamais!...

Figure 6.5 When is a Czar Not a Czar?

dressed in uniform and crown but wearing a server's apron, offering cheese to two "patrons," Franz Joseph of Austria and Wilhelm II of Germany (Figure 6.6). "*Efendiler,*" he says, "May I offer you a savory Balkan." The replies of the two sovereigns suggest their rank-order as threats in the eye of the Ottoman cartoonist. Franz Joseph is a bit finicky. "But," he replies, "it seems a bit maggoty." Wilhelm, however, is undaunted. "We'll have it!!" he says, "For us, maggoty is fine."[47]

This image is, in some ways, a typical Ottoman caricature of the "Great Game." Bulgaria's Ferdinand is demeaned, a servant to the greater powers.[48] Austria, in the person of Franz Joseph, seems willing to exercise some restraint where the consuming of Ottoman territory is concerned. But for Wilhelm, the offering up of the Balkans, however maggoty, and absent the silver platter, is irresistable. The unsettled relations of the Balkans titilate rather than unnerve him. For this Ottoman cartoonist, Wilhelm was poised to gobble down whatever territories were offered him; his appetite was only whetted by the empire's constitutional dilemma.[49]

Other images linked the upstart Bulgaria to the big-time aggressors. One such frame, dated October 8, 1908, suggested that Bulgaria was backed by a duplicitous German emperor who mollified the Ottomans while inflaming the militaristic ambitions of Bulgaria. The frame shows Wilhelm as Caesar, patting two "Young Turks," depicted as youths, on the head (Figure 6.7). "Peace, my dears, peace," he tells them. He then metamorphoses into Wilhelm in military uniform, miniature cannon in hand, and says to the King of Bulgaria, shown drawing his sword, "Zeal, all is ready."[50] This representation of the Ottomans as boys with a toy train suggests the novice status of the new Ottoman order, and its vulnerability. It also suggests that Bulgaria might not be an insignificant opponent. Wilhelm, however, is the power broker, ambitious and anxious to duplicate the conquests of the Caesars.

Ferdinand's subordinate position was suggested in a cartoon in *Alem* that shows him going to meet the czar who cannot decide what to call him: "Emperor of Macedonia !! . . . No, No, King of Bulgaria !! No, Prince . . . ." The czar finally decides upon "*vali* of Eastern Rumelia," thus pointing up both the struggle then going on for control of Eastern Rumelia and the ambiguity of Ferdinand's position.[51] As Barbara Tuchman put it, Ferdinand "annoyed his fellow sovereigns by calling himself Czar and kept in a chest a Byzantine Emperor's full regalia, acquired from a theatrical costumer, against the day when he should reassemble the Byzantine dominions beneath his sceptre."[52]

Elsewhere, Bulgaria was satirized as an ambitious upstart and as a Balkan troublemaker. These topoi are suggested by two satires in *Kalem;* the first is a phony notice advertising a supposed banquet to be served in Sofia, the menu consisting, among other delights, of "*fricasée orientale*" and "*bombe glacée.*"[53] The other is a cartoon of the European "orchestra": Austria, Italy, Germany (with what looks like a real chicken rather than an eagle perched on his helmet), France, Russia, and England. As the musicians prepare to

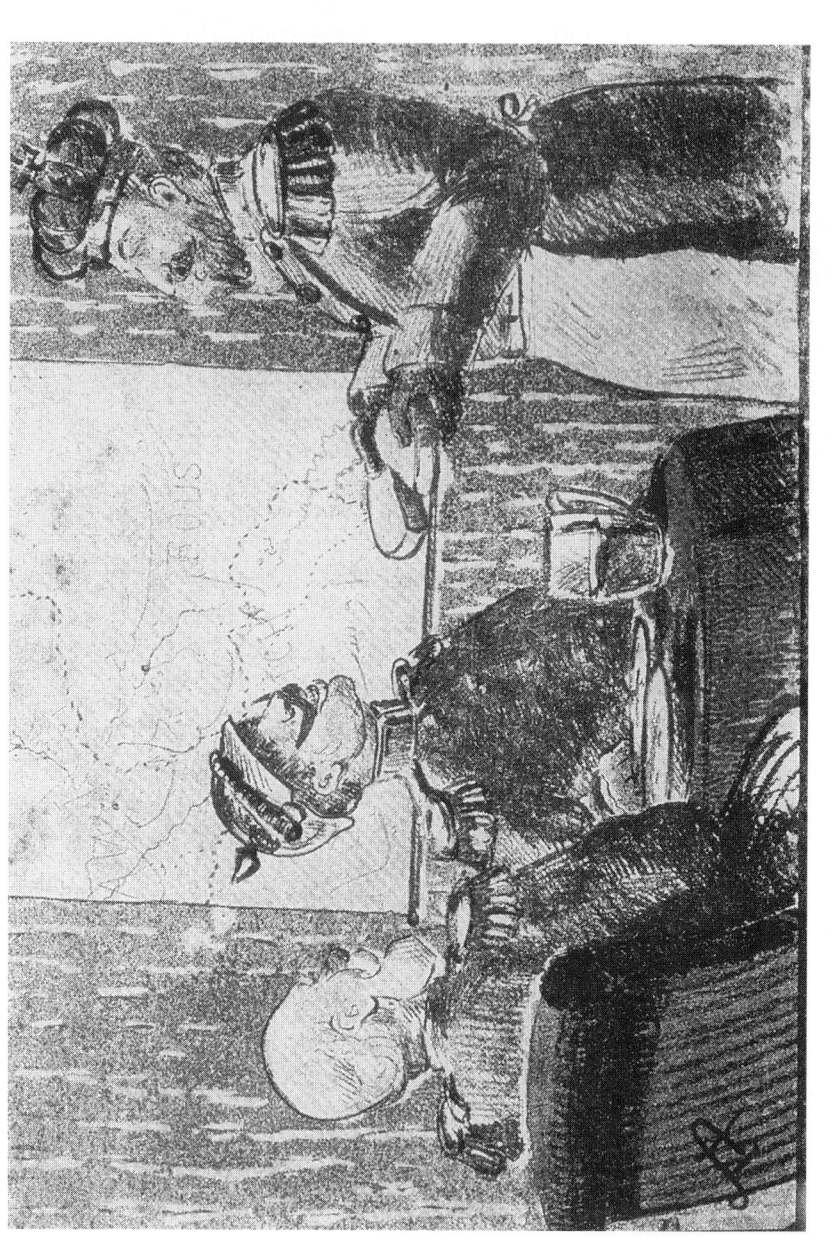

Figure 6.6 Eating the Balkans

L'Empereur { Aux Jeunes Turcs : La paix, mes enfants.
Aux Bulgares : messieurs les Bulgares, tirez les premiers.

Figure 6.7 Austria, Bulgaria, and the Young Turks

blow their horns, a "new Maestro," arrives, a dinky Ferdinand in spurs, cape, and crown. With horn to his lips, he proclaims, in English, "Ta-Ra Ra-Ra! Here I am, Emperor of Bulgaria!"[54] The orchestra members stare at him in amazement. This cartoon is an interesting example of the cultural, linguistic, and iconographic mingling found in the Ottoman cartoon space; it is also a good example of the inclination to draw one's enemies as weak and laughable. Faced with a Europe that was militarily and economically strong, the Ottoman cartoonists looked for opportunities to draw at least parts of that "Europe" as puny and ludicrous.

THE ECONOMIC ORDER

The satire of imperialism targeted the economic as well as the political sphere. According to the satirical press the Ottoman economic order of things was not what it should be.[55] The new "citizens" were victimized and impoverished; the new government was continuing the sellout of Ottoman resources initiated by the sultans in the vain hope of buying foreign friendships; and foreign entrepreneurs were continuing to bully their way into the Ottoman economic space, displacing traditional forms of labor and buying up what they were not given or could not take.[56] Furthermore, the new regime was destined to begin its rule with a budget deficit of six million Turkish pounds.[57] That figure, along with the Ottoman budget problem in general, found its way into many cartoons suggesting both the old regime's corruption and its dependence on Europe.[58]

In the cartoon space, the critique of European economic imperialism centered around four major themes. Already noted was the press's focus on European economic penetration abroad in areas to which the satirical press crafted bonds of sympathy, such as Egypt, Iran, and Morocco. But where Ottoman affairs were concerned, the first and foremost target was the odious capitulatory regime, symbol of the long and gradually intensifying loss of Ottoman economic independence.[59] Next came European business and economic control over the resources and industries of the empire: tobacco, textiles, railroads, steamships. Finally, and a subset of the third theme, was the attack on the tobacco Régie, the organized tobacco monopoly controlled by France, which became the symbol par excellence of the empire's subservience to European economies. Countering these four themes of subordination and dependence was the theme of Ottoman resistance to European economic dominance, a notion that found its most concrete expression in images of the boycott of Austrian goods launched, in retaliation for the annexation of Bosnia and Herzegovina, in fall of 1908. While the capitulations meant subordination, the boycott meant defiance; while the Régie meant dependence, the boycott meant independence. The boycott symbolized the hope of the new regime, a hope that helped sustain the revolution despite the foreign factories on Anatolian shores, the European armies occupying Ottoman territory, and the European steamships monopolizing Ottoman harbors.[60]

The Capitulatory Regime and the Public Debt Administration

The capitulations were economic concessions granted by treaty to European states; these concessions, along with war loans, led the empire into a quagmire of debt. Cartoons equated the capitulatory regime both directly and indirectly with the economic rape of the empire. Prospects for the Ottoman economy were not entirely as grim as the capitulatory regime and the empire's late-nineteenth-century bankruptcy would seem to suggest.[61] Nonetheless, one third of the empire's income by 1870 went to service the foreign debt. After the foreign-run Public Debt Adminstration (*Caisse de la Dette Publique Ottomane*) was founded in 1881, it continued to control a third of the empire's revenues. The Public Debt Administration took over direct administration of many forms of tax and of the salt and tobacco monopolies.[62] After the revolution, the PDA became a significant target of Ottoman satirists. The Public Debt Administration and the Banque Ottomane, which was founded in 1856 to represent Franco-British interests, served as symbols and constant reminders of foreign control over Ottoman affairs and Ottoman weakness in the world economic order.[63] The empire did not control its own finances; it did not even print its own money. Indeed it was not until the beginning of World War I that the new Ottoman regime truly began to assert its economic autonomy.[64] As Çaglar Keyder has noted: "Young Turks abrogated the capitulations when the war began, the Public Debt Administration lost its powers and the government gained the powers to legislate a new tariff and the right to print paper money which until then had been conceded to the Franco-British owned Banque Ottomane."[65]

Harry Stuermer, correspondent for the *Gazette de Cologne* in Istanbul from 1915–1916, probably overstated the case, even in 1917, when he suggested that the abolition of the capitulations literally freed the Ottomans: "*D'abord, la Turquie, après avoir brusquement aboli les Capitulations, s'est entièrement libéré aussi de la tutelle de l'Europe dans le domaine de la politique commerciale.*"[66] But, certainly in the years between the 1908 revolution and the start of the world war, Ottoman journalists, satirists, and politicians saw the capitulations and the institutions of foreign economic control as primary impediments to the success of the new constitutional regime. As long as the capitulations were in place, the empire could not be truly free. The capitulations were named and embodied in many cartoon frames.[67] Their effects, the free or cheap disbursement of Ottoman resources, were represented in many more.

A striking cartoon, which is reminiscent of an Early Modern European engraving of the rape of the Netherlands, shows the empire (*memalik-i osmaniye*) as the milk cow of Europe (Figure 6.8). In this image, however, the Ottomans are no longer victims. The new Ottoman regime is shown reject-

Figure 6.8 The Ottoman Milk Cow

The Comic Aggressor

ing the depredations of the Europeans who have clearly become accustomed to their "milk" privileges. The empire is depicted as a gigantic cow on a hillside. While an Ottoman (identified by dress) milks her, two Ottoman soldiers guard her. They are turning away the European states (shown as tiny men dressed in uniform) who approach the cow, milk pails in hand. The guard tells these would-be exploiters that unless they come with money in hand, they are now out of luck.[68] In effect, the message is no more free lunch, at least not at the expense of Ottoman resources. The costumes of the figures (both the soldiers and the would-be European milk-men are in uniform) suggest that it was military weakness that allowed the exploitation of the empire and military might that must save it from that exploitation. The nation, as cow, is gendered female and is in need of protection. While the outcome of this frame suggests a triumph for the Ottoman state, warding off its aggressors, other cartoons were not so sanguine about the empire's chances against the economic power of Europe.

A compelling caricature of Germany in another cartoon stresses the same links between military might and economic dominance. This cartoon is called "The War Trumpet."[69] It shows an enormous figure of Germany perched upon a building labeled "Bourse" (Exchange), in French and in Ottoman Turkish (Figure 6.9). His cloak encircles the building and the people on its steps. Streaming in and out are tiny, frenzied figures, at least one of whom prepares to shoot himself in the head. Like many other cartoons, this frame relies on the use of size to convey the distribution of power. The military significance of the giant is embodied in his prominent, gleaming cavalry boots and his spiked helmet. His eyes beneath the helmet are not visible; his visage, instead, is dominated by the pointed mustache and the trumpet upon which he blows. Although the pointed mustache and spiked helmet are used somewhat interchangeably in the Ottoman cartoon space to suggest either Austria or Germany, here the single rather than double eagle on the helmet indicates that the threatening figure is Germany; the upward spiked mustache is most frequently an illusion to the Kaiser. Use of the spiked helmet, popularized by the Prussians, spread across the continent in the the nineteenth century. The prominence of the spiked helmet in this frame suggests an 1871 cartoon by Honore Daumier, "*L'Eclipse Sera-t-Elle Totale?* (Will the Eclipse Be Total?)," which shows a huge Prussian spiked helmet eclipsing the sun of liberty so that it may not shine on Europe below.[70] The German giant in the Ottoman cartoon, wearing the same helmet, threatens not merely liberty but economic and political life itself.

It is worth noting here that the actual locale of this cartoon is somewhat murky. The "Bourse," building suggests Paris, but the scene may as well be Istanbul, or any one of a number of European capitals threatened by the prospect of facing the German war machine. The message here is one of power (military and fiscal) and powerlessness; the German juggernaut is the source of general political and economic turmoil. Germany had been partic-

Figure 6.9 The War Trumpet

ularly aggressive in the competition for contol of Ottoman resources, investments, and infrastructural development. The entire frame neatly suggests one view of the Ottoman position early on as the revolutionary regime prepared its elections and as foreign powers mobilized to capitalize on Ottoman weakness. Indeed, the figure of Germany here may be made to stand not only for the German threat to all of its neighbors, but also for the whole range of foreign powers at whose mercy the Ottoman empire lay.

The Boycott

Countless cartoons express the idea of the Ottoman empire as puppet, moved by the hands of Europe on its purse strings. Sovereigns danced to the economic tune of Britain or Germany. As the rulers danced, so did the citizens, individuals shackled to poverty by the corruption and toadying of the old regime and by the economic paralysis of the new. But, when Austria annexed Bosnia and Herzegovina in the aftermath of the revolution, the Ottomans were given the wherewithal to counter their position of powerlessness by means of the boycott of Austrian goods. The boycott was a chance to withhold patronage even when the coins, goods, and merchants might all be "foreign." This image was the natural alternative to those that showed the Ottoman treasury given, sold to, or taken by European interests, the money bags labeled in francs or pounds sterling.

In the Ottoman mind, as envisioned in the satiric press, the 1908 boycott of Austrian goods represented a counterweight to the apparently inexorable invasion of European capital. The boycott began in October 1908, and lasted for about five months, spreading from Istanbul through the empire and even as far as Tripoli in North Africa.[71] It was launched by a call for boycott in the press and became a symbolic drawing of boundaries for an empire that had failed to keep European armies, entrepreneurs, and influence out. The boycott movement involved demonstrations, picketing, the formation of a merchant syndicate, a call to refuse to board and to service Austrian steamships, and the mobilization of the dock porters (*hamals*) and lightermen.[72] The refusal to buy was one of the few weapons the empire had left in the unequal contest to compete and survive in the new twentieth-century world order, although the boycott "hit the Greek and Armenian importers of Austrian goods as much as it hit Austria."[73] While the Ottoman boycott's long-term economic impact was perhaps relatively negligible, it was of great significance in the mobilizing of patriotic sentiment within the empire and in the reinforcing of bonds of Ottoman unity. In some ways, the Ottoman action was reminiscent of the boycott of British goods by Bengali nationalists, just two years before, in 1906.[74] Both enhanced "national" unity. In the press, the boycott became a rallying cry for the refashioned Ottoman citizenry. In the cartoon space, it provided an opportunity to mock the comic aggressor, to applaud revolutionary potential, and to parade the symbols of nation and of revolution. The boycott gave

Ottoman satire one of its few chances to moderate its usually jaundiced view of the revolutionary transformation.

Some of the most dramatic images of the boycott are found in the gazette *Papağan,* which ran large-format, full-page cartoon engravings. *Papağan's* cartoons employ all the patriotic symbolism: the empire as noble lion with a crescent emblazoned on its side, doughty Ottoman citizen boycotters, the intrepid new regime, and a sinister yet hapless Austria, doomed to pay the price, in commercial losses, for its militarism. One image shows the Ottoman lion perched on a stranded Austrian shipment, staring defiance at a fat and unappealing figure of Austria (Figure 6.10). A "Turkish" citizen displays the boycott notice and the other European powers, signified by flags and characteristic military figures, look on from the background.[75]

Other cartoon images were less heroic. The boycott gave the satiric gazettes an opportunity not only to lambast Austria and stir up patriotic sentiments among its readers, but also to poke fun at imperialist ambitions and at Ottoman consumers. Thus, for example, *Geveze* ran a cartoon showing Britian capitalizing on the boycott of Austrian goods by rushing in with its own replacement products.[76] *Dalkavuk,* which regularly mentioned the boycott in its pages, showed a relatively prosperous looking couple bypassing Stein's Department Store in Pera while the shopkeeper tried to urge them to come in.[77] This frame suggests the dependence on foreign goods already well established among Istanbul's elite classes. But even such practiced consumers were taken up in the enthusiasm for the boycott.

The case of the Ottoman boycott demonstrates how foreign economic penetration, labor, the press, and the evolution of socio-political and "nationalist" movements were conjoined in the early twentieth century. Little work has been done on these aspects of Ottoman society at the time, but illuminating comparisons (of urban labor, foreign monopolies, and the articulation of socio-political transformation in the press) could be made, for example, to the cases of India, Brazil, and China.[78]

The Régie

The boycott (as event) and the Régie (as institution) were essential images of European economic dominance in the Ottoman revolutionary press. The Régie (*Societé de la Régie Cointerésée des Tabacs de l'Empire Ottoman*) was a company based on foreign capital that was granted the Ottoman tobacco monopoly in 1883. It controlled tobacco cultivation, purchase, export, and the manufacture of cigarettes for domestic consumption.[79] In return, it paid a lump annual sum (*75 million kuruş*) to the Public Debt Administration; the tobacco producers benefited very little. The Régie, in the Ottoman cartoon space, was a colossal reminder of both the subjugation of the Ottoman state and the misery of the Ottoman worker; it served as a synthesizer for moral, social, political, and economic discontent.

Figure 6.10 The Ottoman Boycott of Austrian Goods

The Régie's role in the political, as well as the economic, affairs of state is clearly indicated in the memoirs of Cemal Pasha. He relates that in the crisis occasioned by the outbreak of the Second Balkan War in 1913, the Ottoman ministers were divided over what action to take. They were also short of cash for military operations. Given the empire's economic straits, the CUP's Talat Bey appealed to Mr. Weyl, the Director-General of the Régie:

> M. Weyl promised the Government a loan of a million and a half on condition that the Régie's concession was extended for fifteen years. Acting on the decision of the Council of Ministers, the Finance Minister, Rifat Bey, and Talat Bey, the Ministers of the Interior accepted these conditions. Such is the explanation of the Régie's business, which for the last two or three years has been denounced in the Chamber of Deputies as a crime of Djavid [the Finance Minister] Bey's. I am convinced that a Government which has accepted these conditions at such a moment cannot undo what has been done.[80]

So Cemal Pasha, in 1913, expressed the same irony found in the cartoons of the revolutionary period. The Ottoman state was, in effect, borrowing its own money from the European owned Régie in order to pay for a crisis spurred on by European political meddling in the Balkans. Like Cemal Pasha, the Ottoman satirists believed that such a regime might not be able to "undo" its fatal dependence.

One image that illustrates the obstacle that the Régie was perceived to constitute is found in *Kalem*. This 1911 cartoon shows Grand Vezir İbrahim Hakkı Paşa as "the acrobat who hurdles all."[81] The "hurdle," in this frame, is two large bales of "second rate," Basra tobacco, labeled with the seals of the Régie (Figure 6.11). Although the grand vezir has successfully leaped the Régie in this cartoon, the frame suggests that, almost three years after the revolution, the new regime has yet to solve its economic problems or to escape European fiscal patronage. Indeed the tobacco monopoly was not bought out until after the empire's demise, in 1925.[82]

The struggle for control of the Ottoman tobacco industry echoed a similar struggle in Iran, where the sale of the tobacco monopoly to British interests by the Qajar Shah had caused the Tobacco Rebellion late in the nineteenth century. It also mirrored a struggle between Western entrepreneurs on a global scale for control of the mineral and agricultural resources of Asia, South America, and Africa. The commentary of Louis Rambert, diplomat and man of affairs, illustrates the position of the Ottoman tobacco industry in the context of the competition for world economic hegemony in 1904.[83] Rambert wrote that when he paid a visit to the Ottoman grand vezir, he was advised that certain American "high officials" and capitalists planned to supplant France's control of the Ottoman tobacco industry. With this objective in mind, a certain very rich St. Louis industrialist had come to Istanbul to urge the Ottoman regime to grant American entrepreneurs a

Cours à obstacle.
le dernier obstacle fremchi je suis veû nepeur sur toute ligue

هرشیدن آتلایان بورجاباز

Figure 6.11 Leaping the Tobacco Régie

new monopoly concession. On hearing this news, Rambert quickly contacted "our friends in Berlin" to demand if this was so. He concluded that the American interests would not succeed in their plans but remained very concerned about the need to protect France's dominant position in the Ottoman economy.

There was indeed some reason to fear competition, as Rambert illustrated with his admiring description of an English cigarette factory and his favorable comparison of that factory to the French factories in Istanbul. Rambert described the M. Wils factory in Bristol in a highly impressionistic fashion:

> a marvel of organization for the methodical extraction of human labor, of attentions given to the workers of both sexes, of the perfecting of implements/plant apparati and of machines. The machines for making cigarettes are comprised of special systems designed especially by this company. They produce in quantities that we have not even imagined. In a vast hall, 52 machines are going at once, each producing 200,000 cigarettes per day. By other machines, the cigarettes are packed in boxes of heavy paper. They introduce a strip of paper into the machine, the box is formed mechanically, filled with cigarettes, closed, and run out the other end of the machine, all neat, labelled and ready for sale . . . Wils employs several thousand workers, among which are a great number of women gathered in the vast halls, well lighted from the ceiling, where they make cigarettes. Everything is admirably neat: the walls, the floors, the furnishings, and the female workers themselves. They are dressed appropriately with a simple and uniform attire, very carefully coifed; the entire aspect creates quite an impression, above all when one imagines our own sloven (*souillons*) Israelite workers in Constantinople.[84]

Rambert's vision of English order and cleanliness compared to the dirty and disordered conditions of cigarette production in Istanbul demonstrates the hierarchical ordering that European imperialism imposed on its economic colonies. European hegemony was not meant to produce equal conditions. Rambert's comparison evoked envy over the English outputs; order and technology meant high production. But it did not provoke an exhortation to alter conditions at the Istanbul factories. The misery of the workers there was the defining characteristic of the Régie regime, one that found its way into Ottoman revolutionary satire.

THE IMAGE OF THE WORKER

The plight of the worker was not a major theme in the Ottoman satirical press, even though, as Eric Zürcher notes, "The freedom of thought, of expression and of association brought about by the constitutional revolution resulted in . . . . widespread labor unrest."[85] Nonetheless, labor problems were linked to European influence and economic imperialism in Ottoman territories and to the dependence of the Ottoman government on foreign loans. When a wave of strikes swept the empire after the revolution, the new regime responded by cracking down vigorously on the labor movement and banning trade unions in the public sector. The new government thus showed itself to be as authoritarian as the old when it came to certain types of expression. Despite this lack of governmental sympathy for organized labor, the image of the ragged poor in general and of the worker in particular, did take varied forms in the revolutionary gazettes.[86] For one thing, there were discussions of socialism in the serious press, which included discussion of workers' conditions.[87] In the cartoon space, the poor man (or woman) in the street was often a symbol of the Ottoman public. The poor, suggested by ragged clothing, skinny bodies, and pitiable aspect, were shown in a variety of frames either targeting the Ottoman elites in social satire or representing the general plight of the empire vis-a-vis foreign powers.[88]

The gazette *Lâklâk*, in particular, employed social satire that brought the poor to the forefront in cartoon frames. It depicted the ragged workers and the greedy owners. In one frame, three skinny workers have the temerity to approach their obese boss. "Mercy Haci Ağa, we're roasting under the sun all day long. We can't fill our stomachs for forty para." They ask for twenty para more, *katık parası*, that is, "relish money," to buy a little something extra to eat with their bread (Figure 6.12). Grinning, he responds with mock astonishment: "What covetous rascals you are! Forty para a day! When was that ever not enough? What more could I give?"[89]

In another image, *Lâklâk* suggested that the poor and the workers were more generous and patriotic than their more prosperous fellow citizens. This cartoon shows a street scene of sorts with a money box affixed to the wall. Lined up on both sides of the box are working stiffs of various types, including one woman; some are ragged but all are dropping money into the box, which bears the star and crescent and represents some type of donation for the navy.[90] In the foreground, three substantial citizens, with frockcoats, fezzes, and walking sticks, pass by unconcerned, ignoring the collection box. The dress of these cartoon figures symbolizes their place in the class hierarchy. The lengthy caption relates how the "workers" all pay a substantial part of their meager salaries while, the "wealthy *sahibs*, the well paid, and the liars' class," pay nothing.[91] This particular frame does not directly target foreign affairs, it is a satire of class, which suggests the poor are more willing (or liable) to do their "patriotic duty" than the wealthy. But the needs of the decrepit Ottoman navy are certainly linked to the fear of foreign attack, and in that regard the European powers are implicated even in this cartoon.

An image that targets both class hierarchy and foreign influence, while simultaneously satirizing conspicuous consumption, is found in a cartoon in *Davul* (Drum) that juxtaposes the fashionable, Westernized, Ist-

Figure 6.12 Asking Haci Ağa For a Raise

anbul elites to a poor Anatolian beggar. The cartoon is entitled, "Returning from the Benefit Ball for Those Striken by Drought and Famine in Anatolia." It shows a beggar approaching a prosperous couple who are leaving the ball; the man is in tuxedo, the woman in low-cut European gown (Figure 6.13). "Be compassionate," says the beggar, "In the country my child is dying of hunger." The smiling woman ignores the petitioner while her escort snarls, "What an ingrate you are! We were just now working for your benefit."[92] Here, the beggar becomes the symbol of the nation. The starving Anatolians are a metaphor for the empire, reduced to beggary by oppression and by the extravagance, ineptitude, and consumerism of its elites. The European threat is not the threat of conquest symbolized by European males in uniform, rather it is the more insidious threat of economic and cultural imperialism symbolized by Western fashions in dress and entertainment. These elite Ottomans become the counterparts of the exploitative Europeans. This is not only a satire of class, but a satire that shows that the Europeanized Ottomans have lost their proper sense of identity. The beggar figure is not a worker but a villager; he symbolizes the poor and all the Ottoman citizens who are exploited and suffering.

Cartoons suggesting the worker per se showed maids and houseservants, often as players in domestic satire; construction workers, often as foils for the satire of new building or transportation projects; drivers commenting on the whims of those they transported; boatmen, muttering over the foibles of steamship travel; and factory workers, usually as characters in frames critiquing the economic holdings and activities of foreigners. In some ways, the *hamal* (porter) served as the quintessential image of the worker, impoverished and downtrodden, yet an ubiquitous symbol of tradition, peasant values, and the persistence of old systems of transport in the face of "modern," foreign inroads. The ineptness of the *hamal*, for example, is lampooned in the French section of the journal *Alem* in an illustrated satire entitled, "*Les Joyeux Hamals.*"[93] The *hamal* signified the changeless nature of the street, the government, and the social order. He also came to be a pivotal figure in the boycott of Austria; Davison suggests that the Ottoman *hamals* paid the greatest personal price for the conduct of the boycott.[94] To a certain extent, workers like the *hamal* and their poverty were taken as a given of society. The workers were poor and they would stay poor. Nonetheless, the Ottoman cartoon recruited the worker, as it recruited other "types," to relay certain messages of the revolutionary era, especially the messages of oppression and defiance.

This oppression could come from the inroads of foreigners or from the persecutions of government and society. In a series of frames, entitled, "Municipal order," in *Kalem,* the worker is shown in different guises, from the street cleaner, to the peddler, to the shop laborer.[95] This cartoon's lengthy caption (given in Ottoman, French, and Arabic) satirizes the rules of the city adminstration, mocking their lack of common sense. The frames juxtapose the dapper Westernized officials and customers to the tradi-

Figure 6.13 The Beggar at the Ball

tionally dressed laborers, suggesting an association between exploitative bureaucracy and European influence. The city's rulings are whimsical for all, but it is the worker who is penalized most by the vagaries of municipal regulation.

There can be little doubt about the precarious economic position of many Ottoman workers. Donald Quataert notes that, in the late nineteenth century, women in Istanbul earned 1.5 *piastres*/day for crocheting lace piecework. At the same time male operators of sewing machines making half shoes earned up to 1.25 *piasters*/day. Quataert estimatês that a family of six, around 1900, would require 35–40 *piasters*/week for minimum bread requirements. This "assumes a per capita consumption of 1.8 lbs./0.83 kg per day at an average price of 1 *kuruş/okka* of bread."[96] By these estimates, in order to survive the family would require other sources of income or the labor of children in addition to the daily wage of husband and wife. In the late nineteenth century, the "Lowest daily wages were paid in the silk and tobacco factories in which mainly women worked."[97] Women dominated the work force of the tobacco processing factories. Still, in early-twentieth-century Salonica for example, the combination of a booming tobacco-processing industry (that competed for relatively scarce labor) and an active worker's movement escalated wages in the cotton mills.[98] Thus, for these workers, the foreign-owned factories were a mixed blessing.

In the Ottoman cartoon space, workers could be represented as merry commentators on the daily scene, critiquing women's hats and the new government with equal aplomb. But most satire of the worker suggested he or she was an exploited citizen/subject. In this regard, the Régie came in for harsh criticism. One particularly effective cartoon shows two emaciated men dressed in ill-fitting and very ragged clothing (Figure 6.14). Both are smoking. One looks sidelong at the other who shrugs his shoulders in a gesture of helplessness. Neither speaks. The frame is entitled, simply, "*Reji grevcileri* (Régie strikers)."[99] The message of this cartoon is a fatalistic one, the workers are exploited and impoverished. They strike; but there is no suggestion that their conditions will improve.

Another cartoon in *Kalem* obliquely brings the United States into the picture of foreign commercial activities in Istanbul. This image shows several workers engaged in producing the "new Tünel adminstration repairs." The Tünel was an innovative underground tramway in Istanbul, constructed and managed by foreign concerns. In the cartoon frame's background are three workers "repairing," a tram car by tacking flattened, empty petrol cans to its sides. A European leans against the car, smoking and watching the work. In the foreground, a supercilious and rather British looking boss, in top hat and spats, speaks to a worker with a saw in one hand and a petrol can in the other (Figure 6.15). The can is labeled "American Refined Petroleum." The foreign "*müdür*" (director) asks, "How's the work going?" The worker tells him, "*Efendim,* to complete the car, four more gas cans are needed." Looking down his very long nose, the boss replies, "Take care of it

Figure 6.14   Régie Strikers

Les grandes répara

Le directeur — Comment vont les travaux
l'ouvrier — Monsieur nous avons besoin encore de quatre caisses à Petrole pour Terminer ce Vagon
Le directeur — Mais ça nous coûtera alors très cher, tachez de vous arranger avec tout ce qu'il ya au dépôt.

Figure 6.15 Tünel Car Construction

with what you've got. Even then, this car will have cost us too much."[100] The boss may not be British, but he is decidedly Western. The worker, for that matter, does not necessarily look Turkish (costume-wise), he might be Armenian or Italian. This could suggest an imported workforce on the Tünel project, but there were plenty of such workers already on site in Pera. This cartoon is both a critique of "modern" and mismanaged transport systems, and of the operations of foreign concerns in Istanbul. The petroleum cans are a symbol of the recent penetration of Standard Oil into the Ottoman market.[101] The patched tram car is a metaphor for the second rate goods and services that, the cartoon suggests, foreign concerns provide. The boss is portrayed as a cheap, cost-cutter, using inferior materials; in this case, he apparently failed to make a quick buck. The worker, here, is not so much oppressed as he is a tool of foreign interests. He has no say in the mode of construction; he merely takes orders. The dandified boss and the imported petrol cans become tropes for foreign investment and intervention. This frame, like that of the Régie strikers, suggests that the Ottoman public was the net loser when it came to foreign capital in Istanbul.

Thus, in the cartoon space, the worker, the Régie, the Public Debt Adminstration, and the capitulatory regime served as symbols, warning the Ottoman reader of the dangers of European imperialism. They were the economic counterparts of the more direct cartoon symbols of Europe, the military personifications of Austria, Russia, Britain, France, Germany, and Italy. For the Ottoman satirist, the revolution meant an enhanced possibility of war; it also meant the European hand could plunge deeper into the Ottoman pocket.

VII

The Comic Culture: The Critique of Society, Culture, and European Influence

There were various types of social satire in the Ottoman revolutionary press: domestic satire, class satire, and lampoons of the timeless failures of men to communicate with one another. In addition, there was a particular focus on the question of change, often couched in terms of a dichotomy between the old (*eski*) and the new (*yeni*).[1] This brand of satire concentrated on the vision of a new, modern, transformed, "progressive" society and on those who attempted, and failed, to make that society a reality. What, the satirists mused, was happening to Ottoman identity in this era of change? They targeted transformations in language, literature, education, entertainment, dress, and lifestyle, examining the ways in which these changes made the Ottomans vulnerable or ridiculous. As in political satire, Europe, to the extent that it served as a model for and instigator of societal change, played a major role in Ottoman social satire.[2] Satirists sketched the Europeanization of Istanbul society and labeled it ludicrous, hilarious, or bewildering. In this regard, the fads of skating and spiritualism were used to show how Western mores had invaded Ottoman society.[3]

Where the evolution of society was concerned, satirists did not necessarily choose between unilaterally supporting the old and unilaterally supporting the new. They both posed and rejected the idea of the "clean slate," the notion that the revolution had cleared the social and political decks, allowing for the development of a new and modern society.[4] There was a clear irony involved in the vision of a new and better society because that vision seemed inevitably tied to subordination to Europe. As they scrutinized the woes of Ottoman society, satirists measured the Ottomans' discontent with both the old system and the new. Ottoman satire grouped the different strands of disaffectedness within society, linking them, for example, to class, exploitative government, unresponsive bureaucracy, and foreign intervention. But disaffection is not the only or even the most prevalent type of social satire; indeed a considerable body of Ottoman social satire might be called a satire of amazement rather than a satire of disaffection.

The satire of amazement was one that marveled at the changes that Ottoman society was undergoing, without evaluating those changes as necessarily or inherently bad or harmful. Thus, cartoon frames could scrutinze the European cultural invasion and celebrate it, laugh at it, scoff at it and, in general, express a certain alternately wry or hilarious bewilderment at its varied ramifications.

The satirists played upon a cartoon terrain that depended upon the typing of European and Ottoman societies, the latter much more elaborately delineated. In particular, Ottoman society was lampooned for its cultural schizophrenia. Its imitations of Europe were neither complete nor successful and, hence, Ottoman society was robbed of its identity. Still, the satirists were intrigued with the new, the modern, and the European. Hence, Ottoman social satire went well beyond a simple critique of European society and its imitators. It expressed, instead, and helped construct, what was, in fact, an evolving Ottoman society, which, by 1908, was already deeply enmeshed in the processes of transformation. At the same time, the satirists did not advocate a return to some idealized Ottoman past; "traditional" Ottoman society was portrayed as alternately backward or at least irretrievable. "Traditional" of course is a highly loaded term; and some elements of the traditional were mythologized. But, in the cartoon space, certain kinds of figure, dress, activity, and point of view were typed as "traditional": the old baba in baggy pants, the frumpy old mother, the sultan and his cadre of syncophants, the peasant, old uniforms, houka smoking, consulting soothsayers, rejecting new forms of entertainment, and so on. These were then made to stand for a highly amorphous "tradition." Thus, the satire of the revolutionary press contained necessarily mixed representations of cultural transformation. Ottoman society was represented, in the cartoon space, as either wedded to old habits and outmoded traditions or deluded by new trends and commodities.

Tradition itself was constructed and manipulated to deliver a complex web of messages. Tradition was the sultans and pashas of an Ottoman golden age, prosperous and leading victorious armies into battle against clearly evil foes. But tradition was also drawn in the form of immobile men, lying about coffee houses and smoking parlors, who could only talk of past martial glories. Meanwhile, the Europeans in their cafe-music halls were gaily celebrating their success. According to the satirists, the Ottomans, in their European-style cafes were, often enough, cheap imitators with nothing to celebrate, morally bankrupt, and squandering the meager resources of the empire. How the social and cultural spaces of a new Ottoman empire would be filled up was a loaded question.

Those in the press who favored the wholesale adaptation of European culture often portrayed it as a type of alliance in progress, suggesting that European political ideology, technology, and fashion would bring with it a share in Europe's dominance. Technological developments were promoted as a means of closing the gap, which had been opened by military and economic disparities, between Ottoman and European societies. So too, in the cultural sphere, enthusiasm for European political theory was coupled with an appetite for European, particularly French, language, arts, and literature—all as vehicles for making the empire competitive in a "modern," European-dominated world. Western-style poetry and short stories, often love stories or patriotic pieces, featured prominently in the revolutionary press. So did reviews of French stage productions.[5] Even historiography was a European art form subject to scrutiny and imitation.[6] The objective of Europeanization was not merely to become "modern," as defined in European terms, but to *appear* modern, and hence competitive, in the eyes of foreign observers.[7]

It was this endeavor to appear modern, in particular, which delighted or disgusted Ottoman satirists, who portrayed the European imitators as hypocritical, pompous, and self deluded. In the satirical press the critique of this enthusiasm for all things European took a range of tones from gentle humor to vitriolic condemnation. It targeted especially Western-style dress, entertainment, language, literature, and the fads of skating and spiritualism. This satire of skepticism was an aggressive way to challenge European cultural hegemony and an alternative to waving the patriotic flag of Turkism, which was to become, somewhat later, the emphasis of choice for segments of the Ottoman press (and for latter-day historical analysts).

In order to understand Ottoman satire's vision of its own Europeanizing society, it is important to take note of the satire of Europe itself. It was against European cultures, in part, that the Ottoman satirists measured the evolution of their own culture. Of course this "European culture" was an imagined culture, distorted, exaggerated, typecast, and molded to identify it as desirable or undesirable. European culture, in the Ottoman cartoon space, was a fashionable, reading, socializing, selling culture. The Europeans were, above all, well dressed, and stylish, their clothes exaggerated. They were accessorized; they had watches, gloves, parasols, and pet dogs. The wealth and prosperity of Europeans was signified by the luxury and variation of their clothing, a readily identifiable marker of success (see chapter 8).

LANGUAGE, LITERATURE, AND CULTURAL DOMINION

If fashion was the outward manifestation of European cultural dominion, language was its implement. Signs and advertisements signaled European intrusions into the Ottoman economic space, while foreign words, slogans, captions, texts, and literature invaded the Ottoman public and private space from the meclis (assembly), to the newspapers, to the harems. French was the primary vehicle for Ottoman intercourse with the Western world. By the late nineteenth century, numerous French–Ottoman dictionaries and conversation guides had been published in Istanbul and abroad; and French novels were an integral part of the educated Ottoman's literary canon.[8] As Demetra Vaka wrote of her upper-class Istanbul harem friends, around 1901, "They read a lot of French novels, without pretending that they did it for the sake of 'culture.' "[9] By the turn of the century, such literary consumption had become a commonplace for elite Ottoman women as well as men. Nor was religious orthodoxy a necessary impediment to the use of French, as illustrated by another of Vaka's friends, Cemileh, (fourth wife of Selim Pasha, a member of Abd ül-Hamid's entourage) who, although married into a pious and conservative household, was fluent in both French and English.[10]

The consumption of foreign literature produced a certain tension between the administration and the consuming public. Under Abd ül-Hamid, there were varied attempts to restrict the consumption of foreign language works by Ottoman readers. Foreign books were indiscriminately seized at the customs stations and, after examinination, might or might not be returned to their owners. Of course innovative publishers, readers, and booksellers conspired to circumvent the censors even before the revolution:

> The list of prohibited books includes also all guide-books and encyclopedias in which mention is made of the sultan, Tasso's *Jerusalem Delivered,* Chateubriand's *Martyrs,* Victor Hugo's *Les Orientales,* la Fontaine's *Fables,* and the works of Shakespeare, Dante, Voltaire, Rabelais, Zola, and several modern French authors. Modern French works are, however, in greater demand by the Turks than any other branch of literature; the booksellers of Pera are sufficiently enterprising; and their initiated customers express no surprise at finding that the contents of the volumes on their shelves do not always correspond with the titles on their covers, Zola's *La Terre* being happily labelled *la Culture Maraichière,* and his *Paris, Traité de la Langue Française!* For the Turkish official considers that he has done his duty in examining the titles of the books which pass through his hands.[11]

This testimony, by a foreign observer, indicates not only the failed attempts of the Ottoman censor but also the familiarity that parts of the Ottoman reading public had with European literatures by the turn of the century. It was a familiarity that then expressed itself in the use of French terms, allusions, and references in Ottoman texts.[12]

The Ottoman revolutionary press embodied the prevalence of the French language in various forms, especially bilingual gazettes, or gazettes with French sections and bilingual captions.[13] In the 1886 edition of İbrahim Şinasi's work on Ottoman proverbs, there were line glosses in French; by the time of the revolution, many Ottoman books and gazettes had such French inserts in one form or another.[14] Şinasi (1824–1871) was a literary pioneer, journalist, social critic, and language innovator who, among many other accomplishments, helped to popularize French poetry.[15] Translations of French-language novels, stories, and plays, not to speak of nonfiction works and essays, were part of the standard repertoire of Ottoman literary gazettes.[16] *Resimli kitab* ran a story, translated from the French by the editor Faik Sabri, complete with illustrations of a fashionable young lady out strolling with her parasol and (the final vignette) in a final embrace with her lover.[17] There were travel accounts, translations of literature like *The Three Musketeers*, reviews of ideas, music, art, plays, manners, and even a picture of the guillotine.[18] Istanbul editors were not content simply to represent Europe to the Ottoman reader, they were also concerned to examine the ways in which European authors represented the empire. Shortly after the revolution, *Aşiyan* published an essay on the nineteenth-century French philosopher and orientalist, Ernest Renan's, life and works.[19] And the August 1909 issue of the gazette, *Resimli kitab*, carried an article on "Eighteenth Century Paintings of the Turks," illustrated almost entirely with Orientalist harem scenes.[20] Gazettes included advertisements for French-Ottoman literary society meetings, French-language instructors, and French-language publications.[21] Thus the revolutionary gazettes at once met and enhanced the demand of an elite, French-literate audience for a French-language voice in Ottoman cultural affairs. Nor was it only French literature that captivated Ottoman audiences; English and American literatures also had their share of space. *Dalkavuk*, for example, beginning in December of 1908, serialized a Twain piece under the title "*Şikago Çiftcisi*" (Chicago Farmer).[22] Cartoons were also reprinted from the foreign language presses of France, England, Italy and Germany.

Educational articles including lists of French words (feminism, communism, constitution) with Ottoman equivalents were very common. Treatments of European politics and economy included Ottoman transliterations of French terms and discussions of the concepts they represented, for example the French notion of sovereignty.[23] In an article by Baha Tevfik, on the language of philosophy, equivalents for Ottoman words were given in French and Greek.[24] In *Tasvir-i efkâr*, the presentation of the French and English languages was coupled with an understanding that Ottoman culture and its milieu had been so altered that an appreciation of French and English was almost a necessity.[25] Other articles discussed the changes the Ottoman language had undergone since the nineteenth century during the process of transformation to a constitutional regime. They had titles like "old language and new."[26]

Indeed, the question of language was crucial to the articulation of what a new Ottoman society might be.[27] A quick look at Celal Nuri's work, *The Turkish Revolution*, indicates the linguistic and comparative prisms through which many of the Young Turks viewed their revolution. Nuri's book included sections on Ottomanness between East and West, The New and the Old, Ottoman and Turkish Language, The Alphabet and Romanization, A Comparison of Ottoman and European Literature, Language, and The Literary Revolution.[28] Nuri (1877–1939) was an Ottoman "modernist," writer, and journalist.

Such treatments bore a mixed message. The knowledge of English and French was associated with progress, but also with a sense of being left behind, with a sense of urgency. This latter sense provoked, on the one hand, a sadness and a chagrin that the old language with its own imperialist connotations now might be unable to compete, or, on the other hand, a "patriotic" emphasis on the validity and glory of the Turkish language.[29] An alternative response viewed the freedom associated with a constitutional regime as bringing with it a freedom of linguistic expression, a freedom that manifested itself in the press, in the development of a national theater, and in a great outburst of literature of all kinds.

The production of Ottoman Turkish literature, based in part on the forms of the Western novel, continued and flourished in this period.[30] This literary production could be serious or satirical; often it was associated with the idea that the Ottoman state and society were embarking upon a new form of nationhood. *Cingöz*, for example, presented its own version of the "national" novel (*milli roman*), *Şadiye*, by Mehmed Âsıf, in the fall of 1908.[31] Other gazettes might designate a piece of serialized fiction as a "national" story (*milli hikâye*), and many other gazettes serialized Ottoman fiction.[32]

Meanwhile, the satirical press responded vigorously to the invasion of European language and French culture. *Züğürt* ran a humorous "Language Comparison," contrasting the way things were said in the former era to the speech of the present era. Where one used to say "in the shadow of the sovereign" (*saye-i şahanede*), one now says "in the shadow of freedom" (*saye-i hürriyet*); one says "homeland and nation (*vatan ve millet*), instead of "king and state (*melik ve devlet*);" and where one once said "send to the censor," one now says "look at the press law."[33] The press found the Frenchification of Ottoman Turkish fertile ground for lampoons. *Boşboğaz* ran a humorous dialogue, with French inserts, on a banquet supposedly given by the foreign ministry; it included humorous glosses in Ottoman of French foods.[34]

As with past revolutionary counterparts, the Ottoman revolution's literati were preoccupied with the evolution of a new and transformed language to reflect their transformed situation. David Nokes, in his study of English satire, argues that a significant characteristic of revolutionary prose is "its preoccupation with forging a new purified vocabulary and grammar, purged of the accumulated assumptions inherent in the language of a corrupt society." He contrasts this with the task of the satirist who "trades and revels in the rich accumulations of imaginative resources stored in the language of the past to confront the utopian schemes of the Aeolists, or the Newspeak of Oceania."[35] In the Ottoman case, I would argue that the satirists made apt use of both the linguistic accumulations of the past and the "new" languages and their associations that were transforming Ottoman culture.

One cartoon, which embodies the distinction between the old and new eras as well as that between the old and new languages, is framed on the steps of the museum, a perfect symbol for the symbiotic relationship between past, present, and future. The cartoon shows a group of *hamals* (porters), themselves a symbol of traditional forms of dress, ideology, and transport. They are bearing loads of books up the steps of the museum (Figure 7.1). At the top of the steps, a museum official (*müze memuru*), intercepts one of the hamals, demanding, "What's all this?" The *hamal* replies, "The old *nişan* registers."[36] The word *nişan,* here, functions on a series of levels. On the surface, the *nişan* registers were the records of the decorations that Abd ül-Hamid passed out wholesale to all and sundry, deserving or not.[37] They were a symbol of the corruption of the old regime. *Nişan,* however, also means sign, seal, mark, writing, so that this illustration of the consignment of the old era to the museum can also stand for the setting aside of the writing, language, ceremonies, and ideas of the past. Of course, these signs of the old era are not discarded as such, when they are put in the museum. Rather they are memorialized as part of the empire's history (for better or for worse). In addition to pointing out their class distinction, the dress of the two main characters highlights the image of the transfer from the old to the new eras, because the museum official (the keeper of the past) is dressed in European-style frock coat and trousers, while the *hamal* wears the characteristic and traditional baggy pants, sandals, vest, and wrapped-cap of his profession.

The struggle between "old" and "new" language, in cartoons, could take different forms; it could, for example, manifest itself in the more direct and dramatic struggle for territory based on violence and military might. This relationship was neatly illustrated in a cartoon by Sedad Nuri focusing on Balkan separatism. The cartoon, supposedly set in Albania, showed two men dressed in pseudo-ethnic garb, one with fez, rifle, and boots, the other in cap, cumberbund, and pointed tassled slippers. The first is a caricature of the Ottoman soldier, the second a caricature of the Albanian "mountaineer" (Figure 7.2). Their dress is an example of typical cartoon usage in which "ethno-national" dress was used to type figures. Each stands as symbol of his respective "nation." One asks the other: "Which alphabet do you prefer, the Latin or the Arabic?" The other replies, "Neither one, I prefer my weapon."[38]

The context for this cartoon is the Albanian struggle for autonomy, which had been brewing since the later nineteenth century and which was encouraged by the constitutional revolution and subsequent reorganization of the government. Albanians rose in open revolt in 1910 and the uprising was harshly suppressed by the Ottoman government. As with other "nationalist" movements, the Albanian struggle for political autonomy was accompanied by demands for recognition and development of the Albanian language, including the proposed adoption of the Latin script.[39] Such a change signified a rejection of the empire and an alignment with Europe (just as it did years later when Atatürk forced the Latin script upon the remnant of the empire that remained after World War I). Thus, this cartoon is not merely a simple commentary on the political events in Albania, it is a

Figure 7.1 Consigning the Nişan Defters to the Museum

Voudrais-tu les caractères latin ou Arabes.
Ni l'un ni l'autre... mais mon fusil...

— سن هانکی حروفاتی ایسترسك ؟ لاتین ویاخود عرب ؟
— موری بن برشی ایستەمم .. سلاحمی ایستەرم ..

Figure 7.2   "Which Alphabet Do You Prefer?"

representation of the broad contest for hegemony that played itself out politically, culturally, and militarily. The whole issue of Albanian nationalism and other nationalisms was contested with great passion on the field of language, a field intimately associated with the forging of "national" identities. The Latin vs. Arabic script was an issue that, in part, attempted to draw the boundaries between European dominance and Ottoman dominance, between the supposedly obsolete and the supposedly modern, between new configurations of "us" and "them." In that sense it was an issue that linked the struggle in Albania to that over whether there should be Francophone education in the Ottoman schools. The Ottoman elites were already Francophone and well conversant with the Latin script; but the bulk of the Ottoman masses were light years away from internalizing French language and literature. It was not the illiterate Albanian mountaineers who attended language congresses or conceived the visions of nation published in Albanian separatist gazettes. Yet, the Ottoman cartoonists knew that the battle over script presumed a larger struggle that would affect all the citizens of the empire; they could not help but imagine that the resolution to the language problem might come at the point of a gun.

EDUCATION

Education was another area in which the debate over language and hegemony found expression. The cultural schizopherenia of the revolutionary press was mirrored in its treatment of traditional Ottoman vs. European forms of education. In satire, old style education came to be associated with backwardness, and the oppression of the old education system was associated with the despotism of the sultanic regime. This is illustrated, for example, by a cartoon entitled "Old teacher and students" showing the schoolmaster raging at a dropped ink pot and demanding to know: "Which beast, son of a beast, did this?" A crestfallen and cowed student responds: "Your son, İsmail, Sir."[40] This frame suggests a blind authoritarianism that reproduced itself without being aware of the consequences. Another cartoon, in *Lâklâk*, purports to show "Progress (*terakki*)" in a primary school in Anatolia.[41] In the frame is the turbanned old schoolmaster, and boys sitting on the floor in a circle, reciting. The "progress" seems to be an extra long stick with which the schoolmaster can beat the pupils. This cartoon suggests that progress can be a mixed blessing. The progress associated with education reforms in Istanbul, at least in this frame, appears not to have reached the provinces.

This type of cartoon, satirizing the rigors or inequities of traditional education, was a standard type in Ottoman satire. But there was also a more transitional type, one that directed itself at the ways in which the social transformation of the empire was affecting the idea, very broadly construed, of education.[42] Thus, Ottoman cartoons played upon certain themes that were prevalent in the Ottoman literature of the day: (1) the adoption of European styles of education; (2) new education as a means of producing strong, capable citizens, and (3) women's education (which in turn would contribute to the raising of educated citizens). If there was to be a new woman, a new man, a new child, and a new social order, clearly there would have to be "new" forms of education. And if the cultures of Europe were coming to dominate many areas of elite Ottoman society, then European-style education would be an important part of the empire's metamorphosis, as it had been for at least a century prior to the Young Turk revolution. Ottoman satirists did not necessarily direct their lampoons of these themes at the classroom itself, instead they directed their barbs at the "Westernized" citizens who had been produced by the new-style ideas of education. These citizens took their ideas from the classroom and translated them into social behavior at which the satirists looked askance.

One aspect of European theories of education that struck a sympathetic chord in the Ottoman press was the idea that education should produce strong, healthy, modern citizens. The healthy citizen had to be literate and educated, but he also had to be vigorous. Thus, Ottoman gazettes looked to the examples of physical culture that, along with ideas about nationalism and constitutionalism, were coming out of Europe.[43] These ideas were embodied in the photographs, such as those found in *Resimli kitab*, of boys' school fencing and gymnastics groups.[44] Physical education for girls too had already found its advocates in the empire. *Resimli İstanbul*, for example, which boasted a substantial women's section in each issue, reflected the interest in physical activity for women in its extensive coverage of women's swimming.[45] Also met with enthusiasm in the period after the revolution was the combination of patriotism, athleticism, and skill building symbolized by Baden-Powell's new phenomenon, the Boy Scouts. The first edition of Baden-Powell's, *Scouting for Boys*, coincidentally, appeared in 1908.[46]

European-style education also meant educating women.[47] Women, if nothing else, were the educators of the citizens of tomorrow.[48] As such, they had to be knowledgeable about world affairs; they had to learn the lessons of progress. According to the famous literary figure and Ottoman nationalist, Halide Edib: "Foreign schools also multiplied [in the empire] and in the later part of the nineteenth century the foreign governess; especially the English governess, became an institution. There was a deeply rooted idea in Turkey that the Englishwoman was serious and manly and must therefore be the model for the modern Turkish woman."[49] Edib's image of the English governess as Boy Scout may not be a very apt or comprehensive characterization of Ottoman ideals of education.[50] But it does reflect the growing demand for European-style education in the empire and the associations (among the Ottoman elite classes) which that style of education had with vigor, progress, and the educated mother.

The idea of the educated citizen-mother had been spreading throughout the Middle East. As the Khedive Ismail of Egypt is supposed to have said, "Our nation will never be civilized until we can educate our women; for when the children hear their mothers talk of *afreets* and *ginns* [evil spirits], and such nonsense, so from the earliest age they are imbued with all sorts of foolish superstitions."[51] In Iran too, after the constitutional revolution, a poem celebrating the ultimate triumph of the revolutionaries included the following stanza:

> Henceforth all the girls shall be educated;
> All shall have their share in the Colleges of Science;
> They shall be equal with the boys in their rights of learning.
> Blessed is this participation of the World of Women.[52]

This stanza is interesting both for its association of women's education with the fruits of constitutionalism but also for its designation of education as a right. The same sentiment was echoed, again by Halide Edib, in a statement on Ottoman education after the revolution and especially after the Balkan Wars: "[The state] modernised the entire educational system of Turkey and equalised educational rights. The normal schools were multiplied and conducted on better and modern lines; the Young Tukish regime began to send women students to European universities and colleges; in 1916 the Istamboul University opened its doors to women."[53]

Other observers made the connection between the educated woman and political action. The American, Mary Mills Patrick, President of the Constantinople Woman's College, in a rather idealized account, noted the role of educated women in the constitutional revolution: "Gülistan İsmet, our first Turkish graduate, was then [1908] in Saloniki. She had married one of the young men working for the new Turkey and she herself took part nobly, writing articles for the papers and helping in other ways."[54] For Mills Patrick, women's "helper" role was significant in the revolution; it would be educated women who could face the challenges of a new constitutional era. Halide Edib, a graduate of the Constantinople Women's College, serves as a significant model in Mills Patrick's memoir.

The "modern" Ottoman thus would be an educated Ottoman.[55] And the mothers of the nation must be educated too, although not in the same ways as the men, in order that they be good companions and fit nurturers for their children's minds and bodies.[56]

But "modern" woman, dressed in European style, educated, politically participant, outspoken, and moving freely about in public was not an idea easily integrated into Ottoman or, for that matter, other societal norms. Thus, the satirists seized on this aspect of modernization, suggesting that the newly educated Ottoman men might be getting more than they bargained for and revealing the joys, miseries, and mayhem that might derive from introducing a "new" woman into Ottoman society. The satire of these "new" or "*alafranga*" citizens will be treated in the following section and in chapters 8 and 9.

CONSUMPTION AND THE "MODERN" OTTOMAN

The "modern" Ottoman, in the cartoon space, was a European-style consumer; the consumption of European goods and European-style entertainment were inextricably linked in Ottoman cartoons. Satirists targeted the ways Europeanized Ottomans spoke, dressed, and behaved; they were identified by their attitudes and by their goods. The modern Ottoman was to be well dressed and well entertained. An elegant little vignette, drawn to look like a framed picture, that appeared in *Kalem,* neatly combines the themes of class distinction, entertainment, European fashion, and extravagance that were so often the focus of Ottoman social satire. It shows the fashionable couple, the epitome of European style: he with cane, monocle, tie, cigarette holder, and top coat; she with tailored tight skirt and coat, bag, ruffled front, and huge flowered hat.[57] He warns her that he will not go to the theater again unless she is willing to get rid of the hat. This cartoon is not simply a tongue-in-cheek poke at the affluent. It plays on a series of themes found in different variants in many cartoons. The hat suggests both the silliness and extravagance of women consuming European fashion. The man, however, is the woman's partner in consumption. He takes a wry view of her hat, but he too is dressed to the nines. Together, they are frequenters of the theater; their consumption of European-style entertainment is drawn as a natural complement to their consumption of European fashion.

The Ottoman cartoon consumers were based on real models, taken from the middle and upper classes of Istanbul society. A good example of the mixed culture and the consumption of European goods that characterized elite Istanbul households of the time is found in the journal of Said Bey, an Ottoman official who also taught at Galatasaray College and the School of Commerce. Said Bey, who was fluent in French, kept a meticulous journal, which described his day-to-day activities and illustrated the rather idle and leisured lifestyles of the upper-middle class.[58] His entertainments, his purchases, and even the arrangement of his house indicate the penetration of European culture into Istanbul society. Although Said Bey's house was divided along traditional lines between men's and women's sections, his furnishings reflected a Europeanization of the Ottoman household. They included a piano, purchased in 1902, "*canapés,* armchairs, a pier-table, a European bed (*karyola*), and also a sewing machine, a phonograph, a telescope, and many other objects."[59] Said Bey's was not the only household with a sewing machine in 1908. Singer sewing machine dealerships were spreading throughout the empire in the earlier twentieth century, a forerunner for latter-day American business interests. That machine invasion was in turn reflected in ads and even in cartoons. In 1913, the satirical *Karagöz* depicted a woman (and Karagöz) hard at work with a Singer sewing machine, making "minaret covers."[60]

Said Bey's family consumed large quantities of fashionable clothing and shopped together at the Bon Marché store in Beyoğlu (a fashionable European district of Istanbul).[61] For entertainment, along with the more traditional visits, weddings, and gender-segregated activities, the couple took carriage rides and attended balls together. Their theater tastes suggest the evolving nature of Ottoman leisure activities. Both attended Karagöz plays (although not necessarily together) and Said Bey frequented cafe-concerts, and the *orta oyunu* (a traditional Ottoman comic theater form); they also attended European-type theater performances.[62]

Ottoman men and women shopping together at a department store modeled on the French original (which revolutionized commercial space and the concept of marketing) symbolized a radical (if gradual) transformation in concepts of Ottoman society and Ottoman family, a transformation that has yet adequately to be explored. In Paris, the Bon Marché, its merchandise, its displays, and its catalogs, both reflected and helped to craft bourgeois society, which in turn influenced the culture and consumption of the lower classes.[63] The Bon Marché, like the Ottoman press, made extensive use of images to propose what a society should be. This commercial and cultural institution was then transplanted into the Ottoman social space, to attract and refashion men and women like Said Bey and his wife. In both instances, fashion was a particular marker of changing ideals and changing lifestyles.[64] The difference was that for the French, the Bon Marché was an innovation of their own making; for the Ottomans it was an import. Once imported, the Bon Marché in Istanbul contributed to what might be considered both an Orientalizing and an Occidentalizing project; it produced a vision of European-style society for Ottoman consumption and, by marketing illustrated postcards of the empire, it produced a vision of Ottoman society for Western consumption.[65]

The lifestyle depicted in Said Bey's journals, and its French antecedents, was given literary form in the Ottoman press, for example in a drawing room scene in the satiric gazette *Dalkavuk*. The scene opens in a "salon," complete with chiming clock, gilded mirror, and stuffed armchairs. The male figure pacing the salon has whiskers cut "a little long, according to the Paris fashion."[66] Other examples are found in Ottoman advertising that presented a vision of woman's role as consumer, not only of fashion but of household goods. One such ad, for a fancy stove, dubbed "The Salamander," and invented by "E. Chaboche, *ingénieur à Paris*," shows a two-frame, before-and-after cartoon. In frame one, the frustrated housewife is struggling over an "ordinary" wood stove. In frame two, the same woman relaxes in her chair in front of "The Salamander," warm, happy, and at ease. The stove was marketed in Galata. France, in this ad, stood for the production of superior consumer goods and for the production of female leisure.[67]

In fact, advertising itself was in some ways associated with European culture, as is illustrated by the announcement (in French) in the satirical *Hokkabaz*, that it would begin to publish "artistic advertisements like the European gazettes."[68] Of course, not all observers were enthralled with the advent of the "modern" stove. Lucy Garnett, writing at the turn of the century, had a somewhat different view of imported stoves. After discussing the traditional Ottoman stoves as "an eminently feminine luxury," she wrote that, "The use of American stoves is, however, increasing every year, and the picturesqueness of many of the old *konaks* [traditional wooden houses or mansions] is destroyed by the hideous black stove-pipes which emerge from the windows or walls and climb up to the roofs."[69] Clearly, the Salamander ad would not have persuaded Garnett.

It was to households like Said Bey's that advertisements in gazettes like *Kalem* were directed, advertisements for things like modern stoves, French lessons, German governesses, and ladies' bicycles.[70] Such households, and their consumption, became, in turn, favored targets of Ottoman satirists. The gazette *Alafranga* (its name itself a satire on the consumption of European styles) used as its mascots, in the first page masthead, the figures of a donkey couple (Figure 7.3).[71] Fashionably dressed, they sit opposite each other at a cafe table, wineglasses before them. Here again, the image is one of European-style entertainment, the consumption of which has, perhaps, here turned the Ottomans into asses. This theme of satirizing the *alafranga* Ottoman dated to the nineteenth century and was, in fact, a popular topic in late-nineteenth-century Ottoman theater productions.[72]

Alafranga was often coterminous with modern in the Ottoman satirical press. The "modern" young man and, to a lesser extent, the modern young woman, modern socializing, modern marriage, and modern ideas in general were all fair game for the satirist's pen. They all symbolized European-style consumption, the subordination of the Ottomans to European ways, and the sometimes dizzying effects of the socio-cultural transformation that Istanbul was experiencing.[73]

Alem ran a poem (in French) that satirized the modern young Ottoman. He was, according to the poem, an insouciant and self-satisfied fop, who fancied himself a theater critic, responded with indifference to the war in Bulgaria, and found it inconvenient to support the boycott of Austrian goods.[74] *Kalem* ran another poem, entitled "*Décadent*," in French, which satirized the paradox of the Occidentalized Ottoman who loved European theatre, styles, and food, yet still refused to budge on certain cultural bottom lines.[75]

Still, it was not only the European imitators that the Ottoman satirists took on. They satirized the idea that the revolution and the adaptation of European culture would somehow make the empire better. They caricatured the civilizational contest between the Orient and the Occident. A fake advertisement (in French) in *Kalem*, noted that a huge order for "material for the production of progress," had been sent out to Europe; among the

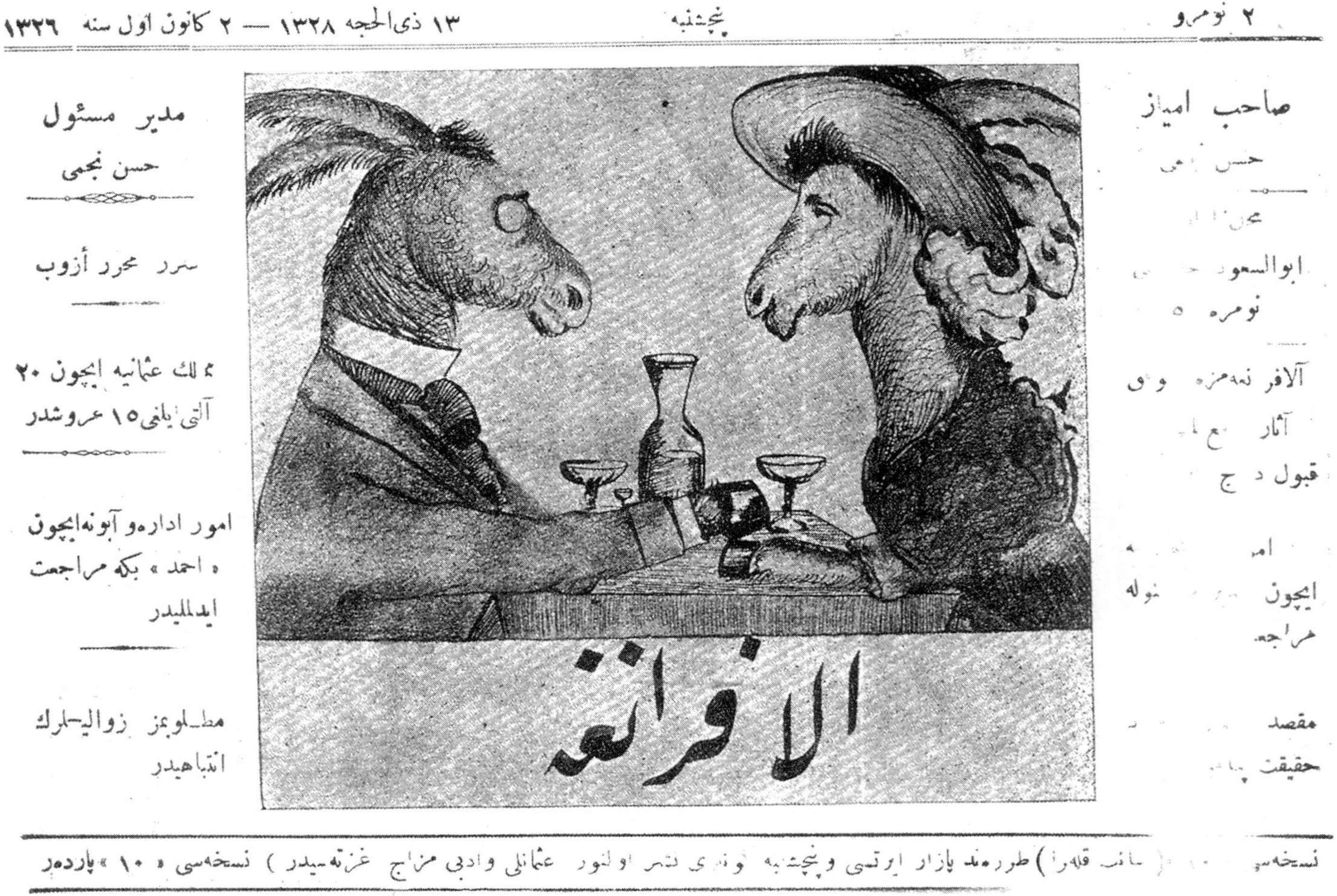

Figure 7.3 Alafranga Couple

materials required were a top quality prime minister and one hundred million pounds sterling.[76] Another humorous piece was attributed to the famous author and Turcophile, Pierre Loti, supposedly a letter to a friend in Istanbul. The letter congratulated the friend on the fact that the empire would no longer be "a stranger to the ideas of progress, the movement of civilization." But, "Loti" reminded his friend that the empire would then lose all its charm, its picturesque character, and its wonderful insouciant lifestyle: "to live without ambition and without ideal, to partake of great cups of coffee, to smoke the narguile, to dream at length, to dream all day and to die, in the end, without regret and without complaint."[77] "Loti" then complained that his dream of the Orient was being slaughtered, that the "Turks" would be subjected to the undignified banality of listening to parliamentary senators and deputies, and that Istanbul would be lost to "the comfort of civilization: large and well paved streets, electric trams, automobiles and a heap of other stupidities."[78] Thus, consuming the "modern," defined as the accoutrements of European culture, was revealed to be a double-edged sword. This passage imagines Ottoman society as a society beleaguered, and reflects the sophistication of the satirists, who mocked the Orientalist's romanticized vision of the empire at the same time as they mocked their own willingness to buy into that vision.

THEATER AND THE ARTS

Perhaps more than any other art form, the theater was a symbol of social change for Ottoman satirists. In the Ottoman cartoon space, the image of the theater, along with that of the cafe, was used to embody the apparent sophistication of culture and entertainment that modern European societies enjoyed. These were the sites where the elites were enlightened, the sexes mixed, and where, in general, the French and their imitators apparently declared their modernity and worldliness. For the Ottomans, who had a long history of consuming plays in traditional forms, the theater seemed to bear a special fascination.[79] Western theater was one of the art forms most readily and vigorously consumed by the Westernizing elites of Istanbul. And, in the satirical gazettes, the stage was a natural metaphor for the empire in this period of transition, caught between what was real and unreal and between its past and present identities so that it barely knew itself. It is no wonder, then, that the Ottoman cartoon space utilized the metaphors of the theater, the actor, and the curtained stage to good effect in its representations of the revolutionary experience.

Cartoon imagery of the theater was a natural offshoot of Ottoman society's interest in theater arts. This interest was, in turn, reflected in and stimulated by the periodical press.[80] By the time of the revolution, elite Ottoman society was already well exposed to European-style entertainment and theater. The nineteenth century had witnessed a burgeoning interest in productions of works by European and Ottoman authors. Talat Halman attributes the first theater construction in Istanbul to Selim III around the turn of the nineteenth century: "The Sultan's active interest encouraged European troupes to perform frequently in the imperial capital."[81] Halman notes that two more theaters were constructed during the reign of Mahmud II (1808–1839), that European troupes performed there regularly, and that "the first Turkish play" (*Şair Evlenmesi* / The Poet's Marriage) was published by İbrahim Şinasi, the famous Young Ottoman writer and publisher, in 1860. In that same year, what was to become "The Ottoman Theater" (*Tiyatro-yu Osmani*) was built; it was reconstructed in 1867 and commonly referred to as the Gedik Pasha Theater. There, a box was set aside for the sultan and there the first Turkish plays were performed under the company direction of an Armenian called Güllü Agop (1840–1902).[82] "The theater advertised in the newspapers for actors who spoke good Turkish and also for anyone who could write, adapt, or translate plays."[83] Once the Taksim Garden in Pera was completed in 1869, it had become a center for promenading and for enjoying beer gardens and cafes, a place where French and Italian companies performed plays and operettas.[84] During the revolutionary era, the theater of Mardiros Mınakyan (d. 1920), known as the Ottoman Theater (*Osmanlı Tiyatrosu*), seems to have served as a national theater of sorts, performing numerous melodramas by foreign and Ottoman playwrights alike.[85]

Istanbul became an important center for the production of adaptations of European works, and its theatrical inclinations seem to have had some influence on the consumption of plays in Iran as well. Western plays, mostly by Molière, were first translated into Persian and performed in Iran in the mid-nineteenth century, and the first play staged at Nasir al-Din Shah's theater was a verse translation of "*Le Misanthrope*," which had been published in Istanbul in 1870.[86] Later, the 1905–1906 Iranian constitutional revolution paved the way for Iranian theater troupes and Tehran public playhouses.

Already in the prerevolutionary era, the Ottoman press had a history of reporting on the theater. *Çıngıraklı Tatar*, published in 1874, ran something in almost every issue on the Gedik Pasha Theater or on other performances. According to Metin And, nineteenth-century gazettes criticized the Ottoman theater for bad acting, the use of artificial language, the failure to adapt plays to Turkish society and cultural themes and, most particularly, for the actors laughing "at their own jokes before the audience did."[87] By 1908, the press had already developed a talent for scathing criticism.

Revolutionary gazettes, in their turn, treated the theater in a variety of ways: they advertised plays, reported on performances at home and abroad, and reproduced scripts, often in serial form. The journal *Aşiyan* serialized a "national play (*milli oyunu*) in four acts," by the well-known playwright Said Hikmet, which took up one of the prevalent themes of the revolutionary era; it was called, "*Mazi ve Âti*" (Past and Future).[88] The same journal carried a piece by Hikmet called, "A Laugh, On Going to the Theater."[89] In other gazettes, there were pictures of famous actors and actresses (like Sarah Bernhardt), reviews, social news, and informational pieces on the thespian arts.[90] The objectives of the revolution were dramatically celebrated with the resurrection of Namık Kemal's (1840–1888) patriotic drama, *"Vatan"* (Homeland), which re-opened to packed and euphoric Istanbul audiences.[91] Kemal (a famous Young Ottoman thinker and writer) first produced *"Vatan"* in 1873, and the response to the play resulted in his imprisonment in Cyprus for three years. And *Kalem,* in a theater piece written shortly after the revolution, applauded the absence of "Madame la Censure," noting that one could at last call "a prince a prince."[92] Meanwhile, satiric gazettes had their own brand of criticism. *Hokkabaz* compared the entertainment of the past (like Karagöz performances under the old sultans) to the French comedies of the present, and the informality of the past to the institutionalization of the theater in the present: "Now, no less than 20,000 lira is required for a theater building."[93] *Züğürt,* also complained of the costs of the "New Theater" in satiric narrative.[94]

Theater coverage in the gazette *Resimli kitab* illustrates how the motifs of European and Ottoman theater were combined in the Ottoman press. Its March 1909 issue carried a photo of the *Üsküb Belediye Tityatrosu* (Üsküb/Skoplje City Theater), testimony to that city's modernity and culture.[95] The same issue contained a long article, "The Artists' Life," on the two French thespians, the Coquelins, complete with photos.[96] The following issue contained an article, by Halide Salih, entitled *Tiyatro Edebiyatı* (Theater Literature), which included a discussion of the influence of foreign, especially French, theater.[97]

These theater pieces were a continuing theme in *Resmli kitab*, which, in its January issue of that year, displayed a photo (by Apollon) of "The celebrated artist, Burhan üd-Din Bey, in the role of Eşber," main character in a tragedy by Hamid Bey (Figure 7.4).[98] This photo of the noble looking Burhan üd-Din as Eşber, an "oriental" lord in a tragedy composed by an Ottoman, illustrates the state of Ottoman theater at the time of the revolution. The photo suggests the evolution of a theater that was uniquely Ottoman, even though some of the framing of that theater was decidely European. Burhan üd-Din symbolizes the continuity of "Turkish" theater, and the synthesis of Ottoman and European forms. Of course the photo (an actor wearing the imagined costume of an imagined king) and the play both suggest the constructed nature of "national" symbols. Nonetheless, the theater critic, İzzet Melih, in an October 1908 issue of *Kalem,* used another performance by Burhan üd-Din to suggest that a glorious future lay in store for the National Ottoman Theater: "The most skeptical could not help but say: 'Now we have the right to hope that our country will one day have great artists and a good Theater'."[99] Burhan üd-Din, on this particular occasion, played the roles of Tarik and of the Marquis de Priola. The critic did note that the actor's diction, in this debut, left something to be desired and that

Photo : Apollon

فوطو : آپولون

صنعتكار شهير برهان الدين بك اشبر رولنده

Le célèbre artiste Burhaneddin Bey, dans le rôle d'Esper, tragédie de Hamid Bey

Figure 7.4　Burhan üd-Din the Actor

his gestures were occasionally excessive. But Melih thought Burhan üd-Din would prove a source of pride for his nation. The satiric gazette *Alem* would seem to have agreed with the critic, judging by its flattering caricature (by Sedad Nuri) of Burhan üd-Din, run with a caption associating him with the advancement of "our" theater.[100] (Even the satiric *Züğürt* illustrated Burhan üd-Din's fame by alluding to him in its humorous announcement to readers on prices.)[101] Both critic and cartoonist, in these evaluations of Ottoman theater, played an active role in constructing notions of what was acceptable and unacceptable or admired and scorned in the new Ottoman order of things.

The revolutionary press also reveals the world of Ottoman theater beyond the ranks of the actors and critics. *Resimli kitab,* in June 1909, ran a photo of sixteen men and two women joined to form what the French caption called "*Troupe Nationale Ottomane Societé d'amateurs;*" but the Ottoman caption, "*milli Osmanlı tiyatrosu heveskâran cemiyeti,*" suggests, rather, The National Ottoman Theater Devotee Society.[102] Ottoman theater did not evolve in a vacuum. Such societies not only mobilized financial support, they also proposed improvements and figured in the popularization of European-style theater and the transmission (in part via the press) of theater tastes and manners to the public.[103]

There were cartoon scenes that gave a surreal air to images of performance. There were also satiric parodies of real theatricals or performers and their foibles.[104] In one such parody, the satirical press fashioned its drama criticism into cartoon form. A frame in *Züğürt* showed a shabby actor being pelted with fruit and other items; he calmly munched one of the offending fruits. The caption read, "In this company, they don't pay much but, thank heaven, the food is free."[105] This cartoon can be read as social satire as well as theatrical criticism. Many actors were ill paid and subject to the sometimes oppressive whims of the managers of theatrical companies.

The most common use of theater in the Ottoman cartoon space was one that took as its premise the notion, popularized by Shakespeare, that all the world is a stage. That is, Ottoman satirists took the foibles of revolutionary politics and society and placed them in theater-like scenes, on stage, thereby playing with the boundaries of reality, creating frames within frames.[106] The satiric *Nekregû ile Pişekâr* ran a repeated section on "At the Theater."[107] *Boşboğaz* ran a cartoon showing two men parading a stage labeled, "National Ottoman Theater."[108] *Falaka* compared the administration of Hakkı Pasha to an *orta oyun* play, advertising it on a playbill; instead of a "two act" play, it was a "two year" play (*iki senelik mufassal oyun*).[109] Even foreign affairs were put on stage as demonstrated by two frames in *Davul* satirizing Pan-Slavism, Bulgaria, and the czar.[110] The stage, in both cartoons is the Balkan Question; and the real political protagonists can be actors or audience.

Other cartoons used the stage as a metaphor for the revolutionary drama. *Dalkavuk,* for example, shows an "actor" on his knees in a scene in which he passionately declares his devotion before a female, dressed in "classical" robes and perched on a pedestal, labeled *Hürriyet* (Freedom).[111] Another frame satirized the idea that the revolution would create liberty, fraternity, and equality. In the foreground is the head of a household. In the background is a "scene" of chaos: destructive children, fighting pets, and a screaming mother. The beleaguered father figure is dressed in some kind of robe (Figure 7.5). He mourns, "Oh, Fraternity, Fraternity, come spend a while with us."[112] One could argue that this image is simply a humorous domestic scene, but it is framed rather like a stage scene, and its play on the element of fraternity (*uhuvvet*) from the French (and then Ottoman) revolutionary slogan, suggests that this drama is also a metaphor for the condition of the empire.

Cartoon satire, like the satire of the puppet theater, often played on the the idea of misunderstandings and taking words too literally. One such frame wove together the themes of the bilingual theater, and the Europeanization of Ottoman culture. The scene shows a chicly dressed gentleman demanding his money back at the box office (Figure 7.6). The playbill announces the appearance of Madeleine Dolley in "*La Femme Nue.*" The cartoon is entitled: "On the occasion of [the showing of] Henri Batayan's [*sic* Bataille's] work entitled *Çaylak Kadın.*" The disgruntled patron says: "You say in the announcement that there will be a naked woman; I waited until the very end of the play and I saw no such woman, on stage or off. Return my money; this is a kind of fraud."[113] This cartoon's humor hinges on the possibilities for word ambiguity and French-Ottoman mistranslations and misunderstandings. Bataille himself commented on the fact that his title intended both the allusion to actual nudity and, more particularly, the idea of instinctual woman, devoid of artifice.[114] The original play, in French, premiered in Paris on February 27, 1908, at The Renaissance Theater, and received rave reviews. The cartoonist is imagining the cultural and linguistic possibilities. Clearly the "new" era of theater and French-Ottoman cultural synthesis produced endless possibilities for confusion and misadventure.

Time and again, the Ottoman cartoon space used the European-style theater as one of the markers of the "new" era, a symbol of the modern, Europeanized lifestyle that was opening up for Ottoman society. Ottoman cartoons suggested that national theater was a natural outcome of the revolution, because that which had been suppressed in the era of *istibdad* (despotism) would now flourish. And the theater, like the press, would both represent and constitute the new nation.[115] Thus, when *Kalem* imagined a street scene in an Istanbul of the future, one of its distinguishing marks was a "Grand Theater."[116]

Nonetheless, there was a darker side to this equation of theater with the newly constituted and modern nation. While celebrating the new Ottoman nation and the possibilities for its citizens, cartoons also satirized the theater (as opposed to shadow plays and other traditional theatrical forms)

— Où es-tu, Fraternité, viens donc passer quelques jours chez nous.

Figure 7.5 Fraternité

هانرى باتايۀنك (چپلاق قادين) نام اثرى مناسبتيله:

Vous allez me rendre mon argent... J'ai payé pour
voir une femme nue... il n'y avait pas de femme nue

— اعلانده چپلاق قادين وار ديورسكز اويونك
نهايتنه قدر صبر ايتدم نه صحنه‌ده و نه ماشاری‌ده بويله بر
قادين كورمدم پاره‌مى اعاده ايديكز بو برنوع دولاندير يجيلقدر.

Figure 7.6 "The Naked Woman"

as an elite, exclusive rather than inclusive, art form. It was a venue to be enjoyed by those who were complicit in the project of Europeanization, a group who, in the cartoon space, represented the Ottoman official classes, the wealthy, and the arrogant, those who were concerned for the forms of fashion rather than for the substance of the nation. In this type of cartoon, the Europeanized Ottoman, as exploitative or unconcerned, was linked, however indirectly, to the exploitative Europeans themselves. He was participant in the European hegemonic project.

BORROWED CULTURE: THE FADS OF SKATING AND SPIRITUALISM

Theater, the cafe-concert, French governesses, the novel—these were the signs of borrowed culture in the Ottoman cartoon space. They represented the combination of lust and fear with which the Ottomans confronted European culture. They suggested intimate connections between borrowed ideas, immorality, the consumption of imported goods, and a deep-seated sense of uncertainty. That uncertainty took "concrete" shape in the Ottoman cartoon space in the form of two other manifestations of borrowed culture, the fads of skating and spiritualism. These fads invaded the empire and captured the imagination of the Ottoman urban public just at the time that the revolution gave freeedom and license to the satirists' pens.

The skating fad sweeping Istanbul in the early twentieth century was an indicator of the opening up of the empire to European and American business interests. This connection was not lost on the American Consul-General, Ernest L. Harris, whose reports in 1910 suggest the intimate relationship between U.S. business and diplomatic activities at a time when American state service in the Middle East was still in its infancy. Echoing the reports of his colleagues in Germany and Russia, Harris noted that the popularity of skating in the Ottoman empire could mean money in American pockets. He also evidenced a firm belief in the superiority of American roller skating products:

> Consul-General Ernest L. Harris reports that in September a roller skating rink was experimentally established in Smyrna, as it was doubtful if it would appeal to the various nationalities in that Asia Minor metropolis. Since that time no less than four have been opened, and the attendance is such that others will be built. The skates used have been chiefly of German and French manufacture, although some English and American makes have lately been imported. The floors are cement, asphalt, and pine. The rollers on the skates most in use are boxwood. What the rinks in this city need are hard maple floors, and skates with steel or aluminum wheels. American manufacturers interested in this trade should send catalogues to this office for distribution to rink owners.[117]

Harris's willingness to distribute roller skating equipment catalogs in Izmir (Smyrna) demonstrates his appreciation of the connection between cultural phenomena and the market. The Consul perceived the Ottoman empire, or at least parts thereof, as an expanding market for American goods. Advertising in the Istanbul revolutionary press suggests that he was right; not only were skating rinks touted in the advertising columns of Istanbul gazettes, but American products were portrayed as both good and desirable.

As for the doubts, which Harris mentioned, about the appeal of skating to "the various nationalitites" of Izmir, it is clear that, by 1910, any moral stigma attached to skating had not prevented numerous Ottoman citizens from getting out on the rink. Women citizens, however, were another matter, at least in Izmir. There, in 1910, an entrepreneur had obtained a permit for a combined cinema and roller skating rink.[118] Two afternoons a week were reserved for women. This drew considerable criticism, particularly in the press: "Articles appeared every day, one after another, to the effect that the sanctity of the home was being endangered, and that women would lose all sense of decency if allowed to view immodest pictures or, worse still, disport themselves on wheels."[119] Apparently fragile female sensibilities, at least to some observers, were not up to the moral challenge of skating; nor was the Ottoman household willing to become "modern" if modern meant rinks and cinemas for the ladies. Nonetheless the rink opened, and ladies, sheltered from the eyes of men, did skate in Izmir, at least for a time.

Ice- and roller-skating were already popular in Istanbul by the time of the Young Turk Revolution.[120] *Kalem* advertised a "Skating Palace" in Beyoğlu, "open every day to families in the morning and at noon times and, in the evenings, to the public."[121] In turn, skating found its way into Ottoman satire, a symbol of something new, precarious, and Western. Skating cartoons were directed at both social and political phenomena; they associated skating with pratfalls but also with the subordination of the Ottoman people, their customs, and their morals.

First, there was always the concern that women out skating were unrestrained women. A cartoon in *Kalem* illustrates the associations of women skating and European fashions with breaches of public morals. In this frame, a dowdy mother calls to her fashionable daughter who is headed out the door, "My daughter, where are you going?" The daughter replies, "Skating, Mama, the chicest men of Beyoğlu [a Europeanized district] gather there every evening."[122] The skating palace, this frame suggests, provided an opportunity for the young to pierce the boundaries of contolled sexual mingling, to see and be seen by strangers (Figure 7.7). It was Western, it was modern, it was "fast." The French caption, interestingly enough, does not duplicate the Ottoman caption, and fails directly to mention the opportunities for young ladies to meet fashionable men.

— Où vas tu ma fille ?
— Tu le vois bien, maman; je vais au Skating... C'est encore là qu'on s'amuse le mieux.

- زوجه كيديیورسك قیزم ...
- ایسكاتینه ، آننه ؛ بك اوغلنده كی الك شیق بكار هر آقشام اوراده طوپلانیور ...

Figure 7.7   Going Skating

The skating rink, then, was a site where Ottoman women could enjoy European-style entertainment and European-style morality. In a similar vein, another cartoon shows two fashionable women conversing. "A perfect cafe-concert is opening nearby in Pera," says one. "What's that to me?" responds her companion. The first woman exclaims, "Really rich men will be going there," to which her companion replies, "What's that to you?"[123] In both cartoons, the women are initiating contact with strange men. In both cartoons, the locale for such encounters is the "European" side of the Golden Horn.

These cartoons employed representations of Ottomans imitating European forms of entertainment with the depiction of exaggerated European-style dress to show that the bounds of propriety had been exceeded. Young women did not go out in public, alone, seeking strange men, chic or otherwise. Skating, as a relatively new form of social intercourse, recently imported, became a metaphor for the relative freedom with which women might mingle with men. Public mingling of the sexes, in 1908 Istanbul, was viewed by some as signifying freedom, modernity, and progress, but by many others it was viewed as signifying license, immorality, and a chaotic disruption of the boundaries of patriarchal and familial authority.[124]

Another cartoon, in *Yeni geveze,* also combined images of European fashion with the setting of a skating parlor, both indicators of European influence. The frame shows the dumpy mascot, *Zevzek* (Silly or Gabby) roller-skating with a fashionable lady in a big feathered hat. *Geveze* (Blabbermouth) stands by, with what looks like a fur stole, and comments: "I'm making you a present of this new fashion costume, it goes well with the skating."[125] Here, despite the light-hearted vein, skating retains it associations with frivolity, consumption of foreign goods, and public mingling of the sexes.

Other satire of skating hinged on the precarious balance and slippery surfaces associated with skating, especially for beginners. A cartoon in *Kalem* shows the government ministers trying unsuccessfully to skate, all having hit the floor with the exceptions of one observer and Hakkı Pasha (the newly appointed grand vezir) who, arms out, was poised immobile (Figure 7.8). The caption reads: "*Yavaş, yavaş kayalım. Zamaneye uyalım.*" (Slowly slowly let us glide; let's get with the times).[126] The frivolity or indignity of skating was only the topical message here because Ottoman society, like the government on the rink, was portrayed as suffering a form of paralysis or at least "learner" status partly under the aegis of Europe. The revolution had not turned the new regime officials into expert skaters. But Hakkı Pasha, distinguished from the others by his dress, seemed to show some potential for adapting to the "modern" age and all that came with it.

Figure 7.8 Getting It Right

İSPİRİTİZMA

> It is indeed curious that this movement, which many of us regard as the most important episode in the history of the world since the Christ episode, has never had a historian from those who were within it, and who had a large personal experience with its development.
> —Arthur Conan Doyle, *The History of Spiritualism*[127]

Gathered around the table are a group of very serious individuals, both men and women, gazing in rapt attention at a figure, often female, who is lost in concentration. She is attempting to conjure a voice or presence from the spirit-world. Sometimes this spirit is even captured in "spirit-photography." This was spiritualism, a movement that intrigued and delighted the satirists and cartoonists of the revolutionary press. Spiritualism was intended to be a serious exploration of alternatives in the realms of science, religion, and medicine; it had made its way eastward from the United States, its original base, to England, to the Ottoman empire.[128] Experiments in "psychic science" had for some time been conducted in Europe and America and had developed a body of "scientific" literature to explain their results. The fact that spiritualism was taken seriously, at least by some members of Ottoman society, is illustrated by the publication of the gazette *İspiritizma*, in Istanbul, from 1910–1912. This publication included articles on the meaning and methods of spiritualism, and presented stories and photographs of famous mediums and their seances.

Spiritualism was an attempt to link science and metaphysics, a way to contact the dead, cure disease, and gain access to the past and future. But, for Ottoman revolutionary satirists, spiritualism was a classic expression of the ridiculous in imported Western culture and politics. This is not to say that belief in the spirit world was in any way anathema to Ottoman society. Quite the contrary, spiritualism struck a sympathetic chord in a society whose literature had long given a special place to jinn, dream visitations, and various spiritual manifestations. Dreams figured prominently in Ottoman literature and were a common device in Karagöz plays.[129] One Ottoman civil servant, late in the nineteenth century, even claimed that his system for regimental accounts had come to him in a dream.[130] Communication with the dead was also certainly not a notion that was foreign to Ottoman culture. But in the satirical press, the idea of spiritualism was associated with superstition, frivolity, bad administration, and the uncritical imitation of European styles.

Before spiritualism became the target of Ottoman satirists, it had been subjected to considerable ridicule by the satirical press in England where it was immensely popular in the nineteenth century. Charles Graves, writing in 1921 noted that "The chief exploiters of credulity, however, were to be found in the ranks of spiritualists, mediums, clairvoyantes and professional somnambulists. Men of science still held aloof from this traffic with the unseen, and its terminology was crude, but the methods and results were strangely familiar."[131] Or, as Halide Edib put it: "Science is no longer so cock-sure. The incalculable, the Unseen has been entering its domain. There is space and room for a belief in the unseen force in creation. . . . . Among the people in the West also there is an obvious curiosity for the Unseen. In the Anglo-Saxon world quack religions and revivalist phenomena are frequent."[132] The satiric gazette, *Punch,* responded with glee to the spiritualists, condemning those who patronized them as dupes and complaining that the police cracked down on the gypsies while the spiritualists plied their trade with impunity.

Ottoman cartoons added some new dimensions to the satire of spiritualism. Seances were shown in the pages of Istanbul satirical gazettes as a reminder of the dreamlike quality of the revolution, which itself suggested a seance attempting to call up independence and prosperity through the medium of the constitutional regime and its attendant social transformation. But, in the cartoon space, the spirits were all too dead, the "spirit-photography" not quite believable, and the mediums perhaps crazy. *Cadaloz,* one of the most imaginative, and sometimes vicious, of the satiric gazettes, picked up on the spiritualism phenomenon with considerable verve, "reporting" on *ispiritizma tecrübeleri* (spiritualism experiments). Its satiric narratives gave the jaundiced view of spiritualism's believers, picturing ten people seated around a table in a broad salon with one of their number putting a question "to the table," calling out *"Ya Ruh"* (Oh Spirit!). *Cadaloz* conjured up an occult meclis with "Reis Beg" officiating, to resolve the dilemmas of the empire.[133] A similar scene can be found eight years later in the gazette *Diken,* suggesting that the fad of spiritualism was still enjoying some popularity even after World War I.[134] *Hande,* in dialogue, satirized the large cadre of men thrown out of work by the new regime's bureaucratic reorganization as "spirits called up by means of *ispiritizma,*" a problem that was, in effect, haunting the administration.[135] *Yeni geveze,* showed Abd ül-Hamid and his eunuchs around a table, calling up the "spirit" of Abu ül-Huda (the sultan's old confidant). The ex-sultan is asking the age old question: "Please, have mercy, tell how many years of life there are." The reply is a knocking sound (lampooning the supposed "spirit" knockings on the table at real seances). The sultan pleads: "a year? a month? a week? a day?" The reply is "Knock? Knock? I don't know." To which the sultan replies, "Please. Reveal the secrets of the devil." To which the "spirit" replies: "Knock! Knock! Knock! A day or a week."[136] This cartoon combines a lampoon of the practice of spiritualism with a satiric meditation on the fleeting nature of life, of custom, and of sovereignty. Abd ül-Hamid is a man like most men, afraid of death, and his conjuring of the spirits will neither ward off the appointed hour, nor satisfy his anxiety. This frame is a good metaphor for the anxieties of the empire in general and for the jaundiced view that the cartoon space was inclined to take of men's strivings and machinations.

Seances were inextricably linked to the nightmares of the paranoid sultan Abd ül-Hamid, who surrounded himself with spies and was supposedly afraid of the disembodied voices of the telephone. In satire, the spiritualism of the new regime, like the dreams and astrologers of the old, suggested all too ephemeral solutions to the time-worn problems of death, bancruptcy, military inadequacy, and the European threat of invasion. The new parlimentary deputies themselves seemed spiritlike, inconsequential, possessing only the voices to debate without the force to implement. The satirists used spiritualism to suggest the disbelief with which they tended to clothe the revolution. Freedom could not be caught and fixed in a photograph. In cartoons, spiritualism was a European "intellectual" movement and the spirits were ultimately harmful, subjecting the empire to ridicule and bringing no relief to its ills, either spiritual or physical. With its female mediums and special appeal to women, the seance also represented the feminization and enervation of the empire, its energies dazzled and drawn off by the cultural pastimes of Europe so that it might be more easily ravished. Spiritualism signified the social ills, seen and unseen, generated by the uncertainty of a state at once in the process of creation and recreation, and subject to the political and cultural domination of Europe.

VIII

Fashion Satire and the Honor of the Nation

To prove we're not barbarians, they dress us up like savages!
To prove we're not barbarians, we wear a funny skirt!
Western people funny, of that there is no doubt.
They feel so sentimental, about the oriental,
They always try to turn us inside down and upside out . . .
—Rogers and Hammerstein, *The King and I*[1]

His name was Chic Bey—well fed, sly, and impeccably dressed in the latest Paris fashion.[2] Chic Bey was a character employed in the cartoon space who merged the critiques of luxury and consumption with the critique of Western styles.[3] The satirist's pen produced Chic Bey to demonstrate that all of Ottoman society was not enamored of the cultural effects of European imperialism. With censorship suspended, cartoon satire aimed at the adaptation of European (particularly French) fashions flourished in *mizah mecmuaları* as well as in the literary and political journals. It mocked the dandification of Ottoman society and the airs it put on in imitation of Europe.[4] Fashion became an implement for critiques of European imperialism and the social ills and cultural transformation contingent upon it. Further, fashion satire was used to highlight the charge that the new parliamentary ministers were exposing the state to the threat of European domination. Imitation in the name of "progress" was an ideology under scrutiny in the revolutionary press.[5] Fashion was the visible manifestation of that ideology of progress.

The 1908–1911 Istanbul gazettes serve to illustrate the forms, content, and anti-imperialist message of fashion satire, fashion, here, meaning dress, furnishings, styles of entertainment, and manners. Its targets were men as well as women, the educated elites more often than not, and members of the government in particular. Chic Bey personified the threat of European cultural hegemony: he might sell out the motherland to pay off his French cook and tailor, all in the name of progress. He stood in direct contrast to the *gazi* warrior, the epic Turkish heroic figure.[6] The *gazi* was strong, courageous, pious, a horseman who enjoyed a good fight and a good song. He was a symbol of Ottoman military success, dominance, and devotion to Islam. Chic Bey was suave, fashionable, a seeker of comfort, a weakling who needed to imitate his rivals rather than challenging them in combat. His loyalties, expertise, accounts, morals, religion, and education were all suspect. At the mercy of various European sovereigns, the Ottoman empire could ill-afford a symbolic hero like the *gazi*. Its authority figures, at least in the satirical press, sought fashion and freedom, not victory. Through figures like Chic Bey, and his female counterparts, fashion provided a readily observable illustration of the apparent conquest of Ottoman identity through European cultural imperialism.

The process of establishing European cultural hegemony in the Ottoman empire followed upon the definitive establishment of European military hegemony in the eighteenth and nineteenth centuries. By the nineteenth century, the Ottoman empire, despite certain valiant successes, was able to defend its territory only with the assistance of European allies, like the British in the Crimean War. Some Ottoman forces were commanded by foreign officers, and foreign instructors staffed the military and professional schools. Nineteenth-century reforms, aimed at European-style modernization, and involving changes in dress such as military uniforms, men's headgear, or women's dresses, provoked a variety of negative responses, from rebellion to mockery, in Ottoman society.[7] European styles were characterized as ridiculous, scandalous, anti-Islamic, or insulting to traditional culture. Fashion was also perceived as constituting a threat to traditional culture in areas of language, education, literature, arts, manners, and morality. Further, the consumption of European goods and services required to imitate European fashion was a marker of European economic dominance.[8] On the other hand, European (particularly French) language, education, books, and plays as well as furnishings, social customs, and dress had become markers of success and advancement among the elite classes of Istanbul society. The Europeanized Ottoman had greater access to positions, world news, and beneficial contacts in a state that was already politically and economically subordinate to European nations. To those for whom European culture had a positive connotation, European fashion symbolized progress, civilization, enlightenment, and a share in world power.

In the satirical press, a juxtaposition of "traditional" and "modern" images drew the battle lines between the collaborators, those willing to sacrifice traditional culture for Western fashion, and the skeptics, those who construed Western fashions as the personification of Western victory. Fashion satire reveals the symbolic repertoire available both to those who wished to preserve sultanic political culture and to those who wished to disestablish it. The task of the collaborators was to delegitimate what the society saw as obviously and eternally legitimate in terms of the old order: sultanic power;

patriarchal gender relations; traditional chains of authority; customary and familiar, if not comfortable, modes of transport; traditional forms of dress, social interaction, and entertainment; and a military whose reputation for ferocity had outlived its combat effectiveness. This struggle for control of the symbolic repertoire was distilled into images of dress that bespoke allegiance and identity without words. Although fashion was also satirized in narrative, the cartoon proved a more effective and pointed vehicle to associate dress with themes like submission, dominance, immobility, and progress.[9] Such images were not employed unilaterally. The same costume could relay a variety of messages depending upon context, aspect, and caption. As a result "traditional" and "modern" costume are not reducible to single polar values of good or bad, progressive or reactionary.[10] Indeed, "traditional" and "modern," as dialogic concepts were restricted neither to single meanings nor to hegemonic symbol sets. The sultan's coat, for example, hanging unoccupied or sold at auction, bespoke the degradation of Ottoman authority. In a different cartoon, the same coat could represent the quintessential symbol of despotism. Veiled women, without benefit of caption, could signify (depending on aspect) either the strong and upright nature of traditional society or the ignorance and submission of a society bypassed in the current world order.

Thus the very symbols of traditional society that were used to represent reaction in some cartoons—the sultan's dress, old military uniforms, covered women, bumpkin peasants, narghile smoking men, turbans and baggy trousers—were also used to clothe the anti-imperialist voice of reason and to warn that European fashion subjected the mind and the body. The fashion symbols of European progess and success—scanty dresses, numerous buttons, frilly skirts, parasols, skates, suits, topcoats, canes, umbrellas, and hats—bespoke arrogance as well as contentment, economic oppression as well as financial success, frivolity as well as fun, and immorality as well as freedom.

In the context of this fashion ambiguity, the satirists posed a question: If European fashions were allowed unequivocally to replace Ottoman traditional forms of dress without challenge, then could the dissolution of Ottoman society be far behind? Such progress might lead to oblivion. The Paris fashions of many constitutional supporters were construed as indicating a willingness to submit to permanent servitude to Europe, giving the West sovereignty in mode and in rule. A prominent example of this type of degradation was the Egyptian royal family.[11] Since 1882, Egypt had been under English control, although the Ottomans still claimed it as part of the sultan's empire and England maintained the fiction that its rule was only temporary. The Egyptian king's family, Europeanized in education, dress, furnishings, and social style, was a highly visible example of the consumption of European fashion.[12] Yet the king was a ruler in name only. He was, in fact, a British puppet. The Khedive's European fashions had not brought him a share in European power or prestige.

Although the satirical press was critical of slavish imitation of European fashions, the wearing of traditional clothing was also problematic. Insistence on traditional forms of dress could be equated with reactionary thinking, in short, with motives not calculated to preserve the integrity of the new Ottoman state.[13] Dress, then, could be used to distinguish the "progressive" from the "reactionary." Still, traditional dress was not simply a marker of reactionary political thinking any more than European fashion was simply a marker of progressive thinking. Both could be charged with subverting the interests of the empire. Some cartoons left the dress of their characters non-descript, that is to say dress was a quiet element in these cartoons. More often, however, dress was either used as an obvious indicator of point of view or it was exaggerated to emphasize the critical message of the cartoon. Dress was an easy way to identify a character or the position of a character before the caption was taken into account; and the messages of many cartoons centered around equations of dress with identity.

FASHION SATIRE PRECEDENTS

Fashion satire was not an innovation of the revolution. There were various cultural precedents.[14] One early Ottoman gazette that combined European and Ottoman styles of cartoon cultural critique was *Çıngıraklı Tatar*.[15] Published in Istanbul by Teodor Kasab, in 1873, it portrayed itself as a new gazette come to shake up the established press, both Ottoman and foreign language.[16] Some of *Çıngıraklı Tatar*'s fashion satire was light-hearted. One cartoon showed an elaborately dressed lady: fan in hand, beribboned full skirts and a plunging neckline revealing lots of bosom. The caption read, "showing the leg is shameful."[17] Clearly shame was a cultural phenomenon with a mixed message in late-nineteenth-century Istanbul. This cartoon critiques European dress style and indicates how cartoonists used dress to reflect their society's failure to form a consensus on what behaviors compromised the honor of the individual or the society. Men were also targets of *Çıngıraklı Tatar*'s fashion satire. A cartoon captioned, "the outcome of a dispute," showed one man dressed in "traditional" military costume, completed incongruously with a silk top hat; he was standing next to a gentleman in European suit and monocle wearing a turban.[18] Both look ridiculous in terms of conventional notions of appropriate dress. This cartoon suggests that there had been no real rapprochement between the old and new. The dispute was "settled" to no one's satisfaction.

In other cartoons, the fashion message was straightforward. One split frame showed a woman dressed in European fashion complete with dipped neckline, fancy bonnet and bustle. The frame was entitled, "in the street." The second frame showed the same woman. Stripped of her finery she was emaciated and bedraggled looking. It was entitled, "in the bedroom."[19] This cartoon graphically suggested that European fashion was an illusion replacing one set of social ills with another. The volume of clothing heaped on the woman gave an impression of beauty and robust health that disguised the fact that she was undesirable and undernourished. This was a pointed critique of the empire itself, clothed in the accoutrements of European culture without the wherewithal to emulate European power.

Another cartoon in *Çıngıraklı Tatar,* symbolizing the disillusionment of lovers, can also be viewed as a metaphor for Ottoman society. The cartoon shows the fashionable female holding hands with her suitor; six months later the couple sits on the same love-seat, backs turned to each other.[20] Like the Ottoman elites enamored of things European, the heroine could not build a lasting relationship on infatuation alone.

Of course Istanbul, as a cosmopolitan city, had a long history of eclectic and varied dress styles. This eclecticism outraged the garrulous Mark Twain when he journeyed to Istanbul in the mid-nineteenth century. He wrote, on Ottoman men: "the men were dressed in all the outrageous, outlandish, idolatrous, extravagant, thunder-and-lightning costumes that ever a tailor with the delerium tremens and seven devils could conceive of. . . . . No two men were dressed alike."[21] And on the women:

> drifting noiselessly about are squads of Turkish women, draped from chin to feet in flowing robes, and with snowy veils bound about their heads, that disclose only the eyes and a vague, shadowy notion of their features. Seen moving about, far away in the dim, arched aisles of the Great Bazaar, they look as the shrouded dead must have looked when they walked forth from their graves amid the storms and thunders and earthquakes that burst upon Calvary that awful night of the Crucifixion. A street in Constantinople is a picture one ought to see once—not oftener.[22]

Twain was not a great admirer of the city of Constantine in its nineteenth century incarnation. But his satire of Istanbul fashion has a certain ring of truth to it.

While the fashion satire of the nineteenth century, at least as embodied in the prose of Twain and the cartoons of *Çıngıraklı Tatar,* was fairly innocent, by 1908 the critical form of Ottoman fashion satire had become more specific, more vitriolic. Twentieth-century satire drew European costume much more thoroughly into the equation whereby dress was a characteristic marker of the plagues afflicting the empire, plagues introduced from or associated with Europe. Revolutionary satire assured the reader that his qualms about Westernization were well founded.[23] Like the Iranian author, Jalal-e Ahmad's 1962 work on *Gharbzadegi* (Westoxication), the Ottoman satirical press conjured an image of Ottoman society stricken by an infectious disease.[24] Cartoons pictured the unsettling effects of societal and political change in the form of incongruous or ludicrous combinations of traditional and European costume.

Fashion Satire

IMPORTED FASHION, THE ECONOMY, AND PUBLIC MORALS

Since the mid-nineteenth century, elite Ottoman women had been importing fashions from Paris on a regular basis and, by the end of the century, dressmakers and Pera shops had made European dress a commonplace for women of the upper classes in Istanbul streets, at least in certain areas. The elite classes in Istanbul had become avid consumers of European fashions, materials, dress makers, patterns, and styles.[25] For the most part, however, public display of these fashions was still restricted, and dresses were usually covered by the two-piece *çarşaf,* usually of black silk, which covered head and body. The face was covered by a light veil called a *yaşmak.*[26]

The association of Europeanized fashion with progress manifested itself in the press. Women read the fashion papers and the revolutionary gazettes catered to Europeanized tastes, picturing "the new fashions of the season," and running advertisements for European-made gowns, corsets, and children's clothing.[27] The 1910 *Karagöz Yearbook* ran a series of satiric sketches showing fashionable women wearing the plumed hats and carrying the ubiquitous parasols that seemed to mark European style.[28] These cartoons showed women scantily clad, women as catty bitches, playful women with pet dogs, saucy women showing their legs, and a woman in a big hat and parasol weeping when confronted with the realities of "father" time. *Resimli kitab* equated the new political freedom of constitutionalism with a new social freedom to imitate French society, "in the streets and in one's home."[29]

Lâklâk, a gazette that is notable for its cartoon representations of women and of the poorer classes, suggested just how far the intrusion of Western styles into Ottoman society had advanced. One of its cartoons showed an older couple out in the park. Seated on a rug and dressed in traditional fashion, they gaze at the passersby (men and women) who are dressed in a set of costumes ranging from traditional to the European-style dress, hat, and jacket worn by one female stroller in the park. "What's all this?" one asks. The other replies, "In the new mode they are living dolls (*canlı kuklalar*) with a light cloak (*yeldirme*) [and] head cover."[30] The point of this cartoon may be that relatively conservative elders do not reject the new modes out of hand. But what is most interesting in this frame is the range of dress styles presented and the notion that these changes are gradually filtering down to achieve some sense of normalcy at all levels of Ottoman society.

The acceptance of European fashion, however, only went so far. Under Abd ül-Hamid, fashion morality had been codified in the form of an imperial edict, as illustrated in a comment by a visiting Frenchman, Louis Rambert, in 1904:

> It is well known that Islam requires women to wear the veil. The *feridje* [long, full coat] and *çarşaf* [floor-length, long-sleeved over-garment] which Muslim

women have always worn have been recently modified in such a manner as to contrast with the usage of the harem. Çarşafs resemble ontari [a long vest]; feridje, garments without sleeves, are cut on a model not in conformity with custom [*moeurs*]. The yaşmak [light veil] is sufficiently filmy that all a woman's tresses are visible. These modifications extend to wearing military style jackets and cloaks and to young girls old enough to wear the veil going about uncovered and dressed in a way antithetical to the prescriptions of Islam. It goes without saying that such a state of affairs would not long be tolerated. So an imperial *irade* [edict] has enjoined women to dress in accordance with the principles of religion. It is announced to the parents and husbands of all those who violate the terms of this edict that it will be duly and rigorously enforced. And so! Poor women![31]

Rambert's story demonstrates that the government placed responsibility for females' fashion violations on their parents and husbands. It may be viewed as reflecting the determination of the regime, four years before the revolution, to enforce restraint in women's public dress. It may also, of course, be viewed as indicating the extent to which European-style disorderly conduct for women had subverted notions of an "Islamic" dress code. As Lucy Garnett pointed out, also in 1904: "A square piece of dark-colored silk or muslin, attached to this [the *çarşaf*] with pins, hangs over and completely conceals the face. This, however, can be thrown back at pleasure, leaving the features of the wearer completely exposed to view. And it is observable that half the women one meets in the streets of the capital without hesitation avail themselves of this facility."[32] Halide Edib also argued that the edict was unenforceable: "Abdul Hamid himself would issue a royal 'Irade,' or ordinance, every Ramazan and the police got busy in the streets cutting the dresses of the women who were not attired according to regulations. But the enforcement of the 'Irade' was never attempted for more than three days."[33]

Of course veiling (a complicated issue on which much has been written) was not a strictly Islamic phenomenon; and veiling and seclusion of women had for centuries been linked to class and economic as well as to moral concerns. Seclusion, in part, signified the financial wherewithal to relieve the women of a household from work and from the necessity to appear in public. Garnett and Edib's observations suggest the porous nature of barriers to women's exposure, while the sultan's edict certifies the effects of the invasion of European fashion and European gender relations and indicates the social imperative to regulate women's public behavior and appearance. But moral concerns were not the sole preoccupation of this regulatory attempt. Rambert's account and, for that matter, much of the historiography on Middle Eastern women, emphasizes religious values as the area of Ottoman social formation most compromised by the importation of European fashion. But these imports also compromised local industry. In the Ottoman cartoon space, they became a symbol of heedless consumption, and of a squandering of economic resources to line foreign pockets which the debt-ridden empire could ill afford.

Linking the consumption of foreign fashion to female extravagance and to class distinctions was a mode of cartoon satire with a history. In European satire of the time, wearing "foreign" fashions and the preoccupation with fashion in general were typically critiqued as female foolishness and romanticism.[34] Fashion consumption was, however, also linked to a general critique of extravagance and lack of fiscal responsibility.[35] In one 1909 English work on fashion, the authors regularly critiqued female extravagance. They noted of the French Empress Eugenie, who had a penchant for "ethnic fashions": "when she went to the opening of the Suez canal [symbol of European imperialism par excellence], which meant an absence in the East of several months, she took two hundred and fifty dresses with her." In this case, however, the authors did provide the empress with something of an excuse: "but these may have been necessary owing to the number of social claims upon her, and the many times she had to appear in public."[36] Others were less charitable. One author, writing in London's *Fortnightly Review*, claimed that "The Empress Eugenie swayed the social world of Europe more effectively than Napoleon III."[37] She was blamed for single-handedly launching "the reign of the hideous crinoline," and her fashion choices were portrayed as having significant economic impacts, particularly on the textile industry.

The economic implications of changes in dress styles were also explored in the Ottoman cartoon space. The dilemma of dress, as Ottoman satirists saw it, extended beyond the realms of class and manners. There was an economic and political messsage that underlay the satirization of women's styles. Istanbul society's submission to French fashion, and its willingness to expend the limited financial resources of the empire on consuming this fashion, indicated a lack of responsibility and of patriotism.

Some fashion images, of course, were merely silly. Fish mongers and *simit* (bread ring) sellers were used to satirize Western styles in women's hats.[38] But, other cartoons reinforced the notion that Istanbul culture, at least in terms of dress, was a mixed if not a schizophrenic culture. A clear illustration of that idea is given in a cartoon entitled "Straight from Paris to Anatolia," showing a woman dressed in half Eastern, half Western fashion (Figure 8.1).[39] This image of recombinant cultures suggested the Ottoman woman and her society were playing the fool, neither retaining their integrity nor succeeding in the imitative project. Ottoman society, embodied as female, was paraded in the streets for the audience's sympathy or ridicule.

The empire's paradoxical economic position is illustrated in the advertising images that inhabited the back pages of the periodical press. One finds, in one gazette, for example, ads showing a scantily clad female advertising imported corsets, "ready made or made to order," from an Austrian shop, and ads showing village women, covered from head to toe, sitting before looms, producing carpets for European entrepreneurs to export

"Combination" modèle Pérote de l'avenir.   پارسدن آناطولی به دوغرو .

Figure 8.1   Straight from Paris to Anatolia

abroad (Figure 8.2).[40] The ubiquitous camel train marched across the top of the carpet ad, intensifying the image of the timeless, "traditional" empire, embodied in the clothing of the women at the loom. Both ads were for businesses that benefited foreign interests in Istanbul. The message in these ads was translated, in cartoons, into a message of exploitation, the Ottomans acquiescing in the stripping of their own dignity and resources.[41]

This image of Ottoman female labor finds a narrative counterpart in a scene depicted by Emine Tugay, who visited an English-owned Ottoman textile factory in Izmir in 1910.

> The frames of the rugs and carpets, all of them hand made, were set up in large, airy sheds, a passage being left in the middle between two rows of frames. Little Turkish girls, fair and blue eyed, wearing white muslin scarves over their hair, sat in rows on one side, and Greek girls, dark with big black eyes, on the other, while older girls supervised the work. The director explained that only children between eight and twelve could be employed to make finely knotted rugs, the hands of the workers having to be very small in order to make it possible for them to tie the knots. . . . As they grew older they were moved to the coarser weaves, but even then the standard of quality insisted on in the factory made it necessary that they should leave the work at the age of fifteen. Great care was taken of their health and the children in fact all looked extremely well.[42]

Needless to say, the English neither invented child labor nor popularized the weaving of carpets by young girls.[43] There was little concern in the Ottoman press for the question of female labor per se, and Tugay, a member of the khedival family, was accustomed to enjoying the fruits of lower-class labor. Nonetheless, the image of Ottoman girls lined up at carpet frames producing profits for Englishmen was one that, when coupled with European fashion images, could conjure a vision of Ottoman production and consumption, both channeled toward the satisfaction of European economic needs and dictates. It was not female labor that provoked a response, but the question of who benefited from it.

For the satirists, the willingness to expend the limited financial resources of the empire on consuming European fashions indicated that the "new" state and society were at risk. They used the idea of the *alafranga* (or Europeanized) Ottoman, male and female, but especially female, to embody that sense of weakness.[44] Consumption of European goods, in and of itself, was not universally condemned or caricatured in the press. But conspicuous consumption was satirized as a weakness to which Ottoman women were particularly prone; their consumption of European styles and the drain on financial resources that it entailed had to be restrained, as did their attraction to the *alafranga* lifestyle. Ads in Ottoman gazettes touted imported hats, parasols, watches, and corsets; while Ottoman cartoons, some-

Figure 8.2 Imported Corsets

times in the same gazettes, lampooned the weakness of the *alafranga* female who consumed them.[45]

Just such a woman can be seen in a cartoon in *Kalem*. It shows a very fashionable *alafranga* couple chatting on the street (Figure 8.3). She wears a chic suit, a big hat, a stole, a parasol, and a muff. The man says, "What a chic outfit, my dear, how much did it cost you?" With a slight, sweet, smile, she replies, "My husband gave me five lira, but it cost twenty."[46] The message in this frame is one of extravagance in the pursuit of European fashion. But it is more than that; the woman has circumvented the household budget and her husband's authority. She is also out in the street; her relationship to the *alafranga* man is unclear, but he is decidedly not her husband.[47]

SEXUAL HONOR AND THE HONOR OF THE NATION

In the cartoon space, the dressing of Ottoman women in European fashion went beyond a critique of consumption and extravagance. Fashion was used to mark those women who upheld and those women who subverted the national honor. Fashion was used to represent the European seduction of the empire and Ottoman resistance to that seduction. In some cartoons, the satirical press transformed Turkey into the whore of Europe, a whore in a flamboyant hat and Parisian gown. The dangers of sex, dress, extravagance, and imperialism were all worked into cartoon images of the fashionably dressed woman and those who looked upon her with desire.[48]

Both sexes could compromise the national honor. Men, too, were shown as dazzled by the allure of European fashion. In that type of representation, the threat to the Ottoman state and society was not an Ottoman woman in European fashion, but the seductive European woman herself. Imagining women of other cultures as seductive temptresses, of course, was nothing new. There had long been genres of literature that classified women according to their "nations" or traits.[49] Orientalist art made a business of imagining Middle Eastern temptresses, as is evident in the frontspiece of E. J. W. Gibb's 1901 *Ottoman Literature,* which depicts a "flower of the Orient," naked, legs akimo, and lounging back in clear invitation.[50] Ottoman cartoons of European women were a bit more restrained. But the message of availability was similar. Some cartoons depicted the Westernized "Young Turks" off in Paris or Vienna, wasting the energies (and money) of the nation on foreign women. These men were dressed *alafranga,* in European styles. Their tastes also ran to European-style entertainments.

One cartoon, by the astute political critic, Sedad Nuri (İleri), showed an Ottoman official strolling with two fashionable Frenchwomen in big hats. The trio are viewed from the rear; the women link arms behind the man, and he rests a casual hand on the curvacious hip of each of his companions (Figure 8.4). The frame is captioned, "At Marienbad—Triple Alliance."[51] The Ottoman in this frame is not an identifiable individual; but the political

— Charmante votre toilette; qu'est ce qu'elle vous a couté.
— Mon mari m'a donné cinq livres; mais ma toilette m'en a couté dix.

Figure 8.3   Conspicuous Consumption

L'une des petites femmes. — Et les Jeunes Turcs ?
Ça marche... ça marche

Figure 8.4 Young Turk at Marienbad

context for the cartoon is certainly the Ottoman government's vigorous efforts to negotiate a loan from France at this time.[52] The satirist, here, suggests that "cultural" alliances may be proceeding more favorably than financial ones. Nuri drew a similar cartoon showing a smiling Westernized "Young Turk," strolling with a fashionable young European, his arm encircling her shoulders and his hand beneath her breast. He jokes, "And there are those who say I'm xenophobic (*ecnebi düşmeni*)."[53] The foreign women, in these frames, were fashionable and enticing, and the Ottoman men willingly susceptible. In other frames, cartoon seductresses, like the many European entrepreneurs who had flooded the empire seeking profit, supposedly worked their wiles in Istanbul, corrupting the young men of the Ottoman nation.[54] One cartoon showed two dapper young Ottomans dressed in the latest Paris fashion eyeing a fashionable young lady out for a stroll with her dog. "Don't ogle too long," warned one, "She's Austrian!"[55] In the cartoon space, then, fashionable European women were a trope for the weakening of the (male) nation.

While the satirists tweaked these chic Ottoman dandies, it was in the figures of women, the mother and the beloved, that they most often embodied the honor of the nation, especially its sexual honor.[56] These figures, as allegorical symbols of the nation or as stand-ins for real Ottoman citizens, were calculated to be provocative. They challenged male and national honor by drawing the gaze of the viewer to images of the Ottoman female threatened by foreign men and in need of protection. The cartoon nation, gendered female, could be strong or vulnerable. She had the potential to be either patriot or subversive depending on how she was framed in the cartoon space: her dress, her manner, her actions, her associates. While some cartoons suggested she was inviolable, others suggested she had already been violated. She could be shown victimized and suffering either at the hands of foreign imperialists or at the hands of squabbling Ottoman politicians.[57] Or, a vulnerable female figure of the nation could be shown as the potential victim of European male sexual desire. "Traditional" dress was used to type these woman figures as truly Ottoman. They called upon the Ottoman male (the primary audience for the cartoon space) to fight, to defend, and to redeem the empire's honor and his own.

A two-page illustration in *Kalem,* for example, graphically expressed the anguish over Ottoman military and sexual honor produced by the confrontation with Europe. This frame was called "The Slave Merchant," and purported to be a copy of a painting from the Luxembourg Museum in Paris (Figure 8.5). The scene is a traditional one with two women (probably representing Bosnia and Herzegovina) presented as gifts by a petitioner to win the favor of the monarch.[58] But the women are no longer initiates, as the setting and postures would suggest, to the sultan's harem. Instead, the Ottoman male has become a syncophant slave-merchant, offering up the (female) bodies of his state and people to the devouring eye of the Austrian emperor, who now sits the throne, in Istanbul, in place of the sultan. The

Figure 8.5 Gift for the Harem

women, in traditional dress, were possessions (stand-ins for Ottoman territory), offered to a foreign master. In this frame, Ottoman sovereignty, patriarchal authority, and masculine honor were all sacrificed on the altar of European dominance. Although this cartoon was captioned, its message required no words—the setting, staging, and characters were all inscribed in the Ottoman memory. Only the male roles had been recast.

Where the empire was envisioned as surrounded by threatening male imperialists, allegorical images of the nation equated women with territory or property.[59] In them, the honor of the nation was embodied; and, because the bodies were female, the military and sexual honor of the nation were confounded. Sexual imagery was used to depict women of the empire confronted by their potential male seducers. Two cartoons of this type show Ottoman women embodying specific regions: Crete, Bosnia, and Herzegovina. In each case, the women are young and alluring "pieces" of the nation. The male figures in these cartoons signify European nations poised to seduce or carry off the objects of their desire, the Ottoman women.

The first example shows Crete, a demure young woman in traditional dress, surrounded by her *duvel-i hamiye* (protector nations): England, Austria, and France. They are larger than she. Arm in arm, they are marching her off. Standing before them, but not confronting them directly, is a noble looking Ottoman soldier (Figure 8.6). The powers say, "Don't trouble yourself; we take full responsibility this time. We hope, now, that she'll behave herself."[60] Here, the "nation" is vulnerable. She is in need of protection, but there is a competition between contending males over who will serve that protective function, the Ottoman empire (here called *Türkiye*), or the imperial powers of Europe. Crete, at this time, is portrayed as Ottoman property and "her" abduction is, in effect, a rape. There is no indication that the Ottoman soldier can stop her so-called protectors and, thereby, preserve the nation's honor. A similar cartoon in *Nekregu ile Pişekâr*, has a happier outcome. It shows the huge hand of a larger-than-life Ottoman soldier rescuing Crete. She is, however, half naked, suggesting that she has already been compromised.[61]

There is, however, another way to read this cartoon. Rather than being abducted, Crete might be running off with her virile companions, all dressed in military costume. In either reading, the Ottoman male is emasculated, his honor compromised. Crete becomes a symbol of Ottoman territorial integrity. But because that territory is embodied in human form, Crete also stands for the "Ottoman" citizen, tempted to violate the sovereignty of the nation by engaging in separatist national projects. Finally, the cartoon Crete is subversive. "She" provides the opportunity for foreign states to penetrate and disarticulate the empire. "She" is a member of the nation who is willing to compromise its integrity for a better offer. Once she is gone, the nation is diminished. Nonetheless, it would be a mistake, here, to suggest that this is a cartoon showing some kind of empowerment of the female "Crete." Although she may be flirting with the new protectors, the

La Turquie et la Crète

تركيا و كريد

Les Puissances protectrices—Nous vous assurons qu'elle sestera desormais tranquille.

دول حاميه — بوسفر بزكفيل اولدق تكدير ايتيك.
اميد ايدرزكه آرتق اوصلو اوطورره

Figure 8.6 Crete and Her Protectors

tacit assumption is that she must have a male protector. There is no question of autonomy. Even though she walks arm in arm with the European powers, she is surrounded and they are, in effect, captors.

A similar cartoon shows Austria as a dirty old man in uniform, attempting to seduce the nubile young Bosnia and Herzegovina who are dressed in traditional clothing (harem pants, fezzes, sashes, and pointed shoes). The young women are standing in a courtyard within the large protective gates of a domestic compound, but the gates are open (Figure 8.7).[62] Austria beckons to them, saying, "Please, Mesdemoiselles, Come. I've been waiting for you too long!" Again, the females signify a part of the nation that threatens to become detached, thus shaming the (here absent) Ottoman men. Here too, the women take on the roles of nation, citizen, and subversive; they have not decisively rejected the advances of the Austrian, even though they are demurely hanging back. In both these seduction scenes, women have the power to honor or shame the nation; their "traditional" dress suggests the empire's claim to them.

These cartoons of Crete, Bosnia, and Herzegovina are characteristic of Ottoman cartooning that often depicted territories that the Ottomans no longer controlled as if they were still "parts" of the nation. There had been a long struggle for control of Crete. The Powers forced Abd ül-Hamid to accept an autonomous regime under Ottoman suzerainty in 1897 and Greece had gained virtual control of the island before it was formally annexed in 1912. Likewise, although Austria only annexed Bosnia and Herzegovina outright on October 5, 1908, it had occupied those territories since the Congress of Berlin in 1878.[63] Nonetheless, in the Ottoman cartoon space, these territories served as symbols of the integrity of the empire and of the insidious and grasping nature of the European powers. This is not to say that the Ottoman satirists were deluded or that they proposed to support the fiction of possession embodied in nominal claims of Ottoman suzerainty. Rather, they used the formal instances of territorial loss to caricature the European aggressors and to bemoan the Ottoman weakness that led to the dislocation, and becoming "other," of one-time Ottoman citizens and territories. Thus Crete or Bosnia, feminized as the land, could still stand for the empire, even though the empire did not have the power to possess them. They were an accusation and a warning. Cartoons, after all, were not solely a reflection of the events of the day, they were also a calling up of images of the past and visions of the future.

There were East-West seduction scenarios in theater satire as well as in the cartoon space. The Karagöz plays, always topical, juxtaposed images of foreign fashion, on the one hand, and foreign men making off with Ottoman women, on the other. One observer, in 1897, described a shadow play featuring one Ottoman woman in European dress and another in traditional dress. She of the European fashion, a married woman, was carrying on an affair with an Ottoman dandy. The European-style clothing of both dandy and *hanım* denoted their "natural" moral decadence. This was a

Psst... Psst.. Mesdemoiselles écoutez moi donc!!   بكوردم: دوشيزكان بفرمائيد مرا كوش بدهيد دمادم

Figure 8.7 Dirty Old Man Austria

common theme in Karagöz plays. In the next scene, however, after the dandy triumphed over the woman's husband and Karagöz and Hacivat triumphed over the dandy, the French ambassador entered the room. Both women rushed towards him and, arm in arm, he began to escort them off. Whereupon, Hacivat attacked the ambassador, tore up his gold-laced coat, and chased him while the orchestra played a few bars "vaguely recalling the Marseillaise."[64] In this particular play, the moral of the story is twofold: the woman in European fashion is sexually available and, where the French ambassador is concerned, not even the woman in traditional dress can be considered either trustworthy or safe from his charms. Thus, the often lascivious shadow play used the figures of the Europeanized dandy and the French ambassador to symbolize male rivals invading the Ottoman moral and sexual space.

Sedad Nuri, one of the most innovative cartoonists in the press of the revolutionary period, summed up the equation for women, torn between old values and European styles, in a cartoon lampooning women's options. It was titled: "Either prisoner of the harem or slave to fashion."[65] The message of Nuri's dichotomy is that women were either subordinate to traditional constraints of dress, space, and morality or they were parading their imported fashions in the streets and violating public propriety, slaves to the new masters of Europe and consumption. There was no middle ground.

But there was a third option for Ottoman women in revolutionary cartoons, that of symbolizing the honor of the nation and the unity of the Ottoman people against the unjust aggressions of the European "other."[66] Such options are found in images of women as noble symbols of the nation, and in cartoons on the boycott of Austrian goods launched in autumn of 1908 as a response to Austria's annexation of Ottoman territory. In this latter setting, the image of women as thoughtless consumers of European fashion was converted into another image of women as patriotic consumers, preserving the honor of the state.

An idealized female figure came to represent the strength, unity, and endurance of the nation in some cartoons, just as it represented weakness and humiliation in others.[67] In such images, however, the female embodiment of the nation was clothed either in traditional or in classical costume. A characteristic cartoon shows a female empire as the idealized "*Hürriyet*" (Liberty) dressed in classical draperies and diaposed to the male demon, "*İstibdad* (Depotism)."[68] Her "classical" dress makes her appear timeless; but it also asserts her identity as distinct from those who are dressed in the costume of their conquerors (Figure 8.8). Of course this dress is not "classical" for all peoples. It is an imagined "Western" classical or Greek drapery, used to stand in for non-modern, non-national dress

A similar image, in *Falaka*, shows *Hürriyet* in a representation that combines the figure of Marianne in French revolutionary art with a set of traditional Ottoman (or Perso-Turkish) icons. This romanticized frame

Figure 8.8 Liberty and Despotism

Fashion Satire

shows the classical musician mascot of the gazette, playing to the half-naked "*Peri Hürriyet*" (The Fairy, Liberty), who floats in the sky over the Bosphorus with a star and crescent behind her.[69] Here, the figure of freedom is a figure of the nation, she is the beloved, hovering somewhat beyond men's reach. This particular image demonstrates the synthetic nature of Ottoman cartooning, in many ways very European in artistic style but also using traditional iconography and calling to mind figures from Persian miniatures and the fairy lovers of epic literature.

One of the most dramatic images of the mother or beloved nation is a cartoon that might take the title "Türkiye Unchained." Here, woman as symbol of the nation dons "traditional" dress (Figure 8.9).[70] Around her neck and on her legs are shackles labeled "ignorance" and "capitulations," the latter suggesting the debilitating economic concessions that the empire had for centuries granted to European powers. Towering over the landscape, this female Türkiye, a figure representing "Ottoman Constitutionalism," has at her feet a group of men, each representing a European nation, and each made insignificant by his miniscule size. The female nation, has already broken some of the chains of dependency, forged by her captors. She says: "I can no longer bear these old iron balls; I will break the fetters that bind my legs!" Surrounded by uniformed great powers, and weighed down by the chains of the European capitulatory regime, Türkiye might yet break those chains and attempt to strike a balance of power between the men fighting to possess her. But she would not do it dressed in Paris fashion.[71] This cartoon figure of the nation is the antithesis of her consuming, imitating, dependent, stylish cartoon sister, the *alafranga* woman, she of the feathered hat and Austrian corset with ice skates in hand. This Türkiye rejects the uncritical acceptance of Western culture as an unqualified good; suggesting that with the benefits of material culture come economic subservience and social disarticulation. Her dress is a symbol of her resistance.

The theme of general resistance to European economic dominance found more specific expression in cartoons of the Ottoman boycott of Austrian goods, which was launched in fall of 1908 after Austria's annexation of Bosnia and Herzegovina. The boycott, as already noted, provided a concrete symbol around which Ottoman patriotic sentiments and patriotic imagery could be mobilized. The revolutionary press exhorted Ottoman citizens to support the boycott, and Ottoman satirists produced both humorous and inspirational cartoons to illustrate the effects of this significant brand of Ottoman resistance. *Kalem*, for example, ran a series of boycott vignettes, among them a cartoon that showed a parade of rejected goods, including a stack of fezzes, returning to Austria.[72] *Resimli kitab* invoked the fashion image by showing an "Austrian Madame," confronting her counterpart, Mrs. Ottoman, or "*Hanım*." Each woman was dressed in a cartoon approximation of elite "national" costume. The Austrian lady complains to her friend that all her acquaintances have been shunning her, refusing to look her in the eye. The Ottoman lady responds, "Well, its a political ques-

Figure 8.9 Breaking Her Chains

tion, they're boycotting you."[73] *Resimli kitab* was a gazette that advocated the consumption of European culture, but the subject of the boycott was irresistable. It was a question of asserting Ottoman sovereignty, not necessarily of rejecting all things European.

Other cartoonists combined representations of the boycott with female figures of the Ottoman nation, evoking sentiments of love and loyalty for the nation and love and protection for the female embodiment thereof. One such image was an allegory of Türkiye as both nation and citizen. In this cartoon (one segment of a large frame showing the boycott and a triumphant procession in which Türkiye is the central figure), the proud Ottomans and their allies are the heroic figures, resisting the evil interloper, Austria. Türkiye appears as a mother, here, rather than a beloved; she is serene, beautiful, yet strong (Figure 8.10).[74] She has supporters, rather than male protectors, bearing her along in a cart. This female centerpiece of the frame is peaceful, and still in need of assistance, but she will not submit to the violence of Austrian dominance, just like the earlier figure of Türkiye would not submit to the violence of the capitulations. Next to her is Marianne, as France personified, but this Marianne has also been made into an older, more motherly figure. They are mother nations, alongside England (in uniform) and Russia (in peasant costume) as father nations. Türkiye's simple and conservative dress, with hair, neck, and arms covered, suggests her dignity and the honor and respect due her. In her lap she bears the slogan, "Liberty, Peace, Progress."[75] Above all, she is a patriot, signifying the endurance and stability of the nation that will survive the onslaught of European imperialism.[76] She accepts Europeans who will support her and rejects those who threaten her. This cartoon is somewhat unusual in that its producers were willing to make a distinction (which many Ottoman revolutionary cartoons would have rejected) between good and bad European imperialists. In most cartoons, Britain and France, like Austria, were also cast in the role of grasping imperial powers. *Papağan*, however, tended to cast Britain and France in a friendly light.

A contrasting image is that of the Ottoman woman (not the allegorical Türkiye) responding to the boycott. Unlike the serene mother nation, the woman in one boycott cartoon is a wife figure, accompanying her husband. Rejecting the temptation to consumerism, she passes by the Pera shopkeeper who is offering Western goods. She is not the nation, instead she is the citizen-patriot, who has put aside her own wishes to serve the interests of the country. The caption suggests that the couple is still bypassing the store even though the boycott is over.[77] The woman, at least for a time, has resisted the temptation to continue being the subverted citizen, consumer of imported goods, and symbol of European dominance. This theme of sacrifice was intimately associated with the boycott as it would later be associated with women's participation in the war effort in World War I.[78] The citizen-patriot in this cartoon wears Europeanized costume, suggesting the degree of influence Europe has already exerted on Ottoman fashion

Figure 8.10 The Mother Nation

and culture. But now, the frame proposes, the consumption of European goods can be moderated and subordinated to higher goals.

Thus woman, in the cartoon space, symbolized both the honor of the nation compromised and the honor of the nation defended. Clothed in European fashion she usually represented subordination, consumption, and dishonor. Clothed in classical or traditional costume she represented patriotism, honor, and resistance.

WOMEN'S PLACE

> In Turkey we have a saying, 'Women are all one nation.' . . . . Though men may belong to differentiated groups called races and nations, the female of the human species remains the same.
> —Halide Edib, *Conflict of East and West in Turkey*.[79]

The question of woman's place in Ottoman society was a theme that was intimately associated in the cartoon space with the questions of imperialism, fashion, and consumption. Cartoons were populated by male characters more often than by females; but images of women suggested the crisis of the Ottoman social and political order. One element of this crisis was the debate over women's place. The cartoon space provided a forum for this debate, and fashion was used to get the message across. In the Ottoman press, the question of women's "place" was treated as part of the greater question of how Ottoman society would be transformed in the face of European-style "modernization." As a piece in *İnkılâb* put it: "These days, the question of Eastern women (*şark kadınları*) has provoked lengthy discussion among Eastern and Western men of the pen."[80] Those men of the pen included Ottoman satirists. The "woman question," as it is sometimes called, involves a complicated set of issues and it is not within the scope of this study thoroughly to explore them.[81] What follows is, rather, an attempt to show some of the ways that the "woman question" was linked to fashion and how it played in the press and in the Ottoman cartoon space.

Deniz Kandiyoti has noted that "treatments of the 'woman question' in novels of the late Ottoman and early republican periods served as a vocabulary to debate the questions of cultural and national integrity, notions of order and disorder, and finally conceptions of the indigenous relative to the foreign."[82] Cartoons debated these same questions. Woman's place was an issue of identity and of survival. It was a subset of the larger questions of the place of the empire in the world and the place of Ottomans in Westernizing society.[83] The Ottoman press's treatment of the woman question might be divided roughly into the categories of feminism, the vote, and woman's political roles; the modern citizen and women's education; and marriage, the family, and women's domestic roles.

Feminism, of course, was only one element in the Ottoman press's treatment of the woman question. As a movement, feminism was treated in the press, although frequently as a foreign phenomenon, and often as an oddity rather than a serious political concern.[84] Its treatment does, however, reflect the fact that feminism and the rights of women were pertinent and contested issues of the day. Various gazettes showed pictures of suffragette activities abroad.[85] *İstişare,* in a section entitled "Laughing and Weeping," considered the problematic effects of feminism for Ottoman women.[86] Elsewhere, critical essays examined the status of Western women as an avenue for exploring the social and educational possibilities of the newly imagined Ottoman constitutional order. And the press functioned as a forum for debate on the woman question.[87] *Beyan ül-hak,* a conservative gazette, in its October 1908 issue, for example, contained a discussion of European ("Frank") women in its politics section and a discussion of Muslim women in its society section.[88] *İştirak,* a socialist journal, carried an exhortative article on the "working girl" as the lead piece in its sixth issue. This piece finished with a dramatic vision of the miserable female laborer, working endlessly and facing misery and oppression: "Work, for two *kuruş.* And the manufacturer, in one day, from your efforts, earns ten *kuruş.*"[89]

Some of the ambiguities inherent in the position of women are evident in the themes and images of women's gazettes or women's sections in the periodicals of the revolutionary era. *Mahasin* (Charms) an illustrated women's gazette that began publication in September 1908, in a single issue, for example, contained all of the following: dramatic romanticized images of women, ads for clothing patterns, and a "hymn to liberty," in French and Ottoman. A good proportion of the articles were written by women, but the article on the laws and duties of women was written by a man.[90] "Feminist," as a simple designation for such gazettes, would be an anachronism; but *Mahasin* illustrates the placing of women as participants in the revolutionary project and the degree to which women as authors and contributors to the press had already become institutionalized.[91] Other gazettes targeted women in special sections. *Muhit* ran European-style fiction along with soup recipes; and *Resimli İstanbul* showed a female military volunteer in Thessaly on one page and young Parisian ladies in a hot air balloon club on the opposite page. The latter gazette also gave advice on modern child care.[92]

The situation for the women of Istanbul after the Young Turk revolution was perhaps analogous to that posed by one author for mid-nineteenth-century America: "Though some women were marching out into fields sacred to men and in 1848 dared organize the first Women's Rights Convention, most knew and cherished their place."[93] The "cherished," of course, for many women, would be difficult to document. But, judging by discussions in the Ottoman press, it is clear that the male authors, on one side and the other, were quite certain they knew what woman's place should be.

After the Young Turk regime was established, the debate over the woman question intensified and became institutionalized. In 1913, Celal Nuri (a noted writer and journalist) published a work on the woman question, entitled *Kadınlarımız* (Our Women), which discussed the history and position of women, their education and role as nurturers of the next generation, marriage, the family, and gender relations.[94] In 1914 the University was opened to women. Cemal Pasha, writing of his term as governor of Istanbul just before World War I, wrote: "Nevertheless the Women's Movement which began with my term of office not only did not die out as time went on, but extended and developed continuously and rendered the greatest service during the war. I am absolutely convinced that the civilizing agencies of a country can best and soonest be promoted with the help of woman, and that those nations which keep their womankind in a state of slavery are on the high road to inevitable decay."[95] By the early 1920s, Halide Edib, in a published lecture on "Turkish Women," was tracing the history of the feminist movement in Turkey and in the West to its antecedents in Sparta, Rome, and Islam.[96] The issue of women's place in Islamic society and the imitation of European ways was also raised in gazettes like *Hikmet*.[97]

These discussions were not directly a function of the revolution; they were, rather, part of a complex and continuing debate on the place of women in modern society, in Muslim societies and, specifically, in the empire.[98] They were part of what Kandiyoti has called, "a painful and bitter process of negotiation and compromise between the pressures of foreign powers, the requirements of modernity as perceived by different sections of the Ottoman elite, and the resistance of those most threatened by changes in the Ottoman order."[99]

The revolution would not bring an immediate or dramatic transformation in the position of women; what it did do was open up various forums for debate on the woman question. Neither the constitutional revolution in the empire nor that in Iran brought women the vote; the struggle for Ottoman women's suffrage, as in contemporaneous struggles in the West, was slow going. The Iranian constitution of 1909 specifically named women as the first group "absolutely disqualified from electoral functions." Other excluded groups were bankrupts, apostates, murderers, children, foreigners, and "persons not of full understanding."[100] While the Ottoman empire was, in many ways, closer than Iran to Westernizing influences, it was not yet ready to give serious consideration to women's suffrage.

This lack of readiness was neatly expressed in the satirical press, its coverage, in many ways, a direct reflection of the debate over the woman question in the serious press. Right after the revolution, *Kalem* published a farce on, "Our Women," a long speech, signed "White Cat," about the new things women wanted.[101] Humorous pieces, stories, and dialogues depicted women's meetings, clubs, discussions, and pretensions to a political voice. *Boşboğaz*, for example, in a piece entitled "Women's Deputy," depicted a gathering of women in the house of Baha Efendi, a handkerchief seller. "There were women of all sorts: young, old, elaborately dressed, unpretentious. Nearly a third of the crowd consisted of children. In order to deliver themselves from the tumult, the mischievous ones were placed in another room and told, 'Play here.' Only those from a month or two old to two or two and a half remained at [their mothers'] knees or clasped to their breasts."[102] Other satirists lampooned the idea of women meeting for political purposes. *Davul* showed a woman addressing a conference on the question of veiling. While her hair, face, and body were covered, the lower part of her jaw was exposed. This, she claimed, was "progress—thanks to Europeanization!"[103] *Kalem* ran a humorous essay, in French, on the supposed formation of a "*syndicat féminin*," which had to resolve the problem that the word "*syndicat*" was masculine.[104] *Karakuş Ezop*, in one of its Karagöz-type dialogues, linked frivolous, money-squandering women to clubs, concerts, and newspapers.[105]

Five years after the revolution, in 1913, women's associations were still the target of humor and sexual innuendo in the cartoon space. In one cartoon, Karagöz suggested that the modernization of women was a puzzling proposition. The frame shows a two-story building packed with women; women and their children are also gathered outside its door, conversing (Figure 8.11). The sign on the building says "Women's World Bureau." The comic hero and his sidekick are walking by:

Karagöz: Mercy, what's this here, Hacivat?
Hacivat: Didn't you see the sign? Its the Women's World Bureau.
Karagöz: Really! I would have thought it was a wedding house.[106]

This cartoon plays upon the idea of the ways that women could be imagined. For Karagöz, such a house overflowing with women meant only one thing, a "hen-party" to celebrate a wedding. The notion of women gathering to organize politically was not yet a familiar thought. The context for this cartoon is undoubtedly the proliferation of women's associations, including one called The Defense of the Rights of Women. Its gazette, called *Kadınlar Dünyası* or *Women's World,* began publication in 1913.[107]

The cartoon space was sometimes outspoken and sometimes reserved on the debate over women's place. There, possibilities could be explored, positions ridiculed, theories advanced, boundaries tested. This is not to say that Ottoman cartoon satire advocated any type of radical transformation in the roles of women.[108] Quite the contrary, satire of women's place tended to stick to relatively conventional areas of politics and of domestic life. But on the themes of gender and society, Ottoman cartoons both reflected and shaped the concerns, the preoccupations, and the speculations of a society in rapid transition.

Even though the idea of Ottoman women deputies was held up as laughable rather than as a distinct possibility, cartoons show that the idea of women's political participation was certainly not considered unthinkable. After all, women in Iran were writing to newspapers urging the government

Figure 8.11 Women's World Bureau

to take steps in the process of emancipating women and, in 1911, three hundred women marched into the public galleries of parliament, "with pistols hidden under their long veils, and threatened to shoot any deputy willing to submit" to Russian threats.[109] But the great mass of Ottoman women, like the great mass of Iranian women, was not rising up and demanding equal rights.[110] That some did seek such rights was often attributed to the deleterious effects of Western influences; and European dress was the symbol of those influences. It is here that the question of fashion is critical because, as shown, the same women who advocated Western dress were often depicted as violating political and social boundaries. They represented the possible encroachment of women into previously male-only spheres. Those concerns had been exacerbated by the political transformation of the revolution, by the advances in female education, and by the influence of Europeans (and educated Ottomans) agitating for the liberation of women, however that might be construed.[111] Concern over fashion in the Ottoman press echoed the same fears that had been expressed in London, a generation earlier, in an 1883 *Fortnightly Review* article entitled "Modern Dress," fears that female fashion was inextricably linked to social disorder: "As our social conditions grow more and more chaotic and disturbed, so do many women claim to be a law to themselves and their followers in dress. This is helped partly by that absence of authoritiative models already referred to; partly by the increased yearning in a large section of the sex for emancipation from all trammels."[112]

In France too, the prospect of unrestrained women was intimately associated with shopping and fashion consumption. European observers linked the advent of the department store in Europe to a sort of moral degradation deriving from the inability of women to control themselves when they were left untended and faced with dazzling arrays of fashionable goods. This view is illlustrated by Miller in his study of the Bon Marché. Miller cites Pierre Gifford describing the female shopper in 1882. The wife is left for long hours, "to go on and on in the wonderful storehouse of attractions where she empties her purse, her eyes on fire, her face reddened, her hand shivering, placed on that of the gloves salesman," while her husband goes off to patronize the whorehouses.[113]

The debate over fashion was, at its core, a debate over morals, social order, and women's place.[114] In the Ottoman cartoon space, European fashion stood as metaphor for the various challenges to the traditional orders of things. Thus, even though the position of women was not necessarily a major issue in the Ottoman revolutionary press, it was an issue that lurked on the fringes of many other issues, an issue that would not go away. Often it expressed itself in treatments of the effect of fashion on the moral and family order and on the hierarchy of patriarchy. More often it found expression in issues of extravagance, honor, social inequity, and political and economic subordination.

An interesting example of the combining of images of fashion and

Fashion Satire

women's morality can be found in the pages of *Falaka*. This cartoon shows a large balance scale, one side labeled "East" (Şark), and one side labelled "West" (Garb). On the "Western" side are two fashionably dressed woman and a crying child. On the "Eastern" side, there are also two women and a child holding a doll (Figure 8.12). The "Eastern" women are dressed in bastardized or partly Western style but one wears a filmy veil. The scale is tipped in favor of the "East." The caption reads: "The women of a nation should not simply be a measure of the degree of its progress, but a proof of the degree of its moral purity (*iffet*)." The gazette's two mascots are smiling and pointing at the tipped scale The falakacı says excitedly, "Look, Deli Oğlan! Ours again, ours are still heavier! [Life and] love to you!"[115]

This cartoon can be interpreted in a number of ways. First of all, it clearly demonstrates the conscious and continuous weighing in the Ottoman press of the empire against Europe. It also shows the Eurpeanization of women's styles that was at once marked, incomplete, and the target of satire. Finally, it points up the inclination in the satirical press to conflate immorality and Westernized progress and to use *alafranga* dress as suggestive of moral decline. Beyond those representations, the cartoon proposes that progress (*terakki*) remains an area in which Ottoman women fall short of their European counterparts. But, when it came to a choice between progress or chastity, Ottoman men are shown to be clearly more enthusiastic about the latter.

FASHION, IDENTITY, AND THE SOCIAL ORDER

Fashion was a metaphor for the social order. It was used not only to attack foreign intervention and differentiate the Europeanized from the traditional, but also directly to satirize social problems associated with the old and new regimes. The symbolic function, then, of fashion satire in the Ottoman revolutionary press was not so much to urge or to reject a social leveling, but rather to distinguish those who either bolstered or threatened the values of the nation, as each satirist interpreted them. In this sense, the points of concern of the Ottoman press were not directly analogous to those, for example, of the French revolutionary press. Ribiero, in a study of French fashion images, has elaborated upon the self-conscious way in which the French revolutionaries linked dress and ideology. "From the beginning of the revolution . . . much consideration was given to the question of dress and how far appearances should contribute to the concept of equality."[116] The Ottomans were also self-conscious about dress, but neither the reformist codes of the nineteenth century nor the revolution obliterated customary associations of dress with social position.[117] The class of occupants of Ottoman cartoon frames was readily apparent from their dress and accoutrements. While Ottoman cartoons can certainly be compared to the infamous plates of Daumier, satirizing the French bourgeoisie in the nineteenth cen-

Figure 8.12 The Balance of Chastity

tury, the fashion preoccupations of Ottoman satire were not directed solely at delegitimizing one particular class within Ottoman society.

Unlike French revolutionary satire's clothes-branding of the three estates, Ottoman revolutionary cartoons focused on fashion satire to target the political inequity of Europe versus the "East." Certainly the "crown" was targeted; but the turban of the "clergy" did not figure prominently as a threat to Ottoman society.[118] At worst, religion symbolized social backwardness. Often, however, it was considered a force for "traditional" social solidarity. Faced with the threat of conquest, the Ottoman satirists could ill afford to undermine any such forces for strength or unity. Conversely, foreign domination, dressed in top hat or silk petticoats, was an obvious target.

The economic, moral, and social challenge of imported European fashions and associated mores was thus portrayed in the press as a threat to the integrity of the nation. Dress, in the construction of national identity posed the same dilemma for the Ottomans that it had for the French in the aftermath of revolution. Neither the garb of an idealized past nor that of a subjugated or subjugating "other" quite fit. In 1799, when Napoleon returned from Egypt, he appeared in Paris in Mamluk costume, donning the garb of the defeated Egyptian military caste as a symbol of his claimed "triumph."[119] Later, seizing power in France, Napoleon dispersed the French deputies whose togas, donned in appreciation of an heroic age, became "melancholy symbols of departed dignity."[120] Were the newly "liberated" Ottoman revolutionaries to celebrate their own success by assuming the garb of those who wished to conquer them? Their own symbols of the heroic past had been humiliated by the economic and military superiority of Russia, Austria, England, and France. European dress had been intended, by Selim III in his eighteenth-century reforms, to transform the Ottoman military—cloth imbued with a certain animistic prowess. But, like the "emperor's new clothes," those uniforms had proved a deception. European-style uniforms, when finally adopted, had not brought victory to Ottoman armies. Nor would European topcoats and Parisian gowns necessarily bring success to a constitutional Ottoman society. Thus, for the satirists, the costumes available to clothe the new Ottoman constitutional identity were tainted by associations either with autocracy or imperialism.

After the revolution, the press satirized both the disposal of the old order (symbolized by its uniforms) and the imitation of European dress as signifying acquiescence to conquest. One revolutionary gazette showed the new ministers conducting a liquidation sale on the uniforms of the old official class (Figure 8.13).[121] This cartoon implied that the old order was being liquidated as well, disrupting Ottoman society and leaving the state, perhaps, at the mercy of outside forces. Would the "shining armor" of the meclis members substitute for ships and a well-equipped and orderly soldiery? The Ottoman satirists thought not, portraying the new government and its arsenal as grossly inadequate to meet the challenge of European power. Fashion satire, during the revolution, revealed this sense of unease. It

Figure 8.13 Uniform Sale

demonstrated that no domestic issues could be interpreted outside of the context of a possible colonial outcome to the unequal struggle between the new Ottoman state and European imperial powers.

Dress would not take down the barriers between Ottoman and European. Fashion satire was used to portray the disruption of social hierarchies that resulted from European hegemony, imported technology dispossessing established labor interests, Western education spreading contempt for "traditional" values, and "new" dress and manners undermining the positions of established elites.[122] It made manifest the notion that European dominance and Ottoman subordination could result in social ills even worse than those associated with the despotic regime of the sultan.[123]

By World War I and the early 1920s, the treatment of political and cultural imperialism in the Ottoman press had become even more sophisticated. Journals like *Diken* satirized the United States, England, and France, which were portrayed as stripping the Ottomans naked, while women's gazettes, like *Sevimli Ay* included articles on everything from women working, to European hats, to European-style kissing.[124] The difference between the satire of the revolution and that written at the end of the war was that in 1908 the Ottoman writers were more optimistic about the empire taking its place in the European dominated world order. By 1918, their attitudes had changed. Atatürk had not yet led the revolt that saved Ottoman Turkey from the post–World War I partition that made the Arab provinces protectorates of Europe; and the Ottoman press had no illusions that western Europe intended a partnership in progress.

IX

Dogs, Crime, Women, Cholera, and Other Menaces in the Streets

Cartoon satire was very conscious of space: territorial, cultural, intellectual and political. Like their French and English counterparts, Ottoman satirists took their fair share of shots at personal space (the private lives of parliamentary ministers and the like), but it was in the realms of the public space that revolutionary satire struck its most telling blows. Much of the Ottoman cartoon revolution took place in the streets of Istanbul. In the streets, the revolution was at its most vulnerable: bungling city services, inviting its women to outrage public propriety, and making itself ridiculous with its hodge-podge parliamentarians—all before the anxious gaze of press and populace. Just as the new street lights were beginning to illumine the city's streets, Ottoman satirists were using the Istanbul streets as a backdrop for their project to illuminate the ills of the empire.

The identity crisis of the revolution was thus reflected in cartoons showing Ottomans in the streets. The ideal Ottoman street, complete with street lights, traffic police, department stores, a national theatre, electric trolleys, and a serene woman aviator was depicted in a cartoon called "Türkiye, Fifty Years Later," from the journal *Kalem*.[1] This fanciful street scene comprises some of the wishes for European-style progress that the press suggested the revolution might fulfill (Figure 9.1). But it also combines many of the targets of revolutionary satire into one cartoon (the streets, the police, transport, women's dress, and the press). This particular euphoric vision of the future is in direct contrast to a more jaundiced vision of the Ottoman street, found in many Ottoman cartoons, which imagines dark and unsafe streets, a corrupt police force, inefficient attempts to modernize transport, and women and men made ridiculous by forcing them into unsuitable European clothes or contexts. One such cartoon, for example, showed a ragged mailman in a dog-pulled postal cart, going nowhere. The cartoon's caption read, "The rapidity of postal service is absolutely assured."[2] Through such cartoons, the Ottoman press satirized Ottoman society, Ottoman government, and itself, suggesting that idyllic revolutionary visions of resurrected glory were as far from Ottoman reality as were black clad females soaring through the streets of the capital.

Figure 9.1 Istanbul Fifty Years Later

Menaces in the Streets

In the streets, the Ottoman and his revolution were compromised in a variety of ways. He was subject to a number of menaces, some of which were controllable and some of which were uncontrollable. Images from the Ottoman cartoon space suggest four such menaces: dogs, crime, women in European-style fashions, and cholera; they illustrate how the Ottoman empire's struggle to redefine itself after the revolution combined an assessment of social and cultural ills with the critique of European imperialism.

The press did not attribute all the ills of Istanbul to a European induced "new" social order. Some ills, like "scandalous" women, stray dogs, crime, and cholera were old dilemmas. Yet the images of women, dogs, and disease came to be associated (in cartoons) with European hegemony, as a force that exacerbated and made public and embarrassing the old ills. It was in the streets that Istanbul's social problems were made manifest for native and foreigner alike to see. As European economic dominance brought more outsiders to Istanbul, the Ottomans were subjected to the painful scrutiny of civilizational comparisons that presupposed their own inferiority.[3] One such comparison was penned in 1890 by an American observer: "The barbaric virtues of the [Turkish] invader have given place to a sham civilization, as unlike the European as the Stamboul costume is to that after which it is patterned; and decay and degradation have set their stamp on Stamboul, which nature has done its best to beautify, and man to mar."[4] Sensitive to this scrutiny, the new regime had to decide whether to clean the streets or to proclaim them as a legitimate reflection of Ottoman culture.

Stray dogs, cholera, and crime were social ills whose treatment became inextricably linked to notions of European "progress." In Europe, "scientific" methods had apparently been devised to take care of these plagues and to make urban living more "civilized." There was a certain sense of shame that Ottomans were somehow less "advanced." For the Ottomans, progress in this context could not be viewed as uniquely desirable because it required a concomitant admission, via imitation, of European cultural and technological superiority. It was a progress whose method was defined abroad. European superiority in the Ottoman press took the forms of sanitation committees, dog catchers, or modern police forces. Images of these indicators of progress, of cultural integrity, and of European imperialism were integrated and intertwined in the cartoon space, which suggested that the Ottomans could not generate a unilateral notion of acceptable and happy progress.

In the press, the blame for public nuisances was first apportioned, part to European imperialism, part to civil administrators, and part to public morality. There was unanimity on the need to eradicate a social ill like cholera. Dogs and crime were more complex social phenomena, the dogs because they were sentient beings, represented by some as part of the cherished essence of the old city, crime because it was tied to notions of a tacit partnership between the criminals and corrupt officials. Women were problematic because their dress and behavior was an inescapable reminder that the Ottomans were being subjected to a loss of economic control over fashion, as well as social control over morality. Woman, in the street or the cafe, dressed in European fashion, became a symbol of this humiliation as well as a symbol of liberation. Yet, as noted in the previous chapter, the female form and its drapery, as symbol, were imbedded in a complex web of cultural assumptions not readily reducible to polarizations of occident/ orient, imitation/resistance, or patriarch/subordinate. Class, religion, ethnicity, attempts to articulate the nation, distinctions of urban and rural culture, and the idealized images of literature, poetry, and music, all contributed to the construction of women in the cartoon space of the Ottoman revolutionary press.

DOGS—A MANAGEABLE PLAGUE

Dogs were a plague on the streets of Istanbul in 1908.[5] But street dogs were also part of the literary imagery used to embody the city.[6] Early in the century, one resident described the city's sounds in this way: "To the conglomeration of advertising tunes was added the shrill monotonous barking of the world-famed dogs, who bark, apparently, with the simple desire of adding to the noises of the hot city; for they bark even when eating."[7]

In this image, the chronic aggravation of Istanbul's dog packs is combined with the notion that the dogs are a characteristic, and familiar part of the traditional Istanbul urban landscape. Other sympathetic observers pointed out that the dogs were useful for their role in the disposal (or consumption) of garbage. Or, as one satirist in the gazette *Alem* put it, "The municipality seems to feel that it can clean the streets without recourse to these precious auxiliaries."[8] Less sympathetic observers, however, saw the dogs, like the garbage, as a municipal cleaning problem. In cartoons, the dog-packs came to symbolize the dilemma of how the new constitutional regime would control and order the social space. They became a measure of its efficiency. The dogs were a nuisance, and the task of the regime was to get rid of them. If the revolutionary government could not hold off the dogs of Europe maneuvering for territorial spoils, it could at least demonstrate its effectiveness by removing the dogs from Istanbul, a manageable domestic task in an unmanageable world.

The new government did, in fact, manage to eradicate the dogs. A 1909 Ottoman almanac showed barefoot workers using pitchforks to throw Istanbul street-dog carcasses from carts onto a boat for dumping.[9] The workers grinned for the camera. This photograph evokes an ordered form of street cleaning. Its inclusion in an almanac, along with schools and other indicators of "progress," suggests that the revolutionary regime considered the elimination of the dogs a triumph of municipal government. A.V. Williams Jackson, a professor of Indo-Iranian Languages at Columbia, traveling through Istanbul in 1907, described the streets as a place "where hurrying feet can scarce find space to avoid the packs of mangy curs that do duty as town scavengers."[10] On his return in 1911, Jackson noted approvingly that the dogs had been eliminated. Mary Mills Patrick, an American professor at the Constantinople Woman's College, lauded the Young Turk regime for having eradicated the dogs that, she noted, "were rightly considered to be out of place in a civilized city."[11]

In the eyes of some European observers, however, this effort was a symbol not of progressive government but of Ottoman barbarism. A British officer, Sir Mark Sykes, regretted the passing of the dogs as he regretted the passing of the old sultanic regime. He characterized the regime of Abd ül-Hamid as one where everything and everyone had its place: "there was a grand and noble toleration—the harmless idiot, the dogs, the poor, the beggars, the orphans, each had their place."[12] Place was a very important concept for British imperialists like Sykes, and also for those attempting to reconstruct the Ottoman empire after the revolution.[13] The new constitutional order disrupted a sense of place: getting rid of the old bureaucratic organization, getting rid of the dogs, defining new roles for women. Just as the nineteenth-century planners altered the landscape of Istanbul to make way for French-style flats and boulevards, the revolutionary regime saw itself sweeping the old political, social, and urban spaces to make room for a new order. For Sykes, the revolution disrupted the "proper" order of things in the streets of the Ottoman capital. It was not his concern that the dogs were a nuisance; they were a symbol of his romantic notion of a timeless Istanbul. Hence their removal, for him, was indicative of the insensitive nature of the Ottoman authorities. Dogs were still viewed as a plague in much of the Middle East, but the European elite classes had already discovered pet-culture.[14] After the revolution, Sykes noted: "The dogs were killed in 1909 with the same cruel fury, ruthless and senseless stupidity as the honest [Ottoman] soldiers were thrown away in 1912 [fighting in the Balkan and Libyan wars]."[15] Sykes returned to Istanbul in 1913 to report that the dogs were gone but that cholera had come to stay, an outcome that symbolized for him the misplaced priorities of the constitutional regime.

Ultimately, the Ottoman government came around to Sykes point of view where dogs and "progress" were concerned. By 1913, the Ottoman police gazette held up Paris and New York as exemplars for proper canine control. No more dirty laborers forking dead dogs. The police gazette showed the latest in technology and animal humane treatment: a fine French dog catcher equipped with shining uniform, new truck, serious visage, and individual cages for captured strays.[16]

Sykes's critique of the revolution, sympathy for the dogs, and romanticization of the old regime are representative both of European scorn and of the paradoxical position of the new Ottoman regime. Both the cur-infested streets and the Ottoman government's efforts to alleviate the problem drew the contempt of foreign observers. The Ottoman regime, anxious for British and French support and approval, was faced with swallowing this scorn and seeking methods more palatable to European notions of progress.

There was, indeed, a certain incongruity in the Ottoman position—unable to remain romantic, progressive, and intact at the same time. For Sykes, an ideal Istanbul was one that most closely approximated a certain English notion of the proper ordering of "Oriental" political and cultural space. For Ottoman cartoonists, that political and cultural space housed an empire that appeared helpless, unable to defend itself from the external threats of European imperialism or from the internal threat of domestic disorder and chaos. The apparent helplessness of the empire led cartoonists to equate the Istanbul street dogs with the Ottoman people.

Dogs became a metaphor for Ottoman society itself. Associated with images of eating, dogs also symbolized notions of choice and subordination, who ate and who did not. This dichotomy was presented in a striking cartoon showing two dogs watching a poor man eat his bread. The caption was an oft cited Ottoman proverb:

"*Biri [yi]yer, biri bakar, kıyamet ondan kopar.*" (When one eats and one watches, tumult will soon follow)[17]

This same proverb was repeated in the slogan for the journal, called *İştirak*, of the Ottoman Socialist Party, founded in 1910. In cartoons, the dogs of Istanbul came to represent the empire itself, as beggar, whose eradication was demanded in the name of progress, yet whose resourcefulness in attempting to survive evoked a certain sympathy.[18] After the revolution, the dog packs of Istanbul, long tolerated, would be subjected to systematic annihilation, just like the empire in the face of European imperial ambitions. In the world of "eat or be eaten," both were prey. This identifying with the "underdogs" brought into the press images equating the dogs with the Ottoman people: starving, oppressed, and at the mercy of foreign entrepreneurs and an unsympathetic government. Dogs were shown presenting a petition to the municipality protesting their own eradication (Figure 9.2). The caption reads, "Unlawful Assembly: A Protest to the City Government."[19] This frame echoed many similar images that showed various groups within Ottoman society petitioning the unsympathetic or unhearing officials of government to hear their demands and address their needs.

The dogs thus engendered sympathy as a symbol of resistance to changing an old, traditional, and perhaps more humane order.[20] Cartoons showed that the comfortable old order of things had been subverted. In these images, the old sultanic order, ideologically rooted in the notion of the circle of justice (a system whereby the prosperity of the state depended upon just rule responsive to the needs of the people), had been overturned. Abd ül-Hamid's tyranny had subverted the political and social order, reducing his subjects to the low status of dogs, fighting for their livelihood and with no legitimate avenue to seek redress for their ills. Only unwillingly did a

Figure 9.2 Petitioning Against Their Eradication

man equate himself with a dog; but, under conditions of despotism and imperialism, animals were transformed into spokesmen for the people, as they were in classical folktales like *Kalilah wa Dimna*.[21] Dogs and asses would demand justice in Ottoman satire, if there was no one else to do so.

The equation of human beings, especially the poor, with dogs is a theme that also appeared obliquely in the shadow puppet theater. In one such shadow play, a drunkard informs Karagöz, "One has to earn one's livelihood albeit by cleaning the streets of dead dogs."[22] The drunkard, in this scene, had been attempting to persuade Karagöz (who had described himself as "a highly qualified loafer") to accept a job. Their repartee paired the poor man in the street (Karagöz) with the street dogs who might also be classified as highly qualified loafers. It also suggests that the removal of dog carcasses was one avenue the city municipality had for giving employment to the urban poor. Thus, the shadow play, like the revolutionary press, drew bonds of sympathy and humor between the dogs of Istanbul and the man on the street. In the end, the dog packs, besides creating a public nuisance, symbolized the inability of the regime to provide for the basic order and security of its citizens.

CRIME AND THE POLICE

Where dogs were a solvable problem for the new regime, crime apparently was not. The satirization of crime took several forms. For one thing, it was suggested that the revolution and its associated disorders produced a crime spree. Many accounts associate the revolution and the interregnum that followed it (through the counter-revolution of April 1909) with a dramatic increase in urban crime and lawlessness, not only in the capital but throughout the empire.[23] Indeed the new order was accompanied by a release of both political prisoners and criminals.[24] The same reconfiguration of law that permitted the flourescence of the long-gagged press permitted a reordering of the structures of authority including the police. The proposed metamorphosis of the police, for example, was a hot topic in the press in the months after the revolution. But cartoon satire associated this reordering with confusion and license. The failure of the constitutional government to control crime symbolized the similarity of the new regime to the old and affirmed the notion that political reform could not produce domestic tranquility any more than it could create secure foreign relations. The press suggested that efforts to control crime, like those to revitalize the military, were merely cosmetic. Finally, crime, as a plague in the streets, was inextricably linked to the police force as a plague on the citizens. *Volkan*, for example, published an article entitled: "Police or Robber (*Polis mi Hırsız mı*)?"[25]

In the cartoon space, satires of crime were often satires of the police. Cartoonists of the revolutionary press gleefully depicted a revamped police force sporting new Western-style uniforms but caught in the old quagmire of corruption and indifference. There were some cartoons that celebrated the "new" police, contrasting young, noble-looking officers to old-style officers, slovenly and inefficient. Such images are found, for example, under the rubrics "*yeni*" (new) and "*eski*" (old), in *Alem*, showing an alert young officer gazing askance at a sloppy, nose-picking old officer, and in *Şakaa*, showing a neat and alert "new" officer contrasted to a squinty-eyed, unbuttoned, "old" policeman who looks more like a crook than like an enforcer of the law.[26] But many more cartoons showed the new regime's police as merely a reincarnation (in new clothes) of the old. The police, in these images were accused of brutality, inefficiency, laziness, taking bribes, and looking the other way while citizens were victimized by criminals.[27] *Protesto*, for example, ran a cartoon showing a policeman smoking a cigarette while a robber stalked an affluent-looking man with packages and, in the background, two men stabbed a victim.[28]

As in other forms of satire, costume was used as a target in caricatures of the police. *İncili çavuş* announced the new uniforms in its "news" section: "It has been learned that three hundred new uniforms for the police were delived to the Ministry of Police yesterday"; and commented: "Mercy, let us see no more of the old."[29] This "announcement" equated the uniforms with their wearers and expressed relief at the idea that the old police force was a thing of the past. But some satirists suggested that the new uniforms of the police simply served to delude citizen and criminal alike into imagining that things had changed. The serious press, too, expressed its thoughts on police reform and uniform changes; *Serbesti* clucked: "It is our hope that [the administration] will not content itself simply with changing the [police] uniforms."[30] Meanwhile, *Al-Üfürük* posed the image of the (old) police uniforms being placed in the "imperial museum," where they would be exposed to the public as a symbol of the era of despotism.[31]

New uniforms not only failed to make the police more effective but, acording to one cartoon in *Kalem,* rendered them unrecognizable. This frame, captioned "new police uniforms," showed a thief hollering for forgiveness as a policeman struck him. He protested, "Don't blame me, I wouldn't have done it had I recognized you in your new uniform!"[32] This cartoon symbolized the chaotic conditions associated with administrative change. Change in costume meant change in custom; it meant confusion and disorder. But new uniforms would not solve Istanbul's crime problems.[33]

The satirical gazette that took most consistent aim at the police force was *Alem*, a bilingual gazette in Ottoman and French. It featured a variety of cartoons and narrative satires on the faults and inadequacies of the police. One of its most dramatic and telling images is a caricature of the Minister of Police who is shown in a Napoleonesque pose, hand tucked in his jacket.[34] The minister leans on his long sword, the point of which is peircing the breast of a naked and supine infant. He seems oblivious to the damage he has inflicted. Elsewhere, the gazette depicted the policemen as buffoons or skeletons on horseback. It imagined the Chief of Police touring Istanbul police stations and instructing the officers not to go out on the streets after nine at night for fear of being robbed.[35] In one cartoon, *Alem* showed a policeman, rifle resting over his arm, standing idly by while hooligans beat and robbed a man on the street.[36] This same scene, suggesting police indifference, was repeated in various forms in other satirical gazettes. Another variant of the same theme is suggested in a set of silhouette drawings accompanying a satirical piece on "Our Police."[37] *Alem*, which pursued the question of police corruption most doggedly, suggested that the police were not only ineffectual, but that they harassed and made life miserable for the Ottoman citizen.

Kalem showed a mock vision of instruction in the police academy. The classroom windows are full of spider webs. In the back row of desks, one cadet is asleep while another tries to tickle him (Figure 9.3). In the front row, a standing student responds to the question of a somnolent instructor. "What is the police?" the instructor asks. "It is the means of the enforcement of justice," responds the student. The next question, "What is justice?" draws the following reply: "The regular payment of salary."[38] That answer might draw some sympathy from readers aware of the irregular nature of salary payments to government functionaries during Abd ül-Hamid's reign. But the more cynical message of this cartoon is that the police, at best, are only looking out for their own interests. The classroom also contains a poster that enhances that sinister message. This particular "instructional material" shows a criminal preparing to stab a prostrate and screaming victim while a policeman ambles in the other direction.

The police were often charged with indifference in the satiric gazettes. Cartoons show police officers chatting on the street while thieves slip daggers into unsuspecting passersby, or taking bribes to look the other way while street crime proceeds unchecked.[39] *Malum*, for example, ran a satiric dialogue between two policemen. The first comments on hearing some kind of uproar or tumult. The second says, "Yes, probably they're yelling 'Help!'" The first policeman urges him, "Come on, let's go, let's find out what's going on." But the other is nonchalant: "What's the rush? Tomorrow we'll read about it in the newspaper."[40]

In a similar vein, *Kalem* sketched a dialogue between a policeman and a police superintendent (*komiser*). The *komiser* shakes his finger in exasperation at the policeman while nearby a thief is running off with a bag of loot (Figure 9.4). "Hey policeman. Do you expect to catch this thief?" The policeman, who is seated and smoking his water-pipe, replies: "It'll be easier to catch him when he's in custody."[41] In another cartoon, *Alafranga* shows a citizen demanding that a policeman pursue a fleeing killer while another culprit with a long knife lurks in the police-box right behind the policeman's back.[42] Other frames emphasized the absence of the police rather than their lackadaisical performance. *Kalem*, for example, in a frame entitled "Old-Style Security," showed one man approaching another on a

Ecole de Police.

LE PROFESSEUR. — Qu'est-ce que la police ?
L'ÉLÈVE. — C'est l'instrument de la justice.
LE PROFESSEUR. — Et qu'est-ce que la justice ?
L'ÉLÈVE — La régularité des appointements.

Figure 9.3 Police Academy

— Est-ce que vous ne pouvez pas arrêter ce voleur qui fuit?
— Oui, mais après qu'il aura été attrapé.

Figure 9.4 Pursuing a Thief

darkened street (Figure 9.5). A knife hidden behind his back, the first enquires: "Sir, have you by chance come across a policeman hereabouts?" When the other answers in the negative, the first exclaims, "Well then, hand over your money!"[43]

Charges of failing to serve the public and represent justice were used to illustrate the continuity between the police forces of the old and new regimes. The police under Abd ül-Hamid had also been associated with punitive actions against the populace. As one foreign observer wrote in 1904: "The extraordinary interference by the police and the Government with individual liberty has, indeed, made Turkish life in the capital a somewhat gloomy business."[44] The message in the revoutionary gazettes, then, was that the police remained a force for oppression. They were visible symbols, like tax collectors, of the ways in which the government, despite its rhetorics of freedom, interfered in the day-to-day lives of citizens. Such interference may have been tolerable had the police served their primary function of providing security. But the satirists proposed that the police did not protect the people either. According to the satirists, the revolution had created a demand, a language, and a rhetoric of "citizens" rights that the constitutional regime was unprepared to deliver in the realm of law enforcement.

The police, like the *muhtesib* (a combination market inspector, peace officer, and enforcer of public morality) in the traditional organization of Islamic urban space, were associated with a diverse set of municipal responsibilities. Crime prevention was only one aspect of maintaining the public order. Others were sanitation, which included control of dogs and cholera, and public decency, which included control of women.[45] In the satirical gazettes, the police were shown implementing, or attempting to implement, various forms of social control (chastising improperly dressed women or attempting to negotiate traffic altercations) often to the great annoyance or discomfiture of the populace.[46] This image of an interventionist Istanbul police force is reflected in the memoirs of Cemal Pasha, who served as governor of Istanbul and in several military offices. Cemal Pasha notes, for example, that after the assassination of the grand vezir Mahmud Şevket Pasha, he ordered the police to draw up [and then arrest] "a list of all persons of every class who might be expected to attempt to exploit the situation and start riots in the different quarters of the city."[47] He also notes the use of the police in cracking down on black-market tobacco sales and in controlling sexual harrassment of ladies in the Istanbul streets and bazaars.

A related target of press satire against City Administration agents was the collection of tolls charged to those crossing the Galata Bridge. The bridge tolls, implemented in 1862 and continued until 1926, were satirized in the press and in the Karagöz plays.[48] They were a symbol of the reconstruction of the Istanbul urban space, a reconstruction (and reconception) that included trams, traffic control, utility installations, and building projects. These, along with the "new" constabulary, in the view of the revolution-

— Avez-vous rencontré, Effendi, un agent de police?
— Non.
— Alors, donnez-moi la bourse.
— !!!!

Figure 9.5 Safety in the Streets

ary cartoonists, were indicators that the city streets would remain for the urban citizen a place of disruption and confusion, at least for the foreseeable future.

A final theme associated in Ottoman cartoons with crime control was the illumination of the Ottoman streets with street lamps. Poking fun at the gap between municipal ideals and municipal realities, satirists lampooned the idea that the street lights would lead to a reduction in crime. This notion, in the cartoon space, was just another grandiose "modern" idea that did not live up to its promise. Technological innovations would not automatically solve age-old social problems, like crime.[49] To prove the gullibility of those who thought they would, Ottoman cartoons showed crimes taking place directly under street lamps and citizens amazed that neither the police nor the new illumination could protect them.[50] The criminals and the police, then, survived the attempted modernization of the Ottoman streets more successfully than did the dog packs. Policeman and thief, in the satirist's vision, conspired to make sure that the Ottoman citizen remained unsafe and insecure.

WOMEN—CRISIS OF CULTURE

Insecurity, for the Ottoman citizen, came in many cartoon forms. One of these tropes for insecurity was the figure of woman. Like dogs, women became cartoon symbols of the Ottoman crisis of identity. Literary constructions of woman as temptress or demon, such as those found in the *Arabian Nights* tales, were transformed in cartoon satire into images of woman as pawn of European social and economic power and woman as threat to public morality—woman as menace in the streets.

As noted in the previous chapter, the most characteristic symbol of subversion of Ottoman culture was the dressing of Ottoman women in Paris fashions.[51] The "women's page" of the gazette *Resimli kitab* showed fashions of the season, "desirable, fashionable, elegant."[52] But, in cartoons, the critical message of European fashion went beyond the desirable and the elegant. Ottoman women in European fashions symbolized a challenge to the ability of the empire to control its own social customs. European fashion was used to illustrate the loosing of Ottoman women onto the streets and the exposing of their faces and hair to male gaze.

This was the crux of the dilemma. There had always been women in the Istanbul streets. But the Ottoman revolution, the social and political transformations that the empire was undergoing, and the European cultural invasion were all perceived as contributing to a lack of restraint, a loosing of women on the streets in new and disquieting ways. Deniz Kandiyoti, in her analysis of the Ottoman novel, has expressed the dilemma of Western influence in this way: "in the Ottoman/Turkish novel the point of ultimate degradation is reached when Westernism, in the guise of foolish and feckless young men and 'fashionable' loose women, enters the home, corroding the moral fabric of the family and by extension the society as a whole."[53] Although the fashionable young men are represented as compromising the moral order of Ottoman society, it is, in the cartoon space as in the novel, the *alafranga* women who constitute the real threat to Ottoman morality; it is they who can corrupt absolutely. Such women's behavior runs the gamut from "frivolous and inconsequential" to "truly corrupt," as illustrated in the late-nineteenth-century Ottoman novels *Felatun Beyle Rakım Efendi* and *Aşk-ı Memnu*.

In the revolutionary cartoon, woman as menace was perhaps more often frivolous than truly corrupt. But because the integrity of Ottoman culture was always contingent upon the sexuality of its women and upon their providing a certain continuity in the ordering of society, the image of the frivolous, Westernized, exposed woman always had certain sinister connotations. She suggested a society at risk and boundaries crossed that might never be regained.

Woman as symbolizing the moral fabric of society and of the family is, of course, a theme that crosses cultural, national, class, and racial boundaries. Much work has been done on the social construction of female identity and the imposition of morality in colonial context, but Ottoman historiography, in general, has left those territories as yet unexplored.[54] Suffice it to say, here, that the Ottoman cartoon space employed a set of models for what constituted respectable behavior and that, in the context of the revolution, women dressed in European fashion and women engaged in European-style entertainments were often made to stand for a breaching of propriety and a violation of sexual boundaries. Further, there is a significant class component to this drawing of the lines between respectable and non-respectable, because it is those women with the financial wherewithal and leisure time to consume European styles and entertainments who often constitute the subjects of cartoons that show women loosed on the streets. This is not to suggest that lower-class women were not portrayed as engaging in disreputable behavior. But the revolution, as already noted, provided the occasion for an elevation of the common man and woman in the Ottoman cartoon space and for the construction of new types of non-respectable behavior among the elite classes that were associated with the importation and imitation of European mores.[55] Much of this association is treated in the previous two chapters.

Perhaps the last word on women in the streets, their virtue, and public authority can be left to a brief, humorous dialogue in *Malum*. This sketch is called "The Policeman and the Woman Culprit." It reads as follows:

> Policeman: [apparently in pursuit] Lady! Lady! Look, Hey . . . . don't you listen?
> Woman: An honorable woman does not reply to strangers hollering at her in the street.

This little vignette is telling. It suggests that the woman is indeed guilty of some offense but that the overarching social order allows her to disregard the authority of the policeman with impunity, at least in her own mind. This dilemma of conflicting systems of authority and contending influences is precisely the dilemma involved in the loosing of women on the streets. In certain ways they were supposed to be unapproachable, in others their very presence in public demanded intervention and suggested impropriety. Women loosed on the streets were one more sign of the Ottoman regime's (and Ottoman society's) loss of control. And, in the cartoon space, this image of woman as menace came ultimately to be confounded with that of another type of menace, cholera.

CHOLERA—ANOTHER FAILURE TO CONTROL THE STREETS

Cholera's invasion of the Ottoman empire was contemporaneous with the launching of the Ottoman language press in Istanbul.[56] Spreading over land and seaborne routes from India, cholera struck Istanbul in 1831, the same year that the Ottoman official gazette, *Takvim-i vekayi*, was first published. The Ottoman press thereafter reported upon the incidence of epidemics and on government attempts to control them. It also used the incidence of cholera as an opportunity to critique rather than inform. The gazette *Perde*, for example, in its "internal affairs' section spoke of cholera as an invited guest in a brief vignette entitled, "Welcome cholera!" (*Hoş geldin kolera*).[57] *Malum* railed against the industrial pollution of the drinking water; it demanded action but suggested that nothing would be done.[58] Cartoonists also conjured an image of Ottoman society stricken by a series of infectious diseases. Cholera was used as a stand-in for Westernization, imperialism, immorality; it was fear itself. In these images, cholera surpassed dogs and fashion as a symbol of the ills of empire and the plagues of Europe.[59]

Although quarantine was a control mechanism employed in the Mediterranean basin since the Middle Ages, the association of cholera with "bad air," poverty, and moral depravity impeded the systematic implementation of controls on its transmission.[60] Some of the "remedies" posed worldwide to counter the cholera plagues of the nineteenth century were temperance, moderation, prayer, resignation to divine will, and massive doses of mercury compounds taken internally or rubbed on the skin. If a person could survive the mercury treatments, he or she might survive the cholera. The virulence, rapid onset, and speedy death that characterized cholera magnified its image as the vengeance and punishment of the unseen. But resignation was not the only factor impeding quarantine measures. Cholera control was also an economic issue. "Germ theory" threatened the status and income of traditional medical pratitioners. Quarantine attempts met with systematic resistance from trading and business interests.[61] Proposals for public health measures such as disinfectant spraying, corpse disposal, and isolation of the infected required a high level of governmental organization. Governmental control also required consistent invasion of private domestic spheres, creating popular resistance when customary burial practices, healing and nursing regimens, and household organization were violated by the state or municipality. As one astute foreign observer, Lucy Garnett, noted:

> Quarantine regulations are certainly observed at Constantinople and the other large seaports. But in the towns of the interior, the Moslem population manifest the greatest dislike to such sanitary regulations, which they regard as a profane interference with the will of Allah, and do their best to avoid carrying out. The doctor of the first quarantine station established at Bursa was, for instance, attacked in the street by several hundred Turkish women, who, save for the intervention of the police, would have beaten him to death for his supposed impiety.[62]

Garnett was right about the difficulties involved in cholera control, but her association of resistance with Islam was misguided, since similar objections to sanitation measures were certainly evident elsewhere among non-Muslim populations.

It was, however, in these realms of economic organization, municipal efficiency, and social control that the representations of cholera in the Ottoman satirical press were constructed. Cholera, like crime, illustrated the gap between revolutionary expectations and the realms of social interaction that the constitutional regime failed to control. As the parliament was charged with clearing the government of old regime corruption and oppression (shown in many cartoons as acts of sweeping or cleaning), the city administration was charged with ridding the municipality of disease (shown as an act of spraying). A twentieth-century version of the old Ottoman chronicles, tallying the death tolls of Istanbul's plagues, the press recounted the efforts of the public health administration to obliterate cholera. But the task was not as simple as banishing Abd ül-Hamid's spies and ministers, who were portrayed in the press as the governmental equivalent of the plague. The satirical press also equated cholera control with other bureaucratic systems like police-work and transport, and portrayed it as ineffective, misdirected, and a ludicrous example of the various "pest control" efforts of the new regime. Those efforts were satirized in the gazette *Falaka*, which showed cholera and his skeleton demons dancing and playing before a row of sickbeds representing the do-nothing offices of the City Security Administration (*Şehir Emniyeti*).[63]

In Istanbul, at the time of the revolution, typical treatment measures for cholera were quarantine and spraying lime. Microbe theory was well known in Istanbul by 1908 and was the subject of both scientific educational articles and cartoons in the press. The idea of the unseen microbe provided bountiful grist for the satirist's mill as evidenced by the anthropomorphization of the microbe and by all sorts of microbe caricatures.[64] Microbe cartoons were used to satirize people's ignorance and anxieties. Thus, *İncili çavuş* depicted a poor mother sweeping. Her ragged son, school books in hand, asks her: "What's going on, Mom, sweeping again?" She replies, "Yes my son, I'll sweep until I've cleaned out these cursed, hidden microbes."[65] Knowing about microbes did not allay people's fears of cholera. Cartoon microbes were also used to represent the threat of European imperialism, the internecine struggles of Ottoman politicians (in the blood of the state), and a whole repertoire of political and social ills. *Kalem* for example, showed a microscopic view of "the new plague microbe," tiny little Austrian (or German) soldiers and cannon.[66] *Alafranga* satirized both the inefficiency of municipal government and the power struggles within the government in a cartoon showing skeleton microbes threatening its terrified donkey-mascot, symbol of Ottoman society.[67] In a cartoon that took aim at the old regime as well as the new, *Falaka* showed Abd ül-Hamid, in exile, preparing to spray his eunuch who had just come in from outside. The eunuch cries: "Mercy, Sire, having escaped from the noise and tumult, do we now have to be fearful of a virulent cholera?"[68] This frame neatly lampoons the anxieties of Abd ül-Hamid while satirizing the failure of his successors to control the plague that might kill them all. *Al-Üfürük* even claimed that the cholera was spreading to the press, and was to blame for killing off various of the new gazettes and sickening others.[69]

These representations of cholera as distilling all the fears of the empire, an undefined and illusory menace, were combined with specific images in which cholera was approximated to various types of social problem that had to be controlled, like the consumption of alcohol and the behavior of women.[70] The same skeletal figure used to embody the cholera "germ" was also used to suggest various forms of moral corruption or pollution.[71] These connections are illustrated in a cartoon in *Cadaloz* that uses skeletons to suggest the dangers of beer consumption. The cartoon shows skeletons beckoning from a brewery and coming out of a big bottle of beer.[72] This cartoon connects the factors of cholera, alcohol consumption, and bad water, suggesting that people are drinking beer with the idea (or the excuse) that it is good for warding off cholera. *Falaka*, in narrative satire, took on a similar subject, the association of cholera with impure water but also, obliquely, with moral turpitude.[73]

In the Ottoman cartoon space, images of women, cholera, and imperialism were intertwined in the context of the empire's struggle to redefine itself and to ward off the dangers of the unseen. Cholera, like Otttoman women, was often clothed in the rich accoutrements of European fashion. Reminiscent of the French satirist Legrand's famous cartoon depicting French prostitution in 1888 (or of James Ensor's skeleton paintings of the same era) cholera was drawn as a social ill, with a voluptuous exterior and a skeletal, spectral shadow.[74] Such images preserved the outmoded notion associating cholera with moral depravity. Images of cholera, like those of women and of European imperialism, share certain characteristics. There is the visible and the invisible about them. The visible could be enticing and beautiful, the invisible was deadly.[75]

In the early-twentieth-century milieu of social and political anxiety, the preoccupation with the visible and invisible found various manifestations. It was at this time that spiritualism became a fad in Ottoman revolutionary society. Spiritualism discarded the insurmountable space between mortality and immortality, attempted to make the invisible visible, and gave the Ottomans insight into Western attempts to control the realms of spirits as well as the territories of humankind.[76] Supplying what purgatory had given medieval Christianity, spiritualism gave the living control of the dead in a time of enormous uncertainty.

In the real, as opposed to the spirit, world and in the cartoon space, woman was a symbol of life and death, the manifestations of each sometimes indecipherable. European hegemony was also life and death, providing the goods of fashion and progress while draining the empire of its resources and will. Cholera was only death, but invisible, so it was anthropomorphized into a spectral female, alive yet dead, clothed in European fashions, as in a 1911 cartoon (Figure 9.6) captioned, "Could it be that cholera has returned?"[77] This same female figure, in another cartoon, becomes the symbol of the new Ottoman era, dressed in European fashion and, by implication, taking on all the corruption and immorality of European culture (Figure 9.7). The "old era" (literally the *sene-i maliye*) dressed in "traditional" clothing, a male "peasant" figure, regards the stylish "new era," an old and ugly (but thin) woman, with suspicion and resignation: "Impure, old and ugly, compared to me," he sighs, "but dressed in the latest fashion."[78] The French caption, here, misses the point of the term *şıllık* in the Ottoman caption, which means a gaudy, vulgar, or unchaste woman; a nice, if somewhat dated, English equivalent might be floozy.[79]

In these two cartoons, the stylish European new order and cholera are both embodied in the same unappealing female form. Although, on the surface, the second cartoon refers to the replacing of the traditional *malî*, or fiscal year, dating system with a system based on the Christian (*milâdî*) era, the change in calendar was also a metaphor for the entire complex of Europeanizing changes then affecting (or infecting) the empire. Many cartoons in this period satirized the changes in the way time was counted. The power to change the calendar was the power to recreate culture. Thus, changing the clocks and the calendar signified confusion, a loss of the familiar and proper order of things. In the cartoon contrasting the old (masculine) and new (feminine) eras, the temporal, social, moral, and physical orders were all intertwined.

In other cartoons, the spectral female cholera is metamorphosed into a spectral male, the grim reaper. In these cartoons, the reaper is the military menace of Europe rather than the (apparently) more insidious European cultural menace. The insidious female cartoon menace of cholera is clothed in superficial beauty and sumptuous clothing. The direct male cartoon

— On dirait que c'est le choléra qui est revenu.

— غبا قولرا عودغى ايتدى ؟

Figure 9.6 The "Look" of Cholera

La querelle des ères.

تاریخ غوغاسی .

L'ère ancienne.—Celle qu'on veut me substituer est plus vieille et plus laide que moi. Mais elle porte l'habit à la mode.

سنۀ مامه . — بم بريه قبول ایتك ایستهدکلری شیلق بندن هم دها اختیار. هم دها جبرکین اما نهیاپارسلك كه صوك موده یه کوره کینمش ...

Figure 9.7 Old Era and New

menace of cholera is clothed in military uniform, as the Russian Czar with his armies threatening to invade in a cartoon entitled "the last gift of the esteemed Czar Nicholas (Figure 9.8)," or as Austria, engaged in the economic rape of the Ottoman state. In this latter example, cholera is a mustachioed skeleton, sneaking out of Istanbul with a valise labeled "booty" (Figure 9.9).[80] Another cartoon played on the theme of equality (*müsavat*) prominent in revolutionary sloganeering, to compare the czar in Russia to cholera, as "equal" ravagers.[81]

In another frame, Sedad Nuri manages to combine the images of the pet dog, the stylish female in a big hat, and the male grim reaper cholera. The lady in the hat looks archly at the viewer, and Cholera, a grinning skeleton, muses: "Should I even bother with this one?" (Figure 9.10).[82] Essentially, this cartoon is another potshot at extravagant fashion, but it pairs, once again, the image of the *alafranga* woman, with the specter of cholera, a pairing that is something more than coincidental.

A final image of cholera comes in the form of a representation of a representation. It is called, "A Play in Two Acts: A Suspicious Encounter." This "two act play" is a double-frame, before-and-after cartoon.[83] The first frame is a street scene that is reminiscent of medieval accounts of the plague (Figure 9.11). Attendants are shown carrying the coffins of cholera victims down the street. Also in the street is the ubiquitous street dog. In the center of the frame, a woman is seized by the abdominal pains characteristic of cholera; she doubles over. Immediately she is surrounded by the male figures of Ottoman authority: the officious looking bureaucrat, giving orders, and the police, who douse her with disinfectant. In frame two, the reason for her disability is revealed, she has delivered an infant (Figure 9.12). Her would-be attackers, with the disinfectant cannister, have become her protectors and their scowls have dissolved into smiles. The woman, as menace, has been brought in from the street and transformed into a mother, much to everyone's satisfaction. She is no longer a deadly threat, but a reassuring promise of the future. A happy ending, true, but first the woman had to be decontaminated. According to Ottoman cartoonists, the empire too had to be decontaminated, rid of the debilitating effects of European domination. Only then could the new nation be born.

Thus, the anxieties of revolution were distilled, in the satirical press, into images of plagues on the city streets: dogs, women, crime, and cholera, all moving in an atmosphere of the greater imminent threat of European imperialism. The plagues in the streets of Istanbul were both visible and invisible. Cholera was the definitive symbol of the unseen menace in the street. The dogs were a success story, despite the moans of the romantics, a triumph for a revolutionary regime that had few victories to count. Crime control was a failure. Women in European fashion were enigmatic— apparently pretty, seductive or silly, but essentially a symbol of cultural crisis. While journalists in the Istanbul press were attempting to redefine the political space, satirists were providing a more utilitarian division of the

Le dernier cadeau de notre grand ami Nicolas II.

Figure 9.8 Gift of Czar Nicholas

Figure 9.9   Austria as Cholera

Le Choléra. — Que voulez-vous que je prenne dans ça, moi?....

Figure 9.10   Cholera and the Lady

Acte I

Figure 9.11 A Play in Two Acts: Act I, Stricken

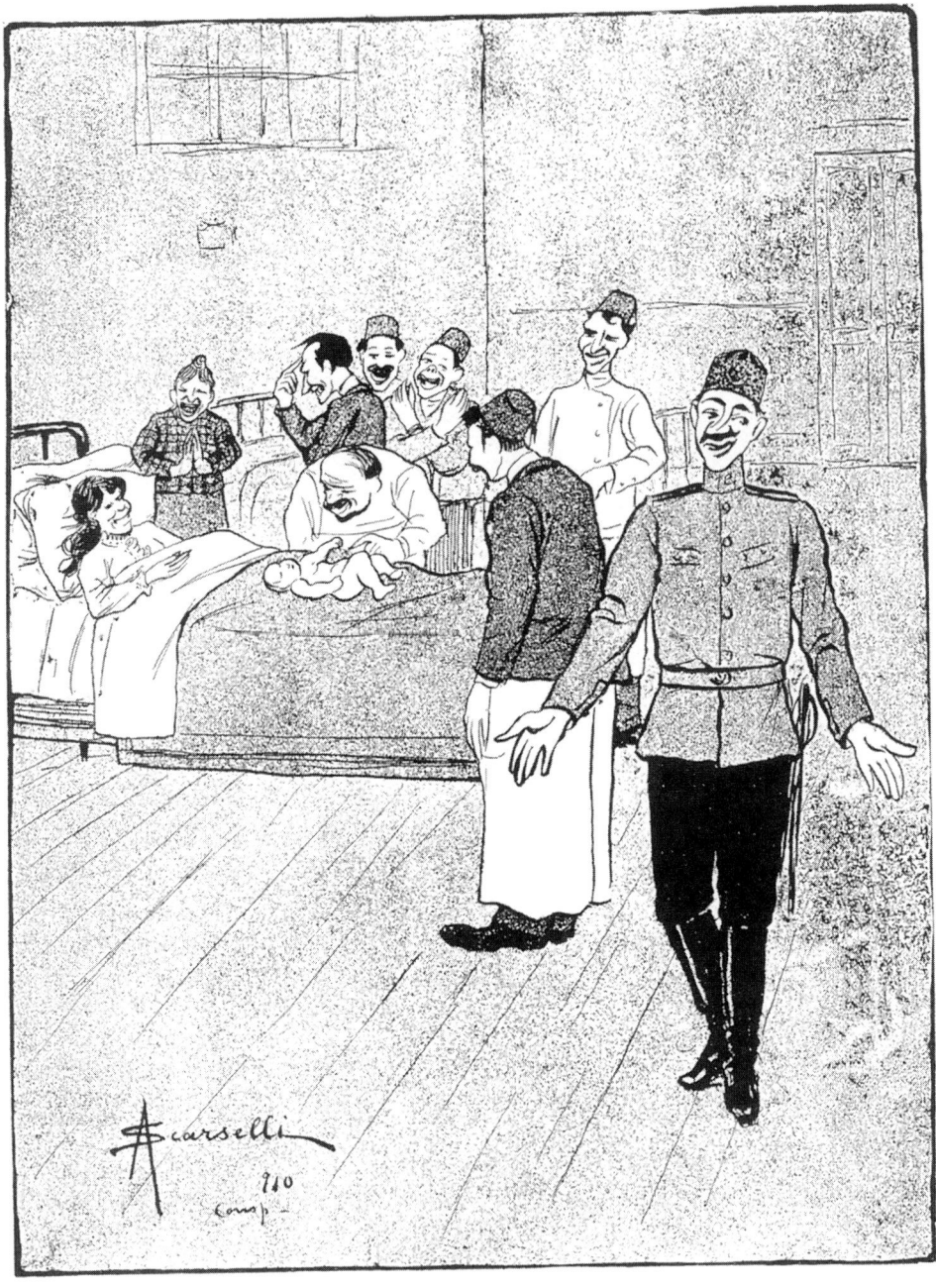

Figure 9.12 A Play in Two Acts: Act II, The Delivery

urban space into controllable or uncontrollable, safe or unsafe, working or not working. Would the cure of European progress save the empire? The cartoonists thought not. They suggested that the Ottomans, like the residents of Hamlin in the fairy tale, were sacrificing their progeny, inviting in one plague to dispose of another.

X

Technology, Transport, and the "Modern" Street

> *Driving across the Galata Bridge . . . was an adventure in itself. In those days there was even less traffic control in Istanbul than there is today—and God knows there is little enough today. That morning, horse-drawn cabs, carts, porters carrying beds or other furniture on their shoulders, gypsies stepping out into the road beneath the very feet of the flying horses, peasants riding their mules—all were in danger of being knocked down or overturned, for Murat, with a fine disregard of human life, drove like the wind and was more autocratic than any Sultan.*[1]

The image of modernity, or rather, to use a less overdetermined, less sophisticated notion, the image of the new (*yeni*), was, as already noted, a preoccupation of the periodical press. The "new," was intimately associated with technologies that were, in turn, intimately associated with European progress. Technologies of transport, of communication, and of production (airplanes, trams, steamships, automobiles, phones, and electric machinery) were associated with innovation and excitement, but also with social disruption and imperialist exploitation. They were perceived as making life exponentially better, but also as assaulting the old ways and dispossessing old forms of labor. Another modern form was the technology of time, expressed in clocks, watches, and the Latin calendar, a way of counting time that would impose itself upon the Ottoman citizenry, making them temporarily unable to "read" time. The satirical press took these "new" technologies and used them both to caricature the obsolescence of the old era, and to paint a picture of turmoil in the new.

In serious literature, automobiles, trams, electric presses, steamships, and other machines were used as concrete symbols of progress, modernity, and power.[2] The success of the West was envisioned as intimately linked to the possession of machines, as was the survival of the empire in the new constitutional era. The illustrated gazette, *Resimli kitab,* for example, included many photos of machines in its various issues. In one single two-page spread, in November 1908, it showed three mechanized transport systems as illustrations of military power: a steam powered naval vessel on maneuvers, a military transport train car (Renard type), and an armed and armored automobile.[3] Some years later the well-known nationalist, Halide Edib, would illustrate her book, *Turkey Faces West,* with two photos embodying the old and the new in transport systems. The first photo, entitled "To Market in the Old Way," shows two farmers riding donkeys and leading camels on the road to Izmir. The second photo, entitled "Road Building, New Style," shows a tractor pulling what looks like an early form of road grader.[4] For Edib, the tractor symbolized progress and the way of the future; the beasts of burden symbolized the ways of the past. Edib's dichotomy between machine power and animal power was one much favored in the satirical press of the revolutionary period, although the satirists were not as optimistic about Western technology as Edib was. The donkey or the mule, especially, served in cartoons as a convenient symbol of people and ways wedded to tradition, slow moving, and oblivious to the possibilities for the social and spatial speed that imported machinery provided. Just as the old bumpkin, Nasr üd-Din Hoca, was associated in Ottoman humor with the donkey, so too was the mascot, *Züğürt,* of the Ottoman gazette of the same name, pictured most often with his donkey, as a generic symbol of the old ways. By 1908, steamships, motorized vehicles, and railroads were already well established as challengers to the various beasts of burden in the empire. But, the extent to which the competition between old and new styles of transport remained a topic of satire indicates the extent to which the shift to new forms of transport continued to disrupt Ottoman society, even after that shift became (or seemed to become) inevitable.

The associations of transport with the old and new eras is strikingly depicted in a cartoon of the sultan in *Kalem* (Figure 10.1). Abd ül Hamid, already deposed and in exile, is a crow (symbol of death) chained to his perch. He watches morosely as an airplane soars by, mute reminder of its freedom and his captivity. The cartoon is captioned, "Jealousy."[5] This image suggests the ways in which new technology made the old era obsolete, an era that would pass unmourned, because it could not compete. It stands in direct contrast to another image, a photograph in *Resimli kitab,* which shows Ottoman deputies of the new regime riding an automobile out of the royal palace in London.[6] Unlike the chained ex-sultan, these "new" men were mobile, they made use of the new technologies, traveled abroad, consorted with Europeans, and wore European dress. The automobile is the symbol of their modernity, just as the airplane in the cartoon is the symbol of Abd ül-Hamid's obsolescence. At least one cartoon, however, suggested that the sultan too had some ideas for using modern technology to make good his escape from Istanbul (Figure 10.2). It showed a set of escape "projects not adopted" employing a dirigible, a submarine, a tunnel and, finally, a piggy-

Figure 10.1 Abd ül-Hamid and the Airplane

Les projets de départ non exécutés.

Figure 10.2 The Sultan's Planned Modes of Escape

back ride on the back of a eunuch.[7] The first three modes of transport suggest the practical uses of "modern" technology, while the eunuch, as in many other cartoons, stands as a symbol of the past era.

Machines were everywhere in the revolutionary press. They stood as indicators of progress, but they bore an underlying message of dependence and subordination. The cover of an issue of the *Ottoman Agriculture and Commerce Gazette* (*Osmanlı ziraat ve ticaret gazetesi*) bears an unintentionally ironic image: a harrow with the single word "EMPIRE" emblazoned across the front.[8] Like many other images in this particular gazette, the picture of the harrow stamped with the name of its English manufacturer, the Empire Company, was intended to display the latest advances in machine technology. Elsewhere in the same gazette were stories and images of the Paris agricultural exhibition, new developments in "radioculture," and innovations in animal husbandry, plowing machinery, and harvesting devices.[9] The paradox of the Empire harrow image lies in the dichotomy between the Ottoman empire, struggling to overcome its financial disabilities through agricultural development, and the British empire (and its Western counterparts) further subordinating the Ottoman state through the control and marketing of technology. The images in the *Osmanlı ziraat ve ticaret gazetesi* were supposed to be images of promise.

Robert Phillipe has argued, in his work on Western political graphics, that the later nineteenth and early twentieth centuries were an era of optimism:

> While pondering the great myths of the century is not its proper concern, political graphic art within its own sphere reveals the basic psychological motives of public opinion in Western society in the second half of the nineteenth century and the early years of the twentieth. The atmosphere is one of joyous optimism; the ideal of progress has put down roots and found confirmation in the general transformation of peoples lifestyles.[10]

That atmosphere of hope and "joy" was also reflected in much of the post-revolutionary, serious, periodical press in Istanbul. The task of reflecting public skepticism was then left to the satirical gazettes, which delivered, instead, the message that all this progress came at a considerable cost. While the *Osmanlı ziraat ve ticaret gazetesi*, and others like it, touted Western technology transfer as empire saving or resurrecting, the satirical gazettes used Western technology transfer as a metaphor for the overturning of Ottoman society by an unholy alliance of foreign machines and inept domestic officials. Echoing the societal compromise that the satirical press found in the Ottoman importation of French culture was the economic and cultural compromise that it found in the Ottoman importation of Western technology. (The term *Western*, here, is meant to suggest both European and American technology.)

TRANSPORT, THE REGIME, AND THE MUNICIPALITY

In the cartoon space, the machine, particularly in the realm of transport, became yet another symbol of misplaced enthusiasm leading to a society worse off than it was under the old regime. Technological developments like steam engines and trams became the "new toys" of the parlimentary regime—a distraction from the serious matters of defense against invasion. The "new toys" symbolized Europe's insidious domestic invasion, paralyzing Ottoman society from within.[11] The transport revolution, as far as the satirists were concerned, meant the displacement of old transport monopolies and the economic position that went with them, the establishment of new economic elites with access to technology, the loss of a sense that the government was controlling the destiny of the state, and plain old chaos in the streets.

The critique of technology, then, was a microcosm of the critique of the meclis. It evoked an image of government, powerless and out of control, accused of slavish imitation of the West with no concomitant certainty of advantage therein. Satire pointed to technological developments, not so much as evil in and of themselves, but as part of the symbolic repertoire of the inability to act: a crippled steamship with a rowboat passing by, a tram pulled by a mule, a train immobile on tracks leading to nowhere. Although this crippling was attributable in most cases to economic problems predating the revolution, the immediate scapegoats were the meclis, the municipality, and the West. It was not coincidental that cartoons depicted the old modes of transport bypassing the new. The boatman and the carter suggested that the old social order could maintain mobility where the new technology could not; it was slow but at least it moved. The implication was that traditional political practice, the hegemonic culture of the sultanate, for all its defects and abuses, was, if not capable, at least functional. The suggestion that the old order may have been more workable than the new only became a satiric option when the old order, at least in part, had been set aside. Then, the new government was blamed for problems with public transportation, whether the perceived problem was impassable streets, foreign exploitation, disgruntled labor, or non-functional conveyances.[12]

One example from this latter genre of transport cartoons is interesting for the fact that it ran a caption in Italian (rather than the common French) alongside its Ottoman caption. The cartoon showed a tramcar, with driver and conductor dozing fore and aft. All the riders inside the curtained windows are also asleep (Figure 10.3). Their somnolence derives from the fact that the tram is being powered by one very large turtle. The top caption reads: "From the Ottoman proverbs." Below the frame, the Ottoman caption notes: "Who goes slowly, arrives at the intended destination." That caption's perfect counterpart, an Italian proverb, reads: "*Chi va piano, va sano*" (He who goes slowly, goes safely.)[13] This image lampoons the supposed speed of "modern" forms of transport. It also implies that the trans-

— Chi va Piano va sano.

Figure 10.3 Turtle-Pulled Tram

port system, like the Ottoman government, cannot utilize the "speed" of modernity while still employing turtle-paced modes of organization.

MODERN TRANSPORT AND THE URBAN SPACE

Henry Ford designed the Model-T in the same year that the Young Turk revolution forced Abd ül-Hamid to reinstate the constitution. Meanwhile, the Wright brothers were flying demonstration flights around Europe. It was a time when the possibilities for a revolution in transportation seemed to have opened wide, just when Ottoman society saw itself as entering a new era of freedom.

That new era meant the modernization of the city and its streets. Modern streets would be reconstructed streets, with new types of buildings, such as the New York skyscrapers shown in the April 1909 issue of *Resimli kitab*.[14] But the reconstruction of the streets along European or Western lines came with a price. While the streets were construed as the location of physical and moral corruption in Ottoman cultural and social satire, they were construed as hazardous and chaotic in Ottoman satire of technology. Ottoman cartoonists represented the streets of Istanbul as places where the Ottoman citizen proceeded at his or her own risk. Sometimes the risks were familiar, unlighted, unpaved streets filled with dog packs, dust, or mud. These were problems the empire shared with many other states. An 1892 Iranian press clip, for example, claimed that an entire string of camels had sunk from sight in the mud in the streets of Tabriz.[15] The Ottoman gazette *Boşboğaz* in a humorous series entitled "Freedom Dictionary," defined *mud* as "the glory of the Istanbul streets."[16] But, in addition to complaints about unpaved streets, Ottoman satirists also took aim at the perils produced by attempts to modernize transport and the urban space.[17] The hazards of the streets had a dual nature: physical, in the form of danger to life and limb, and economic (the displacement of Ottomans from their traditional livelihoods and occupations or their exploitation by European entrepreneurs and their clients). Citizens were shown killed or injured by cartoon trams and autos that bore down on unsuspecting pedestrians accustomed to more traditional modes of transport. Other cartoon Ottomans were injured or inconvenienced by construction projects.

The modernizing street could be a dangerous place, as illustrated in a cartoon in *Karagöz* showing pedestrians dismembered by encounters with Istanbul's trams. The frame shows Hacivat barely escaping injury under the wheels of a speeding auto (Figure 10.4). In the background is an electric tram; in the foreground are topless and bottomless citizens as well as assorted body parts. Hacivat gasps, "Mercy Karagöz, hold on, let's get out of here. See the tramway accidents, people cut in two." But Karagöz has an explanation: "Wait, quit [hollering], the population of Istanbul increases in

Figure 10.4 Doubling the Population

this way, everyone divided into two; soon it will be doubled . . ."[18] This is a later cartoon, depicting the trams after they had been converted to electrical power, unlike the horse-drawn trams of the earlier revolutionary period. But Karagöz transport cartoons are quite similar to others appearing in the satirical press shortly after the revolution. Karagöz, of course, had an answer for everything. But in the Ottoman cartoon space, each new form of transport took its turn as a symbol of the perils of modern technology in the Istanbul streets.

Auto

The automobile was satirized in two major ways in the satirical press. First, it was lampooned as a modern form of transport that was a menace, either because it was inefficient and broke down frequently, or because it wrought havoc among pedestrians. Second, the automobile was associated with the affluent and with the "new ways," as a sort of affront to the bulk of Ottoman society.

A cartoon in *Züğürt* neatly combined both of these themes. The frame shows *Züğürt*'s raggedy mascot smiling smugly at three motorists who have had to stop to repair their automobile. Meanwhile, he passes them by on his donkey. This humorous scene becomes a class satire when the caption points out that Züğürt's donkey was passing the "automobile of the wealthy."[19] The affluent bourgeoisie were associated in the cartoon space with the new technologies and new fashions; only the wealthy could afford a car in this early era of auto transport. When their cars broke down it gave the "lesser" citizens of the cartoon space a chance to mock their "betters."

Another cartoon, in the gazette *Karagöz*, also emphasized the dependability of animal over machine transport. It showed a carter leading along his oxen and pulling a disabled automobile (Figure 10.5). Hacivat, watching from the window of a building bordering the street, calls the scene to Karagöz's attention: "What's this, Karagöz? Oxen harnessed to an automobile. . . . " Blasé as usual, Karagöz replies, "That's the way it goes with autos; they're quick to break down."[20] This cartoon is from 1914, suggesting that the reliability of the auto was no more assured then than it had been in 1908.

Ottoman satire of the automobile may, in part, be considered an offshoot of similar satire in the European press, depicting such novelties as faddish and silly. But the automobile, like the airplane, the tram, and the steamship, captured the Ottoman imagination through its associations with modernity, speed, and new modes of existence.[21] As such, it provided a ready means by which satirists might suggest the new, the Europeanized, and the progressive. Autos were still very much a rarity in 1908 Istanbul; *Muhit* ran a photo in December 1908 of what it claimed was the "first automobile in Istanbul."[22] The satirical press, in turn, proposed that the Ottoman streets were not ready for this new form of transport. Thus the

حیوان — اوه فرګوز اوتومبیلده اوګوز قوشتسلر ... اوتومبیلاه حال بدن.
فرګوز — حایوق یوزوڭدن اوتومبیلاه حال بدن.

Figure 10.5 Broken-Down Auto

automobile was pictured, like the tram, cutting down unsuspecting foot-traffic. Or, as *Boşboğaz* put it, "taking vengeance on its detractors."[23]

Trams and Rail

The tram was satirized for a variety of reasons besides its inefficiency or its threat to pedestrians.[24] It was targeted because it was a foreign product (that is, its construction and management benefited European companies), and it caused "labor problems such as putting horses out of work."[25] Trams, like fashions, were also subject to satire because they combined the old and the new. In its division of space, the Ottoman tram asserted traditional culture in a modern conveyance; it was divided, as was the Ottoman house, into men's and women's sections, *selâmlık* and *harem*.[26] This assertion of culture in the division of space is a neat metaphor for Ottoman adaptations of foreign goods. Technologies and fashions were of foreign origin, but in the process of transfer from Europe to Istanbul, they were culturally conditioned and transformed.

Trams were satirized for their inefficiency, slowness, or failure to work.[27] The slow rate of supposedly "improved" methods of transport was a common target of cartoon barbs. *Nekregû* showed travelers pushing a tram up a hill through the muddy streets, while the conductor, up front, tugged at the horses.[28] Indeed trams became a metaphor for labor-intensive transport; they were depicted being pushed by riders, pulled with ropes, and drawn by various "obsolete" forms of transport like horses.[29]

One of the most frequently satirized forms of transport was the Tünel, the innovative subway which carried passengers up the hill on the Galata side of Istanbul; it was designed and operated by European companies. The Tünel was satirized as an often inefficient form of transport, and as one of the many means by which Europeans got their hands into Ottoman pockets and bamboozled the Ottoman government. *Alem,* in a satirical piece entitled, "*Les Progrès,*" mocked the station building and reconstruction projects of the Tünel Company.[30]

The very site of the subway, at least for one observer, was associated with European corruption and exploitation. Edwin de Leon portrayed the route to the bottom end of the tunnel in Galata as an unsavory experience, a gathering place for "all the scum of the earth . . . from East or West." Once across the Galata Bridge, he portrayed the traveler as emerging into:

> the mean traffic of Maltese and Sicilian and nondescript hucksters of European products, such as bacon, sausages, brandies, and other articles which stink in the nostrils of the faithful, you pass through narrow lanes rather than streets, redolent of all such abominations, with drunken and blasphemous European sailors, and vulgar hucksters barring your way; until you emerge into pure air and wider streets, as you ascend the winding road leading up-hill, towards the tramway and cemetery, which leads to Pera.[31]

Once in Pera, "an imitation European town," however, De Leon found the Grand Rue of Pera a "really fine street," renewed, "on the modern system," after the area was devastated in a fire.[32] He was particularly impressed by the roughly two miles of tramway that traversed Pera's main drag. De Leon, thus had his own social hierarchy of the good and bad deriving from the European impact on Istanbul. The bad Europeans were salesmen and drunkards. The good Europeans brought wide streets and trams.

Foreign observers, however, were not the only ones to bemoan traveling and traffic conditions in Istanbul. A humorous dialogue in *Hande*, outlines the tribulations of traversing the city. The dialogue begins, as many Karagöz-style dialogues do, with a question: "Hey, where are you coming from [looking] so weary?" The traveler replies, "Where would I be coming from . . . ? " He then relates the trials of his journey including a vision of the Tünel, where the "wayfarers are packed into the cars (*vagonlar*) as if pickled in brine."[33] The more modern forms of transport, then, could serve simply to add another, albeit different, layer of chaos and discomfort to the often chaotic conditions of downtown streets. In satiric dialogue and cartoon frame, rail transport did not necessarily make city travel more commodious.

Trains, unlike trams and automobiles, were not regularly caricatured, perhaps because they were less new and because they did not occupy the Ottoman streets in the same ways that other forms of mechanized transport did. Trains appeared in political satire of the Hijaz and Balkan railways (the former as part of the critique of Abd ül-Hamid's caliphal pretensions and the latter as a form of protest over Bulgarian independence and the struggle for control of resources).[34] Trains also played a minor role in the general critique of transport inefficiency, mostly with regard to scheduling. Lucy Garnett noted that few people in Turkey had need of trains and steamships and that timetables were viewed with little concern. "On the majority of Turkish railways there is but one train a day up or down the line, and intending passengers will arrive at the platform at any hour, and seated on their baggage, will wait calmly and patiently—sometimes, it may be, for the best part of a day and night—for the next train."[35] Garnett, here, seems to have suffered from a rather English form of bias when estimating the Ottomans' sense of time and schedule. But her vision of a lack of order, when it came to Ottoman transport, was one that was frequently echoed in the satirical gazettes, where cartoonists often pictured a system that was neither dependable nor comfortable.

Steamships

The impact of steamship transport on Ottoman commerce and society, beginning in the nineteenth century, was profound. Steamship companies, along with their financing, and staff, tended to be foreign, but that fact does not, by any means, suggest that the effects of the steam revolution on the empire were all negative. In fact, steamships greatly expanded Ottoman commerce; the negative effects derived from radical changes in the nature and organization of commercial systems.[36] It was these systemic changes that translated into satire of the steamship in the Ottoman cartoon space.

The steamship, or *vapur*, was a common image in cartoons of the revolutionary era; in fact, the gazette *Ton ton risalesi* (published in just one issue) was devoted to satire of the *vapur*.[37] The steamship became one of those generic symbols of change or the modern era that could be invoked in satire to suggest the "new" way of things. It thus cropped up in poems and in narrative satire, grouped with other things (European-style theater, constitutional government, trams, and *alafranga* dress) which were associated with progress but also subject to criticism. The *vapur* became a symbol of the new Istanbul, sometimes good and sometimes bad.[38]

Like other forms of transport, the steamship was lampooned as subject to the kinds of breakdowns that more primitive conveyances (sailing and rowing boats) did not suffer. Thus, Ottoman cartoons showed boatmen on the Bosphorus rowing past stalled steamships, just as they showed horse drawn vehicles stepping lively past stalled autos.[39] But the image of the traditional boatman and the steamship had another message that reflected the systemic social and economic changes that steam power brought to the Ottoman docks. The steamships directly undermined the place and position of traditional forms of labor: the water taximen, the boatmen who ferried cargo between large ships and the wharf, and the porters and loaders on the docks. Although these men were, in some cases, organized and fought to obtain concessions from the government and the steamship companies (see chapter 6), they still found their livelihoods eroding as ports were restructured, transit boats eliminated, and rail lines brought directly up to the quays.[40] These dilemmas of the traditional worker and the modern transport system took cartoon form in satirical frames juxtaposing foreign shippers (in European dress) and their modern technology to Ottoman workers in traditional clothing standing steadfastly by their more primitive (but familiar and reliable) modes of transport.[41]

The docks also provided one of the many sites at which the foibles and failures of the Public Works Ministry (*Nafia Nezareti*) were satirized. *Davul*, for example, employed a two-page illustration in which it "presented to the Ministry of Public Works" its own diagram for a solution to the problems of loading humans and freight.[42] The frame shows a wharf overlooking the Golden Horn (or possibly the Bosphorus); steamships and sailing craft traverse the waters. On the dock, a catapult has been set up. From it, men with packages strapped to them are being shot out towards the boats. An officer with a spy-glass is setting up the trajectories but his first calculation appears to have been somewhat off; the first man fired from the catapult hits a lamppost a few feet forward on the dock. *Davul*, here, is probably not indicating its sympathies for striking dock-workers, but it is taking to task the administration of the new regime for its waterfront reconstruction projects. *Vapur* facilities were also lampooned in *Ton ton risalesi*, which critiqued the phony promises of officials and the failure to build a waiting room for passengers taking trips to the islands.[43] Efficiency was not judged to be a strong point of the new regime's modernization projects.

There was one final context in which the steamship played a role in Ottoman satire. That was the critique of Ottoman seapower as outmoded, broken-down, and non-competitive. The serious press pointed to the naval power of the empire's enemies as compared to the dilapidated, unfunded, and outmoded conditions of the Ottoman navy.[44] Ottoman satirists looked at the steam-powered vessels of states like England and Germany, and measured that palpable image of power against the miserable military and commercial seaborne capabilities of the empire. This was, in some ways, a reversal of the satirical critique of imported technologies, because it scrutinized the empire in terms of those very technologies of power, and found it wanting.

One target of the cartoonists was the empire's own steamship company, founded in 1851, the *Şirket-i Hayriye* (Auspicious Company). Among its shareholders were members of the royal family, including the sultan, and prominent officials.[45] Like fashion satire, satire of the *Şirket-i Hayriye* focused on the apparently ludicrous effects that resulted when Ottomans tried to imitate or beat the Europeans at their own game. Also a target was the government fleet called the *İdare-i Mahsusa* (or *Mahsusa* for short) which was privately managed but under the administration of the Ministry of the Navy.[46] Where steamships in general could be lampooned for their modernity, their breakdowns, and their foreign ownership, Ottoman steamships were lampooned for their inefficiency, disorganization, and failure to live up to European standards.

Of particular concern in the satirical press's attack on Ottoman steamships were the Ottoman navy and Ottoman seapower in general. Various frames scoffed at the navy-building ambitions of the new regime and the lack of a budget to finance those ambitions. In a caricature (entitled "Our Ministers") of other images that glorified officials of the new regime, *Muhit* showed a cartoon depiction of "Naval Minister Pasha."[47] He appears as a big giant in a tiny dish of water smiling down at a toy-sized ship in his hand; in the water at his feet are four wrecked and half-submerged ships. This cartoon suggests both the sorry state of the Ottoman navy and the inflated expectations that the serious press often imposed on Ottoman officials.

Züğürt suggested that the cost-cutting measures of Ottoman officials got them exactly what they paid for. In one cartoon frame, the ragged and wiley old Züğürt stands on the docks speaking to an official. At the dock is a steamship; what looks like an engine is being lowered onto its deck. Züğürt asks if this is not the recently acquired steamship Midhat Pasha. "Yes," says the official, "But what can we do? It has proved itself a luckless vessel; we were deceived in it."[48] The punchline in this cartoon hinges on the ship having been named after the ill-starred nineteenth-century Ottoman statesman, Midhat Pasha, who was assassinated. But the underlying message of the cartoon is that the Ottomans are expending limited resources acquiring second-rate ships or worse. The Midhat Pasha was built in 1900 for the Imperial Direct West India Mail Service, was purchased by the Ottoman Naval Aid Society in 1911, and later commissioned as a transport; it may well have seen better days. *Züğürt* suggests that seapower on the cheap is not likely to contribute to the success of the empire.

The satirists' jaundiced vision of Ottoman seapower was in direct contrast to some of the glorifying and nationalistic visions found in the serious press. The periodical, *Resimli İstanbul*, for example is striking for its varied and rather romanticized images of seapower. *Resimli İstanbul* ran a whole series of pictures of modern naval vessels and equipment, commenting on the expectations of the Ottoman navy for acquiring some of these seagoing wonders.[49] Even the satirical *Kalem* was not immune from the kind of naval flag-waving found in *Resimli İstanbul*; it ran a cartoon showing a modern, new, steampowered Ottoman gunboat threatening the shores of Greece.[50] But, in general, the satirists preferred to point out what much of revolutionary rhetoric preferred to downplay, that the new regime did not have the money to make the empire a seapower that could compete in the modern era.

Airplanes

The possible exception to the general tone of transport satire was the airplane, which seemed to have such universal appeal that it was generally exempted from critique and became instead a symbol of the new age and of the optimistic rather than the skeptical view of the press.[51] The airplane remained largely in the realm of fancy in 1908 and did not yet challenge established transport interests. Airplanes did not intersect with day-to-day life as did the tramways, steamships, and street construction that meant aggravation, loss of time, bad air, and the threat of injury. The Ottoman press enthusiastically reported on aviation technology, air shows, and dirigibles.[52] *Resimli İstanbul* showed European women going up in hot air balloons and gatherings of balloon-enthusiasts.[53] Aviation was a fleeting form of entertainment, something to rush out and look at, a scientific wonder, a representation of progress, but progress that was somewhat distant in both time and space. It also held out a certain promise for the reinvigoration of the Ottoman military.[54] This fantasy aspect of aviation expressed itself in cartoons in which airplanes and dirigibles were associated with an idealized yet improbable future. The most striking example of this idealization is a cartoon with an airplane, piloted by a woman, flying over a futuristic Istanbul street scene, with modern ground level transport, traffic control, glitzy modern shops, and a theater.[55] The aviatrix, swathed in hijab, bespeaks the incongruity of the vision—a future not quite imaginable.

Air travel, in its capacity as the imagined transportation of the future, could also be used to satirize the deficiencies of other forms of transport in

Istanbul. One image, in the gazette *Geveze*, for example, used the airship to caricature the condition of the Galata bridge. It shows a tumbling down bridge with a steamship parked up against it; the bridge is broken and parts of the bridge construction float in the Golden Horn. Sailing over the bridge were two dirigibles, one very primitive plane, and two more fanciful types of airship. The caption read: "After the bridge has completely sunk beneath the waves, airships will be employed [to traverse the water]."[56] Dirigibles over the Golden Horn also appeared in another cartoon frame but with a different target: the precarious nature of Ottoman authority in the form of the office of grand vezir (Figure 10.6). This particular cartoon showed a series of airships carrying successive grand vezirs off across the water and away from the capital, each dirigible named for its occupant, the most recent being Kâmil Pasha. In this case, the airship signifies speed, but also a lack of control. The caption reads: "With the wind blowing this way, it's impossible to approach the Sublime Porte."[57]

Besides its associations with modernity, air travel was also intimately associated with foreign powers and foreigners. *Kalem* ran a cartoon of a rather fanciful dirigible, taken from a Berlin gazette.[58] It showed the Emperor Wilhelm II, and a close-up of his flying machine, complete with throne, trumpeter, various insignia, and two black eagles on leashes flying off to the side. Two men dressed like sailors are shown dumping bags of something off the side of the ship. The Ottoman cartoon did not bother to identify these items, apparently content with the amusing vision of the emperor piloting his rather hodge-podge airship. The dirigible was thus turned against its European inventors and used to make them ridiculous.

So, even the airplane was not completely free from the satirical gaze of the Ottoman press. One cartoon showed a glider-type plane apparently being loaded onto a ship at the wharf (Figure 10.7). In the foreground two men discuss the proceedings. "Hey Monsieur," says one, "What's this?" The other replies, "A balloon . . . . it will be eight years before the automobile, the omnibus, and the bicycle will be able to run in Istanbul, so I'm making my trip to Istanbul by air."[59] In this frame, air travel became a vehicle for satirizing the primitive state of Ottoman transport systems and the lousy roads, not fit for overland travel. Yet, even the two characters in this cartoon suggest the connection between modern transportation and the Europeanization of the empire. One is an official, perhaps a policeman, dressed in cloak and fez; the other is clearly a Westerner, in suit, cap, and tie, perhaps a European entrepreneur. In fact, aviation images in the Ottoman cartoon space usually associated air transport with European-style dress.

Karagöz, not surprisingly, could also be depended upon to find the downside of air travel. Rather than associate airplanes with European-style modernization, the gazette *Karagöz* linked them, like other forms of modern transport, to aggravation and inconvenience. One frame showed Karagöz thrashing about his bed, having a nightmare in which a phantom airplane dive-bombed him; another pointed out that air travel exposed pedestrians

Figure 10.6 The Vezirs' Dirigibles

— Un aéroplane pourquoi faire ?...
— Dame, comme c'est seulement dans 5 ans que nous aurons des routes et que d'ici là on ne pourra se servir ni de voitures, ni de bycyclettes, ni d'automobiles pour voyager à l'intérieur.....

Figure 10.7 Circumventing the Empire's Bad Roads

to new types of insult from above. In this latter illustration, Karagöz is doused with what is clearly not "rain" from a passing plane (Figure 10.8):

Karagöz: Ah Hacivat, there's a draft on my head. Does it rain on a clear day?
Hacivat: That's not rain. It's a kind of liquid that comes from an airplane .... Don't you smell its stink?
Karagöz: Oh! God give him his just deserts! .... They've made road laws and sea laws, but still no air laws?[60]

That, indeed, was part of the dilemma of the revolutionary period; its laws had not yet caught up with its realities or its technologies.

COMMUNICATIONS AND TIME

Technologies of communication, the telegraph and telephone, functioned as simple codes for what was new and progressive in the Ottoman cartoon space. They were juxtaposed to the monarchs of the old regimes to provide a visual contrast between the modern and the obsolete. Abd ül-Hamid was supposed to have been superstitious about the disembodied spirit-like quality of telephone communication; and there is a fine irony to the fact that the demand of the revolutionaries for the reinstatement of the constitution came to the sultan via telegraph.[61] Like Parisian gowns and roller skates, the telephone and the telegraph in Ottoman cartoons were simple and readily accessible markers of the new era and of the approximation of the empire to Europe.

Satirical gazettes capitalized upon the idea of the telegraph, and the "instant" and long range opportunities for knowledge it provided, by including phony, humorous, telegraph "news" columns and "news" flashes in their contents. For example, *Alem* included the following under the heading "Today's telegrams": "Very urgent. The government has demanded the lantern from in front of the Tünel at Galata; It is destined for the Chamber [of Deputies] to shed light on the deputies' nocturnal labors."[62] This "telegram" managed simultaneously to satirize two symbols of technology (the Tünel railway and street lighting) and the primary symbol of the new regime, the Chamber of Deputies.

Some years later, the gazette *Karagöz* would satirize the degree to which new communications technologies had invaded and disrupted the Ottoman street (Figure 10.9). One of its cartoons showed a perplexed Karagöz trapped in wires that crisscrossed the Istanbul thoroughfare.

Karagöz: Mercy, Hacivat, I've been caught between the wires, has this place been fortified?
Hacivat: What are you doing Karagöz? This isn't a battlefield, it's Kadiköy. Those are telephone wires!

قره‌گوز — ایواه حاجیواد، اوستم باشم برباد اولدی. آچیق هوادە یاغمور یاغارمی ؟..
حاجیواد — او یاغمور دگل، طیارەدن کلن بر نوع مایع... قوقوسنی حس ایتمیورمیسك ؟..
قره‌گوز — های الله مستحقنی ویرسین... یول قانونی، دکز قانونی پایبلدی‌دە حالا هوا قانونی یاپیلمادی‌می ؟..

Figure 10.8   "Rain" from a Plane

Figure 10.9 Phone Wire War Zone

Karagöz: I've seen telephone wire all over, but I've never seen anything like this![63]

In 1908, the telephone was considered a rare and elite form of communication. But by 1913, this cartoon suggests, telephone technology was becoming a real and intrusive fact of life in the Istanbul streets.

Foreign control of communications technology did not receive the same attention in Ottoman cartoons that foreign control of transport technologies did. But the telegraph, like the tram and the steamship, was also a technology that required foreign equipment, staff, and instructors. As such it provoked a certain envy and resentment as foreign interests profitted from the installation of the systems and from the training of young Ottomans to man the telegraph stations.[64] Communications technologies, like transport technologies brought great benefits in the realm of conquering distance, but those benefits could not be neatly separated from the discomfiture that was the inevitable companion of change.

The telegraph and telephone were technologies that seemed to conquer time as well as space. But, in other ways, the new era and its new technologies were associated with distrupting the old familiar Ottoman sense of time. The metaphor of timelessness, long applied to the Middle East in Western texts, had no place in the literary output of the Ottoman revolution. The dilemma of the revolutionary regime, rather, was expressed in terms of capturing time: time running out or moving too fast, time counted on imported clocks, or time governed, written, and controlled by Europe. Ottoman satire used the European clock and calendar as emblems of ill-considered, bewildering, and unenforceable change, change that was imposed and not integrated into society. Mirroring the image of the old order clothed uncomfortably in Western fashion is the image of the new order bound to a clock that it could not read and to a calendar on which it could not operate.

Who would name the time on which the "new" Ottoman state would run? In the cartoon space, a villager stands bewildered, gazing at a clock indicating noon. "What's this?" He asks, "The clock reads noon but the sun is at the back of my head (Figure 10.10)?"[65] Elsewhere, affairs at the Porte are interrupted because the ministers cannot function on the "European time," embodied in a clock with Roman numerals topping the Sublime Porte (*Bab-ı Âli*).[66] The European-style coats and hats of the ministers in this second clock cartoon did not protect them from looking foolish when presented with an alternative way of measuring time. The cartoon villager, looking askance at the clock, was trying to figure out why its reading did not match his notion of time, which was based on the movement of the sun. Dressed in wrapped fez, short jacket, and baggy trousers, he was a symbol of tradition, conservatism, and Ottoman self-determination. The clock tower, on the other hand, was a symbol of Europe and modernity. A clock tower was erected at Tophane Square at the end of the nineteenth century when

Le paysan.— Depuis quelque temps, je n'y comprends plus rien.

— زو ، بونه ایشدرکه ؟ ... کونش ا کسه‌مده ایکن ساعت اون ایکی اولوور ؟

Figure 10.10 Telling Time

an *irade* (decree) was issued ordering the erection of clock towers, a sign of Westernization and progress.[67] A clock tower was also erected by the Ottoman administration in Jerusalem shortly before the revolution.[68] Such clock towers may have prompted the cartoonist's depiction of the discomfiture of the peasant.

These were the cartoon images of a state whose "oriental" systems would not run on "occidental" time. The dilemma of running the government on European time was a microcosm of the dilemma of running the Ottoman empire with a constitutional system developed in Europe. The short-lived parliament of the first Ottoman constitutional revolution expressed these difficulties, in 1877, when it was proposed that the new meclis meet at eleven A.M. European time in order to avoid calculation of hours based on sunrise and sunset. The proposal was rejected "on the grounds that most deputies would not understand the changed system."[69] Conservative members of parliament opposed Rıza Tevfik's proposal to introduce European time as the state standard.[70] *Kalem* lampooned this very same confusion in a 1909 cartoon that showed two deputies consulting their watches in front of the meclis, one on his way in and the other apparently on his way out, one relieved that he was not late and the other just as certain that he was.[71] Thus, there was clearly ambivalence over whether the Ottoman empire should be run on European time and a European calendar just because it now had a European-style constitution.[72] As Lucy Garnett noted:

> The hours of the day are still reckoned, in ancient Oriental fashion, from sunset to sunset, which is estimated with more or less exactitude. Many of the watches used in Turkey are made with two dials, one for Turkish and the other for European time, the former, to be correct, requiring daily regulation; and one may often hear the seemingly odd question asked: "At what time is noon today?"[73]

The satirical gazettes were not convinced that such "cosmetic" changes in counting time would accomplish the ideological changes they represented, or lead to coherent government rather than confusion. Further, such changes subjected the Ottomans to humiliation at home and abroad. The Europeans were naming the new regime and even creating the time on which it ran. In that context, the Ottomans became, as Garnett put it, "seemingly odd."

In fact, the gazettes themselves symbolize the difficulties of forcing Ottoman systems into a Latin time scheme. Most Ottoman gazettes ran on a *malî* (financial-year) publication schedule not coincident with either Christian era (*milâdî*) or Muslim era (*hicrî*) dating systems. For years, some Western catalogers, assuming that all the publications of "Islamic" states ran on *hicrî* time, mistranslated the dates of Ottoman gazettes into *milâdî* (Christian era) dates, resulting in errors of as much as three years. In the revolutionary period, such muddling also afflicted the gazettes themselves when many attempted to offer both *malî* and *milâdî* dating, resulting, for example, in year changes that occurred at the end of December and at the end of February (*Şubat*). This decision on labeling was based on an anticipated audience and on the cultural modeling that each gazette wished to bring to that audience. *Malî/miladî* dating, went along with bilingual French and Ottoman captioning. Some gazettes resisted the Westernized dating, used *malî/hicrî* dating or even employed only *hicrî* dating (usually an indication of "conservative" content). In any case, the ideal of translating Ottoman time into European time and dating ran afoul of traditional organizational modes in many areas of social intercourse, a minor preview of the gross disruptions that would occur when Atatürk forced the Latin alphabet upon his resurrected empire.

Nor was the affront simply one of a challenge to the ways in which systems functioned. The Ottomans, in the realm of time, were again placed in the role of suppliant and subordinate to Europe. Time had to be learned again as Ottoman society was subjected to the hegemony of European-style knowledge. The choice of what kind of time to use was a question of either resisting or having easy access to dominant European states whose inroads into the military, educational, and economic systems of the empire were well advanced before the revolution. While the armies of Europe threatened to annex Ottoman territory, Ottoman elites tried to run on European time in order to meet the perceived demands of modernization.

ISLAM, TECHNOLOGY, AND SATIRE

There was a complex relationship between Ottoman society and Western technology. Much has been written on the Early Modern Period that suggests that Ottoman Islamic culture was disinterested in, if not downright hostile to, European thought, culture, and technology. This idea of Ottoman society as hostile to Western "progress" is often based on assumptions about Islam, particularly the assumption that Islamic societies naturally reject all forms of innovation (*bid'at*). But characterizations of Ottoman aloofness to Western technology are a grave form of reductionism. They are, in some ways, analogous to similar characterizations of Chinese aloofness in the same period. Joanna Waley-Cohen has argued that Chinese imperial expressions of disdain for Western technology were motivated by internal political agendas, not by actual circumstances and, as a result, "the whole tenor of early Sino-Western relations was based on false premises."[74] She argues, further, that the "Chinese have consistently sought to absorb Western practical technical skills while remaining inimical to Western ideologies."[75] This latter was not the case for the Ottomans, of course, who were ambivalent about the value of Western ideologies and also historically closer to them. Nonetheless, the assessment of Ottoman interest in Western technology must be based more on an evaluation of the empire's economic and political situation and less on cultural assumptions.[76] In the Ottoman case, traditional scholarship suggests that the Ottomans were disinterested in and aloof from Western technology in the Early Modern Era and then, in the early twentieth century, became eager, ready, and willing to imitate and adopt Western technology willy nilly and at all costs. Ottoman satire reveals the middle ground between these two exaggerations of the apparent sentiments of successive eras. That middle ground was characteristically voiced through the skepticism of Karagöz and his cronies, who suggested that Western technology was neither necessarily good nor necessarily bad; it was an historic inevitability that both disrupted Ottoman society and made it more interesting.

In the cartoon space, technology was not pitted against Islam. In fact, the categories of technology satire, discussed above, do not deal directly with Islam at all. This is important because there remains a vague sense that Muslim societies have a natural aversion to "modern," imported technologies. That charge may be partially true, but if one takes the Ottoman satirical press as evidence, that aversion did not derive from Islam, it derived from social, economic, and political competition. It is the case that, in the exchange of the old for the new, Islam, where it was represented at all, tended to fall into the "old" camp. It was familiar, comforting, spiritual, traditional, and unifying unlike those things construed as new, which were unfamiliar, disconcerting, material, foreign, and socially factionalizing. But that association of Islam with the traditional in the satirical press did not tend to extend into the realm of technology. Ottoman cartoons seem to suggest that technology is religiously neutral. It was attacked for practical and economic reasons, not for reasons of faith.

Technology was one element in rhetorics of modernization that were themselves rooted in an often vague notion of the scientific. What was scientific might automatically be construed as antithetical to religion in general (not only to Islam), but that seemed not to be the case in Ottoman satire. Şükrü Hanioğlu, for example, has discussed how the Young Turks used *science,* in their arguments for a constitutional government; but he has also presented the ways in which Islam was represented as a tool of modernization.[77] Various scholars have noted the support of Ottoman Muslim clerics (and others) for technological innovation.[78] In fact, the Ottoman ulema could not be clearly and decisively excluded from the Ottoman impetus to "modernization" and progress. Members of the ulema figured prominently in Ottoman reforms and in, for example, the opening ceremonies for the new telegraph from Istanbul to Edirne in 1855.[79]

Taking another tack, given the precedent of the French revolution, and given Abd ül-Hamid's recourse to the ideology of Pan-Islam to bolster his legitimacy, one might expect the revolutionary press to link the attack on traditional sovereignty to an attack on Islam.[80] But Ottoman satire did not mimic the French Revolution's vehement attack on the second estate; it tended carefully to separate the Islamic ceremonial and legitimation of kingship from the sultan's association with despotism, obsolescence, and treachery. For the most part, the press was not yet even ready to dispense with the idea of the sultanate; much less with the idea of institutional Islam.

The Istanbul revolutionary press, far from denouncing Islam as the root cause of reaction and scientific as well as political inertia, frequently skirted the issue of Islam in general and avoided direct assaults on the clergy. Rather, enlightenment science, rational approaches to knowledge, and language modernization were posed as avenues to progress without attempting to dislodge the ulema from its already seriously weakened position. This reticence in the press, may result from two related factors: (1) the long history of Ottoman state co-optation of the ulema, and the interrelatedness of the political, religious, and literary elites; and (2) the acknowledgment by the press of Islam as a unifying force at a time when Ottoman civilization threatened to succumb to the hegemony of European culture. Especially because European rhetorics of dominance linked the weakness of the Ottoman state to religious inadequacy, embracing all the accoutrements of European culture could suggest that Islam was an innate and fatal civilizational flaw that practically predetermined the empire's subjugation. Conversely, Islam could be perceived as providing a precedent of civilizational glory that could hold the fabric of Ottoman society together in the face of external threat. This past glory was the antithesis to the humiliating alternative of territorial and cultural defeat. The risk of overturning traditional forms of sovereignty and at the same time rejecting the bases for social unity was too great. Instead the press focused its criticism on the external threats and on the failures of the Ottoman authorities (sultan and meclis) to resist them. Given these focuses, it was only natural that the satire of technology found its most characteristic expression in caricatures of foreign inventions that undermined Ottoman society and an inefficient Istanbul metropolitan order that made life difficult, rather than in attacks on "anti-Islamic" innovation.

XI
Conclusion: Revolutionary Options, Satiric Imagery, and the Historiographic Frame

The satire and imagery of the Ottoman revolutionary press do not reveal or define a formed and fixed Ottoman nation. Rather they suggest the boundaries within which the symbols of people, nation, and sovereign were construed. These boundaries, however, were not so much boundaries of religion and ethnicity as they were indices of the realms of the modern and the traditional, the foreign and the native, the threatening and the safe. As I hope these preceding chapters have demonstrated, the traditional historiographic frames by which this early-twentieth-century history has tended to be viewed prove inadequate for expressing the content of the Ottoman cartoon space. In that space, the frames of nationalism, Ottomanism vs. Turkism, and Islam vs. the "secular" West do not take precedence. Rather, satiric imagery focused the viewers' attention on the revolutionary situation, with its paradoxes of old and new, tyranny and freedom, glory and humiliation.

When W. L. Courtney, an eyewitness, tried to explain the unsuccessful Ottoman counter-revolution of 1909 to the literate British public, he was more open minded about Ottoman rationales than is much of twentieth-century historiography.

> Was the mutiny [the counter-revolt] due to the incompatibility of the Sheriat and the Constitution, of Islam and Parliamentary Government? If so, then Turkey is doomed irrevocably, for . . . the Committee's attempt to make the Ottoman Empire a Constitutional State will be as hopeless an undertaking as an attempt to make ropes out of sea-sand or bricks without straw. Happily, however, the matter has still to be decided, for though there was undoubtedly some religious feeling at the bottom of the movement, there was a great deal more of Hamidian gold.[1]

Courtney rightly saw what was going on in Istanbul as a struggle for power rather than an epic contest between heroic secular constitutionalism on the one hand and villainous and backward religious monarchy on the other.

Conclusion

Although Ottoman cartoons were guilty of drawing such simple contrasts between *istibdad* and *hürriyet,* they were equally adept at demonstrating that the symbols, ideas, and institutions of the past were not so readily or happily discarded. In the cartoon space, Islam and the Shariah were not arrayed on one side against the forces of modernity on the other.[2] Nor were the satirists of 1908 concerned to discern nationalism in the same way that latter day historians became concerned to discern it. The satirists did surely embody the nation, but not so much to differentiate Ottoman from Turk, or Turk from Arab; rather they embodied the "nation," as empire, in order to assert its integrity against the foreign powers and internal factionalism that threatened it.[3]

NATIONS

Thoreau might have been thinking of the Ottoman condition when he wrote: "Nations! What are nations? Tartars and Huns, and Chinamen! Like insects, they swarm. The historian strives in vain to make them memorable."[4] Like the task of Thoreau's historians, the task of the Ottoman revolutionary press was to make the "nation" memorable, to reconstruct and defend it; but it was not necessarily the same kind of nation. Great energy has been devoted to the description of Balkan, Turkish, and Arab provincial nationalisms and much agony to the attempt to characterize them as "European type" (inspired, imitated, cloned, suggested, pressured, forced), or not. From the perspective of this debate, the Ottoman empire and its revolution do not necessarily fit the image of the restive nation(s) rising up and fulfilling its destiny. Historiographically, Turkey seems to emerge out of what was left over after the Great Powers, and their created nations and nationalisms, appropriated the empire's citizens and territory. A post–World War I notion of the Turkish nation, spirit quickened by the memory of the French revolution and by the pens of Ziya Gökalp and *Türk Yurdu,* is extended benevolently backward to include the revolt of Abd ül-Hamid's vassals.

But there is no real theoretical consensus on the nature of nationalism in the late Ottoman period. The concept has tended to develop along geographic lines (the Balkans, the Arab provinces, and whatever was left), or has focused on an intellectual history, which gives a determining voice to selected works of selected writers.[5] Some historians have looked for evidence that types of nationalism were mass movements rather than "elitist" intellectual currents and to assess the nature of nationalist options.[6] Still, the debate remains centered on the question of when Ottomanism became Turkism and on the extent to which Ottoman nationalisms were induced by Europe. Further, the rough division of nationalism studies into Balkan, Arab, and Turkish types begs the questions of whether ethno-linguistic nationalism is a functional category for the late Ottoman empire and, if so, in what ways it can be applied to Istanbul.[7]

Perhaps Ottoman historiography has too readily accepted the categories passed down by confident, early-twentieth-century European nationalists. A contemporary observer, David Fraser, expressed the Ottoman "national" paradox in this fashion:

> The extraordinary variety of races within the Turkish Empire, speaking different languages, using different forms of writing, and professing different religions makes the task of evolving a common nationality one of remarkable perplexity. Ideals of existence differ in each region and what suits one community is anathema to another. Moreover, the Turks are hated from Albania to Arabia, and proposals emanating from Constantinople are frequently viewed with suspicion and dislike. Nevertheless, the avowed object of the new règime is the Ottomanisation of the whole.[8]

Fraser had a good sense of the obstacles facing the Young Turk regime but (like other European observers of the time) he was inclined to view multi-"racial" and multi-linguistic existence as a problem to be overcome rather than as the norm it was in the empire of the time. Because his own model began with racial, religious, and national uniformity, he could imagine no alternative option. Fraser can be forgiven for his rather limited vision of the shaping of the modern state, but the frames through which he assessed the empire have been all too readily adopted by modern historiography. Hence, the nation remains the measure by which late Ottoman society is assessed, typed, and identified.

But what is the nation? It is much easier to talk of nationalism and invented national traditions in the twenties than in 1908. In the twenties, empire was no longer an option; but in the Ottoman press of 1908 it is often quite difficult to discern how exactly the "nation" was different from the empire. What made the empire a "nation" seems primarily to have been the acquisition of a constitutional regime and the popularization of the designation *milli* (national). The language of nationalism was being practiced in the empire just as it was being practiced in the various states of Europe.[9] The nation was not, in general, an entity envisioned as having reduced boundaries or ethnic and linguistic homogenization. It was a large, unwieldy empire composed of many communities; the problems of generating allegiance to the "nation" remained the same as those of generating allegiance to the empire.

OTTOMANISM

The revolutionary press clearly reflects the assessment of Roderic Davison that, "To the end of the empire . . . the concept of Ottomanism persisted."[10]

Conclusion

In the cartoon space, Ottomanism was an inclusive, understood, assumed category, a rhetorical category which attempted to provide a locus of unity and, often, to bypass the local identities, which were not an invention of the nineteenth century but which formed the basis for individual and community identity throughout the Ottoman period. This Ottoman identity could be named or unnamed; it was joined, and complicated, in cartoons, by the various designations of Türk, Türkiye, and *milliye*, which could suggest, however vaguely, some type of national identity.

As the Ottoman state attempted to provide for its own continuity against the pressures of European imperialism, the state rhetoric of unity explored various options, a process mirrored in Iran with the reformulation of the Qajar empire. Ottomanism was a default category that did not attempt, for the most part, to bridge the class lines between *askeri* and *reaya*, but rather attempted to resist the exclusionary losses demanded by pan-Islam and by ethnic or linguistic separatist movements. This was a process that, although represented by different legitimizing constructs, had characterized the central government's attempts to retain the allegiances of polyglot provinces for generations. Like other idealist legitimizing concepts, Ottomanism was not primarily an operational category intended to transform all day-to-day interactions among people. That said, it was still meaningful; its articulators intended to create a social consciousness that would preserve both empire and privilege. In the period here studied, the new regime was still engaged in that process of legitimizing and defending the Ottoman nation. The satiric press laughed at that regime's failures, as it had at those of the old regime. But, at the same time, it reinforced the basic identity of Ottoman-ness through its own rhetorics of internal unity and resistance against the forces of fragmentation. Within that assumed Ottoman identity, satirists emphasized the differences of citizen and foreigner, old and new, male and female, Westernized and not Westernized, imperialist and imperialized, and affluent and poor.

The satirical press did imply that there was such a thing as Ottoman culture, even though the culture of the elites might differ considerably from that of the masses. Even those Ottomans accused of being Europeanized were still represented as Ottomans; there was no confusing them with the "real" Europeans.[11] The markers of Ottoman culture, those things that identified people as Ottoman in the cartoon space, have been at least partially elaborated here. They included the very geographic space in which Ottomans lived, the sovereign or regime they served, the clothes they wore, their accoutrements, food, and characteristic behaviors (as distinct from those of Europeans or others), and their seemingly innate desire not to be subsumed into some other "national" entity. All of these things figure into what is often an intangible sense of who is "us" and who is "them," what is "here" and what is "there." Cartoons tried to make these intangibles tangible.

Conclusion

ETHNICITY AS IDENTITY

The cartoon space comprised a range of possibilites where identity was concerned. Specific named (or nameable) individuals were identified; groups or types (politicians, monarchs, workers, middle-class women) were embodied in a single figure; and nations were embodied in figures that were allegorical, like John Bull, or real, like Abd ül-Hamid. Except for politicians and heads of state, most cartoon figures were not named individuals. Thus, most cartoon figures were representative of collective identities and, often, those identities were overlapping. For example, ethno-linguistic identities could overlap with gender or functional identities. This use of overlapping or multiple identities, in Ottoman cartoons, confounds expectations based on simple ethnic dichotomies.

Given the nature of the historiographic discourse on nationalism, I had expected the Ottoman cartoon space to be full of vehement ethnic representations, the reflections of the ethno-linguistic national struggles that would seem to have dominated the late Ottoman period.[12] Surely the cartoons would express a range of violent tensions or hostilities between Turk, Arab, Greek, and Armenian. But I did not find the ethnic satire, in volume or degree, that I expected. Perhaps I was looking in the wrong places; perhaps a study of the Arabic, Greek, or Armenian language gazettes would have produced just the type of "ethnic" caricature I expected. (Certainly it would be useful to compare the satire produced in Istanbul with that produced in the provinces.) Then again, perhaps the Turk, the Arab, the Greek, the Armenian, and others defined as "national" types, so taken for granted in the traditional historiography, did not exist as such in the Ottoman gazettes. They seem to have been imagined differently in the satirical press of the revolutionary era. That is not to say that I did not find ethnic satire (or hostility) in the Ottoman cartoon space; but it was a different sort of ethnic satire, one with a longer history than that based on the image of the modern nation-state and its devotees.

Ethnicity, most often suggested by dress and sometimes by facial type in cartoons, tended to delineate the occupants of different states rather than to differentiate among the various ethnic groups within the boundaries of the empire. That is, a common type of ethnic satire opposed the Ottoman to the Frenchman or the Ottoman to the Austrian. Exaggerated "ethnic" dress separated the Ottoman from the foreigner, or it suggested the traditional identity of the empire in contrast to a proferred "modern" European identity. Cartoons did show "ethnic" Ottomans. But when ethnicity was pointed out, usually through costume, it was often done to produce a comic effect rather than to point up separatist sentiments among members of the Ottoman public.[13] Such cartoons frequently targeted rural or "country" people (the Anatolian peasant, the Albanian villager), in the form of "hick" or bumpkin jokes. Their ethnicity was associated with their naivete, ignorance, or lack of sophistication. Or, ethnic satire caricatured regional differences in much the same way that Americans employ Yankee, Southerner, or "red-neck" jokes. The gazette, *Cadaloz,* for example, frequently ran this type of satire. This was an old genre of humor, one that was exploited fully in traditional Ottoman theater forms like the shadow play.[14] It was certainly not specific to the age of nationalism.

Where "national" dress was used to designate an ethno-linguistic or geographic identity within the empire, it was not typically used to express an overt hostility based on any sort of "national" grounds. Of course hostility comes in many forms, as our literature on stereotyping has made quite clear. Hostility based on class or economic grounds can express itself in ethnic terms and could do so in Ottoman satiric gazettes. Hostility based on what we would call ethno-national grounds was expressed in references to the Balkans, particularly in the case of Bulgaria, which declared its independence shortly after the revolution. Nonetheless, in Ottoman cartoons in Istanbul in the period 1908–1911, the purposeful identification of Ottoman "ethnics" tended to take the less conflictual social forms noted above more often than the angry or rejectionist typing of ethno-linguistic groups within Ottoman society.

This neglect of certain types of ethnic satire does not, of course, prove that the empire was a haven of ethnic tolerance.[15] That would be hard to demonstrate anywhere, although it is useful to point out that polyglot empires like the Ottoman empire had multiculturalism long before it became a late-twentieth-century fashion. We have testimonies, for example, that show that conflicts in the Ottoman schools could manifest themselves through divisions along ethnic lines. Corinne Blake has pointed out the "intensification of ethnic awareness," after 1908, among Arab students at the Mülkiye government training school. She notes that Arab students were angered by attacks in the Istanbul newspapers on Abd ül-Hamid's advisors, Abu ül-Huda and İzzet Pasha, and by the designation "*pis Arab*" (dirty Arab), applied to them.[16] Ten years later, İrfan Orga noted that ethnic tensions in the schools, which he suggests were always a factor, had been greatly exacerbated by the war and by the flood of refugees into Istanbul.[17]

What the distribution of ethnic satire in the Ottoman satirical gazettes does suggest is that (1) Ottoman satire had a long history of humor based on lampooning regional differences in dress and speech; (2) differentiating Ottoman from foreigner was a task that took precedence over making internal ethno-linguistic distinctions at this particular juncture in Ottoman history; (3) rhetorics of unity had a certain priority in the turmoil of the revolutionary era, even in satire that often minimized the ethnic differences *among* Ottomans. It may also be the case that those men who were producing Ottoman satiric gazettes in Istanbul at the time tended to be men with a commitment to Ottomanism and, hence, men whose interests were not served by vitriolic and divisive ethnic satire.

One interesting example of the disparity between the historiographic

Ottoman "ethnic" and the "ethnic" of the cartoon space is the cartoon "Arab." As already noted, revolutionary cartoons drew ties of unity and brotherhood between the Ottomans (not ethnically differentiated) and the "Arabs," particularly those in Egypt and Morocco. The choice of Egypt and Morocco is not, I think, coincidental. These two areas were not functionally part of the empire and were depicted as subjected to the yoke of European imperialism. The Young Egyptians and the Young Ottomans were equated as partners in liberating revolutionary movements. "Arabs" within the empire, in Syria and Palestine for example, were not usually so differentiated, presumably because they *were* Ottomans and part of the empire.

Hence, if there was an Arab nationalism in the cartoon space, it was a "nationalism" aimed at throwing off the British, not at indelibly separating "Turk" from "Arab." Both these designations are, in any case, very ambiguous categories when one considers the considerable ethnic mixing that had existed for centuries within the empire.[18] Other than in this anti-imperialist form, the "Arab" is a bit hard to find in these Ottoman cartoons. He does not appear as a rabid separatist, demanding an Arab nation from the new regime. He does not appear, as he will in a later era in the West, as a catch-all symbol of terrorism and trouble. Indeed, one can scan hundreds of Ottoman cartoons without finding a figure who can be irrevocably tagged as "Arab." For that matter, one can scan hundreds of cartoons without finding a figure tagged as a "Turk," except where "Turk" stands as a synonym for Ottoman in general and particularly for an Ottoman as distinct from a European.

Arabs, then, as a select group, tended to be treated in Ottoman satire only in very specific sets of circumstances, especially in the targeting of Abd ül-Hamid's coterie of "corrupt" cronies.[19] Some Arabs were associated with special privileges under the sultan's regime and hence they were targeted, not only as Arabs per se, but as individuals who represented the abuses of the old regime. It is also important to note that emphasizing ethnic or racial hierarchies did not tend to serve the interests of the new regime or of many of the Young Turk literati. Şükrü Hanioğlu has pointed out that

> the Young Turks refrained from formulating a nationalist theory involving race during the formative years of their movement. Although, in their scientific writings they frequently discussed the importance of race, they proposed no theory evaluating "the Turkish race." There is little doubt that this was because, in the Darwinist racial hierarchy, Turks were always assigned to the lowest ranks. . . . This coupled with the participation of many non-Turk members in the nascent movement, prevented the Young Turks from focusing on the race issue.[20]

This situation, Hanioğlu argues, changed after the first Japanese victories over Russia in 1904: "The Young Turks [then] embraced the race theories except for the placement of Turkish and Asian peoples in the lowest rungs.

With Japanese successes, they achieved a new freedom to use race theories, because now they could rearrange the hierarchical assignments." Hanioğlu goes on to point to the significance of Yusuf Akçura, a Tatar, in advancing Turkism as opposed to Ottomanism.[21] The extent of this commitment to Turkism, however, remains problematic if for no other reasons than that there were not so many "pure" Turks and, furthermore, because fixing ethnic hierarchies might tend to alienate those segments of the Ottoman population that the Young Turks wished to unify and preserve.[22] In any case, I do not propose to solve the race question, or even to propose when the Ottoman satirists began to draw Turks instead of Ottomans. To muddy the waters further, one might say that, in the period from 1908–1911, the Istanbul satirists tended to draw Ottomans, but sometimes they called them *Turks*.[23]

The vision of ethnic identity in the cartoon space is, of course, only one vision among many. It is at once a surreal vision and one firmly rooted in past tropes of caricature. But it does suggest that the "national" framing of the ethnic question in the late Ottoman state is a very restrictive type of framing, one which not only telescopes a complex and evolving social reality but also projects an ideal and very particular European vision of nation onto the peoples of the empire. Some of the Ottoman editors and cartoonists were certainly complicit in the projection of that nationalist ideal. But the Ottoman cartoon space, notorious for its reduction of individuals to types for satirical purposes, did not reduce Ottoman society to a melange of contending "nations."

A final problem, where identity and nation are concerned, is the problem of religious identity. A long debated question that extends well beyond the realm of Ottoman studies is that over the extent to which competing identities are subsumed under the consuming category of "Muslim" in Islamic states. One sometimes gets the impression in reading about the late empire that ethnic identities are paramount as long as one takes for granted that religious identity, for Muslims at any rate, is even more paramount. (This characterization is even now apparent in the one-time Yugoslavia where the Christian citizens are designated ethnically, as Serbs or Croats, and the Muslim citizens are designated communally as if they had no ethnicity.) Muslim identity is often represented as absolutely primary at least until Atatürk attempted to subordinate or mask it in the aftermath of the empire's demise in World War I. If that were truly so, it is difficult to imagine that such a powerful cultural norm could be challenged to the extent that Atatürk managed to challenge it with his radical secularizing ideals.[24] Somewhere there must be an historiographic middle ground between Islam as preeminent in the empire and Islam as subordinate in the republic.[25]

In the cartoon space, Islam was neglected, not because it was unimportant, but as already noted, because it provided a powerful force for social unity in a time when that social unity was being vehemently challenged and threatened. Thus, those forces and ideologies that might have provoked an attack on Islam, organized religion in general, and religious custom were restrained in the cartoon space. The Ottoman satirists tended to leave the second estate alone, contenting themselves, instead, with oblique satire directed at traditionalism and superstition. In fact, one might argue that specific allusions to Islam tended to fall within the category of rhetorics of unity rather than within the category of rhetorics of difference, at least where cartoon satire was concerned.[26] Religious difference, like ethnic difference, did not command the attention of the satirists in the same way that the differences between Ottoman and foreigner did.

HISTORIOGRAPHY—FOUR FRAMES

Theoretical models in history need never match ground level realities, which are themselves always relative unknowns. But it is important to appreciate the ways in which our historigraphic frames have pointed the historian's gaze in very specific and sometimes limiting directions. The late Ottoman period has been viewed through a set of prisms that only sometimes coincide with the prisms employed by Ottoman editors and cartoonists to convey their own sense of revoutionary realities. Having grouped examples of Ottoman satire into my own set of limiting thematic or content frames, I would like to conclude by commenting briefly on what I see as possible historiographic problems and possiblities for reframing.

Despite its survival into the twentieth century, the Ottoman state formation remained an early modern one. Viewing it as such, rather than as a "periphery" in a world capitalist system or as a chronologically modern state in the body of a medieval empire, suggests some of the ways in which it might be profitably analyzed. The satirical press indicates several possible frames. First, the empire can be compared to other agrarian empires with long traditions of kingship: Muslim empires, like Iran, and non-Muslim empires, like Russia. The Ottoman press made these comparisons, and measured itself against those monarchical states that were perceived to have successfully negotiated modernization, like Japan, and those perceived to be indelibly committed to tradition and despotism, like Russia. Economic stability, military power, and "freedom," differentially defined, were important indices in that evaluation of success.

A second frame is the colonial frame, the extent to which the empire is drawn as one of a series of victims or targets of European imperialism. It may seem that this is a frame that has been extensively explored and developed. But that is not the case. Because the empire was not directly conquered or colonized by European states, it has not been such a focus of dependency theory as, for example, India has been; it is separated from those areas like India, Brazil, and Mexico, which were conquered and with which it might legitimately be compared. Where relations with Europe are concerned, the empire has tended to be treated in terms of two historigraphic traditions: one is the continuation of the enduring Islam vs. the West frame (applied to the relations of all Middle Eastern states with Europe from the time of the Crusades to the present); the other is a tradition by which the empire is measured against a model of the industrialized nation-state, based on England and France, and evaluated in accordance with the extent to which it diverges from that model. Neither of these traditions is without value. But, again, the Ottoman cartoon space suggests an alternative mode for evaluating "East–West" relations. That mode starts with a model of the empire, as center, rather than with a model of Britain or France. It assesses Europe in terms of the degree to which it has affected or is capable of affecting Ottoman society, and then values those effects as desirable or undesirable. The margin of tolerance varies from gazette to gazette, but no satirical gazette valued the European impact as either entirely desirable or entirely undesirable. Further, in the cartoon space, cultural synthesis is taken for granted; it is not viewed as a new process. What is different is that the empire, once a great imperial power itself, is viewed as subject to the new imperial powers and compelling cultural influences of Europe. Satirists drew the empire as militarily, economically, and culturally exposed and vulnerable; they critiqued that position, laughed at it, and tried to measure the empire's options for response

A third possible framing technique, related to the second, is that which draws boundaries of association and separation based on the dichotomy of imperialists and imperialized. That is, the satirical press drew bonds of sympathy with those states that seemed to share their position of subordination to Europe, and it drew lines of antipathy against those states that imposed the burdens of subordination. This particular frame is useful because it violates the geographic and ethno-linguistic boundary drawing that is the essential element of the nationalism model.[27] The nationalism model, applied to the turn-of-the-century empire, neatly sorts the peoples of the empire into Arabs, Greeks, Turks, Armenians, and ascribes to them nation-state aspirations. It obscures a complex set of associations, allegiances, alliances, ideologies, identities, language use, and living patterns. The content of the satirical press does not neatly express those ethno-linguistic divisions any more than it fits into ready dichotomies of the Christian West and the Muslim East.

Another frame for the analysis of the late Ottoman empire is that of notable politics, a frame not really dealt with here, but one that has been employed to great advantage in European historiography on the Medieval and Early Modern periods. There has been a type of study of Ottoman notable politics, embodied in the examinations of political parties and factions by such scholars as Ahmad, Hanioğlu, and Zürcher.[28] But what is still required is the pursuit of the lines of inquiry proposed in the works of Niyazi Berkes, Şerif Mardin, and Bernard Lewis, those lines of inquiry that link notable politics to their intellectual, literary, and social contexts.[29] This work, by its very nature, requires the collaboration of historians and of scholars who are well versed in all aspects of late Ottoman literature. The significance of intellectual trends (though these are often exaggerated or held aloof from their economic and social milieus) cannot be discarded. To do so would be to ignore the overlap in literary production and political influence found in the late Ottoman state, particularly in Istanbul.

Ottoman literati often held governmental positions in the revolutionary and constitutional period. They were not generally the first tier of political power like the sultan and state ministers, but they held the second- or third-tier authority of governmental functionary and deputy, often wielded by members of relatively affluent Ottoman families who had the benefit of higher and foreign education. Notable politics translated into access to political power through knowledge of world systems and into a "popular" or public voice through literary production. The education, financial position, network of foreign and domestic contacts, and degree of familiarity with the European aggressor/ally gave these members of the intelligensia avenues for exploring in the press the ambiguities of the Ottoman position, the nature and extent of its integration into a new world order, and the options for meeting or succumbing to the threat of European dominance. This press was searching for options, alternatives to the sultanic order and to that order's integration into the schema of Great Power politics, which the constitutional revolution had rejected. The options articulated in that search, and their form, language, and rhetorics of exclusion or inclusion, constitute revolutionary Ottoman expressions of self. They reveal the points of concern of those Ottoman elites and of the society over which they attempted to exert their influence.

REVOLUTIONARY OPTIONS AND THE ROLE OF THE WEST

How does the content of the Ottoman satiric press diverge from our historiographic expectations? First, it was not exactly a harbinger of the Turkish republic. Second, it did not dismantle the sultanic order with unbridled enthusiasm, in part because foreign powers were perceived as conducting that particular dismemberment themselves, without bothering to consult the Ottomans about their wishes. Ottoman satire was not committed to the inevitable outcomes that later events and historians have bestowed upon the empire. The final era of Ottoman history has to a certain extent been denied the perception of alternatives. This study, through one limited set of sources, has attempted to reveal that perception.

The dialogic form, so favored in the revolutionary press, symbolizes the nature of the press itself. The dialogue suggests a dynamic Ottoman reality, one that presents a series of options and a series of as yet indeterminate outcomes. The dialectical relationship between utopia and the existing order, as expressed by Karl Mannheim, might be applied to the Ottoman case: "Every age allows to arise ... those ideas and values in which are contained the unrealized and unfulfilled tendencies and needs of that age. These are the explosive elements for bursting the limits of the established order."[30] The cartoon space expressed the utopian ideals, the fears, the disappointments, and the desires of the revolutionary era. Both integrative and subversive tendencies can be found in that space; and the balance struck between them was mediated through, but not dictated by, European imperialism. The choices made and the ultimate outcomes decided were in the process of being worked out. The press saw itself as a primary agent of that working out process and European imperialism as a primary impediment.

Of course the decision to pursue any given option is never free and unencumbered. As discussed in this study, the satiric press was constrained by the systems and symbols already in place, no less than by political and economic conditions.[31] Satire, however, and cartoon satire in particular, sometimes operated to simplify the representation of Ottoman alternatives into the good, the bad, and the ugly. Often enough the sultanic order became the bad, the constitutional order became the good, and the European imperial order became the ugly—the latter complicating the easy choice between bipolar goods and evils, and standing in the background waiting to seize the profits while the internal forces for good and evil struggled. At other times, of course, the satirical press seemed to say that Ottoman society's options were the real bad, the bad, and the not so bad, each designation applying alternately to Europe, the old regime, and the new regime. It is not in the nature of satire to paint rosy pictures; if it were, the Ottoman satirists would have had only limited cause for optimism.

Some of the options suggested in the satirical press were conquest and the surrender to Europen culture, tenacious adherence to the imperfect yet familiar old order, or some form of compromise position along with its concomitant anxiety and cultural schizophrenia. The responses to these options in the cartoon space tended toward: some kind of inclusive vison of Ottomanism; the acceptance of a qualified notion of progress that admitted the inevitability of European-style modernization but that challenged the notion that that modernization was desirable; and an insistence on the need to control cultural and economic choices and to defend the nation against foreign invasion.

There remains the question of how to measure the West's role in the transformation of Ottoman state and society in the modern era. This issue has been problematic rather than controversial; it has been delineated mostly in Orientalist and nationalist terms. It has been little disturbed, at least in Ottoman historiography, by the polemical broadside of Edward Said's *Orientalism* and its successors. The notion that the West rose and the East unwillingly knelt and became Westernized as part of the march of progress embodied in Western civilization has been accepted rather unilaterally. But the satirical press represented the European role in Ottoman society's transformation, and in the creation of its desires and resentments, as multilayered and problematic. It cast Europe, all too often in the guise of greedy imperialist rather than in the guise of enlightened role-model. Further, it represented Ottoman society as static only when it wished to mock the nature or speed of its responses to Europen penetration, when it wanted to lampoon its own passive vessels. Otherwise it represented Ottoman society as an active resistor, revisor, recreator, and interpreter of Western culture.

How one draws the border lines between cultures, and discerns whose culture is whose is, of course, a vexed question. The Ottoman satirists called Ottoman culture many things, and, in the cartoon space, the images of that culture sometimes called for vigorous delineation of the borders between the empire and Europe and sometimes for stretching, swirling, or radically altering them.[32] The boundaries of the modern nation-state must be clear but, as the cartoonists well knew, cultural boundaries had no such constraints.

The problem of cultural hegemony is crucial to this study of Ottoman satire, a study that focuses specifically on texts rather than events. I do not pretend to have resolved it. But the work of anthropologists may prove useful in imagining the nature of the Ottoman–European cultural encounter. In his work on the South Seas, Marshall Sahlins expressed the equation as one of encounters through which cultural change, "externally induced," nevertheless becomes "indigenously orchestrated." John and Jean Comaroff, working on Africa, put it this way: "local history, always 'the outcome of a reciprocally determining interaction of local and global forces whose logic must first be comprehended in its own terms,' is best conceptualized as the reflex of a 'dialectic of articulation between a local system and its encompassing context'—that is, in light of how 'internal forms and external forces' condition each other."[33]

I would not argue that we can comprehend the logic of the Ottoman journalist on its own terms. But the problem as stated by Sahlins and by the Comaroffs is one with which Ottoman historians must contend. Once the image of victorious Europe pouring its ideas into the leaky if not empty vessel of the Middle East is relinquished, then the "indigenous orchestrations" of Sahlins can be examined. But that act alone does not settle the question. The Ottoman empire never employed its language and images in a vacuum constructed of some pure native tradition as uniquely discernable from a distinct and increasingly threatening Western "other."[34]

The Ottoman empire was Constantinople, enduring symbol par excellance of the synthesis of material and intellectual traditions of East and West. If Europe and the Ottoman empire evolved as sites of recombinations of linguistic and cultural traditions, sharing certain cultural elements, like Indo-European literary traditions, then how can we possibly accept either the indigenous/exogenous paradigm of the anthropologists or the oriental/occidental paradigm of Said (which granted was never intended to be permanent or fixed). Istanbul was not only the East, it was the West, it was Rum.[35]

Here the "reciprocally determining interaction" of the Comaroffs is a useful idea (although I would still not state the alternatives in terms of "internal forms and external forces" since these oppositional terms suggest inertia vs. determining activity). I have not, here, attempted to evaluate the effects of the Ottoman interaction on Europe. This study, rather, attempts to transmit or perhaps translate the dialogic processes (including those in images) that represented the logic by which some Ottomans expressed their revolutionary vision (an attempt to construct reality) and their notions of revolutionary reality. In the course of that attempt, it becomes apparent that European imperialism was a very important and determining factor in the construction of Ottoman satire. Once that influence is recognized, it still has to be interpreted in terms of representation and meaning. Representation involves the universe of symbols employed in the Ottoman cartoon space and the revolutionary options those symbols suggested. I have here tried to convey at least a small part of that universe of symbols; the interpretation of their meaning, however, is highly subjective.

It is easier to say what the weight given to European imperialism in Ottoman satire does not mean than what it does mean. It does not mean either a wholesale celebration or a wholesale rejection of European culture. Each frame represents a value judgment of the relative validity of Ottoman and European cultural, economic, and political systems. The Ottomans gave value to the European systems insofar as they were thought by each individual satirist or editor to be beneficial. At the same time, there was a resistance to cultural options determined abroad, hence a need to make Western cultural symbols (and the Ottomans who employed them) ridiculous. Certainly, the empire's own imperialist and dominant past lent a romantic, nostalgic, and security-conscious weight to old regime symbols. But, the association of the old regime with oppression, despotism, and failure, and the success of the constitutional revolution moved Ottoman satire in the direction of giving serious consideration to European forms that, were the empire in a position of power, it could have ignored or considered at its leisure.

The Ottoman people and nation, then, could not be defined outside the confines of the conditions of European dominance, but that does not imply an inevitable recognition of the superiority of European political and cultural modes. The forces of cultural assimilation, though they favored the dominant side, were operating in a long process of synthesis that began long before the eighteenth century and that involved other cultures besides the Ottoman and the French. Ottoman historians, then, need not choose between discovering the Ottoman nation and making Ottoman "peasants into Frenchmen," on the one hand, or making them, Ziya Gökalp notwithstanding, prematurely into "Turks" on the other. Like the "Terrible Turk" of the

Renaissance world (the embodiment of the Islam vs. the West paradigm) these identity options only tell part of the story.

The satirical press, like the shadow puppet theater, created a vision of reality, the cartoon celebrating itself as both illusion and reflection of the world, the print image both denying and affirming its relationship to the vicissitudes of day-to-day social and political interaction. The page of the gazette was the curtain of the shadow theater, its images dancing, mocking, translucent, familiar, tempting the viewer to discern the "truth." As Hacivat tells us in one of his many play-opening "curtain poems":

> To the eye of the uninitiated this curtain produces (only) images.
> But to him who knows the signs, symbols of truth. . . .
> It relates the reality of the world through a language of symbols. . . .
> Behold the meanings which are hidden under this (play)!
> It is a show of subtlety intended for the expert ones to understand its subtle points.[36]

Like the viewers of the shadow play, the scholars of the late Ottoman empire and its press take what appear to be "only images" and produce from them a multiplicity of "truths."

Appendix 1
List of Gazettes

Information for these charts is based on physical examination of the gazettes. Many gazettes changed publishing house frequently and this chart reflects the publisher listed for issue 1, or in the case of the following gazettes the publisher listed on the first available issue: Arz-u hâl, Curcuna, Geveze, Gramofon, Hokkabaz, Latife, Nekregû ile Pişekâr, Protesto, Şahika, Şark.

Title	Dates	Frequency	Publisher
Afacan	August 1911	twice weekly	Manzume-i Efkâr
Alafranga	Nov–Dec 1910	twice weekly	Ruşen
Alem	Feb–Jun 1909	weekly	Arif
Arz-u hâl	Feb–Mar 1909	weekly irr.	Karagöz
Aşiyan	Sep 1908–Mar 1909	weekly	Ş. Müretibbiye
Beyan ül-hak	Oct 1908–Nov 1912	weekly	Yeni İkdam
Boşboğaz	Aug–Dec 1908	twice weekly	Osmaniye
Cadaloz	Apr–Sep 1911	twice weekly	Tercüman-ı Hakikat
Cellâd	20 Sep 1908	one only	n.p.
Cingöz	Sep–Oct 1908	twice weekly	Şems
Coşkun kalender	Apr 1909–1911 n.s.	weekly irr.	Hayriye ve Şürekâsı
Curcuna	Feb–Apr 1911	weekly	Mısr
Dalkavuk	Sep 1908–Mar 1909	weekly	Hilal
Davul	Oct 1908–May 1909	weekly	Hilal
Dertli ile garib	Aug–Sep 1910	twice weekly	Manzume-i Efkâr
Devr-i cedid	May–Jul 1909	weekly	Ruşen
Eşek	29 Nov 1910	one only	———
Eşref	Mar–May 1909	weekly	Ahmed Said Bey
Ezop	Sep 1908	twice weekly	Türkiye Kitabhanesi
Falaka	Aug–Oct 1911	twice weekly	Manzume-i Efkâr
Geveze	Nov 1908–Jun 1909	daily irr.	Asr
Gramofon	Mar–Jun 1909	weekly	Ceride-i Şarkiye
Hacivat	Sep 1908	twice weekly	İbn al-Hâkkı
Hande	Apr 1910	weekly	Bakr Efendi
Hikmet	Apr 1910–Sep 1912	weekly	Ahmed Sakı
Hokkabaz	Oct 1908		———
İncili çavuş	Aug–Oct 1908	twice weekly	Karabet
İnkılâb	Jul–Nov 1909	weekly	Hayriye ve Şürekâsı
İspiritizma	Jan–Jul 1910	monthly	

List of Gazettes

Title	Dates	Frequency	Publisher
İştirak	Feb–Sep 1910	weekly	Bakr Efendi
İttifak	Aug–Sep 1908	daily	Hanımlara Mahsus
Kalem	Sep 1908–Jun 1911	weekly	Kalem
Kara kuş	Sep 1908	twice weekly	Cihan
Kibar	6 Dec 1910	one only	———
Lâklâk	Jul–Oct 1909	weekly	Mahmud Bey
Lâla	Dec 1910–Jan 1911	weekly	Amedî
Latife	Jul 1911	twice weekly	Türk
Malûm	Dec 1910–Jan 1911	twice weekly irr.	———
Meram	Nov 1908–Feb 1909	weekly irr.	———
Millet	Aug–Oct 1908	daily	Matbaa-ı Osmaniye
Muhit (Musavver)	Nov 1908–Aug 1909	weekly	Hayriye ve Şürekâsı
Nekregû	Aug–Oct 1908	weekly	Karabet
Nekregû ile Pişekâr	Jun–Jul 1909	weekly	Vatan
Nevsal-ı Osmanî	1910–1911	annual	Kanaat
Osmanlı ziraat ve ticaret gazetesi*	Mar 1909–Sep 1910	weekly	Ruşen
Papağan (Musavver)	Sep 1908–May 1909	weekly irr.	Karabet
Perde	Dec 1911–Feb 1912	twice weekly	Asr
Piyano	1910	weekly	Hürriyet
Protesto	Nov? 1908–Apr 1909	twice monthly irr.	Cihan
Püsküllü belâ	Feb–Apr 1909	weekly	Hayriye ve Şürekâsı
Resimli kitab	Sep 1908–Feb 1913	monthly	Resimli Kitab
Salname-i servet-i fünun	1910–1911	annual	Ahmed İhsan
Serbesti	Nov 1908–Sep 1912	daily	Selanik
Şahika (Musavver)	Dec 1910	weekly irr.	Şems
Şakacı	Oct–Dec? 1908	weekly	Artın Asadurian
Şark	Aug–Sep 1908	daily	Kasbar
Şark ve Kürdistan	Nov–Dec 1908	twice weekly	Kasbar
Şikâyet	Apr 1909	weekly	Cihan
Takvim-i vekayi n.s.	Sep 1908–1922	daily	Sabah
Ton ton risalesi	18 Sep 1908	one only	———
Ulûm-i iktisadiye ve içtimaiye mecmuası	Dec 1908–Dec 1910	monthly	Hilal
Üç gazetesi	Sep 1908	daily	Şirket-i Sahafiye
Al-Üfürük	Sep–Oct 1908	weekly	Hilal
Volkan	Dec 1908–Apr 1909	daily irr.	Ahmed Sakı
Yeni geveze	Mar 1910–Aug 1912	twice weekly	Bakr Efendi
Yuha	15 Dec 1910	one only	———
Zevzek	Sep 1908	twice weekly	İkbal
Züğürt	Mar–Jul 1911	twice weekly	Manzume-i Efkâr

*This is volume 3; vols. 1–2 were published before the revolution: May 1907–Mar 1908.

Appendix 2
Price and Post

Prices: k = kuruş, p = para, f = franc, r = ruble, mec. = mecidiyye, pi = piastre
Subscription prices are given for one year (followed by a slash and the six month subscription price when provided). Where prices changed the initial price is given, followed by a comma, then the second price.
dışarı = outside/provinces/foreign —— = no information given   * = frequency irregular

Title	Issue Price	Subscription: Dar ül-Saadet (Istanbul)	Vilâyet (Provinces)	Ecnebiye (Foreign)
[Twice Weekly]				
Afacan	10 p	30 k		12 f
Alafranga	10 p			
Boşboğaz	20 p	75 k / 40 k		
Cadaloz	10 p	30 k		12 f
Cingöz	20 p	40 k	50 k	60 k
Dertli ile garib	10 p	35 k / 20 k		10 f / 6 f
Ezop	20 p	40 k	55 k	
Falaka	20 p	half lira	half lira	80 k
Hacivat	20 p	65 k / 35 k		80 k
İncili çavuş	20 p	40 k	60 k	
Kara kuş	10 p	20 k	35 k	20 pi
Latife	20 p	50 k / 25 k		15 f
Malûm*	10 p	25 k		
Perde	10 p	25 k / 13 k (100 issues)		10 f / 5 f
Şark ve Kürdistan	10 p	40 k	60 k	80 k
Yeni geveze	10 p	35 k / 20 k (later 25 k / 13 k)		
Zevzek	20 p			
Züğürt	10 p	25 k		
[Weekly]				
Alem	50 p	70 k	80 k	17 f
Arz-u hâl*	20 p	25 k / 15 k		
Aşiyan	——			
Beyan ül-hak	10 p	95 k / 50 k (area not specified)		

335

Price and Post

Title	Issue Price	Subscription: Dar Ül-Saadet (Istanbul)	Vilâyet (provinces)	Ecnebiye (foreign)
Coşkun kalender*	10 p	30 k / 20 k		
Curcuna	10 p	20 k / 12 k	35 k / 25 k	
Dalkavuk	20 p	20 k	30 k (40 issues)	
Davul	1 k	65 k		16 f
Devr-i cedid	50 p	65 k / 35 k		16 f / 9 f
Eşref	20 p	65 k / 35 k		80 k / 45 k
Gramofon	10 p	27 k		
Hande	20 p	40 k		50 f
Hikmet	20 p		35 k / 20 k	10 f / 6 f
Hokkabaz*	20 p	25 k	38 k	8 f
İnkılâb	20 p	40 k / 20 k		
İştirak	20 p	60 k / 40 k (later 40 k / 25 k)		
Kalem	1 k	70 k	80 k	18 f
Lâklâk	10 p	20 k	20 k	5 f
Lâla	10 p	30 k	30 k	
Meram*	—			
Muhit	50 p, 2 k	60 k / 30 k	80 k / 45 k	18 f / 9 f
Nekregû	20 p	30 k		
Nekregû ile Pişekâr	10 p	25 k / 15 k	25 k / 15 k	30 k / 17 k
Osmanlı ziraat ve ticaret gazetesi	40 p	half lira	3 mec. / 30 k	14 f / 7 f
Papağan*	40 p, 20 p			
Piyano	20 p	30 k / 20 k		
Püsküllü belâ	30 p	45 k	50 k (*dışarı*)	
Şahika*	1 k	45 k / 25 k	45 k / 25 k	
Şakacı	20 p	25 k	38 k	
Şikâyet	10 p	40 k		12 f
Al-Üfürük	20 p	35 k / 20 k	35 k / 20 k	7 f or 3 r

[Twice Monthly]

Protesto*	10 p	120 k	120 k	30 f

[Monthly]

İspiritizma	—			
Resimli kitab	5 k	60 k / 30 k	80 k / 40 k	18 f / 9 f
Ulûm-i iktisadiye ve içtimaiye mecmuası	10 k	1 lira		

[One Issue Only]

Cellâd	10 p
Eşek	10 p
Kibar	10 p
Ton ton risalesi	20 p
Yuha	10 p

Price and Post

[Daily]				
Geveze*	10 p	110 k / 55 k	140 k / 70 k	
İttifak	10 p		150 k / 80 k	32 f / 17 f
Millet	10 p		180 k / 95 k	40 f or 15 r
Serbesti	10 p	180 k / 90 k		38 f
Şark	10 p		150 k / 80 k	40 f / 20 f
Takvim-i vekayi n.s.	10 p		120 k (*dışarı*)	
Üç gazete	10 p		150 k / 80 k	30 f / 20 f
Volkan*	10 p	108 k	120 k / 70 k	
[Annual]				
Nevsal-ı Osmaniye	—			
Salname-i servet-i fünun		130 k		150 k

337

Appendix 3
Location of Publishers

The area surrounding Bab-ı Âli Caddesi in the Eminönü District held the highest concentration of publishers in the city. Among the gazettes cited in this study, of the thirty publishers who listed addresses, twenty-six were located in this area: thirteen on Bab-ı Âli Street itself; four on streets branching off Bab-ı Âli Street (Cagaloğlu Caddesi, Divan Yolu, Şeref Efendi Sokak, Abu Su'ud Caddesi); five in the vicincity of the new post office (Yeni Postahane); and four at Çemberlitaşı/Vezir Hanı. Two others were nearby and two were in Beyoğlu.

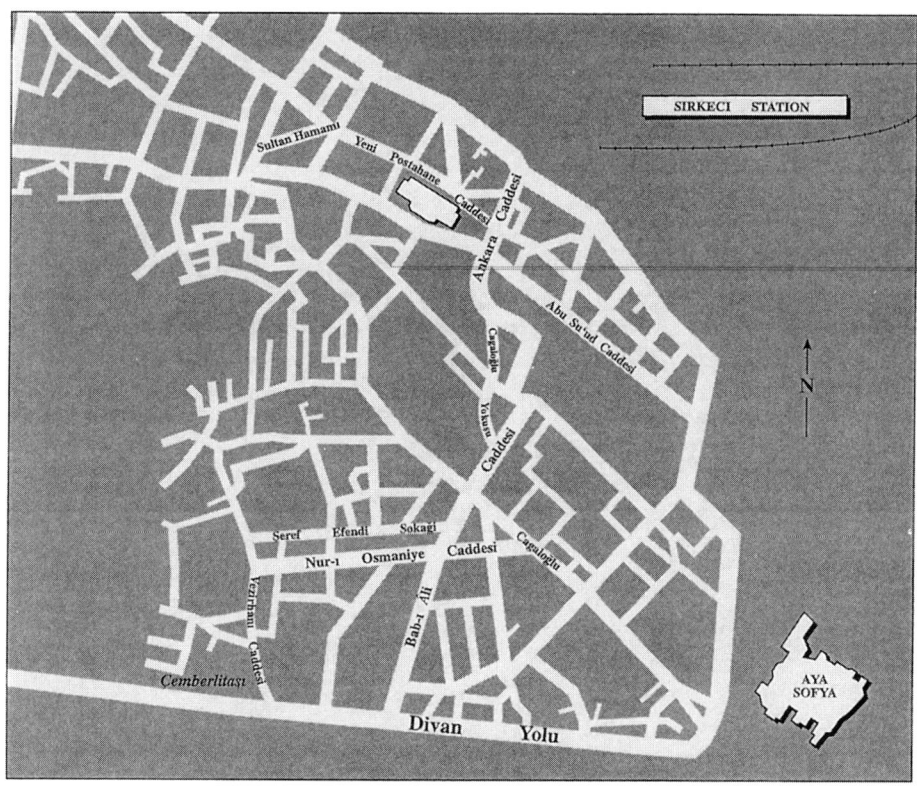

NOTES

Chapter I. Introduction

1. *Hacivat,* 1:1, 13 Şaban 1326 / 27 Ağustos 1324 / 9 Eylül 1908.

2. Feroz Ahmad (personal communication) has noted that after the Balkan Wars some ideologues proposed the Dual Monarchy model for the Ottoman empire (emulating the Hapsburgs), with Turks and Arabs substituting for Germans and Magyars. Ottomanism can be viewed as a form of official nationalism (a reaction to popular nationalism), one of the four types of nationalism outlined by Benedict Anderson, *Imagined Communities: Reflections on the Origin and Spread of Nationalism* (London: Verso Press, 1991), 83–111.

3. *Meşveret* was published in Paris (1895–1908) while Rıza was in exile. On Ahmet Rıza see Sina Akşin, *100 Soruda Jön Türkler ve İttihat ve Terraki* (İstanbul: Gerçek Yayınevi, 1980), 26–28.

4. Feroz Ahmad, *The Young Turks: The Committee of Union and Progress in Turkish Politics 1908–1914* (Oxford: Clarendon Press, 1969). See also David Kushner, *The Rise of Turkish Nationalism 1876–1908* (New York: Frank Cass, 1977); Erik Zürcher, *The Unionist Factor: The Rise of the Committee of Union and Progress in the Turkish National Movement 1905–1926* (Leiden: E.J. Brill, 1984); Niyazi Berkes, *The Development of Secularism in Turkey* (Montreal: McGill University Press, 1964); Bernard Lewis, *The Emergence of Modern Turkey,* 2nd edition, (Oxford: Oxford University Press, 1968); Ernest Ramsaur, *The Young Turks: Prelude to the Revolution of 1908* (Princeton: Princeton University Press, 1957); Yusuf Hikmet Bayur, *Türk İnkılâbı Tarihi* (Ankara: T.T.K., 1963–1964); Zafer Toprak, *"Türkiye'de "Milli İktisat" (1908–1918)"* (Ankara: Olgaç Matbaası, 1982); Tarık Zafer Tunaya, *Türkiye'de Siyasal Partiler,* 2 vols. (İstanbul: Hilal Basımevi, 1984–1986); and M. Şükrü Hanioğlu, *Osmanlı İttihad ve Terakki Cemiyeti ve Jön Türklük (1889–1902)* (İstanbul: İletişim Yayınları, n.d.), and *The Young Turks in Opposition* (New York: Oxford University Press, 1995).

5. A typical example of British approval is found in David Fraser, *Persia and Turkey in Revolt* (London: William Blackwood and Sons, 1910), 422–423.

6. Carla Hesse, "Economic Upheavals in Publishing," in Robert Darnton and Daniel Roche, eds. *Revolution in Print: The Press in France 1775–1800* (Berkeley: University of California Press, 1989), 97: "The number of printing and publishing establishments in Paris easily tripled during the revolutionary period, allowing much broader social initiative and participation in the production of the printed word and, consequently, in the public exchange of ideas."

Notes to Page 4

7. *Salname-i Devlet-i Aliye-i Osmaniye*, v. 64 (İstanbul: Matbaa-ı Ahmet İhsan, 1326 A.H. / 1908), 1050–1063. Enver Koray, ed., *Türkiye Tarih Yayınları Bibliyografyası 1729–1955*, 2nd. edition (İstanbul: Maarif Basımevi, 1959), 82–146, lists 104 publishers, but does not include fourteen of the thirty-four publishers responsible for the sixty-eight gazettes surveyed in this study. See also the later list of publishing houses (117) and publishers in Server İskit, *Türkiyede Neşriyat Hareketleri Tarihine Bir Bakış* (İstanbul: Devlet Basımevi, 1939), 301–306.

8. Selim Nüzhet, ed. *1933 Almanak* (İstanbul: Devlet Matbaası, n.d.), 242–250. See also, for gazette lists, Selim Nüzhet, *Türk Gazeteciliği* (İstanbul: Devlet Matbaası, 1931), 84–92; and *Salname-i Servet-i Fünun*, 2: 70, 1326 rumi, published 1326 / 1911.

9. Carter Findley, *Bureaucratic Reform in the Ottoman Empire: The Sublime Porte, 1789–1922* (Princeton: Princeton University Press, 1980), 253–254, 258. Server İskit, *Türkiyede Matbuat İdareleri ve Politikaları* (Ankara: Başvekâlet Basın ve Yayın Umum Müdürlüğü Yayınları, 1943), contains an elaborate discussion of the pre and post-revolutionary governments' publishing administrations, including biographies of the new regime's publishing officials. See also, İskit, *Türkiyede Neşriyat Hareketleri*, 128–129. Corinne Blake, "Training Arab-Ottoman Bureaucrats: Syrian Graduates of the Mülkiye Mektebi, 1890–1920," PhD. thesis, Princeton University, Near Eastern Studies, 1991, 98–101, 141, sketches the censorship of the Hamidian era and notes its effect on textbooks.

10. See İskit, *Türkiyede Matbuat Rejimleri* (İstanbul: Ülkü Matbaası, 1939), 691–729, for the press laws, beginning with the 1865 law, in effect under Abd ül-Hamid and those implemented in 1909 after the revolution (and counter-revolution). Ali Pasha's edict of 1867 allowed summary suspensions of newspapers. See also Roderic H. Davison, "How the Ottoman Government Adjusted to a New Institution: The Newspaper Press," in Sabrî Akural, ed. *Turkic Culture: Continuity and Change* (Bloomington: Indiana University Press, 1987), 17–26, on the press, state, and censorship in the mid-nineteenth century; and Enver Behnan Şapolyo, *Türk Gazeteciliği Tarihi Her Yöniyle Basın* (Ankara: Güven Matbaası, n.d.), 166–167, 264–270. Şapolyo's work is unfootnoted but contains many interesting tidbits.

11. See Talat Halman, *Modern Turkish Drama: An Anthology of Plays in Translation* (Minneapolis: Bibliotheca Islamica, 1976), 19. This information is taken from Halman's discussion of the *meddah* story performances, one man comedic narratives or burlesques often performed in coffeehouses.

12. Hasan Javadi, *Satire in Perian Literature* (Rutherford: Fairleigh Dickinson University Press, 1988), 138, notes that even after the Iranian constitutional revolution the Persian press was restricted: by the requirement that publication permits had to be obtained from the government, by the continued censorship of foreign publications, and by the fact that "The language at first was florid, archaic, and unsuitable for journalism." On the implementation of the Ottoman press laws under the Egyptian Khedives (1850s and after), see Caesar Farah, "Censorship and Freedom of Expression in Ottoman Syria and Egypt," in William Haddad and William Ochsenwald, eds. *Nationalism in a Non-National State: The Dissolution of the Ottoman Empire* (Columbus: Ohio State University Press, 1977), 151–194.

13. Lucy Garnett, *Turkish Life in Town and Country* (New York: G. P. Putnam's

Sons, 1911), 44–46. Garnett noted around 1903 that Abd ül-Hamid had intensified spying and censorship activities, that all public assemblies, "even cricket matches," required permission from the palace, and that even private balls had been canceled on the sultan's order.

14. Ismail Kemal Bey, *The Memoirs of Ismail Kemal Bey*, ed., William Morton Fullerton (London: Constable and Company, 1920), 279.

15. Ali Haydar Midhat Pasha, *The Life of Midhat Pasha: A Record of His Services, Political Reforms, Banishment and Judicial Murder Derived from Private Documents and Reminiscences* (London: John Murray, 1903), 122–127. Of course Midhat Pasha's son cannot be presumed to have an unbiased opinion of the sultan who, he believed, ordered his father's execution.

16. Also on the press and censorship, see Louis Bazin, "Censure Ottomane et Lexicographie: Le Kamus-i Fransevî de Sâmî Bey," in Jean Louis Bacqué Grammont et Paul Dumont, eds., *Économie et Sociétés dans l'Empire Ottoman (Fin du XVIIIe–Début du XXe siècle)* (Paris: Editions du Centre National de la Recherche Scientifique, 1983), 203–206; Cevdet Kudret, "Birkaç Örnek İle Mütareke Dönemi Sansürü," *Tarih ve Toplum* 9 (1988): 298–301, with some examples from the period 1919–1922; and Turgut Çeviker, "Türk Karikatüründe Kurtuluş Savaşı Dönemi (1918–1923)," *Sanat Dünyamız* 40 (1990): 18–25.

17. Carter Findley, *Ottoman Civil Officialdom: A Social History* (Princeton: Princeton University Press, 1989), 333, basing his argument on a study of Ottoman officials' salaries and costs of living, has argued persuasively for economic causation in the development of the Young Ottoman and Young Turk movements.

18. For the reinstitution of censorship and the hard times to which the press later returned, see: *Karagöz*, 525: 4, 1 Haziran 1329 / 14 June 1913, for a cartoon showing Ottoman journalists led by Karagöz and Hacivat headed for the poorhouse (*dar ül-acize*): Doorkeeper: Who are you? Karagöz: We are journalists. Doorkeeper: But this place isn't the press bureau, its the poorhouse . . . Karagöz: We know, my Dear, we come knowingly! . . . Isn't it here that we'll end up?

19. *Alem*, 1: 4, 29 Kanun-ı sani 1324 / 11 February 1909.

20. For a scissors image of the censor in Ottoman context, see Efthymia Canner, "La Presse Satirique grecque d'Istanbul au lendemain de la révolution jeune-turque: le journal Embros," 111–121, *Revue du Monde Musulman et de la Méditerranée* 77–78 (1996): 115. Robert Justin Goldstein, *Censorship of Political Caricature in Nineteenth Century France* (Kent, Ohio: Kent State University Press, 1989), 35–52, 79–85, 258–262, notes how cartoons were manipulated to ridicule the censor when the intended message was prohibited. The French authorities in 1881–1914 could still ban street sales and display, or prosecute for insult as alternative forms of censorship. For Ottoman cartoon attacks on the censor, see *Kalem*, 5: 1, 18 Eylül 1324 / 1 October 1908; and 8: 9, 9 Teşrin-i evvel 1324 / 22 October 1909. Javadi, *Satire in Persian Literature*, 119, notes tombstone images for censored newspapers in Iranian satire in 1908. *Küçük gazete* 97/673: 1 [no date] in a later satire, uses a tombstone for "*merhûm* (the defunct) *Tanin gazete.*"

21. *Davul*, 5: 5, 11 Teşrin-i sani 1324 / 24 November 1908; *Kalem*, 24: 8, 29 Kanun-ı sani 1324 / 11 February 1909. The *Kalem* cartoon shows Ottoman officials, some

trying to pry off the lid and others trying to hold it down. Hakkı Bey, ambassador to Rome, is featured, jumping on the coffin lid. For other images on the struggle over the Press Law, see *Kalem*, 17: 9, 12 Kanun-ı evvel 1324 / 25 December 1908, and *Musavver Muhit* [?]: 236, [1325] / 1909.

22. *Musavver Muhit* 7: 98–100, 4 Kanun-ı evvel 1324 / 17 December 1908; *Davul*, 15: 13, 4 Şubat 1324 / 17 February 1909. *Musavver* means *illustrated* and was part of the title of many illustrated gazettes; *muhit* means a person's surroundings, circle (of acquaintances), familiar environs.

23. The gazette *İstanbul* pointed out in 1908 that freedom of the press should not mean limitless freedom: Korkmaz Alemdar, *İstanbul 1875–1964 Türkiyede Yayınlanan Fransızca Bir Gazetenin Tarihi* (Ankara: Ankara İktisadî ve Ticari İlimler Akademisi, 1980), 92–96.

24. There is the suggestion (communication from Feroz Ahmad) that the British embassy was subsidizing Vahdeti. Vahdeti was founder of what became the İttihad-ı Muhammedî Party; see Akşin, *Jön Türkler*, 118.

25. For an interesting account of Ottoman press censorship during the Balkan Wars, and of Ottoman military relations with foreign journalists, see E.N. Bennett, "Personal Observations During the Balkan War II, Press Censors and War Correspondents: Some Experiences in Turkey," *The Nineteenth Century: A Monthly Review* 73 (January 1913): 28–40.

26. Turgut Çeviker, *Gelişim Sürecinde Turk Karikatürü*, 3 vols. (İstanbul: Adam Yayınları, 1986–1991). One model for the treatment of Ottoman press history can be found in the recent scholarly study by Ami Ayalon, *The Press in the Arab Middle East: A History* (New York: Oxford University Press, 1995).

27. Hasan Duman, ed. *İstanbul Kütüphaneleri Arap Harfli Süreli Yayınlar Toplu Kataloğu 1828–1928* (İstanbul: Research Centre for Islamic History, Art and Culture, 1986); also *Eski Harfli Türkçe Süreli Yayınlar Toplu Kataloğu*, vol. 1 (Ankara: Milli Kütüphane Başkanlığı, 1987), an updating of the 1963 Milli Kütüphane handlist with the inclusion of other collections.

28. Jack Censer, *Prelude to Power: The Parisian Radical Press 1789–1791* (Baltimore: Johns Hopkins University Press, 1976); Roger Chartier, *The Cultural Uses of Print in Early Modern France* (Princeton: Princeton University Press, 1987); Darnton and Roche, eds. *Revolution in Print;* Richard Terdiman, *Discourse/Counter-Discourse: The Theory and Practice of Symbolic Resistance in Nineteenth Century France* (Ithaca: Cornell University Press, 1985); and Jeremy Popkin, "The Business of Political Enlightenment in France, 1770–1800," 412–435, in John Brewer and Roy Porter, eds., *Consumption and the World of Goods* (London: Routledge, 1993). See also Roger Chartier, *The Culture of Print: Power and Uses of Print in Early Modern Europe* (Cambridge: Polity Press, 1989).

29. Jürgen Habermas, *The Structural Transformation of the Public Sphere: An Inquiry into a Category of Bourgeois Society* (Cambridge: M.I.T Press, 1989); and Eric Hobsbawm, "Mass Producing Traditions: Europe, 1870–1914," in Hobsbawm and Terence Ranger, eds., *The Invention of Tradition* (Cambridge: Cambridge University Press, 1989), 263–307. Habermas focuses on a philosophical sociology of communication while Hobsbawm is concerned with the construction and transmission of symbols of group identity.

Notes to Pages 10–14

30. The development of a stage three commercial/bourgeoisie/capitalist press such as Habermas, *The Structural Transformation,* 184–185, describes, was known in the Ottoman case, but Ottoman press development historically was comparatively primitive. Where Habermas is preoccupied with discerning the public and private spheres and the question of whether the press is addressing public opinion or private "consumers" (193), Terdiman is preoccupied with categories of class and capitalism. Habermas notes that the press once "was able to limit itself to the transmission and amplification of the rational critical debate of private people assembled into a public, now conversely this debate gets shaped by the mass media to begin with . . ." (188). Terdiman, arguing that a hegemonic discourse is always involved in this shaping, would not be persuaded that there was ever such a "simpler" time.

31. Percival Griffiths, *The British Impact on India* (n.p.: Archon Books, 1965), 264–272. The Indian press, in fact, influenced revolutionary literature in Iran and in the Ottoman state in the nineteenth century.

32. See Ayalon, *The Press in the Arab Middle East,* 211–214, on the ways Arab newspapers were funded, their subsidies, and the failure of many of them to break even.

33. The dilemma of its own imperialism was "solved" by the revolutionary press through targeting European imperialism as a particularly menacing form and by focusing on the tyranny of Abd ül-Hamid rather than on the imperial system of the Ottoman state to explain internal weakness. Meanwhile the press used the memory of the Ottoman imperial past as a means to stir up "national sentiments." One is tempted to say that, historically, the other guy's imperialism can always be censored as rapacious while one's own is merely extending the benevolent and just protection of the father-king to weaker neighbors.

34. Edmund Burke, III, and Ira M. Lapidus, *Islam, Politics, and Social Movements* (Berkeley: University of California Press, 1988), 27. Of course, European power was not based only on the local elites, it was multifaceted, taking forms such as the imitation of European dress patterns by middle-class Ottoman seamstresses and the co-optation of Ottoman labor by European companies.

35. On the conflict of discursive systems, Joan Scott, "The Evidence of Experience," *Critical Inquiry* (Summer 1991): 773–797, is useful. In the present study, however, the coexistence and compromise among discursive systems emerges as much as does the conflict that Scott emphasizes.

36. Censer, *Prelude to Power,* 71–72, notes that the Parisian radical press constructed and "believed in" a polarization between a demonic aristocracy and the people and their revolution. "The radicals believed in the reality of this polarization and constructed a political, economic, and cultural ideal to conform to and influence the outcome of the struggle." Although the Ottoman press did demonize the enemies of the "people," such a simple dichotomy cannot be found generally in the Ottoman press where the worst enemies were often foreign powers.

37. David Laitin, *Hegemony and Culture: Politics and Religious Change among the Yoruba* (Chicago: University of Chicago Press, 1986).

38. Feroz Ahmad, "The Young Turks, 1908–1918," *Review* 11, no. 2 (Spring 1988): 267, also uses Gramsci in assessing the new Ottoman regime. The interests of

the old regime "were restricted to those of the Ottoman family and a very small elite that monopolized power in the Palace and in the upper reaches of the civil and military bureaucracy. The Unionists, who constituted the most radical wing of the Young Turk movement, represented what may be described as Gramsci's 'subordinate class.'"

39. The revolutionary era was a period of political and social crisis for the empire and, as noted by Robert Philippe, *Political Graphics: Art as a Weapon* (New York: Abbeville Press, 1982), 13, "Graphic art, flourishes at periods of crisis." It is one way of creating new metaphors. Also on graphic art, see Martin Medhurst and Michael Desousa, "Political Cartoons as Rhetorical Form: A Taxonomy of Graphic Discourse," *Communication Monographs* 48, no. 3 (Sept. 1981): 197–236.

40. Ahmad, *The Young Turks*, 23, notes that the Ottomans asked the English for an alliance in November 1908, using the Anglo-Japanese Alliance as a precedent.

41. Şerif Mardin, "A Note on the Transformation of Religious Symbols in Turkey," *Turcica* 16 (1984): 115–127. Mardin, in his complex and multifaceted analyses of religion in the context of Ottoman intellectual history, notes that, "in the Ottoman Empire, orthodox, state-supported Sunni Islam was highly suspicious of *communitas* as a social force, even though its first thrust had depended on that force, [and] that this denial has basically affected the modalities of the individual's integration into society in the Ottoman Empire and in Turkey. . . . Turkish Islam, which has so often been analyzed in political settings, has a less viable but possibly more important dimension, that of a 'prime mover' in the elaboration of frames of integration for the individual in society (118)." Mardin goes on to argue that Abd ül-Hamid and the Young Turks were "in the same camp as concerns the role of religion as a means of social control (121)." Clearly, one can debate this latter premise as variable across events and issues. It would be difficult, however, to challenge Mardin's conclusion that, "the view that Islam could be used as 'social cement' for the new society continued to prevail for decades among a section of Turkish intellectuals . . ." (123).

42. As Feroz Ahmad has pointed out, Islam became a weapon in the hands of the anti-Unionists (including the British embassy) and was used against the Unionists in October 1908 and April 1909. After the counter-revolution, the Unionists were careful not to permit Islam to be used against them and adopted more conservative social policies.

43. The latter two have been used to present the "outsider's" view of the revolution. See for some treatments of these various other presses I. Groc and İ. Çağlar, *La Presse Française de Turquie de 1795 à nos Jours: Histoire et Catalogue*, Varia Turcica II (İstanbul: Isis Press, 1985); Korkmaz Alemdar, "Türkiye'de Yabancı Dilde Basın," *Tarih ve Toplum* 10 (1988), 166–171; Cavit Orhan Tütengil, *Yeni Osmanlılar'dan bu Yana İngiltere'de Türk Gazeteciliği (1867–1967)* (İstanbul: Belge Yayınları, 1969); and Şevket Beysanoğlu, *Basın ye Yayın Dünyamızda Diyarbakır* (Ankara: İş Matbaacılık, 1970).

44. This type of skepticism has a long history in Middle Eastern literary traditions. It is found not only in the shadow plays but in verse, in narrative, and in oral traditions that came to be written, such as *The Arabian Nights*. Gazettes used charac-

ters from the shadow puppet theatre and from the *Ortaoyunu* comic theatre. For a good summary history of Turkish theatre and its development, see Halman, *Modern Turkish Drama*, 13–51.

45. The cartoons treated here are, by definition, satirical; the genre of satire provides them with their confounding power. Although, as in other genres of literature, the degree to which these dimensions are confounded varies from one type of cartoon to another, I would argue that such confounding is a part of the essence of the cartoon. For discussions of the nature of satire, see Edward I. and Lillian D. Bloom, *Satire's Persuasive Voice* (Ithaca: Cornell University Press, 1979); Robert C. Elliott, *The Power of Satire: Magic, Ritual, Art* (Princeton: Princeton Univeristy Press, 1960); and W. J. T. Mitchell, ed. *The Language of Images* (Chicago: University of Chicago Press, 1980)

46. Mary Lee Townsend, *Forbidden Laughter: Popular Humor and the Limits of Repression in Nineteenth-Century Prussia* (Ann Arbor: University of Michigan Press, 1992), 9–10, has attempted to do so through a social and political contextualization of nineteenth-century Prussian humor. She has analyzed cartoons using a broad, four-part classification: 1) universal or traditional humor, which deals with fundamental human and social problems; 2) innocent humor, which deliberately avoids delicate topics; 3) reflective humor, which articulates perceptions of the surrounding world; 4) political or critical humor, which deliberately addresses public issues.

47. Or, as Chartier, "Texts, Printing, Readings," 171, puts it: "the emphasis on cultural appropriation also enables us to see that texts or words intended to mold thoughts and actions are never wholly effective and radically acculturating. The practices of appropriation always create uses or representations that are hardly reducible to the wills or intentions of those who produce discourses and norms."

48. Press, *The Political Cartoon*, 60–70, poses this model for breaking down cartoon satire into component parts for analysis. Put another way, "As a persuasive art indebted to rhetoric, satire attempts to transmit the strong convictions of its creator to its readers and thus implicate them in a particular set of emotions," Bloom, *Satire's Persuasive Voice*, 59. The Blooms, however, (31–35) make a strong case both for the altruistic sentiments of the satirist and for his/her tendency to associate him/herself with the hurt of others. Neither of these, I would argue, is essential to satire. They argue, further, "Satiric representation, in other words, should be a goad toward positive action, uniting in its readers aesthetic satisfaction and the ache of conscience" (32). A great deal of Ottoman satire is much more fatalistic than this representation would suggest.

49. Terdiman, *Discourse/Counter-Discourse*, 121, also speaks of a society's points of concern while exploring the roles of counter discourses: "With great conjunctural sensitivity, counter-discourses thus map the points of stress within the social system which accompany the slow institutionalization of the new."

50. Terdiman points out that one of the most powerful ways of subverting the dominant (and ubiquitous) discourse is to mimic it, thereby reproducing, mocking, and pointing out its inadequacies all at the same time (210–212). Terdiman focuses on this process in language, but it also takes place through the medium of the cartoon image. Of course the dominant discourse is never as seamless and solid as

Terdiman for example, seems to suggest (199). The dominant discourse is always partially subverted, otherwise there would be no need to point out its dominance.

51. Giulio Carlo Argan, "Ideology and Iconology," in Mitchell, ed. *The Language of Images,* makes this same point about the iconology of art: "Without those conventions which form a sort of code common to artist and spectator, the work would be indecipherable, and art, not acting on a specific and accepted cultural terrain, would not collaborate, as it often does, to modify that terrain" (20). The purpose of many Ottoman cartoons was to help modify the cultural, social, and political terrains, putting traditional images to revolutionary purposes.

52. Philippe, *Political Graphics,* 10–26, argues that political graphics are used either as weapons of groups opposed to authority or as apologias and glorifications of the great and powerful. Hence they are used to support both dominant and counter discourses. Philippe, however, argues that when the audience of the graphic is the public then the symbols are necessarily simple. That is not always the case.

53. Ibn Khaldun, *Muqaddimah: An Introduction to History,* translated by Franz Rosenthal (Princeton: Princeton University Press, 1970), 36–38. Ibn Khaldun notes, "Another reason making untruth unavoidable—and this one is more powerful than all the reasons previously mentioned—is ignorance of the nature of the various conditions arising in civilization" (36).

54. Argan, "Ideology and Iconology," 17, continues the argument: "The image which is discredited or sometimes contaminated by ingenuous associations, combinations, or even by banal confusions (through assonance) with other latent images in the memory is the document of a culture of the diffused image; it is a *significant* to which may be attributed, as to the words of a spoken language, many *signifiés.*" Argan is not here speaking of cartoons; but the worn and contaminated image is a very nice analogy for the cartoon.

55. Argan, "Ideology and Iconology," 20–21, conjures a nice vision of the hodgepodge collage of materials and images that go into the creation of art (junk, props, studies, sketches, notes, casts, reproductions). He argues that it is not necessary for the historian to perceive or be able to trace the connection between an image and its "remote iconic predecessor. . . . Because the fact that the correlation is neither conscious nor direct does not demonstrate that it does not exist at the unconscious level and that it does not function as a profound motivational force."

56. As Townsend, *Forbidden Laughter,* 4, so aptly notes, published popular humor, "occupied a middle ground between the popular and high cultures."

57. Chartier, "Texts, Printing, Readings," 169. Chartier argues that "Thus, a presumed 'popular' spontaneity cannot be simply opposed to the coercions imposed by the authorities; what must be recognized is how liberties that are always restrained (by conventions, codes, constraints) and disciplines that are always upset, articulate with each other" (174).

58. Chartier, *The Cultural Uses of Print,* 4–6. Richard Stites, *Russian Popular Culture: Entertainment and Society since 1900* (Cambridge: Cambridge University Press, 1992), 3–12, has approached the question of popular culture in the Russian empire, which, like the Ottoman empire, was also undergoing radical transformation in the early twentieth century. Stites notes the sometimes temporary nature of popular

Notes to Pages 21–26

culture and argues that, "Mass audiences may differ in tastes and sensibilities from those of people who mainly frequent the temples of exalted art, but the interaction of high and 'low' culture is dense and continuous, especially in countries like Russia with very old and highly revered cultural traditions" (174). Stites, nonetheless, emphasizes the hostile relationship between "popular" and elite cultures (10–12), arguing that various types of elites aligned against the "new" culture of the urban masses, which they associated with vice.

59. On issues of the juxtaposition of image and text, see Christian Jouhard, "Readability and Persuasion: Political Handbills," 235–259, and Alain Boureau, "Books and Emblems on the Public Stage: *Côté jardin* and *côté cour*," 261–289, in Roger Chartier, ed., *The Culture of Print*.

60. Terdiman, *Discourse/Counter-Discourse*, 224–226, associated folk tradition with counter discourse, but we cannot assume that either folk tradition or folk forms of satire are necessarily subversive.

61. I make no attempt here to predict or pronounce upon the direct effect of any of these cartoons. In fact, the debate on the effectiveness of political cartoons has continued throughout the century. Of some interest in this regard are two short pieces: Leroy M. Carl, "Editorial Cartoons Fail to Reach Many Readers," *Journalism Quarterly* 45 (Autumn 1968): 533–535, a study that measured the stated intent of the cartoonists against the interpretation of readers and found a huge disparity; and Del Brinkman, "Do Editorial Cartoons and Editorials Change Opinions?" *Journalism Quarterly* 45 (Winter 1968): 724–726, which attempts to evaluate the effectiveness of cartoons depending upon their placement and their juxtaposition to editorials.

Chapter II. Publishing, Format, Images, and Readers

1. *Mizah* assumes a component of social or political criticism. Other terms, such as *latife* (joke, witicism) or *eğlence* (amusement) were used to identify genres of humor; but the focus here is on *mizah* or satire.

2. Habermas, *The Structural Transformation*, 184–187. The Ottoman press fits roughly into Habermas's categories of "journals cultivating rational-critical debates" and (a somewhat later stage) the "party-bound press," neither geared primarily to profit-oriented enterprise. Habermas uses the incidence and type of advertising, in part, to trace the commercialization of the press (190–192).

3. A recent study that has grappled with the methodological problems of representing a society through its humor and through its struggles for dominance is Townsend, *Forbidden Laughter*. Townsend employs the term popular humor, although she notes that "mass market" humor might be more appropriate given her focus on published, commercial sources (in nineteenth-century Prussia) (4). I would neither call Ottoman satire at the time of the revolution "popular" (because that word is overdetermined and suggests boundaries that I do not acknowledge) nor "mass market" because the Istanbul press was not yet at a stage of development that assumed a "mass" market. See also, Terdiman, *Discourse/Counter-Discourse*, 122–125. The early-twentieth-century Ottoman press is in many ways comparable to the early-nineteenth-century French press in terms of stage of development and commercial-

ization (although I do think that Terdiman's emphasis on the inherently commercial nature of the press is overblown).

4. On the role of the publishers and humorists of the nineteenth-century Prussian press, see Townsend, *Forbidden Laughter,* 35-68.

5. Censer, *Prelude to Power,* xii, 72.

6. Mark Sykes, *The Caliph's Last Heritage* (New York: Arno Press, 1973, reprint of 1915 London edition), 488-489. Sykes, who was a caricaturist himself, was particularly concerned with noting down examples of caricature that he witnessed in his travels. See David Fromkin, *A Peace to End All Peace: Creating the Modern Middle East, 1914-1922* (New York: H. Holt, 1989), 147.

7. Şevket Süreyya Aydemir, *Makedonya'dan Ortaasya'ya Enver Paşa,* v. 2 (1908-1914), (İstanbul: Remzi Kitabevi, 1976), 192. The writer goes on to blame this license for the murder of the young editor of *Saday-ı hak,* Ahmet Samim, in the street on 9 Haziran 1325 (22 June 1909). On the dilemma over liberty vs. license in the French revolutionary press, see Hugh Gough, *The Newspaper Press in the French Revolution* (London: Routledge, 1988), 44-81.

8. See Fraser, *Persia and Turkey in Revolt,* 32-33. Another British observer made similar remarks about the Calcutta press in the late-nineteenth-century: Graham Shaw, *Printing in Calcutta to 1800* (London: Bibliographical Society, 1981), 215. Steven C. Dubin, *Arresting Images: Impolitic Art and Civil Actions* (New York: Routledge, 1992), 13, notes that the late twentieth century revolution/liberation in Hungary brought an explosion of pornography to the newsstands, prompting one teacher to lament that "People are mixing liberty with bad taste."

9. For examples of humorous representations of journalists, see *Kalem,* 56: 8, 24 Eylül 1325 / 7 October 1909 (a raggedy man telling a policeman he is not a vagabond but a publisher, one of the *erkân-ı matbuat*); and *Karagöz,* 267: 1, 1910 (journalists fleeing from the CUP). See also Turgut Çeviker, *İbret Albümü 1908* (İstanbul: Mataş Matbaacılık, 1991), 22-23.

10. On Rıza and *Meşveret,* see Şerif Mardin, *Jön Türklerin Siyasi Fikirleri 1895-1908* (İstanbul: İletişim Yayınları, 1989), 129-162; Mardin also discusses the Young Turk press of the era in general, 104-128.

11. On some of the *mizah* predecessors, see Selim Nüzhet (Gerçek), *Türk Gazeteciliği* (İstanbul: Devlet Matbaası, 1931), 60-63. On Ottoman and later humor gazettes, see *Türkiye'de Dergiler Ansiklopediler (1849-1984),* (İstanbul: Gelişim Yayınları, 1983), 71-84.

12. J. S. Szyliowicz, "Functional Perspectives on Technology: The Case of the Printing Press in the Ottoman Empire," *Archivum Ottomanicum* 11 (1986): 249-259, cites the figure of 116 printing presses in Istanbul in 1875, but also notes that the number of dailies in Istanbul declined from six in 1891 to three in early 1908.

13. The pioneering work on late Ottoman intellectual history and the role of the press and its publishers has been done by Şerif Mardin, *The Genesis of Young Ottoman Thought: A Study in the Modernization of Turkish Political Ideas* (Princeton: Princeton University Press, 1962), and by Bernard Lewis, *The Emergence of Modern Turkey.* No comprehensive analytical work, however, has been done on the evolution of journalists, their connections, their ideologies, and the publishing industry. For one exam-

ple, based on the French press, of the kind of work that still needs to be done, see Robert Darnton, "The High Enlightenment and the Low-Life of Literature in Pre-Revolutionary France," *Past and Present* 51 (1970): 81–115.

14. Ottoman biographical dictionaries are of little use and modern literary compendia devote themselves only to the most prominent figures. Examples are: Mehmed Tahir, *Osmanlı Müellifleri* (İstanbul: Matbaa-ı Amire, 1333 A.H. / 1915); and Nihad Sami Banarlı, *Resimli Türk Edebiyatı Tarihi* (İstanbul: Milli Eğitim Basımevi, 1971). More useful are memoirs, reference works such as *İstanbul Ansiklopedisi* (İstanbul: Neşriyat Kollektif Şirketi, 1959) which was, unfortunately, completed only through the letter *H;* and İbrahim Alaettin Gövsa, *Türk Meşhurları* (İstanbul: Yedigün Neşriyatı, n.d.). Other important references are İskit, *Türkiyede Neşriyat Hereketleri,* which treats of publishers and their locations (97–122) and discusses various aspects of the publishing trade; and Asaf Tugay, *İbret: Abdülhamid'e Verilen Journaller ve Journalciler* (İstanbul: Okat Yayınevi, n.d.), which includes a variety of documents and a list of journalists' names (299–326). Other work on Ottoman journalists can be found in Muzaffer Gökman, *Sedat Simavi* (İstanbul: APA Ofset Basımevi, 1970), on the Ottoman journalist and satirist; Mehmet Ali Beyhan, "Bir II. Abdülhamid Devri Aydını'nın Profili: Lastik Said Bey," *Osmanlı Araştırmaları* 13 (1993): 167–185; Nuri Akbayar and Orhan Koloğlu, *Gazeteci Bir Aile: Mehmet Asım, Hakkı Tarık, Hasan Rasim Us'lar* (Ankara: ÇGD Yayıları, 1996); and the documents and memoirs compiled by Münir Çapanoğlu, *Basın Tarihine Dair Bilgiler ve Hatıralar* (İstanbul: Hür Türkiye Dergisi Yayıları, 1962).

15. Çeviker, *Gelişim Sürecinde Türk Karikatürü,* v. 2.

16. See *İstanbul Ansiklopedisi,* v. 2, 1056–1057; Atilla Özkırımlı, *Türk Edebiyatı Ansiklopedisi,* v. 1 (İstanbul: Cem Yayınevi, 1982), 125.

17. *Kalem,* 7: 1, 2 Teşrin-i evvel 1324/ 15 October 1908.

18. See *Türk Dili ve Edebiyatı Ansiklopedisi,* v. 2 (İstanbul: Dergah Yayınları, 1976), 72–73.

19. See Çeviker, *Gelişim Sürecinde Türk Karikatürü,* 2: 83–88. Çeviker's work contains brief but illuminating sketches on the most well-known Ottoman editors and cartoonists.

20. Çeviker, 2: 116–117. Fazlı also penned cartoons in *Püsküllü belâ,* published 1908–1909.

21. See Çeviker, 2: 99–100, which includes a highly impressionistic description of Faik from a contemporary saying Faik was known more for his intelligence than for his fastidiousness (*"Temizliğe hiç dikkat etmezdi."*).

22. See Gövsa, *Türk Meşhurları,* 103; and M. Ertuğrul Düzdağ, *İkinci Meşrutiyetin İlk Ayları ve 31 Mart Olayı İçin bir Yakın Tarih Belgesi: Volkan Gazetesi, 11 Aralık 1908–20 Nisan 1909* (İstanbul: İz Yayıncılık, 1992); Fuat Süreyya Oral, *Türk Basın Tarihi 1728–1922, 1831–1921,* v. 1, *Osmanlı İmparatorluğu Dönemi* (İstanbul: Yeni Adım Matbaası, n.d.), 186. For a picture and a less than favorable impression of Vahdeti, see Aydemir, *Makedonya'dan Ortaasya'ya Enver Paşa,* 2: 144–147.

23. Çeviker, *Gelişim,* 2: 159, contains a picture of Nazmi.

24. An interesting study of this question, focusing on the Arabic newspaper *Al-Nahla* (published in London in the late nineteenth century) of John Louis Sabunji,

Notes to Pages 31–34

is found in Martin Kramer, "Pen and Purse:—Şābūnjī and Blunt," in C. E. Bosworth, et. al., eds., *Essays in Honor of Bernard Lewis: The Islamic World from Classical to Modern Times* (Princeton: Darwin Press, 1989), 771–780. Kramer notes that the editor in this case was constrained by his dependence for financing on Wilfred Blunt. He also includes references from Sabunji's letters on his costs of publication.

25. W. A. Coupe, "The German Cartoon and the Revolution of 1848," *Comparative Studies in Society and History* 9, no. 2 (January 1967): 137–167, has noted that the big cartoon publishers in Frankfurt and Berlin had staffs of regular contributors and "were prepared to handle both right and left-wing materials indiscriminately" (159). On Ottoman political parties see: Tunaya, *Türkiye'de Siyasal Partiler,* 1: 483–489.

26. See for pioneering attempts, İskit, *Türkiyede Matbuat İdareleri ve Politikaları;* and Ahmed Emin (Yalman), *The Modernization of Turkey as Measured by Its Press* (New York: Columbia University Press, 1914).

27. *Servet-i fünun,* 4, inside front cover, 1328 / 1912. Ahmet İhsan (Tokgöz), *Matbuat Hatıralarım* (İstanbul: İletişim Yayınları, 1993), in his memoirs describes the Ottoman publishing industry, the first days after the revolution (129–134, 151–152), the army's response to the counter-revolution (178–182), and the logistics of gazette production.

28. See "Printing," *Encyclopedia Britannica,* 11th ed., v. 22 (1910), 350–359, which includes illustrations of contemporary printing presses and the notation that "Electricity is supplanting both steam and gas, and is being installed in most large printing houses, including newspaper offices."

29. *Takvim-i Bahar,* 1306 / 1890 (İstanbul: İstepan Matbaası, 1307/1891), 67–69. The description goes on to mention *World*'s huge number of employees, reporters, correspondents and substantial circulation increases.

30. Muhammad as-Saffār, *Disorienting Encounters: Travels of a Moroccan Scholar in France in 1845–1846, The Voyage of Muḥammad as-Saffār,* trans. and edited by Susan Gilson Miller (Berkeley: University of California Press, 1991), 150–151, 201–205. On the development of printing, and its social contexts, in Central Asia, see Adeeb Khalid, "Printing, Publishing, and Reform in Tsarist Central Asia," *International Journal of Middle East Studies* 26 (May 1994): 187–200. This is an interesting study on the use of and reaction to print.

31. On the electrical age and the transformations of the urban space that took place as a result of the use of electric light see, Wolfgang Schivelbusch, *Disenchanted Night: The Industrialization of Light in the Nineteenth Century,* translated by Angela Davies (Oxford: Berg, 1988), esp. 79–154. On the links between electrical lighting, consumption, shopping, nightlife, and the automobile, see Neil McWilliam, *Dreams of Happiness: Social Art and the French Left, 1830–1850* (Princeton: Princeton University Press, 1993), 84–90. Williams emphasizes the ways in which electric lighting radically transformed the public space. Pierre Teilhard de Chardin, *Letters from Egypt 1905–1908* (New York: Herder and Herder, 1965), 227, mentions that a new electric power station was being built in Cairo in 1908, "to supply the future garden cities of the 'Oases,' as well as the hypothetical metropolitan railway. . . ." It had French staff and "turbines of the latest model."

32. See Zeyneb Çelik, "The Impact of Westernization on Istanbul's Urban Form,

Notes to Pages 34–36

1838–1908" (PhD dissertation, University of California, 1984), 99–102, 206, on the use of electricity for Istanbul trams (beginning in 1912) and on the founding of the Istanbul electric company in 1909. Note that Çelik's thesis contains many interesting details not found in her subsequent book. See the photographs in *Boğaziçi Şirket-i Hayriye Tarihçe, Salname* (İstanbul: Ahmet İhsan, 1330/1914), 62, 108, 114, 124, and 17 in the French language section.

33. Shusha Guppy, *Memoirs of a Persian Childhood* (Boston: Beacon Press, 1988), 68, notes that one street near her house in Tehran was named Electricity Avenue because it was one of the first to have electric lights installed under the street improvement program of Reza Shah (who came to power ca. 1924). In 1912, plans for a tramway and electric lighting in Edirne were still merely ideas on the drawing board, see U.S. Dept. of Commerce and Labor, *Daily Consular and Trade Reports,* no. 1 57, 987, March 8, 1912.

34. A comprehensive study of Ottoman print technology remains to be done and I claim no expertise in that area. A double illustration in Ali Seydi, *Resimli Kamus-ı Osmanı* (İstanbul: Cihan Matbaa, 1330 / 1914), 652–653, shows equipment for typographic and lithographic printing. The lithographic presses are all hand presses. The large typographic presses include one single cylinder, one double cylinder, and one rotary machine (all of which could be gas, steam or electric powered; the one and two cylinder presses both appear to have hand cranks).

35. *Salname-i servet-i fünun,* 1328/1912, inside front cover. Even here, the notice did not indicate specifically that the presses themselves were electric but only that the plant was electrified. A separate notice indicated the inauguration of the new plant would take place on April 20, 1912, the twenty-second anniversary of the A. İhsan Publishing House, and that the capital of the company amounted to 10,000 *livres turques.*

36. Habermas, *The Structural Transformation,* 186–187, has noted that plate sharing, and the dependence of parochial and smaller papers on larger ones, resulted in Europe in the formation of newspaper groups and led to editorial homogenization.

37. On the spatial concentration of booksellers and publishers, as mentioned in the work of Ahmet Rasim, see Şerif Aktaş, *Ahmed Rasim'in Eserlerinde İstanbul* (Ankara: Kültür Bakanlığı, 1988), 674–675.

38. Şapolyo, *Türk Gazeteciliği Tarihi,* 147–148. It is not clear exactly what year Şapolyo intends here, although he is speaking in this paragraph of the character of *Tercüman-ı Hakikat* after the 1908 revolution.

39. Pioneering work has been done on Ottoman photography by Nancy Micklewright, "Photographic Memories: Travel Albums compiled by Nineteenth Century British Visitors to the Middle East," paper delivered at the Middle East Studies Association Conference, Washington D.C., November 1991.

40. Çelik, thesis, 255–256. On Abd ül-Hamid's commemorative photographic albums see Charles E. S. Gavin, ed., *Imperial Self-Portrait: The Ottoman Empire as Revealed in the Sultan Abdul Hamid II's Photographic Albums,* special issue of *Journal of Turkish Studies,* 12 (1988). For an interesting work on court photography in India at the same time see Clark Worswick, ed. *Princely India: Photographs by Raja Lala Deen Dayal, Court Photographer (1884–1910) to the Premier Prince of India* (New York: Alfred

A. Knopf, 1980). Dayal's studio, like those of at least some of the Istanbul photographers, provided a woman photographer for portraits of women and children. Engin Çizgen, *Photography in the Ottoman Empire, 1839–1919* (İstanbul: Kervan Kitapçılık Basın Sanayı, 1987), 83, 119, 125, contains some examples of early studio photographs of women in Istanbul.

41. *Resimli kitab,* published by Faik Sabri, had its own publishing house, which also issued the gazette *Musavver Muhit.* Çizgen, *Photography,* 27, contains a map of the Grande Rue and its photographic establishments.

42. *Resimli kitab,* 10: back cover, 10 Temmuz 1325 / 23 July 1909. Apollon was owned by Aşil Samancı (1870–1942) born the son of a painter, in Istanbul. He gained practical experience working with the famous photographer Abdullah Frères and gave photography lessons to the Ottoman princes. On Samancı and other Ottoman photographers see: Çizgen, *Photography,* 144.

43. *Resimli kitab* also published an illustrated supplement, by Kenan Bey, to the eleventh issue of August 1325. This supplement, "a gift to our readers," was on the sultan's "imperial voyage to Bursa."

44. According to F. D. E., *Système des Mesures, Poids et Monnaies de l'Empire Ottoman et des Principaux États* (Constantinople: n.p., 1910), 23–29, the basic unit of Ottoman coinage was the *piastre* or *kuruş.* The gold lira (*livre*) = 100 *piastres;* the silver *medjidié* = 20 *piastres;* and 1 *kuruş/piastre* = .22 *francs.* This source noted that, legally, the *medjidié* = 19 *piastres,* and 1 *piastre* = 38 *para;* but, for convenience sake, the convention was 1 *medjidié* = 20 *piastres;* 1 *piastre* = 40 *para;* and a double *piastre* (*ikilik*) = 80 *para.*

45. *Kalem,* 7: 10, 2 Teşrin-i evvel, 1324 / 15 October 1908: notice published in French and in Ottoman.

46. See ad in *Kalem,* 84: 15, 23 Temmuz 1325 / 5 August 1909. All the cartoons in the Izmir gazette, *Gıdık,* published in 1910 were labeled "*Atelier Terakki,*" in Latin characters, suggesting, perhaps, the functioning of a cartoon production group there as well. I have not been able to find any substantive information on these apparent cartooning shops.

47. Çeviker, *Gelişim,* 2: 101–131.

48. Çeviker, 2: 101, lists thirty-nine others about whom he notes that new data would be necessary in order to say anything: Mehmet Halis, M. Sarım, Mim Naci, Servet İzzet, R. Dupour, Platon, Scham, "e", Fahretto, H. Yan, Mirnurite, Ali, Y. Hikmet, Mahssousa, M. F. Hüseyin Avni, M. E., Selim, Frans, Bonifour, Nurettin Rüştü, M. Haydar, P. A., S., N. Z., N. Fléchs, A. Ménélas, Zeki, A., M. R., Dava Vekili Nazif, Ph. Démétriadis, Ettlagadis, l. Avakyan, Y. B., A. Ruhi, Mehmet Ferit, Agustidi, Hadi, and others whose signatures Çeviker cannot make out.

49. We do not know, for the most part, what Charles Press, *The Political Cartoon,* 60, calls the cartoonists' "inner compass," their loyalties, their "cherished groups." Often, we can only surmise these things from the nuances of their cartoons.

50. For a listing of European satirical gazettes and some coverage on European cartoonists, see R. Geipel, *The Cartoon: A Short History of Graphic Comedy and Satire* (Newton Abbot: David and Charles, 1972), 79, 115–133. One reviewer of an earlier article of mine insisted that cartoons extracted from Ottoman gazettes *had to be* "European," or that, at the very least, the cartoonists had studied in Europe. This is,

of course, incorrect; it presumes the hegemony of European style and the inflexibility of artistic boundaries. It is clear that Ottoman cartoonists were influenced by and copied European cartoons. They also forged their own styles; many clearly did not study art in Europe.

51. For these similar cartoons, see Ralph E. Shikes, *The Indignant Eye: The Artist as Social Critic in Prints and Drawings from the Fifteenth Century to Picasso* (Boston: Beacon Press, 1969), 186–187, 291–292. See *Kalem*, 5: 4, 18 Eylül 1324 / 1 October 1908 (in which the bayonet points are various gazettes). George Grosz' stark pictures of wealthy, piggish industrialists and bourgeois elites (sometimes contrasted to the ragged and hungry poor) in post–WWI Germany are echoes of similar frames found in pre-war Ottoman and European satire. On Daumier, see A. Hyatt Major, *Prints and People: A Social History of Printed Pictures* (Princeton: Princeton University Press, 1971). This latter work includes a useful analysis of the types of print image, from folk art, to engraving, to photography. Major's work is not paginated.

52. Speaking of European cultural influences is of course rather vague. These ranged from the European press, to the European expatriot community, to the Europeanized education (at home and abroad) of Ottoman elites, to the consumption of European, especially French, literatures. I did find one specific reference to European cartooning in the French language section of *Alem*, 6: 2, French section, 5 Mart 1324 / 18 March 1909. In a communication to its readers, the gazette announced that it had secured the collaboration of the "*caricaturiste* Andrès," who had produced cartoons for many gazettes in Istanbul. It is unclear whether Andrès is an Ottoman citizen, but the announcement does go on to mention "*collaborateurs français*." On French narrative and satirical forms of the era see, for example, Roger Shattuck, *The Banquet Years: The Origins of the Avant-Garde in France 1885 to World War I* (Salem, New Hampshire: Ayer Co, 1984, Reprint of 1969 edition), 33–35.

53. See Javadi, *Satire in Persian Literature*; and Paul Sprachman, "Persian Satire, Parody and Burlesque," 226–248, in Ehsan Yarshater, ed., *Persian Literature* (n.p.: Bibliotheca Persica, 1988). Khalid Kishtainy, *Arab Political Humour* (London: Quartet Books, 1985), 69–99, illustrates many humorous dialogues in classical Arab satire and discusses the Arab satirical press. Even the Prophet Muhammad, according to the hadith, appreciated a good joke; see as-Saffār, *Disorienting Encounters*, 148–149. See also, on nineteenth-century theatricals in Ottoman Egypt, Ehud Toledano, *State and Society in Mid-Nineteenth Century Egypt* (Cambridge: Cambridge University Press, 1990), 231–237. Toledano highlights the "open-air" theater, its political critique, and the *karagöz*.

54. Carl Petry, *Twilight of Majesty: The Reigns of the Mamlūk Sultans al-Ashraf Qāytbāy and Qānṣūh al-Ghawrī in Egypt* (Seattle: University of Washington Press, 1993), 102, using the Mamluk chronicles of Ibn Iyās, notes how shadow plays satirizing Ottoman political figures were used in 899/1493–1494 in Cairo during the festivities sending off the Mamluk ambassador to Istanbul. The puppet theater was always topical. Petry also notes that Jamāl al-Dīn al-Salmūnī's satiric ode, targeting the jurist Sarī al-Dīn, circulated throughout the capital and landed him in jail (148). Satiric verse was employed for political purposes long before the advent of the newspaper press and it was taken very seriously.

55. Ismail Kemal Bey, *Memoirs*, 277.

56. See, for example, *Alem*, 4: 2, 19 Şubat 1324 / 4 March 1909, which fixed charges by ad size and the number of times the ad would run.

57. For a comparison with the press of the French revolutionary era, see Jeremy D. Popkin, "The Business of Political Enlightenment in France 1770–1800," 412–435, in Brewer and Porter, *Consumption and the World of Goods*, (423–428) which treats of profit margins and points out the security of subscription based publishing. He notes (424) that publishers often increased their number of presses (wooden hand presses) and workers rather than utilizing newer technologies in response to increased volume. He also notes (426) the difficulties involved in sending provincial subscriptions because it complicated bookkeeping and was plagued by slow mail sevice or subscriptions lost in the mail.

58. *Alem*, 5: 6, 5 Mart 1324 / 18 March 1909; the cartoon is by Ali Cemali. For photos of the main post office, see Ahmet Eken, *Kartpostallarda İstanbul* (İstanbul: Büyükşehir Belediyesi, 1992), 102.

59. For an intersting treatment of readership in the Middle East, see Ayalon, *The Press in the Arab Middle East*, 135–165. Ayalon does pioneering work on the questions of circulation, readership, and cultural contexts.

60. Some early attempts to compile bibliographic information on the output of the Ottoman periodical press are *Takvim-i vekayı*, a twenty-two-page supplementary list published in seven installments between January and March of 1909 and inserted (out of numbering sequence) in the issues between nos. 102 and 167 (12 Kanun-ı sanı 1324 / 25 January 1909 and 18 Mart 1325 / 31 March 1909). See also, *Salname-i servet-i fünun*, 2: 70–80, 1326 rumi; Selim Nüzhet, ed., *1933 Almanak* (İstanbul: Devlet Matbaası, n.d.), 242–250, for gazettes published 1247/1831 through 1927; *Revue du Monde Musulman* (1909), 87–139; and (1925) 44–62. See also J. H. A. Ubicini, *Letters on Turkey: An Account of the Religious, Political, Social and Commercial Condition of the Ottoman Empire* (London: John Murray, 1856), 246–253.

61. İskit, *Türkiyede Matbuat Rejimleri;* and *Türkiyede Matbuat İdareleri ve Politikaları*.

62. See, for example, *Kalem*, 36: 9, 21 Mayıs 1325 / 3 June 1909.

63. Edward G. Browne, *The Press and Poetry of Modern Iran* (Los Angeles: Kalimat Press, 1983, reprint of 1914 edition), 25, notes that the circulation of newspapers went up during the Iranian constitutional period after the revolution of 1905–1906. He gives figures of 3,000 for *Musávát*, 5,000–5,500 for *Şúr-i-Isráfíl*, and 7,000–10,000 for *Majlis*. For comparison purposes, see Townsend, *Forbidden Laughter*, 81–83. Townsend's study of the mid-nineteenth-century press in Berlin notes that circulation figures for satirical gazettes are hard to pin down and varied considerably. The satirical *Die Locomotive*, published in Leipzig "advertised a circulation of 10,000 and then 12,000 in 1842 and 1843, and was considered an amazing success" (82). So these statistics may be considered roughly comparable to the circulation of popular gazettes in Istanbul sixty or so years later. Townsend also points out the problem of counting readers who did not pay for their gazettes, who got them second-hand in some way. One contemporary in Berlin in the early 1840's claimed that each copy of a newspaper reached at least four readers. "Other estimates for central Europe are as high as twenty readers per copy (83)."

64. Şapolyo, *Türk Gazeteciliği Tarihi*, 183. Javadi, *Satire in Persian Literature*, 139, notes that an expatriate Iranian journal called *Shah Seven* was published in Istanbul in 1888–1889, printing three hundred copies, which were placed in envelopes to look like letters and then sent to readers in Iran. The gazette, *Çıngıraklı Tatar*, 1: 13, 24 Mart 1289 / 6 April 1873, ran a list, by language and circulation, of Istanbul gazettes. Ayalon, *The Press*, 145–154, contains circulation figures, ranging from 1,000 to 14,000, for Arab newspapers in the period 1900–1911.

65. Roger Chartier, *Cultural History: Between Practices and Representations* (Ithaca: Cornell University Press, 1988), 164–166. Nor can the impact of the press be readily assessed or assumed to be widespread (as Censer, [124 & 128] is inclined to assume for the Parisian press). Although individual events (the assassination of the journalist Hasan Fehmi in 1909 for example) or reactions can sometimes be linked specifically to press coverage, ordinarily cause and effect are difficult to document. How, for example, does one document that a reaction occurred specifically in response to news communicated in print as opposed to that communicated by word of mouth?

66. Chartier, ibid., 165. For a fascinating examination of the transition to print culture in the Yemen and some of the tensions between oral and print culture, see Brinkley Messick, *The Calligraphic State: Textual Domination and History in a Muslim Society* (Berkeley: University of California Press, 1993), 115–119, which, for example, discusses the advent of printing in the Ottoman Yemen and its effects on methods of education.

67. *Kalem*, 64: 5, 19 Teşrin-i sani 1325 / 2 December 1909. Another cartoon in *Kalem*, 81: 5, 25 Mart 1326 / 7 April 1910, shows the bookseller idle while the cheese seller does a brisk business.

68. *Kalem*, 6: 3, 25 Eylül 1324 / 8 October 1908.

69. For an interesting study of the English countryside and the ways in which the press promoted and exploited markets, see C. Y. Ferdinand, "Selling it to the Provinces: News and Commerce Round Eighteenth-Century Salisbury," 393–411, in Brewer and Porter, *Consumption and The World of Goods*. Ferdinand points out (394, 397–399) the intimate relationship between book publishing and newspaper publishing in England which was also true in the case of Istanbul.

70. Eugen Weber, *Peasants into Frenchmen: The Modernization of Rural France 1870–1914*, (Stanford: Stanford University Press, 1976), 467–469, on the increase in provincial reading, and (453) on "popular libraries" and the existence of a working-class reading public in late-nineteenth-century France.

71. On the women's press, see *İstanbul Kütüphanelerindeki Eski Harfli Türkçe Kadın Dergileri Bibliyografyası* (İstanbul: Metis Yayınları, 1992), a preliminary reference work; *Türkiye'de Dergiler Ansiklopediler (1848–1984)* (İstanbul: Gelişim Yayınları, 1984), 163–168; and Ayfer Stump, "The Emergence of a Feminist/Nationalist Discourse in Pre-Republican Turkey: Case Study of *Kadın* Magazine (1908–1909)," (M.A. thesis, Ohio State University, 1996). Other work on the women's press is done by Elizabeth Frierson (Ph.D. dissertation, Princeton, 1997); and Beth Baron, *The Women's Awakening in Egypt: Culture, Society, and the Press* (New Haven: Yale University Press, 1994). For work on images of women see, Palmira Brummett, "New Woman and Old Nag: Images of Women in the Ottoman Cartoon Space," *Princeton Papers: An*

Notes to Pages 45–46

Interdisciplinary Journal of Middle Eastern Studies (Spring/Summer 1997); Brummett, "Dressing for Revolution: Mother, Nation, Citizen, and Subversive in the Ottoman Satirical Press, in Zehra Arat, ed., *Deconstructing Images of "The Turkish Woman,"* (New York: St. Martin's Press, 1998).

72. At 65 *kuruş*/year for a subscription to a 4–8 page weekly, or around 100 *kuruş*/year for a daily subscription, not all could afford their own paper. Carter Findley, *Ottoman Civil Officialdom: A Social History* (Princeton: Princeton University Press, 1989), 318–367 has published extensive analyses of the salaries and living costs of Ottoman officials in the late nineteenth and early twentieth centuries. He notes (322) official salaries in the 1,000–1,500 *kuruş*/month range as necessary to support a modest household, but also points out that nominal salary was not necessarily indicative of what was actually paid.

73. Literacy rates are very difficult to pin down. See Findley, *Ottoman Civil Officialdom*, 142–145, on education reform and the Ottoman bureaucracy. Ayalon, *The Press*, 143–144, estimates that 0.2 percent of women and 8 percent of men in the settled population of Egypt were literate in 1897 and that, by 1917, only 2.1 percent of Egyptian women were literate. Emel Doğramcı, *Atatürk and the Turkish Woman Today* (Ankara: Atatürk Araştırma Merkezi, 1991), 36, cites statistics indicating in 1935, that 9.81 percent of women in Turkey were literate.

74. Other forms of address (*müslimanlar, müslimin*) may also be ambiguous but others (*vatanperver*/patriot) although not essentially gendered were clearly addressing men. When women were intended as audience, that intention was often specifically indicated by the addition of inclusionary terms like *kadınlar*. See on the inclusion and exclusion of women in the language of the Iranian constitutional revolution: Afsaneh Najmabadi, "Zanhā-yi Millat: Women or Wives of the Nation?" *Iranian Studies* 26 (Winter–Spring 1993): 51–71.

75. Demetra Vaka, *Haremlik: Some Pages from the Life of Turkish Women*, (Boston: Houghton Mifflin Company, 1910), 137–139.

76. Emine Tugay, *Three Centuries: Family Chronicles of Turkey and Egypt* (London: Oxford University Press, 1963), 166–167, 179.

77. Townsend, *Forbidden Laughter*, 85–86, in a chapter on the readers of the Berlin press in the first half of the nineteenth century, has argued that "everyone"—members of all classes—"read and looked at" humorous publications. The factors that contributed to high consumption, according to Townsend, were high literacy rate, innovative publishing and marketing, varied modes of dissemination, and official apprehensions. All these factors were in place in revolutionary Istanbul except a high literacy rate. The primary factor, for Townsend, that moderates consumption of humorous publications, is cost. Unfortunately, I have no information on the market for second-hand periodicals, which must have existed in Istanbul as it did in Berlin.

78. Garnett, *Turkish Life in Town and Country*, 59–60.

79. Edward G. Browne, *The Persian Revolution of 1905–1909* (London: Frank Cass and Co., 1966, reprint of 1910 edition), 143. Browne also notes the establishment by Iranian revolutionaries of a "free library," in Tabriz, designed to "educate the people in patriotic ideas" before the revolution (116–117). On cafes and readers in Egypt, see Ayalon, *The Press*, 156.

80. Findley, *Ottoman Civil Officialdom*, 319, suggests an estimate of laborer's wages at about 350 *kuruş* per month in 1908. Thirty daily papers per month, at the most common (10 *para* per issue) price, would cost him 7.5 *kuruş* per month (although "dailies" were not necessarily published every single day).

81. Ahmet Rasim, *Şehir Mektupları*, v.1 (İstanbul: Milli Eğitim Basımevi, 1971; translation of 1328/1912 edition), 40. Also on the *kıraathaneler*, see Eken, *Kartpostallarda İstanbul*, 182.

82. These processes altered the nature and style of even the most elite publications. As Chartier, *The Cultural Uses of Print*, 238, has pointed out: "When printed matter underwent the process of diffusion, the printed work was no longer a rare possession. Consequently, it lost some of its symbolic value and became an object for somewhat nonchalant consumption." Chartier also notes reading as a collective exercise and the French practices of renting out gazettes and of reading aloud for a small contribution (184, 214).

83. Puzzles were found in Ottoman serials in the prerevolutionary period, for example "*Fenni Eğlenceler*," in *Takvim-i Bahar*, 2: 129–133, 1306 / 1890.

84. For some gazettes that ran the *bilmece*, see *Resimli İstanbul*, *Coşkun kalender*, *Musavver devr-i cedid*, and *Gramophon*.

85. In these cases "*bilmece*" could take on the meaning of little bits of knowledge, rather than strictly a riddle or problem to be solved.

86. This is illustrated on the last puzzle page in *Resimli İstanbul*, 13: 208, 31 Ağustos 1325 / 13 September 1909, which included, in English and Ottoman, the riddle embedded in a story: "Uncles and brothers have I none, but that man's father is my father's son." This particular riddle was not part of a contest but it does illustrate the combination of educational and entertainment objectives in the *bilmece* sections of gazettes.

87. *Resimli kitab*, 8: 846, Mayıs 1325 / May 1909.

88. It would be interesting to see if these types of puzzles were incorporated into school texts or instructional materials employed in the schools of the empire. What exactly was the supply of print materials available in the primary and secondary schools is not clear. A second point is that we cannot assume a priori that the Ottoman audience's only familiarity with such materials came from European publications.

Chapter III. The Voice and Image of the Public, and Its Targets

1. Roger Chartier, *The Cultural Uses of Print*, 10. In another work, Chartier, "Texts, Printings, Readings," 174–175, in Lynn Hunt, ed., *The New Cultural History* (Berkeley: University of California Press, 1989), has argued that the utility of studying what he calls "print practices" in this period is "First, they fix or convey speech, which means that they cement sociabilities and prescribe behavior, cross into both private and public space, and give rise to belief, imagination, and action. They overturn the whole culture, coming to terms with traditional forms of communication and establishing new distinctions. Second they permit the circulation of writing on an unprecedented scale."

2. Quoted in William Feaver and Ann Gould, eds., *Masters of Caricature From Hogarth and Gillray to Scarfe and Levine* (New York: Alfred Knopf, 1981), 95. Boss Tweed was referring to Thomas Nast's cartoons in *Harper's Weekly*. The journal's circulation tripled in 1871 as Nast took on New York's Tammany Hall.

3. For example, Habermas, Terdiman, and Chartier, op. cit. In the Ottoman context, Mardin, *The Genesis of Young Ottoman Thought*, 273–274, has noted the ill-defined nature of Şinasi's conception of public opinion: "it is probable that Şinasi addressed himself to an imaginary anthropocentric man, a type of *homo politicus* similar to the *homo oeconomicus*, a product of the mathematical imagination of the Enlightenment."

4. For one interpretation of the link between press, public, and advertising, see Terdiman, *Discourse/Counter-Discourse*, 122–125, who focuses on the "commoditization" of the nineteenth-century French press.

5. *Beyan ül-hak*, 2: 1, 29 Eylül 1324 / 12 October 1908. This direct form of address was a standard in articles as well as editorials of the time. *Beyan ül-hak*, journal of the Cemiyet-i İlmiye-i Osmaniye, was a religious journal that covered a variety of subjects; it employed *hicrî* along with *malî* dating in its issues. See, on *Beyan ül-hak* and religiously oriented gazettes, *Türkiye'de Dergiler, Ansiklopediler*, 20–21.

6. Laitin, *Hegemony and Culture*, 175–179. Laitin argues that, "A symbol system provides a clue as to what is worth fighting about and also as to what is so common-sensical that attempts to change it seem pointless." I am not sure exactly what Laitin intends by commonsensical, but the radical cultural changes taking place at the time of the Ottoman revolution were subverting what may once have seemed common-sensical. Dubin, *Arresting Images*, 19, has argued in his analysis of late-twentieth-century conflict over the terrain of art that, "whenever a society is overwhelmed by problems and its sense of national identity is shaky or diffuse, a probable response is for states to attempt to exercise control by regulating symbolic expression."

7. Phillipe, *Political Graphics*, 9. On Republican art and the attempt to speak for the people in early-nineteenth-century France, see McWilliam, *Dreams of Happiness*, 267–314.

8. Walter Armbrust, "The National Vernacular: Folklore and Egyptian Popular Culture," *Michigan Quarterly Review* 31, no. 4 (Fall 1992): 525–542, includes an interesting discussion of the connections between print culture, popular culture, and the associations of various types of language with modernity and with high and low culture. In the Ottoman case, while the elite classes in Istanbul were certainly implicated as European collaborators (a common cartoon topic), there was not a rigid differentiation between an elite (rather than classical) and a colloquial language. And, because print culture was still at a rather primitive stage of development, there could be no question of a national vernacular. Ottoman Turkish was already a highly mixed (classical, coloquial, Levantine) language before its invasion by European, primarily French, elements.

9. *Boşboğaz*, 18: 3, 25 Eylül 1324 / 8 October 1908. The play *Vatan* was written by Namık Kemal in 1873, and performed to enthusiastic audiences after the revolution. Note that what is actually printed here seems to read "*mesarrat*." It is probably a misprint; after *adalet* and *uhuvvet* one would expect *meşveret* (consultation).

Notes to Pages 53–54

10. Habermas, *The Structural Transformation*, 254, n. 35, speaks of the significance of dialogue for early versions of the news in Europe. In a dense note, he points out that the sixteenth-century European New Journals and fifteenth century broadsheets were written in dialogue form and meant to be declaimed or sung.

11. The works of Usama, a Syrian writing at the time of the crusades, and Busbecq, the Hapsburg Emperor's envoy to Sultan Suleiman's court, are earlier examples of such comparative arguments. See Usamah ibn Munqidh (d. 1188), *The Autobiography of Ousama* (London: G. Routledge, 1929); and Ogier Ghislain de Busbecq, *The Turkish Letters of Ogier Ghislain de Busbecq, Ambassador at Constantinople 1554–1562*, translated by Edward Foster (Oxford: Clarendon Press, 1968). Europe and European "opinion" were important measures (both positive and negative) for the self-evaluations and strategies of Asian revolutionary movements. Afsaneh Najmabadi, "The Daughters of Qūchān: Re-membering the For-gotten Gender of the Iranian Constitutional Revolution," unpublished paper, 1994, notes the referential nature of debates in the Iranian meclis (after Iran's own early-twentieth-century constitutional revolution). During those debates speakers often appealed to the assembly by asking what would be thought of them in Europe if they followed such and such course of action. Conversely, in India, in 1919, a contributor to a gazette used Europe as the epitomy of all that was undesirable: "the day the Hindu widow, like a European widow, openly sets out on her own to seek a second husband . . . . That very day the heart of Mother India will split asunder in anguish and all of us men will be engulfed in it." See Vir Bharat Talwar, "Feminist Consciousness in Women's Journals in Hindi, 1910–1920," Kumkum Sangari and Sudesh Vaid, eds., in *Recasting Women: Essays in Indian Colonial History* (New Brunswick, N.J.: Rutgers University Press, 1990), 217–218.

12. See, for example, an open letter by one Hüseyin Saad to the military commander, İzzet Pasha, in *Aşiyan*, 1: 20–24, 28 Ağustos 1324 / 10 September 1908. Such open letters were common, written by the journalists themselves, by prominent figures, or by readers.

13. Ahmad, *The Young Turks*, 35–36.

14. This idea was reinforced by section titles like "*Açık Sözler* (Frank Speaking)," a regular column in the gazette *İnkılâb*.

15. *Kalem*, 64: 2, 19 Teşrin-i sani 1325 / 2 December 1909, for example, begins this particular "gossip" section with a series of images of everyone talking, all the gazettes preoccupied, and "public opinion" (*efkâr-ı umumî*). A similar illustration can be found in *Hande*, 1: 3, 22 Mart 1326 / 4 April 1910, in its "Weekly Smile" section, with a dialogue between an old man and woman talking over the fence. Dialogues were used for serious discussion as well, as (for example) in a dialogue about the revolution between an "inhabitant" and an "exile," in the religious daily *Volkan*, 3: 1–2, 30 Teşrin-i sani 1324 / 13 December 1908.

16. On the history of the Karagöz plays, see Metin And, *Karagöz: Turkish Shadow Theatre* (İstanbul: Dost Publications, 1987); the collection of dialogues in Hellmut Ritter, *Karagöz: Türkische Schattenspiele*, 3 vols. (Hanover, Leipzig, Wiesbaden: 1924–1963). See also Cevdet Kudret, *Karagöz*, 3 vols. (Ankara: Bilgi Yayınevi, 1968–1970), an expanded Turkish version of Ritter, which contains many examples of Karagöz

Notes to Page 54

dialogues. For examples, see the gazette entitled *Karagöz* (published 1908–1928); and *Kalem* 57: 5, 1 Teşrin-i evvel 1325 / 14 October 1909, and 72: 6, 14 Kanun-ı sani 1325 / 27 January 1910. On shadow theater, see René Simmen, *The World of Puppets* (New York: Thomas Y. Crowell, 1972), 79–116. Puppet theater was also an important element of theatricals and satire in turn-of-the century Russia: Stites, *Russian Popular Culture*, 17.

17. On Karagöz and comedy, see Michèle Nicolas, "La comédie humaine dans le Karagöz," *Revue du Monde Mussulman et de la Méditerranée* 77–78 (1996): 75–87. For examples of the "Everyman" character in Iranian satire, see Javadi, *Satire in Persian Literature*, 153–154. Javadi notes, for example, the 1906 story "Freedoom in Iran," by Jalil Mamen Quli-Zade whose main character is the poor, naive, and ignorant Baku worker, Karbalay Mohammad 'Ali. See Press, *The Political Cartoon*, 222, on John Q. Public as the Everyman of American cartoons and (208–231) on American symbols like Miss Liberty, Yankee, Uncle Sam, and Columbia. Townsend, *Forbidden Laughter*, 116–129, discusses the figure Nante, a day laborer, social critic, and scamp who was a type of lower-class Everyman figure and a staple of nineteenth-century Prussian satire.

18. See, for example, *Perde*, 4: 1, 3 Kanun-ı evvel 1327 / 18 December 1911, for title vignettes and a cartoon on politics and the press.

19. *Karagöz Salnamesi* (İstanbul: Ahmed İhsan, 1910). Karagöz and Hacivat decorated humorous announcements in *Üç gazete*, 8: 4, 5 Eylül 1324 / 18 September 1908. They were two of several secondary mascots (after Zevzek and Geveze) in *Yeni Geveze*, and the primary mascots in issues 203–214. Karagöz was the cartoon partner of Zevzek (Giddy One) in the gazette of that name; he also appeared in *Cadaloz, Cingöz, Dalkavuk, Ezop, Falaka, Gramofon, Hacivat, Karakuş*, and others. For example, see *Cingöz*, 1: 4, 26 Ağustos 1324 / 8 September 1908, featuring Cingöz welcoming a boatload of satiric characters including a rather primitively drawn Karagöz. Karagöz's name could also be signed to humorous pieces, as in *Ton ton risalesi*, 1, 5 Eylül 1324 / 18 September 1908.

20. And, *Karagöz*, 87–93. In 1911, in Algiers, the authorities banned all political references from Karagöz performances. Shadow theater, originating in the Far East and India, was spread throughout the empire; references to it in the Ottoman sources date from at least the sixteenth century.

21. And, *Karagöz*, 22, on the meaning of *hayal*.

22. See, for example, *Çıngıraklı Tatar*, 7: 1–2, [14] Nisan 1289 / [27] April 1873, for a Karagöz-type dialogue in a nineteenth-century gazette. For just a few of the many, many examples in the revolutionary period; see *Karakuş Ezop* (published 13 Eylül 1324 / 26 September 1908); *Şakacı* (published 1908); *Yeni geveze* (1910–1912); *Üç gazete* 1: 4, 29 Ağustos 1324 / 11 September 1908; *Züğürt*, 7: 2, [22] Mart 1327 / 4 April 1911; and *Resimli kitab*, 3: 277–285, Teşrin-i sani 1324 / November 1908. The gazette *Coşkun kalender* (1909) relied heavily on humorous dialogue for its satire, including three or four regular dialogue sections in each issue.

23. Chartier, "Texts, Printings, Readings," 170, has argued against the radical differentiation of oral and written culture: "Thus formulated, the opposition of oral

and written fails to account for the situation that existed from the sixteenth to the eighteenth century [in Europe] when media and multiple practices still overlapped." I might add that it also fails to account for the situation that existed in the early-twentieth-century Ottoman empire.

24. See also, And, *Karagöz*, 44–45; Mustafa Şahin, "Karagöz'den Punch'a Nazıre," *Tarih ve Toplum* 22, no. 122 (Şubat 1994), 43–47. Javadi, *Satire in Persian Literature*, 187, notes that the "*Monazere*, a kind of debate between two persons or things," was a favorite poetic form of the social satirist Parvin E'tesami.

25. *Yuha*, 1: 2, 2 Kanun-ı evvel 1326 / 15 December 1910. This was one of the ubiquitous dialogues on the press, the plethora of gazettes available after the revolution, censorship, and the press's effects on the public. *Boşboğaz*, 26: 2, 28 Teşrin-i evvel 1324 / 10 November 1908, for example, on "where and when the Ottoman gazettes must be read."

26. *Lâla*, 5: 4, 30 Kanun-ı evvel 1326 / 12 December 1910; *Ton ton risalesi*, 1: 4, 8, 5 Eylül 1324 / 18 September 1908 (dialogues between minor officials); *Geveze* (repeated as a regular category), published 1908–1909); *Karakuş*, 1: 3–4, 9 Eylül 1324 / 22 September 1908; and *Zevzek*, 1: 4, 29 Ağustos 1324 / 11 September 1908.

27. In *Malum*, for example, where he was listed as head writer. In *Piyano*, Don Kişot is listed as a writer in the *mizah* section.

28. This figure had various names: Mulla Naṣru'd-Dīn, Djoha, and Goha. See for example: Jean Dejeux, *Djoha hier et aujourd'hui* (Sherbrooke, Quebec: Editions Naaman, 1978); Browne, *The Press and Poetry of Modern Persia*, front cover, 16, 23, 116; Irène Fenoglio, "Caricature et représentation du mythe: Goha," in *Images d'Egypte, De la fresque à la bande dessiné*, (Cairo: CEDEJ, 1992), 133–143. On the "wise fool" in Iranian satire, see Javadi, *Satire in Persian Literature*, 147–159, 166.

29. The Hoca is found occasionally in revolutionary satire. See, for example: *Malum*, 1: 4, [8] Kanun-ı evvel 1326 / 21 December 1910, in which the hoca is teaching a camel to read; *Boşboğaz*, 17: 2, 22 Eylül 1324 / 5 October 1908; and *Kibar*, 1: 3, 23 Teşrin-i sani 1326 / 6 December 1910.

30. Quoted in Nokes, *Raillery and Rage*, 52.

31. A similar mascot predecessor was the bell-ringer in *Çıngıraklı Tatar* (published 1289/1873).

32. A counterpart to Züğürt is the mounted peasant, "Charro," of Mexican cartoons; Mexican cartoons and "protest art" of the early twentieth century provide a useful comparison to the context and themes of Ottoman cartoons. See Shikes, *The Indignant Eye*, 374–379, and Press, *The Political Cartoon*, 131.

33. *Züğürt*, 8: 1, 19 Nisan 1327 / 2 May 1911. The big purge of bureaucrats, according to Carter Findley (personal communication) came in the *tensikat* (reorganization) after the 1908 revolution, although salary and staff cuts came at various dates after 1876. Unneeded officials were eliminated and placed *kadro haric*. By 1909 these men numbered in the tens of thousands.

34. McWilliam, *Dreams of Happiness*, 313, has noted some of the ironies of the attempt to co-opt the voice of the laboring poor in early-nineteenth-century France: "Such an attitude tended to foster an idealized perception of the people as the

Notes to Pages 60–63

upright but stoical victims of corrupt masters, who sought less revenge for their repression than acceptance as equals in a morally cleansed nation of brothers." Züğürt was, perhaps, a little less optimistic.

35. The revolution and the "new" Ottoman society were staged in the Ottoman press through a careful use of photographic images. Another example is in *Eşref,* 8: 1, 23 Nisan 1325 / 6 May 1909, which showed photos of Enver, Niyazî Bey, and M. Şevket Pasha as heroes of the national struggle for freedom against the counter-revolutionaries.

36. As argued in another context for the women of the Ottoman harem, in Leslie Peirce, *The Imperial Harem: Women and Sovereignty in the Ottoman Empire* (New York: Oxford University Press, 1993).

37. Partha Chatterjee, "The Nationalist Resolution of the Women's Question," 244, in Sangari and Vaid, eds., *Recasting Women,* has noted the association of loudness and quarrelsomeness with the "common" woman, lower class female characters who inhabit nineteenth-century literature: maidservants, washerwomen, barbers, peddlers, procuresses, prostitutes. There are some similarities here to the Ottoman old nag, who is usually dressed and framed as a member of the lower or middle classes, ordinarily not a member of the elite classes.

38. Cadaloz, as the voice of skepticism, had a youthful male counterpart in the "naughty urchin," Afacan, mascot for the publication of the same name; the figure of Cadaloz appeared in two of the cartoons in the gazette *Afacan,* published by Hüseyin Nazmi from July to August 1911.

39. On the patriarchal bargain see Deniz Kandiyoti, "Islam and Patriarchy: A Comparative Perspective," in Nikki Keddie and Beth Baron, eds., *Women in Middle Eastern History* (New Haven: Yale University Press, 1991), 23–44. The model of the patriarchal bargain deemphasizes patriarchy as monolithic and focuses instead on analyzing women's strategies for dealing with male dominance.

40. Recent scholarship on women in Middle Eastern states has focused on silence as a mode by which Islamic systems and androcentric historiography have controlled women. See, for examle, Farzaneh Milani, *Veils and Words: The Emerging Voices of Iranian Women Writers* (Syracuse: Syracuse University Press, 1992); and Leila Ahmed, *Women and Gender in Islam* (New Haven: Yale University Press, 1992), 61.

41. The gazette *Dalkavuk* (September 1908–March 1909), contains various humorous dialogues between *Büyük Hanım* and others including *Kızım* (meaning *my daughter* although it can be applied to any young woman). Büyük Hanım appears in *Boşboğaz,* 13: 2, 8 Eylül 1324 / 21 September 1908. Another such figure is Hanım Nene (mother, nurse, wet-nurse) in *İncili çavuş,* 14: 4, 23 Eylül 1324 / 6 October 1908.

42. *Geveze* was published by Kirkor Faik between fall of 1908 and spring of 1909. The satric gazette *Cingöz,* 1: 2, 26 Ağustos 1324 / 8 September 1908, ran a version of the "*milli roman*" (national novel or story), entitled "*Dedikoducu Kadınlar*" (Gossipy Women), in its first issue.

43. *Diken,* published by Sedat Simavi, began publication in November 1918. Here the old nag is basically the equivalent of the old male, *baba* (meaning father, but also suggesting old fashioned grandpa or bumpkin).

Notes to Pages 66–67

44. Press, *The Political Cartoon*, 75. Geipel, *The Cartoon: A Short History*, divides the forms or styles of cartooning into two very rough groupings: (1) whimsy, burlesque, impudent caricature, and distortion; and (2) "only essential penstrokes," "naturalistic to ornate," and "free and fluid." Phillipe, *Political Graphics*, 10–12, divides political graphics into the following categories: caricature, metamorphosis, or allegory.

45. Phillipe, *Political Graphics*, 94, 216, (who divides the "modes" of political graphic into narrative, inspirational, and inciting to moral meditation) notes the element of fatalism in the graphics of the Mexican revolution. He points, for example, to the artist José Posada who, speaking for the have-nots in 1911 Mexico, portrayed both the haves and the have-nots as skeletons.

46. Terdiman, *Discourse/Counter-Discourse*, 158–159. Ottoman revolutionary satire also blended the destructive and fatalistic modes into what Terdiman has called "organized disaffection." Organizing disaffection had been one of the characteristic tasks of shadow puppet theater; in the press this disaffection took both cartoon and narrative forms.

47. Press, *The Political Cartoon*, 136, 251.

48. Feaver and Gould, eds., *Masters of Caricature*, 74.

49. Philippe, *Political Graphics*, 15, has argued that the "external threat" is critical for the development of internal criticism of a regime. He argues, for example, that criticism of the aristocracy in Italy was less vigorous than elsewhere because the Italian aristocracy sometimes supported "national opposition to foreign domination." In the Ottoman case, too, there seems to be some correlation between the degree of external threat (considerable) and the willingness to tear down hegemonic political and social systems.

50. As Elliot, *The Power of Satire*, 271, has noted regarding early modern European satire, "The pressure of the satirist's art inevitably comes athwart society's efforts to maintain its equilibrium. . . . . an attack by a powerful satirist on a local phenomenon seems to be capable of infinite extension in the reader's mind into an attack on the whole structure of which that phenomenon is part."

51. In other satiric contexts, the sultan could be associated with the evil foreigner, as Stites, *Russian Popular Culture*, 34, has noted. Stites points out a popular Russian satire of 1914 that targeted both Germany and the Ottoman state: "a salacious treatment of the German Kaiser," entitled *Wilhelm in the Sultan's Harem*.

52. Feaver and Gould, *Masters of Caricature*, 71, note that the idea of showing King Louis-Philippe as a rotting pear was Charles Philipon's (editor of *La Caricature*). They argue further that the English *Punch*'s popularity derived from its taking a milder tone than that of many French satirical gazettes.

53. Terdiman, *Discourse/Counter-Discourse*, 118–119, 142–145, has equated newspapers with dominant discourse and satirical gazettes with counter-discourse. He writes, "Newspapers: their ubiquity, their very banality, stand as signs of dominant discourse self-confidently bodied forth" (118). One could argue that, during Abd ül-Hamid's reign, censorship had made the press a reflection of the dominant sultanic discourse. However, Terdiman is talking about the mass dailes of the nineteenth-century French press. The Ottoman case had no such mass press market (either before or after the revolution). Thus, Terdiman's polarization of commercial mass

press culture (dominant discursive) and institutionalized antibourgeois satire (counter discursive) does not work well for the Ottoman situation in 1908 Istanbul. Also, because of the relative novelty, considerable freedom, and (often) high literary style of the Istanbul press after the revolution, there was not the association of the serious press with low-brow or common culture that Terdiman (144–145) suggests was evident in nineteenth-century French characterizations.

54. This phenomenon contrasts directly, for example, with that of the gazette *Mullah Nasr al-Din* in which the mullahs (clerics) were the favored embodiments of ignorance and pomposity: Ernest Tucker, "The Newspaper *Mullah Nasr al-Din* and Satirical Journalism in Early Twentieth Century Azerbaijan," unpublished paper, University of Chicago, 1987.

55. Laitin, *Hegemony and Culture*, 176, does not agree with Clifford Geertz that religions provide a sense of "a general order of existence." But I do. One way that religious satire did enter into the satirical press was in the form of satirization of various folk rituals that were equated with ignorance and superstition. Of course such practices were no more particular to Islam than they were to Christianity, or Judaism; they were widespread among people of many religious beliefs.

56. The Ottoman clergy like others (Muslim and Christian), before and since, had certainly been the object of satirical attack long before the revolution; but the position and treatment of the clergy in the Ottoman empire were not analogous to those of the Catholic clergy during the French Revolution. See, Shikes, *The Indignant Eye*, 84. Attempts selectively to attack religious corruption or the behavior of the clergy could all too readily escalate into general attacks on religion itself, as Elliot, *The Power of Satire*, 273, has noted regarding Swift's, *Tale of a Tub*. For a general treatment of Western religious satire, see Bloom and Bloom, *Satire's Persuasive Voice*, 160–201. On the struggle over images that attack or subvert religion in late-twentieth-century America, see Dubin, *Arresting Images*, 79–101.

57. The Ottoman clergy wielded extensive power but not the direct political and institutional power that they had once had, nor the extensive power that the French and Iranian clergies wielded before (respectively) their late-eighteenth and early-twentieth-century revolutions.

58. For some of the basic literature on nationalism see: Rashid Khalidi, ed., *The Origins of Arab Nationalism* (New York: Columbia University Press, 1991); Albert Hourani, *Arabic Thought in the Liberal Age 1798–1939* (Oxford: Oxford University Press, 1970); William Haddad and William Ochsenwald, *Nationalism in a Non-National State: The Dissolution of the Ottoman Empire* (Columbus: Ohio State University, 1977); Zeine N. Zeine, *The Emergence of Arab Nationalism: With a Background Study of Arab Turkish Relations in the Near East* (Beirut: Khayats, 1966); A. A. Duri, *The Historical Formations of the Arab Nation: A Study in Identity and Consciousness* (London: Croom Helm, 1987); Jacques Berque, *Egypt, Imperialism and Revolution* (New York: Praeger, 1972); and Hamid Enayat, *Modern Islamic Political Thought* (Austin: University of Texas, 1982).

59. This strategy would reflect, for example the political platform of the CUP, which, in the revolutionary period, was still stressing Ottoman (rather than Turkish) nationalism. On this subject see Ahmad, *Young Turks*, Zürcher, *The Unionist Factor*,

and Hasan Kayalı, *Arabs and Young Turks: Ottomanism, Arabism, and Islamism in the Ottoman Empire, 1908–1918* (Berkeley: University of California Press, 1997). Kayalı stresses the commitment to Ottomanism in the central government and in the Arab provinces well into World War I. He also contextualizes the charges of Turkification against the CUP.

60. Ernest Tucker, "Mullah Nasr al-Din," 9, notes that an article in the Azerbaijani gazette, *Mullah Nasr al-Din*, points up the dilemmas of ethnic or national typing. In the article, entitled "Mr. Translator," the author, after making fun of the strange dress and behavior of other nationalities, meets a man whose ethnicity he cannot guess. It turns out that the man's "nationality" is neither Russian, Armenian, Georgian, Turkish, Persian, or French, he is a "*seyyid*," a descendent of the Prophet who considers himself as a completely separate "nationality" from other Muslims.

61. See *Revue du Monde Musulman*, 6, no. 9 (September 1908): 160–179. This piece, published shortly after the revolution, demonstrates an awareness in France of Ottoman cartoons. It contains (166–167) two cartoons of İzzet Pasha, one showing him as a thief and the other (calling him "Arab" İzzet) as a prisoner. Another cartoon using the same designation is in *Musavver Cellâd*, 1: 4, 7 Eylül 1324 / 20 September 1908. İzzet became the image of the quintessential traitor, toady, and enemy of the nation.

62. *Dalkavuk*, 3: 4, 13 Eylül 1324 / 26 September 1908; this issue is misprinted so that the date reads 31 Eylül.

63. Some gazettes, like *Protesto* for example, were particularly concerned with affairs in Egypt and the Arab provinces.

64. This maxim was expressed almost half a century later when a disappointed Nasser admitted that the masses were not ready to play the role he had envisioned for them before the Egyptian revolution succeeded. Gamal Abdel Nasser, *The Philosophy of the Revolution* (Buffalo: Economica Books, 1959), 31–37. Nasser's society sounds a lot like Ottoman revolutionary society; it was afflicted with some of the same dilemmas. As Nasser expressed it, "We live in a society that has not yet crystalized. It is still boiling over and restless" (51).

65. McWilliam, *Dreams*, 317.

66. McWilliam, *Dreams*, 319. The Ottoman revolutionary press was only revolutionary to a limited degree and suffered from the same constraints as the French "radical" artists; as McWilliams puts it: "What is, then, perhaps most striking about art *social* and the politics within which it is framed, is the difficulty faced by middle-class radicals, as well as by artisan intellectuals, in staking out an authentically different moral terrain on which to construct a progressive sociocultural practice" (320). McWilliams, however, seems to see this constraint as a fault; I would, rather, consider it inevitable.

67. *Cadaloz*, 31: 4, [5] Temmuz 1327 / [18] July 1911. Role reversals and the "speaking up" of the lower classes, as in this cartoon, were common in revolutionary satire. There is a somewhat similar cartoon in *Lâklâk* 3: 2, 23 Temmuz 1325 / 5 August 1909, in which a workman is spraying a "pasha," with a hose, although in this case he does not attribute his act to the new freedom, but calls it a free bath on a hot day. For an example from a very different place but similar time, see: Margaret

Lavinia Anderson, "Voter, Junker, *Landrat*, Priest: The Old Authorities and the New Franchise in Imperial Germany," *The American Historical Review* 98, no. 5 (December 1993): 1448–1474, which shows a cartoon (1473) of a poor man arrogantly boarding a limosine the day after the election and informing the chauffer that he will now have a new class of clientele.

Chapter IV. Revolutionary Exemplars: France and Iran

1. This excerpt is from an article that begins with a longer list of grievances by way of introducing the Iranian constitutional movement and events in Iran: *Nevsal-ı Osmanî* (İstanbul: İkbal Kitabhanesi, 1327 / 1911), 159. It goes on to note how "some young men" who completed their education in Europe, worked to establish the idea of constitutionalism in Iran.

2. This preoccupation is recorded in such works as Celal Nuri's, *Türk İnkılâp* (İstanbul: Ahmed Kâmil Matbaası, n.d.), which begins its consideration of the question of writing about the Ottoman revolution with reference to the French and Bolshevik revolutions (3), and begins a discussion of economic, literary and religious revolution (336–381) with the statement that the subject of discussion will be the question of [Ottoman] participation in European civilization. France is a frequent point of reference in this work.

3. These notions had to be created, refashioned, and popularized by the Ottoman intellectuals. See, for example, Berkes, *The Development of Secularism in Turkey*, 194–200, 232–233, 240–260; and Bernard Lewis, "Why Turkey?: The Development of Constitutional and Representative Government in the Ottoman Empire and Turkey in the 19th and 20th Centuries," *Archivum Ottomanicum* 11 (1986/1988): 9–22.

4. Of course, no work has yet surpassed Lewis, *Emergence of Modern Turkey*, as an intellectual history of the late Ottoman period. Bernard Lewis, *The Shaping of the Modern Middle East*, 2nd edition (New York: Oxford University Press, 1994), 46, sees the transmission of culture from West to East as direct: "The tree of liberty bore fruit. The French Revolution was the first great movement of ideas in Europe that was not expressed in more or less Christian terms, and its doctrines could therefore spread, unhampered, through the new channels that were being opened into the world of Islam."

5. An early study, first published in Arabic in 1943, by Ra'īf Khūrī, *Modern Arab Thought: Channels of the French Revolution to the Arab East*, translated by Iḥsān 'Abbās (Princeton: Kingston Press, 1983), attempts systematically to trace the influences of the French revolution in the work of various Arab thinkers and writers.

6. On the nature and channels of French influence on the Ottoman empire, see: Khūrī, op.cit. Randi Deguilhem-Schoem, "The Transmission of French and Other European Revolutionary Ideas in the Ottoman Empire," *British Society for Middle Eastern Studies, Proceedings of the 1989 International Conference on Europe and the Middle East,* Durham 9–12 July 1989, 234–243; Deguilhem-Schoen, "La diffusion des idées révolutionnaires et réformistes française dans l'Empire ottoman: le cas de l'école secondaire Maktab 'Anbar á Damas," *Revue du Monde Musulman et de la Mediterranée* 52/53 (1990): 185–192; Bernard Lewis, "The Impact of the French

Revolution on Turkey: Some Notes on the Transmission of Ideas," *Journal of World History* 1, no. 1 (July 1990): 105-125; Sina Akşin, "La Révolution Française Et La Conscience Révolutionnaire Des Nationalistes Turcs a L'Aube De La Lutte D'Indépendance," in *Collection Turcica*, v. 1, *La Turquie Et La France A L'Époque D'Atatürk*, (Paris: Association Pour Le Développement Des Études Turques, 1981), 45-55; and articles in Hamit Batu and Jean-Louis Bacqué-Grammont, eds. *L'Empire Ottoman, la République de Turquie et la France* (İstanbul: Editions Isis, 1986). On the general debate over the influence of the French Revolution, see Jack Censer, "Commencing the Third Century of Debate," *The American Historical Review* 94, no. 5 (December 1989): 1309-1325.

7. Berkes, *The Development of Secularism in Turkey*, illustrates the evolutionary nature of these discussions.

8. *Üç gazete*, 1: 1, 29 Ağustos 1324 / 11 September 1908; 11: 3, 8 Eylül 1324 / 21 September 1908; 14: 2, 12 Eylül 1324 / 25 September 1908; and 15: 2, 13 Eylül 1324 / 26 September 1908, also ran articles on the Iranian kings from Muzaffar al-Din to Muhammad Ali Shah, and on Iranians in Istanbul.

9. Lynn Hunt, "Discourses of Patriarchalism and anti-Patriarchalism in the French Revolution," 25-49, in John Renwick, ed., *Language and Rhetoric of the Revolution* (Edinburgh: Edinburgh University Press, 1990). Hunt writes on the importance of familial images to the imagination of power: "the family romance of fraternity enabled the French to imagine a complete rupture with their past. . . . . by rejecting their political fathers, French republicans were able to imagine a wholly new future. They hesitated to identity themselves as political fathers in turn because they did not want to fix definitively the revolutionary process (39)." One might argue that, conversely, the Ottoman republicans had no problem identifying themselves as political fathers (Enver comes to mind), nor did they imagine a complete rupture with their past

10. Feroz Ahmad (personal communication) has pointed out that, "The categories of the French Revolution continued to influence the Unionists and the Kemalists, especially the notion of the Third Estate, which excluded the nobles, i.e. the Palace; both Unionists and Kemalists wanted to create the bourgeoisie that would lead this amorphous *Halk* [people, folk] of their Third Estate."

11. *İnkılâb*, beginning 1: 16, 11 Temmuz 1325 / 24 July 1909, for example, ran a long serialized history of the French Revolution in its early issues; *Şark*, 29: 3, 4 Eylül 1324 / 17 September 1908, ran a serialized article on "The History of Revolution in France;" *Ulûm-i iktisadiye ve içtimaiye mecmuası*, beginning 1, 15 Kanun-ı evvel 1324 / 28 December 1908, ran a long serial on the French Revolution over several issues; İstişare, [?] 51-56 [began pub. 4 Eylül 1324 / 17 September 1908], ran an article, by Saad Muhtar, on the French Revolution and the Law of Man; and *Meram*, beginning 1: 20-23, 30 Teşrin-i evvel 1324 / 12 November 1908, ran a serialized article (from the French) on conditions in Europe in 1815.

12. *Volkan*, 28: 1, 15 Kanun-ı sani 1324 / 28 January 1909; and another article, *Volkan*, 35: 1, 23 Kanun-ı sani 1324 / 5 February 1909, in which Vahdeti, asked, "Does the Law Mean Justice? If Not, Does the Law Mean Despotism?"

13. *Davul*, 11: 8, 31 Kanun-ı evvel 1324 / 13 January 1909.

14. See, among others, Lewis, *The Emergence of Modern Turkey*, 104, 117–118; and Ann K. S. Lambton, "Social Change in Persia in the Nineteenth Century," 145–168, in Albert Hourani, et al., eds., *The Modern Middle East: A Reader* (Berkeley: University of California Press, 1993). The *Tercüme Odası* was founded in 1833.

15. On İhsan, see Stanford Shaw and Ezel Kural Shaw, *History of the Ottoman Empire and Modern Turkey*, v. 2, *Reform, Revolution, and Republic: The Rise of Modern Turkey, 1808–1875* (Cambridge: Cambridge University Press, 1977), 254–255; Berkes, *The Development of Secualrism in Turkey*, 295–296; and (on the Servet-i fünun period) Nihad Sâmi Banarlı, *Resimli Türk Edebiyatı Tarihi*, v. 2 (İstanbul: Milli Eğitim Basımevi): 1011–1065; *Türkiye'de Dergiler Ansiklopediler (1849–1984)*, 13, 17–19;

16. See Lewis, *The Emergence of Modern Turkey*, 136–146. Lewis's discussion of these men neatly illustrates that a French education did not produce unequivocal support for French political and literary forms.

17. The play's full title was "*Vatan Yahud Silistre*." Such patriotic works were endemic in the Ottoman press of the time, as for example in the gazette *Aşiyan*, 1: 18–20, 28 Ağustos 1324 / 10 September 1908, which ran many patriotic poems and included a poem entitled "*Vatanım*" (My Homeland), by Ali Said in its first issue. A song called "For My Homeland" (*Vatanım İçin*), composed by "Mademoiselle İhsan Sabrî," (actually İhsan Sabrî Hanım) was published in *Resimli kitab*, 1: 73, Eylül 1324 / September 1908. *Serbesti*, 1: 2, 3 Teşrin-i sani 1324 / 16 November 1908, rhetorically addressed the public ("in the *meydan*") as "*vatandaşlar*," compatriots.

18. Findley, *Ottoman Civil Officialdom: A Social History*, 251, quotes one *Mülkiye* (Istanbul civil service training school) graduate that, "France is what we imitate," and notes that this, "School of Civil Administration was supposed to be a counterpart of the prestigious École libre des Sciences politiques." On the *Mülkiye*, see Blake, "Training Arab-Ottoman Bureaucrats." For a photograph of *Mülkiye* graduates, see *Resimli kitab*, 7: 698, Nisan 1325 / April 1909.

19. Ahmad, *The Young Turks*, 270, has noted that the new Ottoman regime and Unionist methods of mobilization were compared to those of the French Revolution and the Jacobins. One could add the Ottoman revolution to the comparative model of Theda Skocpol, *States and Social Revolutions: A Comparative Analysis of France, Russia, and China* (Cambridge: Cambridge University Press, 1979), 161–171, especially in terms of leadership and the threat of military invasion. But the Ottoman revolution was never completed because WWI ended the empire before the revolutionary outcomes could be worked through. Also there was no real Ottoman mobilization of the masses. Still, Skocpol's observations on revolutionary crisis, ring true for the new Ottoman regime: "In short, ideologically oriented leaderships in revolutionary crises have been greatly limited by existing structural conditions and severely buffeted by the rapidly changing currents of revolutions" (171).

20. See Berkes, *The Devlopment of Secularim in Turkey*, 194, on the assertion of Ottoman as against French culture; and *Meram*, 1: 20–23, 40, 30 Teşrin-i evvel 1324 / 12 November 1908. On Napoleon, see *Resimli kitab*, 6: 565–568, Mart 1325 / March 1909. On Ottoman press coverage of France focusing much more directly on foreign relations and finances than on ideology see Groc, "La Presse Turque Et Son Opinion

Notes to Pages 79–80

Sur la France: Un témoignage du Bulletin de la Presse de l'Ambassade de France (1925–1927)," 479–498, in Batu and Bacqué-Grammont, *L'Empire Ottoman*.

21. In fact, it is notable how the image of Napoleon, as "world" conqueror, was not so very prominent in the Ottoman press, which contented itself with images of Napoleon's imperialistic twentieth-century successors and with the French Revolution. The Revolution became a sort of necessary antecedent; see for example *Piyano*, 6: 63–64, [13] Eylül 1326 / [26] September 1910, in an article entitled "What is the Political." For a cartoon of Napoleon, see *Kalem*, 52: 16, 27 Ağustos 1325 / 9 September 1909.

22. One word of the slogan might be varied and the order of the words was sometimes switched. For the literate Ottoman public, the French language was inscribed in dictionaries as well as in the press. See for example, Samy Bey Fraschery, preparer, *Resmi Kamus Fransevi / Dictionnaire Français—Turc Illustré*, 3rd edition (İstanbul / Constantinople: Mıhran Matbaası, 1318 / 1901). Note that this 1901 edition is the third version of this dictionary. *Liberté* is glossed on 1354 as *serbestlik*, and *égalité* on 878 as *müsavat*. See also *Sevimli Ay*, 6: 1–2, 1341 / 1926, an article on "Bab-ı Âli Lisanı.".

23. Quoted in Paul Imbert, *La Rénovation de l'Empire Ottoman: Affaires de Turquie* (Paris: Librairie Académique, 1909), 288.

24. For example, *Musavver cellâd*, 1: 4, 7 Eylül 1324 / 20 September 1908, in a satirical poem.

25. *Nekregû*, 1: 1, 19 Ağustos 1324 / 1 September 1908. The same gazette ran a set of poems on *hürriyet, adalet, müsavat,* and *uhuvvet* in its third issue: *Nekregû*, 3: 1, 3 Eylül 1324 / 16 September 1908.

26. *Kalem*, 16: 16, 4 Kanun-ı sani 1324 / 17 January 1909. This particular cartoon shows the monument as unstable because the base rests on a stone representing Article 113 of the constitution, which retained for the sultan the right to exile and conferred on the executive the right to proclaim martial law.

27. *Lâklâk*, 1: 4 10 Temmuz 1325 / 23 July 1909. On the use of the terms *meşrutiyet* and *meşveret*, see Berkes, *The Development of Secularism in Turkey*, 232–233.

28. *Kalem*, 56: 11, 24 Eylül 1325 / 7 October 1909, ran a humorous version called "Histoire Negro-Marseillaise," to be sung to the tune of the French anthem.

29. *Kalem*, 66: 1, 3 Kanun-ı evvel 1325 / 16 December 1909.

30. *Boşboğaz*, 14: 2–3, 11 Eylül 1324 / 24 September 1908, and in succeeding issues. The series was penned by Midhat Cemal.

31. *Kalem*, 11:1, 30 Teşrin-i evvel 1324 / 12 November 1908. Marianne figures, in Ottoman cartoons were sometimes named Marianne and sometimes not; they also took on various ages, from youthful to elderly.

32. See Shaw, *History of the Ottoman Empire*, 281–282; Ahmad, *The Young Turks*, 39–46.

33. For French imagery of the female nation, see *La France: Images of Woman and Ideas of Nation, 1789–1989*, the Hayward Gallery, London, 26 January to 16 April 1989 and the Walker Art Gallery, Liverpool, 3 May to 11 June 1989 (London: South Bank Centre, 1989).

34. *Davul*, 6: 16, 19 Teşrin-i sani 1324 / 2 December 1908. This particular cartoon is sexually charged, showing a European male physician (provider of "Constitutionalism Insurance") examining the female *Meşrutiyet*. See also Turgut Çeviker, *İbret Albümü 1908* (İstanbul: Mataş Matbaacılık, 1991), 26, for the female figure as the constitution, wearing a fez.

35. *İncili çavuş*, 4: 4, 19 Ağustos 1324 / 1 September 1908. Maurice Aghulhon, *Marianne Into Battle: Republican Imagery and Symbolism in France, 1789–1880* (Cambridge: Cambridge University Press, 1981), points out the Roman antecedents of the French use of symbols of liberty (11), and then traces the associations of liberty with woman figures in the French revolution (38–42). He goes on to note the confounding of images of Liberty and the Republic, with or without the Phrygian cap, in artistic images and cartoons (82). That confounding was also characteristic in Ottoman imagery.

36. *Musavver Papağan*, 32, 27 Nisan 1325 / 10 May 1909. This image recalls the account of Bayezid I who was caged and hauled off with the army of Timur after his loss to that monarch in 1403.

37. *Kalem*, 130: 9, 16 Haziran 1327 / 29 June 1911. This very same cartoon is attributed to the Armenian gazette *Gavroche*, published in Istanbul, in Anahide Ter-Minassian, "Les dessins satiriques dans le périodique arménien Gavroche (1908–1920)," *Revue du Monde Mussulman et de la Méditerranée* 77–78 (1996): 123–143.

38. See Skocpol, *States and Social Revolutions*, 170. The symbolic power of the sultanate, however, retained much of its resonance within Ottoman society, alongside competing revolutionary ideologies.

39. *Kalem*, 121: 8–9, 31 Mart 1327 / 13 April 1911.

40. *Resimli kitab*, 4: 340, Kanun-ı evvel 1324 / December 1908; 5: 466–467, Kanun-ı sani 1324 / January 1909; and 9: 877, Haziran 1325 / June 1909 ran articles discussing liberty, society, and nationalism in France and America, covered U.S. elections, and ran photos of an election march in Chicago.

41. *Resimli kitab*, 7: 717–730 (begins), Nisan 1325 / April 1909, also 832–841, 930–942, 1039–1045, 1146–1150. See Nuri, *Türk İnkılâbı*, 130–140, for a section titled, "*yenilikler, eskilikler.*" See also, *Resimli kitab*, 1: 53–60, Eylül 1324 / September 1908, for an article by editor Faik Sabrî, entitled "Yesterday and Today;" and *İttifak*, 11: 1, 14 Ağustos 1324 / 27 August 1908.

42. *Resimli kitab*, 5: 423–429, Kanun-ı sani 1324 / January 1909, "Terbiye-i milliye–Terbiye-i beyn ül-milel" (National Development/Education-International Development/Education).

43. *İnkılâb*, 4: 1, 1 Ağustos 1325/ 14 August 1909.

44. *Beyan ül-hak*, 1: 11, 22 Eylül 1324 / 5 October 1908, ran a poem in its first issue, by Şirvani Ali Nazmi, on "national harmony," which examined the notions of *milliyet* (nationalism) and *hürriyet* (freedom). *İttifak*, 1: 3, 3 Ağustos 1324 / 16 Ağustos 1908, ran photos of the armies of *hürriyet*, and a celebratory article in its first issue, by Mehmed Halim, which began, "*Hürriyet, hürriyet, hürriyet!*" *Millet* (published 1908) ran rhetorical articles on *hürriyet, meşrutiyet,* and *istibdad*.

45. *Hokkabaz*, 2: [16], 27 Eylül 1324 / 10 October 1908, included the age of zealotry, the age of ladies, the age of princes, and concluded with a poke at the

Bulgarians and the Greeks. See also, *Dertli ile garib,* 4: 2, 17 Ağustos 1326 / 30 August 1910.

46. *İncili çavuş,* 10: 2, 10 Eylül 1324 / 23 September 1908. For more of the same, see a humorous dialogue in *Karakuş Ezop,* 3: 2, 17 Eylül 1324 / 30 September 1908.

47. *İncili çavuş,* 1: 1, 5 Ağustos 1324 / 18 August 1908.

48. *Kalem,* 2: 12, 28 Ağustos 1324 / 10 September 1908. A cartoon in the next issue shows the constitution balanced on the point of a gun: *Kalem,* 3: 10, 4 Eylül 1324 / 17 September 1908.

49. Emmanuel Sieyes, "Qu'est-ce le tiers état?," Edme. Champion, ed. (Paris: n.p. 1888).

50. *Meram,* 1:2–4, 30 Teşrin-i evvel 1324 / 12 November 1908. It was written by Ali Kemal. On French language publishing in the Ottoman empire, see Orhan Koloğlu, "Alexandre Blacque Défenseur De L'Etat Ottoman par Amour Des Libertés," 179–195, in Batu and Bacqué-Grammont, *L'Empire Ottoman;* Richard Clogg, "A Further Note on the French Newspapers of Istanbul During the Revolutionary Period (1795–1797)," *Belleten* 39, no. 155 (1975): 483–490; and Korkmaz Alemdar, *İstanbul (1875–1964): Türkiyede Yayınlanan Fransızca Bir Gazetenin Tarihi* (Ankara: Ankara İktisadi ve Ticari İlimler Akademisi Yayınlar, 1980).

51. *Resimli kitab,* 5: 466–467, Kanun-ı sani 1324 / January 1909. Comparisons originated from the French side as well as from the Ottoman side. In 1912 a thesis comparing the press regime in the empire to that in France was published by the University of Paris Faculty of Law: A. Djivéléguian, *Le Régime de la Presse en Turquie: Comparison avec le Régime Français* (Paris: Emile Larose, 1912). Djivéléguian, of course, may have been an Ottoman citizen studying in Paris, another indicator, if that is the case, of the intellectual intercourse between the two states.

52. Ahmad, *The Young Turks,* 29.

53. *Kalem* 8: 5, 9 Teşrin-i evvel 1324 / 22 October 1908. The Chamber of Deputies was selected by electors. On the electoral process, see Hasan Kayalı, *Arabs and Young Turks,* esp. 52–68, 121–122.

54. Findley, *Ottoman Civil Officialdom,* 210–215. Dress patterns and the use of French language also symbolized a divergence in officials' career patterns and opportunities. As Garnett, *Turkish Life,* 38, put it, in the bureau, the offical, "learns to despise the costume of his forefathers and to become anxious about the fit of a frock coat cut in the latest Paris fashion . . . ." See Paul Dumont, "Said Bey—The Everyday Life of an Istanbul Townsman at the Beginning of the Twentieth Century," 271–288, in Hourani, *The Modern Middle East;* and Donald Quataert, "Clothing Laws, State, and Society in the Ottoman Empire, 1720–1829," *International Journal of Middle East Studies* 29, no. 3 (August 1997): 403–425.

55. *Alem,* 7: 8 French section pagination, 12 Mart 1325 / 25 March 1909. For more social satire of "freedom," see *Geveze,* 35: 4, 5 Mart 1325 / 18 March 1909.

56. On the delineation of the notion of liberty in France see Linda Orr, *Headless History: Nineteenth–Century French Historiography of the Revolution* (Ithaca: Cornell University Press, 1990), 113–114. The "people," in the historiography of the Ottoman revolution are problematic. As Orr, rather nicely puts it: "the society that seems to lose its author in the Revolution regroups around a new notion, no less symbolic, of

the popular" (75). This "popular" never achieved the exaltation in the Ottoman historiography that it did in the French.

57. Ottoman gazettes often dedicated themselves to these objectives. *Osmanlı ziraat ve ticaret gazetesi,* 1: 1, 22 Mart 1325 / 4 April 1909, noted on its masthead that it was devoted to "the felicity and advancement of the nation [*millet*] and the wealth and prosperity of the homeland [*vatan*]."

58. Cüneyt Ölçer, *Ottoman Coinage During the Reigns of Sultan Mehmed Reşad and Sultan Mehmed Vaheddin* (İstanbul: by the author, 1987), 84. See also, İbrahim and Cevriye Artuk, *İstanbul Arkeoloji Müzeleri Teşhirdeki İslâmî Sikkeler Kataloğu,* v. 2 (İstanbul: Millî Eğitim Basımevi, 1974), 736.

59. This sense of joint oppression is perhaps symbolized by the shutting down of the Persian language gazette *Akhtar,* which was published in Istanbul from 1875 to 1896.

60. Ervand Abrahamian, *Iran Between Two Revolutions* (Princeton: Princeton University Press, 1982), 81–110. See also on the revolution: Edward G. Browne, *The Persian Revolution of 1905–1909* (New York: Barnes and Noble, 1966), which includes pictures and documents; Mangol Bayat, *Iran's First Revolution: Shīʿism and the Constitutional Revolution of 1905–1909* (Oxford: Oxford University Press, 1991); Victor Berard, *Révolutions de la Perse* (Paris: Librarie Armand Colin, 1910); Vanessa Martin, *Islam and Modernism: The Iranian Revolution of 1906* (London: I. B. Tauris, 1989); and Nikki Keddie, "Iranian Revolutions in Comparative Perspective," in Burke and Lapidus, eds., *Islam, Politics, and Social Movements,* 298–313. The first issue of the Ottoman language gazette *İctihad* (Interpretation), 1: 1–2, Temmuz 1906 / July 1906, published in Cairo, covered the Iran question (the constitutionalists' struggle with the shah and the question of Iranian/Ottoman borders) in its two lead stories.

61. Abrahamian, *Iran Between Two Revolutions,* 87, notes that, "the number of papers and journals published within Iran jumped from six on the eve of the revolution to over one hundred during the ten months after the Constituent Assembly." On the press and the constitutional movement in Azerbaican at this same time, see Tadeusz Swietochowski, *Russian Azerbaijan 1905–1920: The Shaping of National Identity in a Muslim Community* (Cambridge: Cambridge University Press, 1985), 26–75. Speaking of the famous Azerbaicani gazette, *Molla Nasr-al-Din,* published 1906–1924, Swietochowski writes: "By far the greatest success story was the immensely popular satirical magazine Molla Nasr al-Din, with subscribers even in such faraway lands as India and Afghanistan. The aficionados of the magazine included illiterates who enjoyed its famous cartoons" (57).

62. Abrahamian, *Iran Between Two Revolutions,* 96, 103–110. The Second National Assembly opened in November of 1909; its Democrat Party included five journalists. But the new regime was plagued by factionalism and tribal warfare; by late 1911, Russia had invaded the north and Britain the south. The Ottoman embassy provided sanctuary, as did the British, for constitutionalists in their struggle with the shah. Browne, *The Persian Revolution,* 271–272, notes that the abortive Ottoman counterrevolution, in spring 1909, termporarily bolstered Muhammad Ali Shah in his battle with the constitutionalists.

63. Abdul-Hadi Hairi, "The Debates Over the Constitutional Revolution," 318–

324, in Seyyed Hossein Nasr et al., eds., *Expectation of the Millennium: Shi'ism in History* (Albany: State University of New York Press, 1989), 323. See also, on Muslim sympathies for the Iranian constitutionalists: Mansour Bonakdarian, "Iranian Constitutional Exiles and British Foreign-Policy Dissenters, 1908–1909," in *International Journal of Middle East Studies* 27, no. 2 (May, 1995): 184.

64. *Lâklâk*, 2: 2, 16 Temmuz 1325 / 29 July 1909, showed Muhammad Ali Shah sheltering behind the protective bars of the Russian embassy, dressed in Russian cap and admitting that he was "A Muscovite, a Cossack, and had worn the *şapka* [Russian hat]." The civil war in Iran and the Russian occupation were a threat to the security of Ottoman borders; see *Yeni geveze*, 84: 4, 1 Teşrin-i sani 1326/ 14 November 1910.

65. *Karagöz*, 5: 4, 11 Ağustos 1324 / 24 August 1908.

66. *Geveze*, 15: 1, [14] Kanun-ı sani 1324 / [27] January 1909. It also sneered at the "tyranny" (*zulüm*) of the shah in a humorous piece, *Geveze*, 17: 4, 1 Kanun-ı sani 1324 / 14 January 1909.

67. The shah's defeat was celebrated in Persian poetry; see Edward G. Browne, *The Press and Poetry of Modern Persia, Partly Based on the Manuscript Work of Mīrzā Muḥammad 'Alī Khān "Tarbiyat" of Tabriz* (Los Angeles: Kalimāt Press, 1983, reprint of 1914 edition), 242–246; and Morgan Shuster, *The Strangling of Persia*, (Washington, D.C.: Mage Publishers, 1987, reprint of 1912 edition), 221, on the "baby" shah.

68. *Lâklâk*, 4: 3, 30 Temmuz 1325 / 12 August 1909, reprinted a cartoon from the Franch gazette *Rire*, showing the little shah in a huge crown, with the caption: "*Küçük baş, büyük tac*" (Little head, big crown). Conversely, *Protesto*, 5: 1, 26 Kanun-ı sani 1324 / 8 February 1909, satirized Muhammad Ali Shah as among the "Big Heads" (*Büyük Başlar*). *Kalem*, 55: 3, 17 Eylül 1325 / 30 September 1909, reprinted a cartoon showing the little shah negotiating with Russia. Ahmad Shah continued to be the butt of Ottoman satire even after he was grown; see, for example, *Diken*, 22: 5, 4 Eylül 1335 / 17 September 1919. But, as M. Reza Behnam, *Cultural Foundations of Iranian Politics* (Salt Lake City: University of Utah Press, 1986), 19, suggests, the revolution "arose primarily out of discontent with inefficient governmental rule, opposition to foreign interference, and a fervent desire for independence from external forces." I would add: and out of a social order marked by a rapidly changing economic situation and by new cultural and intellectual influences.

69. *Al-Üfürük*, 3: 45, 25 Eylül 1324 / 8 October 1908. The cart holds a series of labeled jars, but the labels are illegible.

70. *Püsküllü belâ*, 4: 8, 4 Mart 1325 / 17 March 1909. This cartoon is also interesting for its unusual personification of the poor in Paris.

71. *Kalem*, 62: back cover, 5 Teşrin-i sani 1325 / 18 November 1909. In 1911, a Persian gazette ran a cartoon satirizing a 100,000 toman bounty which Treasurer-General of Iran Morgan Shuster had placed on the head of the former shah; see Janet Afary, *The Iranian Constitutional Revolution, 1906–1911: Grassroots Democracy, Social Democracy, and the Origins of Feminism* (New York: Columbia University Press, 1996), figure 13 placed before 145.

72. *Hikmet*, 1, 8 Nisan 1326 / 21 April 1910. *Hikmet*, with a clear Russian connection and an Islamic tone, covered foreign relations and ran a serialized article, beginning in the first issue, by Doctor Kara Beg Karabakof, called "Why the Situation

in Iran Cannot Easily Be Put Right." There were two gazettes called *Millet*. The one cited here was published by İbrahim Hilmi from August to November 1908.

73. *Salname-i servet-i fünun* 1326, 2: 184, 318–319, published 1327 / 1911; it also ran photos of Muhammad Ali Shah and his son, the "baby" shah.

74. *Musavver Eşref*, 2/28: 9, 10 Eylül 1325 / 23 September 1909.

75. *Resimli kitab*, 2: 166, Teşrin-i evvel 1324 / October 1908; and 15: 210, 213, Kanun-ı evvel 1325 / December 1909.

76. *Resimli kitab*, 6: 568, Mart 1325 / March 1909. A photo of both shahs and of Muhammad Ali Shah and his cabinet are in *Resimli kitab*, 9: 895 Haziran 1325 / June 1909. See also *Resimli İstanbul*, 5: 68, 6 Temmuz 1325 / 19 July 1909, for a photograph of the shah and his suite.

77. Both *Alem* and *Kalem* were fond of satirizing the sultan's eunuchs. There was a tradition of eunuchs in certain high offices in the Ottoman state and two of Abd ül-Hamid's eunuchs, Gânî Ağa and Hafız Behram Ağa had been given the rank of vezir: see Shaw, *The History of the Ottoman Empire*, 174, 214. For a more elaborate treatment of the eunuch corps and the slave trade in the late empire period, see Ehud Toledano, *The Ottoman Slave Trade and Its Suppression* (Princeton: Princeton University Press, 1982.)

78. *Resimli kitab*, 2: 138, Teşrin-i sani 1324 / November 1908. The shah had repaired to a country estate called Bāgh-i Shah, outside the city of Tehran, prior to the June 1908 coup and shelling of the meclis. There he mobilized his troops and prepared his plan of attack. It may be that this is where the prisoners were held. See Rouhollah K. Ramazani, *The Foreign Policy of Iran, A Developing Nation in World Affairs 1500–1941* (Charlottesville: University Press of Virginia, 1966), 96.

79. *Resimli kitab*, 6: 529, 532, Mart 1325 / March 1909.

80. *Resimli kitab*, 9: 895, 902, 914–915, Haziran 1325 / June 1909. See also Browne, *The Persian Revolution*, 113, 148–149, 242, 444–445.

81. The Iranian press, in its turn, paid considerable attention to the Ottoman revolution: examining the conflict with Abd ül-Hamid, covering the Ottoman counter-revolution, and drawing comparisons between the Ottoman, Iranian, and Russian revolutions (personal communication from Camron Amin).

82. *Davul*, 13: 10, 14 Kanun-ı sani 1324 / 27 January 1909.

83. Abu ül-Hüda, Abd ül-Hamid's advisor, remained a characteristic figure of Ottoman satire, a target of pity and scorn alike. On the persona of Abu ül-Hüda see Çeviker, *İbret Albümü*, 118, 149–150; and Ernest Ramsaur, *The Young Turks: Prelude to the Revolution of 1908* (Princeton: Princeton University Press, 1957), 12. Abu ül-Hüda can be found in cartoons and narrative in *Al-Üfürük*, 1: 4, 10 Eylül 1324 / 23 September 1908 (this gazette also lists Abu ül-Hüda as the gazette concessionaire or licensee); *Püsküllü belâ*, 1: 4, 11 Şubat 1324 / 24 February 1909; *Musavver cellad* (published in one issue only), 1: 1, 7 Eylül 1324 / 20 September 1908; and *Ezop*, 2: 3, 23 Ağustos 1324 / 5 September 1908.

84. The affinities between autocrats were portrayed in *Kalem* 56: 13, 24 Eylül 1325 / 7 October 1909 (shah seeking refuge with czar); and *Davul*, 21: 1, 15 Nisan 1325 / 28 April 1909 (shah commiserating with sultan).

85. *Kalem*, 34: 9, 16 Nisan 1325 / 29 April 1909.

86. See, for example, *Karagöz*, 5: 4, 11 Ağustos 1324/ 24 August 1908, a telegraph cartoon; and *Kalem*, 1: 2, 21 Ağustos 1324 / 3 September 1908, in the "*hitab ve cevab* (dialogue)" section.

87. *Boşboğaz*, 11: 3, 1 Eylül 1324 / 14 September 1908. A cartoon in *Musavver cellad*, 1: 2, 7 Eylül 1324 / 20 September 1908, I think, bears a similar message to that in the *Boşboğaz* cartoon. Although large segments of the cartoon are obliterated in the issue I saw, it shows the shah's sun throne and sword, and the caption caricatures "the announcement of *hürriyet* and the implementation of *meşrutiyet* half a century ago in Iran."

88. *Coşkun kalender*, 4: 1, 23 Nisan 1325 / 6 May 1909.

89. For other examples of images and narrative that critique and satirize the shah, see *Cingöz*, 5: 1, 11 Eylül 1324 / 24 September 1908; and 6: 1, 18 Eylül 1324 / 1 October 1908 (*Cingöz* was a regular critic of the shah).

90. For example, *Dalkavuk*, 21: 1, 22 Kanun-ı sani 1324 / 4 February 1909; and *Davul*, 21: 1, 15 Nisan 1325 / 28 April 1909 (the latter provided an Ottoman Turkish gloss on the Persian part of the caption).

91. *Püsküllü belâ*, 6: 1, 18 Mart 1325 / March 31, 1909.

92. *Kalem*, 41: 1, 11 Haziran 1325 / June 24, 1909.

93. *Alem* 8: 4 (French section page number), 19 Mart 1324 / 1 April 1909 shows lions and skulls decorating the shah's throne, which sits on a slab decorated in the style of pre-Islamic Persian stone carving. The sun is associated with Jemshid, the mythological king, and also with Solomon and Alexander.

94. On Iranian images of the shah as collaborator and traitor, selling out his country's resources to foreign interests, see Javadi, *Satire in Persian Literature*, 149, 176–177, 182; also Afary, *The Iranian Constitutional Revolution*, 116–144. For some samples of the charges leveled against Muhammad Ali Shah in Iranian poetry, see Browne, *The Press and Poetry*, 178, 204–205, 269–270.

95. *Alem* 12: 8–9, 21 Mayıs 1325 / 3 June 1909. Cemali did many of the cartoons in *Alem*. He is not included in Çeviker's biographies of cartoonists. Many of his cartoons, such as this one of Abd ül-Hamid, share the dark and brooding quality found today in some of Marvel Comics' figures.

96. This figure is reminiscent of the demon king, Dajjāl (or Zahhak in the *Shahnamah*).

97. Illustrating the shared ideals of the Ottoman and Iranian constitutionalists is a poem published in the gazette *Musavver Muhit*, 9: 138, 18 Kanun-ı evvel 1324 / 31 December 1908. The poem, "composed on the occasion of the opening of the meclis" was by "the most exalted ambassador of Iran, Prince Mirza Reza Daneş Khan." This poem, consisting of noble sentiments, suggested the triumph of constitutional government in Iran, ignoring its vulnerability.

98. *Papağan*, 21: 4, 26 Kanun-ı evvel 1324 / 8 January 1909.

99. *Papağan*, 24: 4, 16 Şubat 1324 / 1 March 1909.

100. On Sattar Khan, see Browne, *The Persian Revolution*, 205, 248–258, 303, and plate after 440. The battle for Tabriz lasted from June 1908 until April 1909. For other satire of the shah and Sattar Khan, see *Alem*, 11: 9, 14 Mayıs 1325 / 27 May 1909 (this cartoon shows the shah kissing Sattar Khan, whom he calls "my pride and joy,"

on the head and swearing that he too is a supporter of *hürriyet*); and *Gramafon*, 6: 4, 28 Mart 1324 / 10 April 1909.

101. *Musavver Muhit*, 4: 62, 13 Teşrin-is ani 1324 / 26 November 1908; and *Eşref*, 1: 3, 5 Mart 1325 / 18 March 1909.

102. *Cadaloz*, 33: 4, 12 Temmuz 1327 / 25 July 1911.

103. *Afacan*, 3: 4, [26] Temmuz 1327 / [8] August 1911 (cartoon and poem; the Iranian sun symbol laughs in the background and M. Ali Shah's flag reads "*zindebad istibdad*" [Long Live, Despotism!]); *and* 6: 3–4, 6 Ağustos 1327 / 19 August 1911. See also Shuster, *The Strangling of Persia*, 85.

104. *Falaka*, 5: 4, 9 Ağustos 1327 / 22 August 1911; and 12: 1, 1 Eylül 1327 / 14 September 1911. *Falaka*, 4: 1, 5 Ağustos 1327 / 18 August 1911, contains another cartoon of the ex-shah as pawn of Russia.

105. *Resimli kitab*, 9: 911, Haziran 1325 / June 1909.

106. The empire served in a variety of ways as a refuge for Iranians. See, for example, Browne, *The Press and Poetry*, 307, on Iranian men of letters resident in İstanbul, especially Ḥusayn Dānish, whose poem "The Ruins of Ctesiphon," was published in Istanbul and dedicated to Dr. Rıza Tevfik (a well known Ottoman writer and journalist). See also Thierry Zarcone and Fariba Zarinebaf, *Les Iraniens D'Istanbul* (İstanbul: Institut Français de Recherches en Iran, 1993).

107. In later years, the gazette *Cem (Djem)* would satirize (along with the CUP) such ideals of patriotism and constitutionalism: *Cem*, 31: 1, 18 Haziran 1327 / 1 July 1911, showing the constitution as a tower of blocks; and 36: 9, 18 Ağustos 1327 / 31 August 1911, which suggests that the ideal patriot is blind, dumb, and immobile.

108. *Yeni geveze*, 90: 1, 15 Teşrin-i sani 1326 / 28 November 1910.

109. *Kalem*, 101: 1, 28 Teşrin-i evvel 1326 / 10 November 1910. The date of this cartoon precedes by one year Russia's outright occupation of Enzeli and Rasht and its delivery of an ultimatum to Iran; see Abrahamian, *Iran, Between Two Revolutions*, 109.

110. *Kalem*, 118: 5, 10 Mart 1327 / 23 March 1911.

111. *Alem*, 2: 6, 5 Şubat 1324 / 18 February 1909.

112. Abrahamian, *Iran Between Two Revolutions*, 105; and Parker Thomas Moon, *Imperialism and World Politics* (New York: The Macmillan Company, 1926), 278–287.

113. *Nevsal-ı Osmanî*, sene 3: 159–168, published 1327 / 1911, (especially 166). These yearbooks were a cross between an almanac and an informational journal.

114. *Kalem*, 104: 7, 2 Kanun-ı evvel 1326 / 15 December 1910. For Iranian press satire of the greed of Russia and Britain, see Afary, *The Iranian Constitutional Revolution*, 131–144.

115. *İncili çavuş*, 12: 4, 2 Teşrin-i evvel 1324 / 15 October 1908. In this particular cartoon, Britain and France are cast as the good guys, trying to throw the Ottoman state a life preserver.

116. Browne, *The Press and Poetry of Modern Persia*, 295–297. See also, 213, for an Iranian cartoon of the British "antique-ing," in Iran.

117. Ibid., 297.

118. See *Kalem*, 99: 14, 14 Teşrin-i evvel 1326 / 27 October 1910, for a cartoon that shows England and Russia preparing to divide and eat "Iran."

119. *Kalem*, 110: 9, 13 Kanun-ı sani 1326 / 26 January 1911.

120. For an English version of the amputation cartoon, circa 1785, by Thomas Rowlandson, see Shikes, *The Indignant Eye*, 78.

121. *Meram*, 4: 113, 27 Teşrin-i sani 1324 / 10 December 1908. Japanese diplomatic life was treated in *Salname-i servet-i fünun* 1326, 2: 200, published 1327 / 1911. Japan also served as a role model for the Iranian constitutionalists; see Keddie, "Iranian Revolutions in Comparative Perspective."

122. *Meram*, 1: 24–27, 40, 30 Teşrin-i evvel 1324 / 12 November 1908, covered the economic history of England and the history of the East India Company in its first issue; the next issue contained an article on England's relations with the Ottoman empire.

123. On the Indian nationalist movement of the time, especially in Bengal, see Lajpat Rai, *Young India: An Interpretation and a History of the Nationalist Movement from Within* (New York: Howard Fertig, 1968, reprint of 1916 edition). On the press in the early 1900's, Rai writes that the newspapers were the "classroom" of the people (176). "In a few months the face and spirit of Bengal was changed. Their press, the pulpit, the platform, the writers of prose and poetry, composers of music and playwrights were all filled with the spirit of nationalism."

124. Edwin De Leon, *Thirty Years of My Life on Three Continents* (London: Ward and Downey, 1890), 275–276. De Leon, as with most Western travelers of the time, focused on communal distinctions, and often projected his own sense of the Christian–Muslim dichotomy onto the populations he evaluated.

125. Bernard Lewis, "Why Turkey is the Only Muslim Democracy," *Middle East Quarterly* (March 1994), 42.

126. *Servet-i fünun* 1326, 2: 43–47, published 1327 / 1911. *Muhit*, 19: front cover, 5 Mart 1325 / 18 March 1909, ran a flattering photo of the Japanese Prince Koni who visited Istanbul.

127. *Kalem*, 57: 3 1 Teşrin-i evvel 1325 / 14 October 1909.

128. Japan did, however, have some direct connections with Ottoman economic realities. See Charles Issawi, "Middle East Economic Development, 1815–1914: the General and the Specific," 177–194, in Hourani, *A Middle East Reader*. Issawi uses the comparison with Japan and India to analyze modern Middle Eastern economic conditions.

Chapter V. The Comic Sovereign: The Satirical Critique of Authority

1. Ahmed Şerif, *Anadolu Tanin* (İstanbul: Tanin, 1325), 336.

2. *Perde*, 4: 4, 3 Kanun-ı evvel 1327 / 16 December 1911, with Hacivat calling on God to aid them.

3. Vaka, *Haremlik*, 5, 21, argued that a Frenchman would require a lifetime to understand things in Turkey. See also Alemdar, *İstanbul (1875–1964)*, 46–48.

4. As Peirce, *The Imperial Harem*, 262–266, puts it, "Whereas no popular depositions had occurred before the reign of Süleyman, of the twenty-seven sultans following him, thirteen were forcibly deposed. . . . . Loyalty of its subjects to the House of Osman appears in the seventeenth century to have become more abstract, a loyalty

more to the dynasty than to the individual. . . . ." Peirce's characterization still applies, to a considerable extent, in the early twentieth century. Thus, the situation in the Ottoman state was not analogous, for example, to England when Cromwell used the public beheading of Charles I to symbolize what he thought was the end of the English monarchy.

5. This is not to say that ravens and crows are synonymous, only that both were symbols of death and that cartoons made no effort to be ornithologically precise. The direct equation of the sultan with the crow can be found in cartoons in *Kalem, Alem*, and *Karagöz*.

6. See Âşıkpaşa, *Âşıkpaşaoğlu Tarihi*, ed. Atsız (İstanbul: Milli Eğitim Basımevi, 1970), 10–11. Such images were a logical extension of the king's power over life and death, on which, for a comparative African perspective, see Bruce Lincoln, *Discourse and the Construction of Society: Comparative Studies of Myth, Ritual, and Classification* (New York: Oxford University Press, 1989), 61–63.

7. See, for example, Bernard Lewis, *The Shaping of the Modern Middle East*, 24–43.

8. For an interesting study of notions of kingship and sovereignty in India, and of the conceptual dilemmas involved in transferring sovereignty from the king to the modern nation state, see André Wink, "Sovereignty and Universal Dominion in South Asia," *The Indian Economic and Social History Review*, 21, no. 3 (1984): 265–292. In Wink's study, universal dominion is an ideal (and idea) used by both Ottomans and Mughuls to forge political unities, which, however, did not necessarily have the same territorial conceptualizations as those of the modern nation state.

9. The Great Power rivalry and the rise of nationalism are still the two primary historiographic prisms through which the Ottoman revolution is viewed. One of the best basic works (if a bit dated) on the political background is J. A. R. Marriott, *The Eastern Question: An Historical Study in European Diplomacy* (Oxford: Clarendon Press, 1917).

10. On that ambivalence see Lewis, *The Emergence of Modern Turkey;* Berkes, *The Development of Secularism in Turkey*, 232–250; and Shaw, *History of the Ottoman Empire*, 55–271.

11. On the eras of certain kinds of monarchy in the European context, see J. H. Burns, *Lordship, Kingship, and Empire: The Idea of Monarchy 1400–1525* (Oxford: Clarendon Press, 1992). Burns has suggested (146–147) that the popularity and success of republican alternatives to monarchy in the Renaissance period has been exaggerated or misrepresented. Just so, the ultimate demise of monarchy in the Ottoman empire and the eventual triumph of constitutionalism should not be taken as a sign that the end of monarchy was either easy or swift. Burns also argues that in the late sixteenth and early seventeenth centuries, a concept of absolute monarchy was firmly established, "which was not only compatible with but in fact inseparable from a framework of fundamental laws." If one qualifies this notion with the statement that "absolute," rule is never in fact really possible, then Burns's characterization certainly applies to the Ottoman state. Nicholas Henshall, *The Myth of Absolutism: Change and Continuity in Early Modern European Monarchy* (London: Longman, 1992), directly addresses the ambiguous nature of absolutism. Henshell differentiates between the absolute monarchies of the early modern period and the autocracies of

the nineteenth century, arguing that the former were, "more consultative, more constitutional, and more patriarchal" (211). This distinction does not work well for the Ottoman monarchy. On the Ottomans as a model for European notions of absolutism see, Lucette Valensi, *Venice and the Sublime Porte: The Birth of the Despot* (Ithaca: Cornell University Press, 1993); and also Patricia Springborg, *Western Republicanism and the Oriental Prince* (Austin: University of Texas Press, 1992).

12. Robert Phillipe, *Political Graphics*, 10. Phillipe characterizes the modern era as one which signaled the advent of "generality" of the "ordinary," namely the man without specific qualities. In this era, the political graphic became the weapon of groups opposed to authority and of those making apologias for and glorifications of the great and powerful (a defensive response). I would not agree, however, that the modern age negated uniqueness, but rather that it substituted alternative forms of uniqueness, in the realms of authority and of print.

13. These links were embodied in some of the covers of the gazette *Musavver devr-i cedid*, which portrayed glorious, past monarchs of the empire, like Fatih Mehmed.

14. The gazette *Dalkavuk*, for example, raised this theme of obsolescence in various contexts, but without the wicked satire and attacks on the monarch found in some other satiric gazettes.

15. In the commitment to monarchy, of course, the Ottomans were not alone. Viscount Grey, writing in 1925, and admitting of alternatives, still insisted on the benefits of constitutional monarchy in England, as long as it was tempered by democracy. Visount Grey, *Twenty Five Years 1892–1916*, v. 1 (New York: Frederick A. Stokes, Co., 1925): 200–201.

16. *Kalem*, 53: 16, 3 Eylül 1325 / 16 September 1909. This cartoon was, no doubt, provoked in part by the military revolt in Athens the preceding month and its context of criticism of the Greek monarchy. See, for a general summay of events in Greece, L. S. Stavrianos, *The Balkans Since 1453* (New York: Holt, Rinehart, and Winston, 1965), 467–482, especially 474.

17. The links between sultan, shah, and czar were drawn by Iranian satirists as well, by the poet Saber, for example, who satirized all three as ruthless. See Javadi, *Satire in Persian Literature*, 145.

18. *Cingöz*, 1: 1, 26 Ağustos 1324 / 8 September 1908.

19. *Davul*, 21: 4, 15 Nisan 1325 / 28 April 1909.

20. *Karagöz*, 82: 4, 27 Nisan 1325 / 10 May 1909.

21. *Karagöz*, 100: 4, 29 Haziran 1325 / 12 July 1909. See also *Hokkabaz*, 2: 12, 27 Eylül 1324 / 10 October 1908. Often enough, the various autocrats were shown dispassionately discussing their own demise.

22. *Alafranga*, 2: 1, 2 Kanun-ı evvel 1326 / 15 December 1910. The East Asian figure could represent the Manchu dynasty in China, which was cast aside in an uprising the following year. The Moroccan ruler is probably Mulla Hâfız but could be the brother he overthrew a couple of years earlier. See also, *Lâklâk*, 1: 1, 10 Temmuz 1325 / 23 July 1909; and *Papağan*, 32: [n.p.], 27 Nisan 1325 / 10 May 1909, on Abd ül-Hamid's exile in Izmir.

23. This cartoon may be a reprint from a European gazette; *Resimli kitab*, 2: 197,

Teşrin-i evvel 1324 / October 1908. *Kalem,* 13: 6, 13 Teşrin-i sani 1324 / 26 November 1908, reprinted a European cartoon, from *Pasquino,* showing Mulla Hafız who is just preparing to sit on his newly acquired throne when he spies the spiked helmet of the Kaiser already in the seat and waiting to spear him.

24. *Kalem,* 1: 5, 21 Ağustos 1324 / 3 September 1908. In this issue, one of the benefits of the constitution is "a refrigerated depot to conserve liberty, fraternity, and equality or to freeze reactionary projects" (7).

25. Benedict Anderson, *Imagined Communities,* 178–185, has demonstrated how the museum synthesizes the imagination of community, imagining and fixing the past and its relationship to the viewing public.

26. The Ottoman yearbook (*salname*) reflected a popular preoccupation with the fate of kingship during the first years of the revolution. Not truly popular, because they targeted at least a semi-literate audience, these yearbooks addressed a wider audience than the often highlty sophisticated political and literary journals. Typical examples are *Salname-i servet-i fünun* 1326, 2: 43–48, published 1327 / 1911; and *Resimli İstanbul,* 4: 56, 29 Haziran 1325 / 12 July 1909.

27. *Davul,* 1: 6, 14 Teşrin-i evvel 1324 / 27 October 1908.

28. *Muhit,* 12: 185, 15 Kanun-ı sani 1324 / 28 January 1909, for "big head" satire on Muhammad Ali Shah of Iran; *Protesto* also used the big head theme. See *Resimli kitab,* 2: 158–159, Teşrin-i evvel 1324 / October 1908, for Ferdinand of Bulgaria and Emperor Franz Joseph.

29. By 1911, Abd ül-Hamid was considered part of a past era; he was history, as witnessed by Osman Nuri and Ahmed Refik (Altınay's), *Abd ül-Hamid-i Sani ve Devr-i Saltanatı* (İstanbul: n.p. 1327 / 1911).

30. The satiric gazettes focus first on the huge foreign debt amassed by the old regime and its wasting of Ottoman resources, then on the new regime's mismanagement of finances and the escalating war budget. See *Kalem,* 5: 3, 18 Eylül 1324 / 1 October 1908; and *Falaka,* 9: 1, 22 Ağustos 1327 / 4 September 1911.

31. *Resimli İstanbul,* 6: 87–88, 13 Temmuz 1325 / 26 July 1909, ran a feature and photos on Abd ül-Hamid's kittens. For images of Mehmed Reşad, see *Resimli kitab,* 7: front page, Nisan 1325 / April 1909 (on accession); 8: most of issue, Mayıs 1325 / May 1909; and the illustrated supplement with issue 12: 2–15, Eylül 1325 / September 1909.

32. As, for example, in *Papağan,* 1: 2, 6 Eylül 1324 / 19 September 1908; or in *Al-Üfürük,* 1: 5, 10 Eylül 1324 / 23 September 1908, which satirized the ministers of the "era of *istibdad*" as greedy opportunists. Despotism, of course, as *Zevzek,* 2: 1, 2 Eylül 1324 / 15 September 1908, pointed out, would not disappear readily or willingly.

33. V. Alfieri, *İstibdad,* translated by Abdullah Cevdet (Geneva: Osmanlı İttihad ve Terakki Cemiyeti, 1317 / 1899); Charles Kools, *Histoire des Parlements à Travers les Siècles* (İstanbul: Imprimerie du Levant Herald—Pera, 1908).

34. *Kalem,* 7: 1, 2 Teşrin-i evvel 1324 / 15 October 1908.

35. *Kalem,* 34: 8, 16 Nisan 1325 / 29 April 1909.

36. *Davul,* 21: 8, 15 Nisan 1325 / 28 April 1909.

37. Shaw, *History of the Ottoman Empire,* 282: "Obtaining a *fetva* that justified the sultan's deposition on the grounds of complicity in the counter-revolution and the

deaths that resulted, as well as of the theft of state funds, the National Assembly declared him deposed in favor of his brother, Mehmet V Reşat."

38. I have András Riedlmayer to thank for this reference. Montêpin (1826?–1902) was a prolific writer of pulp fiction, producing over one hundred novels and thirty plays. Several of his novels were translated into Ottoman Turkish (both in Arabic and in Armenian script). See Xavier de Montêpin, *Kırmızı Değirmen* (İstanbul: Kırk Anbar Matbaası, 1292 / 1872).

39. *Hande,* cover cartoon, 35: 1, 29 Mart 1333 / 11 April 1917, used the image of a pile of skulls with the czar and his symbols of monarchy (throne and crown) perched on top. In this frame, however, the Russian bear was shaking the czar off his grisly pile, a metaphor for the Russian Revolution and its deposition of the monarch.

40. *Geveze,* 34: 1, Mart 2 [or 3] 1325 / March 15 [or 16] 1909. Harvests in Anatolia had been bad and the eastern provinces were plagued by intermittent famine (both natural and created), which continued after the revolution and became quite severe in the winter of 1911. See Shaw, *History of the Ottoman Empire,* 266.

41. Feroz Ahmad, *The Making of Modern Turkey* (London: Routledge: 1993), 42–43, points out that "feudal lords" owned 39 percent of the land and large landholders owned 26 percent in 1913. Land was not scarce, but labor was. The power of the landholders in the Ottoman state was, thus, not broken under the Young Turk regime, just as it was not later broken by the reforms of the British/Waft regime in Egypt or by the "White Revolution," of Muhammad Reza Shah in Iran.

42. On satire of the monarch as ludicrous or incongruous in German revolutionary cartoons, see W. A. Coupe, "The German Cartoon and the Revolution of 1848," *Comparative Studies in Society and History* 9, no. 2 (January 1967): 137–167, especially 155. On caricature of the crown in England, see Diana Donald, *The Age of Caricature: Satirical Prints in the Reign of George III* (New Haven: Yale University Press, 1996).

43. *Kalem,* 38: 1, 21 Mayıs 1325 / 3 June 1909, for balloon cartoon.

44. *Kalem,* 34: 1, 16 Nisan 1325 / 29 April 1909. Cem has another cartoon of Abd ül-Hamid, still hoping to remain in power, on the back page of this same issue. See also, *Kalem,* 122: 1, 7 Nisan 1327 / 20 April 1911, for a "memorial of April 14th" cartoon showing the sultan in exile.

45. In 1907, Hoca Şakir had published a condemnation (using the *fetva* ruling according to Islamic law) denouncing Abd ül-Hamid's claims to be e*mir ül-müminin* and caliph; see Hoca Şakir, *Ulema-i İslâm Enarallahü Berahinehüm Taraflarından Verilen Fetava-yı Şerife* (Egypt: İçtihat Matbaası, 1325 hicrî / 1907).

46. Rennell Rodd, quoted in Denis Mack Smith, *Italy and Its Monarchy* (New Haven: Yale University Press, 1989), 183.

47. On the stages by which the new regime evolved and on its personnel and legislative acts, see Zürcher, *The Unionist Factor;* Ahmad, *The Young Turks,* which carefully details the events of the years 1908–1914; and Shaw, *History of the Ottoman Empire,* 274–275, 282–287.

48. Darnton, "The High Enlightenment and the Low-Life of Literature," 81–115. The exploration of pamphlet and ephemeral Ottoman literature may ultimately make the Ottoman "low" press look more like Darnton's model, but I doubt it. For one thing, the Ottoman press was still at a more primitive level of development and

did not have the extensive "low" literature that Darnton portrays in France. Secondly, the colonial and cultural conditions for the representation of sovereignty during the Ottoman revolution were much different from those in eighteenth-century France and acted against the expression of "hatred of the system," as Darnton portrays it. Nor do we find, to my knowledge, the type of sexual attacks on the "aristocracy" in the Istanbul press, that Darnton finds in the French (105). Whether this makes the Ottoman press more or less sophisticated, I leave to the reader to decide.

49. *Papağan*, 32: 1, 27 Nisan 1325 / 10 May 1909, celebrated the elevation of Mehmed Reşad with a proclamation beginning, "*hür milletin hür padişahi Sultan Mehmed-i hamis hazretlerine.*" "*Hür,*" here should probably be glossed as noble ("the noble padishah of the noble nation, his excellency Mehmed the V"), but "*hür*" is also the word for free, a term thought to be defining for the state, newly relieved of past tyranny. The same issue included the "*fetva*" (instrument of legitimation via religious law) for the deposition of Abd ül-Hamid (2). In fact, after Abd ül-Hamid proclaimed the constitution, his name too had been associated in the press with the notion of *hürriyet* (freedom), with the assumption that the old sovereignty and the new constitutionalism could be combined. See, for example, the celebratory poem and illustration in *Şark*, 13: [1], 19 Ağustos 1324 / 1 September 1908.

50. *Kalem*, 1: 7, 21 Ağustos 1324 / 3 September 1908.

51. W. L. Courtney, "The Constitutional Mutiny of April 13th," *Fortnightly Review*, n.s. 86 (July–December, 1909): 68. Courtney was resident in Istanbul during the revolution and counter-revolution.

52. For one such cartoon, characterizing the palace cadre as dedicated to *istibdad*, see *Dalkavuk*, 13: 1, 22 Teşrin-i sani 1324 / 5 December 1908; also *Dalkavuk*, 1: 4, 30 Ağustos 1324 / 12 September 1908.

53. Ahmad, *The Making of Modern Turkey*, 33–37. On political factions, see Shaw, *History of the Ottoman Empire*, 279, 282–283; and Tunaya, *Türkiyede Siyasal Partiler*, 1: 19–363. For brief summaries of the various grand vezirates and meclis activities in this transitional period, see Ali Fuad Türkgeldi, *Görüp İttiklerim* 3rd edition (Ankara: Türk Tarih Kurumu Basımevi, 1984), 21–49.

54. *Dalkavuk*, 4: 5, 20 Eylül 1324 / 3 October 1908. See also, *Kibar*, 1: 1, 23 Teşrin-i sani 1326 / 6 December 1910.

55. *Eşek*, 1: 1, 16 Teşrin-i sani 1326 / 29 November 1910; *Malum*, 3: 1, 15 Kanun-ı evvel 1326 / 28 December 1910; *Lâla*, 1: 1, 2 Kanun-ı evvel 1326 / 15 December 1910.

56. Ahmad, *The Young Turks*, 30–38. Strong opposition did not prevent Kâmil Pasha from engaging in a prolonged power struggle with the CUP; he led an anti-Unionist government again in 1912. Mahmud Şevket Pasha was assassinated on June 11, 1913, while he was serving as both Grand Vezir and War Minister. For an heroic photo of M. Şevket Pasha, see *Resimli kitab*, 8: 747, Mayıs 1325 / May 1909.

57. *Kalem*, 95: 1, 16 Eylül 1326 / 29 September 1910.

58. *Kalem*, 97: 10–11, 30 Eylül 1326 / 13 October 1910. It is interesting that the French caption mentions Germany as the recipient of the "child's" proposed offerings; the Ottoman caption does not.

59. Donald Blaisdell, *European Financial Control in the Ottoman Empire* (New York: Columbia University Press, 1929), 215-217.

60. For some of the many examples, see *Resimli kitab*, 5: 432-433, Kanun-ı sani 1324 / January 1909; 8: 754-755, Mayıs 1325 / May 1909; 10: 986-987, Temmuz 1325 / July 1909; 11: 1142-1143, Ağustos 1325 / August 1909; and *Salname-i servet-i fünun* 1324-1325, 1: 132-135, published 1326 / 1910. *Nevsal-ı Osmani*, 1: 83-89, 165-196, 216-225, 61-66 (added section at end), 1325-1326 / 1909-1910, ran lists of ministers and meclis members, biographies of important men, and a section, entitled "Deliverance from Despotism," on the officials of the Hamidian regime.

61. These subjects were a clear precoccupation of the press of the time. See: *Beyan ül-hak*, 1: 6-7, 22 Eylül 1324 / 5 October 1908 (including a poem on national harmony); *Serbesti*, 2: 1 (and throughout), 4 Teşrin-i sani 1324 / 17 November 1908, on "National Sovereignty and the Spirit of Constitutionalism."

62. *Boşboğaz*, 7: 1, 18 Ağustos 1324 / 31 August 1908. This particular cartoon is an interesting image because its elements are numbered (rather like some European images which have a key and show the location of things); no key is apparent here. See also, *Kalem*, 1: 1, 21 Ağustos 1324 / 3 September 1908.

63. *Üç gazete*, 2: 3, 30 Ağustos 1324 / 12 September 1908, after the revolution but before the elections.

64. *Boşboğaz*, 13: 1, 8 Eylül 1324 / 21 September 1908, and 34: 4, 24 Teşrin-i sani 1324 / 7 December 1908. For a thematically related cartoon using the metaphor of kite strings, see *Cingöz*, 2: 1, 30 Ağustos 1324 / 12 September 1908.

65. *Kalem*, 4: 6, 11 Eylül 1324 / 24 September 1908.

66. See *Cellad*, 1: 2-4, 7 Eylül 1324 / 20 September 1908, which both advanced and lampooned these sentiments while also providing poetic renditions of Abd ül-Hamid's "age of despotism." *Cellad* was published in one issue only.

67. *Dalkavuk*, 5: 1, 27 Eylül 1324 / 10 October 1908.

68. W. A. Coupe, "The German Cartoon," 162-163.

69. *Alem*, 6: 8-9, 5 Mart 1324 / 18 March 1909. On the Liberal Union, see Ahmad, *The Young Turks*, 28, 32ff., 38ff, 41ff, 45ff, 99-100, 104. A cartoon in *Davul*, 2: 7, 21 Teşrin-i evvel 1324 / 3 November 1908, also outlined the obstacles the new regime had to overcome (although not depicting them so brutally). It showed that the last jump in a game of administrative leap frog was "the Balkan Question," a "jump" bristling with cannons and bayonets.

70. *Cingöz*, 1: 2, 26 Ağustos 1324 / 8 September 1908. This gazette's mascots were Cingöz and Komik. Like many other gazettes, *Cingöz* used the Karagöz dialogue to good effect to satirize the revolution.

71. For an example of the more inspirational image, see a patriotic scene urging on the Ottoman army in battle in *Cadaloz*, 22: 1, 4 Haziran 1327 / 17 June 1911. This scene takes place during tha Balkan Wars, but it is strikingly similar to those found in posters of the 1978-1979 Iranian revolution that picture Ayatollah Khomeini watched over and urged on by various deceased ulema or martyrs who speak down from the clouds.

72. The Ottoman official gazette, *Takvim-i vekayi*, covered the election law, the

elections, and meclis proceedings in detail. *Takvim-i vekayi,* begun in 1831, started a new series of numbering after the revolution, beginning with no. 1, 15 Eylül 1324 / 28 September 1908. There was also regular coverage of the meclis in gazettes like *Ulûm-i iktisadiye ve içtimaiye mecmuası* (published 1908–1910). See also, *İnkılâb* (published in 1909); *Salname-i servet-i fünun* 1326, 2 : insert at end of volume before the ads, published 1327 / 1911; and *Meram,* 4: 108, and 5: 130 [n.d., approximately December 1908]. *Resimli kitab,* 4: 301–305, Kanun-ı evvel 1324 / December 1908, ran a photo of the assembly's meeting room and an article on the Ottoman *"Meclis-i Mebu'san,"* by Selanikli Tevfik, which harked back to the first parliament at the beginning of Abd ül-Hamid's reign.

73. *Resimli kitab,* 4: 348, 384–385, 389, Kanun-ı evvel 1324 / December 1908. See also, *Muhit,* 5: 65, 20 Teşrin-i sani 1324 / 3 December 1908, for a photo by Apollon of the elections at Pera.

74. *Kalem,* 104: 1, 2 Kanun-ı evvel 1326 / 15 December 1910.

75. Ahmad, *The Making of Modern Turkey,* 39, notes regarding the Balkan Wars of 1912–1913: "[The Unionists] saw that the same Great Powers which had guaranteed the territorial status quo at the start of the conflict had abandoned their guarantee as soon as the Turks were in retreat."

76. *Kalem,* 60: 10, 22 Teşrin-i sani 1325 / 4 November 1909.

77. *Resimli İstanbul,* 10: 1, 10 Ağustos 1325 / 23 August 1909. The same photograph is carried in the periodical *Resimli kitab,* 12: 1245, Eylül 1325 / September 1909, a monthly priced at 5 *piastres* per issue, which carried multiple photographs.

78. *Lâklâk,* 7: 1, 20 Ağustos 1325 / 2 September 1909. There could be a play on "iron age" *(demir devri)* here. On Ottoman overtures to London and other foreign capitals see Ahmad, *The Making of Modern Turkey,* 40; see also Ahmad, "Great Britain's Relations with the Young Turks, 1908–1914," *Middle Eastern Studies* (July, 1966), 302–329, and Marian Kent, ed. *The Great Powers and the End of the Ottoman Empire* (London: Frank Cass, 1993).

79. To be fair, the new regime's dilemma was analogous to that of the nineteenth-century reformers, described by Findley, *Bureaucratic Reform in the Ottoman Empire,* 157.

80. This is not to say that the satiric press did not celebrate the installation of the new regime; see the cover of the first issue of *Alem,* 1: 1, 29 Kanun-ı sani 1324 / 11 February 1909, a dramatic rendering of street celebrations with the skyline of Istanbul as background and a huge saber superimposed across the festivities.

81. *Züğürt,* 2: 4, [4] Mart 1327 / [17] March 1911. I do not know if this frame is alluding to one particular ministry or some specific situation of the day. But the fact that the door and building are not labeled suggests that this is a generic complaint.

Chapter VI. The Comic Aggressor: The Critique of European Political and Economic Hegemony

1. Great Britain, Foreign Office, *British Documents on the Origins of the War 1898–1914,* v. 5, *The Near East 1903–1909,* edited by Gooch and Temperley (London: His Majesty's Stationery Office, 1926–1938), 247.

2. Moon, *Imperialism and World Politics*, 248: the quote aptly suggests the feeling of "joyous exaggeration of economic prospects," that characterized thinking about ventures in the Middle East at the turn of the century.

3. I have not run into the word *imperialism* in a cartoon caption. It does, however, crop up periodically in the press. One example is in the gazette *İstişare*, 178, published 4 Eylül 1324–19 Mart 1325 / 17 September 1908–1 April 1909; it appeared in the subhead of an article on the British empire. *İstişare* was in the habit of Ottomanizing French words, like using *capitulation* (in Ottoman script) rather than *imtiyazat* (56). *Resimli kitab*, 4: 338–335, Kanun-ı evvel 1324 / December 1908, in an article on the American elections, inserted the word *impérialisme*, in French, and the words "campaign fund" and "slang" in English.

4. A good symbol of the equation of European systems with progress and prosperity was the interest shown in the Ottoman empire in the Paris (and other European) expositions. Coverage of these expositions was found in the press and in the various Ottoman almanacs and annuals. For example, in the gazette *Resimli kitab*, 4: 388–389, Kanun-ı evvel 1324 / January 1909, are photos of the exposition "*au jardin des Petits-Champs,*" and of the elections for the new assembly in Istanbul.

5. *Kalem*, 3: 12, 4 Eylül 1324 / 17 [labeled 18] September 1908; technically the date in C.E. terms should be thirteen days later but in this case the date (fourteen days later) is given as the eighteenth. For a nineteenth-century Prussian cartoon satirizing the sultan, see Townsend, *Forbidden Laughter*, 156, an 1822 cartoon showing the sultan brutally putting down the Greek rebellion while Austria and Britain look on.

6. Much had been written on the events and diplomacy of what was, in the West, called the Eastern Question, that is the question of the disposition of the Ottoman empire. See Marriott, *The Eastern Question;* and Moon, *Imperialism and World Politics*, 237–259. For a work which has culled some of the documents of Abd ül-Hamid for his statements regarding relations with Europe, see Sultan II. Abdülhamid Han, *Devlet ve Memleket Görüşlerim*, edited by A. Alaaddin Çetin and Ramazan Yıldız (İstanbul: Çığır Yayınları, 1976).

7. Austria had occupied Bosnia and Herzegovina since 1878. On the Balkan situation see Paul Imbert, *La Rénovation de L'Empire Ottoman: Affaires De Turquie* (Paris: Perrin Et Cie., 1909), 276–289. Imbert notes that the positions of the Great Powers had altered considerably between 1878 (when England, Germany, and Austria were all aligned in their desire to contain Russia) and 1908 when the Russians intervened to moderate Austrian expansion in the Balkans (278). See also Stavrianos, *The Balkans*, 74–75, 94–95, 100–114; and Shaw, *History of the Ottoman Empire*, 173, 191–196, on Austria in Bosnia and Herzegovina and 197–199, 276–277, on the move towards independence of Bulgaria.

8. It was in 1853 that the English cartoon gazette, *Punch*, first warned of the fragile condition of the empire by showing it as a seemingly dead turkey in the grasp of the Russian Bear; see Phillipe, *Political Graphics*, 169; and M. H. Spielman, *The History of "Punch,"* (London: Cassell and Co., 1895), 118–119.

9. *Kalem*, 4: 1, 11 Eylül 1324 / 24 September 1908. This call for peace is reminiscent of the eighteenth-century career of the diplomat Ahmed Resmi as recalled in

Notes to Pages 151–158

the biography by Virginia Aksan, *An Ottoman Staesman in War and Peace: Ahmed Resmi Efendi, 1700–1783* (Leiden: E.J. Brill, 1995).

10. Feroz Ahmad, "War and Society under the Young Turks, 1908–1918," *Review* 11 (Spring 1988): 276. Ahmad, however, would not consider the Ottoman situation "colonial."

11. *Meram*, 1: 15–18, 24–27, 30 Teşrin-i evvel 1324 / 12 November 1908; 2: 34, [9] Teşrin-i sani 1324 / [22] November 1908; and 4: cover, 27 Teşrin-i sani 1324 / 10 December 1908.

12. *Beyan ül-hak*, 1: 15–16, 22 Eylül 1324 / 5 October 1908, by Mehmed Fetin, including analysis of Bismarck's politics and the Russian and German interventions in Bulgaria.

13. *İstişare*, 56–61, 603–611, 738–741, published 4 Eylül 1324-19 Mart 1325 / 17 September 1908–1 April 1909 (on the French capitulations).

14. *Serbesti*, 1: 1, 3 Teşrin-i sani 1324 / 16 November 1908.

15. Fraser, *Persia and Turkey in Revolt*, 422–423. For a detailed account of British-Ottoman relations during this period and a description of the day-to-day construction of British policy, see Joseph Heller, *British Policy Towards the Ottoman Empire 1908–1914* (New York: Frank Cass, 1983). On the internal workings of the British government and British press coverage of the late-nineteenth-century Eastern Question, see R. W. Seton-Watson, *Disraeli, Gladstone and the Eastern Question: A Study in Diplomacy and Party Politics* (London: Macmillan and Co. Ltd., 1935). For some interesting treatments on British self-images at the time, see John M. Mackenzie, ed., *Imperialism and Popular Culture* (Manchester: Manchester University Press, 1986), which includes treatments of English juvenile fiction, and of imperialism in British literatures and schoolrooms.

16. *Serbesti*, 7: 2, 10 Teşrin-i sani 1324 / 23 November 1908.

17. Benedict Anderson, *Imagined Communities*.

18. *Kalem*, 55: 12, 17 Eylül 1325 / 30 September 1909. Another cartoon in *Kalem*, 63 :12, 12 Teşrin-i sani 1325 / 25 November 1909, showed a similar figure of Britain, this time armed with a rifle. Also on the British (and Ottomans) in Egypt, see *Arz-u hâl*, 3: 4, [?] Şubat 1325 / [?] late February or early March 1910. Elsewhere, *Resimli kitab* 18: 487–489, Mart 1326 / March 1910, covered the funeral of Butrus Gali Pasha, assassinated in Egypt, and the Suez canal concession to the British.

19. *Züğürt*, 6: 4, [18] Mart 1327 / [31] March 1911.

20. *Kalem*, 109: 9, 6 Kanun-ı sani 1326 / 19 January 1911. As in English, the word used here for tongue (*dil*) can mean tongue or language. On the "reorganization of language," in Egypt at this time and the various foreign language influences there, see Berque, *Egypt: Imperialism and Revolution*, 203–210.

21. See *Salname-i servet-i fünun* 1324–1325, 1: 73–90, published 1326 / 1910, on coinage.

22. Kandiyoti, "The End of Empire," 50.

23. Harry Stuermer, *Deux Ans De Guerre A Constantinople: Études de Morale et Politique Allemandes et Jeunes-Turques* (Paris: Librairie Payot, 1917), 146.

24. *Kalem*, 110: 18, 13 Kanun-ı sani 1326 / 25 January 1911. Another cartoon on

Britain in the Gulf shows England as a magician pulling a rabbit (Kuwait) out of his hat: *Kalem,* 120: 12, 24 Mart 1327 / 6 April 1911.

25. *Diken,* 3: 5, 28 Teşrin-i evvel 1918 / 10 November 1918.

26. *Kalem,* 3: 6, 4 Eylül 1324 / 17 September 1908.

27. *Geveze,* 1: 1, 6 Teşrin-i sani 1324 / 19 November 1908. The first part of this caption is obliterated. The object of the Europeans' urgings wears a fez; he could represent the empire itself, or the Balkan provinces. The foreign powers include Austria, France, England, Italy, and Russia. For an image of Austria "eating" Rumelia, see *Kalem,* 35: 18, 23 Nisan 1425 / 6 May 1909.

28. *Dalkavuk,* 1: 5, 30 Ağustos 1324 / 12 September 1908, in a frame called "The Eastern Question."

29. *Kalem,* 124: 5, 28 Nisan 1327 / 11 May 1911.

30. *Alem,* 2: 16, 5 Şubat 1324 / 18 February 1909. Puppet imagery also suggested relationships of subordination and dominance. See, for example, *Kalem,* 60: 1, 22 Teşrin-i evvel 1325 / 4 November 1909.

31. *Davul,* 13: 8–9, 14 Kanun-ı sani 1324 / 27 January 1909.

32. *Yeniçeri,* 3: 4, 5 Kanun-ı evvel 1327 / 18 December 1911. See Zürcher, *Turkey, A Modern History,* 110. *Alem,* 1: 9, 29 Kanun-ı sani 1324 / 11 February 1909, also shows Franz Joseph as a child engaged in a dangerous game with Bosnia and Herzegovina

33. On Italy's imperial ambitions and their political context, see Smith, *Italy and Its Monarchy,* 182–196; Marriott, *The Eastern Question,* 385–408; Sir Robert Graves, *Storm Centres of the Near East: Personal Memories 1879–1929* (London: Hutchinson & Co., 1975), 253–264; and Ali Abdullatif Ahmida, *The Making of Modern Libya: State Formation, Colonization, and Resistance, 1830–1932* (Albany: State University of New York Press, 1994), 19–41, 103–124. On 27 September, 1911, the Italian king, having acquiesced to the invasion of Libya, sent an ultimatum to Istanbul that resulted in a declaration of war. By that time, as Smith notes, "a group of Italian journalists had already been drafted to Tripoli to be on hand for the attack" (187). During the war, some of the Ottoman gazettes excoriated the Italian press for its role in promoting and reporting the confrontation. See also Orhan Koloğlu, *1911–1912'de Karikatur Savaşı* (Ankara: Engin Yayınlar, 1989) for cartoons of the time.

34. *Kalem,* 125: 3, 5 Mayıs 1327 / 18 May 1911, a cartoon by Sedad Nuri. *Kalem,* 122: 8, 7 Nisan 1327 / 20 April 1911, showed Garibaldi as Don Quixote. Also on Italy: *Alem,* 2: 13, 5 Şubat 1324 / 18 February 1909.

35. *Kalem,* 106: 3, 16 Kanun-ı evvel 1326 / 29 December 1910.

36. *Kalem,* 7: 6, 9 Teşrin-i evvel 1324 / 22 October 1908. The serious gazette, *Resimli İstanbul,* was very interested in events in Morocco, running a series, from August to October 1909, of pieces and romanticized images on the wars there, expecially on Fez and the Spanish intervention. Also on the Moroccan situation and European intervention, see *Nevzad-ı vatan,* 1: 2, 13 Ağustos 1324 / 26 August 1908; and *Boşboğaz,* 21: 3, 6 Teşrin-i evvel 1324 / 19 October 1908. *Resimli kitab,* 6: 524–525, Mart 1325 / March 1909, ran photographs of the two Moroccan sovereigns shortly after Mulla Hafız's coup.

37. See, on postcards, Malek Alloula, *The Colonial Harem* (Minneapolis: University of Minnesota Press, 1984).

38. Wilfrid Blunt, *Desert Hawk: Abd el Kader and the French Conquest of Algeria* (London: Methuen and Co., 1947), 1. The event may have been "famous" but its actual details have been contested.

39. Blunt, *Desert Hawk*, 2.

40. Goldstein, *Censorship of Political Caricature*, plate not paginated.

41. *Kalem*, 7: 7, 2 Teşrin-i evvel 1324 / 15 October 1908. This cartoon appeared only ten days after Austria's annexation of Bosnia and Herzegovina.

42. *Alem*, 1: 6, 29 Kanun-ı sani 1324 / 11 February 1909, shows Franz Joseph as a lion tamer, attempting to tame the lions of Bosnia and Herzegovina. Austria was also charged with instigating the Bulgarian revolt and with encouraging Ferdinand; see, for example, *İncili çavuş*, 16: 4, 2 Teşrin-i evvel 1324 / 15 October 1908; and *Meram*, 4: 1, 27 Teşrin-i sani 1324 / 10 December 1908, for a brief note on the annexation question. Also on Crete (and "national feelings") see *Falaka*, 10: 1, [22] Ağustos 1327 / [4] September 1911. The struggle for Crete drew a lot of comment in the Ottoman press of the time.

43. See the Ottoman yearbook *Salname-i servet-i fünun*, 2: 210–213, 1326, published 1327 / 1911, for an informational series on Russia, including a long article on the Muslims in Russia.

44. The role of the Ottoman empire as a pawn between the powers of England and Russia is reflected in an 1871 British War song, "We've Swept the Seas before Boys," cited in Penny Summerfield, "Patrioism and Empire: Music Hall Entertainment, 1870–1914," 27, in John Mackenzie, ed. *Imperialism and Popular Culture*. Russia had its own satire of its foes; Jahn Hubertus, *Patriotic Culture in Russia During World War I* (Ithaca: Cornell Univeristy Press, 1995), 37–38, notes the emperor and the sultan each garnered a 12 percent share in Russian patriotic cartoons while the kaiser was targeted in one third.

45. *Kalem*, 8: 1, 9 Teşrin-i evvel 1324 / 22 October 1908.

46. See Shaw, *History of the Ottoman Empire*, 285–298; and Marriott, *The Eastern Question*, 361–389.

47. *Alem*, 1: 3, 29 Kanun-ı sani 1324 / 11 February 1909. For later cartoons of Bulgaria and its entanglements in the 1913–1914 period, see the gazette *Karagöz* (published 1908–1928).

48. The princedom of Bulgaria had to be shopped around to the European courts in 1887 to find a prince acceptable to the European powers and the czar. Ferdinand of Saxe-Coburg-Gotha was finally persuaded and took over the government in July of 1887. After the Young Turk Revolution, Ferdinand reached an understanding with Franz Joseph and proclaimed Bulgaria independent on October 5, 1908. Britain tried to play both sides in the Bulgarian question but recognized Ferdinand as king in May of 1909; see Heller, *British Policy*, 43. Filling the throne of Greece (to the satisfaction of the Great Powers) in 1863, had proved a similar dilemma, with the succession finally falling, rather by default, to William, second son of the heir to the throne of Denmark, who ruled (1863–1913) as George I.

49. A later cartoon, in *Diken*, 1: 8, 13 Teşrin-i evvel 1918 / 26 October 1918, suggests the perils of the Ottoman inclination towards Germany. The cartoon, en-

titled "A short history of our friendship with Germany," shows Germany calling upon the empire to come to its aid. The "Turk" bravely fights the Russian foe while Germany stands by cheering him on. Then Germany tells the wounded Ottoman that he has come to his (Germany's) assistance, but if the Ottoman wants help in return he must look to God.

50. *Kalem,* 6: 7, 25 Eylül 1324 / 8 October 1908. The same issue shows Franz Joseph of Austria aiding Bulgaria's Ferdinand as he walks a tightrope toward independence.

51. See *Alem,* 4: 9, 19 Şubat 1324 / 4 March 1909. Also in *Alem,* 5: back cover, 26 Şubat 1324 / 11 March 1909, the Bulgarian king is shown full size but satirized as admiring himself in the mirror, inflated with the idea of being king. *Musavver devr-i cedid,* 5: 73, 1 Haziran 1325 / 14 June 1909, ran a photograph of the "Slav Rulers," in 1909, which included Ferdinand, but which designated him as "prince," not king, of Bulgaria.

52. Barbara Tuchman, *The Guns of August* (New York: Macmillan Company, 1962), 2–3. For further discussion of Ferdinand, his detractors, and the French consul's description of him in 1907, see Stavrianos, *The Balkans Since 1453,* 434–441.

53. *Kalem,* 5: 9, 18 Eylül 1324 / 1 October 1908, in one of the French sections. For other satire of the Bulgarian question, see: *Boşboğaz,* 19: 1, [29] Eylül 1324 / [12] October, 1908.

54. *Davul,* 2: 2, 21 Teşrin-i evvel 1324 / 3 November 1908. This cartoon is "signed" and captioned "from Enver Bay in New York." It is unusual in this regard, as well as for the English balloon caption and for at least one attempt at a verbal Americanization that occurs when the figure representing Czar Nicholas exclaims, "Gee Whishky!" when he sees the new maestro. See also, Çeviker, *İbret Albümü,* 29.

55. On the empire's economic position, see Zürcher, *Turkey, A Modern History,* 67–69, 76–116; Şevket Pamuk, *The Ottoman Empire and European Capitalism, 1820–1913* (Cambridge: Cambridge University Press, 1987); and Shaw, *History of the Ottoman Empire,* 95–105, 122–128, 155–156, 221–227, 234–238, 285.

56. Charges that the regime was selling out to foreign powers were also found in Iranian nationalist literature and cartoons of the time; see Javadi, *Satire in Persian Literature,* 178, and the third plate after 117.

57. Graves, *Storm Centres of the Near East,* 234–235, who served Britian in Salonica before and after the revolution, notes that, when he returned from London to Istanbul in October of 1908, his colleague Block (of the Public Debt Administration) met with the new Ottoman Minister of Finance who informed Block of the six million pound deficit and solicited his advice on "fresh sources of revenue."

58. See, for example, *Boşboğaz,* 43: [?], 20 Ağustos 1324 / 2 September 1908.

59. On the capitulations, see Halil İnalcık, "İmtiyazat," in *Encyclopedia of Islam,* 2nd series, v. 3, 1179–1189 (Leiden: E.J. Brill, 1971); Jacques Thobie, *Intérêts et Impérialisme Français dans l'Empire Ottoman (1895–1914)* (Paris: Publications de la Sorbonne, 1977); Thobie, *La France Impériale, 1880–1914* (Paris: Editions Mégrelis, 1982), 1–53, 205–215, 287–312; Amiya Bagchi, *The Political Economy of Underdevelopment* (Cambridge: Cambridge University Press, 1982), 25–31. On British privilege

and the capitulations in Palestine, see David Kushner, "Ali Ekrem Bey, Governor of Jerusalem, 1906–1908," *International Journal of Middle East Studies* 28 (August 1996): 349–362.

60. Zürcher, *Turkey*, 89–90, notes that around the turn of the century in the empire, "Over 90 percent of the industrial establishments with more than ten workers were owned by non-Muslims." But he does not indicate what percentage of those non-Muslims were not Ottoman citizens. On competition among foreign investors for Ottoman turf and on the foreign-built railroads, see Pamuk, *The Ottoman Empire and European Capitalism*, 55–81; and Moon, *Imperialism and World Politics*, 244–245.

61. See *Salname-i servet-i fünun*, 2: 224, 1327 / 1911, which published a list of companies organized since the revolution.

62. Zürcher, *Turkey*, 67–68, 88–90. For an elaborate treatment of the Public Debt as an instrument of European control of the empire, see Blaisdell, *European Financial Control in the Ottoman Empire*, esp. 1–46, 108–185; also Thobie, *Intérêts et Impérialisme*, 609–631; and "Sur Quelques Sociétés Oubliées à Capitaux Français Dans l'Empire Ottoman," 375–390, in Batu and Bacqué-Grammont, eds., *L'Empire Ottoman*.

63. The Ottoman Bank was used to arrange and guarantee new Ottoman loans from European backers. For a comparison of the Ottoman Bank and the Persian Imperial Bank, see Jacques Thobie, "Banque Impériale Ottomane Et Banque Impériale De Perse Jusque'en 1914," 105–135, in *La France Et l'Est Méditerranéen Depuis 1850*, Analecta Isisiana, v. 5 (İstanbul: Editions Isis, 1993). This article includes a fairly elaborate discussion of Ottoman money standards under the Bank's administration, systems of credit, and associated financier groups. Also on the Ottoman Bank, see Shaw, *History of the Ottoman Empire*, 97, 204–205, 223; and Alemdar, *İstanbul*, 37–39.

64. Ahmad, "The Young Turks, 1908–1918," 277.

65. Çaglar Keyder, *The Definition of a Peripheral Economy: Turkey 1923–1929* (Cambridge: Cambridge University Press, 1981), 8–9.

66. Stuermer, *Deux Ans De Guerre A Constantinople*, 151.

67. For example, *Kalem*, 98: 1, 7 Teşrin-i evvel 1326 / 20 October 1910. The capitulations, as might be imagined, were regularly treated in the serious press as well; see, for example, *İttifak*, 6: 1, 9 Ağustos 1324 / 22 August 1908, on "Germany and the Capitulations."

68. *Kalem*, 45: 1, 9 Temmuz 1325 / 22 July 1909. Pamuk, *The Ottoman Empire and European Capitalism*, 72–81, attempts a quantification of European "shares," in the Ottoman economic "pie" over time, noting that the shares of French, German, and Belgian investors increased between 1881–1914 as the shares of the British declined (73).

69. *Kalem*, 11: 16, 30 Teşrin-i evvel 1324 / 12 November 1908; and 12: 16, 7 Teşrin-i sani 1324 / 19 November 1908 [correct date would be 20 November].

70. Rogers, *Mightier Than the Sword*, 154. Daumier was famous for his caricatures of posturing countries contending for territory. In another cartoon, by John Tenniel, published in *Punch* in 1878, Bismarck is shown wearing a Roman skirt and the spiked helmet on which is mounted a directional weather vane. Burdened by his huge

bundle of "War," he is being buffeted by the wind. See, Phillipe, *Political Graphics,* 169.

71. Roderic Davison, "The Ottoman Boycott of Austrian Goods in 1908 as a Diplomatic Question," in Heath Lowry and Ralph Hattox, eds., *Third Congress of the Social and Economic History of Turkey, Princeton University 24-26 August 1983* (Istanbul: Isis Press, 1990), 1-28. Davison considers the implications of the boycott, focusing on the international crisis over Bosnian annexation.

72. Davison, "The Ottoman Boycott," 5-6, notes that an article calling for boycott in the October 7, 1908 issue of *Servet-i fünun* is most commonly attributed to Dr. Rıza Tevfik (Bölükbaşı). It was followed by anti-Austrian posters and an article in *Tanin* by Hüseyin Cahit (Yalçın).

73. Zürcher, *Turkey,* 109.

74. Rai, *Young India,* 177-178. Rai notes with some humor the indignation that the Superintendant of Police and the Collector in the district of Barisal in Bengal felt when they, "both failed to be able to buy a piece of Manchester shirting." Davison, "The Ottoman Boycott," 10, points out that the Muslim vernacular press in India picked up on the Ottoman boycott and urged Muslims there to join in. He also notes, 6, the possible influences of the Austrian boycott against Serbia, the Iranian Tobacco Rebellion of 1891, and the Chinese boycott against the United States.

75. *Papağan,* 13: 1, 10 Kanun-ı evvel 1324 / 23 December 1908, and 15: 1, 15 Kanun-ı evvel 1324 / 28 December 1908; see also issues 17, 19, and 20, on the boycott. For other cartoons on the boycott see: *Boşboğaz,* 24: 4, 20 Teşrin-i evvel 1324 / 2 November 1908; and *Dalkavuk,* 6: 8, 4 Teşrin-i evvel 1324 / 17 October 1908, and 8: 4, 18 Teşrin-i evvel 1324 / 31 October 1908.

76. *Geveze,* 32: [2], 23 Şubat 1324 / 8 March 1909.

77. *Dalkavuk,* 25: 1, 21 Şubat 1324 / 6 March 1909.

78. On economic intervention in India and China, for example, see Bagchi, *The Political Economy of Underdevelopment,* 78-105. On Brazil, the organization of labor, and the colonial context, see June Hahner, *Poverty and Politics: The Urban Poor in Brazil, 1870-1920* (Albuquerque: University of New Mexico Press, 1986); and Joel Wolfe, "The Rise of Brazil's Industrial Working Class: Community, Work, and Politics in São Paulo, 1900-1955," (Ph.D. dissertation, Dept. of History, University of Wisconsin, Madison, 1990). For a study of later labor movements in Egypt and their associations with Islam, see Ellis Goldberg, "Muslim Union Politics in Egypt: Two Cases," in Burke and Lapidus, *Islam, Politics, and Social Movements,* 228-243, which focuses on sugar and oil workers

79. See Pamuk, *The Ottoman Empire and European Capitalism,* 53-54, 182-190; Blaisdell, *European Financial Control in the Ottoman Empire,* 113-114; and Shaw, *History of the Ottoman Empire,* 233.

80. Cemal Pasha, *Memories of a Turkish Statesman—1913-1919: By Djemal Pasha, Formerly Governor of Constantinople, Imperial Ottoman Naval Minister, and Commander of the Fourth Army in Sinai, Palestine and Syria* (New York: George H. Doran Co., 1922), 46-47. In his memoirs, Cemal defends his own actions in this crisis (p, 47). At this time, when the Ottoman government decided to attempt the recapture of Edirne, the British government, according to Cemal, "showed its true face," and demons-

trated that "the policy pursued by England was utterly hostile to the Turkish Government" (48). He added that Russia favored the Turks but only because they expected to "inherit" Constantinople (48–49).

81. *Kalem*, 128: 5, 26 Mayıs 1327 / 8 June 1911. This cartoon is signed with the initials C. P., an "unidentified" cartoonist, see Çeviker, *Türk Karikatürü*, 2: 130. It is also signed "A. Tatlian," presumably the printing or production house.

82. See Zürcher, *Turkey*, 204

83. Louis Rambert, *Notes et Impressions de Turquie: L'Empire Ottoman sous Abdul Hamid II 1895–1905* (Geneva: Edition Atar, 1910), 279.

84. Rambert, *Notes et Impressions*, 275. Rambert notes that this factory is part of a vast association of the big British tobacco companies, The Imperial Tobacco Company, organized to resist the invasion of the American tobacco trust. Also on cigarette factories, see Donald Quataert, "The Age of Reforms, 1812–1914," 902, in Halil İnalcık and Donald Quataert, eds. *An Economic and Social History of the Ottoman Empire, 1300–1914* (Cambridge: Cambridge University Press, 1994). For an Ottoman image of foreign factory technology and women workers, see *Osmanlı ziraat ve ticaret gazetesi*, 10 : 153, 26 Teşrin-i sani 1325 / 9 December 1909, a picture of a milk "*hane* (house)" in Denmark with women workers.

85. Zürcher, *Turkey*, 98. Zürcher notes that inflation was 20 percent, the workers were demanding wage increases, and there were over one hundred strikes in the first six months after the revolution. On the labor movement and these strikes see Yavuz Karakışla, "The 1908 Strike Wave in the Ottoman Empire," *The Turkish Studies Association Bulletin* 16, no. 2 (September 1992): 153–177; and Peter Mentzel, "Nationalism and the Labor Movement in the Ottoman Empire," esp. 141–170, (Ph.D. dissertation, University of Washington, Department of History, 1994). Davison, "The Ottoman Boycott," 2–3, notes that the largest previous strikes in the empire had been in 1873, 1875, and a dockyard strike in 1876; "but there had been nothing to compare with the wave of strikes that began at the start of August 1908." In the following ten weeks, there were strikes by, "boat crews, stevedores and ship's porters, dockside coalheavers, miners in Ereğli, Istanbul tramway employees, tobacco Régie laborers, bakers, typesetters, salt workers at Izmir, and railway workers. . . ." All this activity suggests considerable unmet demand and the perception of opportunity that derived from the revolution.

86. In England, *Punch* had a long history of playing the role of defender of the poor, sometimes focusing on the abuse of the laborer and other times on the workhouses or child labor. Often this satire targeted the heedlessness of the elites. See Graves, *Mr. Punch's History*, 42–53. For a photo of the Topkapı Paupers Aid Society, in Istanbul, see Eken, *Kartpostallarda İstanbul*, 218.

87. *İştirak*, 5: 79–80, [13] Mart 1325 / [26] March 1909; and 6: 81, [20] Mart 1325 / [2] April 1909, the organ of the Ottoman Socialist Party, addressed the questions of "our workers," and of "working girls." Its pages covered socialism abroad and the meaning of socialism. On socialism see Mete Tunçay and Erik Zürcher, *Socialism and Nationalism in the Ottoman Empire, 1876–1923* (London: British Academic Press, 1994); and *Türkiyede Dergiler, Ansiklopediler*, 23–34. *Resimli kitab*, 14: 117, Teşrin-sani 1325 / November 1909; and 9: 877, Haziran 1325 / June 1909, also

covered socialism, and depicted labor strikes in France, and the arrest of a socialist deputy, "Pablo Galezya" [sic] in Spain. Later, *Perde*, 1: 4, 21 Teşrin-i sani 1327 / 4 December 1911, used Karagöz and Hacivat to satirize the socialists in the context of the war with Italy. See also, Paul Dumont, "20. Yüzyıl Başları Osmanlı İmparatorluğu İşci Hareketleri ve Sosyalist Akımlar Tarihi Üzerine Yayımlanmamış Kaynaklar," *Toplum ve Bilim* 3 (1977): 31–50.

88. On class satire in Iran and France, see Browne, *The Press and Poetry of Modern Persia*, 233, 241; and Ribeiro, *Fashion in the French Revolution*, 113–114.

89. *Lâklâk*, 2: 4, 16 Temmuz 1325 / 29 July 1909; the setting is rural and the boss, or owner, is identified as a "*çiftlik sahibi.*" Forty para is roughly equivalent to 1 *kuruş* (*piastre*). See also *Lâklâk*, 6: 4, 13 Ağustos 1325 / 26 August 1909 (on villagers come to the city). For some other, less-politicized, cartoon images of workers, see *Nekregû ile Pişekâr*, 3: 4, 3 Haziran 1325 / 16 June 1909.

90. Probably this cartoon refers to the proposals for a national susbscription to raise money for warship construction and the subsequent founding of the *Donanmayı [Muavenet-i] Milliye Cemiyeti* (National Naval Aid Society), founded in July 1909, which raised money for the navy and published the gazette *Donanma*. See Bernd Langensiepen and Ahmet Güleryüz, *The Ottoman Steam Navy, 1828–1923*, edited and translated by James Cooper (London: Conway Maritime Press, 1994), 14; Ali Haydar Emir (Alpagut), *Balkan Harbinde Türk Filosu* (İstanbul: Deniz Basımevi, 1932), 29, 60; and Afif Büyüktugrul, *Balkan Harb Tarihi*, v. 7, *Osmanlı Deniz Hareketi, 1912–1913* (Ankara: Genelkurmay Başkan Harb Tarihi Dairesi, 1965), 14–15, 67.

91. *Lâklâk*, 13: 1, 4, 1 Teşrin-i evvel 1325 / 14 October 1909.

92. *Davul*, 16: 8, 11 Şubat 1324 / 24 February 1909. There was indeed famine in the countryside at this time. See also, *Karakuş Ezop*, 3: 3, 17 Eylül 1324 / 30 September 1908, a satirical dialogue.

93. *Alem*, 9: 4 (French section), 26 Mart 1325 / 8 April 1909. For a photo and a postcard image of the *hamal*, see Eken, *Kartpostallarda İstanbul*, 254–255.

94. Davison, "The Ottoman Boycott," 9, 12, 19. *Alem*, 7: 6 (French section), 12 Mart 1325 / 25 March 1909, has a piece satirizing "*la grève des hamals*" (the porters' strike), which also pokes fun at Ottoman forms of negotiation. Selma Ekrem, *Unveiled: The Autobiography of a Turkish Girl* (New York: Ives Washburn, 1934), 114, tells the tale of how her father was made governor-general of Beirut after the revolution. But when they arrived: "The hamals had gone on strike. They shouted liberty and independence in the numerous coffeehouses and sipped the hours away in a dream blue with smoke. Then we looked for a policeman but they too were striking!"

95. *Kalem*, 55: 8–9, 18 Eylül 1325 / 1 October 1909.

96. Donald Quataert, "Ottoman Women, Households, and Textile Manufacturing, 1800–1914," 161–176, in Nikki Keddie and Beth Baron, eds., *Women in Middle Eastern History* (New Haven: Yale, 1991), see especially 169, 171. Quataert's figures on wages and bread consumption, of course, are preliminary, representative of his pioneering work on Ottoman economic history. No systematic survey of either wages, prices, or consumption (even for the city of Istanbul alone) has yet been made. For ads for workers in the revolutionary press, see, for example, *Serbesti*, 3: 4, 5 Teşrin-i sani 1324 / 18 November 1908.

97. Quataert, "Ottoman Women," 164.
98. Ibid., 167.
99. *Kalem,* 123: 5, 21 Nisan 1327 / 4 May 1911.
100. *Kalem,* 78: 5, 4 Mart 1326 / 17 March 1910.
101. See Elena Frangakis-Syrett, "American Trading Practices in Izmir in the Late Nineteenth and Early Twentieth Centuries," 177–184, in Daniel Panzac, ed. *Histoire Économique et Sociale de l'empire Ottoman et de la Turquie (1326–1960),* Actes du sixième congrès international tenu à Aix-en-Provence, July 1992 (Paris: Peeters, 1995), on the Standard Oil Company, which entered the Izmir market in 1911 (182). Standard Oil became the largest U.S. company in the empire.

Chapter VII. The Comic Culture: The Critique of Society, Culture, and European Influence

1. *Modern* was usually glossed *yeni* but also sometimes *moderne.* On the construction of ideas of the old and new Ottoman society in the late nineteenth century (with a comparison to Russia), see Şerif Mardin, "Super Westernization in Urban Life in the Ottoman Empire in the Last Quarter of the Nineteenth Century," 404–446, in Peter Benedict et. al., eds., *Turkey: Geographic and Social Perspectives* (Leiden: E.J. Brill, 1974), especially 408–409.

2. In Ottoman revolutionary satire there was not a shift from focus on the political sphere to focus on the social sphere such as Terdiman shows for the post-Press-Law Daumier cartoons in mid-nineteenth-century France. Terdiman, *Discourse/Counter-Discourse,* 162–166. There may, however, have been such a shift in the history of the later-twentieth-century republic.

3. McWilliam, *Dreams of Happiness,* 302–303, has argued that in France the "call for modernity is perhaps the most distinctive characteristic of republican critical discourse during the 1830s." The call for modernity was also a significant factor in Ottoman discourses of the nineteenth and early twentieth centuries. Walter Andrews, "Time Warps: Through the Transparent Wall as Literature Writes Literary History," paper presented at the MESA conference, Phoenix, 1994, has discussed the difference between Western and Turkish modernity. He characterizes the latter (in part) in this way: "And a number of things came with modernity and its new vocabulary: a unitary and unified nation, a new culture, a national language that presumably transcends class, a secular civil society .... and a number of things were consequently (and necessarily, perhaps) repressed: the old languages, the old culture, a society that saw itself as centered in the sacred, the heterology of a multi-ethnic, multi-cultural, hereoglossic empire, the sense of an unbroken continuous history" (5).

4. The notion of the new (*yeni*) raises this idea of the clean slate, the chance to start over. On the equation of Europe and modernity in the transformation of the empire, see Berkes, *The Development of Secularism in Turkey,* although he focuses more on secularism than on modernity per se. For an interesting treatment of the idea of the modern (in Western settings) and its various uses and contexts, see Stephen Toulmin, *Cosmopolis: The Hidden Agenda of Modernity* (New York: The Free Press,

1990), 5–44: "But the received view of Modernity rested not only on the Quest for Certainty and the equation of Rationality with a respect for formal logic: it also took over the rationalists' belief that the modern, rational way of dealing with problems is to sweep away the inherited clutter from traditions, clean the slate, and start again from scratch" (175).

5. *Resimli kitab,* 6: 583–597, Mart 1325 / March 1909.

6. *Meram,* 1: 20, 30 Teşrin-i evvel 1324 / 12 November 1908, discusses conditions in Europe, from the Napoleonic era on, in an article translated from the original French.

7. Şerif Mardin, *The Genesis of Young Ottoman Thought: A Study of the Modernization of Turkish Political Ideas* (Princeton: Princeton University Press, 1962), 115–117 (for example), has pointed out the complexity of motivations and legitimations involved in the political transformations of the Young Ottoman period. Westernization, in the Young Turk Period, as in the Young Ottoman, cannot be viewed as a simple linear process, its outward manifestations evidence of a simple and evident shift in ideology. Thus, the celebration by certain gazettes of Western styles and the adaptation of those styles by Ottoman elites must be viewed with caution and with the understanding that Europeanization was understood in various ways and experienced at varying levels. Chartier, *The Cultural Uses of Print,* 10, on the circulation of cultural objects, has argued that the processes of imitation and popularization were competitive efforts "in which any instance of dissemination—whether granted or hard-won—was met with a search for new procedures for distinction." See also Edmund Burke, "Islam and Social Movements: Methodological Reflections," 17–35, in Burke and Lapidus, eds., *Islam, Politics, and Social Movements,* esp. 17–25.

8. Two examples were *Mükemmel ve Muvazzah Türkçe ve Fransızca Usûl-i Mükâleme—Nouvelle Méthode Guide Complet de la Conversation Turque—Français* (İstanbul: Ahter Matbaası, 1316 / 1898); and G. A. Nar Bey de Lusignan, *Guide de la Conversation Français—Turque* (Paris: By the Author, 1881). For other examples see "Lisan-i Türki," Catalog 12, November 1995, Librarie de Péra, İstanbul, items 1–933.

9. Vaka, *Haremlik,* 28. She added that Turkish women did not suffer from "unwholesome introspection, that horrible attribute of the average half-educated European and American woman."

10. Vaka, *Haremlik,* 59, 75.

11. Garnett, *Turkish Life,* 206–207. See also İskit, *Türkiyede Matbuat İdareleri ve Politikaları,* 129.

12. Garnett, *Turkish Life,* 209, praises the Ottomans' abandoning of the "ponderous, grandiloquent, and inflated styles of diction formerly in vogue," noting that Ottoman Turkish had taken on a sentence structure more comparable to those of European languages and that new words, "to express the wants of modern civilization," had been adapted from other languages, all of which greatly benefited the nation.

13. Many gazettes had French inserts and captions, for example, *Kalem* and *Muhit.* See G. Groc and İ. Çağlar, *La Presse Française de Turquie de 1795 à nos Jours: Histoire et Catalogue* (İstanbul: Editions Isis, 1985); Jean-Louis Bacqué-Grammont and Edhem Eldem, eds., *De La Révolution Française À la Turquie d'Atatürk: La modernisation*

politique et sociale. Les lettres, les sciences et les arts. Actes des Colloques d'Istanbul (10–12 mai 1989) (İstanbul: Editions Isis, 1990), especially the articles by Davison, Huré, Hanioğlu, and Kuneralp. Alemdar, *İstanbul*, 221–226, also includes a list of French gazettes published in Istanbul and the provinces.

14. İbrahim Şinasi, *Durub-ı Emsal-i Osmaniye* (İstanbul: Matbaa-ı Abu ül-Ziya, 1302 / 1886–1887).

15. On Şinasi, see Berkes, *The Development of Secularism in Turkey*, 197–198; and İbnülemin Mahmut Kemal İnal, *Son Asır Türk Şairleri*, 3rd edition, v. 4 (İstanbul: Dergâh Yayınları, 1988): 1836–1848.

16. For example, Proudhon, in *İştirak* (1909–1910). For an interesting comparison on the consumption of French literature in the United States, see James D. Hart, *The Popular Book: A History of America's Literary Taste* (Berkeley: University of California Press, 1961), 100–101. According to Hart, *The Three Musketeers* was popular in the States in the 1840's even though French literature was associated with immorality. "If a domestic novelist wanted to show a character as evil she had but to insinuate into the character's possession a copy of a French novel and all was perfectly clear to the reader" (100).

17. *Resimli kitab*, 4: 374–379, Kanun-ı evvel 1324 / December 1908. The story, by Michel Pruuns [*sic*] is titled *tenezzüh* (the stroll or excursion). Sabrî (Duran) was active in a variety of publications during this era.

18. See, T*asvir-i efkâr*, 114: 5, 22 Eylül 1325 / 5 October 1909, for the *Three Musketeers* and notices on theater (Sherlock Holmes); and, for the picture of the guillotine, see *Resimli kitab*, 12: 1225, Eylül 1325 / September 1909. On translations and the consumption of novels and foreign literature in the nineteenth and early twentieth centuries see Berkes, *The Development of Secularism in Turkey*, 277–283; Jitka Malecková, "Ludwig Büchner versus Nat Pinkerton: Turkish Translations from Western Languages, 1880–1914," *Mediterranean Historical Review* 9, no. 1 (June 1994): 73–99; and Johann Strauss, "Romanlar, Ah! O Romanlar! Les Débuts De La Lecture Moderne Dans L'Empire Ottoman (1850–1900)," *Turcica* 26 (1994): 125–163.

19. *Aşiyan*, 2, no. 2: 43–58, Eylül 1324 / September 1908.

20. *Resimli kitab*, cilt 2, 11: 1151–1165 (unsigned), Ağustos 1325 / August 1909. The article credits Monsieur Bop [*sic*]; A. Bopp was the French Chargé d'Affaires in Istanbul.

21. For ads for instruction in French, for example, see *Üç gazette*, published September 1908.

22. *Dalkavuk*, 15: 7, 11 Kanun-ı evvel 1324 / 24 December 1908. *Kalem*, 5: 8, 18 Eylül 1324 / 1 October 1908, also reprinted a Twain joke.

23. *Resimli kitab*, 6: 549–554, Mart 1325 / March 1909.

24. *Piyano*, 14: 154–157, [6] Teşrin-i sani 1326 / [19] November 1910. Tevfik was editor-in-chief of *Malum*.

25. Annuals like *Salname-i servet-i fünun 1324–1325*, 1: 143–155, published 1326 / 1910, and 2: 246–259, published 1327 /1911 included coverage of foreign writers in their sections on literature. *Tasviri efkâr*, 114: 4, 22 Eylül 1325 / 5 October 1909, contrasted French-language influence to the Arabic-language influence of former times. On the importance of foreign languages, French and other, for Ottoman civil

officialdom in this period, see Carter Findley, *Ottoman Civil Officialdom*, 167–169. Findley looks at the personnel records for officials of the Foreign Ministry and their self ratings of their language proficiency.

26. *Resimli kitab*, 11: 1083–1085, Ağustos 1325 / August 1909, for *"Eski-Yeni,"* on literature. See also, *Resimli kitab*, 1: 24–29, Eylül 1324 / September 1908, on "The Bases of Our Language and Şams üd-Din Sami Bey;" and *Ulûm-i iktisadiye ve içtimaiye mecmuası*, 1, 15 Kanun-ı evvel 1324 / 28 December 1908. The first three issues of the latter include European articles "in our language." On Sami, see Shaw, *History of the Ottoman Empire*, 253–254. *Boşboğaz*, 27: 1, 30 Teşrin-i evvel 1324 / 12 November 1908, and 14: 2–3, 11 Eylül 1324 / 24 September 1908, satirized the evolution of language in revolutionary context with its "New Dictionary," and "Freedom Dictionary." *Cadaloz*, 31: 3, [5] Temmuz 1327 / [18] July 1911, ran a word play on speaking Turkish that hinged on the use of Arabic and Persian.

27. David Laitin, *Politics, Language, and Thought: The Somali Experience* (Chicago: University of Chicago Press, 1977), for example, 221–224, has argued the powerful impact of the infusion of European language into the cultural spheres of Somalia: "to change a people's language is to change a way of life" (222). He argues further that the transfer of cultural insutitions then impeded the development of political and cultural autonomy in Africa. What is clear from the Ottoman press is that not only were the satirists aware of these processes of cultural transformation through language, they captured, employed, and added to them.

28. Celal Nuri (İleri), *Türk İnkılâbı* (İstanbul: Ahmet İhsan Matbaası, n.d.).

29. On language chauvinism and the intrusion of French literature, see Berkes, *The Development of Secularism*, 188–192, 291–293.

30. On the evolution of the Turkish novel, see Robert P. Finn, *The Early Turkish Novel 1872–1900* (İstanbul: Isis Press, 1984); and Ahmet Evin, *Origins and Development of the Turkish Novel* (Minneapolis: Bibliotheca Islamica, 1983). Both authors address the satire of the Westernized Ottoman in Ottoman novels. Both demonstrate (Finn, 2–3; Evin 23–40) the ways that Ottoman narrative forms shaped the evolution of the Ottoman novel. Just so, traditional Ottoman satirical forms, in tandem with Western influences, shaped the evolution of the Ottoman cartoon.

31. *Cingöz*, 2: 2, 30 Ağustos, 1324 / 12 September 1908, and on. The street dogs of Istanbul are conjured up as denizens of the city in this novel. *Musavver devr-i cedid* (published May–July 1909) serialized a *"milli roman,"* entitled *"Bir Az Dâvacık Tarihi,"* by Safvet Nazih. Nazih also translated novels by European authors, like Maxime Gorky (the famous Russian writer and revolutionary) in the gazette *İnkılab*, 10: 153, 12 Eylül 1325 / 25 September 1909. One of Gorky's plays, *Gariblık* (Strangeness), set in the "Deputies Club," was published in *Resimli kitab*, 6: 617–628, Mart 1325 / March 1909.

32. For example, the story, "Journalism" (*Gazetecilik*), unsigned, in the satirical *Nekregû*, 4: 2, 10 Eylül 1324 / 23 September 1908, and 5: 2, 24 Eylül 1324 / 7 October 1908.

33. *Züğürt*, 4: 3, 12 Mart 1327 / 25 March 1911, entitled *"Mukayese-i Lûgat."*

34. *Boşboğaz*, 12: 1–2, 4 Eylül 1324 / 17 September 1908. Word play, after all, was one of the basic foundations of Ottoman humor. The satiric gazettes also took on

Notes to Pages 194–199

other languages, like Arabic and Persian. See *Cadaloz* 31: 3, [5] Temmuz 1327 / [18] July 1911, for a word play on speaking Turkish.

35. Nokes, *Raillery and Rage,* 19.
36. *Kalem,* 44: 12, 2 Temmuz 1325 / 15 July 1909.
37. Thanks to Eric Zürcher for information on the *nişan defterleri.*
38. *Kalem,* 93: 3, 2 Eylül 1326 / 15 September 1910.
39. See on the Albanian nationalist struggle Shaw, *History of the Ottoman Empire,* 288–293; Stavro Skendi, *The Albanian National Awakening 1878–1912* (Princeton: Princeton University Press, 1967), 335–463, esp. 366–390, on the language question; Georges Castellan, *History of the Balkans* (Boulder: East European Monographs, 1992), 363–367; and Marriott, *The Eastern Question,* 382–417. Albania achieved autonomy after another period of revolt and negotiation in 1912.
40. *Kalem,* 54: 8, 10 Eylül 1325 / 23 September 1909. This cartoon is interesting in that it gives the caption in Arabic as well as French and Ottoman, a nod, I suppose to the language traditions of the system. The Arabic reads, "What ass, son of an ass . . . ." Blake, "Training Arab-Ottoman Bureaucrats," 81, has noted that violence was a commonplace of instruction in the Ottoman primary schools (as it tended to be in many traditional school systems), as illustrated in numerous memoirs.
41. Also *Lâklâk,* 4: 4, 30 Temmuz 1325 / 12 August 1909.
42. Şerif Mardin, "Religion and Secularism in Turkey," 347–374, in Hourani, ed., *The Modern Middle East,* speaking of the late-nineteenth- and early-twentieth-century Ottoman education reforms, notes that, "The model of social reality constructed from the school vision of the world had, therefore, an additional element: that of a hypothetical future which could be shaped at will" (361). This "progressive" notion of socially ordering the future was one of which the satirists were skeptical. Also on the "modernization" of Ottoman education, see Findley, *Ottoman Civil Officialdom,* 51–56, 131–173; Blake, "Training Arab-Ottoman Bureaucrats," 63–69, on curriculum and staffing, and 151, on Abd ül-Mecid's donation of five hundred volumes in French to the Mülkiye government training school; Szyliowicz, "Functional Perspectives on Technology," 252; and Martin Strohmeier, "Muslim Education in the Vilayet of Beirut, 1880–1918," 215–241, in Caesar Farah, ed., *Decision Making and Change in the Ottoman Empire* (Kirksville, Missouri: Thomas Jefferson University Press, 1993).
43. On athletic and sports clubs as a vehicle for nationalization in Germany at this time, see George Mosse, *The Nationalization of the Masses* (Ithaca: Cornell University Press, 1991), 127–160. Germany seems to have been a significant source for such influences in the empire.
44. *Resimli kitab,* 5: 413, Kanun-ı sani 1324 / January 1909. See for example, *Resimli İstanbul,* 9: 137, 3 Ağustos 1325 / 16 August 1909, for a photo of a boys' gymnastics program. Such photos were also ubiquitous in almanacs. I have found no photos of female gymnasts, but Elizabeth Frierson, "Unimagined Communities: Women and Education in the Late-Ottoman Empire, 1876–1909," *Critical Matrix* 9, no. 2 (Fall 1995): 77, notes that gymnastics was part of the curriculum in girl's secondary schools during Abd ül-Hamid's reign. Later, the annual, *Resimli Yıl,* 103–110, 1341 / 1924, would cover "The 1924 Sport Life," including the Olympics. On

sport gazettes, see *Türkiye'de Dergiler Ansiklopediler,* 203-208, which makes mention of the German and Austrian influences on late Ottoman athleticism.

45. *Resimli İstanbul,* 5: 77, 6 Temmuz 1325 / 19 July 1909, 9: 141, 3 Ağustos 1325 / 16 August 1909, 10: 157, 10 Ağustos 1325 / 23 August 1909; and 16: 253, 21 Eylül 1325 / 4 October 1909, on women swimming and swimming lessons in England. *Resimli İstanbul,* 1: 3, 8 Haziran 1325 / 21 June 1909, also contained a piece on when girls should begin piano lessons.

46. See Allen Warren, "Citizens of the Empire: Baden-Powell, Scouts and Guides and an Imperial Ideal, 1900-1940," 232-257, in John Mackenzie, ed., *Imperialism and Popular Culture.*

47. See Raif Necdet, "The Education of Women," *Resimli kitab,* 5: 439-447, Kanun-ı sani 1324 / January 1909, which is addressed to "The Honored Sisters of the Nation," and which treats of *"terbiye"* (education) in the broad sense of development.

48. Zehra Arat, "Turkish Women and the Republican Reconstruction of Tradition," 57-80, in Müge Göçek and Shiva Balaghi, eds., *Reconstructing Gender in the Middle East* (New York: Columbia University Press, 1994), has pointed out how important the training of girls as model citizens and mothers was to Atatürk's Republican programs. These ideas dated from the nineteenth century and were being tested during the revoutionary era. See also: Akram Khater, "'House' to 'Goddess of the House': Gender, Class, and Silk in Nineteenth Century Mount Lebanon," *International Journal of Middle East Studies* 28 (August 1996): 340, n. 348. On the citizen-mother in Iran, see Afsaneh Najmabadi, "Hazards of Modernity and Morality: Women, State, and Ideology in Contemporary Iran," 663-687, in Hourani, ed., *The Modern Middle East.*

49. Halide Edib Adıvar (1885-1964), *Conflict of East and West in Turkey,* 2nd. ed. (Lahore: S. M. Ashraf, 1935), 261, on governesses for educating young Ottoman girls; also Garnett, *Turkish Life,* 205.

50. Other observers, more rightly, noted that it was French governesses who were considered chic among the elites of the empire. De Leon, *Thirty Years of My Life,* v. 2, 224: "The young girls learn, therefore, to speak and write French and to read French novels. I have known these fine ladies to make no better use of education than to write love letters to European men."

51. Quoted in de Leon, *Thirty Years,* v. 2, 223. This quote is probably a paraphrase, but it illustrates the sentiment all the same.

52. Browne, *The Press and Poetry,* 239-240. On women's education and demand for rights in the Iranian Constitutional Revolutionary period, see Afary, *The Iranian Constitutional Revolution,* 177-208.

53. Edib Adıvar, *Conflict of East and West in Turkey,* 263.

54. Mary Mills Patrick, *Under Five Sultans* (New York: The Century Company, 1929), 203-204.

55. See Nur Bilge Criss, "A Facet of Muslim Womanhood: The Turkish Case," *Turkish Review of Middle East Studies* 7 (1993): 237-257, which contains a very brief (241-243) outline of some of the educational advances for women in the late Ottoman period.

56. Little has been done on this subject of the changing values of wife and mother in the Ottoman context outside of the work of Duben and Behar, *Istanbul Households;* and they do not specifically develop the images of woman in the press, advertising, school texts, and moral literature.

57. *Kalem,* 64: 12, 19 Teşrin-i sani 1325 / 1 December 1909. On the question of European civilization and the transformation of Ottoman society, see Fatma Müge Göçek, *Rise of the Bourgeoisie, Demise of Empire: Ottoman Westernization and Social Change* (New York: Oxford University Press, 1996), 118–127. Göçek looks at consumption, notions of class, and the "new Ottoman social vision," in the nineteenth century.

58. Dumont, "Said Bey," 271–288. See also, on the almanacs of Said Bey, dated 1901–1909, François Georgeon, "Note Sur le Budget d'Une Famille Ottoman au Debut du XXème Siècle," *Revue d'Histoire Maghrebine* 10, no. 31–32 (December 1983): 210–218. Said Bey's monthly income from his various employments was about 9,000 *kuruş* (*piastres*) per month.

59. Dumont, "Said Bey," 284–285.

60. *Karagöz,* 572: 1, 26 Teşrin-i evvel 1329 / 8 November 1913. For a Singer Sewing Machine ad in the Ottoman press, see *Salname-i servet-i fünun* 1326, 2: (ad pages not numbered), published 1327 / 1911. On Singer's markets, see Robert Davies, *Peacefully Working to Conquer the World: Singer Sewing Machines in Foreign Markets, 1854–1920* (New York: Arno Press, 1976), 206–220.

61. Garnett, *Turkish Life,* 30, commented unfavorably on the mixing of traditional and Western furnishings in the Ottoman household. On the availability of Western goods in Middle Eastern capitals, in a somewhat earlier era, see Mary Whately, *Letters from Egypt to Plain Folks at Home* (London: Seeley, Jackson and Halliday, 1876), 156–157, 169, 171–172.

62. Dumont, "Said Bey," 277, 281–283. Georgeon, "Note Sur le Budget," 214–218, includes some of Said Bey's notes on his expenses. He spent considerably on clothing and also purchased newspapers and journals. His domestic and clothing budget dropped to austerity levels in 1909 in response to official restructuring after the revolution. His budget was also constrained by having spent somewhere in the vicinity of 63,000 *piastres* in June 1908 for expenses associated with the marriage of his daughter.

63. On the Bon Marché, see Michael B. Miller, *The Bon Marché: Bourgeois Culture and the Department Store, 1869–1921* (Princeton: Princeton University Press, 1981), who argues that this revolutionary department store "became a bourgeois instrument of social homogenization" (182–183). The Bon Marché created values and then "translated those values into marketable goods" (185). Khater, "'House' to 'Goddess,'" 325–348, notes that by the late nineteenth century in Lebanon, "Even watches and clocks, which were unheard of before, were making an inroad into peasants' pockets and houses" (334).

64. Miller, *The Bon Marché,* 185, makes the point: "It was not simply that clothing styles varied from year to year or that complete changes occurred . . . . There were also entirely new kinds of clothing to fit entirely new kinds of wants." These wants included cycling and automobile clothing.

65. For Galata and Pera scenes and Bon Marché postcards, see Eken, *Kart-*

postallarda İstanbul, 193–197, plates 230, 239, and 251; and Behzat Üskiden, "Beyoğlu'nda Resimli Kartpostal Yayımcıları," *Tarih ve Toplum* 100 (Nisan / April 1992): 27–34.

66. *Dalkavuk,* 17: 2, 25 Kanun-ı evvel 1324 / 7 January 1909. It is entitled *"Parisde Neler Oluyor Etti?"*

67. *Kalem,* 13: 2, 13 Teşrin-i sani 1324 / 26 November 1908. For a discussion of commodity ads and the idea of making female work vanish, see Anne McClintock, *Imperial Leather: Race, Gender and Sexuality in the Colonial Contest* (New York: Routledge, 1995), 222.

68. *Hokkabaz,* 2: 11, 27 Eylül 1324 / 10 October 1908. This announcement went on to advise readers how they could find out the conditions of insertion of such ads (or announcements).

69. Garnett, *Turkish Life,* 29,

70. *Kalem,* 14: 2, 20 Teşrin-i sani 1324 / 3 December 1908 (French lessons), and 7: 10, 2 Teşrin-i evvel 1324 / 15 October 1908.

71. *Alafranga,* 1: 1, 30 Teşrin-i sani 1326 / 13 December 1910.

72. See Metin And, *A History of Theatre and Popular Entertainment in Turkey* (Ankara: Forum Yayınları, 1963–1964), 80. Frierson, "Unimagined Communities," 76, points out that *alafranga* modernity was a major target in the Ottoman women's gazette, *Hanımlara Mahsus Gazete* (1895–1909). Findley, *Bureacratic Reform,* 165–167, 208–211, distinguishes between true "modernists" and those "for whom modernity meant little more than glibness in French and the aping of Parisian manners and fashions" (210). Findley, *Ottoman Civil Officialdom,* 174–210, contains a fairly elaborate discussion of the cultural dualism and intellectual orientations of the Ottoman official class.

73. On "modern" notions of marriage, see *Alem* 12: 14 (French section), 21 Mayıs 1325 / 3 June 1909, reporting on a purported marriage in Chicago at the top of the Auditorium Tower (the couple had to take the elevator to get there). For later satire on "modern" marriage see the gazette *Diken,* published 1918–1920.

74. *Alem,* 2: 15 (French section), 5 Şubat 1324 / 18 February 1909.

75. *Kalem,* 2: 11, 28 Ağustos 1324 / 10 September 1908.

76. *Kalem,* 5: 9, 18 Eylül 1324 / 1 October 1908.

77. *Kalem,* 2: 9–10, 28 Ağustos 1324 / 10 September 1908. The piece ends by noting that copies are available from İzzet Melih, who was a writer and theater critic.

78. Ibid., 9. For a rather different and much more serious version of European civilization and its origins, see *Hikmet,* 3: 3, 22 Nisan 1326 / 5 May 1910.

79. On the Ottoman theater, players, and playwrights, see And, *A History of Theatre,* 65–89. A bibliography of works on Ottoman and Turkish theater can be found in Talat Sait Halman, ed., *Modern Turkish Drama: An Anthology of Plays in Translation* (Minneapolis: Bibliotheca Islamica, 1976). Halman, 28, argues that, "All traditional theater among Turks—peasant plays, court entertainment, shadow plays, *meddah, ortaoyunu*—seems to have been in the comic vein. There is a conscious absence of serious drama, particularly tragedy."

80. Representations of the theater and of Istanbul social life of the time can be found in the works of the famous literary figure and satirist Ahmed Rasim, whose

Şehir Mektubları (İstanbul: Kadır Matbaası, 1328 / 1912), consists of a series of vignettes on life in the city. See also Ahmet Rasim, *Ciddiyet ve Mizah* (Earnestness and Satire) (İstanbul: Kurtiş Matbaası, 1989, reprint of *Cidd ü Mizah*, 1336 / 1920 edition).

81. Halman, *Modern Turkish Drama*, 29–32; see also And, *A History of Theatre*, 66.

82. Halman, *Modern Turkish Drama*, 32. Agop, whose name was Agop Vartovyan, converted to Islam and used the name Yakub. The Gedik Pasha produced a large repertoire of plays in Turkish, and it was at this theater that Namık Kemal's play, *Vatan Yahut Silistre* was produced in 1873. By 1880 the theater was closed. For reminiscences about the Gedik Pasha Theater, and theater and cultural life of the period in general, see Halid Ziya Uşaklıgil, *Kırk Yıl* (İstanbul: Sulhi Garan Matbaası, 1969), 33–34, passim.

83. And, *A History of Theatre*, 68–69, 76. Sultan Abd ül-Hamid also had his own theater, built in 1889, at Yıldız palace. And provides many details on the struggle to monopolize theater in Istanbul and on the processes by which European plays were transformed, often radically, into Turkish language adaptations (often without crediting the originals).

84. Zeyneb Çelik, *The Remaking of Istanbul: Portrait of an Ottoman City in the Nineteenth Century* (Berkeley: University of California Press, 1993), 69–70. Ahmet Rasim frequently mentions the beer-gardens of Istanbul in his works.

85. Halman, *Modern Turkish Drama*, 35–36; And, *A History of Theatre*, 78, 88–89. The Istanbul Municipal Theater was not founded until 1914.

86. See Javadi, *Satire in Persian Literature*, 256–257, 262–263. "The first professional troupe was formed in Tabriz in 1909 and performed a play in honor of Sattar Khan [hero of the revolution] at the Garden of Arg" (262). Molière was popular for Ottoman adaptations; see Halman, *Modern Turkish Drama*, 34.

87. *Çingiraklı Tatar*'s editor, Teodor Kasab, had a running feud with Agop over the attribution of translations and the selection and content of his productions: see And, *A History of Theatre*, 70–72.

88. *Aşiyan*, 2: 225–232, 257–272, 289–297 (published 28 Ağustos 1324 / 10 September 1908 to 27 Şubat 1325 / 12 March 1909); 10: beginning 290, 6 Teşrin-i sani 1324 / 19 November 1908, also serialized a play by Huseyin Saad, "*Şehbal Yahud İstibdadın Son Perdeyi*" (*Şehbal*, or Despotism's Last Act). *Şehbal* means pinion feather, but it could also refer to the wealth of the ruler. Theater announcements can also be found in other gazettes, like *Millet*, published daily August–October 1908. There is an ad in *Şark*, 6: 4, 12 Ağustos 1324 / 25 August 1908, mentioning *Vatan* by Namık Kemal, "arranged by the "*Osmanlı Kadınları Cemiyet-i İttihadiye*" (Ottoman Women's Unity Society).

89. *Aşiyan*, 4: 117–120 (approximately 19 Eylül 1324 / 2 October 1908). See also *Serbesti*, 8: 4, 11 Teşrin-i sani 1324 / 24 November 1908, on "Our Theatres," and the idea of a national theater.

90. Sarah Bernhardt gave numerous performances in Istanbul in 1888; see Halman, *Modern Turkish Drama*, 33. *Muhit*, 4: 49, 13 Teşrin-i sani 1324 / 26 November 1908, published a photo of Bernhardt in the role of "l'Aiglon." *Eşref* (published 1325–1328 /1909–1912) featured pictures of actresses in its later issues; and *Kalem*,

Notes to Page 207

13: 12–13, 13 Teşrin-i sani 1324 / 26 November 1908, has a piece on Bernhardt. *Piyano*, 11: 117–120, 25 Teşrin-i evvel 1326 / 7 November 1910, included photographs of actors and artistes, and articles on the theater by Kemal Emin. See *Alem*, 1: 12 (French section), 29 Kanun-ı sani 1324 / 11 February 1909, for a humorous theater and entertainment report.

91. For a reference to "*Vatan*" (glossed as "*Patrie*" in French), and the theater, see *Kalem*, 6: 10, 25 Eylül 1324 / 8 October 1908. The revamping of the Ottoman theater in the prerevolutionary and revolutionary periods echoes a similar theatrical revolution in France's prerevolutionary and revolutionary periods, a revamping in which journalists played an active role. See, for example, Gelbart, *Feminine and Opposition Journalism*, 208–212, 297–298, on the role of *frondeur* journalists in promoting theatrical evolution and their approval "of *drames* as instruments of propaganda, as weapons in the fight for greater freedom." For the revamping of Russian theater and its perceived role in uplifting the masses, see Richard Stites, *Russian Popular Culture: Entertainment and Society since 1900* (Cambridge: Cambridge University Press, 1992), 17–22; the first "native feature" was shown in 1908 (28).

92. *Kalem*, 4: 11, 11 Eylül 1324 / 24 September 1908.

93. *Hokkabaz*, 2: 15, 27 Eylül 1324 / 10 October 1908.

94. *Züğürt*, 5: 4, [16] Mart 1327 / [29] March 1911; see also 6: 2, [19] Mart 1327 / [1] April 1911.

95. *Resimli kitab*, 6: 581, Mart 1325 / March 1909. Üsküb, or Skoplje is a town in Macedonia, on the Vardar River, south-southeast of Belgrade.

96. *Resimli kitab*, 6: 582–597, Mart 1325 / March 1909. See also on the roles (and funeral of one of) the Coquelins, Aîné, *Muhit* 16: 248, 12 Şubat 1324 / 25 February 1909, and 15: 232, 5 Şubat 1324 / 18 February 1909. The Ottomans, of course, had their own comic tradition. See the photo of Abdi Efendi, "celebrated Turkish comic," in *Devr-i cedid* (New Era), 9: 141, Haziran 1325 / June 1909. For Ottoman cartoons of comic and Karagöz performances, see François Georgeon, "Rire dans l'Empire ottoman?," *Revue du Monde Musulman et de la Méditerranée* 77–78 (1996): 89–110.

97. *Resimli kitab*, 7: 699–703, Nisan 1325 / April 1909. "*Edebiyat*" can also refer to philology, and the arrangement of language.

98. *Resimli kitab*, 5: 477, Kanun-ı sani 1324 / January 1909. This tragedy in verse, *Eşber*, by Abd ül-Hak Hamid Tarhan (1852–1937) was first published in 1881. See Abdülhak Hamid Tarhan, *Eşber: Manzum Bir Facia-yı Tarihiyedir* (İstanbul: Halk Kütüphanesi, 1922); and I. H. Danişmend, ed. *Abdülhak Hamit Külliyatı*, v. 3 (İstanbul: Kanaat, 1945). Thanks for these references to Irvin Schick and Andras Riedlmayer. Edib Adıvar, *Conflict of East and West in Turkey*, 261, suggests that, "In the tragedies of Abdul Hak Hamid, especially, women are given a most important part. His saying that 'The measure of a people's civilization is the standard of their women,' is the motto of the Women's Training College now."

99. *Kalem*, 7: 13, 2 Teşrin-i evvel 1324 / 15 October 1908. There was nothing unusual about a satirical gazette serving the role of cultural critic. On the English satrical gazette, *Punch's*, vigorous theater critcism, see Graves, *Mr. Punch's History of Modern England*, 290–299. *Punch*, like *Kalem*, critiqued not only the performances but

the social, moral, and economic implications of individual pieces and of the theater and music halls in general.

100. *Alem,* 10: 5, 7 Mayıs 1325 / 20 May 1909. *Alem*'s publication was interrupted in the immediate aftermath of the spring 1909 counter-revolution; it ceased altogether after issue twelve. For pictures of Burhan üd-Din, his company, and "Susan Hanım, the premier actress of his company," see *Piyano,* 9, 11 Teşrin-i evvel 1326 / 24 October 1910; and *Muhit,* 18: 281, 26 Şubat 1324 / 11 March 1909, and 3: 33, 6 Teşrin-i sani 1324 / 19 November 1908. For a dialogue scene, entitled "The Return," written by Burhan üd-Din, and a photo of the author, see *Resimli kitab,* 2: 177–179, Teşrin-i evvel 1324 / October 1908; also 1: 66, 87; 2: 177; 3: 232.

101. *Züğürt,* 1: 4, 1 Mart 1327 / 14 March 1911.

102. *Resimli kitab,* 9: 907, Haziran 1325 / June 1909.

103. And, *A History of Theatre,* 69, 74, 84, mentions several theater improvement committees and devotee societies.

104. *Davul,* 14: 4, 28 Kanun-ı sani 1324 / 10 February 1909.

105. *Züğürt,* 4: 4, 12 Mart 1327 / 25 March 1911. I do not have further information on this company. The frame is labeled, "in the theater of Behran Altın (or Altıyan) [sic] Bey."

106. See *Alem* 5: 8 (French section), 26 Şubat 1324 / 11 March 1909, for a cartoon playing on the masks of theater hiding the realities beneath.

107. *Nekregû ile Pişekar,* published June–July 1909.

108. *Boşboğaz,* 19: 4, 29 Eylül 1324 / 12 October 1908.

109. *Falaka,* 16 : 1, [15] Eylül 1327 / [28] September 1911.

110. *Davul,* 7: 10, 26 Teşrin-i sani 1324 / 9 December 1909, and 17: 13, 12 Şubat 1324 / 25 February 1909. The stage and setting is the same in both cartoons. The medallion over the stage reads "Balkan . . ." (the rest of the inscription is unreadable).

111. *Dalkavuk,* 17: 8, [25] Kanun-ı evvel 1324 / [7] January 1909 .

112. *Kalem,* 9: 16, 13 Teşrin-i evvel 1324 / 29 October 1908.

113. *Kalem,* 66: 16, 3 Kanun-ı evvel 1325 / 16 December 1909..

114. Henri Bataille (1872–1922), *La femme nue, piece en quatre actes,* (Paris: L'Illustration, 1908), un-numbered introductory page. The play, a treatment of infidelity, focuses on the themes of being natural and free. As Bataille explained his title: "*C'est le nu, non point obscène ou déchu, c'est le nu grave et sacré. Le titre est même triplement métaphorique, car il fautencore ajouter à l'inconsciente héroïne, qui traverse ma pièce, cette nudité primitive et originelle d'une âme riche seulement de son instinct, sans autre parure que cette mystériuse et précaire beauté.*" The play received rave reviews.

115. Loren Krueger, "Attending (to) the National Spectacle: Instituting National (Popular) Theatre in England and France," 243–265, in Jonathan Arac and Harriet Ritvo, eds., *Macropolitics of Nineteenth-Century Literature: Nationalism, Exoticism, Imperialism* (Philadelphia: University of Pennsylvania Press, 1991), comments on the realities and expectations in France and England for popular theater constituting the nation.

116. *Kalem,* 17: 8, 12 Kanun-ı evvel 1324 / 25 December 1908.

117. United States Foreign Tariff Notes, Department of Commerce, Bureau of

Foreign and Domestic Commerce, *Daily Consular and Trade Reports,* no 3683, 12–13, January 12, 1910. Consul John H. Grout, in the same report, notes that the roller skating craze, "which has been rapidly spreading over various parts of Western Europe," had finally reached Odessa in Russia.

118. *Kalem,* 100: 11, 21 Teşrin-i evvel 1326 / 3 November 1910, advertised an Ottoman "Cinema Orientaux," located at 164, Grand Rue de Péra, in Istanbul, in 1910. The cinema would show "sensational events, the Portuguese revolution, William II at Brussels, art films."

119. Tugay, *Three Centuries,* 176–277. Tugay was a member of the Khedival family; her father supported the cinema-skating rink proposal. Her mother bought up all the tickets for the first ladies' performance to avoid public criticism. Emine and her brothers received private skating lessons at home from the rink's owner. The concession for the rink and cinema was later canceled. See also Pierre Teilhard de Chardin, *Letters from Egypt 1905–1908* (New York: Herder and Herder, 1965), 229–230, which narrates a film screening in Cairo by the Jesuits in 1908 with a second screening given to "an assembly of ladies or women (mainly Syrian) who came, of course, with their whole families."

120. *Resimli kitab,* 7: 702, Nisan 1325 / April 1909, shows a photo of another variant of skating, a man ice-skating on a lake or river using a hand-held sail. De Chardin, *Letters,* 246, notes that roller skating was also "all the rage" in Cairo in 1908.

121. *Kalem,* 53: 15, 3 Eylül 1325 / 16 September 1909.

122. *Kalem,* 109: 10, 6 Kanun-ı sani, 1326 / 19 January 1911. For a 1909 image of the fashionable woman and ice-skating in the European context, see Max von Boehn and Oskar Fischel, *Modes and Manners of the Nineteenth Century as Represented in the Pictures and Engravings of the Time,* v. 3, *1843–1875* (London: J. M. Dent and Co., 1909), 114.

123. *Kalem,* 102: 3, 4 Teşrin-i sani 1326 / 17 November 1910.

124. These images suggest that boundaries were being crossed; but they also suggest the fear and humor directed at the *possibility* that such boundaries might be crossed. See Mardin, "Super Westernization," 404–446, on the depiction of boundary-crossing behavior in Ottoman novels as a form of social control. De Leon, *Thirty Years,* v. 2, 217–218, in a chapter written by Mrs. De Leon, notes that one of the Egyptian princesses remarked on foreign women riding spirited horses and "conversing with men in public with uncovered faces. Doubtless she thought both actions highly improper, although too polite to say so."

125. *Yeni geveze,* 99: 4, 2 Kanun-ı evvel 1326 / 15 December 1910.

126. *Kalem,* 70: 7, 31 Kanun-ı evvel 1325 / 13 January 1910. Carter Findley, *Ottoman Civil Officialdom,* 195–209, has pointed out the great expectations awakened by the Grand Vezirate of Hakkı Pasha.

127. Arthur Conan Doyle, *The History of Spiritualism,* 2 vols, (New York: George H. Doran Co., 1926, 1): vii. The spiritualist movement created considerable debate in the scientific community in the United States and England. Doyle, who was President of the London Spiritualist Alliance and President of the British College of Psychic Science, cites the "brave" work of Professor Hare on spiritualism and

deplores the response to that work: "The professors at Harvard—a university which has a most unenviable record in psychic matters—passed a resolution denouncing him and his 'insane adherence to a gigantic humbug' " (137).

128. On the phenonmenon of spiritualism, see, for example, Alex Owen, *The Darkened Room: Women, Power and Spiritualism in Late Victorian England* (Philadelphia: University of Pennsylvania Press, 1990); and Ann Braude, *Radical Spirits: Spiritualism and Women's Rights in Nineteenth Century America* (Boston: Beacon Press, 1989).

129. Colin Imber, "Ideals and Legitimation in Early Ottoman History," 138–153, in Metin Kunt and Christine Woodhead, eds. *Süleyman the Magnificent and His Age* (London: Longman, 1995), especially 141–142, 148; and Robert Dankoff, *The Intimate Life of an Ottoman Statesman: Melek Ahmed Pasha (1588–1662) as Portrayed in Evliya Çelebi's Book of Travels (Seyahat-name)* (Albany: State University of New York Press, 1991). Dreams and their interpretation have a significant and continuing role in Evliya's story here as they do in other Ottoman literature and in earlier Turkish literature. See Faruk Sumer, trans., *The Book of Dede Korkut* (Austin: University of Texas Press, 1972). See also Toledano, *State and Society*, 235–237, on fortune telling and the occult in nineteenth-century Ottoman Egypt. See And, *A History of Theatre and Popular Culture*, 35–36, on the Karagöz dream devices. There is a distinct link between shadow puppetry and spirit communication. Ruud Spruit, *The Land of the Sultans: An Illustrated History of Malaysia* (Amsterdam: The Pepin Press, 1995), 34, notes that in carly Malaysian shadow plays, "The silhouettes represent the ancestors who are summoned by the *dalang* (puppeteer), who acts as a medium between mortals and gods."

130. This was the sufi, Aşçı Dede, as related in Findley, *Ottoman Civil Officialdom*, 234.

131. Graves, *Mr. Punch's History of Modern England*, 202–206.

132. Edib Adıvar, *Conflict of East and West*, 280. The above quote is taken from a discussion that focuses primarily on mysticism and sufism in the East.

133. *Cadaloz*, 1: 3, 22 Mart 1327 / 4 April 1911, and 2: 3, 26 Mart 1327 / 8 April 1911.

134. *Diken*, 6: 1, 9 Kanun-ı sani 1335 / 22 January 1920.

135. *Hande*, 1: 6, 22 Mart 1326 / 4 April 1910 (those put out of work were called *kadro haric*); see also *Züğürt*, 8: 1, 19 Nisan 1327 / 2 May 1911.

136. *Yeni geveze*, 3: 4, 8 Mart 1326 / 21 March 1910, and 121: 1, 14 Şubat 1326 / 27 February 1911.

Chapter VIII. Fashion Satire and the Honor of the Nation

1. Richard Rogers and Oscar Hammerstein, "Western People Funny," 115–116, from the vocal score for "The King and I," (New York: Williamson Music, 1952). This lyric predated Edward Said's *Orientalism* by quite a few years.

2. Chic Bey was found in various cartoons and in various forms, see: *Cadaloz*, 14: 4, 3 Mayıs 1327 / 16 May 1911. The gazette *Lâla* (published December 1910–January 1911), shows him as a dandy with fez, cane, and glasses. He is found in the form of

Notes to Pages 221–223

Zarifi Çelebi (Mr. Elegant) in a dialogue in *Nekregû*, 1: 1, 18 Ağustos 1324 / 31 August 1908. Mardin, "Super Westernization in Urban Life in the Ottoman Empire," 404–446, discusses at length the idea of the Westernized dandy (the "Bihruz Bey syndrome") in Ottoman literature and its social and political contexts. There was a novel by Hüseyin Rahmi Gürpınar, entitled *Şik* (Chic), published in 1887. See Deniz Kandiyoti, "Slave Girls, Temptresses, and Comrades: Images of Women in the Turkish Novel," *Feminist Issues* 8 (Spring 1988): 35–50. Kandiyoti notes that *Şik*, "is in the familiar mold of burlesque depictions of the Western-struck male" (42).

3. Chic Bey can be considered, in part, a print version of the shadow puppet character, the dandy or *Çelebi*. See Andreas Tietze, *The Turkish Shadow Theatre and the Puppet Collection of the L.A. Mayer Memorial Foundation*, The L.A. Mayer Memorial Studies in Islamic Art and Civilization, v. 4 (Berlin: Gebr. Mann Verlag: 1977), plates 7–11; and And, *Karagöz*, 71. For the figure of the dandy in another type of oral tradition, the minstrel show, see Eric Lott, *Love and Theft: Blackface Minstrelsy and the American Working Class* (Oxford: Oxford University Press, 1993), 25; like the dandy in the Karagöz theater, this dandy was directly associated with sexual themes. Chic Bey also looked very much like a similar character, "The Modern Patriot," found in the Indian press; see Abu Abraham, *The Penguin Book of Indian Cartoons* (New Delhi: Penguin Books, 1988), xvii. See also Williams, *Dream Worlds*, 107–153, which discusses the notion of dandyism and its link to critiques of class, manners, luxury and consumption in Europe, especially France.

4. For one example, see *Yeni geveze*, 78: 4, 18 Teşrin-i sani 1326 / 1 December 1910, in which one of the gazette's mascots mocks the other's dressing up and fashionable strolling.

5. David Nokes, *Raillery and Rage*, 17, suggests, regarding English satire: "yet on closer investigation there is reason to suggest that satire tends to be an instrument not for change but for grumbling acquiescence by allowing anger and indignation to vent themselves in laughter rather than build into action, satire may be a substitute for, not a summons to revolution." Other analysts argue that newspaper satire took an active role in prompting revolutionary action, for example Press, *The Political Cartoon*, 11–12, 51.

6. In fact, the confusion between a "progressive" and a "traditional" image of political authority is demonstrated by the names of two of the sultan's boats in 1909: "*Ertuğrul*," for the mythical Turkish tribal hero, and "*Hürriyet*," for freedom. *Resimli kitab*, 9: 950, Haziran 1325 / June 1909, (*Ertuğrul*); and 11: 1112, Ağustos 1325 / August 1909, (*Hürriyet*).

7. Lewis, *The Emergence of Modern Turkey*, 187–194; and Berkes, *The Development of Secularism in Turkey*, 296–304.

8. See Donald Quataert, *Social Disintegration and Popular Resistance in the Ottoman Empire 1881–1908: Reactions to European Economic Penetration* (New York: New York University Press, 1983), 116–142.

9. See Javadi, *Satire in Persian Literature*, 264–265, on modern Persian literature using a French poodle as a symbol of the dandified Iranian returning from Europe minus his identity.

10. Roland Barthes, *The Fashion System* (New York: Hill and Wang, 1983), 27–28, 59–61, 156–163, 230–267, has proposed a method for "reading" fashion based on the compound nature of the fashion message. Barthes notes the rhetorical construction of meaning in fashion and the divergences between meaning and function: "the cultural object possesses, by its social nature, a sort of semantic vocation: in itself, the sign is quite ready to separate itself from the function and operate freely on its own, the function being reduced to the rank of artifice or alibi: the ten gallon hat (rainproof, sunproof) is nothing more than a sign of what is 'Western' " (265). See also, Joanne Finkelstein, *The Fashioned Self* (Cambridge: Polity Press, 1991), on the valuing of appearance in history and the conceptualization of self.

11. Davison, *Essays in Ottoman Turkish History*, 91, "though European manners and Parisian modes came to Istanbul via the Levantines during the Crimean War via an influx of Europeans, free spending members of the Egyptian ruling family were exemplifying such fashions in Istanbul at an early date."

12. In her husband's book, De Leon, *Thirty Years*, v. 2, 211–222, Mrs. De Leon described the European fashions and affectations of the Khedival women in the nineteenth century.

13. See Aileen Ribeiro, *Fashion in the French Revolution* (New York: Holmes and Meier, 1988), 68, 134, on the French monarchists.

14. For some examples of nineteenth-century Prussian fashion satire and how it was censored, see Townsend, *Forbidden Laughter*, 88–89.

15. Another was *Hayal*, published 1289–1293 / 1873–1877. For an early treatment of the evolution of women's fashion and Western influence in the empire, from the Tanzimat to World War I, see Muhaddere Taşcıoğlu, *Türk Osmanlı Cemiyetinde Kadının Sosyal Durumu ve Kadın Kıyafetleri* (Ankara: Akın Matbaası, 1958), 26–54. See on nineteenth century satire of Ottoman women: Nora Şeni, "19. Yüzyıl Sonunda İstanbul Mizah Basınında Moda ve Kadın Kıyafetleri," in Şirin Tekeli, ed. *Kadın Bakış Açısından 1980'ler Türkiye'sinde Kadınlar* (İstanbul: İletişim, 1990), 43–68.

16. *Çıngıraklı Tatar*, 1: 3, 24 Mart 1289 / 6 April 1873.

17. *Çıngıraklı Tatar*, 13: 3, 9 Mayıs 1289 / 22 May 1873. *Diken*, 8: 7, 6 Şubat 1919 / 19 February 1919, takes another view of this same question in a cartoon satirizing a police commissioner's decision on veiling. It shows a policeman correcting a woman for showing her ankles.

18. *Çıngıraklı Tatar*, 19: 3, 30 Mayıs 1289 / 12 June 1873.

19. *Çıngıraklı Tatar*, 2: 3, 28 Mart 1289 / 10 April 1873.

20. *Çıngıraklı Tatar*, 6: 3, 14 Nisan 1289 / 27 April 1873.

21. Mark Twain, *Innocents Abroad or the New Pilgrim's Progress* (New York: Harper and Brothers, 1911), 67. The original was published in 1869.

22. Twain, *Innocents Abroad*, 68. This observation, however overstated, suggests that relatively full veiling, complete with the semi-see-through veil, was the most common dress style for women in mid-nineteenth-century Istanbul. Of course, it could mean that these were merely the most compelling images upon which Twain could focus his prose. In any case, the association of veiled woman with ghosts is one that later-day women writers have used to characterize the oppressive nature of the veil.

23. See *Kalem*, 2: 11, 28 Ağustos 1324 / 10 September 1908, for a poem by Ali Sami, in French, mocking an Ottoman whose associate accuses him of being occidentalized.

24. The Iranian writer, Jalâl Al-e Ahmad (1923–1969), *Gharbzadegi* = *(Weststruckness)* (Lexington, Kentucky: Mazda Publishers, 1982), wrote a 1950's satire accusing the Middle East of "Westoxication," following a satirical tradition of portraying Westernization as analogous to catching an infectious disease.

25. Nancy Micklewright, "Woman's Dress in Nineteenth Century Istanbul: Mirror of a Changing Society," (Ph.D. dissertation, History of Art, University of Pennsylvania, 1986), 155–205; Tugay, *Three Centuries,* 222. Tugay was a member of an Ottoman pasha and Egyptian royal-family-linked household: "Our clothes, made in the current French fashion, were rather fussy."

26. Tugay, *Three Centuries,* 206. Flimsy *yaşmak* veils were no impediment to the flirtations conducted in the park and from small boats on the Bosphorus. For one elite Ottoman woman's memories of the first *veiling* and her resistance to it as fashions changed, see Ekrem, *Unveiled,* 178–181, 267–268.

27. See Micklewright, "Women's Dress," 203–205, on fashion papers; there were advertisements in many gazettes for Pera clothing shops. See *Salname-i servet-i fünun* 1326 2: 124–125, published 1327 / 1911, for sketches of the year's Paris fashions; and *Resimli İstanbul,* 4: 62, 29 Haziran 1325 / 12 July 1909, on the latest English fashions for women. Ribiero, *Fashion in the French Revolution,* 20, notes that, in France, high quality fashion magazines emerged in the prerevolutionary decade of the 1780s, educating their readers in fashion and politics, "albeit—with regards to the latter—in a somewhat simplified form."

28. *Karagöz salnamesi,* v. 1, 1326 / 1910. Tight sleeves were also the subject of humor, as in a cartoon in *Geveze,* 29: 4, 12 Şubat 1324 / 25 February 1909, which compared fashions in women's sleeves to the bandages on a broken arm.

29. *Resimli kitab,* 1: 79, Eylül 1324 / September 1908, and 3: 202–212, Teşrin-i evvel 1324 / October 1908, on promenading, social life, and freedom. This same notion was reflected in *Diken,* 23: 5, 18 Eylül 1335/ 1 October 1919, in a frame that purports to show the "history of flirting," beginning with the Janissary era when men could only dream of seeing women, to the "pre-constitutional period," when discreet flirtations could take place with veiled ladies, to the post-revolutionary period when a man could stand in the street speaking to a woman behind a latice, to the "present" (1919), when fashionably dressed men and women promenaded openly, arm in arm, on the street.

30. *Lâklâk,* 6: 4, 13 Ağustos 1325 / 26 August 1909. For some other cartoons of women in traditional dress, see *Lâklâk,* 10: 4, 3 Eylül 1325 / 16 September 1909, and 9: 3 Eylül 1325 / 16 September 1909 (date misprinted).

31. Rambert, *Notes et Impressions de Turquie,* 279. See also Lucy Garnett, *Turkish Life in Town and Country* (New York: G.P. Putnam's Sons, 1904), 95: "The reason for this separation of the sexes out-of-doors is sufficiently obvious; for a father or brother could not frequent the public promenades in company with his womenkind without bringing them directly under the notice of his men acquaintances, and thus infringing the fundamental principle of the harem system." *Ontari* is actually *antari;* and *feridje* is *ferace*.

32. Garnett, *Turkish Life*, 102–104.

33. Edib Adıvar, *The Conflict of East and West in Turkey*, 260. See also, Leila Ahmed, *Women and Gender in Islam: The Historical Roots of a Modern Debate* (New Haven: Yale Unviersity Press, 1992), 152–164, on unveiling and women's place.

34. Satirization of women's extravagance in dress was a well-worn standard of English and French satirical gazettes. See, for example, von Boehn and Fischel, *Modes and Manners*, v. 3; Graves, *Mr. Punch's History*, v. 2, *1857–1874*, 320–338; and Ribeiro, *Fashion in the French Revolution*.

35. On the theme of women as "consumers whose natural fickleness and extravagance ensured an insatiable appetite and market for costumes, decorations and embellishments," see Gelbart, *Feminine and Opposition Journalism in Old Regime France*, 299. See also, M. H. Spielman, *The History of 'Punch,'* 483.

36. Von Boehn and Fischel, *Modes and Manners*, v. 3, 67, 81, 94–98. The Empress Eugenie, for example, went through "ethnic" styles like the Arab burnoose faster than her admirers could keep up. The *New York Times* of October 13, 1898, remarked on the German empress's impressive baggage train on the Kaiser's trip to Jerusalem: noted in Amy Landis, "The Kaiser Visits the 'Holy Land': Perceptions and Representations," 7, unpublished paper, 1995.

37. G. Armytage, "Modern Dress," *Fortnightly Review*, 34 n.s. (July 1–December 1, 1883): 344–353, especially 346.

38. In *Kalem*, 89: 6, 5 Ağustos 1326 / 18 August 1910, hats are compared to umbrellas and, 90: 14, 12 Ağustos 1326 / 25 August 1910, to *simit* sellers' trays. In *Kalem* 53: 6, 3 Eylül 1325 / 16 September 1909, the fish monger says, "The women do not resemble us but they copied their styles from us." See also, for hat satire, *Kalem*, 64: 12; 90: 14; 96: 8; 109: 12. Men were the targets of fashion satire: *Falaka*, 10: 1 (male), 26 Ağustos 1327 / 8 September 1911, and 3: 4 (female), 1 Ağustos 1327 / 14 August 1911. In English satire, see Graves, *Punch*, v. 2, 327; *Punch* compares an overloaded laborer to a woman with a gigantic hairdo. *Lâklâk*, 3: 3, 23 Temmuz 1325 / 5 August 1909, juxtaposed a veiled woman and European "madames," in a spoof on how women's dragging skirts cleaned the streets.

39. *Kalem*, 126: 12, 12 Mayıs 1327 / May 25, 1911.

40. *Kalem*, 125: 14, 5 Mayıs 1327 / 18 May 1911 and 64: 15, 19 Teşrin-i sani 1325 / 2 December 1909. For a postcard image of young Ottoman girls at the loom, see Eken, *Kartpostallarda İstanbul*, 226.

41. On Ottoman women and the textile industry, see Quataert, "Ottoman Women, Households, and Textile Manufacturing," 161–176.

42. Tugay, *Three Centuries*, 275–276.

43. On child-labor in Ottoman factories, see Quataert, "The Age of Reforms," 904.

44. On the consumption and marketing of goods in Paris and on the consumption of elite-type goods by the lower classes, see Cissie Fairchilds, "The Production and Marketing of Populuxe Goods in Eighteenth-Century Paris," 228–248, in Brewer and Porter, *Consumption and the World of Goods*. Fairchilds traces (e.g., 230, 235–239), the consumption of such goods as watches, pets, umbrellas, canes, and stockings. All of these goods were used to identify European-style fashion in the Ottoman cartoon space.

45. Ottoman gazettes are full of ads for European and American products that are equated with the fashionable, the progressive, and the modern. American made timepieces, for example, were advertised, "for 80 kuruş, from the most famous American factories," in *Serbesti*, 144: 4, 28 Mart 1325 / 10 April 1909. *Reklâm* (or *Reclame*, a supplement to the gazette *Piyano*), 1: 2–3, 1326 / 1910, featured a two-page ad for watches and clocks of Swiss, American, and German make. Shaw, *History of the Ottoman Empire*, 238, notes that watches, at 7 million kuruş worth per year, in 1897, were a major Ottoman import. Watches were a primary Western trade good well before 1908; Göçek, *Rise of the Bourgeoisie*, 106–107, notes clocks and watches (some extremely valuable) as one of the most common kinds of Western good found in eighteenth-century Ottoman inheritance records.

46. *Kalem*, 115: 6, 17 Şubat 1326 / 2 March 1911; the French caption says ten instead of twenty. See also *Kalem*, 114: 10, 10 Şubat 1326 / 23 February 1911, for a cartoon lampooning an *alafranga* woman who shows up at a ball shortly after her husband dies rather than staying home in mourning.

47. Ribeiro, *Dress and Morality*, quotes the 1931 publication, "Modest Apparel," as follows, "Suggestive dress means in the end the ruin of a people" (146). Ribeiro also cites the 1906 work of a Jesuit, Father Bernard Vaughan, entitled *The Sins of Society*, which, "castigated those in the 'Smart Set,' whose craving for sports, pleasures, travel and immodest dress indicated a reversal to paganism" (146).

48. Images of states embodied as women continued in the Ottoman press after the fall of the empire, as illustrated on the cover of *Papağan*, 38: 1, 7 Kanun-ı sani 1341 / 20 January 1925, where the female is the object of a lustful "Red" Russia. For other images of rape and empire, see Sam Keen, *Faces of the Enemy: Reflections of the Hostile Imagination* (San Francisco: Harper and Row, 1986), 58–64, 76–79.

49. For example, the Ottoman poet, Fazıl Bey (ca. 1757–1810), who wrote a "Book of Women," describing the women of about forty different races and regions; see Bernard Lewis, *Race and Slavery in the Middle East: An Historical Enquiry* (New York: Oxford University Press, 1990), 93.

50. Elias J. W. Gibb, *Ottoman Literature* (New York: M. Walter Dunne, 1901), frontspiece.

51. *Kalem*, 92: 10, 26 Ağustos 1326 / 8 September 1910. Findley, *Ottoman Civil Officialdom*, 224, points out that Abd ül-Hamid had forbidden Muslim dependents to accompany Ottoman ambassadors abroad; "This prohibition may have increased the frequency of marriages—and less formal liaisons—between Ottoman diplomats and foreign ladies, some of them unsuitable choices, with the result that a decree issued after the 1908 revolution required all Foreign Ministry officials to obtain approval from the ministry for their marriages."

52. Ahmad, *The Young Turks*, 76–81, discusses these financial negotiations. Cavid Bey, the finance minister, had just returned from Paris when this cartoon was printed, but the figure in the cartoon cannot be Cavid who was thin. Hakkı Pasha was in France at the time, but this cartoon figure does not closely resemble his usual caricatures either. It seems, rather, to be a generic "Young Turk."

53. *Kalem*, 100: 10, 21 Teşrin-i evvel 1326 / 3 December 1910. "Xenophobic" has other connotations than what is said here, literally "enemy of foreigners," or "anti-

foreign," but it does express the notion of hostility to people and things non-Ottoman. This cartoon looks like a bit of ink may have been added to obscure the exact position of the "gentleman's" hand beneath the "lady's" breast.

54. Such themes were also reflected in the novels of the late Ottoman period, as suggested by Deniz Kandiyoti, "Slave Girls, Temptresses," 42. Kandiyoti mentions the novel *Mürebbiye* (The Governess) by Hüseyin Rahmi (Gürpınar), published in 1898, "where the importation of Mlle Angèle, a French governess, for the sake of fashion, into a traditional Ottoman household results in a farcical denoument where family honor and propriety are totally compromised." The eroticization of the West, the Ottoman dandy, and the old/new (father/son) cultural struggle in Ottoman novels is also addressed in Jale Parla, *Babalar ve Oğullar: Tanzimat Romanının Epistemolojik Temelleri* (İstanbul: n.p. 1991). A Moroccan diplomat in mid-nineteenth-century Paris, remarking on the fashions and (corset induced) figures of the Parisian women, suggested they were almost irresistable: "If one of them is close to you, you are seized with the desire to grab her by the waist." See aṣ-Ṣaffār, *Disorienting Encounters*, 182–183. See also, Mohamad Tavakoli-Targhi, "The Persian Gaze and Women of the Occident," *South Asia Bulletin* 11, nos. 1–2 (1991), 21–31.

55. *Kalem*, 8: 10, 9 Teşrin-i evvel 1324 / 22 October 1908.

56. The idea of *vatan* was more often personified as a motherland than a fatherland in the cartoon space. Although one might argue that *vatan* is gendered female in Ottoman Turkish, the Arabic *waṭan* from which it derives is often glossed fatherland. James W. Redhouse, *A Turkish and English Lexicon* (Beirut: Librairie du Liban, 1974 reprint), 2141, does not gender *vatan*, choosing the gender neutral translation "homeland."

57. See the sick mother constitution (*Kanun-ı esasî*) in *Kalem*, 76: 5, 18 Şubat 1325 / 2 March 1910.

58. *Kalem*, 23: 8–9, 22 Kanun-ı sani 1324 / 4 February 1909. The slave merchant figure, here, might be Hüseyin Hilmi Pasha, a significant Ottoman political figure who became grand vezir later that February, but I am not sure it is he. For a photo of Hilmi Pasha, "the new Grand Vezir," see *Muhit*, 15: 225, 5 Şubat 1324 / 18 February 1909. For a treatment of this question of the challenge to male sexual and national honor posed by imperialist aggression and unjust rule in Iran at this same time, see Afsaneh Najmabadi, "Zanhā-yi Millat: Women or Wives of the Nation?" *Iranian Studies* 26 (Winter–Spring 1993): 51–71; and "The Erotic Vatan [Homeland] as Beloved and Mother: To Love, to Possess, and To Protect," *Comparative Studies in Society and History* 39, no. 3 (July 1997): 442–467.

59. For studies on nationalism and sexuality that discuss the equation of the land or territory with the female body, see Andrew Parker et. al., eds., *Nationalisms and Sexualities* (New York: Routledge, 1992).

60. *Kalem*, 52: 8, 27 Ağustos 1325/ 9 September 1909. I have translated "*bu sefer*" here as "this time." But "*sefer*" also carries the meanings of stage (of an endeavor) or campaign, both of which would also be appropriate here. I cannot be absolutely positive that the third figure is France, it could be Greece. Also on the struggle for Crete, see *Malum*, 4: 1, 19 Kanun-ı evvel 1326 / 1 January 1911. The Powers had withdrawn their troops from Crete in July 1909, basically signaling the end of any

pretense at protecting Ottoman "rights," on the island; see Marriott, *The Eastern Question*, 370–371.

61. *Nekregû ile Pişekar*, 3: 1, 3 Haziran 1325 / 16 June 1909. Much has been written on colonial rape imagery, especially for the Indian Subcontinent. Of particular interest here, because it focuses on fiction thus suggesting the analogies between the genres of satire and fiction, is Jenny Sharpe, *Allegories of Empire: The Figure of Woman in the Colonial Text* (Minneapolis: University of Minnesota, 1993). Sharpe notes the recombinant nature of "colonial" rape imagery that, as is the case with Ottoman satire, employs allegories from both European and Asian contexts.

62. *Kalem*, 10: 7, 23 Teşrin-i sani 1324 / 6 November 1908. Their positioning, poised at the gateway, also suggests a violation of the boundary between the public and domestic spheres. Austria is a stranger, encouraging them to leave the "sacred" precincts of their domicile or to violate the "sacred" trust of loyalty to the nation. A similar cartoon, *Kalem*, 22: 4, 15 Kanun-ı sani 1324 / 28 January 1909, shows Bosnia and Herzegovina as counterparts to Alsace and Lorraine, all as female bodies representing contested territory.

63. See Shaw, *History of the Ottoman Empire*, 191–196, 206–207, 276–277; Marriott, *The Eastern Question*, 307–340, 370–380.

64. Quoted in And, *A History of Theatre*, 37–38.

65. *Kalem*, 94: 7, 9 Eylül 1326 / 22 September 1910.

66. Kandiyoti, "Slave Girls, Tempresses," 38, 45, mentions just such a dichotomy in the late Ottoman novel where, "women came to occupy a privileged place as the bearers of potential moral decay or, on the contrary, national redemption." Female figures could also be used to represent European imperial ambitions, even though, in Ottoman cartoons, European states were customarily gendered male. See *Boşboğaz*, 21: 3, 6 Teşrin-i evvel 1324 / 19 October 1908.

67. For images of woman as nation and the patriot-citizen in the context of the American Revolution, see Linda K. Kerber, *Women of the Republic: Intellect and Ideology in Revolutionary America* (Chapel Hill: University of North Carolina Press, 1988). See also *La France: Images of Woman*, which speaks of the image of woman as redeemer. "French culture, deprived of those values which had held it together, looked for a sign sufficiently powerful to maintain itself in a secular and utopian age and found it in the image of a beloved woman, often contrasted to a darker *femme fatale*" (19).

68. *Kalem*, 10: 1, 23 Teşrin-i evvel 1324 / 5 November 1908. The renowned French satirist, Daumier, was famous for his images of women citizens and the female nation. See Kirsten Powell and Elizabeth C. Childs, *Femmes d'esprit: Women in Daumier's Caricature* (Middlebury, Vermont: The Christian A. Johnson Memorial Gallery and Middlebury College, 1990), 135–144.

69. *Falaka*, 8: 1, 15 Ağustos 1327/ 28 August 1911.

70. *Lâklâk*, 12: 1, 24 Eylül 1325 / 7 October 1909. The caption of this cartoon was in Ottoman and Arabic, unlike the cartoons in *Kalem*, which were usually in Ottoman and French. Of course, in cartoons, dress is itself a caricature; and "traditional" dress is often suggestive of ethnic or national types rather than an exact copy of what "traditionally" dressed women might wear.

71. For another version of a female nation, dressed in "classical" robes, resisting

the blandishments of foreign (male) nations, see *Malum,* 2: 1, 10 Kanun-ı evvel, 1326 / 23 December 1910.

72. *Kalem,* 9: 5, 7, 16 Teşrin-i evvel 1324 / 29 October 1908. Austria was the main supplier of Istanbul's fezzes, the conventional headgear for men at the time.

73. *Resimli kitab,* 2: 198, Teşrin-i evvel 1324 / October 1908

74. On the construction of motherhood, and womanhood in Western contexts, see E. Ann Kaplan, *Motherhood and Representation: The Mother in Popular Culture and Melodrama* (London: Routledge, 1992), 17–26, who attempts an historical schematization of representations of motherhood.

75. *Papağan,* 20: 4, 19 Kanun-ı evvel 1324 / 1 January 1909.

76. Similar images of the Ottoman woman as patriot are found during and after World War I, images of women at the front, at the homefires, making sacrifices for the cause, and upholding morale. For one vivid example see Edib Adıvar, *Conflict of East and West in Turkey,* 264, 268–269.

77. *Dalkavuk,* 25: 1, 21 Şubat 1324 / 6 March 1909. The woman laughs as she passes the storekeeper by.

78. Similarly the theme of sacrifice is found in the Iranian boycott of Russian tea in 1911, a symbol of resistance to the Anglo-Russian occupation. Shops selling Russian goods in Tehran were vandalized in the course of demonstrations in that year. See Abrahamian, *Iran Between Two Revolutions,* 109.

79. Edib Adıvar, *Conflict of East and West in Turkey,* 235.

80. *İnkılab,* 10: 153, 12 Eylül 1325 / 25 September 1909. This article, entitled "Eastern Women," was reproduced and translated from the gazette, *al-Mufid;* it evaluated the ways in which Eastern women (and men) were measured against Europeans in terms of their advancement in things like science and education. See also *Piyano,* 1: 3–4 and 2: 12 [no dates, approximately September 1910], written by İsmail Hamî, "Concerning Women, a Comparison." On the woman question and comparison with the West, see Berkes, *The Development of Secularism,* 385–389; and Carter Findley, "An Ottoman Occidentalist in Europe: Ahmed Midhat Meets Madame Gülnar, 1889," *American Historical Review* 103, no. 1 (February 1998): 15–49.

81. See Kandiyoti, "End of Empire: Islam, Nationalism, and Women in Turkey," 22–47, in Deniz Kandiyoti, ed., *Women, Islam, and the State* (London: Macmillan, 1991).

82. Kandiyoti, "Slave Girls, Temptresses," 35. Kandiyoti's notion of the distinctions between indigenous and foreign is, however, different from the contrast between Ottoman and European utilized here in my study.

83. Garnett, *Turkish Life in Town and Country,* 14–18, gives a more balanced interpretation of women's place in the empire at the turn of the century than do many Western accounts. Lauding the rights Islamic law grants women, she adds that the emancipation of women is hampered by social usage, by the linkage between the harem system and domestic slavery, and by the fact that many Ottoman women had neither the education nor the work skills that would enable them to be employed or self-sufficient.

84. For example, see *Salname-i servet-i fünun* 1326, 2: 150–151, published 1327 / 1911, reporting on women's "activism" in England. Of course, whether women were

to be taken seriously or not was not a uniquely Ottoman problem. According to Graves, *Mr. Punch's England*, 236–237, writing in 1921, "Feminism in the modern sense . . . is, in English, at any rate, a twentieth century word. . . . But from 1860 onward one notes an increasing readiness to take women seriously." Ahmad, *Young Turks*, 279–281, writing on the Ottoman state during World War I, argues that there was a certain amount of "liberation—if liberation is the appropriate term—for urban Turkish women, especially in the capital, as a result of war [World War I]."

85. See *Salname-i servet-i fünun* 1326, 2: 150–152, published 1327 / 1911.

86. *İstişare*, 1: 84–85, 4 Eylül 1324 / 17 September 1908, an imaginary speech. Edib Adıvar, *The Conflict of East and West in Turkey*, 266, idealizes the differences between Ottoman Turkish women's emancipation and that of their Western sisters.

87. Kandiyoti, "End of Empire," 25, notes how Namık Kemal used his journal, *İbret* (1288–1289 / 1873–1874) in the late nineteenth century to discuss the position of Ottoman women. For a report in the Ottoman press on American women's gazettes, see *Resimli İstanbul*, 10: 159, 10 Ağustos 1325 / 23 August 1909. Women's gazettes cannot be assumed necessarily to have taken "liberal" positions on the woman question. In the Ottoman empire, as in France in an earlier era, the women's gazettes evolved along with the woman question. Irène Fenoglio—Abd El Aal, *Défense et Illustration de l'Égyptienne* (Cairo: Centre d'Etudes et de Documentation Economique, Juridique et Sociale, 1988), 9–47, writes on the Cairo women's gazette, *L'Égyptienne*, its female journalists, and the range of opinions on the woman question. See also, Gelbart, *Feminine and Opposition Journalism*, 8–14, 91–93, on the conservative nature of French old regime literature for women and on the evolution of *Le Journal des Dames*.

88. *Beyan ül-hak*, 3: 20–25, 192–194, Teşrin-i evvel 1324 / October 1908. This gazette was used by certain members of the ulema, like Mustafa Sabrî and Musa Kâzım, to express Islamist views on the position of women; see Kandiyoti, "End of Empire," 32.

89. *İştirak*, 6: 1, 20 Mart 1326 / 2 April 1910.

90. *Mahasin*, 6, Şubat 1324 / February 1909. The communist gazette, *Şark Kadını* (Eastern Woman), published in Baku in 1923, is a later example of a gazette targeting women but primarily written by men.

91. On the evolution of women's gazettes in Istanbul, see Serpil Çakır, *Osmanlı Kadın Hareketi* (İstanbul: Metis Yayınları, 1994), 22–42; and Stump, "The Emergence of a Feminist/Nationalist Discourse," 4–5, 42–53, 75–78, who provides a thoughtful analytical framework for evaluating Ottoman "feminism."

92. For example, *Muhit* 16: 254–255, 12 Şubat 1324 / 25 February 1909; and *Resimli İstanbul* 4: 60, 29 Haziran 1325 / 12 July 1909.

93. Hart, *The Popular Book*, 86. Hart does own that the heroines of popular fiction were much changed but notes a striking resemblance of the "ideal woman" of the time to past ideals. Stump, "The Emergence of a Feminist/Nationalist Discourse," 48–53, 78–87, shows that all women clearly did not cherish their assigned place and illustrates the women's debates over that question in the pages of *Kadın* magazine.

94. Celal Nuri, *Kadınlarımız* (İstanbul: Matbaa-ı İctihad, 1331 hicrî / 1913). Nuri takes as his main categories Muslim women and Turkish women. See Fenoglio-Abd

El Aal, *Défense et Illustration*, 48–55, on the liberal and conservative treatments of the question of marriage in early-twentieth-century Egypt. See also Zafer Toprak, "Osmanlı'da Alafranga: Evlenme Ilânları," *Tarih ve Toplum*, 9 (1988), 44–46.

95. Djemal [Cemal] Pasha, *Memories of a Turkish Statesman—1913–1919* (New York: George H. Doran Company, 1922), 18. On the education and development of women, with reference to Europe, see *Resimli kitab*, 5: 439–447, Kanun-ı sani 1324 / January 1909, "*Terbiye-i Nisvan*," by Raif Necdet. Almanacs and gazettes regularly showed pictures of girls in school as a sign of Ottoman progress; for example the Üsküdar Füyuzat Mektebi in *Muhit*, 4: 53, 13 Teşrin-i sani 1324 / 26 November 1908.

96. Edib Adıvar, *Conflict of East and West in Turkey*, 247–249, traces the worldwide movement in favor of women's rights to 1848 (247) and gives a brief history of Western feminism (247–249). Edib argues that originally the Turkish or Ottoman woman was of the "manly type. That is, her virtues are those of strength of character and straightforwardness" (252).

97. See for example, *Hikmet*, 13: 4–5, 1 Temmuz 1326 / 14 July 1910, for a serialized article under the heading "*ictimaiyat*" (sociology), entitled "Islam and Women: Past, Present, and Future."

98. In 1913, a former secretary of the Pan-Islamic Society of London, S. Mushir Hosain Kidwai, who had received a decoration from Abd ül-Hamid, published a book called *Islam and Socialism*, which argued that Islam was essentially socialistic, and that Muhammad had greatly improved the condition of women. See, Stephen Trowbridge's review of Mushir Hosain Kidwai, "Islam and Socialism," in *Muslim World* 4, no. 1 (1914): 432–433. Edib Adıvar, *The Conflict of East and West in Turkey*, 265, argued that the Tanzimat had given a limited religious sanction to women's equality but that the foundation of the Turkish *Ocak* (hearth) organizations after the 1908 revolution gave "national," sanction to women's equality.

99. Kandiyoti, "End of Empire," 27.

100. E. G. Browne, *The Persian Revolution*, 386–387. See also, Javadi, *Satire in Persian Literature*, 208–213, on satire of the woman question, including ridicule of woman as superstitious and associations of woman's education with moral decadence. Stump, "The Emergence of a Feminist/Nationalist Discourse," 63, 70, notes Ottoman-Iranian affinities; an article on women in the Iranian revolution in the Ottoman women's gazette *Kadın*; and the critique of women as superstitious.

101. For another humorous piece called the "marriage club," see *Kalem*, 3: 3–5, 11, 4 Eylül 1324 / 17 September 1908. The same issue includes an ad for a new woman's gazette (5).

102. *Boşboğaz*, 18: 1–2, 25 Eylül 1324 / 8 October 1908.

103. *Davul*, 1: 12, 14 Teşrin-i evvel 1324 / 27 October 1908.

104. *Kalem*, 7: 4, 3 Teşrin-i evvel 1324 / 16 October 1908. On women's associations, see Çakır, *Osmanlı Kadın Hareketleri*, 43–78.

105. *Karakuş Ezop*, 2: 1, 13 Eylül 1324 / 26 September 1908. On the inherent linking of the woman question and the critique of Western influences, frivolous consumption, and immorality, see Mardin, "Super Westernization," 432–435.

106. *Karagöz*, 533: 4, 29 Haziran 1329 / 12 July 1913.

107. For an extensive treatment of *Kadınlar Dünyası*, see Çakır, *Osmanlı Kadın*

Hareketleri, 80–312. Çakır discusses the social context of the gazette and its treatment of themes such as women's rights, the law, the family, dress, and education.

108. Ahmad, *The Young Turks,* 279, has pointed out that despite the new regime's efforts, its opening of schools, and the liberal ulema's pronouncements after 1908 that the Prophet had opposed polygamy, "Turkish-Muslim society as a whole remained conservative, and in some towns in Anatolia a man speaking to a woman in public was still liable to be fined and the woman flogged."

109. Abrahamian, *Iran Between Two Revolutions,* 109.

110. Mary Louise Roberts, "Samson and Delilah Revisited: The Politics of Women's Fashion in 1920's France," *American Historical Review* 98, no. 3 (June 1993), 657–684, in a study of fashion imagery in post–World War I France, has noted the role of fashion in testing and establishing the boundaries of women's place.

111. Weber, *Peasants into Frenchmen,* 290, in considering changes in the French countryside, has argued for an intimate connection between fashion and politics: "Changes in dress, manners, diet, the gradual rise in expectations (especially among women), the very breakdown of isolation, may well have counted more than radical politics. Nor, possibly, would politics have been much radicalized without them."

112. G. Armytage, "Modern Dress," *Fortnightly Review* 34, n.s. (July 1–Dec. 1, 1883): 344–353, see 352.

113. Miller, *The Bon Marché,* 192.

114. One cartoon vision of the Europeanized Ottoman suggested that the imitation of French culture would be accompanied by a certain sexual license and by women abandoning their domestic responsibilities: *Boşboğaz,* 12: 4, 4 Eylül 1324 / 17 September 1908.

115. *Falaka,* 3: 4, 1 Ağustos 1327 / 14 August 1911. *İffet* can be translated as chastity, uprightness, or purity. The *falakacı* was a traditional figure in the sultan's retinue who administered the bastinado punishment to various offenders.

116. Ribeiro, *Fashion in the French Revolution,* 101. On a later period, see Weber, *Peasants into Frenchman,* 229–231, who notes that costume was a marker of local and class identity as well as of consumption patterns. He points to a homogenization of dress in France at the turn of the twentieth century as urban styles spread to the countryside: "Peasants were beginning to look like everybody else."

117. On dress reform see Findley, *Ottoman Civil Officialdom,* 212–213.

118. Ribeiro, *Fashion in the French Revolution,* 110, discusses the rapidity with which civic religion lost popularity, as the public associated it with a discredited regime, and the speed with which the Christian churches were reinstated. In the Ottoman case, civic religion was never really a competing option.

119. Of course Napoleon's victory in Egypt was ephemeral, but the triumph, as in similar celebrations in other places and other times, served to divert attention from the celebrator's problems. C. E. Bosworth, ed., *The Islamic World from Classical to Modern Times* (Princeton: Darwin Press, 1989), 415, notes that after the Ottoman conquest of 1517, the *awlād al-nās* (sons of the Mamluks) discarded the characteristic Mamluk headgear, the *takhfīta* and *zamṭ* hats, in order to disassociate themselves from the defeated, formerly elite class.

120. Ribeiro, *Fashion in the French Revolution,* 94–96, 136, 140. Costume was ma-

nipulated by the regime and by Napoleon to reinforce authority, order society, and link the revolution to an admired classical past.

121. *Kalem*, 5: 12, 18 Eylül 1324 / 1 October 1908. For an example of the official dress uniform, see Findley, *Ottoman Civil Officialdom*, 198. Old regime uniforms could stand for the discarding of the old order in general, as suggested by a cartoon in *Davul*, 3: 19, 28 Teşrin-i evvel 1324 / 10 November 1908, which showed a raggedy old *baba* hauling a cartload of notables' coats, those of the "*ayan*," as he tells a young *efendi*.

122. See Barthes, *The Fashion System*, 27–31, on word vs. picture signifiers.

123. *Resimli kitab*, 1: 11, Eylül 1324 / September 1908, on the political climate in Europe; and 2: 198, Teşrin-i evvel 1324 / October 1908, for a cartoon of Austrian and Turkish women (fashion and politics).

124. *Diken*, 19: front cover [undated but published in July 1919]; and 21: cover, 21 Ağustos 1335 / 3 September 1919.

Chapter IX. Dogs, Crime, Women, Cholera, and Other Menaces in the Streets

1. *Kalem*, 17: 8, 12 Kanun-ı evvel, 1324 / 25 December 1908.

2. *Kalem*, 103: 9, 11 Teşrin-i sani 1326 / 24 November 1910.

3. See Mark Girouard, *Cities and People: A Social and Architectural History* (New Haven: Yale University Press, 1985), 233–254, on "the city as export." It was to European architects or foreign planners, often, that the Ottoman government appealed to redesign Istanbul in the nineteenth and early-twentieth centuries. See Çelik, *The Remaking of Istanbul*, 102–153.

4. De Leon, *Thirty Years*, v. 2, 141.

5. Dogs were a common urban problem. The sanitation committee of nineteenth-century New York, for example, struggled for years not only with dog packs but with hogs (in the streets and in apartment houses), the latter of which provided both garbage control and food for the poor. See Charles E. Rosenberg, *The Cholera Years, The United States in 1832, 1849, and 1866* (Chicago: University of Chicago Press, 1987), 110–113. For scavenger imagery, see *Arz-u hâl*, 2: 1, 8 Şubat 1325 / 21 February 1910.

6. See for example, *Boşboğaz*, 22: 3, 9 Teşrin-i evvel 1324 / 22 October 1908, for a column entitled "Our Streets," a sort of newsy narrative that included mention of Istanbul's street dogs; and *Şakacı*, 6: 7, 29 Teşrin-i evvel 1324 / 11 November 1908, for a ditty on "Street Dogs." For a generic example of street dogs in cartoons, see *Hokkabaz*, 2: 11, 27 Eylül 1324 / 10 October 1908.

7. Vaka, *Haremlık*, 30. An additional source, which I have been unable to consult, is Abdullah Cevdet, *İstanbul'da Köpekler* (Cairo: n.p., 1909). The street dogs turned up in various images of Istanbul. See Ekmeleddin Ihsanoğlu, *Istanbul: A Glimpse into the Past* (İstanbul: Research Centre for Islamic History, Art and Culture, 1987), 36; Çizgen, *Photography in the Ottoman Empire*, 101; and I. Gündağ Kayaoğlu, *Eski İstanbul'da Gündelik Hayat*, Kültür İşleri Daire Bakanlığı Yayınları, no. 7 (İstanbul: İstanbul Büyükşehir Belediyesi, 1992), 138–143.

8. *Alem*, 8: 5 (French secion), 19 Mart 1325 / 1 April 1909.

9. *Salname-i servet-i fünun* 1326, 2: 128, published 1327 / 1911. See Eken, *Kartpostallarda İstanbul*, 243, for a photo of the garbage man and the dogs. The dogs were also rounded up and dumped on an off-shore island to starve, as satirized in *Dertli ile garib*, 1: 3, 6 Ağustos 1326 / 19 August 1910.

10. A.V. Williams Jackson, *From Constantinople to the Home of Omar Khayyam: Travels in Transcaucasia and Northern Persia for Historic and Literary Research* (New York: Macmillan, 1911), 2.

11. Mary Mills Patrick, *Under Five Sultans* (New York: The Century Company, 1929), 67–68, 228.

12. Mark Sykes, *The Caliph's Last Heritage* (New York: Arno Press, 1973), 507, 512.

13. Sykes was not the only one who valued a sense of place and associated that value with Europe. Muḥammad aṣ-Ṣaffār, *Disorienting Encounters*, 193, on a diplomatic mission to France in the mid-nineteenth century noted that one of the things that made the French so powerful was their ability to have everything in its "proper" place.

14. In the Ottoman press, pet toy-size dogs were frequently pictured in cartoons of women done up in Paris fashions, a readily identifiable sign of the imitation of European mores. Pet culture is here viewed as distinct from the keeping of hunting dogs and exotic pets, customs that the Ottoman palace shared with the palaces of Europe. See also, Kathleen Kete, *The Beast in the Boudoir: Petkeeping in Nineteenth Century Paris* (Berkeley: University of California Press, 1994). See also, Ferdinand, "Selling It to the Provinces," 393–411, in Brewer and Porter, *Consumption and the World of Goods*.

15. Sykes, *The Caliph's Last Heritage*, 507, 512.

16. *Polis mecmuası*, 5: 1, 109, 15 Eylül 1329 / 28 September 1913.

17. *Kalem*, 65: 5, 26 Teşrin-i evvel 1325 / 8 November 1909. While this proverb in modern Turkish would ordinarily read *yer* rather than *yiyer*, here the initial letter is clearly doubled. I believe this form is a common alternate spelling rather than a misprint; there are other instances of an additional written *ya* in the first sylables of Ottoman verbs. Additionally, it might be used to provide a poetic balance of syllables with *bakar*. In any case, my transliteration here serves to indicate the doubled *ya*.

18. The analogy of men to dogs was not lost on the American observer Edwin De Leon who noted that the main street of Pera was fine from a carriage, but on descending one had to "pick your way among dogs and vagabonds of the human species." See De Leon, *Thirty Years*, v. 2, 132–133. Or as Twain, *Innocents Abroad*, 82, put it in his travel account published originally in 1869, "these dogs are the scavengers of the city. . . . But for their usefulness in partially cleansing these terrible streets, they would not be tolerated long. They eat anything and everything that comes in their way, from melon rinds and spoiled grapes up through all the grades and species of dirt and refuse to their own dead friends and relatives—and yet they are always lean, always hungry, always despondent." I have Ginny Aksan to thank for this reference.

19. *Kalem*, 33: 14, 9 Nisan 1325 / 22 April 1909. Anthropomorphized animals were commonly used in cartoons at this time, both in Ottoman and European presses (the gazette *Eşek* is a characteristic example). But *Kalem*'s direct equation of

men with dogs is a bit different, a pointed critique rather than a humorous device. See also: *Yuha,* 1: 1, 2 Kanun-ı evvel 1326 / 15 December 1910, where journalists are transformed into animals; and *Hande,* 3: 1, 5 Nisan 1326 / 18 April 1910.

20. *Alem,* 8: 5 (French section), 19 Mart 1325 / 1 April 1909.

21. In the animal tales, as in the satirical press, making animals speak critically of the dominant system either suggested that the critique had a humorous purpose or helped avert retaliation against the author.

22. Tietze, *The Turkish Shadow Theatre,* 41.

23. Similar charges were made about the early-twentieth-century Russian revolution, see Engelstein, *The Keys to Happiness,* 264. Also Phil Billingsley, *Bandits in Republican China* (Stanford: Stanford University Press, 1988), xi–xviii, 226–243, which treats rural banditry in the context of the 1911 Chinese revolution. Billingsley writes of China (227–228): "'After the revolution' was another concept that appeared differently to bandits and to revolutionaries. For ordinary people, it made no difference that the new 'revolutionary' government claimed to rule on their behalf when bullies continued to bully, taxes continued to be demanded, and so on."

24. Shaw, *History of the Ottoman Empire,* 274–275, 306. After the counter-revolution, a new "Law on Vagabonds and Suspected Criminals," was passed (May 8, 1909) to crack down on lawlessness especially in the provinces (285–286). This was part of a general cracking down that took place at that time.

25. *Volkan,* 42: 4, 20 Kanun-ı sani 1324 / 2 February 1909, (taken from *Yeni gazete*). In the end, the police got back at *Volkan;* it was shut down in the aftermath of the counter-revolution. *Volkan,* 110: 1, 7 Nisan 1325 / 20 April 1909, published a summons from the Ministry of Public Security, for items "published contrary to the truth in such a way as to disturb or confuse [*teşviş*] public opinion [*ezhan-ı umumiye*]." *Volkan* published an impassioned reply, calling upon God, but this was its last issue.

26. *Alem,* 10: 8, 7 Mayıs 1325 / 20 May 1909; and *Şakaa,* 7: 4–5, 5 Teşrin-i sani 1324 / 18 November 1908 (this latter illustration follows on a short satire on the "old and new police"); also *Şakacı,* 5: 3, 22 Teşrin-i evvel 1324 / 4 November 1908. There were other comparisons as well; *İttifak* (Harmony), 18: 2, 21 Ağustos 1324 / 3 September 1908, ran an article by Mehmed Rauf comparing the Ottoman police and the English police, with special attention to expenditure and appropriations.

27. Satire of law enforcement officers was of course nothing new. For an example in the satire of nineteenth-century Prussia, see Townsend, *Forbidden Laughter,* 112. Townsend also points out (11–12) the common image of the police as harrassers of the people who are simply going about their business.

28. *Protesto,* 10: 1, 4 Mart 1324 / 17 March 1909.

29. *İncili çavuş,* 11: 2, 12 Eylül 1324 / 25 September 1908.

30. *Serbesti,* 7: 3, 10 Teşrin-i sani 1324 / 23 November 1908. See also *Üç gazete,* 13: 4, 10 Eylül 1324 / 23 September 1908, "Concerning the Gendarme."

31. *Al-Üfürük,* 3: 5, 25 Eylül 1324 / 8 October 1908

32. *Kalem,* 15: 14, 28 Teşrin-i sani 1324 / 11 December 1908.

33. For crime statistics from August 1909 to February 1910 in Istanbul, Beyoğlu, and Üsküdar, see *Salname-i servet-i fünun* 1326, 2: 71–72, published 1327 / 1911. See also, for crime reports beginning in 1913, the bimonthly *Polis mecmuası,* for example,

5: 118–120, 15 Eylül 1329 / 28 September 1913, showing mug shots of domestic and international criminals.

34. *Alem*, 1: 8, 19 Kanun-ı sani 1324 / 1 February 1909. Other satire directed at the Ministry of Police can be found in *Ezop*, 3: 4, 27 Ağustos 1324 / 9 September 1908.

35. *Alem*, 3: 11, 12 Şubat 1324 / 25 February 1909; 6: 5 (French section), 5 Mart 1324 / 18 March 1909; and 4: 13, 19 Şubat 1324 / 4 March 1909.

36. *Alem*, 2: 1, 5 Şubat 1324 / 18 February 1909. This cartoon is captioned, "tranquility in Istanbul."

37. *Alem*, 6: 4 (French section), 5 Mart 1324 / 18 March 1909.

38. *Kalem*, 13: 9, 13 Teşrin-i sani 1324 / 26 November 1908.

39. *Dalkavuk*, 2: 4–5, 6 Eylül 1324 / 19 September 1908, shows (in one frame) a prosperous-looking lady with a fat pet dog and puffed sleeves being robbed of her watch.

40. *Malum*, 4: 3, 19 Kanun-ı evvel 1326 / 1 January 1911. *Malum* was fond of poking fun at the police and the City Administration. *Malum*, 1: 3, [8] Kanun-ı evvel 1326 / [21] December 1910. *Geveze*, 23: 1, 23 Kanun-ı sani 1324 / 5 February 1909, also focused on the theme of lazy officials.

41. *Kalem*, 12: 12, 7 Teşrin-i sani 1324 / 20 November 1908.

42. *Alafranga*, 1: 4, 30 Teşrin-i sani 1326 / 13 December 1910.

43. *Kalem*, 45: 16, [9 Temmuz] 1325 / [22 July] 1909.

44. Garnett, *Turkish Life*, 45. On the organization of the police under Abd ül-Hamid, see Shaw, *History of the Ottoman Empire*, 215; there was another reorganization of the police in 1913 (306)

45. The police force in New York City was crucial in the implementation of cholera control in the nineteenth century, enforcing sanitation laws, for example, keeping a complaint-book, and providing communication assistance in the enforcement of disease controls: Rosenberg, *The Cholera Years*, 202.

46. In 1917, the Istanbul police were still harrassing women over improper dress, or "shameful fashions" as they were called in a police bulletin. But, in 1917, this harrassment was moderated by influential protests; see Kandiyoti, "End of Empire," 31.

47. Djemal [Cemal] Pasha, *Memories of a Turkish Statesman*, 296. De Chardin, *Letters from Egypt 1905–1908*, 167, reports that there was a cab strike in Cairo because the police were responsible for impounding the cabs of all drivers whose horses were not properly cared for. A large fine was then imposed and the policeman received a bounty for each offender he brought in. The British instituting some sort of society for the protection of animals seems to have been instrumental in mobilizing this regulation.

48. In one play, Karagöz informs his companion that he won't go to Galata with him to eat tripe soup because the bridge toll of 10 para is too much money; see Tietze, *The Turkish Shadow Theatre*, 39. See *Dalkavuk*, 6: 8, 4 Teşrin-i sani 1324 / 17 November 1908, for a cartoon in which paying the bridge tolls is humorously confused with alms giving; *Alafranga*, 2: 3, 2 Kanun-ı evvel 1326 / 15 December 1910, where it is equated with a judicial penalty or means of atonement; and *Lâklâk*, 5: 3, 6

Ağustos 1325 / 19 August 1909, which satirized dodging the bridge tolls. Rasim, *Şehir Mektupları,* Turkish edition, v. 1, 36, also satirized the bridge tolls and toll takers in a passage that ends, "through the zeal of the government, those without money were unable to pass." The bridge was a favored site for Rasim's literary images. For a photo of the bridge toll-takers, see İhsanoğlu, *İstanbul: A Glimpse into the Past,* 27.

49. Nonetheless, electric lights were still regarded as a marvel of technology in early-twentieth-century Istanbul. See Simon Schaffer, "The Consuming Flame: Electrical Showmen and Tory Mystics in the World of Goods," 489–526, in Brewer and Porter, *Consumption and the World of Goods.*

50. *Dalkavuk,* 2: 4–5, 6 Eylül 1324 / 19 September 1908.

51. Micklewright, "London, Paris, Istanbul, and Cairo," has demonstrated the prevalence of Western fashion among Istanbul's upper and even upper-middle classes by the second half of the nineteenth century.

52. *Resimli kitab,* 2: 190, Teşrin-i evvel 1324 / October 1908.

53. Kandiyoti, "Slave Girls, Temptresses," 38, 41–42. Kandiyoti uses the concept of the *alafranga* woman to good effect in her treatment of literary "heroines." *Felatun Beyle Rakım Efendi* was published in 1875 by Ahmed Midhat and *Aşk-ı Memnu* (Forbidden Love) in 1900, by Halit Ziya (Uşaklıgil). Domestic dramas, such as those treated by Kandiyoti, and stories were popular in the periodical press of the revolutionary period. They could be either serious or satirical.

54. Some steps have been taken in this direction by Duben and Behar, *Istanbul Households,* 194–238. For examples on other areas of the world, see Parker, *Nationalisms and Sexualities;* Kumkum Sangari and Sudesh Vaid, eds., *Recasting Women: Essays in Indian Colonial History* (New Brunswick: Rutgers University Press, 1990); Valentine Moghadam, ed., *Identity, Politics, and Women* (Boulder: Westview Press, 1994); Haleh Afshar, ed., *Women, State and Ideology: Studies from Africa and Asia* (London: Macmillan, 1987).

55. Engelstein, *The Keys to Happiness,* 217, 253, points out some of the ambiguities associated with literary imagery of revolution, political ideology, and the lower classes (and their unruly sexual conduct) in the context of 1905 Russia.

56. See Daniel Panzac, *La Peste dans l'Empire ottoman 1700–1850* (Leuven: Éditions Peeters, 1985), 411–413, 445–459, 478–492. On the ravages of cholera in late nineteenth-century Egypt, see Berque, *Egypt, Imperialism and Revolution,* 124–126, which includes stories of suspicions concerning physicians.

57. *Perde,* 4: 7, 3 Kanun-ı evvel 1327 / 16 December 1911.

58. *Malum,* 3: 3, 15 Kanun-ı evvel 1326 / 28 December 1910.

59. See *Geveze,* 34: 1, 3 Mart 1325 / 16 March 1909; *Kalem,* 97: 20, 30 Eylül 1326 / 13 October 1910. Associations of disease, immorality, urban elite life, and Western culture were not, of course limited to the Ottoman context. For a treatment of these questions (focusing on disease, prostitution, and fashion) in early-twentieth-century Russia, see Engelstein, *The Keys to Happiness,* 128–164, 210–211.

60. On cholera as a social and moral construct in Europe and the United States in the nineteenth century see, Rosenberg, *The Cholera Years;* and Michael Durey, *The Return of the Plague, British Society and the Cholera 1831–1832* (Dublin: Gill and Macmillan Press, 1979). See also La Verne Kuhnke, *Lives at Risk: Public Health in*

Nineteenth-Century Egypt, Comparative Studies in Health Systems and Medical Care, no. 24 (Berkeley: University of California Press, 1990).

61. Rosenberg, *The Cholera Years,* 199-200, proposes that only one in seven physicians in the United States supported "germ theory" in 1866. De Leon, *Thirty Years,* 127-128, in his discussion of nineteenth-century visits to Egypt, has suggested some other economic associations of quarantine. De Leon says that quarantine was imposed on the least excuse. "All but those bearing the official stamp have to put up with this nuisance to gratify the avarice of port officials who make no inconsiderable sum out of the fees they are permitted to charge."

62. Garnett, *Turkish Life,* 152. Garnett was not devoid of Eurocentric biases, but she was a careful and astute observer of village life and social custom.

63. *Falaka,* 11: 4, 29 Ağustos 1327 / 11 September 1911. This particular gazette carried a variety of barbs aimed at cholera control. There were also more humorous allusions to cholera, even though any reference to cholera had a certain edge to it because of the fear the disease prompted. See *Piyano,* 8: 88-89, 4 Teşrin-i evvel 1326 / 17 October 1910, for a narrative piece entitled "The Advantages of Cholera," supposedly written by "Don Kişot" (Don Quixote), a "regular contributor" of pieces to satiric gazettes. For serious coverage of cholera in the empire, see *Salname-i servet-i fünun* 1326, 2: 185, published 1327 / 1911.

64. See, for example, *Alem,* 2: 7, 5 Şubat 1324 / 18 February 1909; and the cover story in *Boşbogaz,* 35: 1, 27 Teşrin-i sani 1324 / 10 December 1908, on "the microbe conference." Persian satire also critiqued microbe theory; see Javadi, *Satire in Persian Literature,* 264, on a satirical play by Hasan Moqaddam that lampoons a Europeanized Iranian's preoccupation with "microbes" in the air.

65. *İncili çavuş,* 5: 3, [22] Ağustos 1324 / [4] September 1908.

66. *Kalem,* 7: 2, 2 Teşrin-i evvel 1324 / 15 October 1908.

67. *Alafranga,* 1: 1, 30 Teşrin-i sani 1326 / 13 December 1910.

68. *Falaka,* 9: 4, 22 Ağustos 1327 / 4 September 1911. The spray canister also appeared in *Yeni geveze,* 146: 4, 1 Eylül 1327 / 14 September 1911; and 90: 4, 15 Teşrin-i sani 1326 / 28 November 1910, along with images of cholera, typhus, and fever as dancing skeletons, and barbs aimed at quarantine control.

69. *Al-Üfürük,* 1: 4, 10 Eylül 1324 / 23 September 1908. This satiric narrative claimed that *Hürriyet,* (published 2-16 Ağustos 1324), *Nevzad-ı Vatan* (one issue only), and *İttifak* (17 Ağustos-21 Eylül 1324) were all "sacrificed" to the cholera. *İttifak,* in fact, still had a few issues to go when this piece was published.

70. *Kalem,* 111: 10, 20 Kanun-ı sani 1326 / 2 February 1911, in a rather unusual cartoon, satirized a drunkard coming out of a shop labeled, in French, "Liquers, Vins, Cognac." See also Toledano, *State and Society,* 243-248, on the commonality of alcohol consumption in mid-nineteenth-century Egypt, the critique of taverns, government regulation, and the relative toleration (no criminal charges) of instances of public drunkenness. For nineteenth-century Prussian alcohol satire, see Townsend, *Forbidden Laughter,* 110-112. Hogarth's famous 1750 etching, "Gin Lane," was a vision of all the social ills of drink; see Shikes, *The Indignant Eye,* 72.

71. Skeletons were often used to represent cholera. See *Karagöz,* 542: 4, 29 Temmuz 1329 / 11 August 1913.

72. *Cadaloz*, 44: 4, 23 Ağustos 1327 / 5 September 1911. The brewery is labeled "*niktar bira fabrikası.*" "*Niktar,*" brand could mean: good-dark, better (*nikter*), or even nectar.

73. *Falaka*, 12: 3, 1 Eylül 1327 / 14 September 1911. Perhaps there were specific charges against various bottlers at this time.

74. Robert Goldstein, *Censorship of Political Caricature in Nineteenth-Century France* (Kent, Ohio: Kent State University Press, 1989), 246. On Ensor, see Xavier Tricot, *James Ensor: Catalogue Raisonné of the Paintings*, v. 1 (Antwerp: Pandora, 1992), 251, 284, 312–313; Ensor also employed the images of puppet theatre and the masque in his paintings. See also: William Feaver, *Masters of Caricature: From Hogarth and Gilray to Scarfe and Levine* (New York: Knopf, 1981), 71; M. H. Spielman, *The History of "Punch"* (London: Cassell and Co., 1895), 139–143, 152, 187.

75. Images of death, as clad enticingly but actually corrupt and skeletal on the inside, can be traced back at least as far as the Middle Ages in art iconography where they were used in allegorical and moralizing literature. Death figures in Western art history have been male, female, and sexless. See, for example, Philippe Ariès, *The Hour of Our Death* (Oxford: Oxford University Press, 1991), plates between pages 204 and 205; A. Hyatt Mayor, *Prints and People*, plates 54, 55, 129, 667. Skeletons take another form in late-nineteenth- and early-twentieth-century Mexican satire, see: Keen, *Faces of the Enemy*, 64–66.

76. In an interesting article on the use of images and on image as communication, Barbara Stafford, "Presuming Images and Consuming Words: The Visualization of Knowledge from the Enlightenment to Post-Modernism," 462–477, in Brewer an Porter, *Consumption and the World of Goods*, argues that in the eighteenth century a "pedagogical struggle to comprehend the full power of visual arrays" was initiated (467). In this struggle "the determining desire was to get a glimpse of the unseen." One might argue that all eras are characterized by attempts to get a glimpse of the unseen; spiritualism was one particularly popular such attempt at the turn of the twentieth century.

77. *Kalem*, 111: 14, 20 Kanun-ı sani 1326 / 2 February 1911.

78. *Kalem*, 112: 8, 27 Kanun-ı sani 1326 / 9 February 1911.

79. French captions are often more or less discrepant from their Ottoman counterparts. On more than one occasion I have found a French caption that simply notes that the Ottoman is "untranslatable."

80. *Kalem*, 97: 20, 30 Eylül 1326 / 13 October 1910; *Geveze*, 34: 1, 3 Mart 1325 / 16 March 1909.

81. *Kalem*, 8: 6, 9 Teşrin-i evvel 1324 / 22 October 1908.

82. *Kalem*, 98: 8, 7 Teşrin-i evvel 1326 / 20 October 1910.

83. *Kalem*, 107: 10–11, 23 Kanun-ı evvel 1326 / 5 January 1911.

Chapter X. Technology, Transport, and the "Modern" Street

1. This vision of the Istanbul streets, near the Galata Bridge, before World War I, is from İrfan Orga, *Portrait of a Turkish Family* (London: Victor Gollancz, 1950), 41.

2. For an overview of the question of transportation in the late Ottoman period, see Donald Quataert, "The Age of Reforms, 1812–1914," 759–946, in Halil İnalcık

Notes to Pages 289–296

and Donald Quataert, eds., *An Economic and Social History of the Ottoman Empire 1300–1914* (Cambridge: Cambridge University Press, 1994), 796–823.

3. *Resimli kitab*, 3: 224–225, Teşrin-i sani 1324 / November 1908. Also for a photo of the Renard locomotive and cars, see *Muhit*, 2: 1, 30 Teşrin-i evvel 1324 / 12 November 1908. For other photos of innovative or modern machines, see *Resimli İstanbul*, 6: 105, 20 Temmuz 1325 / 2 August 1909; and 18: 281, 5 Teşrin-i evvel 1325 / 18 October 1909 (a cannon carriage, and a huge spherical spinning cage for bike riding).

4. Edib Adıvar, *Turkey Faces West*, plate after page 10. Most of the machinery, according to the caption, was American made.

5. *Kalem*, 65: 1, 26 Teşrin-i sani 1325 / 9 December 1909. The top caption reads: "The Istanbul Air Racers." See also *Kalem*, 35: 1, 23 Nisan 1325 / 6 May 1909 and 38: 1, 21 Mayıs 1325 / 3 June 1909.

6. *Resimli kitab*, 12: 1188, Eylül 1325 / September 1909. Same view in *Resimli İstanbul*, 10: 148, 10 Ağustos 1325 / 23 August 1909.

7. *Kalem*, 36: 5, 7 Mayıs 1325 / 20 May 1909.

8. *Osmanlı ziraat ve ticaret gazetesi*, sene 3, 13: 1, 24 Kanun-ı evvel 1325 / 6 January 1910.

9. *Osmanlı ziraat ve ticaret gazetesi*, sene 3, 2: 1–9, 22 Mart 1325 / 4 April 1909. On agricultural technology of the time, see Quataert, "The Age of Reforms," 853; and Shaw, *History of the Ottoman Empire*, 232, on imported machinery from the United States, England, and Germany. See *Alem*, 10: 3, 7 Mayıs 1325 / 20 May 1909, for an announcement of a regional industrial and commercial exposition, "sponsored by His Majesty the Sultan," in Bursa, featuring works of art, diverse arts, crafts and machines, mining and foresty products and equipment, agriculture, and provisioning. Prizes to be awarded were gold and silver medals, diplomas, honorable mentions, and money.

10. Robert Phillipe, *Political Graphics*, 194–197. See Findley, "An Ottoman Occidentalist in Europe," 42–44, on Ahmed Midhat's, visit to the Palace of Machines at the 1889 Paris exposition.

11. See *Kalem*, 10: 5, 23 Teşrin-i evvel 1324/ 15 November 1908, on the "new toys" of constitutionalism.

12. *Alem*, 11: 16, back cover, 14 Mayıs 1325 / 27 May 1909, shows a carriage driver with his carriage on a raft. The caption suggests the drivers (*arabacılar*) were unhappy with new regulations (*nizamname-i cedid*).

13. *Kalem*, 47: 8, 23 Temmuz 1325 / 5 August 1909.

14. *Resimli kitab*, 7: 686–687, Nisan 1325 / April 1909.

15. Javadi, *Satire in Persian Literature*, 139, 142, 152, on the terrible condition of Iranian streets. See Browne, *The Press and Poetry of Modern Persia*, 275–276, for a poetic satire from the gazette *Tūs* on the muddy streets in Mashhad. See Quataert, "The Age of Reforms," 811, on Ottoman roads.

16. *Boşboğaz*, 14 : 2–3, 11 Eylül 1324 / 24 September 1908. The author here is apparently playing with the ambiguity of the word *âbruy*, which can mean modesty or shame as well as glory or radiance. On paved roads in the empire, see Shaw, *History of the Ottoman Empire*, 227–228.

Notes to Pages 296–301

17. On satire of transport see François Georgeon, "La Presse Satirique Ottomane Miroir de la Ville."

18. *Karagöz*, 609: 1, 29 Mart 1330 / 11 April 1914.

19. *Züğürt*, 3: 4, 8 Mart 1327 / 21 March 1911.

20. *Karagöz*, 614: 4, 16 Nisan 1330 / 29 April 1914.

21. The automobile was of interest for its military uses as well as for its passenger transport capabilities. For two photographs of early automobiles in revolutionary gazettes, see *Resimli kitab*, 8: 773, 799, Mayıs 1325 / May 1909; and *Resimli İstanbul*, 16: 249, 21 Eylül 1325 / 4 October 1909. See also the "year in science" section of *Salname-i servet-i fünun* 1324–1325, 1: 156–158, published 1326 / 1910, which included coverage on flight, new inventions, and "*lokomotivsiz vagonları* (locomotiveless carriages)."

22. *Muhit*, 6: 93, 27 Teşrin-i sani 1324 / 10 December 1908. See also, *Resimli İstanbul*, 12: 249, 21 Eylül 1325 / 4 October 1909. I have no indication of the number of automobiles actually running in the empire at this time. But automobiles were still considered a novelty in Europe, the Model-T was only just being launched in the United States, and Ford was still a few years away from starting assembly-line processes.

23. *Boşboğaz*, 9: 4, 25 Ağustos 1324 / 7 September 1908. For a humorous "car ad," see *Kalem*, 12: 2, 7 Teşrin-i sani 1324 / 20 November 1908.

24. See Çeviker, *Gelişim Sürecinde Türk Karikatürü*, 2: 218–219, for tram cartoons.

25. The first tramway was a horse-drawn tram, established by the Société des Tramways de Constantinople, founded in 1870. This society was part of the financial empire of a long-established Ottoman Jewish family, the Camondos, and their partners. See Nora Şeni, "The Camondos and Their Imprint on Nineteenth Century Istanbul," *International Journal of Middle East Studies* 26, no. 4 (1994): 663–675. On tram horses lazing in their depot, see *Nekregû*, 5: 1, 24 Eylül 1324 / 7 October 1908. A little more than five years after the revolution, *Karagöz*, 588: 4, 15 Kanun-ı sani 1329 / 28 January 1914, ran a cartoon showing the tram horses pleading for salvation to the boss after the trams had been electrified.

26. Garnett, *Turkish Life*, 36. Garnett says that "Moslem women and girls may, for instance, occasionally avail themselves of a tramcar when on an expedition."

27. See *Üç gazete*, 7: 2, 5 Eylül 1324 / 18 September 1908, for a serious article on the tram situation.

28. *Nekregû*, 4: 1, 10 Eylül 1324 / 23 September 1908.

29. These tram problems were also used as a metaphor for other types of difficult or futile tasks, see, for example, *Boşboğaz*, 25: 3, 23 Teşrin-i evvel 1324 / 5 November 1908.

30. *Alem*, 5: 4–5 (French section), 26 Şubat 1324 / 11 March 1909. *Kalem*, 93: 18, 2 Eylül 1326 / 15 September 1910, mocked the municipal administration of the Galata tram system.

31. De Leon, *Thirty Years*, v. 2, 131–132.

32. De Leon, *Thirty Years*, v. 2, 133.

33. *Hande*, 1: 3–4, 22 Mart 1326 / 4 April 1910. The word for pickled is *salamura*, probably from the Italian.

34. See, for example, *Kalem,* 5: 6, 10, 18 Eylül 1324 / 1 October 1908. Most railways within the empire were built with foreign capital, which also caused conflict over sovereign control of rail transport. See *Üç gazete,* 1: 4, 29 Ağustos 1324 / 11 September 1908, for ads for advance ticket purchases for train travel to Sofya and Filibe; prices ranged from 170 and 130 *kuruş* respectively for third class to 365 and 275 *kuruş* for first class. This same gazette ran a series on the Hicaz Railway.

35. Garnett, *Turkish Life,* 12.

36. See Quataert, "The Age of Reforms," 800–804, 828–841, on the steamship, commerce, and Ottoman ports.

37. *Ton ton risalesi,* 1: 1–8, 5 Eylül 1325 / 18 September 1908. It had the following sections: "on passengers waiting for the vapur," "on the Kadıköy vapurs," "on the bridge," and so on.

38. *Dalkavuk,* 8: 8, 18 Teşrin-i evvel 1324 / 31 October 1908. Steamships also appeared in many cartoons as part of the Istanbul scene. See, for example, *Geveze,* 39: 1, 19 Mart 1325 / 1 April 1909.

39. See for example, *Kalem,* 96: 20, 23 Eylül 1326 / 7 October 1910; also 49: 6, 11; and 51: 16.

40. On the traditional boatmen, see Cengiz Orhonlu, "Boat Transportation in Istanbul: An Historical Survey," *Bulletin of the Turkish Studies Association* 13, no. 1 (March 1989): 1–21. It was not only on the docks that European dominance of the new transport industries and government attempts to regulate transport workers caused labor unrest. There were strikes and protests among the rail workers and others in the Ottoman empire and in Egypt at this time. See Quataert, "The Age of Reforms," 811. De Chardin, *Letters From Egypt,* 167, noted cab driver strikes in Cairo in 1907. Drivers and carters, as they are today, were sometimes cast in the role of lazy or treacherous rascals in satire; see *Piyano,* 9: 102–103, 11 Teşrin-i evvel 1326 / 24 October 1910.

41. *Hamals* (porters) were also shown fighting over travelers' luggage. See for example, *Lâklâk,* 4: 2, 30 Temmuz 1325 / 12 Ağustos 1909.

42. *Davul,* 15: 8–9, 4 Şubat 1324 / 17 February 1909. On the Public Works Adminstration and technology transfer, see İlhan Tekeli and Selim İlkin, "The Public Works Program and the Development of Technology in the Ottoman Empire in the Second Half of the Nineteenth Century," *Turcica* 28 (1996): 195–234.

43. *Ton ton risalesi,* 1: 1, 5 Eylül 1325 / 18 September 1908

44. See for example *Salname-i servet-i fünun* 1324–1325, 1: 185–189, published 1326 / 1910, which examined the naval budgets of states like Russian, Austria, France, America, Germany, and England.

45. Şeni, "The Camondos," 673. These ships provided transport on the Bosphorus.

46. *İdare-i Mahsusa* literally means special or reserved administration; it evolved into the National Maritime Line. See *Hande,* 1: 6, 22 Mart 1326 / 4 April 1910 (*Hande* contained a variety of *vapur* satire); *Cingöz,* 5: 2, 11 Eylül 1324 / 24 September 1908; *Karakuş Ezop,* 3: 3, 17 Eylül 1324 / 30 September 1908 (in satiric dialogues); and *Kalem,* 89: 8, 5 Ağustos 1326 / 18 August 1910. *Kalem,* 67: 12, 10 Kanun-ı evvel 1324 / 23 December 1909, pointed out that the Ottoman steamship adminstration could

always be counted upon to run its ships on a very tardy schedule; and 49: 11, 6 Ağustos 1325 / 19 August 1909, published a satiric song on the *Mahsusa*. On the *Şirket-i Hayriye* and the *Mahsusa*, see Shaw, *History of the Ottoman Empire*, 228; Shaw notes that, by 1905, 68,769 vessels (4,756 steam powered) were flying the Ottoman flag.

47. *Muhit*, 12: 185, 15 Kanun-ı sani 1324 / 28 January 1909.

48. *Züğürt*, 12: 4, 21 Mayıs 1327 / 3 June 1911. Thanks to Bill Blair for information on the Midhat Pasha. See Langensiepen and Güleryüz, *The Ottoman Steam Navy, 1828–1923*, 21, 45, 178.

49. For example, *Resimli İstanbul*, 2: front page, 15 Haziran 1325 / 28 June 1909; 4: 49, 29 Haziran 1325 / 12 July 1909; 7: 104, 20 Temmuz 1325 / 2 August 1909.

50. *Kalem*, 93: 12, 2 Eylül 1326 / 15 September 1910. Shaw, *History of the Ottoman Empire*, 285–286, 308–309, notes that Ottoman naval expenditures increased from 50.06 to 115.2 million *kuruş* between 1901 and 1910, and that the Ottoman deficit increased steadily through the Young Turk period.

51. Peter Fritzsche, "Machine Dreams: Airmindedness and the Reinvention of Germany," *American Historical Review*, 98, no. 3 (June 1993): 685–709, explores the ideological and political implications of airmindedness. He notes: "Victor Hugo counterposed the steamship, symbol for an industrial system of exploitation and destitution certain to run aground, with an imaginary airship, which would inaugurate an era of social peace and global prosperity" (685). In a very different context, the air age provided the post-revolutionary Ottoman empire with a symbol for its own possibilities of reinvention in the modern world.

52. See, for example, the photos in *Resimli kitab*, 5: 475, Kanun-ı sani 1324 / January 1909, of airplanes and dirigibles at the Grand Palace exposition in Paris and of the biplane of Henri Farman. *Resimli kitab*, 14: 135–139, Teşrin-i sani 1325 / November 1909, also covered aviation accidents, showing that the hazards of air travel were of interest even if they did not dampen the apparent enthusiasm of the press for airpower.

53. *Resimli İstanbul*, 4: 60, 29 Haziran 1325 / 12 July 1909; and 8: 125, 27 Temmuz 1325 / 9 August 1909.

54. As suggested in a political cartoon in *Arz u-hâl*, 5: 1, 26 Şubat 1325 / 11 March 1910.

55. *Kalem*, 17: 8, 12 Kanun-ı evvel 1324 / 25 December 1908. For other aviation satire, see *Kalem*, 66: 12, 3 Kanun-ı evvel 1325 / 16 December 1909, which links European-style dress to the consumption of aviation technology.

56. *Geveze*, 22: 1, 19 Kanun-ı sani 1324 / 1 February 1909.

57. *Kalem*, 35: 1, 23 Nisan 1325 / 6 May 1909.

58. *Kalem*, 66: 3, 3 Kanun-ı evvel 1325 / 16 December 1909. The word for plane or flying machine, *tayara*, is not specific to airplanes; it can simply mean something that flies or even a swift mare. See also, *Hacivat*, 2: 1, 30 Ağustos 1324 / 12 September 1908.

59. *Alem*, 9: 8, (French section), 26 Mart 1325 / 8 April 1909. Note that there is a fair amount of variation between the French caption and the Ottoman caption. The use of *balon* to describe a picture of an airplane might suggest that *balon* was a generic

for air travel or it could suggest that the caption was prepared apart from the cartoon itself and envisioned a hot air balloon in the frame rather than an airplane.

60. *Karagöz*, 573: 1, 30 Teşrin-i evvel 1329 / 12 November 1913, and 579: 4, 14 Kanun-ı evvel 1329/ 27 Decmber 1913.

61. See Ahmad, *The Young Turks*, 6-13; Davison, *Essays in Ottoman and Turkish History*, 156; and Shaw, *History of the Ottoman Empire*, 230. Cambridge University Library's manuscript collection includes a set of Iranian telegraph forms with the lion and sun on them: Cambridge Library, ms. Or. 2152, piece no. 51.

62. *Alem*, 5: 2 (French section), 26 Şubat 1324 / 11 March 1909.

63. *Karagöz*, 524: 4, 29 Mayıs 1329 / 11 June 1913; see Shaw, *History of the Ottoman Empire*, 306, on the municipal modernization, including electricity, of Istanbul after Abd ül-Hamid's reign ended.

64. On the evolution of the Ottoman telegraph system and on telegraph training, see Davison, *Essays in Ottoman and Turkish History*, 135-165; and Findley, *Ottoman Civil Officialdom*, 165-166.

65. *Kalem*, 106: 12, 16 Kanun-ı evvel 1326 / 29 December 1910.

66. *Kalem*, 13: 10, 13 Teşrin-i sani 1324 / 26 November 1908 (*Bab-ı Âli*). This cartoon on the "new ministerial schedule," was from an original in *Yeni gazete*, 8 Teşrin-i sani 1324 / 21 November 1908.

67. Zeyneb Çelik, "The Impact of Westernization on Istanbul's Urban Form," 253-254. The setting-up of public clocks disordered the conventions of measuring time. The conflict between "scientific" and "natural" time, of course, was not a new dilemma; see Anthony Grafton, *Defenders of the Text: The Traditions of Scholarship in an Age of Science, 1450-1800* (Cambridge: Harvard University Press, 1991), 104. Grafton tells of Philipp Melanchthon who castigated a physician dinner companion for not appreciating the scientific measurement of time. The physician said his peasants knew perfectly well, "when it was day, when it was night, when it was winter, when it was summer and when it was noon," without any mathematical knowledge.

68. Kushner, "Ali Ekrem Bey," 355, notes that the governor (1906-1908) had the clock tower built and also completed a new customs pier at Jaffa, another symbol of both modernity and European penetration.

69. Davison, *Essays in Ottoman and Turkish History*, 156.

70. Ahmad, "The Young Turks, 1908-1918," 283.

71. *Kalem*, 40: 16, 4 Haziran 1325 / 17 June 1909.

72. *Kalem*, 13: 10, 13 Teşrin-i sani 1324 / 26 November 1908. Of course, the publishing industry, by the time of the revolution was running on a combination of Ottoman and European times and calendars. For *alafranga* and *alatürka* time and dating, see *Salname-i servet-i fünun* 1324-1325, 1: 22-27, published 1326 / 1910; and Findley, "An Ottoman Occidentalist in Europe," 26, n. 51.

73. Garnett, *Turkish Life*, 12. Garnett, of course, was being a bit silly when she designated traditional timekeeping as "Oriental." I have no further evidence concerning the two-dial watches.

74. Joanna Waley-Cohen, "China and Western Technology in the Late Eighteenth Century," *American Historical Review* 98, no. 5 (December 1993): 1525-1544. "Europeans specifically equated this apparent lack of [Chinese] interest in what the

West had to offer with a lack of interest in science and practical technology, because at that time the West had come to define itself in terms of, and derive a strong sense of superiority from, its undoubted technological power. From such a perspective it was an easy step to regarding the Chinese as inferior in an overall sense. These views took firm hold as the nineteenth century unfolded and have remained tenacious to this day. Although scholars have recently exploded the myth of China's "opposition" to Western science, it remains widely believed, and, in the case of technology, neither the conviction of the Chinese lack of interest nor the assumptions on which it rested have been subjected to serious inquiry" (155–156).

75. Waley-Cohen, "China and Western Technology," 1527

76. For an elaborate discussion of modernization, religious ideals, and Ottoman culture, see Berkes, *The Development of Secularism in Turkey*, 253–366, especially 337–347.

77. M. Şükrü Hanıoğlu, *The Young Turks in Opposition* (New York: Oxford University Press, 1995), 10–13, 200–203.

78. For example, Bernard Lewis, *The Emergence of Modern Turkey*. Also on the question of adoption of Western technology, see Rhoads Murphey, "The Ottoman Attitude Towards the Adoption of Western Technology: The Role of the *Efrencî* Technicians in Civil and Military Applications," 287–298, in *Contributions à l'histoire économique et sociale de l'Empire ottoman*, Collection Turcica III (Louvain: Éditions Peeters, 1983).

79. Davison, *Essays*, 138–140. By 1914, approximately 5,500,000 telegrams were sent yearly in the empire.

80. On Abd ül-Hamid's Pan-Islamic program, see Shaw, *History of the Ottoman Empire*, 259–260.

Chapter XI. Conclusion: Revolutionary Options, Satiric Imagery, and the Historiographic Frame

1. W. L. Courtney, "The Constitutional Mutiny of April 13th," 58–59. The value of ascribing economic (or mercenary) causes to events taking place in the Asian and Muslim world is that it acts as a counterweight to reductionism of various sorts: religious, nationalist, etc.

2. Şerif Mardin, "A Note on the Transformation of Religious Symbols in Turkey," *Turcica* 16 (1984): 115–127, has discussed the contest for a universe of "national" symbols in 1923: "The new focus of *communitas* was the nation, and the experiment with this frame of allegiance was a success. In the process the entire stock of symbolic resources for social interaction that were available in Islamic culture were set aside: Durkheimian intellectuals who were willing to use Islam were upstaged by the radical secularism of the founding fathers of the Turkish Republic" (123). In 1908, the symbolic resources available in Islam had not been set aside; revolutionary gazettes, satirical and serious, were exploring exactly what it meant to have the nation as a frame of allegiance, how the nation and the empire could be differentiated, and if such differentiation was desirable.

3. Clearly a part of this perceived foreign threat was the threat of separatist movements inspired by European nationalisms, but this element of the foreign

threat was not couched in terms of nation against empire or nation against nation. The foreign nations were significant not so much because they embodied some new form of nationalism but because they were a military, economic, and cultural threat. Mahmoud Haddad, "The Rise of Arab Nationalism Reconsidered," *International Journal of Middle East Studies*, 26, no. 2 (May 1994), 201–222, has made a compelling argument for the complexity and colonial context of nationalisms in the late Ottoman period. He argues, of the Syrian Arabists, that they "continued to regard the Ottoman state as the ultimate repositiory of political legitimacy because it was regarded paradoxically as a bulwark against the Western colonial powers (217)." He also argues against any simple construction of ethnic nationalism.

4. Henry David Thoreau, "Life Without Principle," *The Writings of Henry David Thoreau*, v. 4, *Cape Cod Miscellanies* (Boston: Houghton Mifflin, 1906), 473. Walter Andrews, "Speaking of Power: The 'Ottoman Kaside,'" in Stephen Sperl and Christopher Shackle, eds., *Qasidah Poetry in Islamic Asia and Africa*, v.1 (Leiden: E.J. Brill, 1996), 281–300, has addressed the problem of ascribing national identities to the Ottomans in another (but highly relevant) context, that of Ottoman literature.

5. William W. Haddad, "Nationalism in the Ottoman Empire," in Haddad and Ochsenwald, eds., *Nationalism in a Non-National State*, 22–23; William Cleveland, *Islam Against the West: Shakib Arslan and the Campaign for Islamic Nationalism* (Austin: University of Texas Press, 1985), and *The Making of an Arab Nationalist: Ottomanism and Arabism in the Life and Thought of Sati' al-Husri* (Princeton: Princeton University Press, 1971); Lewis, *The Emergence of Modern Turkey;* George Antonius, *The Arab Awakening: The Story of the Arab National Movement* (Beirut: Librarie du Liban, 1969); François Georgeon, *Aux Origines du Nationalisme Turc: Yusuf Akçura (1876–1935)*, Synthèse no. 2, Institut d'Études Anatoliennes (Paris: ADPF, 1986).

6. Rashid Khalidi, "Arab Nationalism in Syria: The Formative Years, 1908–1914," in Haddad and Ochsenwald, *Nationalism in a Non-National State*, 207–237.

7. Kayalı, *Arabs and Young Turks*, bridges the gap between Anatolia and the Arab provinces by looking at the evolving relationship between the Arab provinces and the Ottoman central government from 1908–1918. Kayalı concludes (207–212), and I concur, that the Turkification policy of the CUP has been exaggerated, that government language policy was linked primarily to centralization (and was nothing new), and that there was not a clear split along ethno-linguistic lines in support of Arabism or Turkism in the empire (even after 1913).

8. Fraser, *Persia and Turkey in Revolt*, 221–225. Although Fraser admits of tribal and self-interested positions, for example, in various groups' assessments of the new regime, he is inclined to think that there is an Arab position and that that position is determined primarily by Islam. That sort of argument becomes a bit tenuous when one recalls the general commitment to Islam of most of the new regime. Race is important to Fraser, and he suggests that Oriental-style governmental corruption has been passed down in the "blood" of the "Turks." He does, however, admit the profit motive, noting that various elites in the Arab provinces saw themselves as having been better off under Abd ül-Hamid, especially in terms of political and economic power.

9. Berkes, *The Development of Secularism in Turkey*, 197–198, credits İbrahim Şinasi

(1824–1871) with popularizing much of the language of constitutionalism and with "the first use of the word *millet* in the sense of 'nation'." Certainly some writers envisioned the empire as a soon-to-be France or Britain. But the European-inspired ideals of the nation diverged considerably from the ground level social and administrative realities of the Ottoman state (just as they diverged from ground level realities in Europe). Not only that, there was the dilemma of posing an ideal of nation in a state with a glorious imperial tradition, quite a different task from posing that same ideal to peoples with a long history of weakness or subordination.

10. Roderic Davison, "Nationalism as an Ottoman Problem and the Ottoman Response," in Haddad and Ochsenwald, *Nationalism in a Non-National State*, 52. For more on this argument see: Kayalı, *Arabs and Young Turks;* Zürcher, *The Unionist Factor;* Zeine, *The Emergence of Arab Nationalism*, who argues the force of Islam as a determining factor; and Duri, *The Historical Formation of the Arab Nation*.

11. Those who adopted European styles wholesale were treated in the press to a certain extent as having sold-out their identities; but more often they were treated as either frivolous or as opportunists. They made what Laitin, *Hegemony and Culture*, 100, has called, "strategic identity readjustments by self-interested individuals."

12. Western observers were fond of focusing on racial or ethnic divisions within the empire. To what extent this was a reflection of the observers' own ethnic preoccupations and to what extent it was a reflection of identities within the empire is, I think, a question that requires considerably more study and discussion.

13. Photos (usually clearly staged) of Istanbul public spaces can give some sense of the variety of costume, associated with both region and function, worn by Istanbul's citizens. One such photo, of tradesmen, soldiers, and waiters at a coffee shop, can be found in İhsanoğlu, *İstanbul*, 74. Photos made for foreign consumption often focused on costume variety and "ethnic" type, although ethnicity in this particular form of Orientalist art could be highly questionable.

14. On ethnic and regional stereotypes in the Karagöz, see And, *A History of Theatre*, 46–48. The "Turk," is a rough but good-hearted bumpkin, a woodcutter; the "Arab" is a merchant or traveler, the "Kurd" a night watchman, the "Laz" a boatman, and so on. Each is characterized by a certain dress, a certain profession, and most particularly by certain patterns of speech.

15. Osman Okyar, "The Union and Progress Committee and the Turkish Republic (Ottomanism and Nationalism)," 287–299, in Jean-Louis Bacqué-Grammont and Emeri van Donzel, eds., *Comité International D'Études Pré-Ottomanes et Ottomanes, VIth Symposium, Cambridge, 1–4 July 1984*, Varia Turcica IV (İstanbul: Editions d'Amérique et d'Orient, 1987), among others, has pointed out the ethnic divisions within the new Ottoman parliament and the tensions that played themselves out along ethnic lines. There was a clear consciousness of ethnic divisions against which the rhetoric of Ottomanism was shaped, that rhetoric, in turn, pointed up those divisions. See Zeine, *The Emergence of Arab Nationalism*, 85–86, 100–115: and Kayalı, *Arabs and Young Turks*, 60–71, 82–100, 121–122, 138–140.

16. Corinne Blake, "Training Arab-Ottoman Bureaucrats," 264–267. It is important to note, however, that Blake also emphasizes the success of schools like the Mülkiye in creating an esprit de corps and sense of social cohesion that transcended

ethnic divisions (106–107). Eugene Rogan, "Aşiret Mektebi: Abdülhamid II's School for Tribes (1892–1907), *International Journal of Middle East Studies* 28, no. 1 (1996): 83–107, has looked at the graduates of the sultan's Istanbul school for the sons of tribal provincials (Arabs and Kurds specifically) and noted its success in producing apparently loyal Ottoman civil servants. The integrative processes of Abd ül-Hamid's reign are just as important as the disintegrative processes in determining the relative value of categories of ethnicity in the late empire period, but the latter have received a lot more press.

17. Orga, *Portrait of a Turkish Family*, 208–213. Orga speaks of the Kurdish and Armenian refugees as "hordes from the East" (209), and characterizes the Armenians as smug, the Kurds as spoiling for a fight, and the Arabs as "excitable" (212–213).

18. One could make a linguistic argument that the Arab is the person who speaks Arabic and the Turk is the person who speaks Turkish, but of course Ottoman is not some pure form of Turkish anymore than the Turkish speaker or the Arabic speaker is somehow ethnically pure Turk or Arab.

19. Also of interest on the efforts of "Arabs" within Abd ül-Hamid's court, see Ş. Tufan Buzpınar, "Abdülhamid II and Sayyid Fadl Pasha of Hadramawt: An Arab Dignitary's Ambitions (1876–1900)," *Osmanlı Araştırmaları* 13 (1993): 227–239.

20. Hanioğlu, *The Young Turks in Opposition*, 209–210. Lewis, *Race and Slavery in the Middle East*, 17–20, discusses some of the antecedents of such racial hierarchies in the Middle East.

21. See François Georgeon, *Aux Origines du Nationalisme Turc;* and Masami Arai, *Turkish Nationalism in the Young Turk Era* (Leiden: E.J. Brill, 1992), 48–82, on Akçura. Berkes, *The Development of Secularism in Turkey*, esp. 313–322, 347–366, 427–430, discusses the interplay of Westernization, Islam, nationalism, and Turkism as forces in the late Ottoman era. Berkes, among others, argues that Turkish nationalism was in part a reaction or defense against European imperialism and ethno-nationalist separatism. He speaks of economic nationalism as aiming to "make the Turks economically independent of internal and external rivals" (335).

22. Of course there were not so many "pure" Germans either, so that is not always an obstacle to ethno-nationalist programs. Also there were the competing identities of Islam, see Hanioğlu, *The Young Turks in Opposition*, 211–212. Kayalı, *Arabs and Young Turks*, 87–88, 208, argues that opponents of centralization policy used the charge of Turkification as a red flag against the CUP; he thus points to Turkification as a rhetorical issue.

23. For an interesting comparison during the same era on the questions of nationalism, race, and the role of the periodical press, see Walter Adamson, "Modernism and Fascism: The Politics of Culture in Italy (1903–1922), *American Historical Review* 95, no. 2 (April 1990): 359–390.

24. Mardin, *The Genesis of Young Ottoman Thought*, 404, pointed out, in 1962: "It is often forgotten, however, that Young Ottoman theories were partly of Islamic origins." He continued, "The significant link to follow, then, in establishing the link between the Young Ottomans, the Young Turks, and Atatürk is the weakening of Islamic content." The cartoons (of the Young Turk period) examined here neither

affirm nor deny that proposal. Islam was neither a particular target nor a banner waved by the satirists; but it was a factor lurking, usually, around the edges of the cartoon space.

25. One possible answer is that the traditional power of the Muslim establishment could not compete against the success and influence of Westernization, see: Hanioğlu, *The Young Turks in Opposition*, 10. But the history of Turkey in the late twentieth century suggests the connections between economic position and religious ideology and also the degree to which Islamic orientations remained strong within Turkish culture. Hence, the nature and degree of the Ottoman, and then Turkish, embracing of Westernization is still at issue. On the ways in which Islam can be treated as one element of social formation rather than as the defining element of a culture, see Burke, "Islam and Social Movements: Methodological Reflections," 17–35. Said Arjomand, "Religion and Constitutionalism in Western History and in Modern Iran and Pakistan," 69–99 in, Said Arjomand, ed., *The Political Dimensions of Religion* (Albany: State University of New York Press, 1993), has written compellingly of the tensions and the connections between Islam and constitutionalism in Iran. See also Zeine, *The Emergence of Arab Nationalism*, 35–115, 143–150, for an integrated treatment of the contending and overlapping Muslim, Ottoman, and Arab identities during this period; and Duri, *The Historical Formation of the Arab Nation*, 215–228, on Arab societies and nationalist identity.

26. Kayalı, *Arabs and Young Turks*, 211, argues that the Unionists' model of Ottomanism evolved and, from 1913 on, increasingly emphasized Islam in its rhetorics of unity. His model suggests, perhaps, that a comparison of cartoons before and after 1913 might be revelatory. Still, what remains to be explored is the extent to which the Islamic (and caliphal) rhetorics of either Abd ül-Hamid or the CUP struck a sympathetic chord, in the general populace or with Muslims abroad, and the extent to which such sympathy might have translated into political action.

27. There are, of course, also communal connotations in the nationalism model, particularly in the notion that Christian subjects of the Ottoman state had natural affiliations with Europe because the Europeans were Christians. In no way am I suggesting here that communal allegiances are not significant; but I do propose that the ramifications of those allegiances be traced out rather than taken for granted, and that competing identities not be neglected in the course of privileging religious ones.

28. Ahmad, *The Young Turks*; Hanioğlu, *The Young Turks in Opposition*; Zürcher, *The Unionist Factor*.

29. Berkes, *The Development of Secularism in Turkey*; Mardin, *The Genesis of Young Ottoman Thought*; and Lewis, *The Emergence of Modern Turkey*. James Gelvin, "The Social Origins of Popular Nationalism in Syria: Evidence for a New Framework," *International Journal of Middle East Studies* 26, no. 4 (1994): 645–661, has critiqued the use of the politics-of-notables model for post–World War I Syria, the area where it has been most usefully applied.

30. Gelbart, *Feminine and Opposition Journalism*, 15–16, uses the thought of Karl Mannheim, (*Ideology and Utopia*), to express the types of options perceived and employed by the French press. Mannheim posited ideological thought, which "re-

mains integrated within the order of things," and utopian thoughts, which "translate into action and threaten to break the bonds of the existing order." Gelbart notes the mixture of integrative and subversive tendencies in "*frondeur* journalism."

31. See Laitin, *Hegemony and Culture,* 19–20. Laitin speaks about the change from one system to another during the revolutionary period. During this time "meaning in a society" is in transition causing insecurity just as, in a more concrete fashion, the government is in transition in terms of political factions (on an internal level), and society is made insecure (on an external level) because of the threat of foreign invasion.

32. Laitin, *Hegemony and Culture,* 104, 145, has noted not only the role of the revolutionary press in shaping identities, but also, in the Yoruba case, the "fluidity of the social definition of society."

33. Sahlins and the Comaroffs are both quoted in Aletta Biersack, "Local Knowledge, Local History," in Hunt, *The New Cultural History,* 93.

34. It is here that both Said, *Orientalism,* and Timothy Mitchell, *Colonising Egypt,* (Cambridge: Cambridge University Press, 1988), tell only part of the story, one because he seems to assume a rather unitary historical hostility and the other because he seems to imagine a rather pristine native past.

35. On the dilemma of categorizing Islam as oriental and Christianity as occidental, see Bryan S. Turner, "Orientalism, the Problem of Civil Society in Islam," in Asaf Hussein et. al., eds., *Orientalism, Islam, and Islamists* (Brattleboro, Vermont: Amana Books, 1984), 23–42.

36. Excerpted from the translation of the curtain poem (*perde gazeli*), "Muddleheaded Night Watchman," by Tietze, *The Turkish Shadow Theatre,* 31. The *perde gazeli* was a convention of the shadow play that equated the scenes of the play with the goings on of the world; see And, *Karagöz,* 44; and (for other versions of the curtain poem in the Turkish), Kudret, *Karagöz,* 1: 65–66, 3: 12.

BIBLIOGRAPHY

Abdullah Cevdet. *İstanbul Köpekler.* Cairo: n.d., 1909.
Abdülhamid Han. *Devlet ve Memleket Görüşlerim.* Edited by Alaaddin Çetin and Ramazan Yıldız. İstanbul: Çığır Yayınları, 1976.
Abrahamian, Ervand. *Iran Between Two Revolutions.* Princeton: Princeton University Press, 1982.
Abu Abraham. *The Penguin Book of Indian Cartoons.* New Delhi: Penguin Books, 1988.
Adamson, Walter. "Modernism and Fascism: The Politics of Culture in Italy, 1903–1922," *American Historical Review* 95, no. 2 (April 1990): 359–390.
Adıvar, Halide Edib. *The Conflict of East and West in Turkey.* 2nd. edition. Lahore: S. M. Ashraf, 1935.
Afary, Janet. *The Iranian Constitutional Revolution, 1906–1911: Grassroots Democracy, Social Democracy, and the Origins of Feminism.* New York: Columbia University Press, 1996.
Afshar, Haleh. *Women, State, and Ideology: Studies from Africa and Asia.* London: Macmillan, 1987.
Aghulhon, Maurice. *Marianne Into Battle: Republican Imagery and Symbolism in France, 1789–1880.* Cambridge: Cambridge University Press, 1981.
Ahmad, Feroz. "Great Britain's Relations with the Young Turks, 1908–1914." *Middle Eastern Studies* (July 1966): 302–329.
———. *The Making of Modern Turkey.* London: Routledge, 1993.
———. *The Young Turks: The Committee of Union and Progress in Turkish Politics 1908–1914.* Oxford: Oxford University Press, 1969.
———. "War and Society under the Young Turks, 1908–1918." *Review* 11 (Spring 1988): 265–286.
Ahmed, Leila. *Women and Gender in Islam.* New Haven: Yale University Press, 1992.
Ahmed Rasim. *Ciddiyet ve Mizah.* İstanbul: Kurtiş Matbaası, 1989 reprint of 1336/1920 edition.
———. *Şehir Mektubları.* İstanbul: Kadır Matbaası, 1328/1912.
———. *Şehir Mektupları.* Vol. 1. İstanbul: Milli Eğitim Basımevi, 1971. Turkish version of 1912 Ottoman edition.
Ahmed Şerif. *Anadolu Tanin.* İstanbul: Tanin, 1325/1909.
Ahmida, Ali. *The Making of Modern Libya: State Formation, Colonization, and Resistance, 1830–1932.* Albany: State University of New York Press, 1994.
Akbayar, Nurhan, and Orhan Koloğlu. *Gazeteci Bir Aile: Mehmed Asım, Hakkı Tarık, Hasan Rasim Us'lar.* Ankara: ÇDG Yayınları, 1996.

Bibliography

Aksan, Virginia. *An Ottoman Statesman in War and Peace: Ahmed Resmi Efendi, 1700–1783.* Leiden: E. J. Brill, 1995.

Akşin, Sina, "La Révolution Française et la Conscience Révolutionnaire des Nationalistes Turcs a L'Aube de la Lutte D'Independence." In *La Turquie et la France a L'Époque D'Atatürk*, Collection Turcica, 1: 45–55. Paris: Association Pour Le Développement Des Études Turques, 1981.

———. *100 Soruda Jön Türkler ve İttihad ve Terakki.* İstanbul: Gerçek, 1980.

Alba, Victor."The Mexican Revolution and the Cartoon." *Comparative Studies in Society and History* 9, no. 2 (January 1967): 121–136.

Alemdar, Korkmaz. *İstanbul (1875–1964): Türkiye'de Yayınlanan Fransızca Bir Gazetenin Tarihi.* Ankara: Ankara İktisadi ve Ticari İlimler Akademisi, 1980.

———. Türkiye'de Yabancı Dilde Basın." *Tarih ve Toplum* 10 (1988): 166–171.

Alfieri, V. *İstibdad.* Translated by Abdullah Cevdet. Geneva: Osmanlı İttihad ve Terraki Cemiyeti, 1317/1899.

Ali Haydar Emir (Alpagut). *Balkan Harbinde Türk Filosu.* İstanbul: Deniz Basımevi, 1932.

Ali Haydar Midhat Pasha. *The Life of Midhat Pasha: A Record of his Services, Political Reforms, Banishment and Judicial Murder Derived from Private Documents and Reminiscenses.* London: John Murray, 1903.

Ali Seydi. *Resimli Kamus-ı Osmanî.* İstanbul: Cihan Matbaa, 1330/1914.

Alloula, Malek. *The Colonial Harem.* Minneapolis: University of Minnesota Press, 1984.

And, Metin. *A History of Theatre and Popular Entertainment in Turkey.* Ankara: Forum Yayınları, 1963–1964.

———. *Karagöz: Turkish Shadow Theatre.* İstanbul: Dost Yayınları, 1987.

Anderson, Benedict. *Imagined Communities, Reflections on the Origin and Spread of Nationalism.* London: Verso Press, 1991.

Anderson, Margaret. "Voter, Junker, Landrat, Priest: The Old Authorities and the New Franchise in Imperial Germany." *American Historical Review* 98 (December 1993): 1448–1474.

Anderson, Patricia. *The Printed Image and the Transformation of Popular Culture 1790–1860.* Oxford: Clarendon Press, 1991.

Andrews, Walter. "Speaking of Power: The Ottoman Kaside." In *Qasidah Poetry in Islamic Asia and Africa*, edited by Stephen Sperl and C. Shackle, 1: 281–300. Leiden: Brill, 1996.

———. "Time Warps: Through the Transparent Wall as Literature Writes Literary History." Paper presented at the Middle East Studies Association Conference, Phoenix, November, 1994.

Antonius, George. *The Arab Awakening: The Story of the Arab National Movement.* Beirut: Librairie du Liban, 1969.

Arai, Masami. *Turkish Nationalism in the Young Turk Era.* Leiden: E. J. Brill, 1992.

Arat, Zehra. "Turkish Women and the Republican Reconstruction of Tradition." In *Reconstructing Gender in the Middle East,* edited by Müge Göçek and Shiva Balaghi, 57–80. New York: Columbia University Press, 1994.

Ariés, Philippe. *The Hour of Our Death.* Oxford: Oxford University Press, 1991.

Bibliography

Arjomand, Said, ed. *The Political Dimensions of Islam*. Albany: State University of New York Press, 1993.
Armbrust, Walter. "The National Vernacular: Folklore and Egyptian Popular Culture." *Michigan Quarterly Review* 31, no. 4 (Fall 1992): 525–542.
Armytage, G. "Modern Dress." *Fortnightly Review* 34 (July 1–December 1, 1883): 344–353.
Arslan, Amir Shakib. *Our Decline and Its Causes*. Translated by M. A. Shakoor. Lahore: Ashraf, 1968.
Artuk, İbrahim and Çevriye. *İstanbul Arkeoloji Müzeleri Teşhirdeki İslâmî Sikkeler Kataloğu*. Vol 2. İstanbul: Milli Eğitim Basımevi, 1974.
Âşıkpaşa. *Âşıkpaşa Tarihi*. Edited by Atsız. İstanbul: Milli Eğitim Basımevi, 1970.
Ayalon, Ami. *Language and Change in the Arab Middle East: The Evolution of Modern Political Discourse*. Oxford: Oxford University Press, 1987.
———. *The Press in the Arab Middle East*. New York: Oxford University Press, 1995.
Aydemir, Şevket. *Makedonya'dan Ortaasya'ya Enver Pasha* . Vol. 2. İstanbul: Remzi Kitabevi, 1976.
Bacqué-Grammont, Jean-Louis, and Paul Dumont, eds. *Économie et Sociétés dans L'Empire Ottoman (Fin du XVIIIe—Début du XXe siécle)* Paris: Editions du Centre National de la Recherche Scientifique, 1983.
Bacqué-Grammont, Jean-Louis and Edhem Eldem, eds. *De La Révolution Française À la Turquie d'Atatürk: La modernisation politique et sociale. Les lettres, les sciences et les arts. Actes des Colloques d'Istanbul (10–12 mai 1989)*. İstanbul: Editions Isis, 1990.
Bagchi, Amiya Kumar. *The Political Economy of Underdevelopment*. Cambridge: Cambridge University Press, 1982.
Banarlı, Nihad. *Resimli Türk Edebiyatı Tarihi*. İstanbul: Milli Eğitim Basımevi, 1971.
Baron, Beth. *The Women's Awakening in Egypt: Culture, Society, and the Press*. New Haven: Yale University Press, 1994.
Barthes, Roland. *The Fashion System*. Translated by Mathew Ward and Richard Howard. New York: Hill and Wang, 1983.
Bataille, Henri. *La femme nue, piece en quatre actes*. Paris: L'Illustration, 1908.
Batu, Hamit, and Jean-Louis Bacqué-Grammont, eds. *L'Empire Ottoman, la République de Turquie et la France*. İstanbul: Editions Isis, 1986.
Bayat, Mangol. *Iran's First Revolution: Shi'ism and the Constitutional Revolution of 1905–1909*. Oxford: Oxford University Press, 1991.
Bayur, Yusuf Hikmet. *Türk Inkilabı Tarihi*. Ankara: T. T. K., 1963–1964.
Bazin, Louis. "Censure Ottomane et Lexicographie: Le Kamus-i Fransevî de Sâmi Bey." In *Économie et Sociétés dans l'Empire Ottoman*, edited by Jean-Louis Bacque-Grammont and Paul Dumont, 203–206. Paris: Editions du Centre National de la Recherche Scientifique, 1983.
Behnam, M. Reza. *Cultural Foundations of Iranian Politics*. Salt Lake City: University of Utah Press, 1986.
Bennet, E. N. "Personal Observations During the Balkan War II." *The Nineteenth Century* 73 (January 1913): 28–40.
Bérard, Victor. *La Révolution Turque*. Paris: Librairie Armand Colin, 1909.

Bibliography

Berkes, Niyazi. *The Development of Secularism in Turkey*. Montreal: McGill University Press, 1968.

Berque, Jacques. *Egypt, Imperialism and Revolution*. New York: Praeger, 1972.

Beyhan, Mehmed Ali. "Bir II. Abdülhamid Devri Aydını'nın Profili: Lastik Said Bey." *Osmanlı Araştırmaları* 13 (1993): 167–185.

Beysanoğlu, Şevket. *Basın ve Yayın Dünyamızda Diyarbakır.* Ankara: İş, 1970.

Bianchi, T. X. *Notice sur le Premier Ouvrage d'Anatomie et de Médecine, imprimé en Turc, a Constantinople, en 1820 . . . ; suivie Du Catalogue des Livres Turcs, Arabes et Persans, Imprimés à Constantinople, depuis l'Introduction de l'Imprimerie, en 1726–27, jusqu'en 1820*. Paris: Imprimerie L.T. Cellot, 1821.

Billingsley, Phil. *Bandits in Republican China*. Stanford: Stanford University Press, 1988.

Black, Jeremy. *The English Press in the Eighteenth Century*. Philadelphia: University of Pennsylvania Press, 1987.

Blaisdell, Donald. *European Financial Control in the Ottoman Empire*. New York: Columbia Univerity Press, 1929.

Blake, Corinne. "Training Arab-Ottoman Bureaucrats: Syrian Graduates of the Mülkiye Mektebi, 1890–1920." Ph.D diss., Princeton University, 1991.

Bloom, Edward and Lillian Bloom. *Satire's Persuasive Voice*. Ithaca: Cornell University Press, 1979.

Blunt, Wilfrid. *Desert Hawk: Abd el Kader and the French Conquest of Algeria*. London: Methuen and Co., 1947.

Boğaziçi Şirket-i Hayriye Tarihçe, Salname. İstanbul: Ahmet İhsan, 1330/1914.

Bonakdarian, Mansour. "Iranian Constitutional Exiles and British Foreign Policy Dissenters." *International Journal of Middle East Studies* 27, no. 2 (May 1995): 175–191.

Bosworth, C. E. et al., eds. *Essays in Honor of Bernard Lewis: The Islamic World from Classical to Modern Times*. Princeton: Darwin Press, 1989.

Boureau, Alan. "Books and Emblems on the Public Stage: Côté jardin and côté cour." In *The Culture of Print*, edited by Roger Chartier, 261–289. Princeton: Princeton University Press, 1989.

Braude, Ann. *Radical Spirits: Spiritualism and Women's Rights in Nineteenth Century America*. Boston: Beacon Press, 1989.

Brewer, John, and Roy Porter, eds. *Consumption and the World of Goods*. London: Routledge, 1993.

Brinkman, Del. "Do Editorial Cartoons and Editorials Change Opinions?" *Journalism Quarterly* 45 (Winter 1968): 724–726.

Browne, Edward G. *The Persian Revolution of 1905–1909*. London: Frank Cass, 1910.

———. *The Press and Poetry of Modern Persia*. Los Angeles: Kalimat Press, 1983 reprint of 1914 edition.

Brummett, Palmira. "Dressing for Revolution: Mother, Nation, Citizen and Subversive in the Ottoman Satirical Press." In *Deconstructing Images of "the Turkish Woman,"* edited by Zehra Arat, 37–64. New York: St. Martin's, 1998.

———. "New Woman and Old Nag: Images of Women in the Ottoman Cartoon Space." *Princeton Papers* (Spring/Summer 1997): 13–57.
Buheiry, Marwan R., ed. *Intellectual Life in the Arab East, 1890–1939*. Beirut: American University of Beirut, 1981.
Burke, Edmund III, and Ira M. Lapidus, eds. *Islam, Politics and Social Movements*. Berkeley: University of California Press, 1988.
Burns, J. H. *Lordship, Kingship, and Empire: The Idea of Monarchy 1400–1525*. Oxford: Clarendon Press, 1992.
Busbecq, Ogier Ghislaine de. *The Turkish Letters of Ogier Ghislain de Busbecq, Ambassador at Constantinople 1554–1562*. Translated by Edward Foster. Oxford: Clarendon Press, 1968.
Buzpınar, Ş. Tufan. "Abdülhamid II and Sayyid Fadl Pasha of Hadramawt: An Arab Dignitary's Ambitions (1876–1900)." *Osmanlı Araştırmaları* 13 (1993): 227–239.
Büyüktuğrul, Afif. *Balkan Harb Tarihi*, vol. 7, *Osmanlı Deniz Hareketi, 1912–1913*. Ankara: Genelkurmay Başkan Harb Tarihi Dairesi, 1965.
Canner, Ethymia. "La Presse Satirique grecque d'Istanbul au lendemain de la révolution jeune-turque: le journal Embros." *Revue du Monde Musulman et de la Méditerranée* 77–78 (1996): 111–122.
Carl, Leroy. "Editorial Cartoons Fail to Reach Many Readers." *Journalism Quarterly* 45 (Autumn 1968): 533–535.
Castellan, Georges. *History of the Balkans*. Boulder: East European Monographs, 1992.
Celal Nuri (İleri). *Kadınlarımız*. İstanbul: Matbaa-ı İctihad, 1331 hicrî/1913.
———. *Türk İnkılâbı*. İstanbul: Ahmet İhsan Matbaası, n.d.
Cemal Pasha. *Memories of a Turkish Statesman 1913–1919*. New York: George A. Duran Co., 1922.
Censer, Jack Richard. "Commencing the Third Century of Debate." *American Historical Review* 94, no. 5 (December 1989): 1309–1325.
———. *Prelude to Power: The Parisian Radical Press*. Baltimore: Johns Hopkins University Press, 1976.
———, and Jeremy D. Popkin, eds. *Press and Politics in Pre-Revolutionary France*. Berkeley: University of California Press, 1987.
Chardin, Pierre Teilhard de. *Letters from Egypt 1905–1908*. New York: Herder and Herder, 1965.
Chartier, Roger. *Cultural History: Between Practices and Representations*. Ithaca: Cornell University Press, 1988.
———. *The Cultural Uses of Print in Early Modern France*. Princeton: Princeton University, 1987.
———, ed. *The Culture of Print: Power and the Uses of Print in Early Modern Europe*. Cambridge: Polity Press, 1989.
Chaudhuri, Nupur and Margaret Strobel, eds. *Western Women and Imperialism: Complicity and Resistance*. Bloomington: Indiana University Press, 1992.
Childers, Thomas. "The Social Language of Politics in Germany: The Sociology of Political Discourse in the Weimar Republic." *American Historical Review* 95, no. 2 (April 1990): 331–358.

Bibliography

Cleveland, William. *Islam Against the West: Shakib Arslan and the Campaign for Islamic Nationalism.* Austin: University ot Texas Press, 1985.

———. *The Making of an Arab Nationalist: Ottomanism and Arabism in the Life and Thought of Sati' al-Husri.* Princeton: Princeton University, 1971.

↙ Clogg, Richard. "A Further Note on the French Newspapers of Istanbul During the Revolutionary Period (1795-97)." *Belleten* 39, no. 155 (1975): 483-490.

Coupe, W. A. "The German Cartoon and the Revolution of 1848." *Comparative Studies in Society and History* 9, no. 2 (January 1967): 137-167.

Courtney, W. L. "The Constitutional Mutiny of April 13th." *Fortnightly Review*, n.s. 86 (July-December 1909): 66-68.

Criss, Nur Bilge. "A Facet of Muslim Womanhood: The Turkish Case." *Turkish Review of Middle East Studies* 7 (1993): 237-257.

Çakır, Serpil. *Osmanlı Kadın Hareketi.* İstanbul: Metis Yayınları, 1994.

Çapanoğlu, Munir. *Basın Tarihine Dair Bilgiler ve Hatıralar.* İstanbul: Hür Türkiye Dergisi Yayınları, 1962.

Çelik, Zeyneb. "The Impact of Westernization on Istanbul's Urban Form 1838-1908." Ph.D. diss., University of California, 1984.

———. *The Remaking of Istanbul: Portrait of an Ottoman City in the Nineteenth Century.* Berkeley: University of California Press, 1993.

Çeviker, Turgut. *Gelişim Sürecinde Türk Karikatürü*, 3 vols. İstanbul: Adam Yayınları, 1986-1991.

———. *İbret Albümü 1908.* İstanbul. Mataş Matbaacılık, 1991.

———. "Türk Karikatüründe Kurtuluş Savaşı Dönemi (1918-1923)." *Sanat Dünyamız* 40 (1990): 18-25.

Çizgen, Engin. *Photography in the Ottoman Empire, 1839-1919.* İstanbul: Kitapçılık Basın Sanayı, 1987.

Danişmend, I. H., ed. *Abdülhak Hamit Külliyatı.* Vol. 3. İstanbul: Kanaat, 1945.

Dankoff, Robert, ed. and trans. *The Intimate Life of an Ottoman Statesman: Melek Ahmed Pasha (1588-1662) As Portrayed in Evliya Çelebi's Book of Travels (Seyahat-name).* Albany: State University of New York Press, 1991.

Darnton, Robert. "The High Enlightenment and the Low-Life of Literature in Pre-Revolutionary France." *Past and Present* 51 (1970): 81-115.

Darnton, Robert and Daniel Roche, eds. *Revolution in Print: The Press in France, 1775-1800.* Berkeley: University of California Press, 1989.

Davies, Robert. *Peacefully Working to Conquer the World: Singer Sewing Machines in Foreign Markets, 1854-1920.* New York: Arno Press, 1976.

Davison, Roderic H. "How the Ottoman Government Adjusted to a New Institution: The Newspaper Press." In *Turkic Culture: Continuity and Change*, edited by Sabri Akural, 17-26. Bloomington: Indiana University Press, 1987.

———. *Essays in Ottoman Turkish History 1774-1923: The Impact of the West.* Austin: University of Texas Press, 1990.

———. "The Ottoman Boycott of Austrian Goods in 1908 as a Diplomatic Question." In *Third Congress of the Social and Economic History of Turkey*, edited by Heath Lowry and Ralph Hattox, 1-28. İstanbul: Editions Isis, 1990.

Bibliography

De Leon, Edwin. *Thirty Years of My Life on Three Continents, with a Chapter on the Life of Women in the East by Mrs. De Leon*. 2 vols. London: Ward and Downey, 1890.

De Lusignan, G. A. Nar Bey. *Guide de la Conversation Français-Turque*. Paris: By the author, 1881.

Dede Korkut. *The Book of Dede Korkut*. Translated by Faruk Sumer. Austin: University of Texas Press, 1972.

Deguilhem-Schoem, Randi. "La diffusion des idées révolutionnaires et réformistes françaises dans l'Empire ottoman: le cas de l'école secondaire Maktab 'Anbar à Damas." *Revue du Monde Musulman de la Méditerranée* 52/53 (1990): 185-192.

———. "The Transmission of French and Other European Revolutionary Ideas in the Ottoman Empire." *Proceedings of the British Society for Middle Eastern Studies*, 1989, International Conference on Europe and the Middle East, pp. 234-243.

Deny, J. "État de la Presse turque en juillet 1925." *Revue de Monde Musulman* (1925, pt. 3): pp. 44-74.

———. "La Presse Musulman." *Revue du Monde Musulman* (1909): pp. 7-139.

Djivélguian, A. *Le Régime de la Presse en Turquie: Comparison avec le Régime Français*. Paris: Emile Larose, 1912.

Doğramcı, Emel. *Atatürk and the Turkish Woman Today*. Ankara: Atatürk Araştırma Merkezi, 1991.

Donald, Diana. *The Age of Caricature: Satirical Prints in the Reign of George III*. New Haven: Yale University Press, 1996.

Doyle, Arthur Conan. *The History of Spiritualism*. 2 vols. New York: George H. Doran Co., 1926.

Duben, Alan and Cem Behar, eds. *Istanbul Households: Marriage, Family and Fertility, 1880-1940*. Cambridge: Cambridge University Press, 1991.

Dubin, Steven C. *Arresting Images: Impolitic Art and Uncivil Actions*. New York: Routledge, 1992.

Duman, Hasan. *Eski Harfli Türkçe Süreli Yayınlar Toplu Kataloğu*. Vol. 1. Ankara: Milli Kütüphane Başkanlığı, 1987.

———. *İstanbul Kütüphaneleri Arap Harfli Süreli Yayınlar Toplu Kataloğu 1828-1928*. İstanbul: Research Centre for Islamic History, Art and Culture, 1986.

Dumont, Paul. "20. Yüzyıl Başları Osmanlı İmparatorluğu İşci Hareketleri ve Sosyalist Akımlar Tarihi Üzerine Yayımlanmamış Kaynaklar." *Toplum ve Bilim* 3 (1977): 31-50.

Durey, Michael. *The Return of the Plague, British Society and the Cholera 1831-1832*. Dublin: Gill and Macmillan Press, 1979.

Duri, A. A. *The Historical Formation of the Arab Nation: A Study in Identity and Consciousness*. London: Croom Helm, 1987.

Düzdağ, M. Ertuğrul. *İkinci Meşrutiyetin İlk Ayları ve 31 Mart Olayı İçin bir Yakın Belgesi: Volkan Gazetesi*. İstanbul: İz Yayıncılık, 1992.

Eken, Ahmed. *Kartpostallarda İstanbul*. İstanbul: Büyükşehir Belediyesi, 1992.

Ekrem, Selma. *Unveiled: The Autobiography of a Turkish Girl*. New York: Ives Washburn, 1934.

Bibliography

bert C. *The Power of Satire: Magic, Ritual, and Art*. Princeton: Princeton rsity Press, 1960.

rol. *Jön Türklere Dair Vesikalar I Edebiyatçı Jön Türklerin Mektupları (Ali Kemal ve ว‍yman Nazif'den Mizancı Murad Beye)*. İstanbul: İstanbul Üniversitesi, Edebiyat Fakültesi, 1982.

Emin, Ahmed. *The Modernization of Turkey as Measured by its Press*. New York: Columbia University Press, 1914.

Enayat, Hamid. *Modern Islamic Political Thought*. Austin: University of Texas Press, 1982.

Engelstein, Laura. *The Keys to Happiness: Sex and the Search for Modernity in Fin-de-Siècle Russia*. Ithaca: Cornell University Press, 1992.

Ersoy, Osman. *Türkiye'ye Matba'aın Girişi ve İlk Basılan Eserler*. Ankara: Güven Basımevi, 1959.

Ertug, Hasan Refik. *Basın ve Yayın Hareketleri Tarihi*. 2 vols. İstanbul: Yenilik Basımevi, 1970.

Evans, Richard J. "Epidemics and Revolution: Cholera in Nineteenth Century Europe," *Past and Present* 120 (August 1988): 123–146.

Evin, Ahmet. *Origins and Development of the Turkish Novel*. Minneapolis: Bibliotheca Islamica, 1983.

F. D. E. *Système des Mesures, Poids et Monnais de l'Empire Ottoman et des Principaux États*. Constantinople: n.p., 1910.

Farah, Caesar. "Censorship and Freedom of Expression in Ottoman Syria and Egypt." In *Nationalism in a Non-National State*, edited by William Haddad and William Ochsenwald, 151–194. Columbus: Ohio State University Press, 1977.

Feaver, William and Ann Gould. *Masters of Caricature from Hogarth and Gillray to Scarfe and Levine*. New York: Alfred Knopf, 1981.

Fenoglio-Abd El Aal, Irène. *Défense et Illustration de l'Egyptienne Aux débuts d'une Expression Féminine*. Cairo: CEDEJ, 1988.

———. "Caricature et représentation du mythe: Goha." In *Images d'Egypte, De la fresque à bande dessiné*. Cairo: CEDEJ, 1992.

Findley, Carter. *Bureaucratic Reform in the Ottoman Empire: The Sublime Porte, 1789–1922*. Princeton: Princeton University Press, 1980.

———. *Ottoman Civil Officialdom: A Social History*. Princeton: Princeton University Press, 1989.

———. "An Ottoman Occidentalist in Europe: Ahmed Midhat Meets Madame Gülnar, 1889." *American Historical Review* 103, no. 1 (February 1998): 15–49.

Finklestein, Joanne. *The Fashioned Self*. Cambridge: Polity Press, 1991.

Finn, Robert P. *The Early Turkish Novel 1872–1900*. İstanbul: Isis Press, 1983.

Fischel, Oskar and Max von Boehn. *Modes and Manners of the Nineteenth Century as Represented in the Pictures and Engravings of the Time*. Vol. 3, *1843–1878*. London: J. M. Dent and Company, 1909.

Frangakis-Syrett, Elena. "American Trading Practices in Izmir in the Late Nineteenth and Early Twentieth Centuries." In *Histoire Économique et Sociale de l'empire Ottoman et de la Turquie (1326–1960)*, editedby Daniel Panzac, 177–184. Paris: Peeters, 1995.

Bibliography

Fraschery, Samy Bey. *Resmi Kamus Fransevi / Dictionnaire Français-Turc Illustré.* 3rd. Edition. İstanbul/Constantinople: Mıhran Matbaası, 1318/1901.

Fraser, David. *Persia and Turkey in Revolt.* London: William Blackwood and Sons, 1910.

Frierson, Elizabeth. "Unimagined Communities: Women and Education in the Late-Ottoman Empire, 1876–1909." *Critical Matrix* 9, no. 2 (Fall 1995): 55–90.

Fritzsche, Peter. "Machine Dreams: Airmindedness and the Reinvention of Germany." *American Historical Review* 98 (June 1993): 685–709.

Fromkin, David. *A Peace to End All Peace.* New York: H. Holt, 1989.

Furet, François. *Interpreting the French Revolution.* Translated by Elborg Forster. Cambridge: Cambridge University Press, 1981.

Garnett, Lucy. *Turkish Life in Town and Country.* New York: G.P. Putnam's Sons, 1911.

Gavin, Charles E. S., ed. *Imperial Self-Portrait: The Ottoman Empire as Revealed in the Sultan Abdul Hamid II's Photographic Albums.* Special Issue, *Journal of Turkish Studies* 12 (1988).

Geipel, John. *The Cartoon: A Short History of Graphic Comedy and Satire.* London: David and Charles, 1972.

Gelbart, Nina Rattner. *Feminine and Opposition Journalism in Old Regime France: Le Journal des Dames.* Berkeley: University of California Press, 1987.

Gelvin, James. "The Social Origins of Popular Nationalism in Syria: Evidence for a New Framework." *International Journal of Middle East Studies* 26, no. 4 (1994): 645–661.

Georgeon, François. *Aux Origines du Nationalisme Turc: Yusuf Akçura (1876–1935).* Paris: ADPF, 1986.

———. "Note Sur le Budget d'Une Famille Ottoman au Debut du XXème Siècle." *Revue d'Histoire Maghrebine* 10, no. 31–32 (December 1983): 210–218.

———. "La Presse Satirique Ottomane Miroir de la Ville." *Les Cahiers de Tunisie* 30, no. 137–138 (1986): 309–323.

———. "Rire dans l'Empire ottoman?" *Revue du Monde Musulman et de la Méditeranée* 77–78 (1996): 89–110.

Gerçek, Selim Nüzhet. *Türk Gazeteciliği.* İstanbul: Devlet Matbaası, 1931.

———. *Türk Matba'acılığı,* 2 vols. İstanbul: Devlet Basımevi, 1939.

Gibb, Elias. *Ottoman Literature.* New York: M. Walter Dunne, 1901.

Girouard, Mark. *Cities and People: A Social and Architectural History.* New Haven: Yale University Press, 1985.

Goldstein, Robert Justin. *Censorship of Political Caricature in Nineteenth-Century France.* Kent, Ohio: Kent State University, 1989.

Gooch, G. P., and Harold Temperley. *British Documents on the Origins of the War 1898–1914.* Vol. 5, *The Near East: the Macedonian Problem and the Annexation of Bosnia 1903–1909.* London: His Majesty's Stationery Office, 1928.

Gough, Hugh. *The Newspaper Press in the French Revolution.* London: Routledge, 1988.

Göçek, Müge. *Rise of the Bourgeoisie, Demise of Empire: Ottoman Westernization and Social Change.* New York: Oxford University Press, 1996.

Gökalp, Ziya. *The Principles of Turkism.* Translated by Robert Devereux. Leiden: E. J. Brill, 1968.

Bibliography

Gökman, Muzaffer. *Sedat Simavi*. İstanbul: APA Ofset Basımevi, 1970.

Gökyay, Orhan, trans. *Türklerde Karagöz*. İstanbul: Bürhaneddin Basımevi, 1938.

Gövsa, İbrahim Alaettin. *Türk Meşhurları*. İstanbul: Yedigün Neşriyatı, n.d.

Grafton, Anthony. *Defenders of the Text: The Traditions of Scholarship in an Age of Science, 1450–1800*. Cambridge: Harvard University Press, 1991.

Graves, Charles L. *Mr. Punch's History of Modern England*. Vol. 2, *1857–1874*. London: Cassell and Company, 1921.

Graves, Sir Robert. *Storm Centres of the Near East: Personal Memories 1879–1929*. London: Hutchinson and Co., 1975.

Grey, Viscount of Fallodon. *Twenty-Five Years 1892–1916*. 2 vols. New York: Frederick A. Stokes Co., 1925.

Griffiths, Percival. *The British Impact on India*. N.P.: Archon Books, 1965.

Groc, G. "La Presse Turque Et Son Opinion Sur la France." In *L'Empire Ottoman*, edited by Hamit Batu and Bacqué-Grammont, 479–498. İstanbul: Editions Isis, 1986.

Groc, G. and İ Çağlar. *La Presse Française de Turquie de 1795 à nos Jours*. İstanbul: Editions Isis, 1985.

Guppy, Shusha. *Memoirs of a Persian Childhood*. Boston: Beacon Press, 1988.

Gündağ, Kayaoğlu. *Eski İstanbul'da Gündelik Hayat*. İstanbul: İstanbul Büyükşehir Belediyesi, 1992)

Habermas, Jürgen. *The Structural Transformation of the Public Sphere: An Inquiry into a Category of Bourgeois Society*. Cambridge: M.I.T. Press, 1989.

Haddad, Mahmoud. "The Rise of Arab Nationalism Reconsidered." *International Journal of Middle East Studies* 26, no. 2 (May 1994): 201–222.

Haddad, William and William Ochenswald, eds. *Nationalism in a Non-National State: The Dissolution of the Ottoman Empire*. Columbus: Ohio State University Press, 1977.

Hahner, June. *Poverty and Politics: The Urban Poor in Brazil, 1870–1920*. Albuquerque: University of New Mexico Press, 1986.

Hairi, Abdul-Hadi. "The Debates Over the Constitutional Revolution." In *Expectation of the Millenium: Shi'ism in History*, edited by Seyyed Hossein Nasr et al., 318–324. Albany: State University of New York Press.

Halman, Talat. *Modern Turkish Drama: An Anthology of Plays in Translation*. Minneapolis: Bibliotheca Islamica, 1976.

Hanioğlu, M. Şükrü. *Bir Siyasal Örgüt Olarak 'Osmanlı İttihad ve Terakki Cemiyeti ve "Jön Türklük."* 2 vols. İstanbul: İletişim Yayınları, n.d.

———. *The Young Turks in Opposition*. New York: Oxford U. Press, 1995.

Hart, James. *The Popular Book: A History of America's Literary Taste*. Berkeley: University of California Press, 1961.

Heidegger, Martin. *The Question Concerning Technology and Other Essays*. Translated by William Lovitt. New York: Harper, 1969.

Heller, Joseph. *British Policy Towards the Ottoman Empire 1908–1914*. London: Frank Cass, 1983.

Henshall, Nicholas. *The Myth of Absolutism: Change and Continuity in Early Modern European Monarchy*. London: Longman, 1992.

Hesse, Carla. "Economic Upheavals in Publishing." In *Revolution in Print: The Press in France 1775–1800,* edited by Robert Darnton and Daniel Roche, 69–97. Berkeley: University of California Press, 1989.

Hitchens, Robert. *The Near East: Dalmatia, Greece and Constantinople.* New York: The Century Co., 1913.

Hobsbawm, Eric. "Mass Producing Traditions: Europe, 1870–1914." In *The Invention of Tradition.* Edited by Hobsbawm and Terrance Ranger, pp. 263–307. Cambridge: Cambridge University Press, 1989.

Hoca Şakir. *Ulema-i İslâm Enarallahü Berahinehüm Taraflarından Verilen Fetava-yı Şerife.* Egypt: İctihat Matbaası, 1325 hicrî/1907.

Hourani, Albert. *Arabic Thought in the Liberal Age.* Oxford: Oxford University Press, 1970.

———. et al., eds. *The Modern Middle East: A Reader* (Berkeley: University of California Press, 1993.

Hubertus, Jahn. *Patriotic Culture in Russia During World War I.* Ithaca: Cornell University Press, 1995.

Hunt, Lynn. "Discourses of Patriarchalism and anti-Patriarchalism in the French Revolution." In *Language and Rhetoric of the Revolution,* edited by John Renwick, 25–49. Edinburgh: Edinburgh University Press, 1990.

———. ed. *The New Cultural History.* Berkeley: University of California, 1989.

Ibn Khaldun, *Muqaddimah: An Introduction to History.* Translated by Franz Rosenthal. Princeton: Princeton University Press, 1970.

Imber, Colin. "Ideals and Legitimation in Early Ottoman History." In *Süleiman the Magnificent and His Age,* edited by Metin Kunt and Christine Woodhead, 138–153. London: Longman, 1995.

Imbert, Paul. *La Rénovation de l'Empire Ottoman, Affaires de Turquie.* Paris: Perrin Et Cie., 1909.

Ismail Kemal Bey. *The Memoirs of Ismail Kemal Bey.* Edited by William Morton Fullerton. London: Constable and Company, 1920.

İhsan, Ahmet. *Matbuat Hatıralarım.* İstanbul: İletişim Yayınları, 1993.

İhsanoğlu, Ekmelledin. *Istanbul: A Glimpse into the Past.* İstanbul: Research Centre for Islamic History, Art, and Culture, 1987.

İnal, İbnülemin Mahmut Kemal. *Son Asır Türk Şairleri.* 3rd edition. Vol. 4. İstanbul: Dergâh Yayınları, 1988.

İnalcık, Halil. "İmtiyazat." In *Encyclopedia of Islam.* 2nd series, 3: 1179–1189. Leiden: E. J. Brill, 1971.

İnalcık, Halil, and Donald Quataert, eds. *An Economic and Social History of the Ottoman Empire, 1300–1914.* Cambridge: Cambridge University Press, 1994.

İskit, Server. *Türkiyede Matbuat İdareleri ve Politikaları.* Ankara: Başvekalet Basın ve Yayın Umum Müdürlüğü Yayınları, 1943.

———. *Türkiyede Matbuat Rejimleri.* İstanbul: Ülkü Matbaası, 1939.

———. *Türkiyede Neşriyat Hareketleri Tarihine Bir Bakış.* İstanbul: Devlet Basımevi, 1939.

İstanbul Ansiklopedisi. İstanbul: Neşriyat Kollektif Şirketi, 1959.

Bibliography

Jackson, A. V. Williams. *From Constantinople to the Home of Omar Khayyam: Travels in Transcaucasia and Northern Persia for Historic and Literary Research*. New York: Macmillan, 1911.

Javadi, Hasan. *Satire in Persian Literature*. Rutherford: Farleigh Dickinson Press, 1988.

Jouhard, Christian. "Readability and Persuasion: Political Handbills." In *The Culture of Print*, edited by Roger Chartier, 235–259.

Kadın Eserleri Kütüphanesi Bibliyografya Oluşturma Komisyonu. *İstanbul Kütüphanelerindeki Eski Harfli Türkçe Kadın Dergileri Bibliyografyası (1869–1927)*. İstanbul: Metis Yayınları, 1992.

Kandiyoti, Deniz. "Islam and Patriarchy." In *Women in Middle Eastern History*, edited by Nikki Keddie and Beth Baron, 23–44. New Haven: Yale University Press, 1991.

———. "Slave Girls, Temptresses, and Comrades: Images of Women in the Turkish Novel." *Feminist Issues* 8 (Spring 1988): 35–50.

———. ed. *Women, Islam, and the State*. London: Macmillan, 1991.

Kaplan, E. Ann. *Motherhood and Representation: The Mother in Popular Culture and Melodrama*. London: Routledge, 1992.

Karabekir, Kazim. *İttihat ve Terakki Cemiyeti 1896–1909*. İstanbul: Türdav, 1982.

Karakışla, Yavuz. "The 1908 Strike Wave in the Ottoman Empire." *Bulletin of the Turkish Studies Association* 16, no. 2 (September 1992): 153–177.

Kayalı, Hasan. *Arabs and Young Turks: Ottomanism, Arabism, and Islamism in the Ottoman Empire, 1908–1918*. Berkeley: University of California Press, 1997.

Keen, Sam. *Faces of the Enemy: Reflections of the Hostile Imagination*. San Francisco: Harper and Row, 1986.

Kent, Marion, ed. *The Great Powers and the End of the Ottoman Empire*. London: Frank Cass, 1993.

Kerber, Linda. *Women of the Republic: Intellect and Ideology in Revolutionary America*. Chapel Hill: University of North Carolina Press, 1988.

Kete, Kathleen. *The Beast in the Boudoir: Petkeeping in Nineteenth Century Paris*. Berkeley: University of California Press, 1994.

Keyder, Çağlar. *The Definition of a Peripheral Economy: Turkey 1923–1929*. Cambridge: Cambridge University Press, 1981.

Khalid, Adeeb. "Printing, Publishing, and Reform in Tsarist Central Asia." *International Journal of Middle East Studies* 26 ((May 1994): 187–200.

Khalidi, Rashid, ed. *The Origins of Arab Nationalism*. New York: Columbia University Press, 1991.

Khater, Akram. "'House' to 'Godess of the House': Gender, Class, and Silk in Nineteenth Century Mount Lebanon." *International Journal of Middle East Studies* 28 (August 1996): 325–348.

Khūrī, Ra'īf. *Modern Arab Thought: Channels of the French Revolution to the Arab East*. Translated by Iḥsān ʿAbbās. Princeton: The Kingston Press, 1983.

Kishtainy, Khalid. *Arab Political Humor*. London: Quartet, 1985.

Kodaman, Bayram. "La Présence Culturelle et Religieuse de la France en Anatolie Orientale de 1878 à 1914." In *L'Empire Ottoman, la République de Turquie et la France*, edited by Hamit Batu and Jean-Louis Bacque-Grammont, 391–400. İstanbul and Paris: Editions Isis, 1986.

Bibliography

———. *Şark Meselesi Işığı Altında Sultan II. Abdülhamid'in Doğu Anadolu Politikası.* İstanbul: Orkun, 1983.

Koloğlu, Orhan. "Alexandre Blacque Défenseur de l'État Ottoman par Amour des Libertés." In *L'Empire Ottoman, la République de Turquie et la France*, edited by Batu and Bacque-Grammont, 179–195. İstanbul and Paris: Editions Isis, 1986.

Koray, Enver, ed. *Türkiye Tarih Yayınları Bibliyografyası 1729–1955*, 2nd ed. İstanbul: Maarif Basımevi, 1959.

Korkmaz Alemdar. *İstanbul 1875–1964 Türkiyede Yayınlanan Fransızca Bir Gazetenin Tarihi.* Ankara: Ankara İktisadi ve Ticari İlimler Akademisi, 1980.

Koss, Stephen E. *The Rise and Fall of the Political Press in Britain.* 2 vols. Chapel Hill: University of North Carolina Press, 1981–1984.

Kramer, Martin. "Pen and Purse: Şābūncī and Blunt." In *Essays in Honor of Bernard Lewis*, edited by C. E. Bosworth. Princeton: Darwin Press, 1989.

Kreiser, Klaus. "Le Role de la Langue Française en Turquie et la Politique Culturelle Allemande au Début du XXe Siècle." In *L'Empire Ottoman, la République de Turquie et la France*, 405–417. İstanbul and Paris: Editions Isis, 1986.

Krueger, Loren. "Attending (to) the National Spectacle: Instituting National (Popular) Theatre in England and France." In *Macropolitics of Nineteenth Century Literature: Nationalism, Exoticism, Imperialism*, edited by Jonathan Arac and Harriet Ritvo, 243–265. Philadelphia: University of Pennsylvania Press, 1991.

Kudret, Cevdet. "Birkaç Örnek İle Mütareke Dönemi Sansürü." *Tarih ve Toplum* 9 (1988): 298–301.

———. *Karagöz*, 3 vols. Ankara: Bilgi Yayınevi, 1968–1970.

Kuhnke, la Verne. *Lives at Risk: Public Health in Nineteenth-Century Egypt.* Berkeley: University of California Press, 1990.

Kuran, Ahmed Bedevi. *İnkılâp Hareketleri ve Milli Mücadele.* İstanbul: Tan, 1950.

———. *İnkılâp Tarihimiz ve İttihat ve Terakki.* İstanbul: Tan, 1948.

Kushner, David. "Ali Ekrem Bey, Governor of Jerusalem, 1906–1908." *International Journal of Middle East Studies* 28 (August 1996): 349–362.

———. *The Rise of Turkish Nationalism 1876–1908.* London: Frank Cass, 1977.

La France: Images of Women and Ideas of Nation, 1789–1989. London: South Bank Centre, 1989.

Laitin, David. *Hegemony and Culture: Politics and Religious Change Among the Yoruba.* Chicago: University of Chicago Press, 1986.

———. *Politics, Language and Thought: The Somali Experience.* Chicago: University of Chicago Press, 1977.

Landau, Jacob. *The Hejaz Railway and the Muslim Pilgrimage: A Case of Ottoman Political Propaganda.* Detroit: Wayne State University Press, 1971.

Langensiepen, Bernd and Ahmet Güleryüz. *The Ottoman Steam Navy, 1828–1923.* Edited and translated by James Cooper. London: Conway Maritime Press, 1994.

Laroui, Abdallah. *The Crisis of the Arab Intellectual: Traditionalism or Historicism?* Translated by Diarmid Cammell. Berkeley: University of California Press, 1976.

Laurens, Henry. *Les Origines Intellectuelles de l'Expedition d'Égypte: l'Orientalisme Islamisant en France (1698–1798).* İstanbul and Paris: Editions Isis, 1987.

———. "Le Siècle des Lumeères Face a l'Empire Ottoman: L'Élaboration d'une

Image." In *L'Empire Ottoman, la République de Turquie et la France*, 119–126. İstanbul and Paris: Editions Isis, 1986.

Lewis, Bernard. *The Emergence of Modern Turkey*. Oxford: Oxford University Press, 1968.

———. "The Impact of the French Revolution on Turkey: Some Notes on the Transmission of Ideas." *Journal of World History* 1, no. 1 (1990): 105–125.

———. *Race and Slavery in the Middle East: An Historical Enquiry*. New York: Oxford University Press, 1990.

———. *The Shaping of the Modern Middle East*. 2nd edition. New York: Oxford University Press, 1994.

———. "Why Turkey? The Development of Constitutional and Representative Government in the Ottoman Empire and Turkey in the Nineteenth and Twentieth Centuries." *Archivum Ottomanicum* 11 (1986/1988): 9–22.

Lincoln, Bruce. *Discourse and the Construction of Society: Comparative Studies of Myth, Ritual, and Classification*. New York: Oxford University Press, 1989.

Lott, Eric. *Love and Theft: Blackface Minstrelsy and the American Working Class*. Oxford: Oxford University Press, 1993.

Mackenzie, John M. ed. *Imperialism and Popular Culture*. Manchester: Manchester University Press, 1986.

Major, A. Hyatt. *Prints and People: A Social History of Printed Pictures*. Princeton: Princeton University Press, 1971.

Malecková, Jitka. "Ludwig Büchner versus Nat Pinkerton: Turkish Translations from Western Languages, 1880–1914." *Mediterranean Historical Review* 9, no. 1 (June 1994): 73–99.

Mardin, Şerif. *The Genesis of Young Ottoman Thought: A Study in the Modernization of Turkish Political Ideas*. Princeton: Princeton University Press, 1962.

———. *Jön Türklerin Siyasi Fikirleri 1895–1908*. İstanbul: İletişim, 1989.

———. "A Note on the Transformation of Religious Symbols in Turkey." *Turcica* 16 (1984): 115–127.

———. *Religion and Social Change in Modern Turkey: The Case of Bediüzzaman Said Nursi*. Albany: State University of New York Press, 1989.

———. "Super Westernization in Urban Life in the Ottoman Empire in the Last Quarter of the Nineteenth Century." In *Turkey: Geographic and Social Perspectives*, edited by Peter Benedict et al., 404–446. Leiden: Brill, 1974.

Marriot, J. A. R. *The Eastern Question: An Historical Study in European Diplomacy*. Oxford: Clarendon Press, 1917.

Martin, Vanessa. *Islam and Modernism: The Iranian Revolution of 1906*. London: I. B. Tauris, 1989.

McClintock, Anne. *Imperial Leather: Race, Gender, and Sexuality in the Colonial Contest*. New York: Routledge, 1995.

McWilliam, Neil. *Dreams of Happiness: Social Art and the French Left, 1830–1850*. Princeton: Princeton University Press, 1993.

Medhurst, Martin, and Michael Sesousa. "Political Cartoons as Rhetorical Form: A Taxonomy of Graphic Discourse." *Communication Monographs* 48, no. 3 (September 1981): 197–236.

Mehmed 'Asım. *Karikatur.* İstanbul: Tanin Matbaası, 1327/ 1911.
Mehmed Tahir. *Osmanlı Müellifleri.* İstanbul: Matbaa-i Amire, 1333 A.H./1915.
Melman, Billie. *Women's Orients: English Women and the Middle East, 1718–1918.* Ann Arbor: University of Michigan Press, 1992.
Mentzel, Peter. "Nationalism and the Labor Movement in the Ottoman Empire." Ph.D. diss., University of Washington, 1994.
Messick, Brinkley. *The Calligraphic State: Textual Domination and History in a Muslim Society.* Berkeley: University of California Press, 1993.
Micklewright, Nancy. "Photographic Memories: Travel Albums Compiled by Nineteenth Century British Visitors to the Middle East." Paper delivered at the Middle East Studies Association Conference, Washington D.C., November 1991.
———. "Woman's Dress in 19th Century Istanbul: Mirror of a Changing Society." Ph.D. diss., University of Pennsylvania, 1986.
Milani, Farzaneh. *Veils and Words: The Emerging Voices of Iranian Women Writers.* Syracuse: Syracuse University Press, 1991.
Miller, Michael B. *The Bon Marché: Bourgeois Culture and the Department Store, 1869–1921.* Princeton: Princeton University Press, 1981.
Miller, William. *The Ottoman Empire and Its Successors 1801–1927.* New York: Octagon Books, 1966.
Mitchell, Timothy. *Colonising Egypt.* Cambridge: Cambridge University Press, 1988.
Mitchell, W. J. T., ed. *The Language of Images.* Chicago: University of Chicago Press, 1980.
Moghadam, Valentine M., ed. *Identity Politics and Women: Cultural Reassertions and Feminisms in International Perspective.* Boulder: Westview Press, 1994.
Montêpin, Xavier de. *Kırmızı Değirmen.* İstanbul: Kırk Anbar Matbaası, 1292/1872.
Moon, Parker. *Imperialism and World Politics.* New York: Macmillan, 1926.
Mosse, George. *The Nationalization of the Masses.* Ithaca: Cornell University Press, 1991.
Muhammad as-Saffār. *Disorienting Encounters: Travels of a Moroccan Scholar in France in 1845–1846.* Translated by Susan Miller. Berkeley: University of California Press, 1991.
Murphey, Rhoads. "The Ottoman Attitude Towards the Adoption of Western Technology: The Role of the *Efrencî* Technicians in Civil and Military Applications." In *Contributions à l'histoire économique et sociale de l'Empire ottoman,* 287–298. Collection Turcica III. Louvain: Éditions Peeters, 1983.
Mükemmel ve Muvazzah Türkçe ve Fransızca Usûl-i Mükâleme—Nouvelle Méthode Guide Complet de la Conversation Turque-Français. İstanbul: Ahter Matbaası, 1316/1898.
Najmabadi, Afsaneh. "The Daughters of Qūchān: Re-membering the For-Gotten Gender of the Iranian Constitutional Revolution." Unpublished paper, 1994.
———. The Erotic Vatan [Homeland] as Beloved and Mother: To Love, to Possess, and to Protect." *Comparative Studies in Society and History* 39, no. 3 (July 1997): 4: 442–467.
———"Zanhā-yi Millat: Women or Wives of the Nation?" *Iranian Studies* 26 (Winter-Spring 1993): 51–71.

Nasser, Gamal Abdel. *The Philosophy of the Revolution*. Buffalo: Economica Books, 1959.

Nicolas, Michéle. "La comédie humaine dans le Karagöz." *Revue du Monde Mussulman et de la Méditerranée* 77–78 (1996): 75–87.

Nokes, David. *Raillery and Rage: A Study in Eighteenth Century Satire*. New York: St. Martin's Press, 1987.

Nüzhet, Selim, ed. *1933 Almanak*. İstanbul: Devlet Matbaası, n.d.

———. *Türk Gazeteciliği*. İstanbul: Devlet Matbaası, 1931.

Okyar, Osman. "The Union and Progress Committee and the Turkish Republic (Ottomanism and Nationalism)." In *Comité International D'Etudes Pré-ottomanes et ottomanes, VIth Symposium, Cambrige 1–4 July 1984*. Varia Turcica IV. İstanbul: Editions d'Amérique et d'Orient, 1987.

Oral, F. Süreyya. *Türk Basın Tarihi*. 2 vols. Ankara: Yeni Adım Matbaası, n.d.

Orga, İrfan. *Portrait of a Turkish Family*. London: Victor Gollancz, 1950.

Orhonlu, Cengiz. "Boat Transportation in Istanbul: An Historical Survey." *Bulletin of the Turkish Studies Association* 13, no. 1 (March 1989): 1–21.

Orr, Linda. *Headless History: Nineteenth-Century French Historiography of the Revolution*. Ithaca: Cornell University Press, 1990.

Owen, Alex. *The Darkened Room: Women, Power, and Spiritualism in Late Victorian England*. Philadelphia: University of Pennsylvania Press, 1990.

Ölçer, Cüneyt. *Ottoman Coinage During the Reigns of Sultan Mehmed Reşad and Sultan Mehmed Vaheddin*. İstanbul: by the author, 1987.

Özkırımlı, Atilla. *Türk Edebiyatı Ansiklopedisi*. Vol. 1. İstanbul: Cem, 1982.

Pamuk, Şevket. *The Ottoman Empire and European Capitalism, 1820–1913*. Cambridge: Cambridge University Press, 1987.

Panzac, Daniel. *La Peste dans l'Empire Ottoman 1700–1850*. Leuven: Éditions Peeters, 1985.

Parker, Andrew, et al., eds. *Nationalisms and Sexualities*. New York: Routledge, 1992.

Parla, Jale. *Babalar ve Oğullar: Tanzimat Romanının Epistemolojik Temelleri*. İstanbul, n.p., 1991.

Patrick, Mary Mills. *Under Five Sultans*. New York: The Century Company, 1929.

Pears, Edwin. *Forty Years in Constantinople: The Recollections of Sir Edwin Pears, 1873–1915*. Freeport, New York: Books for Libraries Press, 1971.

Peirce, Leslie P. *The Imperial Harem: Women and Sovereignty in the Ottoman Empire*. Oxford: Oxford University Press, 1993.

Petry, Carl. *Twilight of Majesty: The Reigns of Sultans al-Ashraf Qāytbāy and Qānsūh al-Ghawri in Egypt*. Seattle: University of Washington Press, 1993.

Philippe, Robert. *Political Graphics: Art as Weapon*. New York: Abbeville Press, 1982.

Powell, Kirsten and Elizabeth Childs. *Femmes d'esprit: Women in Daumier's Caricature*. Middlebury, Vermont: The Christian A. Johnson Memorial Gallery, 1990.

Press, Charles. *The Political Cartoon*. Rutherford: Fairleigh Dickinson University Press, 1981.

Quataert, Donald. "Clothing Laws, State, and Society in the Ottoman Empire, 1720–1829." *International Journal of Middle East Studies* 29, no. 3 (August 1997): 403–425.

———. "Ottoman Women, Households, and Textile Manufacturing, 1800–1914." In

Bibliography

Women in Middle Eastern History, edited by Nikki Keddie and Beth Baron, 161–176. New Haven: Yale University Press, 1991.

———. *Social Disintegration and Popular Resistance in the Ottoman Empire, 1881–1908: Reactions to European Economic Penetration.* New York: New York University Press, 1983.

Quirk, Michael J. "The Decline and Fall of Nihilism." Review of *The Banalization of Nihilism: Twentieth-Century Responses to Meaninglessness,* by Karen Carr. *Soundings* 77, no. 1–2 (1994): 211–231.

Rai, Lajpat. *Young India: An Interpretation and a History of the Nationalist Movement from Within.* New York: Howard Fertig, 1968.

Rajan, Rajeswari Sunder. *Real and Imagined Women: Gender, Culture, and Postcolonialism.* London: Routledge, 1993.

Ramazani, Rouhollah. *The Foreign Policy of Iran: A Developing Nation in World Affairs 1500–1914.* Charlottesville: University Press of Virginia, 1966.

Rambert, Louis. *Notes et Impressions de Turquie: L'Empire Ottoman sous Abdul Hamid II 1895–1905.* Geneva: Edition Atar, 1910.

Ramsaur, Ernest E. *The Young Turks: Prelude to the Revolution of 1908.* Princeton: Princeton University Press, 1957.

Redhouse, James W. *A Turkish and English Lexicon.* Beirut: Librarie du Liban, 1974.

Ribeiro, Aileen. *Fashion in the French Revolution.* New York: Holmes and Meier, 1988.

Ritter, Hellmut. *Karagöz: Türkische Schattenspiele.* 3 vols. Hanover: n.p., 1924–1963.

Roberts, Mary Louise. "Samson and Delilah Revisited: The Politics of Women's Fashion in 1920s France." *American Historical Review* 98 (June 1993): 657–684.

Rogan, Eugene. "Aşiret Mektebi: Abdülhamid II's School for Tribes (1892–1907)." *International Journal of Middle East Studies* 28, no. 1 (1996): 83–107.

Rogers, William G. *Mightier than the Sword: Cartoon, Caricature, Social Comment.* New York: Harcourt, Brace, and World, 1969.

Rose, Richard B. "The Ottoman Fiscal Calendar." *Middle East Studies Association Bulletin* 25, no. 2 (1991): 157–167.

Rosenberg, Charles E. *The Cholera Years, The United States in 1832, 1849, and 1866.* Chicago: University of Chicago Press, 1987.

Said, Edward. *Orientalism.* New York: Pantheon Books, 1978.

Sangari, Kumkum and Sudesh Vaid, eds. *Recasting Women: Essays in Indian Colonial History.* New Brunswick, N.J.: Rutgers University Press, 1990.

Schivelbusch, Wolfgang. *Disenchanted Night: The Industrialization of Light in the Nineteenth Century.* Translated by Angela Davis. Oxford: Berg, 1988.

Scott, Joan. "The Evidence of Experience." *Critical Inquiry* (Summer 1991): 773–797.

Setton-Watson, R. W. *Disraeli, Gladstone and the Eastern Question: A Study in Diplomacy and Party Politics.* London: Macmillan and Co., 1935.

Sharabi, Hisham. *Neopatriarchy: A Theory of Distorted Change in Arab Society.* Oxford: Oxford University Press, 1988.

Sharpe, Jenny. *Allegories of Empire: The Figure of Woman in the Colonial Text.* Minneapolis: University of Minnesota Press, 1993.

Shattuck, Roger. *The Banquet Years: The Origins of the Avant-Garde in France 1885 to World War I.* Salem, New Hampshire: Ayer Co, 1984; reprint of 1969 edition.

Shaw, Graham. *Printing in Calcutta to 1800.* London: Bibliographic Society, 1981.
Shaw, Stanford and Ezel Shaw. *History of the Ottoman Empire and Modern Turkey.* Vol. 2. Cambridge: Cambridge University Press, 1977.
Shikes, Ralph E. *The Indignant Eye: The Artist as Social Critic in Prints and Drawings from the Fifteenth Century to Picasso.* Boston: Beacon Press, 1969.
Shuster, Morgan. *The Strangling of Persia.* Washington, D.C.: Mage Publishers, 1987 reprint of 1914 edition.
Sieyes, Emmanuel. "Qu'est-ce le tiers état." Edited by Edmund Campion. Paris: n.p., 1888.
Simmen, René. *The World of Puppets.* New York: Thomas Crowell, 1972.
Skendi, Stavro. *The Albanian National Awakening 1878–1912.* Princeton: Princeton University Press, 1967.
Skocpol, Theda. *States and Social Revolutions: A Comparative Analysis of France, Russia, and China.* Cambridge: Cambridge University Press, 1979.
Smith, Dennis Mack. *Italy and Its Monarchy.* New Haven: Yale University Press, 1989.
Spielmann, M. H. *The History of "Punch."* London: Cassell and Company, 1895.
Sprachman, Paul. "Persian Satire, Parody and Burlesque." In *Persian Literature,* edited by Ehsan Yarshater, 226–248. N.P.: Bibliotheca Persica, 1988.
Springborg, Patricia. *Western Republicanism and the Oriental Prince.* Austin: University of Texas Press, 1992.
Spruit, Ruud. *The Land of the Sultans: An Illustrated History of Malaysia.* Amsterdam: Pepin Press, 1995.
Stavrianos, L. S. *The Balkans Since 1453.* New York: Holt, Rinehart, Winston, 1965.
Stites, Richard. *Russian Popular Culture: Entertainment and Society Since 1900.* Cambridge: Cambridge University Press, 1992.
Strauss, Johann. "Romanlar, Ah! O Romanlar! Les Débuts de la Lecture Moderne dans L'Empire Ottoman (1850–1900)." *Turcica* 26 (1994): 125–163.
Strohmeier, Martin. "Muslim Education in the Vilayet of Beirut, 1880–1918." In *Decision Making and Change in the Ottoman Empire,* edited by Ceasar Farah, 215–241. Kirksville, Missouri: Thomas Jefferson University Press, 1993.
Stuermer, Harry. *Deux Ans de Guerre a Constantinople: Etudes de Morale et Politique Allemandes et Jeunes-Turques.* Paris: Librarie Payot, 1917.
Stump, Ayfer. "The Emergence of a Feminist/Nationalist Discourse in Pre-Republican Turkey: Case Study of *Kadin* Magazine (1908–1909)." Master's thesis, Ohio State University, 1996.
Swietochowski, Tadeusz. *Russian Azerbaijan 1905–1920: The Shaping of National Identity in a Muslim Community.* Cambridge: Cambridge University Press, 1985.
Sykes, Mark. *The Caliph's Last Heritage.* New York: Arno Press, 1973.
Szyliowicz, J. S. "Functional Perspectives on Technology: The Case of the Printing Press in the Ottoman Empire." *Archivum Ottomanicum* 11 (1986): 249–259.
Şapolyo, Enver B. *Türk Gazeteciliği Tarihi Her Yöniyle Basın.* Ankara: Güven Matbaası, 1969.
Şeni, Nora. "19. Yüzyıl Sonunda İstanbul Mizah Basınında Moda ve Kadın Kıyafetleri," In *Kadın Açısından 1980'ler Türkiye'sinde Kadınlar,* edited by Şirin Tekeli, 43–68. İstanbul: İletişim, 1990.

———. "The Camondos and Their Imprint on Nineteenth Century Istanbul." *International Journal of Middle East Studies* 26, no 4 (1994): 663–675.

Şimşir, Bilal N. *The Turkish Minority Press in Bulgaria, Its History and Tragedy 1865–1985*. Ankara: n.p., 1986.

Şinasi, İbrahim. *Durub-ı Emsal-i Osmaniye*. İstanbul: Matbaa-ı Abu ül-Ziya, 1302/1886–1887.

Tahsin Paşa. *Abdülhamid, Tahsin Paşa'nın Yıldız Hatıraları*. İstanbul: Boğaziçi Yayınlar, 1990.

Talwar, Vir Bharat. "Feminist Consciousness in Women's Journals in Hindi, 1910–1920." In *Recasting Women: Essays in Indian Colonial History*, edited by Kumkum Sangari and Sudesh Vaid. New Brunswick, N.J.: Rutgers University Press, 1990.

Tarhan, Abdülhak Hamid. *Eşber: Manzum Bir Facia-yı Tarihiyedir*. İstanbul: Halk Kütüphanesi, 1922.

Taşcıoğlu, Muhaddere. *Türk Osmanlı Cemiyetinde Kadının Sosyal Durumu ve Kadın Kıyafetleri*. Ankara: Akın Matbaası, 1958.

Tavakoli-Targhi, Mohammad. "The Persian Gaze and Women of the Occident." *South Asia Bulletin* 11, no. 1–2 (1991): 21–31.

———. "Women of the West Imagined: The Farangi Other and the Emergence of the Woman Question in Iran." In *Identity Politics and Women*, edited by Valentine M. Moghadam, 98–120. Boulder: Westview, 1994.

Taylor, Miles. "John Bull and the Iconography of Public Opinion in England c. 1712–1929." *Past and Present* 134 (February 1992): 93–128.

Tekeli, İlhan and Selim İlkin. "The Public Works Program and the Development of Technology in the Ottoman Empire in the Second Half of the Nineteenth Century." *Turcica* 28 (1996): 195–234.

Temo, İbrahim. *İttihad ve Terraki Cemiyetinin Teşekkülü ve Hıdematı Vataniye ve İnkılâbı Milliye Dair Hatıratım*. Romanya: Mecidiye, 1939.

Terdiman, Richard. *Discourse/Counter-Discourse: The Theory and Practice of Symbolic Resistance in Nineteenth Century France*. Ithaca: Cornell University Press, 1985.

Thobie, Jacques. "Banque Impériale Ottomane et Banque Impériale de Perse jusque'en 1914." In *La France et l'Est Méditerranéen Depuis 1850*. Analecta Isisiana. Vol. 5. İstanbul: Editions Isis, 1993.

———. *Intérêts et Impérialisme Français dans l'Empire Ottoman (1895–1914)*. Paris: Publications de la Sorbonne, 1977.

———. *La France Impériale, 1880–1914*. Paris: Editions Mégrelis, 1982.

———. "Sur Quelques Sociétés Oubliées à Capitaux Français dans l'Empire Ottoman." In *L'Empire Ottoman, la République de Turquie et la France*, 375–390. İstanbul and Paris: Editions Isis, 1986.

Thoreau, Henry David. "Life Without Principle." In *The Writings of Henry David Thoreau*, vol. 4, *Cape Cod Miscellanies*. Boston: Houghton Mifflin, 1906.

Tietze, Andreas. *The Turkish Shadow Theatre and the Puppet Collection of the L.A. Mayer Memorial Foundation*. Berlin: Gebr. Mann Verlag, 1977.

Toledano, Ehud. *The Ottoman Slave Trade and Its Suppression*. Princeton: Princeton University Press, 1982.

———. *State and Society in Mid-Nineteenth Century Egypt*. Cambridge: Cambridge University Press, 1990.
Toprak, Zafer. *Türkiyede "Milli İktisat" (1908–1918)*. Ankara: Olgaç Matbaası, 1982.
Toulmin, Stephen. *Cosmopolis: The Hidden Agenda of Modernity*. New York: The Free Press, 1990.
Townsend, Mary Lee. *Forbidden Laughter: Popular Humor and the Limits of Repression in Nineteenth Century Prussia*. Ann Arbor: University of Michigan Press, 1992.
Tricot, Xavier. *James Ensor: Catalogue Raisonné of the Paintings*. Vol. 1. Antwerp: Pandora, 1992.
Trowbridge, Stephen. Review of *Islam and Socialism*, by Mushir Hosain Kidwai. *Muslim World* 4, no. 1 (1914): 432–433.
Tuchman, Barbara. *The Guns of August*. New York: Macmillan Co., 1962.
Tucker, Ernest, "The Newspaper Mullah Nasr al-Din and Satirical Journalism in Early Twentieth Century Azerbaijan." Unpublished paper, Chicago, 1987.
Tugay, Asaf. *İbret: Abdülhamid'e Verilen Journaller ve Journalciler*. İstanbul: Okat Yayınevi, n.d.
Tugay, Emine Foat. *Three Centuries: Family Chronicles of Turkey and Egypt*. London: Oxford University Press, 1963.
Tunaya, Tarik Zafer. *Türkiyede Siyasal Partiler*. 2 vols. İstanbul: Hilal Matbaası, 1982.
Tuncay, Mete and Erik Zürcher. *Socialism and Nationalism in the Ottoman Empire, 1876 1923*. London: British Academic Press, 1994.
Turner, Bryan S. "Orientalism, the Problem of Civil Society in Islam." In *Orientalism, Islam, and Islamists*, edited by Asaf Hussein et al., 23–42. Brattleboro, Vermont: Amana Books, 1984.
Tülbentçi, Feridun Fazıl. *Cümhuriyetten Sonra Çıkan Gazeteler ve Mecmualar: 29 İlkteşrin 1923–31 İlkkanun 1940*. Ankara: Başvekalet Matbuat, 1941.
Türk Dili ve Edebiyatı Ansiklopedisi. Vol. 2. İstanbul: Dergah, 1976.
Türkgeldi, Ali. *Görüp İttiklerim*. 3rd ed. Ankara: Türk Tarih Kurumu Basımevi, 1984.
Türkiye'de Dergiler Ansiklopediler (1848–1984). İstanbul: Gelişim Yayınları, 1984.
Tütengil, Cavit. *Yeni Osmanlılar'dan bu Yana İngiltere'de Türk Gazeteciliği (1867–1967)*. İstanbul: Belge, 1985.
Twain, Mark. *Innocents Abroad or the New Pilgrim's Progress*. New York: Harper and Brothers, 1911.
Ubicini, J. H. A. *Letters on Turkey: An Account of the Religious, Political, Social, and Commercial Condition of the Ottoman Empire*. London: John Murray, 1856.
Unat, Faik Reşit. *Hicri Tarihleri Miladi Tarihe Çevirme Kılavuzu*. Ankara: T. T. K. Basımevi, 1984.
United States. Department of Commerce and Labor. *Daily Consular and Trade Reports*. no. 157: 987, March 8, 1912.
———. Department of Commerce. Bureau of Foreign and Domestic Commerce. *Tariff Notes. Daily Consular and Trade Reports*. no. 3683: 12–13, January 12, 1910.
Uşaklıgil, Halid Ziya. *Kırk Yıl*. İstanbul: Sulhi Garan Matbaası, 1969.
Üskiden, Behzat. "Beyoğlu'unda Resimli Kartpostal Yayımcıları." *Tarih ve Toplum* 100 (Nisan/April 1992): 27–34.

Bibliography

Vaka, Demetra. *Haremlik: Some Pages from the Life of Turkish Women.* Boston: Houghton Mifflin, 1910.

Valensi, Lucette. *Venice and the Sublime Porte: The Birth of the Despot.* Ithaca: Cornell University Press, 1993.

Waley-Cohen, Joanna. "China and Western Technology in the Late Eighteenth Century." *American Historical Review* 98, no. 5 (December 1993): 1525–1544.

Weber, Eugen. *Peasants into Frenchmen: The Modernization of Rural France 1870–1914.* Stanford: Stanford University Press, 1976.

Whately, Mary. *Letters from Egypt to Plain Folks at Home.* London: Seeley, Jackson, and Halliday, 1876.

Williams, Rosalind H. *Dream Worlds: Mass Consumption in Late Nineteenth Century France.* Berkeley: University of California Press, 1982.

Wink, André. "Sovereignty and Universal Dominion in South Asia." *The Indian Economic and Social History Review* 21, no. 3 (1984): 265–292.

Wolfe, Joel. "The Rise of Brazil's Industrial Working Class: Community, Work, and Politics in São Paolo, 1900–1955." Ph.D. diss., University of Wisconsin, 1990.

Worswick, Clark, ed. *Princely India: Photographs by Raja Lala Deen Dayal, Court Photographer (1884–1910) to the Premier Prince of India.* New York: Alfred A. Knopf, 1980.

Zarcone, Thierry and Fariba Zarinebaf. *Les Iraniens D'Istanbul.* İstanbul: Institut Français de Recherches en Iran, 1993.

Zeine, Zeine N. *The Emergence of Arab Nationalism with a Background Study of Arab-Turkish Relations in the Near East.* Beirut: Khayats, 1966.

Zürcher, Erik Jan. *The Unionist Factor: The Role of the Committee of Union and Progress in the Turkish National Movement 1905–1926.* Leiden: E. J. Brill, 1984.

INDEX

Note that Ottoman Turkish names, as in the Bibliography, are alphabetized in their conventional order and not divided into "first" and "last" names (Sedad Nuri instead of Nuri, Sedad). Names are listed as they appear in the text and sometimes include honorifics, such as "Bey" or "Pasha."

A
Abd al-Aziz IV, king of Morocco, 118, 162
Abd ül-Hak Hamid Bey, 207, 405n. 98
Abd ül-Hamid, Ottoman sultan
    as caliph, 12, 92, 149, 301
    caricature of, 4, 27, 66–67, 83–85,
        114–32, 321
    cats of, 128, 382n. 31, 436n. 26
    despotism of, 2, 5, 67, 98, 100, 102,
        152
    in exile, 130–32, 144, 219–20, 264,
        276–77, 290
    rule of, 1–2, 16, 29, 45, 54, 113, 226–
        27, 239, 268, 271, 315, 317, 323
Abu ül-Hüda Efendi, 95, 130–31, 219, 322,
    376n. 83
Abdullah Frères, 36
advertising, 11, 13, 21, 32, 35–36, 43, 48, 53,
    193, 202–3, 226, 228–31, 248, 262
Africa, 160, 178
Ahmad, shah of Iran, 92–93
Ahmed Rasim, 28, 47
Ahmed Rıza, 2, 28
Ahmed Şerif, 113, 121
Ahmet İhsan, 32, 34, 78
'Ain al-Dawla, 96
aircraft, 130, 258–59, 289–92, 304–8
Albania, 69, 161, 195, 197–98, 319, 321,
    400n. 39
Algeciras Conference, 162–63
Algeria, 12, 164
America, 10, 178, 180, 188, 218, 248, 261,
    322
    goods of, 203, 213–14, 293, 396n. 101,
        413n. 45

Anatolia, 117, 128, 170, 198, 321
    starvation in, 139–140, 183
animals, images of, 171–73
Apollon, 36–37, 207
Arabia, 11, 140, 319
Arabs, 321
    satire of, 69–70, 322–23
    as victims of imperialism, 70
Armenia, 139
Armenians, 175, 188, 206, 321
army. *See* military. *See also* soldiers
Aşıkpaşa, 114
audience of press, 19, 26–27, 41–50, 124,
    314, 317. *See also* readers
Austria, 68, 281
    satire of, 70, 140, 235–40, 277
    territorial aggression of, 9, 13, 109, 150
See also imperialism, Austrian
autocracy, 25, 29, 77
    critique of, 10, 65, 95, 113–30
    in Iran, 75, 91–93, 96–105
automobiles, 290, 296–99
    satire of, 68, 205
Azerbaican, 106

B
Baha Tevfik, 29, 193
Balkans, 9, 150, 178
    Balkan Wars, 9, 151, 161, 178, 200, 263
    satire of, 68–69, 140, 164, 195, 209,
        301, 318, 322
Banque Ottomane, 171, 392n. 63
Basra, 158, 178

461

Berlin, 46, 305
    Congress of, 239
Bernhardt, Sarah, 207, 404n. 90
Beyoğlu, 35, 50, 202, 214–15
bicycles, 203,
Blunt, Wilfrid, 162, 164
Bon Marché, 202, 252, 402n. 63
Bosnia-Herzegovina, 2, 138–40, 150, 152, 161, 164, 170, 183, 235–36, 239–40
Bouchire, 106
boycott of Austrian goods, 153, 170, 175–77, 183, 203, 243, 245–46
Boy Scouts, 199
Brazil, 10, 13, 176
Britain
    as model, 75
    satire of, 70, 153
    territorial aggression of, 2, 9, 13, 105–9, 303
    See also imperialism, British
Bulgaria, 2, 9, 69, 121, 138–40, 152–54, 160, 165–68, 203, 209, 301, 322
bureaucracy, Ottoman
    nature of, 14, 147, 263, 266–67, 271, 276
    satire of, 147, 189, 276, 302–3
bureaucrats
    kadro haric, 60–61, 363n.33
    Ottoman, 3, 281
    Western educated, 5, 78
Burhan üd-Din Bey, 207–9, 406n. 100
Bursa, 27

C
Cadaloz, 56, 63–65, 71, 322
Caesar, images of, 167
cafes, 153, 190, 202, 204, 206, 213, 216
Cairo, 160
    press in, 28, 30
calendar. *See* dating systems
caliphate, Ottoman claims to, 12, 92, 149, 301
capitulations, 152, 170–71, 391n. 59
captions
    language of, 21, 96, 98, 140, 173, 183, 192, 214, 294, 397n. 13, 400n. 40
    types of, 21, 26, 39
cartoonists
    ateliers, 37
    ethnicity of, 37
    French, 164
    Ottoman, 19, 37–38

cartoons
    analysis of, 17–23, 347n. 48, 365nn. 44–45
    effects of, 19–22
    European influence on, 39, 67
    foreign, 37, 39, 111, 136, 305
    functioning of, 14
    and identity, 321–24
    selection of, 16–17
    styles, 37–39
Cavid Bey, finance minister, 133–35, 178
Celal Esad, 30
Celal Nuri, 193, 249
Cemal Pasha, 178, 249, 271
Cemil Cem, 38–39
censorship, 343nn. 16, 18, 20
    under Abd ül-Hamid, 3–5, 16, 29, 40, 45–46, 54, 73–74, 87, 152, 192, 194, 342nn. 9–10
    after revolution, 9, 25, 31, 207, 343n. 18
Chamber of Deputies, 2, 75, 87, 133, 178, 308. *See also* deputies
Charles I, king of France, 116
Chartier, Roger, 20–21
China, 176, 314
cholera, 261, 263, 271, 275–87, 424n. 60
Christians, 68, 110, 324, 326
circle of justice, 114
citizen
    notion of, 26, 199–200, 320, 324
    as patriot, 175–76, 245
    satire of, 141, 144, 146–47, 170, 185, 235, 237, 266, 273, 296–97
civilization, idea of, 153, 203, 205, 261, 263, 316, 328
class, 12, 20, 26–27, 45, 271, 320
    elite, 20–21, 46, 57, 69, 87, 113, 176, 181, 263, 274
    lower, 57–60, 70, 181–87, 202, 226
    satire of, 189, 201, 221, 253, 298, 367n. 67
coffee-houses, 46–47, 190
coinage, 91, 158, 354n. 44, 374n. 58
colonial context, 10, 12–15, 89, 257, 274, 325
communications technology, 308, 310–11
constitutional government, 319
    European, 13, 60
    Iranian, 91–92, 100
    Ottoman, 5, 13, 79, 86, 89, 100, 113, 132–47, 262–63, 266, 313, 315, 317, 328
constitutionalism
    idea of, 3, 73, 75, 79–80, 86, 123–24, 132, 136–37, 140, 143–47, 199, 226
    Ottoman sympathies for Egyptian, 154–56

462

Index

Ottoman sympathies for Iranian, 77, 100, 103–6, 109
consumers
　satire of, 228, 221–47, 412n. 44
　of Western goods, 176, 181, 183, 201–5, 221–33, 243, 247
　women as, 202, 221, 226–33, 241, 243, 245, 252
copyright, 28
counter-revolution
　Iranian, 77, 92
　Ottoman, 2, 9–10, 31, 124, 266, 317–18
Crete, 140, 152, 164, 237–39
crime, 266–73, 276, 281, 422nn. 24, 33
crows or ravens, images of, 114, 130
culture
　elite, 21, 26
　popular, 21, 26, 360n. 8
See also European culture
CUP, 2, 28, 30–31, 100, 123
　rule of, 16, 132–33, 158
　satirized, 66–67, 142, 178
Cyprus, 2, 152, 207
czar, 92, 106–7, 117, 121, 128, 161, 165–67, 209

D
dating systems, xv-xvi, 278, 313–14
Daumier, Honore, 66, 173, 253, 415n. 68
De Leon, Edwin, 110, 301
de Montêpin, Xavier, 124
death, images of, 7, 96–97, 100, 105–7, 114, 124–28, 150, 219, 276–78, 281–85, 291, 426n. 75
debt, Ottoman. *See* Public Debt, Ottoman
department stores, 176, 202, 259, 402n. 63
deputies, Ottoman, 9, 133–44, 205, 220, 250, 290, 313, 327
Derviş Vahdeti (Kıbrıslı), 31, 68, 77
despotism, 22–23, 86, 92, 96–107, 210, 241, 266, 276, 316, 324, 330
dialogue, 47, 84, 327, 330, 361nn. 10, 15
　satiric, 21, 23, 28, 52, 86, 95, 140, 149, 250, 268, 301
　traditions of, 52–56
dictionaries, 191, 371n. 22
dirigibles (balloons), 130, 164
dogs, 259, 262–66, 271, 420nn. 5–7
　as pets, 191, 263, 281, 296, 421n. 14
Don Quixote, 56
Doyle, Sir Arthur Conan, 218

dreams and visions, 95, 205, 218–20, 408n. 129
dress
　and ethnic typing, 70, 195, 322
　European style, 87, 189–91, 216, 222–32, 253, 257, 290, 305, 311
　and identity, 83, 195, 223–24, 322, 419n. 116
　and morality, 222–24, 226–28, 239, 241, 252–55, 261, 271, 413n. 47
　satire of, 67, 69, 141, 144, 183–85, 221–26, 228–35, 267
　"traditional," 15, 69, 87, 190, 195, 223, 239–46, 302
See also fashion

E
East-India Company, 151
East-West comparisons, 43, 53, 74, 83–84, 86, 193, 203, 228, 253–55, 261–62, 300–2, 308, 320, 326, 329–31, 361n. 11, 373n. 51, 416n. 80, 417n. 86
eating, images of, 109, 160, 167–68, 262, 264, 389n. 27
editorials, 21, 32, 35, 53
editors, Ottoman, 25, 35, 37
education, 12, 14, 27, 198–200, 269
　French language, 12, 25, 30, 78, 222
　physical, 199, 400nn. 43–44
　Western, 46–47, 78, 189, 327
　of women, 45–46, 199–200, 247, 249, 252, 401n. 48, 418nn. 95, 100
Egypt, 70, 255, 323
　British occupation of, 155–57, 160, 164, 170, 223
　royal family of, 121, 223
elections, 16, 87, 123, 140–42
electricity, 33–34, 259, 289, 296–98, 424n. 49
England. *See* Britain
entertainment
　European style, 84, 189–91, 202–5, 222, 274
　mixed sex, 84, 153, 202–4, 216
Enver Bey, 60, 62
Enver Şapolyo, 35, 43
ethnicity, 27, 320, 434nn. 12–16
　satire of, 23, 68–70, 321–24, 434n. 14
Eugenie, empress of France, 228
eunuchs, 95, 128, 219, 277, 292–93, 376n. 77

463

Index

Europe, territorial aggression of, 9, 12–13, 25, 105–9, 150–75, 220. *See also* imperialism
European culture
    influences of, 70, 74, 115, 150, 189–91, 213, 221–32, 273, 293, 313, 315–16, 326, 329
        satire of, 191, 201–5, 212–19
        See also imperialism

F
Faik Sabri, 193, 354n. 41
falakacı, 56, 105, 253–54, 419n. 115
fashion
    European style, 14, 153, 183–85, 191, 201–5, 213–14, 216, 221–41, 253, 273–74, 277, 311, 410n. 15, 411n. 27
    French, 15, 84, 202, 221, 223, 226, 228–29, 243, 245, 255
    Western, satire of, 141, 153, 201–5, 214–16, 221–32, 247, 279–80
    See also dress
femininity, 63, 220, 278,
feminism, 84, 193, 247–49
Ferdinand, king of Bulgaria, 140, 153–54, 165–68, 170, 390n. 48
Fırka-ı Ahrar, 138–40
France
    cultural influences of, 83, 241
    as model, 15, 22, 33, 73–91, 110–11, 368nn. 4–6
    territorial aggression of, 153, 162–64, 237, 255
    See also imperialism, French
Franz Josef, emperor of Austria, 160–61, 164, 167–69
freedom
    idea of, 52, 56, 63, 71, 75, 79, 88–90, 136, 243, 324
    promise of, 22, 25, 105, 210,
furnishings, household, 201–3, 222

G
games and toys, images of, 136–37, 160–61, 165
Galata bridge, 47, 56, 84, 300
    tolls on, 271, 289, 305, 423n. 48
Garibaldi, Giuseppe, 161
Garnett, Lucy, 203, 227, 276, 301, 313

gazettes, 333–34
    circulation of, 34, 43–44, 356n. 63
    contests in, 35, 37, 47–50
    demand for, 40–41
    foreign, 37, 45–46
    format of, 35–36,
    frequency of publication, 16
    illustrations in, 36–39
    letters to, 35, 43, 53
    price of, 26, 36, 40–41, 335–37
    satirical, 9, 25
    subscriptions to, 36–37, 40–41, 43, 46, 335–37
    women's, 417n. 87
    See also press; satire
Gedik Pasha Theater, 206
gender, 27, 45, 50, 67, 153, 202, 222, 227, 321
    in cartoons, 23, 158–59
Germany, territorial aggression of, 109, 153, 161–62, 164–65, 167–68, 173–75, 277, 303
    See also imperialism, German
governesses, 203, 213
Gramsci, Antonio, 14
Greece, 69, 121, 239, 304
Greeks, 175, 321

H
Hacivat, 1, 3, 54–55, 113, 241, 250, 296–99, 308–10, 331
Halide Edib, 199–200, 219, 227, 247, 249, 290
Halil Menteşe Bey, 60–61
hamals, 175, 183, 195, 302
harem, 192–93, 235–36, 239–41, 300
Hasan Fehmi, 53
Hijaz, 301
historiography
    of Europe, 10
    of Ottoman empire, 10, 317–19, 325–30
honor
    national, 67, 80, 232, 234–41, 247
    sexual, 67, 80, 232, 234–41
hürriyet. See freedom
Husein Hassib Beg, 93
Hüseyin Hilmi Pasha, grand vezir, 79, 128–29, 414n. 58
Hüseyin Nazmi, 31
Hüseyin Rahmi, 28

I

Ibn Khaldun, 19
İbrahim Hakkı Pasha, grand vezir, 178, 209, 216–17
İbrahim Şinasi, 78, 192, 206, 433n. 9
İdare-i Mahsusa, 303, 429n. 46
identity, 331
    national
        Egyptian, 155, 157–58
        European, 321
        idea of, 10, 23, 198, 247
        Ottoman, 11, 15, 255, 273, 317, 320
    political, 14
    religious, 12, 14, 324–25
    social, 16, 223–24, 247, 273–74
images, interpreting, 18–23
imperialism
    American economic, 178, 180, 185, 187–88, 241, 257
    Austrian, 160–61, 164–65, 167–70, 173, 175–76, 228, 235–40, 243, 245, 281, 283
    British, 77–78, 89, 105–9, 158–61, 165, 175, 237–38, 245, 257, 263–64, 323
        economic, 133–35, 144–46, 151, 154, 171, 180, 185, 187–88, 230, 293
    European, 5, 9, 23, 26, 50, 115, 152–88, 325
        critique of, 65–67, 106–9, 128, 261, 277, 296, 301–2
        economic, 1, 5, 11, 98, 133–36, 141, 144–46, 170–81, 185–88, 232, 241, 243–45 301–3, 311
        threat of, 9, 22, 150, 220, 255, 257, 275, 278, 281
    French, 79, 89, 133–34, 161–64, 170–71, 180, 237–38, 257
    German, 143, 161–62, 164–65, 167–68, 173–75
    idea of, 149
    Ottoman, 12, 123
    Russian, 77–78, 92, 106–9, 133–34, 160, 164–67, 245, 281
India, 10, 12, 176
    as colonized, 13, 151, 175
    as model, 15, 110–11, 115
Iran, 117, 128, 249, 252, 325
    as model, 15, 22, 73, 91–110
    National Assembly of, 92, 136
    shah of, 4, 27, 91–109, 121, 375n. 68
    as target of imperialism, 12, 73, 170
Islam, 63, 226–27, 313, 318, 324–26, 331
    bonds of sympathy among Muslims, 100, 103, 105, 110, 162, 393n. 74
    ideology of, 12, 74, 91, 222, 248–49, 271, 435n. 24, 436n. 25, 437n. 35
    and technology, 314–15
    as unifying factor, 15, 316, 346n. 41
Istanbul, streets of, 23, 31, 35, 259–87, 296–301
istibdad. See despotism
Italy, 109, 130, 153, 161, 167, 188
İttihad ve Terraki Atelyesi, 37
İttihad ve Terraki Cemiyeti. See CUP
İzzet Melih, 207, 209
İzzet Pasha, 70, 322, 367n, 61
Izmir, 27, 214, 230
    press in, 29

J

Jalal-e Ahmad, 225
Japan, 15, 110–11, 121, 151, 323
Jerusalem, 110
Jews, 68, 428n. 25
Joallier, 36
John Bull, 108, 158–61, 321
journalists
    backgrounds of, 29–32, 351n. 14
    Ottoman 3, 25–28, 78, 329
    Parisian, 26
journals. *See* gazettes; press

K

Kâmil Pasha, 53, 305
Karagöz, 1, 3, 18, 54–57, 66, 71, 77, 202, 207, 218, 239, 241, 250, 266, 296–99, 301, 305, 308–10, 315, 361n. 16, 362n. 17
    See also shadow puppet theater
Karabet, 83
Karagapoulos, 36
Kasab, Teodor, 224
Kenan Bey, 36–37, 48, 50
kingship. *See* sovereignty; sultan
Kirkor Faik, 30

L

La Caricature, 67
labor
    Ottoman, 67, 170, 175–78, 180–83, 185–88, 248, 257, 294, 300, 302

Index

strikes, 87, 181, 186, 394n. 85, 395n. 94, 429n. 40
Laitin, David, 14, 17–19
language
    Arabic, 155, 157
    English, 157–58, 192–94
    French, 140, 155, 158, 161, 173, 191–94, 203, 210, 222, 250, 373n. 50, 398n. 25
    German, 132
    Greek, 193
    Ottoman Turkish, 158, 194–98
    See also captions, language of
Libya, 263, 389n. 33
literacy, 26, 45–47, 50–51, 358n. 73
literature, 232
    American, 193
    English, 193
    European, 73–74, 189
    French, 78, 191–94
    Ottoman, 194, 273, 327, 383n. 48, 414n. 54
    Persian, 243
London, 46, 144–46, 149
Loti, Pierre, 204
Louis XVI, king of France, 116

M
Macedonia, 11, 167
machines, 289–93, 427n. 9. *See also* technology
Mahmud Nedim, 28
Mahmud Sadık Bey, 32, 86
Mahmud Şevket Pasha, 271, 384n. 56
Mahmut Hakkı, 30
malî year. *See* dating systems
Marianne, images of, 79–81, 83, 133–34, 160–61, 241, 245
mascots, cartoon, 18, 54–65, 121, 140, 216, 243, 253, 290
    lower-class, 57–60, 298
masculine imagery, 162, 183, 235–37, 243, 245, 250, 278
mastheads, 31, 63, 152, 203
meclis
    Iranian, 100, 252
    Ottoman, 4, 87–89, 100, 385n. 60
    as target, 5, 9, 15, 54, 132–47, 152, 255, 276, 294, 313
    See also deputies
Mehmed Âsıf, 194

Mehmed Fazlı, 28, 30, 37, 39
Mehmed Rauf, 29
Mehmed V Reşad, Ottoman sultan, 2, 84, 121, 123, 130, 132
Mexico, 10
Midhat Pasha, 303–4,
military, the
    European, 83, 150, 175, 277–78, 290, 314
    Ottoman, 78, 133, 153, 222, 304
    weakness of, 13, 173, 223, 235, 263, 314
Mınakyan, Mardiros, 206
ministers, Ottoman, 133–35, 137, 144–46, 178, 221, 255, 303, 311
mizah, 3, 16–18, 25, 47, 65, 133
modern vs. traditional
    dialogues, 53, 223
    idea of, 12, 14, 135, 189–91
    images of, 124, 214–16, 222, 315–16
modernity, 396nn. 1–4
    associated with Europe, 15, 84, 116, 149, 153, 165, 201–5, 289, 321
    symbols of, 96, 140, 200, 210, 223–24, 249, 290, 298, 302, 311, 318
modernization, 34, 200, 247, 296, 305, 315–16, 325, 328, 400n. 42
Molière, Jean Baptiste, 206
monarchy, 25, 114, 116, 121, 380nn. 8, 11, 383n. 42
    European, 114, 116, 121, 128
    Iranian, 73, 117–18
    Ottoman, 1, 12, 113–32
    satire of, 57, 63, 96–107, 116–32, 165–67
    See also czar; shah; sultan
Montenegro, 2, 160
morality, 277–78
    threatened, 222–24, 226–28, 271
    and women, 214–16, 253–54, 261, 271, 273–75, 278
Morocco, 118–19, 121, 153, 162–64, 170, 323, 389n. 36
mother figures, 63, 75–76, 113–34, 199, 214–15, 243–46, 250, 277, 364n. 40
Mughul empire, 110, 115–16
Muhammad Ali, shah of Iran
    as despot, 15, 75, 91–101, 103–6, 117–19
    satirized, 66, 91–101, 103–6, 117–19, 121, 128
Muhammad as-Saffār, 33
Muhammad Reza, shah of Iran, 100
Mulla Hâfız, king of Morocco, 118, 162–63

Index

municipality, satire of, 54, 262, 267, 271–73, 276, 281
museums, images of, 118, 120, 195–96, 382n. 25
Muslims, 68, 96, 110–11, 162, 248–49, 276, 315, 326
Mustafa Kemal Atatürk, 314, 324
Muzaffar al-Din, shah of Iran, 77, 91, 94–95

N

Naib al-Saltana, 95
Namık Kemal, 78, 207
Napoleon, 79, 255, 267
Nasir al-Din, shah of Iran, 206
Nasr üd-Din Hoca, 57, 66, 290, 363n. 28
nation
    as female, 67, 80–83, 89, 235–41, 243–46
    idea of, 10, 136, 317–19
    satire of, 69
    symbols of, 175–76, 183, 207, 317–19
National Assembly, Ottoman, 124, 136
nationalism, 11, 23, 176, 341n. 2
    Arab, 74, 318, 322–23, 433n. 3, 433n. 7
    Egyptian, 154
    ethno-linguistic, 69, 195, 197–98, 317–18
    European, 319, 324, 326, 329, 433n. 3
    Indian, 110–11
    Ottoman, 11, 194, 199, 235, 245, 318–19, 328, 432n. 2, 433nn. 3, 5
    shared sympathies for, 154–55, 170, 323, 326
    Turkish, 318–19, 321, 323–24, 435n. 21
navy, Ottoman, 181, 290, 303–4, 395n. 90, 430n. 50
New York City, 33, 263, 296
news, 21
newspapers. *See* gazettes; press
Nicholas, czar of Russia, 96, 106–7, 117, 128, 281–82
North Africa, 9, 153, 162–64, 175

O

old and new (*eski ve yeni*)
    idea of, 19, 22–23, 77, 84, 189–91, 193–96, 266–67, 271, 290

regimes, 5, 65–66, 144, 147, 210, 222, 263, 328, 330
    as target, 66, 255, 264, 271, 290, 300, 311
    satire of, 54, 136–37, 140, 194, 196, 267, 278, 294, 317
    See also sultan
Osman, Ottoman sultan, 114
Ottoman empire
    economic weakness of, 13, 293, 303–4
    military weakness of, 1–2, 13, 150–51, 264
    political thought of, 115
Ottoman Publishing Association, 31–32
Ottoman Translation Bureau, 78
Ottomanism, 318–22, 324, 328
Ottomans, Westernized (Europeanized), 30, 87, 132, 290
    satire of, 28, 71, 84, 141, 181, 183–84, 189–95, 198–206, 209–10, 212–17, 221–23, 228–35, 274, 320, 326, 397n. 7, 399n. 30, 408n. 2, 414n. 54, 434n. 11

P

Pahlavi monarchy, 15
Palestine, 110, 323
Pan-Islam, 2, 105, 315, 320
Pan-Slavism, 209
Paris, 75, 93, 173, 202, 210, 263
    Ottomans in, 28, 46, 78, 135, 232
    press in, 33
parliament. *See* meclis
Patrick, Mary Mills, 200, 263
people, voice and image of
    Iranian, 100, 103–5
    Ottoman, 51–71, 86–87, 144–47, 317, 373n. 56
Pera, 35–37, 158, 176, 188, 192, 206, 216, 226, 300–301
Persian Gulf, 158–59
Phoebus, 36
photographers, 36, 48, 50
photographs, 36–37, 41, 48, 50, 60, 87, 93–95, 121, 128, 130, 135, 140, 142, 144–45, 207, 219–20, 262,
physician-patient images, 109–10, 160
police, 219, 259–60, 266–74, 281
political parties, 32, 133, 136–40
poor, images of, 128–29, 181–84, 226, 266, 277
postcards, 50, 132, 162, 202

467

press
    in Azerbaican, 374n. 61
    critique of, 27
    expatriate, 16, 27
    freedom of, 3, 5–6, 9, 27, 45, 79, 87, 136–37, 194
    French, 11, 15, 26, 45, 342n. 6, 345n. 36
    Indian, 11, 350n. 8, 379n. 123
    Iranian, 27–28
    Islamic, 31
    Italian, 27, 389n. 33
    language of, 38–40, 267
    Ottoman, 3, 11, 16, 39, 57
        coverage of Iran in, 91–109
        French language in, 86–87, 89, 267, 314
        pre-revolutionary, 28–29
        resurrection of, 5
        revolutionary discourses of, 14
    output of, 25, 29
    rhetorics of unity in, 70–71
    role of, 28
    serious (non-satirical), 14, 18, 144–45, 293, 304
    stages of development of, 11, 53, 345n. 30, 349nn. 2–3
    symbolic repertoire of, 14, 67
    women's, 357n. 71
    See also gazettes; satire
Press, Charles, 19, 66–67
Press Bureau, Ottoman, 4
Press Law, Ottoman, 4–5
printing, 32–34, 37–39, 352nn. 28, 30, 353nn. 34–35, 356n. 57
progress, idea of, 14–15, 132, 165, 190, 198, 221, 223, 250, 257, 259, 261, 263–64, 278, 287, 289, 304, 311, 316, 328, 387n. 4
Public Debt, Ottoman, 1, 133, 137, 144, 171, 176, 178, 188, 392n. 62
public opinion, Ottoman, 5, 53, 360n. 3, 422n. 25
public, the, 25, 41, 65, 130
    defining, 51–53
    idea of, 19, 21
    Ottoman, 22, 65, 130, 144
publishers, 3, 12, 19, 27–32, 158, 342n. 7, 350n. 13
publishing
    European, 11
    location of, 35, 339
    Ottoman, 11, 18, 30–35, 40
Punch, 39, 67, 219

Q
Qajars, 109, 178, 320

R
race, 319, 322–23, 435n. 23
railroads, 167, 170, 290, 300–301
Rambert, Louis, 178, 189, 226–27
readers, 19, 21, 41–50, 54, 193, 268
    female, 43–46
Régie, 176, 178–80, 185–86
religion, 27, 68, 192, 227–28, 255, 317, 325
    satire of, 15, 68, 366n. 55
    as unifying factor, 69, 255, 315, 432n. 2
    See also Islam
religious authorities. *See* ulema
revolution
    comparative, 56–57, 73
    French, 3, 22, 69, 73–91, 115–16, 368nn. 4–6, 369nn. 10–11, 370n. 19
        slogans of, 15, 63, 77, 79, 84–85, 87, 89, 91, 123, 210
    Iranian constitutional, 15, 22, 46, 91–109, 206
    Ottoman constitutional, second, 1–2, 10, 22, 113, 199, 203, 271
        aftermath of, 14–15, 25, 34, 68, 180–81, 183, 248–51, 255–57
        context of, 12
    Russian, 57
Reza Daneş Khan, 93
Rıza Tevfik Bey, 118–19, 313, 378n. 106
Rumania, 2
Rumelia, Eastern, 167
Russia, 2, 281, 323, 325
    in Iran, 92, 96, 105–11, 164–67, 252
    satire of, 70, 117, 128, 136
    territorial aggression of, 9, 13, 15, 151
    See also imperialism, Russian

S
Said Bey, 201–2
Said Hikmet, 206–7
Salah Cimcöz, 30
salnames, 16, 33, 54, 106, 111, 121, 226
Salonica, 86
satire
    analysis of, 17–23, 330–31
    Arabic, 39, 355n. 53
    Armenian, 39
    British, 39, 67

cartoon, 3, 10, 22
  ethnic, 321–24
  fashion, 15, 141, 153, 201–5, 214–16, 221–32, 247, 279–80
  French 5, 39, 67
  German, 67
  Greek, 39
  Italian, 67
  nature of, 21, 26, 347n. 45, 409n. 5
  Persian (Iranian), 39, 66, 355n. 53
  political, 132–42, 149–89
  pre-revolutionary, 224–25,
  social, 9, 54, 67, 189–90, 198, 209, 224, 259–87
  styles of, 66
  targets of, 8–9, 18, 22, 65–71, 259
  of the West, 13, 189–257
Sattar Khan, 96, 100, 103–5, 377n. 100
Sedad Nuri, 38–39, 141, 195, 232, 241, 281
Selim I, Ottoman sultan, 73
Selim III, Ottoman sultan, 206, 255
Serbia, 2, 160
Servet-i fünun, 32, 34, 78
sewing machines, Singer, 2, 201–2, 402n. 63
sex and sexuality, 63, 153, 235–40, 250, 252–53, 271, 274, 409n. 3
shadow puppet theater, 22, 54–57, 65, 77, 114, 210, 239, 266, 331, 355n. 54
  female characters in, 56–60, 63–64
  influence on satire of, 39, 322
  See also Karagöz
shah, 27, 91–109, 121, 375n. 68. *See also* Muhammad Ali
Shariah, 77, 317–18
skating, 189, 191, 213–17
social order, 27, 50, 66–67, 183, 253, 274–75, 294
socialism, 26, 394n. 87
Sofia, 167
soldier figures
  European, 106, 173, 195, 197
  Ottoman, 75–76, 80, 86, 106, 108, 173, 195, 197
Soresco, 37
Southeast Asia, 10
sovereignty
  European ideas of, 193
  Ottoman, 152–53
  popular, 73, 115
  symbols of, 165–66
  See also czar; shah; sultan
Spain, 162
spiritualism, 189, 191, 213, 218–20, 278, 407n. 127, 408n. 128

steamships, 34, 170, 175, 183, 290
  satire of, 68, 301–4
sultan, 45
  authority of, 13–14
  compared to other monarchs, 117–18, 121
  deposition of, 83–84, 96, 117, 130–31, 152, 379n. 4
  as symbol, 4–5, 20, 114, 122–23, 130, 190
  as target, 5, 30, 66–67, 114–32, 152
  See also Abd ül-Hamid
sultanic order, 66, 73, 144, 222, 264, 294, 316, 323, 326–28
  symbols of, 98, 100, 102, 105, 124–25, 135–37
Süleiman I, Ottoman sultan, 13, 73, 114
Sykes, Mark, 27, 263–64
symbols, 14, 19, 38
  cartoon, 19–20, 23, 26
  of the public, 51–53
Syria, 110, 323
Şirket-i Hayriye, 303
Şuray-ı Devlet, 133. *See also* ministers

T
Tabriz, 95, 100, 103–4, 296
Takvim-i vekayi, 275, 385n. 72
Talat Bey, 158, 178
technology, 14, 23, 273, 289–316
  European, 26, 149, 180, 190, 305, 314–15
  imported, 15, 34, 257, 431n. 74, 432n. 78
Tehran, 27–28, 93, 98, 105, 206
telegraph, 308, 311, 315, 431n. 64
telephone, 96, 220, 311–12,
Tevfik Efendi (Selanikli), 31
theater, 403n. 79
  coverage of, 35, 193
  European, 202, 205–7, 209–10, 212
  French, 71, 193–94, 207, 222
  Iranian, 206
  Ottoman, 194, 202, 205–13
  plays, 4, 30, 52
  satire of, 67, 201, 205, 209–13, 281, 285–86
  as symbol of freedom, 84, 259, 304
  See also shadow puppet theater
time, ideas of, 301, 308, 311–14
timepieces, 191, 230, 278, 289, 311–14
tobacco, 98, 170, 176, 178–80, 271, 394n. 84

469

Index

Trabzon, 93
tradition, idea of, 190, 223–24. *See also* modernity
trams, 18, 68, 185, 187–88, 205, 295–98, 300–301
transport, 13, 67–68, 289–316
Tripoli, 161
Tunis, 2
Tünel, 34, 185, 187–88, 300–301, 308
Twain, Mark, 193, 225

U

ulema
    Ottoman, 2, 12, 15, 69, 315–16
    Iranian, 77, 92, 105
uniforms, 95, 109
    as markers of identity, 83, 118–19, 161–62, 172–73, 183, 190, 223–24, 243–45, 255–56, 266–67, 281
United States. *See* America
unseen, idea of, 276–78, 426n. 76

V

Vaka, Demetra, 45–46
Vartovyan, (Güllü) Agop, 206
vatan (homeland), idea of, 93
Vatan (play), 52, 78, 207
veil, 46, 132, 226–27, 250, 253
Victoria, queen of England, 110
Vienna, 46, 153, 232
Vittorio Emanuele, king of Italy, 130
Volkan, 31, 68

W

watches. *See* timepieces
Wilhelm II, king of Germany, 160–61, 167, 305

women
    as embodying the nation, 67, 80–83, 235–41, 243–46, 371n. 33, 414n. 59, 415n. 67 foreign, images of, 132, 232–34, 243, 248
    in Iran, 249, 252
    modern (the "new"), 200, 214–16, 247–52, 403n. 72
    and morality, 214–16, 226–27, 273–75
    Ottoman, images of, 235–47, 364n. 37
    See also consumers; dress; fashion; workers
women's organizations, 249–51
women's place, 247–53, 416nn. 80–84
workers
    conditions of, 180–85
    images of, 87, 175–78, 180–83, 185–88, 302
    women, 180, 185, 230, 248, 394n. 87
World War I, 3, 9, 63, 132, 158, 195, 219, 318, 324

Y

yearbooks. *See* salnames
Young Turks, 78, 128
    administration of, 138–40, 171, 200, 263, 315, 319
    ideas of, 132–33, 193, 323–24
    satire of, 84, 118, 141, 162, 232, 234–35
Yusuf Akçura, 324

Z

Ziya Gökalp, 318, 330
Ziya Pasha, 78
Züğürt, 56–57, 59–61, 144, 146, 155, 194, 207, 209, 290, 298, 303–4

It would have been helpful to have dates of cartoons